James D. McCabe, Jr.

LIGHTS AND SHADOWS
OF NEW YORK LIFE;
OR, THE
SIGHTS AND SENSATIONS
OF THE GREAT CITY

A Facsimile Edition

Andre Deutsch

PUBLISHED IN THIS EDITION IN 1971
BY ANDRE DEUTSCH LIMITED
105 GREAT RUSSELL STREET
LONDON W C 1
ISBN 0 233 96321 9
PRINTED IN THE UNITED STATES OF AMERICA

VAN INGEN. SNYDER.

GENERAL VIEW OF NEW YORK CITY, SHOWING THE BRIDGE CONNECTING IT WITH BROOKLYN.

GRAND CENTRAL RAILWAY DEPOT.

LIGHTS AND SHADOWS

OF NEW YORK LIFE;

OR, THE

SIGHTS AND SENSATIONS

OF

THE GREAT CITY.

A WORK DESCRIPTIVE OF THE

CITY OF NEW YORK IN ALL ITS VARIOUS PHASES;

WITH FULL AND GRAPHIC ACCOUNTS OF

ITS SPLENDORS AND WRETCHEDNESS; ITS HIGH AND LOW LIFE;
ITS MARBLE PALACES AND DARK DENS; ITS ATTRACTIONS AND
DANGERS; ITS RINGS AND FRAUDS; ITS LEADING MEN
AND POLITICIANS; ITS ADVENTURERS; ITS CHARI-
TIES; ITS MYSTERIES, AND ITS CRIMES.

By JAMES D. McCABE, Jr.,

AUTHOR OF "PARIS BY SUNLIGHT AND GASLIGHT," "HISTORY OF THE WAR BETWEEN GERMANY AND
FRANCE," "GREAT FORTUNES," "THE GREAT REPUBLIC," ETC., ETC.

ILLUSTRATED WITH NUMEROUS FINE ENGRAVINGS OF NOTED PLACES, LIFE
AND SCENES IN NEW YORK.

———•◇•———

Issued by subscription only, and not for sale in the book stores. Residents of any State desiring
a copy should address the Publishers, and an Agent will call upon them. See page 851.

———•◇•———

NATIONAL PUBLISHING COMPANY,
PHILADELPHIA, Pa.; CINCINNATI, Ohio; CHICAGO, Ill.;
ST. LOUIS, Mo.

A. OAKEY HALL, MAYOR OF NEW YORK.

WILLIAM M. TWEED.

PREFACE.

—————

It is the desire of every American to see New York, the largest and most wonderful city in the Union. To very many the city and its attractions are familiar, and the number of these persons is increased by thousands of new comers every year. A still greater number, however, will know the Great City only by the stories that reach them through their friends and the newspapers. They may never gaze upon its beauties, never enjoy its attractions in person. For their benefit I have written these pages, and I have endeavored to present to them a faithful picture of the "Lights and Shadows" of the life of this City, and to describe its "Sights and Sensations" as they really exist.

This Great City, so wonderful in its beauty, so strange to eyes accustomed only to the smaller towns of the land, is in all respects the most attractive sight in

America, and one of the most remarkable places in the
world, ranking next to London and Paris in the extent
and variety of its attractions. Its magnificence is remarkable, its squalor appalling. Nowhere else in the
New World are seen such lavish displays of wealth,
and such hideous depths of poverty. It is rich in
historical associations and in treasures of art. It presents a wonderful series of combinations as well as
contrasts of 'individual and national characteristics. It
is richly worth studying by all classes, for it is totally
different from any other city in the world. It is always
fresh, always new. It is constantly changing, growing
greater and more wonderful in its power and splendors,
more worthy of admiration in its higher and nobler
life, more generous in its charities, and more mysterious
and appalling in its romance and its crimes. It is indeed a wonderful city. Coming fresh from plainer and
more practical parts of the land, the visitor is plunged
into the midst of so much beauty, magnificence, gayety,
mystery, and a thousand other wonders, that he is
fairly bewildered. It is hoped that the reader of these
pages will be by their perusal better prepared to enjoy
the attractions, and to shun the dangers of New York.
It has been my effort to bring home to those who cannot see the city for themselves, its pleasures and its
dangers, and to enable them to enjoy the former with-

out either the fatigue or expense demanded of an active participant in them, and to appreciate the latter, without incurring the risks attending an exploration of the shadowy side of the Great City.

To those who intend visiting New York, whether they come as strangers, or as persons familiar with it, the writer has a word to say, which he trusts may be heeded. An honest effort has been made in this work to present the reader with a fair description of the dangers to which visitors and citizens are alike exposed. For the purpose of performing this task, the writer made visits, in company with the police officials of the city, to a number of the places described in this work, and he is satisfied that no respectable person can with safety visit them, unless provided with a similar protection. The curiosity of all persons concerning the darker side of city life can be fully satisfied by a perusal of the sketches presented in this volume. It is not safe for a stranger to undertake to explore these places for himself. No matter how clever he may consider himself, no respectable man is a match for the villains and sharpers of New York, and he voluntarily brings upon himself all the consequences that will follow his entrance into the haunts of the criminal and disreputable classes. The city is full of danger. The path of safety which is pointed out in these pages is the only one for either citizen or stranger—an absolute avoidance of the vicinity of sin.

Those who have seen the city will, I am sure, confirm the statements contained herein, and will acknowledge the truthfulness of the picture I have drawn, whatever they may think of the manner in which the work is executed.

J. D. McC., Jr.

New York,
    March 21*st*, 1872.

HENRY WARD BEECHER.

HORACE GREELEY.

CONTENTS.

18 CONTENTS.

CONTENTS.

PETER COOPER.

CORNELIUS VANDERBILT.

H. SEBALD

LIST OF ILLUSTRATIONS.

JAMES GORDON BENNETT.

ROBERT BONNER.

OFFICES OF THE TRIBUNE, TIMES, AND WORLD.

LIGHTS AND SHADOWS

OF

NEW YORK LIFE.

I.

THE CITY OF NEW YORK

I.

HISTORICAL.

On the morning of the 1st of May, 1607, there knelt at the chancel of the old church of St. Ethelburge, in Bishopsgate street, London, to receive the sacrament, a man of noble and commanding presence, with a broad intellectual forehead, short, close hair, and a countenance full of the dignity and courtly bearing of an honorable gentleman. His dress bespoke him a sailor, and such he was. Immediately upon receiving the sacrament, he hastened from the church to the Thames, where a boat was in waiting to convey him to a vessel lying in the stream. But little time was lost after his arrival on board, and soon the ship was gliding down the river. The man was an Englishman by birth and training, a seaman by education, and one of those daring explorers of the time who yearned to win fame by discovering the new route to India. His name was HENRY HUDSON, and he had been employed by "certain worshipful merchants of London" to go in search of a North-*east* passage to India, around the Arctic shores of Europe, between Lapland and Nova Zembla, and frozen Spitzbergen. These worthy gentlemen were convinced that since the effort to find a North-*west* passage had

3

failed, nothing remained but to search for a North-*east* passage,
and they were sure that if human skill or energy could find it,
Hudson would succeed in his mission. They were not mistaken
in their man, for in two successive voyages he did all that mortal could do to penetrate the ice fields beyond the North Cape,
but without success. An impassable barrier of ice held him
back, and he was forced to return to London to confess his failure. With unconquerable hope, he suggested new means of
overcoming the difficulties ; but while his employers praised his
zeal and skill, they declined to go to further expense in an undertaking which promised so little, and the " bold Englishman,
the expert pilot, and the famous navigator " found himself out
of employment. Every effort to secure aid in England failed
him, and, thoroughly disheartened, he passed over to Holland,
whither his fame had preceded him.

The Dutch, who were more enterprising, and more hopeful
than his own countrymen, lent a ready ear to his statement of
his plans, and the Dutch East India Company at once employed
him, and placed him in command of a yacht of ninety tons,
called the *Half Moon*, manned by a picked crew.   On the 25th
of March, 1609, Hudson set sail in this vessel from Amsterdam,
and steered directly for the coast of Nova Zembla.   He succeeded in reaching the meridian of Spitzbergen ; but here the ice,
the fogs, and the fierce tempests of the North drove him back,
and turning to the westward, he sailed past the capes of Green-
land, and on the 2nd of July was on the banks of Newfound-
land.   He passed down the coast as far as Charleston Harbor,
vainly hoping to find the North-*west* passage, and then in despair
turned to the northward, discovering Delaware Bay on his voyage.   On the 3rd of September he arrived off a large bay to
the north of the Delaware, and passing into it, dropped anchor
"at two cables' length from the shore," within Sandy Hook.
Devoting some days to rest, and to the exploration of the bay,
he passed through The Narrows on the 11th of September, and
then the broad and beautiful " inner bay " burst upon him in all
its splendor, and from the deck of his ship he watched the swift
current of the mighty river rolling from the north to the sea.
He was full of hope now, and the next day continued his pro-

gress up the river, and at nightfall cast anchor at Yonkers. During the night the current of the river turned his ship around, placing her head down stream; and this fact, coupled with the assurances of the natives who came out to the *Half Moon* in their canoes, that the river flowed from far beyond the mountains, convinced him that the stream flowed from ocean to ocean, and that by sailing on he would at length reach India—the golden land of his dreams.

Thus encouraged, he pursued his way up the river, gazing with wondering delight upon its glorious scenery, and listening with gradually fading hope to the stories of the natives who flocked to the water to greet him. The stream narrowed, and the water grew fresh, and long before he anchored below Albany, Hudson had abandoned the belief that he was in the Northwest passage. From the anchorage, a boat's crew continued the voyage to the mouth of the Mohawk. Hudson was satisfied that he had made a great discovery—one that was worth fully as much as finding the new route to India. He was in a region upon which the white man's eye had never rested before, and which offered the richest returns to commercial ventures. He hastened back to New York Bay, took possession of the country in the name of Holland, and then set sail for Europe. He put into Dartmouth in England, on his way back, where he told the story of his discovery. King James I. prevented his continuing his voyage, hoping to deprive the Dutch of its fruits; but Hudson took care to send his log-book and all the ship's papers over to Holland, and thus placed his employers in full possession of the knowledge he had gained. The English at length released the *Half Moon*, and she continued her voyage to the Texel.

The discovery of Hudson was particularly acceptable to the Dutch, for the new country was rich in fur-bearing animals, and Russia offered a ready market for all the furs that could be sent there. The East India Company, therefore, refitted the *Half Moon* after her return to Holland, and despatched her to the region discovered by Hudson on a fur trading expedition, which was highly successful. Private persons also embarked in similar enterprises, and within two years a prosperous and important fur trade was established between Holland and the country along the Mauritius, as the great river discovered by Hudson had been named, in honor of the Stadtholder of Holland. No government took any notice of the trade for a while, and all persons were free to engage in it.

Among the adventurers employed in this trade was one Adrian Block, noted as one of the boldest navigators of his time. He made a voyage to Manhattan Island in 1614, then the site of a Dutch trading post, and had secured a cargo of skins with which he was about to return to Holland, when a fire consumed both his vessel and her cargo, and obliged him to pass the winter with his crew on the island. They built them log huts on the site of the present Beaver street, the first houses erected in New York, and during the winter constructed a yacht of sixteen tons, which Block called the *Onrust*—the " Restless." In this yacht Block made many voyages of dis- covery, exploring the coasts of Long Island Sound, and giving his name to the island near the eastern end of the sound. He soon after went back to Europe.

Meanwhile, a small settlement had clustered about the trad- ing post and the huts built by Block's shipwrecked crew, and had taken the name of New Amsterdam. The inhabitants were well suited to become the ancestors of a great nation. They were mainly Dutch citizens of a European Republic, "composed of seven free, sovereign States—made so by a struggle with des- potism for forty years, and occupying a territory which their ancestors had reclaimed from the ocean and morass by indomi- table labor. It was a republic where freedom of conscience, speech, and the press were complete and universal. The effect of this freedom had been the internal development of social beauty and strength, and vast increment of substantial wealth and power by immigration. Wars and despotisms in other parts of Europe sent thousands of intelligent exiles thither, and those free provinces were crowded with ingenious mechanics, and artists, and learned men, because conscience was there un- disturbed, and the hand and brain were free to win and use the rewards of their industry and skill. Beautiful cities, towns, and villages were strewn over the whole country, and nowhere

FIRST SETTLEMENT OF NEW YORK.

in Europe did society present an aspect half as pleasing as that
of Holland.   Every religious sect there found an asylum from
persecution, and encouragement to manly effort, by the kind respect of all.   And at the very time when the charter of the
West India Company was under consideration, that band of
English Puritans who afterward set up the ensign of free institutions on the shores of Massachusetts Bay, were being nurtured
in the bosom of that republic, and instructed in those principles

of civil liberty that became a salutary leaven in the bigotry
which they brought with them.

"Such were the people who laid the foundations of the Com-
monwealth of New York. They were men of expanded views,
liberal feelings, and never dreamed of questioning any man's
inalienable right to 'life, liberty, and the pursuit of happiness'
among them, whether he first inspired the common air in Holland, England, Abyssinia, or Kamtschatka. And as the population increased and became heterogeneous, that very toleration
became a reproach; and their Puritan neighbors on the east,
and Churchmen and Romanists on the south, called New Amsterdam 'a cage of unclean birds.' "

The English, now awake to the importance of Hudson's discoveries, warned the Dutch Government to refrain from making
further settlements on "Hudson's River," as they called the
Mauritius; but the latter, relying upon the justice of their claim,
which was based upon Hudson's discovery, paid no attention to
these warnings, and in the spring of 1623 the Dutch West India
Company sent over thirty families of Walloons, or 110 persons
in all, to found a permanent colony at New Amsterdam, which,
until now, had been inhabited only by fur traders. These
Walloons were Protestants, from the frontier between France
and Flanders, and had fled to Amsterdam to escape religious
persecution in France. They were sound, healthy, vigorous,
and pious people, and could be relied upon to make homes in
the New World. The majority of them settled in New Amsterdam. Others went to Long Island, where Sarah de Rapelje,
the first white child born in the province of New Netherlands,
saw the light.

In 1626, Peter Minuit, the first regular Governor, was sent
over from Holland. He brought with him a *Koopman* or
general commissary, who was also secretary of the province,
and a *Schout*, or sheriff, to assist him in his government. The
only laws to which he was subject were the instructions of the
West India Company. The colonists, on their part, were to
regard his will as their law. He set to work with great vigor
to lay the foundations of the colony. He called a council of
the Indian chiefs, and purchased the Island of Manhattan from

them for presents valued at about twenty dollars, United States coin. He thus secured an equitable title to the island, and won the friendship of the Indians. Under his vigorous administration, the colony prospered ; houses were built, farms laid off; the population was largely increased by new arrivals from Europe ; and New Amsterdam fairly entered upon its career as one of the most important places in America. It was a happy settlement, as well; the rights of the people were respected, and they were as free as they had been in Holland. Troubles with the Indians marked the close of Minuit's administration. The latter were provoked by the murder of some of their number by the whites, and by the aid rendered by the commander at Fort Orange (Albany) to the Mohegans, in one of their forays upon the Mohawks. Many of the families at Fort Orange, and from the region between the Hudson and the Delaware, abandoned their settlements, and came to New Amsterdam for safety, thus adding to the population of that place. Minuit was recalled in 1632, and he left the province in a highly prosperous condition. During the last year of his government New Amsterdam sent over $60,000 worth of furs to Holland.

His successor was the redoubtable Wouter Van Twiller, a clerk in the company's warehouse at Amsterdam, who owed his appointment to his being the husband of the niece of Killian Van Rensselaer, the patroon of Albany. Irving has given us the following admirable portrait of him :

" He was exactly five feet six inches in height, and six feet five inches in circumference. His head was a perfect sphere, and of such stupendous dimensions, that dame Nature, with all her sex's ingenuity, would have been puzzled to construct a neck capable of supporting it; wherefore she wisely declined the attempt, and settled it firmly on the top of his back bone, just between the shoulders. His body was oblong, and particularly capacious at bottom; which was wisely ordered by Providence, seeing that he was a man of sedentary habits, and very averse to the idle labor of walking. His legs were very short, but sturdy in proportion to the weight they had to sustain : so that, when erect, he had not a little the appearance of a beer barrel on skids. His face, that infallible index of the mind, presented a vast expanse, unfurrowed by any of those lines and angles which disfigure the human countenance with what is termed expression. Two small gray eyes twinkled feebly in the midst, like two stars of lesser magnitude in a hazy firmament; and his full-fed cheeks, which seemed to have taken toll of everything that went into his mouth, were curiously mottled and streaked with dusky red, like a Spitzenberg apple. His habits were as regular as his person. He daily took his four stated meals, appropriating exactly an hour to each; he smoked and doubted eight hours, and he slept the remaining twelve of the four-and-twenty."

Van Twiller ruled the province seven years, and, in spite of his stupidity, it prospered. In 1633, Adam Roelantsen, the first school-master, arrived—for the fruitful Walloons had opened the way by this time for his labors—and in the same year a wooden church was built in the present Bridge street, and placed in charge of the famous Dominie Everardus Bogardus. In 1635, the fort, which marked the site of the present Bowling Green, and which had been begun in 1614, was finished, and in the same year the first English settlers at New Amsterdam came into the town. The English in New England also began to give the Dutch trouble during this administration, and even sent a ship into "Hudson's River" to trade with the Indians. Influenced by De Vries, the commander of the fort, the Governor sent an expedition up the river after the audacious English vessel, seized her, brought her back to New York, and sent her to sea with a warning not to repeat her attempt. The disputes between the English and the Dutch about the Connecticut settlements, also began to make trouble for New Amsterdam. Van Twiller possessed no influence in the colony, was laughed at and snubbed on every side, and was at length recalled by the company in 1638. The only memorial of Van Twiller left to us is the Isle of Nuts, which lies in the bay between New York and Brooklyn, and which he purchased as his private domain. It is still called the "Governor's Island."

Van Twiller's successor in the government of the province

was William Kieft.   He was as energetic as he was spiteful, and as spiteful as he was rapacious.   His chief pleasure lay in quarrelling.   He and his council made some useful reforms, but as a rule they greatly oppressed the people.   During this administration agriculture was encouraged, the growing of fruit was undertaken, and several other things done to increase the material prosperity of the town.   The fort was repaired and strengthened, new warehouses were built, and police ordinances were framed and strictly executed.   The old wooden church was made a barrack for troops, and a new and larger edifice of stone was constructed by Kuyter and Dam within the walls of the fort.   Within the little tower were hung the bells captured from the Spanish by the Dutch at Porto Rico.   The church cost $1000, and was considered a grand edifice.   In 1642 a stone tavern was built at the head of Coenties Slip, and in the same year, the first " city lots " with valid titles were granted to the settlers.

The latter part of Kieft's administration was marked by contests with the citizens, who compelled him, in 1641, to grant them a municipal council, composed of twelve of the most prominent residents of New Amsterdam, which council he arbitrarily dissolved at the first opportunity.   He also stirred up a war with the Indians, in which he was the principal aggressor.   This war brought great loss and suffering upon the province, and came near ruining it.   Kieft, alarmed at the results of his folly, appointed a new municipal council of eight members, and this council at once demanded of the States General of Holland the removal of Kieft.   Their demand was complied with, and in 1647, Peter Stuyvesant was made Governor of New Netherlands, and reached New Amsterdam in the same year.

Stuyvesant was essentially a strong man.   A soldier by education and of long experience, he was accustomed to regard rigid discipline as the one thing needful in every relation of life, and he was not slow to introduce that system into his government of New Amsterdam.   He had served gallantly in the wars against the Portuguese, and had lost a leg in one of his numerous encounters with them.   He was as vain as a peacock, as fond of display as a child, and thoroughly imbued with the most aristocratic ideas—qualities not exactly the best for a Governor of New Amsterdam. Yet, he was, with all his faults, an honest man, he had deeply at heart the interests of the colony, and his administration was mainly a prosperous one.

He energetically opposed from the first all manifestations in favor of popular government. His will was to be the law of the province. "If any one," said he, "during my administration shall appeal, I will make him a foot shorter, and send the pieces to Holland, and let him appeal in that way." He went to work with vigor to reform matters in the colony, extending his efforts to even the morals and domestic affairs of the people. He soon brought about a reign of material prosperity greater than had ever been known before, and exerted himself to check the encroachments of the English, on the East, and the Swedes, on the South. He inaugurated a policy of kindness and justice toward the Indians, and soon changed their enmity to sincere friendship. One thing, however, he dared not do—he could not levy taxes upon the people without their consent, for fear of offending the States General of Holland. This forced him to appoint a council of nine prominent citizens, and, although he endeavored to hedge round their powers by numerous conditions, the nine ever afterwards served as a salutary check upon the action of the Governor. He succeeded, in the autumn of 1650, in settling the boundary disputes with the English in New England, and then turned his attention to the Swedes on the Delaware, whom he conquered in 1654. His politic course towards them had the effect of converting them into warm friends of the Dutch. During his absence on this expedition, the Indians ravaged the Jersey shore and Staten Island, and even made an attack on New Amsterdam itself. They were defeated by the citizens, and Stuyvesant's speedy return compelled them to make peace. This was the last blow struck by the savages at the infant metropolis.

In 1652, the States General, much to the disgust of Stuyvesant, granted to New Amsterdam a municipal government similar to that of the free cities of Holland. A Schout, or

Sheriff, two Burgomasters, and five Schepens, were to constitute a municipal court of justice. The people, however, were denied the selection of these officers, who were appointed by the Governor. In February, 1653, these officers were formally installed. They were, Schout Van Tienhoven, Burgomasters Hattem and Kregier, and Schepens Van der Grist, Van Gheel, Anthony, Beeckman, and Couwenhoven, with Jacob Kip as clerk.

During Stuyvesant's administration, the colony received large accessions from the English in New England. "Numbers, nay whole towns," says De Laet, "to escape from the insupportable government of New England, removed to New Netherlands, to enjoy that liberty denied to them by their own countrymen." They settled in New Amsterdam, on Long Island, and in Westchester county. Being admitted to the rights of citizenship, they exercised considerable influence in the affairs of the colony, and towards the close of his administration gave the Governor considerable trouble by their opposition to his despotic acts.

In 1647, the streets of New Amsterdam were cleared of the shanties and pig-pens which obstructed them. In 1648, every Monday was declared a market-day. In 1650, Dirk Van Schellyne, the first lawyer, "put up his shingle" in New Amsterdam. In 1652, a wall or palisade was erected along the upper boundary of the city, in apprehension of an invasion by the English. This defence ran from river to river, and to it Wall street, which occupies its site east of Trinity Church, owes its name. In 1656, the first survey of the city was made, and seventeen streets were laid down on the map; and, in the same year, the first census showed a "city" of 120 houses, and 1000 inhabitants. In 1657, a terrible blow fell upon New Amsterdam—the public treasury being empty, the salary of the town drummer could not be paid. In that year the average price of the best city lots was $50. In 1658, the custom of "bundling" received its death blow by an edict of the Governor, which forbade men and women to live together until legally married. In that year the streets were first paved with stone, and the first "night watch" was organized and duly provided with rattles.

A fire department, supplied with buckets and ladders, was also established, and the first public well was dug in Broadway. In 1660, it was made the duty of the Sheriff to go round the city by night to assure himself of its peace and safety.   This worthy official complained that the dogs, having no respect for his august person, attacked him in his rounds, and that certain evil-minded individuals "frightened" him by calling out "Indians" in the darkness, and that even the boys cut *Koeckies*.   The city grew steadily, its suburbs began to smile with boweries, or farms, and in 1658 a palisaded village called New Harlem was founded at the eastern end of Manhattan Island for the purpose of " promoting agriculture, and affording a place of amusement for the citizens of New Amsterdam."   " Homes, genuine, happy Dutch homes, in abundance, were found within and without the city, where uncultured minds and affectionate hearts enjoyed life in dreamy, quiet blissfulness, unknown in these bustling times.   The city people then rose at dawn, dined at eleven, and went to bed at sunset, except on extraordinary occasions, such as Christmas Eve, a tea party, or a wedding.   Then those who attended the fashionable soirées of the ' upper ten' assembled at three o'clock in the afternoon, and went away at six, so that daughter Maritchie might have the pewter plates and delf tea-pot cleaned and cupboarded in time for evening prayer at seven. Knitting and spinning held the places of whist and flirting in these 'degenerate days;' and *utility* was as plainly stamped on all their pleasures as the maker's name on our silver spoons."

But the period of Dutch supremacy on Manhattan was approaching its close.   Charles II. had just regained the English throne.   In 1664, with characteristic disregard of right and justice, he granted to his brother James, Duke of York and Albany, the whole territory of New Netherlands, including all of Long Island and a part of Connecticut—lands to which he had not the shadow of a claim.   In the same year, a force of four ships and 450 soldiers, under the command of Colonel Richard Nicholls, was sent to New Amsterdam to take possession of that city.   It arrived at the Narrows about the 29th of August, and on the 30th, Nicholls demanded the surrender of the town.

NEW YORK IN 1664.

Stuyvesant, who had made preparations for defending the place, endeavored to resist the demand, but the people refused to sustain him, and he was obliged to submit. On the 8th of September, 1664, he withdrew the Dutch garrison from the fort, and embarked at the foot of Beaver street for Holland. The English at once took possession of the town and province, changing the name of both to New York, in honor of the new proprietor.

The English set themselves to work to conciliate the Dutch residents, a task not very difficult, inasmuch as the English settlers already in the province had to a great degree prepared the way for the change. In 1665, the year after the conquest, the city was given a Mayor, a Sheriff, and a board of Aldermen, who were charged with the administration of municipal affairs, and in the same year jury trials were formally established. In July, 1673, the Dutch fleet recaptured the town, drove out the English, and named it New Orange. The peace between Great Britain and Holland, which closed the war, restored the town to the English, November 10th, 1674, and the name of New York was resumed. The Dutch Government was replaced by the English system under a liberal charter, and during the remainder of the seventeenth century the town grew rapidly in population and size.   In 1689 there was a brief disturbance known as Leislers' Rebellion.   In 1700 New York contained 750 dwellings and 4500 white and 750 black inhabitants.   In 1693 William Bradford established the first printing press in the city. In 1696 Trinity Church was begun, and in 1697, the streets were first lighted, a lamp being hung out upon a pole extending from the window of every seventh house.   In 1702 a terrible fever was brought from St. Thomas', and carried off 600 persons, one-tenth of the whole population.   In 1711, a slave market was established.   In 1719 the first Presbyterian Church was built; in 1725 the New York *Gazette*, the fifth of the colonial newspapers, was established; and in 1730 stages ran to Philadelphia once a fortnight, and in 1732 to Boston, the latter journey occupying fourteen days.   In 1731 the first public library, the bequest of the Rev. Dr. Wellington, of England, was opened in the city.   It contained 1622 volumes.   In 1734 a workhouse was erected in the present City Hall Park.   In 1735 the people made their first manifestation of hostility to Great Britain, which was drawn forth by the infamous prosecution by the officers of the crown, of Rip Van Dam, who had been the acting Governor of the town.   The winter of 1740–41 was memorable for its severity.   The Hudson was frozen over at New York, and the snow lay six feet on a level.   In 1741, a severe fire in the lower part of the city destroyed among other things the old Dutch Church and fort, and in the same year the yellow fever raged with great violence.   The principal event of the year, however, was the so-called negro plot for the destruction of the town. Though the reality of the plot was never proved, the greatest alarm prevailed; the fire in the fort was declared to be the work of the negroes, many of whom were arrested; and upon the sole evidence of a servant girl a number of the poor wretches were convicted and hanged.   Several whites were charged with being the accomplices of the negroes.   One of these, John Ury, a Roman Catholic priest, and, as is now believed, an innocent man, was hanged in August.   In the space of six months 154 negroes and twenty whites were arrested, twenty negroes were hanged, thirteen were burned at the stake, and seventy-eight were transported. The rest were released. In 1750 a theatre was opened, and in 1755 St. Paul's Church was erected. In 1754 the "Walton House," in Pearl street (still standing), was built by William Walton, a merchant. It was long known as the finest private residence in the city. In 1755 the Staten Island ferry, served by means of row boats, was established, and in the same year Peck Slip was opened and paved. In 1756 the first lottery ever seen in the city was opened in behalf of King's (now Columbia) College.

New York bore a prominent part in the resistance of the colonies to the aggressions of the mother country, and in spite of the efforts of her royalist Governor and the presence of a large number of Tories, responded cordially to the call of the colonies for men and money during the war. On the 14th of April, 1776, the city was occupied by the American army, the British force stationed there being obliged to withdraw. On the 26th of August, 1776, the battle of Long Island having been lost by the Americans, New York was occupied by the British, who held it until the close of the war. It suffered very much at their hands. Nearly all the churches, except the Episcopal, were used by them as prisons, riding schools, and stables; and the schools and colleges were closed. On the 21st of September, 1776, a fire destroyed 493 houses, including Trinity Church— all the west side of Broadway from Whitehall to Barclay street, or about one-eighth of the city; and on the 7th of August, 1778, about 300 buildings on East River were burned. The winter of 1779–80 was very severe; there was a beaten track for sleighs and wagons across the Hudson; the ice in that river being strong enough to bear a horse and man as late as the 17th of March; eighty sleighs, with provisions, and a large body of troops, crossed on the ice from the city to Staten Island. On the 25th of November, 1783, the British evacuated the city, which was at once occupied by the American army.

In 1785 the first Federal Congress met in the City Hall, which stood at the corner of Wall and Nassau streets, and on the 30th of April, 1789, George Washington was inaugurated first President of the United States on the same spot. By 1791

New York had spread to the lower end of the present City Hall Park, the site of the new Post Office, and was extending along the Boston road, or Bowery, and Broadway.   In 1799, the Manhattan Company for supplying the city with fresh water was chartered. On the 20th of September, 1803, the corner-stone of the City Hall was laid.   The city fathers, sagely premising that New York would never pass this limit, ordered the rear wall of the edifice to be constructed of brown stone, to save the expense of marble. Free schools were opened in 1805. In the same year the yellow fever raged with violence, and had the effect of extending the city by driving the population up the island, where many of them located themselves permanently.   In 1807, Robert Fulton navigated the first steamboat from New York to Albany.

The war of 1812–15 for a while stopped the growth of the city, but after the return of peace its progress was resumed. In August, 1812, experimental gas lamps were placed in the City Hall Park, though the use of gas for purposes of lighting was not begun until 1825. In 1822 the yellow fever again drove the population up the island, and caused a rapid growth of the city above Canal street. In 1825 the Erie Canal was completed. This great work, by placing the trade of the West in the hands of New York, gave a powerful impetus to the growth of the city, which was at that time spreading at the rate of from 1000 to 1500 houses per year. In 1832 and 1834, the cholera raged severely, carrying off upwards of 4484 persons in the two years. In 1835, the "great fire" occurred. This terrible conflagration broke out on the 16th of December of that year, and swept the First Ward of the city east of Broadway and below Wall street. It laid almost the entire business quarter in ashes, destroyed 648 houses, and inflicted upon the city a loss of over $18,000,000. New York rose from this disaster with wonderful energy and rapidity, but only to meet, in 1837, the most terrible financial crisis that had ever burst upon the country. Even this did not check the growth of the city, the population increasing 110,100 between 1830 and 1840. In 1842 the Croton water was introduced. In 1849 and 1854 the cholera again appeared, killing over 5400 persons.   In 1852, the first street railway was built.   In 1858, the Central Park was begun.

The Civil War checked the growth and trade of the city, which languished during the entire struggle, but upon the return of peace New York resumed its onward progress.   The growth of the city since 1865 has been most marked, especially in the immediate vicinity of the Central Park. Not less marked has been the improvement of the older portions.   The city is rapidly increasing in size, population, and magnificence, and is fully maintaining its position as the brilliant metropolis of the New World.

II.

DESCRIPTIVE AND STATISTICAL.

THE city of New York, the largest and most important in the United States, is situated in New York County, on Manhattan Island, at the mouth of the Hudson River, eighteen miles from the Atlantic Ocean.   The city limits comprise the entire county of New York, embracing Manhattan Island, Randall's, Ward's, and Blackwell's Islands, in the East River, and Governor's, Bedloe's, and Ellis' Islands, in the bay.   The last three are occupied by the military posts of the United States Government.   Manhattan Island is bounded on the north by Spuyten Duyvel Creek and the Harlem River—practically the same stream ; on the east by the East River, on the west by the Hudson, and on the south by New York Bay.   It is nine miles long on the east side, thirteen and a half miles long on the west side, and two and a half miles wide at its greatest breadth, the average breadth being a mile and a half.   It is but a few feet in width at its southern extremity, but spreads out like a fan as it stretches away to the northward.   The southern point is but a few inches above the level of the bay, but the island rises rapidly to the northward, its extreme northern portion being occupied by a series of bold, finely wooded heights, which ter-

4

minate at the junction of the Hudson River and Spuyten Duyvel Creek, in a bold promontory, 130 feet high. These hills, known as Washington Heights, are two or three miles in length. The southern portion of the island is principally a sand-bed, but the remainder is very rocky. The island covers an area of twenty-two square miles, or 14,000 acres. It is built up compactly for about six miles, along the east side, and irregularly to Harlem, three miles farther. Along the west side it is built up compactly to the Central Park, Fifty-ninth street, and irregularly to Manhattanville, One hundred and twenty-fifth street, from which point to Spuyten Duyvel Creek it is covered with country seats, gardens, etc. Three wagon, and two railroad bridges over the Harlem River connect the island with the mainland, and numerous lines of ferries afford communication with Long and Staten Islands, and New Jersey. The island attains its greatest width at Fourteenth and Eighty-seventh streets.

The city is finely built, and presents an aspect of industry and liveliness unsurpassed by any place in the world. Lying in full sight of the ocean, with its magnificent bay to the southward, and the East and Hudson Rivers washing its shores, the city of New York possesses a climate which renders it the most delightful residence in America. In the winter the proximity of the sea moderates the severity of the cold, and in the summer the heat is tempered by the delightful sea breezes which sweep over the island. Snow seldom lies in the streets for more than a few hours, and the intense " heated terms " of the summer are of very brief duration. As a natural consequence, the city is healthy, and the death rate, considering the population, is small.

The southern portion is densely built up. Between the City Hall and Twenty-third street New York is more thickly populated than any city in America. It is in this section that the " tenement houses," or buildings containing from five to twenty families, are to be found. The greatest mortality is in these over-crowded districts, which the severest police measures cannot keep clean and free from filth. The southern portion of the city is devoted almost exclusively to trade, comparatively few persons residing below the City Hall.   Below Canal street the streets are narrow, crooked, and irregular.   Above Houston street they are broad and straight, and are laid out at regular intervals.   Above Houston street, the streets extending across the island are numbered.   The avenues begin in the vicinity of Third street, and extend, or will extend to the northern limit of the island, running parallel with the Hudson River. There are twelve fine avenues at parallel distances apart of about 800 feet.   Second and Eighth are the longest, and Fifth, Madison and Lexington the most fashionable.   They commence with Avenue D, a short street, near the East River.   West of this, and parallel with it, are three avenues somewhat longer, called Avenues C, B, and A, the last being the most westerly. Then begin the long avenues, which are numbered First, Second, and so on, as they increase to the westward.   There are two other avenues shorter than those with numbers, viz: Lexington, lying between Third and Fourth, and extending from Fourteenth street on the south to Sixty-ninth street on the north ; and Madison, between Fourth and Fifth, and extending from Twenty-third street at Madison Square to Eighty-sixth street.   Madison and Lexington are each to be prolonged to the Harlem River.   These avenues are all 100 feet wide, except Lexington and Madison, which are seventy-five feet wide, and Fourth avenue, above Thirty-fourth street, which is 140 feet wide.   Third avenue is the main street on the east side above the Bowery, of which it is a continuation, and Eighth avenue is the principal highway on the west side.   Fifth and Madison avenues are the most fashionable, and are magnificently built up with private residences below the Park.   The cross streets connecting them are also handsomely built.

The numerical streets are all sixty feet wide, except Fourteenth, Twenty-third, Thirty-fourth, Forty-second, and eleven others north of these, which are 100 feet wide.   The streets of the city are well laid off, and are paved with an excellent quality of stone.   The sidewalks generally consist of immense stone " flags."   In the lower part of the city, in the poorer and business sections, the streets are dirty and always out of order.

In the upper part they are clean, and are generally kept so by private contributions.

The avenues on the eastern and western extremities of the city are the abodes of poverty and want, and often of vice, hemming in the wealthy and cleanly sections on both sides. Poverty and riches are close neighbors in New York. Only a stone's throw back of the most sumptuous parts of Broadway and Fifth avenue, want and suffering, vice and crime, hold their courts. Fine ladies can look down from their high casements upon the squalid dens of their unfortunate sisters.

Broadway is the principal thoroughfare. It extends from the Battery to Spuyten Duyvel Creek, a distance of fifteen miles. It is built up compactly for about five miles, is paved and graded for about seven miles, and is lighted with gas along its entire length. There are over 420 miles of streets in the patrol districts, and eleven miles of piers along the water. The sewerage is generally good, but defective in some places. Nearly 400 miles of water-mains have been laid. The streets are lighted by about 19,000 gas lamps, besides lamps set out by private parties. They are paved with the Belgian and wooden pavements, cobble stones being almost a thing of the past. For so large a city, New York is remarkably clean, except in those portions lying close to the river, or given up to paupers.

The city is substantially built. Frame houses are rare. Many of the old quarters are built of brick, but this material is now used to a limited extent only. Broadway and the principal business streets are lined with buildings of iron, marble, granite, brown, Portland, and Ohio stone, palatial in their appearance; and the sections devoted to the residences of the better classes are built up mainly with brown, Portland, and Ohio stone, and in some instances with marble. Thus the city presents an appearance of grandeur and solidity most pleasing to the eye. The public buildings will compare favorably with any in the world, and there is no city on the globe that can boast so many palatial warehouses and stores. Broadway is one of the best built thoroughfares in the world. The stores which line it are generally from five to six stories high above ground,

BROADWAY, LOOKING UP FROM EXCHANGE PLACE.

with two cellars below the pavement, and vaults extending to
near the middle of the street. The adjacent streets in many
instances rival Broadway in their splendors. The stores of the
city are famous for their elegance and convenience, and for the
magnificence and variety of the goods displayed in them. The
streets occupied by private residences are broad, clean and well-
paved, and are lined with miles of dwellings inferior to none in
the world in convenience and substantial elegance. The amount

of wealth and taste concentrated in the dwellings of the better classes of the citizens of New York is very great.

The population of New York, in 1870, according to the United States census of that year, was 942,337. There can be no doubt that at the present time the island contains over 1,000,000 *residents*. Thousands of persons doing business in New York reside in the vicinity, and enter and leave the city at morning and evening, and thousands of strangers, on business and pleasure, come and go daily. It is estimated that the actual number of people in the city about the hour of noon is nearly, if not fully, one million and a half. According to the census of 1870, the actual population consisted of 929,199 white and 13,153 colored persons. The native population was 523,238, and the foreign population 419,094. The nationality of the principal part of the foreign element was as follows:

From Germany	151,222	persons.
" Ireland	201,999	"
" England	24,432	' "
" Scotland	7,554	"
" France	8,267	"
" Belgium	328	"
" Holland	1,237	"
" British America and Canada	4,338	"
" Cuba	1,293	"
" China	115	"
" Denmark	682	"
" Italy	2,790	"
" Mexico	64	"
" Norway	373	"
" Poland	2,392	"
" Portugal	92	"
" Russia	1,139	"
" South America	213	"
" Spain	464	"
" Sweden	1,569	"
" Switzerland	2,169	"
" Turkey	38	"
" Wales	587	"
" West Indies	487	"

Besides those mentioned in this table, are representatives of every nationality under heaven, in greater or less strength. It will be seen that the native population is in the excess. The increase of natives between 1860 and 1870, was 93,246. The Germans increased in the same period at the rate of 32,936 ; while the Irish population fell off 1701 in the same decade. The foreign classes frequently herd together by themselves, in distinct parts of the city, which they seem to regard as their own. In some sections are to be found whole streets where the inhabitants do not understand English, having no occasion to use it in their daily life.

In 1869, there were 13,947 births, 8695 marriages, and 24,-601 deaths reported by the city authorities. The authorities stated that they were satisfied that the number of births was actually over 30,000 ; the number reported by them being very incomplete, owing to the difficulty of procuring such information.

Its mixed population makes New York a thoroughly cosmopolitan city, yet at the same time it is eminently American. The native element exercises a controlling influence upon all its acts, and when the proper exertion is made rarely fails to maintain its ascendancy.

The number of buildings in the city is from 60,000 to 70,000. In 1860, out of 161,000 families only 15,000 occupied entire houses. Nine thousand one hundred and twenty dwellings contained two families each, and 6100 contained three families each. After these come the tenement houses. At present, the number of houses occupied by more than one family is even larger.

It has been well said that " New York is the best place in the world to take the conceit out of a man." This is true. No matter how great or flattering is the local reputation of an individual, he finds upon reaching New York that he is entirely unknown. He must at once set to work to build up a reputation here, where he will be taken for just what he is worth, and no more. The city is a good school for studying human nature, and its people are proficients in the art of discerning character.

In point of morality, the people of New York, in spite of all that has been said of them, compare favorably with those of any other city. If the darkest side of life is to be seen here, one

THE CITY HALL PARK AS IT APPEARED IN 1869.

may also witness the best. The greatest scoundrels and the purest Christians are to be found here. It is but natural that New York, being the great centre of wealth, should also be the great centre of all that is good and beautiful in life. It is true that the Devil's work is done here on a gigantic scale, but the will of the Lord is done on an equally great, if not a greater scale.

In its charities, New York stands at the head of American communities—the great heart of the city throbs warmly for suffering humanity. The municipal authorities expend annually about one million of dollars in public charities. The various religious denominations spend annually about five millions more, and private benevolence disburses a sum of which no record is to be had—but it is large. Besides this, the city is constantly sending out princely sums to relieve want and suffering in all parts of our broad land. New York never turns a deaf ear to an appeal for aid.

The people of New York are very liberal in matters of opinion. Here, as a general rule, no man seeks to influence the belief of another, except so far as all men are privileged to do so. Every religious faith, every shade of political opinion, is protected and finds full expression. Men concern themselves with their own affairs only. Indeed this feeeling has been carried to such an extreme that it has engendered a decided indifference between man and man. People live for years as next door neighbors without ever knowing each other by sight. A gentleman once happened to notice the name of his next door neighbor on the door-plate. To his surprise he found it the same as his own. Accosting the owner of the door-plate one day, for the first time, he remarked that it was singular that two people bearing the same name should live side by side for years without knowing each other. This remark led to mutual inquiries and statements, and to their surprise the two men found they were brothers— sons of the same parents. They had not met for many years, and for fully twelve years had lived side by side as neighbors, without knowing each other. This incident may be overdrawn, but it will illustrate a peculiar feature of New York life.

Strangers coming to New York are struck with the fact that there are but two classes in the city—the poor and the rich. The middle class, which is so numerous in other cities, hardly exists at all here. The reason of this is plain to the initiated. Living in New York is so expensive that persons of moderate means reside in the suburbs, some of them as far as forty miles in the country. They come into the city, to their business, in crowds, between the hours of seven and nine in the morning, and literally pour out of it between four and seven in the evening. In fair weather the inconvenience of such a life is trifling, but in the winter it is absolutely fearful. A deep snow will sometimes obstruct the railroad tracks, and persons living outside of the city are either unable to leave New York or are forced to spend the night on the cars.   Again, the rivers will be so full of floating ice as to render it very dangerous, if not impossible, for the ferry boats to cross.   At such times the railroad depots and ferry houses are crowded with persons anxiously awaiting transportation to their homes.   The detention in New York, however, is not the greatest inconvenience caused by such mishaps.

To persons of means, New York offers more advantages as a place of residence than any city in the land.   Its delightful climate, its cosmopolitan and metropolitan character, and the endless variety of its attractions and comforts, render it the most delightful home in America.   Its people are warmly attached to and proud of it, and even strangers feel drawn towards it as to no other city save their own homes.   Few persons care to leave it after a twelve-months' residence within its limits, and those who are forced to go away generally find their way back at the earliest opportunity.

II.

THE HARBOR OF NEW YORK.

THE bay and harbor of New York are noted the world over for their beauty. When the discoverer, Henry Hudson, first gazed upon the glorious scene, he gave vent to the impulsive assertion that it was "a very good land to fall in with, and a pleasant land to see," and there are few who will venture to differ from him.

To enjoy the wonderful beauty of the bay, one should enter it from the ocean; and it is from the blue water that we propose to begin our exploration.

Nineteen miles from the City of New York, on the western side of the bay, is a low, narrow, and crooked neck of sand, covered in some places with a dense growth of pine and other hardy trees. This neck is called Sandy Hook, and its curve encloses a pretty little bay, known as the Cove. On the extreme end of the point, which commands the main ship channel, the General Government is erecting a powerful fort, under the guns of which every vessel entering the bay must pass. There is also a lighthouse near the fort, and within the last few years a railway depot has been built on the shore of the Cove. Passengers from New York for Long Branch are transferred from the steamer to the cars at this place, the road running along the sea-shore to Long Branch. To the westward of Sandy Hook, on the Jersey shore, are the finely wooded and picturesque Highlands of Nevesink, and at their feet the Shrewsbury River flows into the bay, while some miles to the eastward are the shining sands and white houses of Rockaway Beach and Fire Island. Seven miles out at sea, tosses the Sandy Hook Light Ship, marking the point from which vessels must take their course in entering the bay.

THE HARBOR OF NEW YORK, AS SEEN FROM THE NARROWS.

Leaving Sandy Hook, our course is a little to the northwest.
The New Jersey shore is on our left, and we can see the dim
outlines of Port Monmouth and Perth Amboy and South
Amboy in the far distance, while to the right Coney Island and
its hotels are in full sight.   Back of these lie the low shores of
Long Island, dotted with pretty suburban villas and villages.
A few miles above Sandy Hook we pass the Quarantine station
in the Lower Bay, with the fleet of detained vessels clustering
about the hospital ships.

Straight ahead, on our left, is a bold headland, sloping away
from east to west, towards the Jersey coast.   This is Staten
Island, a favorite resort for New Yorkers, and taken up mainly
with their handsome country seats.   The bay here narrows
rapidly, and the shores of Staten and Long Islands are scarcely
a mile apart.   This passage is famous the world over as *The
Narrows*, and connects the Inner and Lower Bays.   The shores
are high on either side, but the Staten Island side is a bold

headland, the summit of which is over one hundred feet above the water. These high shores constitute the protection which the Inner Bay enjoys from the storms that howl along the coast. It is to them also that New York must look for protection in the event of a foreign war. Here are the principal fortifications of the city, and whichever way we turn the shores bristle with guns. On the Long Island shore is Fort Hamilton, an old but powerful work, begun in 1824, and completed in 1832, at a cost of $550,000. The main work mounts eighty heavy guns; but since the Civil War, additional batteries, some of them armed with Rodman guns, have been erected. A little above Fort Hamilton, and a few hundred yards from the shore, is Fort Lafayette, built on a shoal known as Hendricks' Reef. It was begun during the war of 1812, cost $350,000, and was armed with seventy-three guns. It was used during the Civil War as a jail for political prisoners. In December, 1868, it was destroyed by fire, and the Government is now rebuilding it upon a more formidable scale. The Staten Island shore is lined with guns. At the water's edge is a powerful casemated battery, known as Fort Tompkins, mounting forty heavy guns. The bluff above is crowned with a large and formidable looking work, also of granite, known as Fort Richmond, mounting one hundred and forty guns. To the right and left of the fort, are Batteries Hudson, Morton, North Cliff, and South Cliff, mounting about eighty guns of heavy calibre. It is stated that the new work on Sandy Hook will be armed with two hundred guns, which will make the defensive armament of the Lower Bay and Narrows over six hundred and thirteen guns, which, together with the fleet of war vessels that could be assembled for the protection of the city, would render the capture of New York by an enemy's fleet a hazardous, if not impracticable, undertaking.

Passing through *The Narrows*, we enter the Inner Bay. New York, Brooklyn and Jersey City are in full sight to the northward, with the Hudson stretching away in the distance. The bay is crowded with shipping of all kinds, from the fussy little tug-boat to the large, grim-looking man-of-war. As we sail on, the scene becomes more animated. On the left are the picturesque heights of Staten Island, dotted thickly with country-seats, cottages, and pretty towns, and on the left the heavily-wooded shores of Long Island abound with handsome villas.

Soon Staten Island is passed, and we see the white lighthouse standing out in the water, which marks the entrance to the Kill Van Kull, or Staten Island Sound; and, far to the westward, we can faintly discern the shipping at Elizabethport. We are now fairly in the harbor of New York, with the great city directly in front of us, Brooklyn on our right, and Jersey City on our left. To the northward, the line of the Hudson melts away in the distant blue sky, and to the right the East River is lost in the shipping and houses of the two cities it separates. The scene is gay and brilliant. The breeze is fresh and delightful; the sky as clear and blue as that of Italy, and the bay as bright and beautiful as that of Naples, and even more majestic. As far as the eye can reach on either side of the Hudson extend the long lines of shipping, while the East River is a perfect forest of masts. Here are steamboats and steamships, sailing vessels, barges, and canal boats—every sort of craft known to navigation. The harbor is gay with the flags of all nations. Dozens of ferry boats are crossing and recrossing from New York to the opposite shores. Ships are constantly entering and leaving port, and the whole scene bears the impress of the energy and activity that have made New York the metropolis of America.

At night the scene is indescribably beautiful. The myriad stars in the sky above are reflected in the dark bosom of the harbor. The dim outlines of the shores are made more distinct by the countless rows of lights that line them, and the many colored lamps of the ferry-boats, as they dart back and forth over the waters, give to the scene a sort of gala appearance.

There are several islands in the harbor, which have been entirely given up to the United States Government for military purposes. The largest of these is Governor's Island, formerly the property of the redoubtable Wouter Van Twiller, and still called after him. It lies midway between New York and Brooklyn, at the mouth of the East River. It embraces an area of seventy-two acres, and is one of the principal military posts in the harbor.   Fort Columbus, in the centre of the island, is the principal work.   Castle William, on the west end, is a semi-circular work, with three tiers of guns.   Two strong batteries defend the passage known as Buttermilk Channel, between the island and Brooklyn.   In the early days of the Dutch colony, this passage could be forded by cattle; now it is passable by ships of war.   These works are armed with upwards of 200 heavy guns.   Ellis Island, 2050 yards southwest from the Battery Light-House, contains Fort Gibson, mounting about twenty guns.   Bedloe's Island, 2950 yards southwest of the Battery Light-House, contains Fort Wood, which is armed with eighty guns.

The best point from which to view the Inner Bay is the Battery Park, from the sea-wall of which an uninterrupted view of the bay and both rivers may be obtained.

III.

THE CITY GOVERNMENT.

By the terms of the charter of 1870, the government of the City of New York is vested in a Mayor, Common Council, consisting of Aldermen and Assistant Aldermen, a Corporation Counsel, and Comptroller, all elected by the people. There are also a Department of Public Works, which has charge of the streets of the city, and the Croton Aqueduct and Reservoirs; a Department of Docks, charged with the construction of new piers, etc., along the harbor front; a Department of Public Parks; a Fire Department; a Health Department; and a Police Board. The heads of all these Departments are appointed by the Mayor of the city. Previous to 1870 the city was governed by a series of commissions appointed by the Governor of the State, and the citizens were deprived of all voice in the management of their own affairs. It was urged by the friends of the New Charter, that that instrument restored to the citizens of New York the right of self-government. Had its provisions been honestly carried out, New York might have had a good government; but we shall see that they were perverted by a band of corrupt men into the means of the grossest oppression of the citizens.

For many years it was the habit of the respectable and educated classes of New York to abstain from voting. Many, indeed, boasted that they were utterly indifferent to politics; that it was immaterial to them which party elected its candidates. Others thought that they could not spare the time; and others still would not spare it. Again, there were those whose refined tastes made them shrink from the coarse rabble that surrounded the voting places. The reasons were almost as numerous as the delinquents, and the result was that the best portion of the voters

of the city—those who were most interested in a good government—left the control of public affairs entirely in the hands of
the worst and most vicious classes.   As a natural consequence,
the suffrage being exercised chiefly by the ignorant and degraded, corrupt men availed themselves of the opportunity afforded them, and, by bribery and kindred practices, managed to
secure their election to power.   Once in office, they exerted
themselves to remain there.   They were the rulers of the great
Metropolis of the Union, and, as such, possessed power and influence unequalled in any city in the world.   They controlled
the public funds, and thus had an opportunity of enriching
themselves by robbing the people.   They held in their grasp all
the machinery of elections, and, by filling the ballot-boxes with
fraudulent votes, and throwing out those which were legally
cast, they could, they believed, perpetuate their power.   If their
strength in the Legislature of the State was inadequate to the
passage of the laws they favored, they robbed the city treasury
to buy up the members of the Legislature opposed to them, and
it was found that rural virtue was easily purchased at city
prices.   In this way they secured the enactment of laws tending
not only to enlarge and perpetuate their powers, and to increase
their opportunities for plunder, but also to bar the way of the
people should they awake from their criminal carelessness, and
seek to overthrow and punish them.   It mattered very little to
the men who ruled the city of New York how the elections were
decided in the rural districts.   They could always swell their
vote in the city to an extent sufficient to overcome any hostile
majority in the State ; and they even boasted that they cared not
how many votes were cast against them in the city, as long as
they " had the counting of them."   In this way they filled the
statute-book with laws for the oppression and injury of the
people, and in this way they passed the New Charter of 1870,
which they declared was meant to restore self-government to
New York, but which was really designed to continue themselves in power, and break down the last obstacles between
themselves and the city treasury.

In well-regulated municipal governments, the popular branch,
5

the Common Council, is designed to act, and does act, as a check upon the Executive branch. In New York, a Common Council which thoroughly represented the people of the city—the great commercial, social, and political Metropolis of the Union—would have given the Executive branch of the City Government no little trouble; but the respectable citizens were indifferent to the selection of Councilmen, and the " Ring " took care that the majority of the " City Fathers " were creatures of their own, under obligations to them, and ready to sustain them in any outrage upon the people.

The Common Council of the City of New York can hardly be termed a representative body. It does not represent the honestly gotten wealth of the city; for, though many of its members are wealthy, people look with suspicion upon a rich Councilman. It does not represent the proud intellectual character of New York; for there is scarcely a member who has intellect or education enough to enable him to utter ten sentences in good English. For many years the Councils have been composed of small tradesmen, who found politics more profitable than their legitimate callings, of bar-keepers, of men without social position in the city they professed to represent, and many of whom were suspected of dishonest and corrupt practices by their fellow-citizens. Indeed, it may be said, that, with a very few exceptions, there was not a man in this important body who possessed the respect or confidence of the citizens of New York. They were elected by bribery and corruption, maintained their positions by the same means, and enjoyed the favor and protection of the leaders of their party, only by aiding the execution and covering up from investigation the schemes of those men for their mutual engorgement at the expense of the public treasury.

Mr. James Parton gives the following account of the proceedings of this worshipful body:

" Debates is a ludicrous word to apply to the proceedings of the Councilmen. Most of the business done by them is pushed through without the slightest discussion, and is of such a nature that members cannot be prepared to discuss it. The most reckless haste marks every part of the performance. A member proposes that certain lots be provided with curbstones; another, that a free drinking hydrant be placed on a certain corner five miles up town; and another, that certain blocks of a distant street be paved with Belgian pavement. Respecting the utility of these works, members generally know nothing, and can say nothing; nor are they proper objects of legislation. The resolutions are adopted, usually, without a word of explanation, and at a speed that must be seen to be appreciated.

.   .   .   .

"At almost every session we witnessed scenes like the following: A member proposed to lease a certain building for a city court at $2000 a year for ten years. Honest Christopher Pullman, a faithful and laborious public servant, objected on one or two grounds; first, rents being unnaturally high, owing to several well-known and temporary causes, it would be unjust to the city to fix the rent at present rates for so long a period; secondly, he had been himself to see the building, had taken pains to inform himself as to its value, and was prepared to prove that $1200 a year was a proper rent for it even at the inflated rates. He made this statement with excellent brevity, moderation, and good temper, and concluded by moving that the term be two instead of ten years. A robust young man, with a bull neck and of ungrammatical habits, said, in a tone of impatient disdain, that the landlord of the building had 'refused' $1500 a year for it. 'Question!' 'Question!' shouted half a dozen angry voices; the question was instantly put, when a perfect war of *noes* voted down Mr. Pullman's amendment. Another hearty chorus of *ayes* consummated the iniquity. In all such affairs, the visitor notices a kind of ungovernable propensity to vote for spending money, and a prompt disgust at any obstacle raised or objection made. The bull-necked Councilman of uncertain grammar evidently felt that Mr. Pullman's modest interference on behalf of the tax-payer was a most gross impertinence. He felt himself an injured being, and his companions shared his indignation.

"We proceed to another and better specimen: A resolution was introduced, appropriating $4000 for the purpose of present-

ing stands of colors to five regiments of city militia, which were
named, each stand to cost eight hundred dollars. Mr. Pullman, as usual, objected, and we beg the reader to mark his
objections. He said that he was a member of the committee
which had reported the resolution, but he had never heard of
it till that moment, the scheme had been 'sprung' upon him.
The chairman of the committee replied to this, that, since the
other regiments had had colors given them by the city, he did
not suppose that any one could object to these remaining five
receiving the same compliment, and therefore he had not thought
it worth while to summon the gentleman. 'Besides,' said he,
'it is a small matter anyhow;'—by which he evidently meant
to intimate that the objector was a very small person. To
this last remark, a member replied, that he did not consider
$4000 so very small a matter. 'Anyhow,' he added, 'we
oughter save the city every dollar we kin.' Mr. Pullman
resumed. He stated that the Legislature of the State, several
months before, had voted a stand of colors to each infantry
regiment in the State; that the distribution of these colors had
already begun; that the five regiments would soon receive
them; and that, consequently, there was no need of their having
the colors which it was now proposed to give them. A member roughly replied, that the colors voted by the State Legislature were mere painted banners, 'of no account.' Mr. Pullman denied this. 'I am,' said he, 'captain in one of our city
regiments. Two weeks ago we received our colors. I have
seen, felt, examined, and marched under them; and I can
testify that they are of great beauty, and excellent quality,
made by Tiffany & Co., a firm of the first standing in the city.'
He proceeded to describe the colors as being made of the best
silk, and decorated in the most elegant manner. He further
objected to the price proposed to be given for the colors. He
declared that, from his connection with the militia, he had
become acquainted with the value of such articles, and he could
procure colors of the best kind ever used in the service for
$375. The price named in the resolution was, therefore, most
excessive. Upon this, another member rose and said, in a

peculiarly offensive manner, that it would be two years before Tiffany & Co. had made all the colors, and some of the regiments would have to wait all that time. 'The other regiments,' said he, 'have had colors presented by the city, and I don't see why we should show partiality.' Whereupon Mr. Pullman informed the board that the *city* regiments would all be supplied in a few weeks; and, even if they did have to wait awhile, it was of no consequence, for they all had very good colors already. Honest Stephen Roberts then rose, and said that this was a subject with which he was not acquainted, but that if no one could refute what Mr. Pullman had said, he should be obliged to vote against the resolution.

"Then there was a pause. The cry of 'Question!' was heard. The ayes and noes were called. The resolution was carried by eighteen to five. The learned suppose that one-half of this stolen $4000 was expended upon the colors, and the other half divided among about forty persons. It is conjectured that each member of the Councilmen's Ring, which consists of thirteen, received about forty dollars for his vote on this occasion. This sum, added to his pay, which is twenty dollars per session, made a tolerable afternoon's work.

"Any one witnessing this scene would certainly have supposed that *now* the militia regiments of the City of New York were provided with colors. What was our surprise to hear, a few days after, a member gravely propose to appropriate $800 for the purpose of presenting the Ninth Regiment of New York Infantry with a stand of colors. Mr. Pullman repeated his objections, and recounted anew the generosity of the State Legislature. The eighteen, without a word of reply, voted for the grant as before. It so chanced that, on our way up Broadway, an hour after, we met that very regiment marching down with its colors flying; and we observed that those colors were nearly new. Indeed, there is such a propensity in the public to present colors to popular regiments, that some of them have as many as five stands, of various degrees of splendor. There is nothing about which Councilmen need feel so little anxiety as a deficiency in the supply of regimental colors. When, at last, these extravagant banners voted by the corporation are pre-sented to the regiments, a new scene of plunder is exhibited. The officers of the favored regiment are invited to a room in the basement of the City Hall, where city officials assist them to consume $300 worth of champagne, sandwiches, and cold chicken—paid for out of the city treasury—while the privates of the regiment await the return of their officers in the unshaded portion of the adjacent park.

" It is a favorite trick with these councilmen, as of all poli-ticians, to devise measures, the passage of which will gratify large *bodies* of voters. This is one of the advantages proposed to be gained by the presentation of colors to regiments ; and the same system is pursued with regard to churches and societies. At every one of the six sessions of the Councilmen which we at-tended, resolutions were introduced to give away the people's money to wealthy organizations. A church, for example, is assessed $1000 for the construction of a sewer, which enhances the value of the church property by at least the amount of the assessment. Straightway, a member from that neighborhood proposes to console the stricken church with a 'donation' of $1000, to enable it to pay the assessment; and as this is a pro-position to vote money, it is carried as a matter of course. We select from our notes only one of these donating scenes. A member proposed to give $2000 to a certain industrial school,—the favorite charity of the present time, to which all the benevo-lent most willingly subscribe. Vigilant Christopher Pullman reminded the board that it was now unlawful for the corporation to vote money for any object not specified in the tax levy as finally sanctioned by the Legislature. He read the section of the Act which forbade it. He further showed, from a statement by the Comptroller, that there was no money left at their dis-posal for any *miscellaneous* objects, since the appropriation for 'city contingencies' was exhausted. The only reply to his re-marks was the instant passage of the resolution by eighteen to five. By what artifice the law is likely to be evaded in such cases, we may show further on. In all probability, the indus-trial school, in the course of the year, will receive a fraction of

this money—perhaps even so large a fraction as one half. It
may be that, ere now, some obliging person about the City Hall
has offered to buy the claim for $1000, and take the risk of the
hocus-pocus necessary for getting it—which to *him* is no risk
at all.

"It was proposed, on another occasion, to raise the fees of
the Inspectors of Weights and Measures—who received fifty
cents for inspecting a pair of platform scales, and smaller sums
for scales and measures of less importance.   Here was a subject
upon which honest Stephen Roberts, whose shop is in a street
where scales and measures abound, was entirely at home.   He
showed, in his sturdy and strenuous manner, that, at the rates
then established, an active man could make $200 a day.
'Why,' said he, 'a man can inspect, and does inspect, fifty
platform scales.in an hour.'   The cry of 'Question!' arose.
The question was put, and the usual loud chorus of *ayes*
followed.

"As it requires a three-fourths vote to grant money—that is,
eighteen members—it is sometimes impossible for the Ring to
get that number together.   There is a mode of preventing the
absence, or the opposition of members, from defeating favorite
schemes.   It is by way of 'reconsideration.'   The time was
when a measure distinctly voted down by a lawful majority was
dead.   But, by this expedient, the voting down of a measure is
only equivalent to its postponement to a more favorable occasion.   The moment the chairman pronounces a resolution lost,
the member who has it in charge moves a reconsideration; and,
as a reconsideration only requires the vote of a majority, *this* is
invariably carried.   By a rule of the board, a reconsideration
carries a measure over to a future meeting—to any future meeting which may afford a prospect of its passage.   The member
who is engineering it watches his chance, labors with faltering
members out of doors, and, as often as he thinks he can carry it,
calls it up again, until at last the requisite eighteen are obtained.   It has frequently happened that a member has kept a
measure in a state of reconsideration for months at a time, waiting for the happy moment to arrive.   There was a robust young

Councilman, who had a benevolent project in charge of paying $900 for a hackney-coach and two horses, which a drunken driver drove over the dock into the river one cold night last winter. There was some disagreement in the Ring on this measure, and the robust youth was compelled to move for many reconsiderations. So, also, it was long before the wires could be all arranged to admit of the appointment of a 'messenger' to the City Librarian, who has perhaps less to do than any man in New York who is paid $1800 a year; but perseverance meets its reward. We hear that this messenger is now smoking in the City Hall at a salary of $1500.

"There is a manœuvre also for preventing the attendance of obnoxious, obstructive members, like the honest six, which is ingenious and effective. A 'special meeting' is called. The law declares that notice of a special meeting must be left at the residence *or* the place of business of every member. Mr. Roberts's residence and Mr. Roberts's place of business are eight miles apart, and he leaves his home for the day before nine in the morning. If Mr. Roberts's presence at a special meeting, at 2 P. M., is desired, the notice is left at his shop in the morning. If it is not desired, the notice is sent to his house in Harlem, after he has left it. Mr. Pullman, cabinet-maker, leaves his shop at noon, goes home to dinner, and returns soon after one. If his presence at the special meeting, at 2 P. M., is desired, the notice is left at his house the evening before, or at his shop in the morning. If his presence is not desired, the notice is left at his shop a few minutes after twelve, or at his house a few minutes past one. In either case, he receives the notice too late to reach the City Hall in time. We were present in the Councilmen's Chamber when Mr. Pullman stated this *inconvenience*, assuming that it was accidental, and offered an amendment to the rule, requiring notice to be left five hours before the time named for the meeting. Mr. Roberts also gave his experience in the matter of notices, and both gentlemen spoke with perfect moderation and good temper. We wish we could convey to our readers an idea of the brutal insolence with which Mr. Pullman, on this occasion, was snubbed and defrauded by a young bar-keeper who chanced to be in the chair.   But this would be impossible without relating the scene at very great length.   The amendment proposed was voted down, with that peculiar roar of *noes* which is always heard in that chamber when some honest man attempts to put an obstacle in the way of the free plunder of his fellow-citizens.

"These half-fledged legislators are acquainted with the device known by the name of the ' previous question.'   We witnessed a striking proof of this.   One of the most audacious and insolent of the Ring introduced a resolution, vaguely worded, the object of which was to annul an old paving contract, that would not pay at the present cost of labor and materials, and to authorize a new contract at higher rates.   Before the clerk had finished reading the resolution, honest Stephen Roberts sprang to his feet, and, unrolling a remonstrance with several yards of signatures appended to it, stood, with his eye upon the chairman, ready to present it the moment the reading was concluded. This remonstrance, be it observed, was signed by a majority of the property-owners interested, the men who would be assessed to pay for one-half of the proposed pavement.   Fancy the impetuous Roberts, with the document held aloft, the yards of signatures streaming down to his feet, and flowing far under his desk, awaiting the time when it would be in order to cry out, ' Mr. President.'   The reading ceased.   Two voices were heard shouting, ' Mr. President.'   It was not to Mr. Roberts that an impartial chairman could assign the floor.   The member who introduced the resolution was the one who caught the speaker's eye, and that member, forewarned of Mr. Roberts's intention, moved the previous question.   It was in vain that Mr. Roberts shouted ' Mr. President ;' it was in vain that he fluttered his streaming ribbon of blotted paper.   The President could not hear a word of any kind until a vote had been taken upon the question whether the main question should now be put.   The question was carried in the affirmative by a chorus of *ayes,* so exactly timed that it was like the voice of one man.   Then the main question *was* put, and it was carried by another emphatic and simultaneous shout."

Under the rule of such a Council the public money disappeared. Men who went into the Council poor came out of it
rich. Taxes increased, the cost of governing the city became
greater, crime flourished, and the chief city of the Union became
noted for its corrupt government.

IV.

"THE RING."

I.

THE HISTORY OF THE RING.

WE have spoken of the outrages practised upon the citizens of New York by the Common Council of that city. We must now turn our attention to the other branches of the City Government, and investigate the conduct of the real rulers of New York.

For several years the political power and patronage has been lodged in the hands of, and exercised by a set of men commonly known as " *The Ring.*" They rose to power in consequence of the neglect of their political duties by the respectable citizens of New York, and, having attained power, were not slow in arranging affairs so that their ill-gotten authority might be perpetuated. They controlled the elections by bribery, and the fraudulent counting of votes, and so filled the elective offices with their own creatures. Having done this, they proceeded to appoint to the other offices only such men as were bound to them, and whom they could trust to cover up their mutual dishonesty. Competency to discharge the duties of the offices thus given was not once considered. The Ring cared only for men who would unite in plundering the public treasury, and be vigilant in averting the detection of the theft. They wanted to exercise political power, it is true, but they also desired to enrich themselves at the public expense.

Having secured the city offices, with the control of the finances, the police, the fire department, and the immense patronage of the city, they believed themselves strong enough to hold all they had won. They did not believe that the people of New York would ever awake to a true sense of their public duties, and, if they did, the Ring felt confident that they could control any election by filling the ballot-boxes with fraudulent votes. In many cases money was taken from the city treasury, and used to purchase votes for the Ring or Tammany Hall ticket. It was also used to bribe inspectors of elections to certify any returns that the leaders of the Ring might decide upon; and it came to be a common saying in New York that the Tammany ticket could always command a majority in the city sufficient to neutralize any hostile vote in the rest of the State. If the leaders of the Ring desired a majority of 25,000, 30,000, or any number, in the city, that majority was returned, and duly sworn to by the inspectors of election, even by those of the party opposed to the Ring; for money was used unsparingly to buy dishonest inspectors.

As a matter of course, no honest man took part in these disgraceful acts, and the public offices passed, almost without exception, into the hands of the most corrupt portion of the population. They were also the most ignorant and brutal. The standard of education is, perhaps, lower among the public officials of New York than among any similar body in the land. Men whose personal character was infamous; men who were charged by the newspaper press, and some of whom had been branded by courts of justice with felonies, were elected or appointed to responsible offices. The property, rights and safety of the greatest and most important city in the land, were entrusted to a band of thieves and swindlers. The result was what might have been expected. Public interests were neglected; the members of the Ring were too busy enriching themselves at the expense of the treasury to attend to the wants of the people. The City Government had never been so badly administered before, and the only way in which citizens could obtain their just rights was by paying individual members of the Ring or their satellites to attend to their particular cases. It was found almost impossible to collect money due by the city to private parties; but, at the same time, the Ring drew large sums from the public treasury. Men who were notoriously poor when they went into office were seen to grow suddenly and enormously rich. They made the most public displays of their suddenly acquired magnificence, and, in many ways, made themselves so offensive to their respectable neighbors, that the virtue and intelligence of the city avoided all possible contact with them. Matters finally became so bad that a man laid himself open to grave suspicion by the mere holding of a municipal office. Even the few good men who retained public positions, and whom the Ring had not been able, or had not dared, to displace, came in for a share of the odium attaching to all offices connected with the City Government. It was unjust, but not unnatural. So many office-holders were corrupt that the people naturally regarded all as in the same category.

In order to secure undisturbed control of the city, the Ring took care to win over the Legislature of the State to their schemes. There was a definite and carefully arranged programme carried out with respect to this. The delegation from the City of New York was mainly secured by the Ring, and agents were sent to Albany to bribe the members of the Legislature to vote for the schemes of the Ring. Mr. Samuel J. Tilden, in his speech at Cooper Institute, November 2, 1871, says that $1,000,000, stolen from the treasury of the city, were used by the Ring to buy up a majority of the two Houses of the Legislature. By means of these purchased votes, the various measures of the Ring were passed. The principal measure was the Charter of the City of New York. " Under the pretence of giving back to the people of the City of New York local self-government, they provided that the Mayor then in office should appoint all the heads of Departments for a period of at least four years, and in some cases extending to eight, and that when those heads of Departments, *already privately agreed upon*, were once appointed they should be removable only by the Mayor, who could not be impeached except on his own motion, and then must be tried by a court of six members, every one of whom must be present in order to form a quorum. And then they stripped every legislative power, and every executive power from every other functionary of the government, and vested it in half a dozen men so installed for a period of from four to eight years in supreme dominion over the people of this city." *

Besides passing this infamous charter, the Ring proceeded to ,fortify their position with special legislation, designed to protect them against any effort of the citizens to drive them from office, or punish them. This done, they had unlimited control of all the public affairs, and could manage the elections as they pleased, and they believed they were safe.

The "Committee of Seventy," appointed by the citizens of New York to investigate the charges against the municipal authorities, thus speak of the effect of the adoption of the New Charter, in their report presented at the great meeting at Cooper Institute, on the 2d of November, 1871 :

"There is not in the history of villainy a parallel for the gigantic crime against property conspired by the Tammany Ring. It was engineered on the complete subversion of free government in the very heart of Republicanism. An American city, having a population of over a million, was disfranchised by an open vote of a Legislature born and nurtured in Democracy and Republicanism, and was handed over to a self-appointed oligarchy, to be robbed and plundered by them and their confederates, heirs and assigns for six years certainly, and prospectively for ever. A month's exhumation among the crimes of the Tammany leaders has not so familiarized us with the political paradox of the New Charter of the City of New York, that we do not feel that it is impossible that the people of this State gave to a gang of thieves, politicians by profession, a charter to govern the commercial metropolis of this continent—the great city which is to America what Paris is to France—to govern it with a government made unalterable for the sixteenth part of a century, which substantially deprived the citizens of self-control, nullified their right to suffrage, nullified the principle of representation—which authorized a handful of cunning and resolute robbers to levy taxes, create pub-

---

* Samuel J. Tilden's speech.

lic debt, and incur municipal liabilities without limit and without check, and which placed at their disposal the revenues of the great municipality and the property of all its citizens.

"Every American will say: 'It is incredible that this has been done.' But the history of the paradox is over two years old. And it is a history of theft, robbery, and forgery, which have stolen and divided twenty millions of dollars; which have run up the city debt from $36,000,000 in 1869 to $97,000,000 in 1871, and which will be $120,000,000 by August, 1872; which have paid to these robbers millions of dollars for work never performed and materials never furnished; which paid astoundingly exorbitant rents to them for offices and armories, many of which were never occupied and some of which did not exist—which remitted their taxes, released their indebtedness, and remitted their rents, to the city due and owing—which ran the machinery for widening, improving and opening streets, parks and boulevards, to enable these men to speculate in assessed damages and greatly enhanced values—which created unnecessary offices with large salaries and no duties, in order to maintain a force of ruffianly supporters and manufacturers of votes—which used millions of dollars to bribe and corrupt newspapers, the organs of public opinion, in violation of laws which narrowly limited the public advertising—which camped within the city a reserve army of voters by employing thousands of laborers at large pay upon nominal work, neither necessary nor useful—which bought legislatures and purchased judgments from courts both civil and criminal.

. . . .

"Fellow-citizens of the City and State of New York, this report of the doings of the Committee of Seventy would be incomplete if it did not fully unfold to you the perils and the difficulties of our condition. You know too well that the Ring which governs us for years governed our Legislatures by bribing their members with moneys stolen from their trusts. That, seemingly, was supreme power and immunity. But it was not enough. A City Charter to perpetuate power was needed. It was easily bought of a venal Legislature with the proceeds of a

new scoop into the city treasury. Superadded to this the
Ring had devised a system, faultless and absolutely sure, of
counting their adversaries in an election out of office and of
counting their own candidates in, or of rolling up majorities by
repeating votes and voting in the names of the absent, the
dead, and the fictitious. Still their intrenched camp of villainy
was incomplete. It was deficient in credit. This is a ghastly
jest, the self-investment of the robbers of the world with a
boundless financial credit. And yet the Ring clothed themselves
with it. They entrenched themselves within the imposing limits
of some of our most powerful bank and trust companies. They
created many savings banks out of the forty-two which exist in
the city and county of New York. This they did within the
last two years. The published lists of directors will enable
you to identify these institutions. Now the savings bank is a
place to which money travels to be taken care of; and if the
bank has the public confidence, people put their money in it
freely at low rates of interest, and the managers use the funds
in whatever way they please. In the Ring savings banks there
are on deposit to-day, at nominal rates of interest, many millions
of dollars. It is believed that into these banks the Ring have
taken the city's obligations and converted them into money, which
has been sent flowing into the various channels of wasteful administration, out of which they have drawn into their pockets
millions on millions. The craft of this contrivance was profound. It wholly avoided the difficulty of raising money on
the unlawful and excessive issues of city and county bonds, and
took out of public sight transactions which, if pressed upon the
national banks, would have provoked comment and resistance,
and have precipitated the explosion which has shaken the country.
I think that among the assets of the savings banks of this city,
county and State will be found not far from $50,000,000 of
city and county debt taken for permanent investment. For the
first time in the history of iniquity has the bank for the saving
of the wages of labor been expressly organized as a part of a
system of robbery; and for the first time in the history of felony
have the workmen and workwomen, and the orphans and the

children of a great city unwittingly cashed the obligations issued by a gang of thieves and plunderers."

Having made themselves secure, as they believed, the Ring laughed at the idea of punishment, if detected. They not only controlled the elections, but they also controlled the administration of justice. The courts were filled with their creatures, and were so distorted from the purposes of the law and the ends of justice, that no friend of the Ring had any cause to fear punishment at their hands, however great his crime. The majority of the crimes committed in the city were the acts of the adherents of the Ring, but they escaped punishment, as a rule, except when a sacrifice to public opinion was demanded. If the criminal happened to be a politician possessing any influence among the disreputable classes, he was sure of acquittal. The magistrate before whom he was tried, dared not convict him, for fear of incurring either his enmity, or the censure of the leaders of the Ring to whom his influence was of value. So crime of all kinds increased in the city.

Under the protection of the New Charter, the Ring began a systematic campaign of robbery. Section four of the County Tax Levy, one of their measures, provided that liabilities against the county, the limits of which coincide with those of the city, should be audited by the Mayor, the Comptroller and the President of the Board of Supervisors, or in other words, Mayor Hall, Comptroller Connolly, and Mr. William M. Tweed, and that the amount found to be due should be paid. "These Auditors," says Mr. Tilden, "met but once. They then passed a resolution, which stands on the records of the city in the handwriting of Mayor Hall. It was passed on his motion, and what was its effect? It provided that all claims certified by Mr. Tweed and Mr. Young, Secretary of the old Board of Supervisors, should be received, and, on sufficient evidence, paid." Thus the door was thrown open to fraud, and the crime soon followed. "Mayor Hall," continues Mr. Tilden, "is the responsible man for all this. He knew it was a fraudulent violation of duty on the part of every member of that Board of Audit to pass claims in the way they did."

6

The door being thus thrown open to fraud, the thefts of the public funds became numerous. All the appropriations authorized by law were quickly exhausted, and large sums of money were drawn from the treasury, without the slightest warrant of law.

The new Court House in the City Hall Park was a perfect gold mine to the Ring. Immense sums were paid out of the treasury for work upon this building, which is still unfinished. Very little of this money was spent on the building, the greater part being retained, or stolen by the Ring for their own private benefit. The Court House has thus far cost $12,000,000, and is unfinished. During the years 1869, 1870, and a part of 1871, the sum of about $8,223,979.89 was expended on the new Court House. During this period, the legislative appropriation for this purpose amounted to only $1,400,000. The Houses of Parliament in London, which cover an area of nearly eight acres, contain 100 staircases, 1100 apartments and more than two miles of corridors, and constitute one of the grandest architectural works of the world, cost less than $10,000,000. The Capitol of the United States at Washington, the largest and most magnificent building in America, will cost, when completed, about $12,000,000, yet, the unfinished Court House in New York has already cost more than the gorgeous Houses of Parliament, and as much as the grand Capitol of the Republic.

The Court House was not the only means made use of to obtain money. Heavy sums were drawn for printing, stationary, and the city armories, and upon other pretexts too numerous to mention. It would require a volume to illustrate and rehearse entire the robberies of the Ring. Valid claims against the city were refused payment unless the creditor would consent to add to his bill a sum named by, and for the use of, the Ring. Thus, a man having a claim of $1500 against the city, would be refused payment until he consented to make the amount $6000, or some such sum. If he consented, he received his $1500 without delay, and the $4500 was divided among the members of the Ring. When a sum sufficient for the de-

THE NEW COUNTY COURT HOUSE.

mands of the Ring could not be obtained by the connivance of actual creditors, forgery was resorted to. Claims were presented in the name of men who had no existence, who cannot now be found, and they were paid. The money thus paid went, as the recent investigations have shown, into the pockets of members of the Ring. Further than this, if Mr. John H. Keyser is to be believed, the Ring did not hesitate to forge the endorsements of living and well-known men. He says: "The published accounts charge that I have received upwards of $2,000,000 from the treasury. Among the warrants which purport to have been paid to me for county work alone *there are upwards of eight hundred thousand dollars which I never received nor saw, and the endorsements on which, in my name,* ARE CLEAR AND UNMISTAKABLE FORGERIES."

Another means of purloining money is thus described by Mr. Abram P. Genung, in a pamphlet recently issued by him:

"A careful examination of the books and pay-roll (of the Comptroller's Office) developed the important fact that the titles of several accounts might be duplicated by using different phraseology to convey the same meaning; and that by making up pay-rolls, by using fictitious names of persons alleged to be temporarily employed in his (the Comptroller's) department, he could even cheat the 'heathen Chinee,' who had invited him to take a hand in this little game of robbery. Hence, Mr. 'Slippery' set about finding additional titles for several of the accounts, and in this way 'Adjusted Claims' and 'County Liabilities' became synonymous terms, and all moneys drawn on either account, instead of being charged to any appropriation, became a part of the permanent debt of the city and county. Under the same skilful manipulation, 'County Contingencies,' and 'Contingencies in the Comptroller's Office' meant the same thing, as did also the amount charged to 'Contingencies in the Department of Finance,' generally charged in the city accounts to make it less conspicuous. Again, there are three distinct pay-rolls in the County Bureau. One of these contains the names of all the clerks regularly employed in the Bureau, and about a dozen names of persons who hold sinecure positions,

or have no existence. The other two rolls contain about forty
names, the owners of which, if, indeed, they have any owners,
have never worked an hour in the department. The last two
rolls are called 'Temporary Rolls,' and the persons whose
names are on them are said to be 'Temporary Clerks' in the
Comptroller's Office. One of them is paid out of the regular
appropriation of 'Salaries Executive,' but the other is paid out
of a fund raised by the sale of 'Riot Damages Indemnity
Bonds,' and becomes a part of the permanent debt of the county.
Again, there are no less than five different accounts to which
repairs and furniture for any of the public offices, or the
armories of the National Guard, can be charged; while more
than half of the aggregate thus paid out, is not taken out of
any appropriation, but is raised by the sale of revenue bonds or
other securities, which may be converted at the pleasure of the
Comptroller into long bonds, which will not be payable until
1911—forty years after many of the frauds which called them
into existence shall have been successfully consummated by
Connolly and his colleagues. . . . .
  " When it becomes necessary to place a man in an important
position, or a position where he must necessarily become acquainted with the secrets of the office, some one who is already
in the confidence of the thieves throws out a hint that their intended victim can make $100 or $200 a month, in addition to
his salary, by placing one or two fictitious names on one of the
rolls, and drawing the checks for the salaries to which actual
claimants would be entitled at the end of each month. This
involves the necessity of signing the fictitious names on the pay-
roll or voucher, when the check is received, and endorsing the
same name on the check before the bank will cash it. . . .
So long as he is willing to do their bidding, and to embark in
every description of rascality at their dictation, he can go along
very smoothly; but if he should become troublesome at any
time, or if he should show any conscientious scruples when
called upon to execute the will of his masters, they would turn
him adrift without an hour's warning, and crush him, with the
evidence of his guilt in their possession, if he had the hardihood

to whisper a word about the nefarious transactions he had witnessed."

We have not the space to enumerate the various methods of plundering the city adopted by the Ring. What we have given will enable the reader to obtain a clear insight into their system. During the years 1869 and 1870, the following sums were paid by the Comptroller:

Keyser & Co	$1,561,619.42
Ingersoll & Co	3,006,391.72
C. D. Bollar & Co	951,911.84
J. A. Smith	809,298.96
A. G. Miller	626,896.74
Geo. S. Miller	1.568,447.62
A. J. Garvey and others	3,112,590.34
G. L. Schuyler	463,039.27
J. McBride Davidson	404,347.72
E. Jones & Co	341,882.18
Chas. H. Jacobs	164,923.17
Archibald Hall, jr	349,062.85
J. W. Smith	53,852.83
New York Printing Co	2,042,798.99
Total	$15,457,063.65

These are the figures given by the "Joint Committee of Supervisors and Aldermen appointed to investigate the public accounts of the City and County of New York." * In their report, presented about the 9th of October, 1871, they say: "Your Committee find that immense sums have been paid for services which have not been performed, for materials which have not been furnished, and to employés who are unknown in the offices from which they draw their salaries. Also, that parties having just claims upon the city, failing to obtain payment therefor, have assigned their claims to persons officially or otherwise connected with different departments, who have in

---

* The Committee of citizens consisted of the leading merchants of New York—such men as Royal Phelps, Robert Lenox, P. Bissinger, Paul N. Spofford, Samuel Willets, H. B. Claflin, Seth B. Hunt, T. F. Jeremiah, R. L. Cutting, W. A. Booth, Jas. Brown, B. L. Solomon, Courtlandt Palmer, J. K. Porter, W. E. Dodge, T. W. Pearsall.

many instances fraudulently increased their amounts, and drawn fourfold the money actually due from the city. Thus it appears in the accounts that hundreds of thousands of dollars have been paid to private parties who positively deny the receipt of the money, or any knowledge whatever of the false bills representing the large sums paid to them. These investigations compel the belief that not only the most reckless extravagance, but frauds and peculations of the grossest character have been practised in several of the departments, and that these must have been committed in many instances with the knowledge and co-operation of those appointed, and whose sworn duty it was to guard and protect the public interests."

Under the management of the Ring, the cost of governing the city was about thirty millions of dollars annually. The city and county debt (practically the same, since both are paid by the citizens of New York,) was doubled every two years. On the 1st of January, 1869, it was $36,000,000. By January 1st, 1871, it had increased to $73,000,000. On the 14th of September, 1871, it was $97,287,525, and the Citizens' Committee declare that there is grave reason to believe that it will reach $120,000,000 during the present year (1871).

For several years the Ring continued their robberies of the treasury, enriching themselves and bringing the city nearer to bankruptcy every year. Taxes increased, property was assessed for improvements that were never made, and the assessments were rigorously collected. Large sums were paid for cleaning the streets, which streets were kept clean only by the private subscriptions of the citizens residing in them, as the writer can testify from his personal experience. The burdens of the people became heavier and heavier, and the members of the Ring grew richer and richer. They built them palatial residences in the city, and their magnificent equipages were the talk of the town. They gave sumptuous entertainments, they flaunted their diamonds and jewels in the eyes of a dumbfounded public, they made ostentatious gifts to the poor, and munificent subscriptions to cathedrals and churches, *all with money stolen from the city;* and with this same money they endeavored to control the operations of Wall street, the great financial centre of the Republic. They built them country seats, the beauty and magnificence of which were duly set forth in the illustrated journals of the day; and they surrounded themselves with every luxury they could desire—all with money stolen from the city. Did any man dare to denounce their robberies, they turned upon him with one accord, and the whole power of the Ring was used to crush their daring assailant. They encouraged their adherents to levy black mail upon the citizens of New York, and it came to be well understood in the great city that no man, however innocent, arrested on a civil process, could hope to regain the liberty which was his birthright, without paying the iniquitous toll levied upon him by some portion of the Ring. Even the great writ of Habeas Corpus—the very bulwark of our liberties—was repeatedly set at defiance by the underlings of the Ring, for the purpose of extorting money from some innocent man who had fallen into their clutches.

The Ring was all-powerful in the great city, and they there built up an organized despotism, the most infamous known to history. No man's rights, no man's liberties were safe, if he ventured to oppose them. They even sought to strike down freedom of speech and the liberty of the press. Mr. Samuel J. Tilden, in the speech from which we have quoted before in this chapter, makes this distinct charge against them. He says : " Mr. Evarts went to Albany last year, and carried with him my protest against the passage of the law giving to the judges a power unknown in the jurisprudence of this State—unknown in the jurisprudence of the United States for the last thirty years— *whereby it was secured that any member of the City Government that might be offended, could put his hand upon the city press, and suppress its liberties and freedom of speech.*"

How long all this would have continued, it is impossible to say, had it not pleased God that there should be jealousies and dissensions amongst the members of the Ring strong enough to break even the infamous bonds that had so long bound them together.

The citizens of New York had for some time been slowly

coming to the conclusion that they were losing their rights and property, and had been seeking for some legal means of attacking and overthrowing the Ring. Their great necessity was absolute and definite proof of fraud on the part of certain individuals. This was for a long time lacking, but it came at length. In July, 1871, a former prominent member of the Ring, having quarrelled with the Ring over a claim of three or four hundred thousand dollars, which Mr. Tweed had refused to allow, avenged himself by causing the publication of a series of the public accounts, transcribed from the books of the Comptroller. These accounts showed the millions that had been fraudulently paid away for work which had never been done, and furnished the first definite evidence of fraud on the part of the members of the Ring that had been given to the public. The press, with the exception of a few unimportant sheets owned or controlled by the Ring, denounced the frauds, and demanded an investigation of the public accounts. Mayor Hall, William M. Tweed, Richard B. Connolly, and all the greater and lesser magnates of the Ring were implicated in the terrible story told by the published accounts. The respectable citizens, without regard to party, at once joined in the demand, and expressed their determination to put an end to the power of the Ring. The whole land—nay the whole civilized world —rang with a universal cry of indignation. The temper of the citizens was such as admitted of no trifling.

The publication of the Comptroller's accounts, which revealed the stupendous system of fraud they had practised so successfully, burst upon the Ring like a clap of thunder from a clear sky. It not only surprised them, but it demoralized them. They were fairly stunned. At first they affected to treat the whole matter as a partisan outburst which would soon "blow over." Some of the more timid took counsel of their fears and fled from the city, some even quitting the country. The more hardened endeavored " to brave it out," and defiantly declared that the citizens could not molest them. All the while the wrath of the people grew hotter, and the demand for the publication of the Comptroller's accounts became more urgent. Comptroller

Connolly, conscious of his guilt, met this demand with vague promises of compliance. Mayor Hall set himself to work to prove that the whole affair was a mistake, that no money had been stolen, that the City Government had been unjustly assailed, and by his ill-advised efforts drew upon himself a larger share of the public indignation and suspicion than had previously been accorded to him. The great object of the Ring was to gain time. They meant that the Comptroller's accounts should not be published, and to accomplish this they began the attempt to get possession of the Comptroller's office, the records of which contained the evidence of their crimes. With this important department in their hands they could suppress this evidence, or, if driven to desperation, destroy it. A council of the leaders of the Ring was called, at which it was resolved to get Mr. Connolly out of the Comptroller's office, and to put in his place a creature of their own. They did not dare, however, to make an effort to oust Connolly, without having some plausible pretext for their action. They feared that he would expose their mutual villainy, and involve them in his ruin, and they wished to prevent this. Still, they resolved to get rid of him, and their plan was first to crush him, and thus prevent his exposing them. We shall see how their plan worked.

Meanwhile the public indignation had been growing stronger daily. On the 4th of September, 1871, a large and harmonious meeting of citizens, without regard to party, was held at Cooper Institute. At this meeting it was resolved to compel an exposure of the frauds practised upon the people, and to punish the guilty parties; and committees were appointed, money subscribed, and the best legal talent in the city retained for that purpose. A reform movement to carry the November elections in the interest of the citizens and tax-payers was inaugurated, and the power of the courts was invoked to put a stop to the further expenditure of the city funds. The popular sentiment was too strong to be mistaken, and some of the leading officials, and several journals which had previously supported the Ring, took the alarm and entered the ranks of the party of Reform. The Democratic party of the State repudiated the Ring, and it was plain that the Tammany ticket would be supported only by the lowest classes of the city voters. The members of the Ring were now thoroughly aroused to the danger which threatened them; but, true to their corrupt instincts, they endeavored to meet it by fraud. They appointed a Committee of Aldermen to act with the Citizens' Committee in the investigation of the alleged frauds, and then withheld from them all evidence that could be of service to them.

The Comptroller's office contained not only the accounts of moneys paid out, but also the vouchers for all sums expended, properly signed and sworn to by the parties receiving the money, and these vouchers constituted the principal proof of the frauds. On Monday, September 11th, the city was startled by the announcement that the office of the Comptroller had been forcibly entered during the previous day, Sunday, and that the vouchers covering the principal transactions of the Ring had been stolen. It was a bold deed, and was so thoroughly characteristic of the Ring, that the public at once attributed it to that body. The Ring on their part endeavored to produce the belief that the Comptroller had stolen the vouchers to screen himself. Mayor Hall immediately wrote a peremptory letter to Mr. Connolly, asking him to resign his position as he (the Comptroller) had lost the confidence of the people. Mr. Connolly was not slow to perceive that the Ring were determined to sacrifice him to secure their own safety, and he declined to become their victim. He not only refused to resign his position at Mayor Hall's demand, but set to work vigorously to discover and bring to light the persons who had stolen the vouchers. To have stolen the vouchers himself, or to have countenanced the robbery, would have been worse than folly on the part of the Comptroller. It would have damaged him fatally with the citizens, who were disposed to deal lightly with him if he would aid them in getting at and punishing the villainies of his former confederates. There was no reason why he should seek to screen the Ring, for they made no secret of their intention to destroy him. In view, therefore, of the facts as at present known, it seems certain that the theft was brought about by the

Ring for the purpose of throwing the suspicion of the crime upon the Comptroller, and thus giving them a pretext for crushing him.

Wisely for himself, Mr. Connolly determined to let the Ring shift for themselves, and throw himself upon the mercy of the Reform party. He withdrew from the active discharge of the duties of his office, and appointed Mr. Andrew H. Green—an eminent citizen, possessing the respect and confidence of all parties—his deputy, with full powers, and avowed his determination to do his utmost to afford the Citizens' Committee a full and impartial investigation of his affairs. The Ring made great efforts to prevent his withdrawal, or, rather, the appointment of Mr. Green. Says Mr. Samuel J. Tilden, who was the real cause of this action on Mr. Connolly's part, and who was the acknowledged leader of the Reform Democracy during the contest:

" When Mr. Connolly came to my house on that morning on which he executed an abdication in favor of Mr. Green, he was accompanied by two counsel, one of whom was half an hour behind time, and I learned, not from him, but from other sources, that he spent that half hour at the house of Peter B. Sweeny. When the conference went on, he said, not speaking for himself individually, but still he would state the views taken by other friends of Mr. Connolly as to what he should do. He said he was assured that some respectable man would be put in the office of Comptroller, and that then he would say to Mr. Booth, of the Common Council Committee, and to the Committee of Seventy: 'I am competent to make every necessary investigation myself.' And that then everything that would hurt the party would be kept back; and that was the consideration presented to Mr. Connolly in my presence, and in the presence of Mr. Havemeyer and the two counsel. I told Mr. Connolly that the proposition was wrong, and would fail, and ought to fail; that no man had character enough to shut off the injured and indignant citizens from the investigation desired; and if he attempted to do it, it would ruin everybody concerned in it, and plunge him in a deeper ruin. That his only chance and hope was in doing right from that day, and throwing himself upon the charity and humanity of those who had been wronged."

Failing to prevent the appointment of Mr. Green, the Ring endeavored to ignore it. The Mayor professed to regard the Comptroller's withdrawal from his office as a resignation of his post. He at once announced his acceptance of this resignation, and proceeded to appoint a successor to Mr. Connolly. Here, however, the Ring met with another defeat. During the early part of 1871, Mr. Connolly had some idea of visiting Europe, and, in order to keep prying eyes from his official records, had procured the passage of a law by the Legislature, authorizing him to appoint a Deputy-Comptroller, who " shall, in addition to his other powers, possess every power, and perform every duty belonging to the office of Comptroller, whenever the said Comptroller shall, by due written authority, and during a period to be specified in such authority, designate and authorize the said Deputy-Comptroller to possess the power and perform the duty aforesaid." Mr. Connolly thus had the legal power to appoint Mr. Green, and the Mayor's refusal to recognize the appointment was mere bombast. The best legal talent in New York sustained Mr. Connolly, and the Mayor's own law officer advised him that he must respect the appointment; and so the statute that had been framed for the protection of the Ring was unexpectedly used for their destruction.

Still another discomfiture awaited the Ring. A few days after the appointment of Mr. Green, a servant girl employed in the family of the janitor of the new Court House, unexpectedly revealed, under oath, the manner in which the vouchers were stolen from the Comptroller's office, and the names of the thieves. Her sworn statement is as follows:

"*City and County of New York, ss.*—Mary Conway, being duly sworn, doth depose and say : I have lived with Mr. and Mrs. Haggerty, in the County Court-House, for over fourteen months, as cook; for about three or four months I did general housework; on Sunday morning, September 10th, I got out of bed with the child that slept with me, wanting to get up; I

THE ROBBERY OF THE VOUCHERS FROM THE COMPTROLLER'S
OFFICE.

don't know whether it was half-past six or seven o'clock; Mrs. Haggerty came into the room in her night-dress; and said to me, ' it is too early to get up yet; ' I said to her, ' being as I am up I guess I will dress myself; ' as I was dressed I went out into the hall ; I heard a knocking down stairs; I said to Mrs. Haggerty, ' it sounds as if it was at the Comptroller's door ; ' I went over to the kitchen, unlocked the kitchen door, and went down stairs to the head of the stairs that leads to the Comptroller's hall ; I saw Charley Baulch knocking at the Comptroller's door, and calling, ' Murphy, are you there ? ' Murphy is a watchman ; I came up stairs and went back to the kitchen ; shortly after I went down stairs again and saw Charley Baulch with the door of the Comptroller's office open, he holding it back on the outside, and I saw Mr. Haggerty come out of the door with bundles of papers in his arms and bring them up to his bedroom ; the door where he came out is at the foot of the stairs, where the glass is broken, going into the County Bureau; I came back, and did not go down any more; each bundle of papers was tied with either a pink tape or a pink ribbon round them ; the next thing, I went over from the kitchen out into the hall for a scuttle of coal ; in this hall Mr. Haggerty's bedroom door faced me ; I saw a man with gray clothes going in there with another bundle of papers like what Mr. Haggerty had ; then I brought back the coal to the kitchen, and put it on the fire ; the next I saw was this man with the gray clothes going down with a pillow-case on his back, full, that looked as though filled with papers, shaped like the bundles Mr. Haggerty had ; at the same time he went down the stairs Charley Baulch said to him, ' This way ; ' I kind of judged there was something up, and I went to look in the drawer where the pillow-cases were, and I missed one of the linen pillow-cases ; I did this soon afterward ; soon after the man went down with the pillow-case, Mrs. Haggerty came into the kitchen, giving me a key, and telling me to go over to the drying-room ; that is a room separate from the bedrooms ; there was a chest there full of linen, table linen and bed linen, and silver right down in the bottom ; she told me to get a nut-picker and bring it over, as Mr. Haggerty wanted one; I took all the clothes out of the trunk, and got the nut-picker and brought it back to her, and before I got into the kitchen I said to Mrs. Haggerty, 'What is the matter? The kitchen's all black with smoke, and the dining room's all black with smoke.' She saïd, 'Mr. Haggerty wanted these papers burned, I told him not to put them in, but he wants them burned;' I went over to the range to cook some eggs for breakfast; it was full of burned papers on the top and in the bottom; there lay a bundle of papers on the top that were about half burned, with a piece of pink tape around them; I put on the cover again; they were partly smothered, going out; Mrs. Haggerty had a poker stirring up the papers on the top and underneath, where the ashes were; the bottom of the range was full of burning papers, and Mrs. Haggerty had the poker stirring them up so that they would burn faster; from underneath the range and the top she took three or four pailfuls of burned papers and emptied them up stairs on the attic floor, in a heap of ashes.

"On Tuesday next, when Mrs. Haggerty came home from the market, she asked me if there was anything new about this robbery in the Comptroller's office; I told her I did not know; I didn't hear nothing, no more than a man came up stairs to-day, and asked me if I let anybody in on Sunday, or if I knew anybody to come into the building on Sunday; I told him I did not know who came in; I didn't attend to the front door; I was cooking, and had nothing to do with the front door; and I asked the man who sent him up stairs; and he said a man down in the hall sent him up stairs to inquire; next, I told Mrs. Haggerty that if I had known it was Charley Baulch sent him up stairs to find any information from me, I should have told the man to go down stairs, that Charley Baulch knew as much about it as I did, and more, for he was one of the men that helped to rob it; she said to me, 'Christ! If Charley Baulch knowed that, he'd run into the East River and drown himself—if he knowed you saw him;' this was on Tuesday night I told her this; Mr. Haggerty left town on Tuesday, saying he was going to Saratoga with Hank Smith, and he

would be home on Thursday or Friday, and on Wednesday
night he got home from Saratoga; Mrs. Haggerty told him the
remarks that I made to her on Tuesday night about the robbery; that I saw all that passed; she told me on Thursday
morning that she told Mr. Haggerty about it all, last night;
that he was going to wash his feet, but he felt so bad over it;
they sat up for two hours in the room talking, and he didn't
wash his feet; on Thursday morning when Mr. Haggerty came
into the kitchen, he came to me, running in, and said, 'Mary!'
I said, 'Sir!' Said he, 'I don't want you to speak of what you
saw passed here on Sunday morning; I don't want you to tell
these old women or old men in the building; Charley Baulch
done it for me, and I done it for another man;' I said, 'I
haven't told it to anyone;' he said, 'You did tell it to Kitty'
(his wife); I said, 'She knew as much about it as I did; she
saw the papers burning;' on next Friday of that same week I
saw Mark Haggerty, Mr. Haggerty's brother, who is a detective in the Mayor's office, I think; I called him up stairs and
asked him to come in; he said, 'No, I am afraid to come in;
I am afraid of Ed.,' that is, Mr. Haggerty; they have not been
on speaking terms in a year; I then told him the occurrences
that happened in the Court-House on Sunday morning; I told
him I didn't feel like staying there; that I was almost crazy
about it; he told me to keep it still; that if anybody would hear
about it outside they would be collared; I asked him would it
be prison; he said certainly.

"On Saturday night I went down to the market where Mrs.
Haggerty keeps a stand, and told her that I was going to leave
for a few days until this mess would be settled, for fear there
would be any arrest, and I should be a witness; she told me
all I had to say was that I knew nothing about it; I told her a
false oath I would not give; what I saw with my eyes I would
swear to; she told me I could do as I chose about it; that I
might go against Mr. Haggerty if I chose; she said, 'It's foolish of you to think so; you ought to go to headquarters and
consult Mr. Kelso about it;' I told her no, it was none of my
business to go and consult him about Mr. Haggerty's robbery;

7

then she and I came together to the Court-House; I got a couple
of dresses and a night dress; I went down stairs; she went
with me; I met a policeman at the door, and he asked me where
I was going; I told him I was going to see my uncle's wife;
she was sick; I then went down to Washington street; I came
up for my clothes yesterday (Tuesday); the rooms were locked;
I went down to the market to where Mrs. Haggerty does business, and the first thing she said to me was, ' By Christ
Almighty, Mr. Haggerty will take your life!' I says to her,
' What for?' she said, ' What you told Mark;' I said, ' I've
told him the truth about the robbery;' she says, ' Your life
will be taken, by Christ Almighty!' I said, ' I want my
clothes;' She said, ' You can get your clothes any time, what
belongs to you;' she did not come up, and did not open the
door; I left my trunk in the hall of the Court-House, that I
brought to put my clothes in; they are over there yet; on that
day, before I saw Mrs. Haggerty, Mr. Murphy came to me and
asked me if I knowed anything about the robbery; if I did,
please to tell the Comptroller; I kind of smiled, and said I
knew nothing about it; ' Well,' said he, ' I know you know
something about it;' I was making the bed in Mr. Haggerty's
room when Mr. Murphy came up and asked me if I knew anything about it; I kind of smiled, and said ' No;' Mr. Murphy says, ' I know better, you do;' I says, ' Why?' says he,
' Suppose you should be arrested, then you'd have to prove
about it whether you knew anything about it or not;' that was
in the hall; said I, ' When I'm arrested, it's time enough to
prove it then;' I then promised to see him on the stoop on
Saturday night, but I did not; I came up on Sunday morning,
and left word at the Hook and Ladder House to have Mr.
Murphy come and see me on Sunday night at No. 95 Washington street; Murphy came to me, and I told him I would go up
to the Comptroller's house with him and tell the Comptroller
all I knew about it, and that I was not doing it for any reward
or money; I was doing it to clear the Comptroller in the eyes
of the people; I went on Tuesday morning with Murphy to the
Comptroller's house, and made the above statement; this morn-

ing there was a policeman came into the house where I was
staying at No. 95 Washington street; the woman in the house
told me he would give me advice about the clothes I had
left in the Court-House; he asked me if I had any charge
against Haggerty; I told him no, no more than what happened
there and what I saw on Sunday morning week, and I explained
it to him; he asked me, 'Have you been speaking to Mr. Connolly?' I said, 'Yes, certainly;' the policeman went out of the
house; the captain (as the woman called him) came to the door
and knocked, and asked the woman about me; she said I had
stepped out; he brought her out on the sidewalk, and was talking to her a little while, and as I was in the room I heard him
speak Hank Smith's name to her once; when she came in she
said he told her that he would like to see me and have a talk
with me, because they would do as much for me as Mr. Connolly
would in this business.   " MARY CONWAY.

"Sworn to before me, Sept. 20th, 1871.

                    " THOS. A. LEDWITH, Police Justice."

In consequence of this disclosure, Baulch and Haggerty
were arrested on the charge of stealing the vouchers. Search
was made in the Court-House, and the half-charred fragments
of the vouchers were found in a room used for the storage
of old lumber. Naturally, the Ring endeavored to treat this
discovery as a trick of the Comptroller's, and they furnished the
men charged with the theft with able counsel to defend them.

The citizens on their part endeavored to bring matters to a
satisfactory termination and secure the punishment of the Ring;
but the members of that body met them at every step with defiance and effrontery. They used every means in their power to
prevent an investigation of the public accounts, and to defeat
the efforts that were made to recover the money they had stolen
from the city. Meanwhile the Citizens' Committee labored
faithfully, and, through the efforts of Mr. Tilden, evidence was
obtained sufficient to cause the arrest of Mr. Tweed. Garvey,
Woodward, and Ingersoll sought safety in flight. Mayor Hall
was arrested on the charge of sharing the plunder obtained by
the Ring, but the examining magistrate declined to hold him on

the charge for lack of evidence against him, and the Grand Jury refused to indict him, for the same reason. Mr. Tweed had been nominated for the State Senate by a constituency composed of the most worthless part of the population, and, in spite of the charges against him, he continued to present himself for the suffrages of these people, by whom he was elected at the November election. In due time the various committees appointed by the citizens made their reports, presenting the facts we have embodied in this chapter. The guilt of the members of the Ring was proven so clearly that no reasonable person could doubt it; but still grave fears were expressed that it would be impossible to bring these men to justice, in consequence of the arts of shrewd counsel and legal quibbles. The determination of the citizens grew with the approach of the elections. Their last great victory over the Ring was achieved at the polls on the 7th of November, when the entire Ring ticket in the city, with but one or two exceptions, was overwhelmingly defeated.

Whether the guilty parties will be punished as they deserve, or whether the citizens will allow the prosecutions they have instituted to flag, the future alone can decide. At the present there is reason to fear that the guilty will escape. Should this fear be realized, the citizens of New York will have abundant cause to regret it. The Ring is badly beaten, but it is not destroyed. Many of its members are still in office, and there are still numbers of its followers ready to do its bidding. Until the last man tainted with the infamy of an alliance with the Ring is removed from office, the people of New York may be sure that the danger is not at an end.

II.

PERSONNEL OF THE RING.

GENERALLY speaking, the Ring may be said to include every office-holder in the city, and it is very certain that of late every official has come in for a share of the suspicion with which the people regard the transactions of the Ring. It would be impossible to give an accurate and complete list of the members of that body, for many of them are not yet known to the public; but the recent investigations have shown that it is not composed exclusively of Democrats. A number of Republicans, while openly acting with their party, have been found to be allied with and in the pay of the Ring.

The men who are supposed to have played the most conspicuous parts in the doings of the Ring, and who are believed by the public to be chiefly responsible for its acts, are Mayor A. O. Hall, Richard B. Connolly, William M. Tweed, Peter B. Sweeny, J. H. Ingersoll, Andrew J. Garvey, and E. A. Woodward.

A. OAKEY HALL, Mayor of the city, was born in New York, is of American parentage, and is about forty-six years old. He received a good education, and at an early age began the study of the law. He removed to New Orleans soon after, and was for a while in the office of the Hon. John Slidell. He subsequently returned to New York, where he became associated with the late Mr. Nathaniel Blunt, as Assistant District-Attorney. Upon the death of Mr. Blunt, he was elected District-Attorney by the Whig party, and held that position for about twelve years. At the end of that time, he was elected Mayor of New York, to succeed John T. Hoffman, now Governor of the State. For some years he has been a member of the law firm of Brown, Hall & Vanderpoel, which firm enjoys a large and lucrative practice. He is said to be a lawyer of considerable ability, and has undoubtedly had great experience in criminal practice. As a politician, his experience has also been extensive and varied. He began life as a Whig, but became a prominent Know-Nothing in the palmy days of that party. Finding Know-Nothingism a failure, however, he became a Republican, from which party, about nine or ten years ago, he passed over to the Democrats.

A writer in *Every Saturday* thus speaks of him:

"His Honor has some facility as a writer, and for twenty years has maintained a quasi or direct connection with the press. He is not lacking in the culture of desultory reading, and when he chooses to do so can bear himself like a gentleman. Of such a thing as dignity of character, he appears to have but a faint conception. Pedantry is more to him than profundity, and to tickle the ear of the town with a cheap witticism, he deems a greater thing than to command it with a forcible presentation of grave issues. The essential type of the man was presented to public gaze about two years ago, when he stood on the City Hall steps dressed from head to foot in a suit of green to review a St. Patrick's procession. He is a harlequin with the literary ambition of a Richelieu. He affects an intimacy with the stage, and has done something in the way of producing plays. He can write clearly and concisely when he will, but prefers to provoke with odd quips and far-fetched conceits. He patronizes journalists and magazine writers with a sort of grotesque familiarity, and readily makes himself at home among the Bohemians of Literature."

Since his union with the Democracy, Mr. Hall has been the constant and intimate associate of the men who have brought disgrace and loss upon the city, and of late years he has been regarded as one of the leading members of the Ring. It is said openly in New York that he owes his election to the Mayoralty entirely to William M. Tweed. As Mayor of the city, he has been officially connected with many of the transactions by which the city has been defrauded of large sums of money. Some of the most prominent newspapers of the city have denounced him as a thief and a sharer of the stolen money. His friends, on the other hand, have declared their belief that his worst fault was his official approval of the fraudulent warrants. They state that he has never in his manner of living, or in any other way, given evidence of possessing large sums of money, and his legal partner made oath before the Grand Jury that Mr. Hall was not worth over $60,000 or $70,000. It is certain that when the proprietor of the *New York Times*, which journal had been loud in denouncing Hall as a thief, was called on by the Grand Jury to furnish them with the evidence upon which this charge was based, he was unable to do so, and the Grand Jury was unable to obtain any evidence criminating Mr. Hall personally. His friends declare that his signing the fraudulent warrants was a purely ministerial act, and that having many thousands of them to sign in a year, he was compelled to rely upon the endorsements of the Comptroller and auditing officers.

In the present state of affairs, there is no evidence showing that Mr. Hall derived any personal pecuniary benefit from the frauds upon the treasury. Public sentiment is divided respecting him; many persons believing that he is a sharer in the plunder of the Ring, and others holding the opposite opinion. The most serious charges that have been made against him, have been brought by Mr. John Foley, and Mr. Samuel J. Tilden. The former is the President of the Nineteenth Ward Citizens' Association, and the latter the leader of the Reform Democracy. Mr. Tilden, in his speech at the Cooper Institute, November 2d, 1871, thus spoke of Mayor Hall:

"These three Auditors met but once. They then passed a resolution which now stands on the records of the city in the handwriting of Mayor Hall. It was passed on his motion, and what was its effect? Did it audit anything? Did it perform the functions? Did it fulfil the trust committed to the Board? Not a bit of it. It provided that all claims certified by Mr. Tweed and Mr. Young, Secretary of the old Board of Supervisors, should be received, and, on sufficient evidence, paid. Mayor Hall is the responsible man for all this. He knew it was a fraudulent violation of duty on the part of every member of that Board of Audit to pass claims in the way they did.

. . . .

"Fellow-citizens, let me call your attention for a moment to the after-piece of these transactions. Our friend, Mayor Hall, is a very distinguished dramatist, and he would consider it a very serious offence to the drama to have the after-piece left out. Now, what was that after-piece? When the statements were published in regard to these frauds, Mayor Hall published a card, wherein he said that these accounts were audited by the old Board of Supervisors, and that neither he nor Mr. Connolly was at all responsible for them. A little later—about August

16th—Mayor Hall said it was true they were audited by the
Board of Audit, and, in doing so, they performed a ministerial
function, and would have been compelled by mandamus to do
it, if they hadn't done it willingly.   I do not deem it necessary
in the presence of an intelligent audience and the lawyers sitting
around me on this stage, to present any observations upon the
idea that 'to audit and to pay the amount found due' was a
ministerial function.   .   .   .   .   .   .

"So we pass to Mr. Hall's fourth defence.   On the burning
of the vouchers he made a raid on Mr. Connolly.   He wrote
him a public letter, demanding his resignation in the name of
the public because he had lost the public confidence; and at the
same time he was writing to Mr. Tweed touching and tender
epistles of sympathy and regret.   You might at that time, if
you were a member of the Club, have heard Mr. Hall in his
jaunty and somewhat defiant manner; you might have seen Mr.
Tweed, riding in the midnight hour, with countenance vacant
and locks awry, and have heard dropping from his lips, 'The
public demands a victim.'   And so he proposed to charge upon
Connolly, who had legal custody of the vouchers, the stealing and
burning of them.   He proposed to put some one else in the office
of the Comptroller when Connolly should be crushed out of it,
and so reconstruct the Ring and impose it a few years longer
upon the people of this city.   .   .   .   .   .

"The sequel showed that the vouchers were taken by Haggerty, whom Mr. Connolly sought out and found, and prosecuted.
Then, again, a little later, when it happened that Mr. Keyser
swore that indorsements for $900,000 on warrants made in his
name were forgeries, there was another raid made on the Comptroller's office.   It was then filled by Mr. Green.   The object
was not to get rid of Mr. Connolly but of Mr. Green, and the
men who caused the raid were Mayor Hall and Peter B. Sweeny.
Now, what was the result of that?   And I will say to this meeting that the sense of alarm that I had that morning lest the
movement should mislead the public, was the motive that induced me to lay aside my business, go to the Broadway Bank
and make a personal examination.

PETER B. SWEENY.

RICHARD B. CONNOLLY.

" What was the result of that? Why, that every one of these forged warrants were deposited, except one, to Woodward's account, and only one to Ingersoll, and that the proceeds were divided with Tweed.

" Now, gentlemen, these revelations throw a light upon what? Upon three false pretences in regard to these transactions, made by Mayor Hall under his own signature before the public, and two attempts to mislead the public judgment as to the real authors of the crime. I do not wish to do injustice to Mayor Hall. He is a man experienced in criminal law. (Laughter.) He is a man who is educated both in the drama and in the stirring scenes that are recorded in the actual crimes of mankind in this country and in England, for I understand this has composed the greatest part of his business. Now I say that there is nothing in the melo-dramatic history of crime more remarkable than these two successive attempts of his to lay the crime to innocent men, if the object was not to screen men whom he knew to be guilty. And while I would not do any wrong or the slightest injustice to Mayor Hall, I say to him, as I do to you, that the history of these transactions puts him on his explanation, and draws upon him a strong suspicion that he knew whereof he was acting. Did he mistake when he got the City Charter? Did he mistake when he acted in the Board of Audit? Did he mistake when he accused Connolly of burning the vouchers? Has he been subject to a misfortune of mistakes at all times? Why does he stand to-day endeavoring to preserve that power? I will only say that if he was mistaken on these occasions he is a very unfortunate man, and has not acquired by the six years of practice in the District-Attorney's office that amount of sagacity in the pursuit of crime which we would naturally ascribe to him."

RICHARD B. CONNOLLY was born in the county of Cork, in Ireland. His father was a village schoolmaster, and gave him a good common school education. He was brought over to this country by an elder brother who had been here for several years. He embarked in politics at an early day, and was elected County Clerk before he could legally cast his vote. He soon made himself noted for his facility in making and breaking political promises, in consequence of which he was popularly called "Slippery Dick." He gave considerable dissatisfaction to his party as County Clerk, and soon dropped out of politics. A few years later, taking advantage of the divisions of the Democratic party, he put himself forward as a candidate for the post of State Senator, and was elected, as is charged by the newspaper press, by the liberal use of bribery and ballot-box stuffing. He was charged with using his position to make money, and during his term at Albany was fiercely denounced for his course in this and other respects.

About three years ago, he was appointed Comptroller of the Finance Department of the City of New York. At that time the real heads of the Finance Department were Peter B. Sweeny, City Chamberlain, and the late County Auditor Watson, the latter of whom has been shown by the recent investigations to have been a wholesale plunderer of the public funds. The Comptroller was then a mere ornamental figure-head to the department. In a short while, however, Watson was accidentally killed, and Sweeny resigned, leaving Connolly master of the situation. He was suspected by Tweed, and in his turn distrusted the "Boss." It is said that he resolved, however, to imitate his colleagues, and enrich himself at the cost of the public. He did well. In the short period of three years, this man, who had entered upon his office poor, became a millionaire. He made his son Auditor in the City Bureau, and gave the positions of Surrogate and Deputy Receiver of Taxes to his two sons-in-law. All these three were men of the lowest intellectual capacity, and all three share in the suspicion which attaches to Connolly's administration of the office. The *New York Tribune,* of October 25th, 1871, stated that a short time before he became Comptroller, Connolly was sued for debt by Henry Felter, now a liquor merchant on Broadway, and *swore in court that he owned no property at all.* Under this statement the *Tribune* publishes a list of *a part* of Connolly's transactions in property since he became Comptroller, covering the sum of $2,300,691.

PETER B. SWEENY is the "modest man" of the Ring, and is popularly believed to carry the brains of that body in his head.   He is regarded by the public as the real leader of the Ring, and the originator of, and prime, though secret mover in all its acts.

Mr. Sweeny is of Irish parentage, though born in New York. His father kept a drinking saloon in Park Row, near the old Park Theatre, and it was in this choice retreat that the youth of Sweeny was passed.   He began his career as an errand boy in a law office.   He subsequently studied law, and, in due time, was admitted to the bar.

A writer in *Every Saturday* thus sums up his career :   "He never obtained, and perhaps never sought, much business in his profession ; but very soon after reaching manhood turned his attention to politics.   The first office he held was that of Counsel to the Corporation, to which position he was elected by a handsome majority.   This station did not so much require in its occupant legal skill and legal ability, as an apt faculty for political manipulation ; and in the work he had to do, Mr. Sweeny was eminently successful.   From the Corporation office he went into the District Attorneyship, obtained leave of absence for some time, treated himself to a term of European travel, came home, and resigned the post to which he had been chosen, and soon became City Chamberlain by the Mayor's appointment.

"It was in this office that he did what gave him a national standing, and led many people into the notion that some good had come from the Tammany Nazareth.   The Chamberlain was custodian, under the old charter, of all city moneys.   Such portions of these funds as were not required for immediate use, this official deposited in some of the banks, and the banks allowed interest, as is customary, on the weekly or monthly balance to his credit.   Previous to Sweeny's time the Chamberlain had put this interest money into his own pocket—and a very handsome thing Mr. Devlin and his predecessors made out of the transaction.   But Sweeny startled the political world, and caused a great sensation, by announcing that he should turn these interest receipts into the City Treasury.   Tammany made a notable parade of his honesty and public spirit, and the capital he gained in this way has been his chief stock-in-trade for the last two or three years.

" But in the light of recent developments, Mr. Sweeny's course does not seem so purely disinterested as it once did. He was in full control of the city funds on the memorable Black Friday of two years ago last summer, and sworn testimony taken by a committee of Congress shows that he had a share in the doings of that eventful day. To what extent the money in his official charge was put at the service of the Wall street Ring, the country probably never will know; but the common belief of New York is that Mr. Sweeny made a good deal of money out of his speculations on that occasion. That he has been more or less concerned with Fisk and Gould in various Erie Railway stock operations, is matter of general notoriety; as it is also that most of the lately-exposed fraudulent transactions in connection with the so-called new Court-House and other public buildings occurred during his incumbency of the Chamberlain's office. The greater part of those transactions yet brought into daylight refer to county affairs, it is true; but city and county are one except in name, and we have only just begun to get at what are designated the city accounts.

" As has been already stated, he values himself on his brains, and the Ring adherents take him at that valuation. They believe him capable of finding a way out of the closest corner, and we suppose it is not to be doubted that he is a man of considerable ability. He has not many of the qualities of a popular politician; years ago he cut loose from his early engine-company associations; he is reserved and reticent at all times, and rarely seeks contact with the Democratic masses; he covets seclusion and respectability; apparently he has sought to be Warwick rather than King, and his followers credit him with a masterly performance of the part. One of his earliest acts as President of the Park Commission was to oust Fred. Law Olmstead, and shelve Andrew H. Green, the actual creators of Central Park; but the whirligig of time has now put him into such a position that he cannot get a dollar of public money without the signature of Andrew H. Green."

Since the disastrous defeat of Tammany and the Ring in the November elections, Mr. Sweeny has resigned his Presidency of the Department of Public Parks, and has retired to private life. He is a man of considerable wealth, and, though there is no evidence to convict him of complicity with Tweed and Connolly in their frauds, the public suspect and distrust him, so that altogether, his retirement was a very wise and politic act.

The " head devil" of the Ring is WILLIAM M. TWEED, or, as he is commonly called, "Boss Tweed." He is of Irish descent, and was born in the City of New York. He was apprenticed to a chair-maker, to learn the trade, but never engaged legitimately in it after he became his own master. He finally became a member of Fire Company No. 6—known as " Big Six," and " Old Tiger "—the roughest and worst company in the city. He soon became its foreman. His attention was now turned to politics, and as he possessed considerable influence over the " roughs," he became a valuable man to the city politicians. As a compensation for his services, they allowed him to receive a small office, from which he pushed his way into the old Board of Supervisors, and eventually into the State Senate. Upon the inauguration of the New Charter, he became President of the Board of Public Works, and the most prominent leader of the Ring. He is a man of considerable executive ability, and has known how to use his gifts for his own gain. In March, 1870, the *New York World* spoke of him as follows :

" Mr. Tweed was worth less than nothing when he took to the trade of politics. Now he has great possessions, estimated all the way from $5,000,000 to twice as much. We are sorry not to be able to give his own estimate, but, unluckily, he returns no income. But at least he is rich enough to own a gorgeous house in town and a sumptuous seat in the country, a stud of horses, and a set of palatial stables. His native modesty shrinks from blazoning abroad the exact extent of his present wealth, or the exact means by which it was acquired. His sensitive soul revolts even at the partial publicity of the income list. We are tossed upon the boundless ocean of conjecture. But we do know from his own reluctant lips that this public servant, who entered the public service a bankrupt, has become, by an entire abandonment of himself to the public good, 'one of the largest tax-payers in New York.' His influence is co-extensive with his cash. The docile Legislature sits at his feet, as Saul at the feet of Gamaliel, and waits, in reverent inactivity, for his signal before proceeding to action. He thrives on percentages of pilfering, grows rich on the distributed dividends of rascality. His extortions are as boundless in their sum as in their ingenuity. Streets unopened profit him—streets opened put money in his purse. Paving an avenue with poultice enriches him—taking off the poultice increases his wealth. His rapacity, like the trunk of an elephant, with equal skill twists a fortune out of the Broadway widening, and picks up dishonest pennies in the Bowery."

In 1861, Mr. Tweed appeared in the courts of the city as a bankrupt. In 1871, his wealth is estimated at from $15,000,-000, to $20,000,000. The manner in which he is popularly believed to have amassed this immense sum is thus described in a pamphlet recently issued in New York:

" While holding the position of State Senator he also held the position of Supervisor—was the leading spirit and President of the old Board of Supervisors, that has been denounced as the most scandalously corrupt body that ever disgraced a civilized community—and also the position of Deputy Street Commissioner. The first two he used to put money in his pocket, but the last was used mainly to enable him to keep a set of ruffians about him, who were paid out of the city treasury, and to afford lucrative positions to men who might be of service in promoting his political and pecuniary interests. By employing the same agencies that he had used to secure his own election, he gradually worked his particular friends into positions where he could use them, and then commenced a scheme for surrounding every department in the government of the city and county with a perfect network, which would enable himself and his confederates to appropriate to their own use the greater part of the city and county revenues. The new Court-House has been a mine

of wealth to these thieves from its very inception. The quarry
from which the marble was supplied was bought by the gang
for a mere nominal price, and has since netted them millions of
dollars. The old fire engine-houses were turned over to 'Andy'
Garvey and other cronies of Tweed's at rents ranging from
$50 to $150 a year, and some of them have been let by these
fellows as high as $5000 a year. The public schools, the dif-
ferent departments of the government, and the public institutions under the control of the city authorities, all needed furniture, and Tweed started a furniture manufactory in connection
with James H. Ingersoll, who has since achieved a notoriety as
the most shameless thief among the fraternity of scoundrels
whom we are now describing. Tweed's next step was to get
control of a worthless little newspaper called *The Transcript,*
and then to introduce a bill into the Legislature making this
miserable little sheet the official organ of the City Government.
This sheet receives over a $1,000,000 a year for printing the
proceedings of the Common Council, but the proceedings of
the corrupt Board of Supervisors are studiously concealed from
the public.

    " Tweed's next step was to establish ' The New York Print-
ing Company.' This gives Tweed a pretext for rendering enormous bills for printing for the different departments of the City
Government; and although the amount of work actually performed is only trifling, and consists mainly in printing blank
forms and vouchers, still the amount annually paid out of the
treasury to this company is something enormous—amounting
during the year 1870 to over $2,800,000. Nor is this all.
When this company was first started, a portion of a building
on Centre street was found sufficient for its accommodation.
Since then it has absorbed three of the largest printing establishments in the city, and also three or four smaller ones, and a
lithographing establishment. Why have these extensive establishments been secured ? Simply this : Insurance Companies,
Steamboat Companies, Ferry Companies, and other corporations require an enormous amount of printing. Each of these
associations may be subjected to serious loss and inconvenience,

by the passage of legislative enactments abridging the privileges they now enjoy, or requiring them to submit to some vexatious and expensive regulation. Hence, when they receive notice that ' The New York Printing Company ' is ready to do their printing, they know that they must consent, and pay the most exorbitant rate for the work done, or submit to Tweed's exactions during the next session of the Legislature.

"In addition to the Printing Company, Tweed has a ' Manufacturing Stationers' Company,' which furnishes all the stationery used in the public schools, the public institutions, and the several departments of the City Government. This concern receives not less than $3,000,000 a year out of the city treasury. As an illustration of the way they do things, we will cite one instance : During the month of April of the present year, an order was sent to this company for stationery for the County Bureau. In due time it was delivered, and consisted of about six reams of cap paper, and an equal quantity of letter paper, with a couple of reams of note paper. There were, also, about two dozen penholders, four small ink bottles, such as could be bought at retail for thirty-five or forty cents, a dozen small sponges for pen-wipers, half a dozen office rulers, and three dozen boxes of rubber bands of various sizes—the entire amount worth about fifty dollars at retail. For this stationery, a bill of *ten thousand dollars* was rendered soon after, and was duly paid; and similar claims are presented for stationery for every bureau and department of the government, almost every month throughout the year—and are always promptly paid, although persons having legitimate claims against the same appropriation could not obtain a dollar. . But not content with the enormous amounts that are thus obtained under false pretences, Tweed even charges the city with the wages of the different persons employed in these several establishments, and makes a large percentage on the amounts thus drawn from the Treasury. For instance : Charles E. Wilbour is President of the Printing Company and also of the Stationers' Company, while Cornelius Corson is the Secretary of both companies. Wilbour receives $3000 a year as Stenographer to the Bureau of Elections, $2500 as Stenographer in the Superior Court, and $3500 a year for ' examining accounts ' that he has never seen. These several sums are drawn out of the County Bureau alone, and he holds an equal number of sinecure positions in the City Bureau. Corson is Chief of the Bureau of Elections, for which he receives $6000 a year; and he also receives $3500 for 'examining' the same accounts, for which Wilbour receives a similar sum; while, like Wilbour, he has never seen the accounts."

In order to carry on his immense operations, Tweed has had to avail himself from time to time of the assistance of his partners. He has always found them willing accomplices. These were J. H. Ingersoll, Andrew J. Garvey, and E. A. Woodward, all of whom have sought safety in flight.

J. H. Ingersoll is the son of a chair-dealer in the Bowery, and was Tweed's principal tool in defrauding the citizens. He in his turn " operated " through sub-firms, and was paid in 1869 and 1870 the enormous sum of $5,691,144.26 for furniture and repairs to the new Court House and the militia armories of the city. Much of this work was never done. For the work actually done only the legitimate price was paid; the rest of the enormous sum was divided between Tweed and Ingersoll.

Andrew J. Garvey is a plasterer by trade, and had a shop in the Third avenue. He is also an Irishman, and was a "bunker" of the old fire department. During the years 1869 and 1870 he was paid $2,905,464.06 for repairing, plastering, painting and decorating the militia armories and the new Court-House. But a small part of this sum represents work honestly done. The rest is stolen money, of which Tweed received his share. At the very first discovery of the frauds, Garvey fled from the city, and it is believed sailed for Europe to escape the punishment he dreaded.

E. A. Woodward was a deputy clerk to the Board of Supervisors, and as such received a moderate salary. As far as is known, he had no other means of acquiring money. He was at the beginning of the investigations the owner of a magnificent estate near Norwalk, Connecticut, a partner in the firm of Vanderhoef & Beatty, to the extent of $75,000; and the owner of

8

property variously estimated at from $500,000 to $1,000,000. It was charged by the New York papers that the endorsements of the name of Keyser & Co. on warrants amounting to over $817,000, and which endorsements Mr. Keyser pronounced *forgeries*, were mainly the work of Woodward. The money drawn on the fraudulent warrants was divided between Woodward and Tweed. Conclusive evidence of this was afforded by Mr. Samuel J. Tilden, who, by a happy inspiration, made a personal examination of Tweed's bank account at the Broadway Bank, and there discovered that Tweed, Garvey, Ingersoll, and Woodward had divided $6,095,319.17 of the public funds between them.

Commenting upon this discovery, the New York *Tribune* remarks : " Of the total amount of these warrants,$6,312,541.37, three dependents and tools of Mr. William M. Tweed deposited $5,710,913.38, and the New York Printing Company deposited $384,395.19, making $6,095,319.17. Further, $103,648.68 is believed to have been deposited by Ingersoll in a different bank, so that the whole amount of the audit, except $113,583.52, was really collected by persons in connection with or in collusion with Tweed. Ingersoll collected $3,501,584.50 of the warrants, and he received from Garvey, out of his collections, $47,744.68. Of that aggregate he paid over to Woodward $1,817,467.49, or a little more than half of his whole receipts.

"Garvey deposited warrants amounting to $1,177,413.72. He, Garvey, paid to Woodward $731,871.01, or over two-thirds of the whole amount of his receipts. Woodward deposited $1,032,715.76, and he received in checks from Ingersoll and Garvey enough of these collections to make a total of $3,582,054.26. Of this amount he paid over $923,858.50 to Tweed.

" Woodward was then, and is now, a deputy clerk to Young of the Board of Supervisors, on whose certification, according to Mayor Hall's resolution, as well as on that of Mr. Tweed, the bills were to be paid. It is unknown to whom Woodward made other payments, but those he made to Tweed are established beyond doubt. The tickets accompanying the deposits are in the handwriting of Woodward, and the teller in the

Broadway Bank swore that they were generally made by Woodward in person.

"Including $104,333.64, Tweed received a handsome aggregate of $1,037,192.14.

"The manner in which the city warrants were identified is explained in the affidavit of Mr. Tilden. The first table is headed, 'County Liabilities.' That is made up from the records in the Comptroller's office and the warrants. The last contains all that there is (memoranda and endorsements) on the back of the warrants. Nearly all the vouchers of these bills were among those stolen on Sunday, September 10th, but the warrants were kept in a different place, and are now in the Comptroller's office. The next table headed, 'Identification of Parties who received the Proceeds of the Warrants,' is made up, as to the description of the warrants, from the books of the Comptroller's office, and from the warrants themselves, and the identification of the persons who deposited the warrants is made out from accounts of the entries in the National Broadway Bank. The asterisks against the amounts of the warrants in the fifth column indicate those of the Keyser warrants on' which John H. Keyser alleges the endorsements were forged.

"All those warrants which fell within the period of this account were collected by Woodward, *except one, and that one by Ingersoll.*

"Undoubtedly the transactions, taken together, were in the opinion of the Acting Attorney-General, a conspiracy to defraud the county by means of bills exaggerated many times, for work or services received, or for work and services already paid for, or for accounts that were fictitious.

"The result throws great light both on the stealing and burning of the vouchers by Haggerty, the janitor of the building, appointed by the Chamberlain, and also upon the Keyser forgeries."

Woodward did not wait for the accumulation of evidence against him. He followed the example of Ingersoll and Garvey, and took flight, and at present his whereabouts is unknown.

Mr. Tilden's affidavit relating the facts of his discovery furnished evidence sufficient to justify the arrest of Mr. Tweed. The Sheriff performed the farce of arresting the "Boss" in his office at the Department of Public Works. Bail was offered and accepted. The Sheriff treated the great defaulter with the utmost courtesy and deference, appearing before him, hat in hand, with a profusion of servile bows. No absolute monarch could have been treated with greater reverence. The moral sense of the community was outraged. On the same day a poor wretch who had stolen a loaf of bread to keep his sick wife from starving was sentenced for theft.

Mr. Tweed attempted to explain away Mr. Tilden's discovery, but was met at once by that gentleman, who more than fastened his guilt upon him. Said Mr. Tilden:

"The fourth act in the conspiracy was the collection of the money and its division. (Laughter.) Who collected that money? We found upon investigation that every time Garvey collected $100,000 he paid 66 per cent. to Woodward, who paid Tweed 24 per cent. of it. (Laughter.) Sometimes Woodward paid a fraction above 24 per cent. to Tweed, sometimes a fraction below, but it never reached 25 per cent. nor fell to 23 per cent. (Laughter.)

"Every time Woodward collected money he paid over 24 per cent. to Tweed. The investigations in the Broadway Bank having begun without knowledge of the specific transactions to which they would relate, extend back through the whole of the year 1870, and it appears that about the same transactions were going on in the four months of that year, and about the same division was made. Something like $200,000 or $240,000 was paid over to Tweed during those four months.

"Now, I have heard it said in some of the public presses that a gentleman who had an interview with Mr. Tweed had received the explanation that Mr. Woodward owed him large sums of borrowed money, and that when, in the course of his business arrangements with the city, he received these sums of money from the city, he simply paid it over to Mr. Tweed in satisfaction of his debts. That is a very fine theory. There is only one difficulty about it, and that is, these loans are not entered on the bank account. Examine Mr. Tweed's bank account, and there is not $1000 in it except in city transactions. His whole private business during this time when he was depositing it— checks drawn upon city warrants amounted to $3,500,000—did not amount to $3000; therefore it results inevitably that whatever is taken from that account is city money, for there was nothing but city or county money in that bank. There were no private funds there. Where his 42 per cent. went I am unable to find out. It was probably transferred to some other bank in large checks for subdivision among the parties entitled thereto; but about that we know not. Now, gentlemen, that disposes of the fourth act in the conspiracy, and the events justify me in saying that at the time the City Charter was passed I had no suspicion that the principal object in passing it was not to preserve political power, with the ordinary average benefits that usually accrue to its possessors. I had no suspicion that affairs were going on in this way. But it seems that these transactions were about one-half through; that there was about as much to be done after the new charter as had been done for sixteen months previous under the old law; and that therefore the motive and object of the new charter was not only to secure political power with its ordinary average advantages, but also to conceal the immense amounts that had been already stolen, and to secure the opportunity of stealing an immense amount that was in prospect before its passage. I say, then, that by the ordinary rules and principles of evidence, looking back to the beginning of the transactions, no man can doubt that all this series of acts were parts of one grand conspiracy, not only for power, but for personal plunder."

We have not the space to dwell further upon the villainies from which the city has suffered, but in parting with the Ring we cannot but regret, in the forcible language of the Committee of Seventy, that, "Not an official implicated in these infamies has had the virtue to commit suicide."

V.

BROADWAY.

I.

HISTORICAL.

To write the history of Broadway would require a volume, for it would be the history of New York itself. The street was laid out in the days of the Dutch, and then, as now, began at the Bowling Green. By them it was called the "Heere Straas," or High street. They built it up as far as Wall street, but in those days only the lower end was of importance. The site of the Bowling Green was occupied by the Dutch fort and the church, and on the west side of it was the parade and the market place. Ere long several well-to-do merchants erected substantial dwellings on the same side, one of these belonging to no less a personage than the Schout-Fiscal Van Dyck. The east side of Broadway, during the rule of the Dutch, was thickly built up with dwellings of but one room, little better than hovels. Eventually, however, some of the better class mechanics came there to reside, and erected better houses. Their gardens extended down to the marsh on Broad street, and they cultivated their cabbages and onions with great success, where now the bulls and bears of the stock and gold markets rage and roar.

Under the English rule Broadway improved rapidly. Substantial dwellings clustered around the Bowling Green. The first, and by far the most elegant of these, was the edifice still known as "No. 1, Broadway," at present used as a hotel. It was built by Archibald Kennedy, then Collector of the Port of

New York, and afterwards Earl of Cassilis, in the Scotch Peerage.   In the colonial times it was frequented by the highest fashion of the city, and during the Revolution was the headquarters of the British General, Sir Henry Clinton.   Other noted personages afterwards resided in it.   This portion of Broadway escaped the destruction caused by the great fire of 1776, and until about forty years ago preserved its antecolonial appearance.

This fire destroyed all that part of the street that had been built above Morris street.   After the Revolution it was rebuilt more substantially, and many of the most elegant residences in the city were to be found here, between Wall street and the Bowling Green.   General Washington resided on the west side of Broadway, just below Trinity Church, during a portion of his Presidential term.

In 1653, the Dutch built a wall across the island at the present Wall street.   One of the main gates of this wall was on Broadway, just in front of the present Trinity Church.   From this gate a public road, called the "Highway," continued up the present line of the street to the "Commons," now the City Hall Park, where it diverged into what is now Chatham street.   In 1696 Trinity Church was erected.   The church-yard north of the edifice had for some time previous been used as a burying ground.

Along the east side of Broadway, from Maiden lane to a point about 117 feet north of Fulton street, was a pasture known as the "Shoemaker's Pasture."   It covered an area of sixteen acres, and was used in common by the shoemakers of the city for the manufacture of leather, their tannery being located in a swampy section, near the junction of Maiden lane and William street.   About 1720 the pasture was sold in lots, and Fulton and John streets were extended through it.   That part of the tract bounded by the present Broadway, Nassau, Fulton and Ann streets, was for many years occupied by a pleasure resort, known as " Spring Garden."   The tavern occupied the site of the present *Herald* office.   It was here, during the excitement preceding the Revolution, that the " Sons of

Liberty" had their head-quarters. They purchased the building, and named it "Hampden Hall." It was the scene of many a riot and public disturbance during those stirring times. It was occupied as a dwelling house from the close of the Revolution until 1830, when it was converted into a Museum by John Scudder. In 1840 Phineas T. Barnum became the owner of the building and Museum. After the destruction of the Museum by fire in 1864, Mr. James Gordon Bennett purchased the site, and erected upon it the magnificent office of *The Herald*.

Trinity Church Farm lay along the west side of Broadway, north of Fulton street. It was divided into lots in 1760, and between that time and 1765, the present St. Paul's Church was erected on the lower end of it. The street forming the northern boundary of the churchyard was named Vesey, in honor of a former pastor of Trinity.

In 1738 a public market, 156 feet long, and 20 feet $3\frac{1}{2}$ inches wide, was erected in the middle of Broadway, opposite the present Liberty, then Crown street. It remained there until 1771, when it was removed as a public nuisance.

By the opening of the present century, Broadway had extended above the present City Hall Park, which had been enclosed as a pleasure ground in 1785. It was taken up along its upper portion mainly with cottages, and buildings of a decidedly rustic character. In 1805 the street was paved in front of the Park, and in 1803 the present City Hall was begun on the site of the old Poor House. It was completed in 1812. The principal hotels, and many of the most elegant residences, were to be found at this time on both sides of Broadway between Chambers street and Wall street. In 1810–12 Washington Hall was erected on the southeast corner of Reade street. It was the head-quarters of the old Federal Party, and was subsequently used as a hotel. It was afterwards purchased by Mr. A. T. Stewart, who erected on its site his palatial wholesale store, which extends along Broadway to Chambers street. About the year 1820, the dry goods merchants began to locate themselves on the west side of Broadway near Reade street.

On the west side of Broadway, above Duane street, was the celebrated Rutgers' estate, consisting of a fine mansion and large and elaborately laid out grounds. The house was built by Anthony Rutgers in 1730, and occupied by him until his death in 1750. After his death the property was converted into a pleasure garden, known as "The Ranelagh." It was kept by a Mr. John Jones until a few years before the Revolution. It was a famous resort for the better classes. A complete band was in attendance every Monday and Thursday evening during the summer, and dancing was carried on in a large hall which had been erected in the garden. In 1770, the estate was sold. Five acres, embracing the orchard, were purchased by an association, and in 1773, the New York Hospital was begun on this site. In 1869 the hospital was removed higher up town, the land was sold, and Pearl street was extended through the hospital grounds.

Between 1774 and 1776 a reservoir for supplying the city with water was erected on the east side of Broadway, near the southeast corner of White street. The water was pumped into the reservoir from wells, and was distributed through the city in wooden pipes. At this time the streets were not opened in this vicinity, and the reservoir is described as standing on an "elevated hill." In 1810 the reservoir property was sold in lots, the highest price paid per lot being $3000.

By 1818 Broadway was built up to above Duane street, and in 1826 the Free Masons erected a handsome Gothic Hall, on the east side, between Duane and Pearl streets. The street continued to grow, and about 1830 extended above Canal street. In 1836-39, the Society Library erected a handsome building on the west side, between Howard and Grand streets. In 1853, they sold the building, which fronts sixty feet on Broadway, to D. Appleton & Co., Publishers. By the year 1825, when gas was introduced into the city south of Canal street, the west side of Broadway above Chambers street was the fashionable shopping mart. The cross streets were used mainly for residences, and these daily poured a throng of pedestrians into Broadway, making it the fashionable promenade. At this time long rows of poplar trees lined the sidewalks. The principal hotels and theatres, restaurants, and pleasure resorts were to be found along the street, and Broadway became what it has since been, a miniature of the great city of which it is the chief artery.

After passing Canal street, along which, in the early part of the present century, a considerable stream, spanned at Broadway by a stone bridge, flowed across the island to the Hudson, Broadway grew rapidly. In 1820 the site of the St. Nicholas Hotel was occupied by a store, four dwelling houses, and a coach factory, the last of which was sunk below the level of the street. Back of the present hotel was a hill on which were the remains of an earthwork, thrown up during the Revolution. The hotel was erected in 1852. In 1823 the site of the Metropolitan Hotel was vacant. The block between Prince and Houston streets, on the west side, was occupied by two large houses, a garden, and several shanties.

On the east side of Broadway, above Bleecker street, was a fine pleasure resort, called " Vauxhall Garden." It was opened by a Frenchman named Delacroix, about the beginning of this century. The location was then beyond the city limits. The Bible House and Cooper Institute mark its eastern boundary. Lafayette Place was cut through it in 1837. Astor Place was its northern boundary, and the site of the Astor Library was within its limits. The entrance to the grounds was on Broadway.

From Astor Place, originally known as Art street, the progress of Broadway was rapid. By the year 1832, it was almost entirely built up to Union Square. In 1846, Grace Church was erected, the original edifice, built about 1800, having stood at the corner of Broadway and Rector streets, just below Trinity Church. In 1850, the Union Place Hotel, corner of Broadway and Fourteenth street, and in 1852, the St. Denis Hotel, corner of Broadway and Eleventh street, were built. Union Square was laid off originally in 1815, and in its present shape in 1832.

Above Union Square, Broadway was originally known as the Bloomingdale road, and was lined with farms and country seats.

Madison Square was laid off about 1841. The Fifth Avenue Hotel was built about fifteen years later, and the remainder of the street is of very recent growth, possessing but little local interest.

Broadway has grown with the extension of the city northward. The upper blocks of buildings have always been dwelling houses or shanties, and these have given way steadily to the pressure of business below them. In a few years the entire street, from the Central Park to the Bowling Green, will be taken up with substantial and elegant structures suited to the growing needs of the great city. From the imperfect sketch of its history here presented, the reader will see that the growth of the street is divided into distinct periods. Under the Dutch it was built as far as Wall street. The next 100 years carried it to the Park, from which it extended to Duane street, reaching that point about the close of the Revolution. By the opening of the present century it had reached Canal street. Its next advance was to Astor Place. Thence it passed on to a point above Union Square, and thence by a rapid growth to the neighborhood of the Central Park.

II.

DESCRIPTIVE.

THE most wonderful street in the universe is Broadway. It is a world within itself. It extends throughout the entire length of the island, and is about sixty feet in width. Its chief attractions, however, lie between the Bowling Green and Thirty-fourth street.

It begins at the Bowling Green. From this point it extends in a straight line to Fourteenth street and Union Square. Below Wall street it is mainly devoted to the " Express " business, the headquarters and branch offices of nearly all the lines in the country centring here. Opposite Wall street, and on the west side of Broadway, is Trinity Church and its graveyard. From Wall street to Ann street, Insurance Companies, Real

BROADWAY, AT THE CORNER OF ANN STREET.

Estate Agents, Banks, Bankers and Brokers predominate. At
the southeast corner of Ann street is the magnificent *Herald*
office, and adjoining it the Park Bank. Both buildings are of
white marble, and the latter is one of the grandest in the Union.
Immediately opposite are St. Paul's Church and graveyard, just
above which is the massive granite front of the Astor House,
occupying an entire block, from Vesey to Barclay streets. On
the right hand side of the street, at the lower end of the Park,
is the unfinished structure of the new Post Office, which will
be one of the principal ornaments of the city. In the rear of
this are the Park, and the City Hall. Back of the City Hall,
and fronting on Chambers street, is the new County Court-
House, which proved such a gold mine to the " Ring." Across
the Park you may see Park Row and Printing-House Square,
in which are located the offices of nearly all the great " dailies,"

A. T. STEWART'S WHOLESALE STORE.

and of many of the weekly papers. Old Tammany Hall once stood on this square at the corner of Frankfort street, but its site is now occupied by the offices of *The Sun* and *Brick Pomeroy's Democrat—Arcades ambo.*

Beyond the City Hall, at the northeast corner of Chambers street and Broadway, is " Stewart's marble dry goods palace," as it is called. This is the *wholesale* department of the great house of A. T. Stewart & Co., and extends from Chambers to Reade street. The *retail* department of this firm is nearly two miles higher up town. Passing along, one sees in glancing up and down the cross streets, long rows of marble, iron, and brown stone warehouses, stretching away for many blocks on either hand, and affording proof positive of the vastness and success of the business transacted in this locality. To the right we catch a distant view of the squalor and misery of the Five Points. On the right hand side of the street, between Leonard street and Catharine lane, is the imposing edifice of the New York Life Insurance Company, one of the noblest buildings ever erected by private enterprise. It is constructed of white marble.

Crossing Canal street, the widest and most conspicuous we have yet reached, we notice, on the west side, at the corner of Grand street, the beautiful marble building occupied by the *wholesale* department of Lord & Taylor, rivals of Stewart in the dry-goods trade. The immense brown stone building immediately opposite, is also a wholesale dry-goods house. Between Broome and Spring streets, on the west side, are the marble and brown stone buildings of the St. Nicholas Hotel. Immediately opposite is the Theatre Comique. On the northwest corner of Spring street is the Prescott House. On the southwest corner of Prince street is Ball & Black's palatial jewelry store. Diagonally opposite is the Metropolitan Hotel, in the rear of which is the theatre known as Niblo's Garden. In the block above the Metropolitan is the Olympic Theatre. On the west side, between Bleecker and Amity streets, is the huge Grand Central Hotel, one of the most conspicuous objects on the street. Two blocks above, on the same side, is the New York Hotel, immediately opposite which are Lina Edwin's and the Globe Theatres. On the east side of the street, and covering the entire block bounded by Broadway and Fourth avenue, and Ninth and Tenth streets, is an immense iron structure painted white. This is Stewart's retail store. It is always filled with ladies engaged in "shopping," and the streets around it are blocked with carriages. Throngs of elegantly and plainly dressed buyers pass in and out, and the whole scene is animated and interesting. Just above "Stewart's," on the same side, is Grace Church, attached to which is the parsonage. At the southwest corner of Eleventh street, is the St. Denis Hotel, and on the northwest corner is the magnificent iron building of the "Methodist Book Concern," the street floor of which is occupied by McCreery, one of the great dry-goods dealers of the city. At the northeast corner of Thirteenth street, is Wallack's Theatre. The upper end of the same block is occupied by the Union Square Theatre and a small hotel.

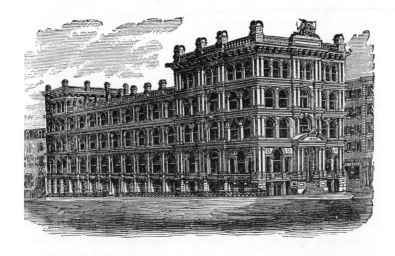

NEW YORK LIFE INSURANCE COMPANY'S BUILDING, CORNER OF
BROADWAY AND LEONARD STREET.

At Fourteenth street we enter Union Square, once a fashionable place of residence, but now giving way to business houses
and hotels.   Broadway passes around it in a northwesterly direction.   On the west side of Union Square, at the southwest
corner of Fifteenth street, is the famous establishment of Tiffany
& Co., an iron building, erected at an immense cost, and filled
with the largest and finest collection of jewelry, articles of *vertu*,
and works of art in America.   In the middle of the block
above, occupying the ground floor of Decker's Piano Building,
is *Brentano's*, the " great literary headquarters" of New York.

Leaving Union Square behind us, we pass into Broadway
again at Seventeenth street.   On the west side, occupying the
entire block from Eighteenth to Nineteenth streets, is a magnificent building of white marble used by a number of retail
merchants.   The upper end, comprising nearly one half of the
block, is occupied by Arnold, Constable & Co., one of the most
fashionable retail dry-goods houses.   At the southwest corner
of Twentieth street, is the magnificent iron *retail* dry-goods
store of Lord & Taylor—perhaps the most popular house in the

city with residents. The "show windows" of this house are always filled with a magnificent display of the finest goods, and attract crowds of gazers.

At Twenty-third street, Broadway crosses Fifth avenue obliquely, going toward the northwest. At the northwest corner of Twenty-third street, and extending to Twenty-fourth street, is the Fifth Avenue Hotel, built of white marble, one of the finest and handsomest buildings of its kind in the world. Just opposite is Madison Square, extending from Fifth to Madison avenues. The block from Twenty-fourth to Twenty-fifth streets is occupied by the Albemarle and Hoffman Houses, in the order named, both of white marble. Just opposite, at the junction of Broadway and Fifth avenue, is a handsome granite obelisk, with appropriate ornaments in bronze, erected to the memory of General W. J. Worth. Immediately beyond this is the Worth House, fronting on Broadway and Fifth avenue. The vicinity of Madison Square is the brightest, prettiest, and liveliest portion of the great city. At the southwest corner of Twenty-sixth street is the St. James' Hotel, also of white marble, and just opposite is the "Stevens' House," an immense building constructed on the French plan of "flats," and rented in suites of apartments. Between Twenty-seventh and Twenty-eighth streets, on the west side, is the Coleman House. At the southeast corner of Twenty-ninth street is the Sturtevant House. At the northeast corner of Twenty-ninth street is the Gilsey House, a magnificent structure of iron, painted white. Diagonally opposite is Wood's Museum. At the southeast corner of Thirty-first street is the Grand Hotel, a handsome marble building. The only hotel of importance above this is the St. Cloud, at the southeast corner of Forty-second street.

At Thirty-fourth street, Broadway crosses Sixth avenue, and at Forty-fourth street it crosses Seventh avenue, still going in a northwesterly direction. It is but little improved above Thirty-fourth street, though it is believed the next few years will witness important changes in this quarter.

There are no street car tracks on Broadway below Fourteenth street, and in that section "stages," or omnibuses, monopolize

BROADWAY, AS SEEN FROM THE ST. NICHOLAS HOTEL.

the public travel. Several hundreds of these traverse the street from the lower ferries as far as Twenty-third street, turning off at various points into the side streets and avenues.

Below Twenty-ninth street, and especially below Union Square, the street is built up magnificently. From Union Square to the Bowling Green, a distance of three miles, it is lined on each side with magnificent structures of marble, brown,

9

Portland, and Ohio stones, granite, and iron. No street in the
world surpasses it in the grandeur and variety of its architectural display. Some of the European cities contain short streets
of greater beauty, and some of our American cities contain
limited vistas as fine, but the great charm, the chief claim of
Broadway to its fame, is the *extent* of its grand display. For
three miles it presents an unbroken vista, and the surface is
sufficiently undulating to enable one to command a view of the
entire street from any point between Tenth street and the
Bowling Green. Seen from one of the hotel balconies, the effect
is very fine. The long line of the magnificent thoroughfare
stretches away into the far distance. The street is thronged with
a dense and rapidly moving mass of men, animals, and vehicles
of every description. The effect is unbroken, but the different
colors of the buildings give to it a variety that is startling and
pleasing. In the morning the throng is all pouring one way—
down town; and in the afternoon the tide flows in the opposite
direction. Everybody is in a hurry at such times. Towards
afternoon the crowd is more leisurely, for the promenaders and
loungers are out. Then Broadway is in its glory.

Oftentimes the throng of vehicles is so dense that the streets
are quickly "jammed." Carriages, wagons, carts, omnibuses,
and trucks are packed together in the most helpless confusion.
At such times the police are quickly on hand, and take possession of the street. The scene is thrilling. A stranger feels sure
that this struggling mass of horses and vehicles can never be
made to resume their course in good order, without loss of life
or limb to man or beast, or to both, and the shouts and oaths
of the drivers fairly bewilder him. In a few minutes, however,
he sees a squad of gigantic policemen dash into the throng of
vehicles. They are masters of the situation, and wo to the
driver who dares disobey their sharp and decisive commands.
The shouts and curses cease, the vehicles move on one at a time
in the routes assigned them, and soon the street is clear again,
to be "blocked" afresh, perhaps, in a similar manner in less
than an hour. Upwards of 20,000 vehicles daily traverse this
great thoroughfare.

It is always a difficult matter for a pedestrian to cross the lower part of Broadway in the busy season. Ladies, old persons, and children find it impossible to do so without the aid of the police, whose duty it is to make a passage for them through the crowd of vehicles. A bridge was erected in 1866 at the corner of Fulton street, for the purpose of enabling pedestrians to pass over the heads of the throng in the streets. Few persons used it, however, except to witness the magnificent panorama of the street, and it was taken down.

Seen from the lofty spire of Trinity Church, the street presents a singular appearance. The perspective is closed by Grace Church, at Tenth street. The long lines of passers and carriages take distinct shapes, and seem like immense black bands moving slowly in opposite directions. The men seem like pigmies, and the horses like dogs. There is no confusion, however. The eye readily masses into one line all going in the same direction. Each one is hurrying on at the top of his speed, but from this lofty perch they all seem to be crawling at a snail's pace.

The display in the windows of the Broadway stores is rich, beautiful, and tempting. Jewels, silks, satins, laces, ribbons, household goods, silverware, toys, paintings, in short, rare, costly, and beautiful objects of every description greet the gazer on every hand. All that is necessary for the comfort of life, all that ministers to luxury and taste, can be found here in the great thoroughfare. And it is a mistake to suppose, as many persons do, that " Broadway prices " are higher than those of other localities. The best goods in the city are to be found here, and they bring only what they are worth, and no more. Yet it must not be supposed that all Broadway dealers are models of honesty. Everything has its price in the great street—even virtue and honesty. By the side of merchants whose names are synonymous for integrity are to be found some of the most cunning and successful scoundrels. Broadway is an eminently cheerful street. On every hand one sees evidences of prosperity and wealth. No unsuccessful man can remain in the street. Poverty and failure have no place there. Even sin shows its most attractive guise in Broadway.

SATURDAY AFTERNOON CONCERT AT CENTRAL PARK.

The side-walks are always crowded, even in the summer, when "everybody is out of town," and this throng of passers-by constitutes one of the most attractive features of the scene. Every class, every shade of nationality and character, is represented here. America, Europe, Asia, Africa, and even Oceanica, each has its representatives. High and low, rich and poor, pass along at a rate of speed peculiar to New York, and positively bewildering to a stranger. No one seems to think of any one but himself, and each one jostles his neighbor or brushes by him with an indifference amusing to behold. Fine gentlemen in broadcloth, ladies in silks and jewels, and beggars in squalid rags, are mingled in true Republican confusion. The bustle and uproar are very great, generally making it impossible to converse in an ordinary tone. From early morn till after midnight the throng pours on.

At night the scene is different, but still brilliant. The vehicles in the street consist almost entirely of carriages and omnibuses, each with its lamps of different colors. They go dancing down the long vista like so many fire-flies. The shop-windows are brightly lighted, and the monster hotels pour out a flood of radiance from their myriads of lamps. Here and there a brilliant reflector at the door of some theatre, sends its dazzling white rays streaming along the street for several blocks. Below Canal street Broadway is dark and silent, but above that point it is as bright as day, and fairly alive with people. Those who are out now are mostly bent on pleasure, and the street resounds with cheerful voices and merry laughter, over which occasionally rises a drunken howl. Strains of music or bursts of applause float out on the night air from places of amusement, not all of which are reputable. Here and there a crowd has collected to listen to the music and songs of some of the wandering minstrels with which the city abounds. Gaudily painted transparencies allure the unwary to the vile concert saloons in the cellars below the street. The restaurants and cafés are ablaze with light, and are liberally patronized by the lovers of good living. Here and there, sometimes alone, and sometimes in couples, you see women, mainly young, and all flashily dressed, walking rapidly, with a peculiar gait, and glancing quickly but searchingly at every man they pass. You can single them out at a glance from the respectable women who happen to be out alone at this time. They are the "street walkers," seeking companions from among the passers-by. Some of them are mere children, and the heart aches to see the poor creatures at their fearful work. The police do not allow these women to stop and converse with men on Broadway, and when they find a companion they turn off promptly into a side street, and disappear with him in the darkness.

Towards eleven o'clock the theatres pour out their throngs of spectators, who come to swell the crowd on Broadway, and for a little while the noise and confusion are almost as great as in the day. Then the restaurants will close, and the street will gradually become deserted and dark, tenanted only by the giant police-men; and for a few hours the great city will be wrapped in silence and slumber.

VI.

SOCIETY.

I.

ANALYTICAL.

ALL the world over, poverty is a misfortune. In New York it is a crime. Here, as in no other place in the country, men struggle for wealth. They toil, they suffer privations, they plan and scheme, and execute with a persistency that often wins the success they covet. The chief effort of every man and woman in the great city is to secure wealth. Man is a social being—woman much more so—and here wealth is an absolute necessity to the enjoyment of social pleasures. Society here is organized upon a pecuniary basis, and stands not as it should upon the personal merits of those who compose it, but upon a pile of bank-books. In other cities, poor men, who are members of families which command respect for their talents or other admirable qualities, or who have merit of their own suffi- cient to entitle them to such recognition, are welcomed into what are called the "Select Circles" with as much cordiality as though they were millionaires. In New York, however, men and women are judged by their bank accounts. The most illite- rate boor, the most unprincipled knave finds the door of fash- ion open to him, while St. Peter himself, if he came "without purse or scrip," would see it closed in his face.

Society in New York is made up of many elements, the principal of which it is proposed to examine, but, unfortunately, wealth is the one thing needful in most of the classes into which it is divided. Nor is this strange. The majority of fashionable people have never known any of the arts and refinements of civilization except those which mere wealth can purchase. Money raised them from the dregs of life, and they are firm believers in it. Without education, without social polish, they see themselves courted and fawned upon for their wealth, and they naturally suppose that there is nothing else "good under the sun."

Those who claim precedence base their demand upon their descent from the original Dutch settlers, and style themselves "the old Knickerbockers." The majority of these are very wealthy, and have inherited their fortunes from their ancestors. They are owners of valuable real estate, much of which is located in the very heart of the city. The incomes derived from such property are large and certain. They are frequently persons of cultivation, and were it not for their affectation of superiority, would, as a class, be decidedly clever people, even if many of them are stupid. They make an effort to have their surroundings as clumsy and as old-fashioned as possible, as a mark of their Dutch descent. They sport crests and coats of arms such as the simple old Dutchmen of New Amsterdam never dreamed of, and rely more upon the merits of their forefathers than upon their own. They are extremely exclusive, and rarely associate with any but those who can "show as pure a pedigree." Their disdain of those whose families are not as "old" as their own is oftentimes amusing, and subjects them to ridicule, which they bear with true Dutch stolidity. They improve in their peculiar qualities with each generation, and the present pompous Knickerbocker who drives in the Park in solemn state in his heavy chariot, and looks down with disdain upon all whose blood is not as Dutch as his own, is a very different personage from his great ancestor, the original Knickerbocker, who hawked fish about the streets of New Amsterdam, or tanned leather down in "the swamp."

Strange to say, the Knickerbocker class receives fresh additions every year. Each new comer has a *Van* to his name, and can show a string of portraits of yellow-faced worthies, in leather breeches, and ruffles, and wigs, which he points to with

A FASHIONABLE PROMENADE ON FIFTH AVENUE.

pride as his "ancestors." The statistician would be sorely perplexed in attempting to ascertain the number of Dutch settlers in New Amsterdam were he to trace back the pedigrees of the present Knickerbockers, for if the claims of the present generation be admitted, one of two things is sure—either the departed Dutchmen must have been more " numerous fathers " than they cared to admit at the time, or the original population has been underestimated.

The next in order are those who, while making no boast of family, are persons who have inherited large wealth from several generations of ancestors. Freed from the necessity of earning their livings, they have an abundance of leisure in which to cultivate the " small sweet courtesies of life." They are neither shoddyites nor snobs, and while there are many who do no credit to their class, they constitute one of the pleasantest portions of metropolitan society. They furnish some of the most agreeable men, and some of the most beautiful and charming women in the city. Their homes are elegant, and abound in evidences of the taste of their owners, who spend their money liberally in support of literature and the arts. Here are to be found some of the rarest works of European and American masters. Unfortunately this class of New Yorkers is not very large. It is destined to increase, however, with the growth of wealth in the city. Good men, who have begun where the forefathers of these people started, will constantly contribute their children to swell this class, in which will always be collected those who unite true merit to great wealth, those who are proud of their country and its institutions, contented with its customs, and possessed of too much good sense to try to add to their importance by a ridiculous assumption of " aristocratic birth," or a pitiful imitation of the manners of the great of other lands.

The third class may be said to consist of those who value culture and personal excellence above riches. There is not much individual wealth in this class, but its members may be regarded as " persons in comfortable circumstances." They are better educated, have more correct tastes, and do the most to give to New York society its best and most attractive features.

It is a class to which merit is a sure passport. It is modest and unassuming, free from ostentatious parade, and, fortunately, is growing rapidly. It is made up of professional men of all kinds, clergymen, lawyers, poets, authors, physicians, painters, sculptors, journalists, scientific men, and actors, and their families. Its tone is vigorous and healthy, and it is sufficiently free from forms to make it independent, and possessed of means enough to enable it to pursue its objects without hindrance.

The remainder of those who constitute what is called society are the " New Rich," or as they are sometimes termed, the " Shoddyites." They constitute the majority of the fashionables, and their influence is felt in every department of domestic life. They are ridiculed by every satirist, yet they increase. Every year makes fresh accessions to their ranks, and their follies and extravagances multiply in proportion. They occupy the majority of the mansions in the fashionable streets, crowd the public thoroughfares and the Park with their costly and showy equipages, and flaunt their wealth so coarsely and offensively in the faces of their neighbors, that many good people have come to believe that riches and vulgarity are inseparable. They make themselves the most conspicuous, and are at once accepted by strangers as the " best society " of the metropolis.

They are almost without exception persons who have risen from the ranks. This is not to their discredit. On the contrary, every American is proud to boast that this is emphatically the land of self-made men, that here it is within the power of any one to rise as high in the social or political scale as his abilities will carry him. The persons to whom we refer, however, affect to despise this. They take no pride in the institutions which have been so beneficial to them, but look down with supreme disdain upon those who are working their way up. They are ashamed of their origin, and you cannot offend one of them more than to hint that you knew him a few years ago as a mechanic or a shopkeeper.

Some of the " fashionables " appear very unexpectedly before the world. But a short while ago a family may have been living in the humbler quarter of the city, or even in a tenement

house.   A sudden fortunate speculation on the part of the husband, or father, may have brought them enormous wealth in the
course of a few days.   A change is instantly made from the
humble abode to a mansion on Fifth or Madison avenue.   The
newly acquired wealth is liberally expended in "fitting up,"
and the lucky possessors of it boldly burst upon the world of
fashion as stars of the first magnitude.   They are courted by all
the newly rich, and invitations to the houses of other "stars"
are showered upon them.   They may be rude, ignorant, uncouth
in manner, but they have wealth, and that is all that is required.
They are lucky indeed, if they hold their positions long.   A few
manage to retain the wealth which comes to them thus suddenly,
but as a rule those who are simply lucky at the outset, find Dame
Fortune a very capricious goddess, and at the next turn of her
wheel pass off the stage to make room for others who are soon
to share the same fate.

During the oil speculations, and during the war, the shoddy
class was largely increased by those who were made suddenly
and unexpectedly rich by lucky ventures in petroleum lands and
stocks, and by army contracts.   Now other speculations provide recruits for this class, to which Wall street is constantly
sending fresh "stars" to blaze awhile in the firmament of
society, and then to make way for others.   The shoddy element
is not, however, confined to those who acquire wealth with
rapidity or by speculations.   There are many who rise very
slowly and painfully in the world, who, when blessed with fortune, throw themselves headlong into the arms of "shoddy."

It is not difficult to recognize these persons.   They dress not
only handsomely, but magnificently, making up in display what
they lack in taste.   They cover themselves with jewels, and
their diamonds, worn on ordinary occasions, might in some
instances rival the state gems of European sovereigns.   Their
rough, hard hands, coarse faces, loud voices, bad English, and
vulgar manners contrast strikingly with the splendors with
which they surround themselves.   They wear their honors
uneasily, showing how little they are accustomed to such things.
They look down with disdain upon all less fortunate in wealth

than themselves, and worship as demi-gods those whose bank accounts are larger than their own.   They are utterly lacking in personal dignity, and substitute for that quality a supercilious hauteur.

II.

FASHIONABLE EXTRAVAGANCE.

EXTRAVAGANCE is the besetting sin of New York society. Money is absolutely thrown away.   Fortunes are spent every year in dress and in all sorts of follies.   Houses are fitted up and furnished in the most sumptuous style, the building and its contents being sometimes worth a million of dollars.   People live up to every cent of their incomes, and often beyond them. It is no uncommon occurrence for a fine mansion, its furniture, pictures, and even the jewels of its occupants, to be pledged to some usurer for the means with which to carry on this life of luxury.   Each person strives to outdo his or her acquaintances. Those who have studied the matter find no slight cause for alarm in the rapid spread of extravagance among all classes of the city people, for the evil is not confined to the wealthy. They might afford it, but people of moderate means, who cannot properly make such a heavy outlay, are among those most guilty of the fault.

In no other city of the land is there to be seen such magnificent dressing on the part of the ladies as in New York.   The amount of money and time expended here on dress is amazing. There are two objects in view in all this—the best dressed woman at a ball or party is not only sure to outshine her sisters there present, but is certain to have the satisfaction next day of seeing her magnificence celebrated in some of the city journals. Her vanity and love of distinction are both gratified in this way, and such a triumph is held to be worth any expense. There is not an evening gathering but is graced by the presence of ladies clad in a style of magnificence which reminds one of the princesses in the fairy tales.   Says a recent writer:

"It is almost impossible to estimate the number of dresses a very fashionable woman will have. Most women in society can afford to dress as it pleases them, since they have unlimited amounts of money at their disposal. Among females dress is the principal part of society. What would Madam Mountain be without her laces and diamonds, or Madam Blanche without her silks and satins? Simply commonplace old women, past their prime, destined to be wall-flowers. A fashionable woman has just as many new dresses as the different times she goes into society. The *élite* do not wear the same dresses twice. If you can tell us how many receptions she has in a year, how many weddings she attends, how many balls she participates in, how many dinners she gives, how many parties she goes to, how many operas and theatres she patronizes, we can approximate somewhat to the size and cost of her wardrobe. It is not unreasonable to suppose that she has two new dresses of some sort for every day in the year, or 720. Now to purchase all these, to order them made, and to put them on afterward, consumes a vast amount of time. Indeed, the woman of society does little but don and doff dry-goods. For a few brief hours she flutters the latest tint and *mode* in the glare of the gas-light, and then repeats the same operation the next night. She must have one or two velvet dresses which cannot cost less than $500 each; she must possess thousands of dollars' worth of laces, in the shape of flounces, to loop up over the skirts of dresses, as occasion shall require. Walking-dresses cost from $50 to $300; ball-dresses are frequently imported from Paris at a cost of from $500 to a $1000; while wedding-dresses may cost from $1000 to $5000. Nice white Llama jackets can be had for $60; *robes princesse*, or overskirts of lace, are worth from $60 to $200. Then there are travelling-dresses in black silk, in pongee, velour, in piqué, which range in price from $75 to $175. Then there are evening robes in Swiss muslin, robes in linen for the garden and croquet-playing, dresses for horse-races and for yacht-races, *robes de nuit* and *robes de chambre*, dresses for breakfast and for dinner, dresses for receptions and for parties, dresses for watering-places, and dresses for all possible occasions. A lady going to the Springs takes from twenty to sixty dresses, and fills an enormous number of Saratoga trunks.   They are of every possible fabric—from Hindoo muslin, 'gaze de soie,' crape maretz, to the heavy silks of Lyons.

"We know the wife of the editor of one of the great morning newspapers of New York, now travelling in Europe, whose dress-making bill in one year was $10,000!   What her dry-goods bill amounted to heaven and her husband only know. She was once stopping at a summer hotel, and such was her anxiety to always appear in a new dress that she would frequently come down to dinner with a dress basted together just strong enough to last while she disposed of a little turtle-soup, a little Charlotte de Russe, and a little ice cream.

"Mrs. Judge ——, of New York, is considered one of the 'queens of fashion.'   She is a goodly-sized lady—not quite so tall as Miss Anna Swan, of Nova Scotia—and she has the happy faculty of piling more dry-goods upon her person than any other lady in the city; and what is more, she keeps on doing it.   To give the reader a taste of her quality, it is only necessary to describe a dress she wore at the Dramatic Fund Ball, not many years ago.   There was a rich blue satin skirt, *en train*.   Over this there was looped up a magnificent brocade silk, white, with bouquets of flowers woven in all the natural colors.   This over-skirt was deeply flounced with costly white lace, caught up with bunches of feathers of bright colors.   About her shoulders was thrown a fifteen-hundred dollar shawl.   She had a head-dress of white ostrich feathers, white lace, gold pendants, and purple velvet.   Add to all this a fan, a bouquet of rare flowers, a lace handkerchief, and jewelry almost beyond estimate, and you see Mrs. Judge —— as she appears when full blown.

"Mrs. General —— is a lady who goes into society a great deal.   She has a new dress for every occasion.   The following costume appeared at the Charity Ball, which is *the* great ball of the year in New York.   It was imported from Paris for the occasion, and was made of white satin, point lace, and a profusion of flowers.   The skirt had heavy flutings of satin around the bottom, and the lace flounces were looped up at the sides with bands of the most beautiful pinks, roses, lilies, forget-me-nots, and other flowers.

"It is nothing uncommon to meet in New York society ladies who have on dry-goods and jewelry to the value of from thirty to fifty thousand dollars. Dress patterns of twilled satin, the ground pale green, pearl, melon color, or white, scattered with sprays of flowers in raised velvet, sell for $300 dollars each; violet poult de soie will sell for $12 dollars a yard; a figured moire will sell for $200 the pattern; a pearl-colored silk, trimmed with point appliqué lace, sells for $1000; and so we might go on to an almost indefinite length."

Those who think this an exaggerated picture have only to apply to the proprietor of any first-class city dry-goods store, and he will confirm its truthfulness. These gentlemen will tell you that while their sales of staple goods are heavy, they are proportionately lighter than the sales of articles of pure luxury. At Stewart's the average sales of silks, laces, velvets, shawls, gloves, furs, and embroideries is about $24,500 per diem. The sales of silks alone average about $15,000 per diem.

A few years ago the dwelling of a wealthy citizen of New York was consumed by fire. The owner of the mansion soon after applied to a prominent Insurance Company for the payment of the sum of $21,000, the amount of the risk they had taken on the wearing apparel of his daughter, a young lady well known in society for the splendor of her attire. The company refused to pay so large a sum, and protested that the lady in question could not have possessed so costly a wardrobe. Suit was brought by the claimant, and, as a matter of course, an enumeration of the articles destroyed and their value was made to the court. The list was as follows, and is interesting as showing the mysteries of a fashionable lady's wardrobe:

6 silk robes—red, enamelled, green, blue, yellow, pink, black—with fringes, ruches, velvets, lace trimmings, etc.................$950
1 blue Marie Louise gros-de-Naples, brocaded with silver taken from the looms of Lyons; cost, without a stitch in it............. 300
Silver bullion fringe tassels and real lace to match............. 200

1 rose-colored satin, brocaded in white velvet, with deep flounce
ot real blonde lace, half-yard wide; sleeves and bertha richly
trimmed with the same rose-colored satin ribbon ; satin on each
side, with silk cord and tassel; lined throughout body, skirt and
sleeves with white silk ....,..............................$400
1 white satin of exceedingly rich quality, trimmed with blonde
and bugles; two flounces of very deep point d'Alençon, sleeves of
the same, reaching down to the elbows, and bertha to match, with
white bugles and blonde to match..........................2500
1 royal blue satin dress, trimmed, apron-shape, with black Brussels lace and gold and bugle trimmings, with one flounce, going all
around the skirt, of black Brussels lace; body and sleeves to
match; sleeves looped up with blue velvet roses set in lace, to
imitate a bouquet................... 1500
1 dove-colored satin dress, trimmed with velvet, half-yard deep ;
a long trail with the velvet going all around, with llama fringe and
dove-colored acorns, forming a heading to the velvet, and going all
up the skirt and around the long Greek sleeves ; the sleeves lined
with white satin and quills of silver ribbon going around the throat ;
lined throughout with white silk, having belonging to it a cloak
and hood, lined and trimmed to match; made in Paris........... 425
1 black Mantua velvet robe, long train, sleeves hanging down as
far as the knees, open, lined with white satin, and trimmed all
round with seed-pearls, as well as all round the top of low body—
the seed-pearls forming clusters of leaves going down front of
skirt and all round the skirt and train........................ 500
1 rich moire-antique dress, embroidered in gold from the body to
the skirt and sleeves and all round, taken up and fastened up with
gold embroidery to imitate the folds and wrinkles of the dress,
trimmed round the edge with white Brussels lace, having an underskirt of amber satin trimmed with Brussels lace, to show underneath ; lined throughout with silk............................. 400
1 large Brussels shawl, of exquisite fineness and elegance of
design, to go with it....................................... 700
1 crimson velvet dress, lined throughout with rose-colored silk;
train very long, trimmed with rich silk, blonde lace covering the
entire train, being carried around and brought up the front of the
dress and body, forming the bertha ; and sleeves looped up with
white roses ; turquoise fan and slippers to match............... 400
1 blue mercantique (lined), low body, trimmed with Honiton
lace, body and sleeves ; one piece of silk to match, unmade, intended for high body, and bons ; sleeves slashed open and lined
with white satin....................................... 200
1 rose-colored robe, with flounces ; high and low body, having
10

fringe and trimming woven to imitate Russian fur; both bodies
trimmed with fringe ribbons and narrow lace....................$250

1 mauve-colored glacé silk, braided and bugled all around the
bottom of skirt, on the front of body, around the band of Garibaldi
body, down the sleeves and round the cuffs of Garibaldi body; the
low body, with bertha deeply braided and bugled, with sleeves to
match; long sash, with end and bows and belts, all richly braided
and bugled with thread lace.. 180

1 vraie couleur de rose gros-de-Naples, with flounces richly brocaded with bouquet in natural size and color, made to represent the
same in panels, trimmed with gimp and fringe to match; also, high
and low body, with bertha and trimmings to match.............. 300

1 pink morning robe, very superb, trimmed down the side with
white satin a quarter of a yard wide, sleeves trimmed to match,
satin-stitched, with flounces in pink silk on edge of satin, passemen-
terie cord and tassels.. 250

1 gold-colored silk aersphane, with three skirts, each skirt
trimmed with quillings of yellow satin ribbon, looped up with pink
roses: body to match, trimmed with silk blonde; white blonde
round the neck; satin quillings; silk blonde on the sleeves, and lace
and yellow satin; rich underskirt to match..................... 100

2 very richly embroidered French cambric morning-dresses, with
bullion and heavy satin ribbons running through; one lined
throughout with pink, the other with blue silk.................. 100

1 rich black silk glacé, trimmed with bugles and black velvet... 200

1 blue-black Irish silk poplin, made in Gabrielle style, trimmed
with scarlet velvet all round the skirt; sleeves and body-belt and
buckle to match.. 125

1 Cashmere, shawl pattern, morning-dress, lined; sleeves and flies
lined with red silk, cord and tassels to match; not twice on....... 100

1 white Swiss muslin, with double skirt and ribbon running
through the upper and lower hems of each skirt, of pink satin; body
with Greek sleeves to match... 90

1 straw-colored silk dress, trimmed with black velvet, and body
of the same.. 80

1 white Swiss muslin robe, with one plain skirt and one above,
graduated by larger and smaller tucks, to imitate three flounces;
the sleeves with puffs, and long sleeves with tucks, down and across
to match skirts, and Garibaldi body made to match; one pink satin
under-body to go with it... 95

1 white Swiss muslin dress, with three flounces, quilled and
tucked, graduated one above the other, with headings of lace on the
top of each flounce; low body, with tuck, bretelles and broad colored
sarsnet ribbon... 90

1 India muslin dress, very full, embroidered to imitate three flounces; and Greek body and sleeves, also embroidered to match sky-blue skirt and body to go underneath........................$110

1 India muslin dress, double skirt, richly embroidered, with high jacket and long sleeves embroidered to match.................... 90

1 pink satin skirt and bodice, to go underneath................ 25

1 white long morning dress, embroidered round the skirt and up the front, in two flounces, one hanging over the other; sleeves and cuffs to match... 60

1 white muslin, with white spots, skirt and bodice trimmed with bullion and narrow real Valenciennes lace....................... 80

2 white cambric morning-dresses, one very richly embroidered, in wheels and flounces; and jacket to match....................... 275

1 white Swiss muslin jacket, very richly embroidered; skirt and bodice to match.. 100

3 cambric tight-fitting jackets, with collar and sleeves very richly embroidered, to imitate old Spanish point....................... 120

5 Marie Antoinettes, made entirely of French muslin, with triple bullion and double face; pink satin ribbon running through. Cost $60 each.. 300

1 piqué morning dress and jacket, richly embroidered.......... 75

1 piqué skirt, richly embroidered............................ 50

6 fine Swiss muslin skirts, four yards in each, trimmed with two rows of real lace, to set in full, finely finished.................... 55

2 very rich bastistes, for morning-dresses.................... 120

2 very fine cambric skirts, delicately embroidered, to wear with open morning-dresses... 60

2 fine linen skirts, embroidered in open work................ 40

2 silk grenadine dresses, trimmed with Maltese lace and velvet; two bodices to match, blue and green........................... 200

2 silk baréges, trimmed with velvet and fringe, and bodice to match.. 200

1 Scotch catlin silk full dress, Stewart, trimmed with black velvet and fringe, made to match colors of dress....................... 100

3 Balmoral skirts, very elegant, embroidered in silk............ 90

1 ponceau silk dress, trimmed with llama fringe and gold balls; body and sleeves very richly trimmed to match.................. 250

1 blue silk to match, trimmed with steel fringe and bugles; body and sleeves richly trimmed...................................... 250

1 French muslin jacket, with lapels and sleeves to turn back, very heavily embroidered.. 40

1 set point d'Alençon, consisting of shirt sleeves, handkerchief, and collar.. 120

1 point d'Alencon extra large handkerchief.................... 100

1 set Honiton lace, consisting of handkerchief, collar, and sleeves $80

1 set Maltese lace, consisting of handkerchief, collar, velvet cape 300

1 set Irish point lace, very rich, consisting of wide, deep sleeves, handkerchief and collar... 80

1 cape of ditto, going up to the neck and shut at the back...... 35

2 black lace mantillas.. 40

1 black lace jacket.. 15

1 cape, composed of Valenciennes lace....................... 75

2 dozen very rich embroidered cambric chemises, with lace..... 120

6 ditto, with puffed bullions in front....................... 100

18 Irish linen chemises, with very rich fronts................ 200

7 Irish linen, embroidered.................................. 40

1 dozen night-dresses, very rich fronts...................... 216

3 linen ditto, very rich.................................... 75

1 dozen embroidered drawers................................ 72

2 very rich ditto... 50

11 new pairs silk stockings, in box......................... 40

1 dozen Lisle thread stockings.............................. 20

9 pairs boots and shoes.................................... 45

3 pairs embroidered slippers, very rich, in gold............. 40

1 pair Irish point lace sleeves (extra)..................... 30

1 black velvet embroidered mantilla, imported............... 450

1 ditto, silk, embroidered with bugles, imported............ 100

1 glacé silk, tight-fitting basque, with black zeplore lace cape; trimmed in every width with narrow lace to match............. 65

1 black silk Arab, with two tassels........................ 25

1 dust-wrapper, from Cashmere.............................. 18

4 magnificent opera-cloaks................................. 175

1 red scarlet cloth cloak, trimmed with yellow cord......... 12

1 cloth, drab-color cloak 8

1 cloak, with hood lined with silk......................... 10

2 dozen cambric, embroidered, with name Fanny.............. 24

1 set Russian sable muffs, cape and boa.................... 100

1 tortoise shell comb, made in one piece and very rich...... 50

6 fancy combs... 30

1 very rich mother-of-pearl, gold inlaid, and vol. feathers beautifully painted by hand................................ 85

1 fan of mother-of-pearl, inlaid in gold, with silk and white and Job's spangles.. 45

1 blue mother-of-pearl, with looking-glass; imitation ruby and emeralds... 35

6 other fans, of various kinds............................. 25

1 parasol, all ivory handle throughout, engraved with name in full, covering of silk and Irish point lace, very fine, covering the entire parasol.. 100

Several other parasols...$ 25
1 real gold head-ornament, representing the comet and eclipse
appearing... 100
About twenty hair-nets, silver, gold, and all colors and pearls...   40
4 ladies' bonnets, some exceedingly elegant.................... 100
1 box marabout feathers, for dressing the hair.................   50
1 box artificial flowers..   15
1 lot new ribbon, for sashes; velvet, silk, and satin.............   35
1 small miniature model piano, played by mechanism, from
Vienna...   50
1 lady's writing-desk, inlaid with tortoise-shell and mother-of-
pearl, lined with silk velvet, with compartments and secretary;
carved mother-of-pearl paper-knife, gold seal, gold pencil, case full
of fancy writing paper; made in Paris.......................... 200
1 bula work-box, elegant; inlaid with silver and lined with
ci-satin, fitted with gold thimble, needle, scissors, pen-knife, gold
bodkin, cotton winders; outside to match French piano.......... 125
1 long knitting-case to match the above, fitted with needles, beads
and silk of every description....................................   40
1 papier-maché work-box, and fitted up......................   5
1 morocco work-bag, ornamented with bright steel; fitted up with
scissors, thimble, etc..   3
1 lady's Russia leather shopping-bag, with silver and gilt clasps
for chain and key...   15
1 18-karat gold filigree card-case.............................   20
1 set gold whist-markers, in hands on little box, a present unto
her..   50
1 lady's small work-bag, silk fittings.........................   5
1 solid silver porte-monnaie....................................   19
1 little blue port-monnaie; velvet, and cords and tassel.........   3
1 ladies' companion, with fixings in silver; a present...........   45
1 hair-pin stand; a small book-case, with small drawers and
mirror..   14
1 basket of mother-of-pearl, and gilt and red satin, full of wax-
flowers...   35
1 elegant Bible in gilt, edge mounted in gold...................   30
43 volumes various miniature books, bound most elegantly in
morocco, and brought as a present from Europe................. 100
1 silver pin-cushion and sewer for fastening on the table........   23
1 elegant, richly carved ivory work-table, brought from Mexico,
inside fitted up with silk and different compartments, standing three
feet high.. 400
1 lady's solid silver rutler, from Mexico......................   25
1 gilt head-ornament, representing a dagger....................   3

1 lady's English dressing-case, solid silver fittings, English make and stamp, rosewood, bound with brass and gilt, fitted and lined with silver $250

1 pair rich carved ivory hair brushes, engraved with name and crest.. 155

1 ditto engraved and crest... 55

1 small ivory hair-brush... 12

1 ebony hair-brush, inlaid with mother-of-pearl..................... 20

1 Berlin-wool worked cushion... 50

1 sewing-chair, elegantly embroidered seat and back............. 75

1 Berlin-wool Affghan... 100

1 fire-screen, Berlin work, beads, representing Charles II. hunting 125

1 large sole-leather trunk, about four feet long and three feet deep, lined with red morocco, handsomely ornamented in gold, embossed on the red morocco, with seven compartments; very scientifically constructed for the necessities of a lady's wardrobe, with springs to hold open each compartment; and the lace compartment could, at pleasure, be rested on two steel legs, covered with gilt embossed morocco, representing a writing table, with a portfolio, containing writing materials; it had two large French patent locks 250

1 lady's travelling trunk, with cover, containing a quantity of worn dresses, zouave cloth and gold, druided jacket cloaks, woollen ditto, opera cloak, etc.. 73

Total $21,000

Such lavish expenditure is a natural consequence of a state of society where wealth is the main distinction. Mrs. John Smith's position as a leader of the *ton* is due exclusively to her great riches and her elaborate displays. Mrs. Richard Roe will naturally try to outshine her, and thus rise above her in the social scale. Many persons seeking admission into such society, and finding wealth the only requisite, will make any sacrifice to accomplish their end. If they have not wealth they will affect to have it. They could not counterfeit good birth, or high breeding, but they can assume the appearance of being wealthy. They can conduct themselves, for a while at least, in a manner utterly disproportioned to their means, and so they go on, until their funds and credit being exhausted, they are forced to drop out of the circles in which they have moved, and the so-called friends who valued them only for their supposed wealth, instantly forget that they ever knew them. No more invitations are left for them, they are not even tolerated in "good society," and are "cut" on the street as a matter of course.

Not a year passes but records the failure of some prominent business man in New York. His friends are sorry for him, and admit that he was prudent and industrious in his business. "His family did it," they tell you, shaking their heads. "They lived too fast. Took too much money to run the house, to dress, and to keep up in society." Only the All Seeing Eye can tell how many men who stand well in the mercantile community are tortured continually by the thought that their extravagance or that of their families is bringing them to sure and certain ruin; for not even in New York can a man live beyond his actual means. They have not the moral courage to live within their legitimate incomes. To do so would be to lose their positions in society, and they go on straining every nerve to meet the demands upon them, and then the crash comes, and they are ruined.

Those who dwell in the great city, and watch its ways with observant eyes, see many evils directly attributable to the sin of extravagance. These evils are not entirely of a pecuniary nature. There are others of a more terrible character. Keen observers see every day women whose husbands and fathers are in receipt of limited incomes, dressing as if their means were unlimited. All this magnificence is not purchased out of the lawful income of the husband or father. The excess is made up in other ways—often by the sacrifice of the woman's virtue. She finds a man willing to pay liberally for her favors, and carries on an intrigue with him, keeping her confiding husband in ignorance of it all the while. She may have more than one lover—perhaps a dozen. When a woman sins from motives such as these, she does not stop to count the cost. Her sole object is to get money, *and she gets it.* It is this class of nominally virtuous married and unmarried women that support the infamous houses of assignation to be found in the city.

The curse of extravagance does not manifest itself in dress alone. One cannot enter the residence of a single well-to-do person in the city without seeing evidences of it.   The house is loaded with the richest and rarest of articles, all intended for show, and which are oftentimes arranged without the least regard to taste.   The object is to make the house indicate as much wealth on the part of its owner as possible.   It makes but little difference whether the articles are worth what was paid for them, or whether they are arranged artistically—if the sum total is great, the owner is satisfied.   It is a common thing to see the walls of some elegant mansion disfigured with frescoes, which, though executed at an enormous cost, are utterly without merit or taste.   Again one sees dozens of paintings, bought for works of the old masters, lining the walls of the richest mansions of the city, which are the merest daubs, and the works of the most unscrupulous Bohemians.   Not long since a collection of paintings was offered for sale in New York, the owner being dead.   They had been collected at great expense, and were the pride of their former owner.   With a few exceptions they were wretched copies, and in the whole lot, over five hundred in number, there were not six genuine " old masters," or " masters " of any age.

Entertainments are given in the most costly style.   From ten to twenty thousand dollars are spent in a single evening in this way.   At a fashionable party from twelve to fifteen hundred dollars' worth of champagne is consumed, besides other wines and liquors.   Breakfasts are given at a cost of from one to three thousand dollars; suppers at a still higher cost.   This represents the expense to the host of the entertainment; but does not cover the cost of the toilettes to be provided for the family, which make up several thousand dollars more.

Suppers or dinners are favorite entertainments, and the outlay required for them is oftentimes very heavy.   The host frequently provides nothing but viands imported from foreign lands.   Sets of china of great cost, or of silver equally expensive, or even of gold, are displayed ostentatiously.   Sometimes the supper-room is entirely refitted in red, blue, or gold, everything, even the lights and flowers, being of one color, in order that the affair may be known as Mrs. A—'s red, blue, or gold supper. Some of the most extravagant entertainers will place at the side of each cover an exquisite bouquet inside of which is a costly present of jewelry.

All this reckless expenditure in the midst of so much sorrow and suffering in the great city! "The bitter cold of winter," says the Manager of the 'Children's Aid Society,' in his appeal for help, "and the freezing storms have come upon thousands of the poor children of this city, unprepared. They are sleeping in boxes, or skulking in doorways, or shivering in cellars without proper clothing, or shoes, and but half-fed. Many come bare-footed through the snow to our industrial schools. Children have been known to fall fainting on the floor of these schools through want of food. Hundreds enter our lodging-houses every night, who have no home. Hundreds apply to our office for a place in the country, who are ragged, half-starved, and utterly unbefriended."

III.

FASHIONABLE FOLLIES.

WE have spoken of the women of fashion. What shall we say of the men? They are neither refined nor intellectual. They have a certain shrewdness coupled, perhaps, with the capacity for making money. Their conversation is coarse, ignorant, and sometimes indecent. They have not the tact which enables women to adapt themselves at once to their surroundings, and they enjoy their splendors with an awkwardness which they seek to hide beneath an air of worldly wisdom. They patronize the drama liberally, but their preference is for what Olive Logan calls "the leg business." In person they are coarse-looking. Without taste of their own, they are totally dependent upon their tailors for their "style," and are nearly all gotten up on the same model. They are capital hands at staring ladies out of countenance, and are masters of all the arts of insolence. Society cannot make gentlemen out of them do what it will. As John Hibbs would say, "they were not brought up to it young." They learn to love excitement, and finding even the reckless whirl of fashion too stale for them, seek gratification out of their own homes. They become constant visitors at the great gaming-houses, and are the best customers of the bagnios of the city.

If men have their dissipations, the women have theirs also. Your fashionable woman generally displays more tact than her husband. She has greater opportunities for display, and makes better use of them. If the ball, or party, or sociable at her residence is a success, the credit is hers exclusively, for the husband does little more than pay the bills. Many of these women are "from the ranks." They have risen with their husbands, and are coarse and vulgar in appearance, and without refinement. But the women of fashion are not all vulgar or unrefined. Few of them are well educated, but the New York woman of fashion, as a rule, is not only very attractive in appearance, but capable of creating a decided impression upon the society in which she moves. She is thoroughly mistress of all its arts, she knows just when and where to exercise them to the best advantage, she dresses in a style the magnificence of which is indescribable, and she has tact enough to carry her through any situation. Yet, in judging her, one must view her as a butterfly, as a mere creature of magnificence and frivolity. Don't seek to analyze her character as a wife or mother. You may find that the marriage vow is broken on her part as well as on her husband's; and you will most probably find that she has sacrificed her soul to the demands of fashion, and "prevented the increase of her family" by staining her hands in the blood of her unborn children. Or, if she be guiltless of this crime, she is a mother in but one sense— that of bearing children. Fashion does not allow her to nurse them. She cannot give to her own flesh and blood the time demanded of her by her "duties in society;" so from their very birth the little innocents are committed to the care of hirelings, and they grow up without her care, removed from the ennobling effect of a mother's constant watchful presence, and they add to the number of idle, dissolute men and women of fashion, who are a curse to the city.

Your fashionable woman is all art. She is indeed " fearfully and wonderfully made." She is a compound frequently of false hair, false teeth, padding of various kinds, paint, powder and enamel. Her face is " touched up," or painted and lined by a professional adorner of women, and she utterly destroys the health of her skin by her foolish use of cosmetics. A prominent Broadway dealer in such articles sells thirteen varieties of powder for the skin, eight kinds of paste, and twenty-three different washes. Every physical defect is skilfully remedied by " artists ;" each of whom has his specialty. So common has the habit of resorting to these things become, that it is hard to say whether the average woman of fashion is a work of nature or a work of art. Men marry such women with a kind of " taking the chances" feeling, and if they get a natural woman think themselves lucky.

IV.

FASHIONABLE CHILDREN.

As it is the custom in fashionable society in New York to prevent the increase of families, it is natural no doubt to try to destroy childhood in those who are permitted to see the light.

The fashionable child of New York is made a miniature man or woman at the earliest possible period of its life. It does not need much labor, however, to develop " Young America " in the great metropolis. He is generally ready to go out into the world at a very tender age. Our system of society offers him every facility in his downward career. When but a child he has his own latch-key ; he can come and go when he pleases ; he attends parties, balls, dancing-school, the theatre and other evening amusements as regularly and independently as his elders, and is rarely called upon by " the Governor," as he patronizingly terms his father, to give any account of himself. He has an abundance of pocket-money, and is encouraged in the lavish expenditure of it. He cultivates all the vices of his grown-up friends; and thinks church going a punishment and religion a bore. He engages in his dissipations with a recklessness that makes old sinners envious of his "nerve." His friends are hardly such as he could introduce into his home. He is a famous "hunter of the tiger," and laughs at his losses. He has a mistress, or perhaps several; sneers at marriage, and gives it as his opinion that there is not a virtuous woman in the land. When he is fairly of age he has lost his freshness, and is tired of life. His great object now is to render his existence supportable.

Girls are forced into womanhood by fashion even more rapidly than boys into manhood. They are dressed in the most expensive manner from their infancy, and without much regard to their health. Bare arms and necks, and short skirts are the rule, even in the bleakest weather, for children's parties, or for dancing-school, and so the tender frames of the little ones are subjected to an exposure that often sows the seeds of consumption and other disease. The first thing the child learns is that it is its duty to be pretty—to look its best. It is taught to value dress and show as the great necessities of existence, and is trained in the most extravagant habits. As the girl advances towards maidenhood, she is forced forward, and made to look as much like a woman as possible. Her education is cared for after a fashion, but amounts to very little. She learns to play a little on some musical instrument, to sing a little, to paint a little—in short she acquires but a smattering of everything she undertakes. She is left in ignorance of the real duties of a woman's life—the higher and nobler part of her existence. She marries young, and one of her own set, and her married life is in keeping with her girlhood. She is a creature in which nothing has been fully developed but the passions and the nerves. Her physical constitution amounts to nothing, and soon gives way. Her beauty goes with her health, and she is forced to resort to all manner of devices to preserve her attractions.

It is a habit in New York to allow children to give large

entertainments at fashionable resorts, without the restraining presence of their elders.   Here crowds of boys and girls of a susceptible age assemble under the intoxicating influence of music, gas-light, full dress, late suppers, wines and liquors. Sometimes this juvenile dissipation has been carried so far that it has been sharply rebuked by the public press.

V.

A FASHIONABLE BELLE.

An English writer gives the following clever sketch of a fashionable young lady of New York, whom he offers as a type of the " Girl of the Period : "

"Permit me to present you to Miss Flora Van Duysen Briggs.   Forget Shakspeare's *dictum* about a name; there is a story attached to this name which I shall tell you by and by Miss Flora is a typical New York girl of the period ; between sixteen and seventeen years old ; a little under the medium height; hair a golden brown ; eyes a violet blue ; cheeks and lips rosy ; teeth whiter and brighter than pearls ; hands and feet extremely small and well-shaped ; figure *petite* but exquisitely proportioned ; *toilette* in the latest *mode de Paris ;* but observe, above all, that marvellous bloom upon her face, which American girls share with the butterfly, the rose, the peach and the grape, and in which they are unequalled by any other women in the world.

"Miss Flora's biography is by no means singular.   Her father is Ezra Briggs, Esq., a provision merchant in the city. Twenty-five years ago, Mr. Briggs came to New York from one of the Eastern States, with a common-school education, sharp sense, and no money.   He borrowed a newspaper, found an advertisement for a light porter, applied for and obtained the situation, rose to be clerk, head-clerk, and small partner, and fagged along very comfortably until the Civil War broke out, and made his fortune.   His firm secured a government contract, for which they paid dearly, and for which they made the Gov-

ernment pay dearer.   Their pork was bought for a song, and
sold for its weight in greenbacks.   Their profits averaged 300
per cent.   They were more fatal to the soldiers than the bullets
of the enemy.   One consignment of their provisions bred a
cholera at Fortress Monroe, and robbed the Union of 15,000
brave men.   Their enemies declared that the final defeat of the
Southerners was owing to the capture of 1000 barrels of
Briggs's mess beef by General Lee.   But Briggs was rolling in
wealth, and could afford to smile at such taunts.

"Flora's mother had been a Miss Van Duysen.   She was a
little, weak, useless woman, very proud of her name, which
seemed to connect her in some way with the old Dutch aristocracy.   In point of fact, Briggs married her on this account;
for, like most democrats, he is very fond of anything aristocratic.
Mrs. Briggs, *née* Van Duysen, has nothing Dutch about her but
her name.   The Knickerbockers of New York were famous for
their thrift, their economy, their neatness, and, above all, their
housewifely virtues.   Mrs. Briggs is thriftless, extravagant,
dowdy in her old age, although she had been a beauty in her
youth, and knows as little about keeping a house as she does
about keeping a horse.   During the war, at a fair given for the
benefit of the Sanitary Commission, in Union Square, several
Knickerbocker ladies organized a kitchen upon the old Dutch
model, and presided there in the costumes of their grandmothers.
Mrs. Briggs was placed upon the committee of management, but
declined to serve, on account of the unbecoming costume she
was invited to wear, and because she considered it unladylike to
sit in a kitchen.   But Mrs. Briggs preserved her caste, and
benefited the Sanitary Commission much more than she would
have done by her presence, by sending a cheque for $500
instead.

"Do we linger too long upon these family matters?   No; to
appreciate Miss Flora, you must understand her surroundings.
She has never had a home.   Born in a boarding-house, when
her parents were not rich, she lives at a hotel now that her
father is a millionaire.   Mr. Briggs married the name of Van
Duysen, in order to get into society.   Miss Van Duysen mar-

ried Briggs's money, in order to spend it.   Miss Flora Van Duysen Briggs combines her mother's name and her father's money; her mother's early beauty and her father's shrewdness; her mother's extravagance and her father's weakness for the aristocracy.   She has good taste, as her *toilette* shows; but she does not believe that anything can be tasteful that is not expensive.   Her aim is to run ahead of the fashions, instead of following them; but she is clever enough to so adapt them to her face and figure, that she always looks well-dressed, and yet always attracts attention.   Her little handsome head is full of native wit, and of nothing else.   Her education has been shamefully neglected.   She has had the best masters, who have taught her nothing.   Like all other American girls, she plays on the piano, but does not play the piano—you will please notice this subtle but suggestive distinction.   She has picked up a smattering of French, partly because it is a fashionable accomplishment, and partly because she intends to marry; but I will not yet break your heart by announcing her matrimonial intentions. Compared with an English or French girl of the same age, she has many and grave deficiencies; but she atones for them by a wonderful tact and cleverness, which blind you to all her faults and lend a new grace to all her virtues.

"Truth to say, the admirers of Miss Flora, whose name is Legion, give her the credit for all her own virtues, and blame her father and mother, and the system, for all her faults.   Born, as we have said, in a boarding-house, left entirely in charge of the nurse-maid, educated at a fashionable day-school, brought into society before fifteen, living in the whirl, the bustle, the luxury, and the unhomeliness of a hotel, what could you expect of Miss Flora but that she should be, at seventeen years of age, a butterfly in her habits, a clever dunce as regards solid knowledge, and a premature woman of the world in her tastes and manners?   The apartments which the Briggs family occupy at the Fifth Avenue Hotel are magnificently decorated and furnished, but they do not constitute a home.   Several times Mr. Briggs has offered to purchase a house in a fashionable thoroughfare; but his wife objects to the trouble of managing unruly

servants, and terrifies Mr. Briggs out of the notion by stories
of burglars admitted, and plate stolen, and families murdered in
their beds, through the connivance of the domestics.   What
more can any one desire than the Briggs family obtain at the
hotel for a fixed sum per week, and a liberal margin for extras?
The apartments are ample and comfortable ; the *cuisine* and the
wines are irreproachable ; there is a small table reserved for
them, to which they can invite whom they choose ; an immense
staff of servants obey their slightest wish ; their carriages, kept
at a neighboring livery stable, can be sent for at any moment ;
they are as secluded in their own rooms as if they lived in another street, so far as the family in the next *suite* is concerned ;
they are certain to meet everybody, and can choose their own
company ; the spacious hotel parlors are at their disposal whenever they wish to give an evening party, reception, or *thé dansant*.
What more could they gain by setting up a private house?   Mr.
Briggs, having never tried the experiment, does not know.
Mrs. Briggs, whose only reminiscence of a private residence is
the one in which her mother let lodgings, does not know.   Miss
Flora Van Duysen Briggs, having never been used to any other
way of life than the present, neither knows nor cares, and 'does
not want to be bothered.'

"The Briggs family spend their winters in town, their sum-
mers at Newport, Saratoga, or some other watering-place, at
which nobody cares anything about the water.   The frequenters
of these rural or seaside retreats are presumed to come for their
health, but really come to show their dresses.   Thus Miss
Flora's life varies very little all the year round ; she rises late,
and is dressed for breakfast ; after breakfast she practises upon
the piano, shops with her mamma, and returns to be dressed for
luncheon ; after luncheon she usually takes a brief nap, or lies
down to read a novel, and is then dressed for the afternoon
promenade, as you have just seen her ; after the promenade she
is dressed for a drive with mamma in the Central Park ; after
the drive she is dressed for dinner, or dines in her out-of-door
costume, preparatory to being dressed for the opera, the theatre,
a ball, or a party.   Every Tuesday she receives calls ; every

Thursday she calls upon her acquaintances. Whenever she has
a spare moment, it is bestowed upon her dressmaker. If she
thinks, it is to design new trimmings; if she dreams, it is of a
heavenly *soirée dansante*, with an eternal waltz to everlasting
music, and a tireless partner in paradisiacal Paris.

"As all the best and—in a double sense—the dearest things
of Miss Flora's life come from Paris, it is quite natural that she
should look to Paris for her future. The best of all authorities
declares that 'where the treasure is there will the heart be also.'
Miss Flora's treasures are in the Parisian *magasins*, and her
heart is with them. Although scores of young men kneel at
her feet, press her hands, and deride the stars in comparison
with her eyes, she cares for none of her worshippers. She
smiles upon them, but the smile is no deeper than the lips; she
flirts with them, but stops at that sharp, invisible line which
separates a flirtation from a compromising earnestness; she is a
coquette, but not a jilt. If she encourages all, it is because she
prefers none. Her heart has never been touched, and she knows
that none of her admirers in her own country can hope to touch
it. Her rivals scornfully assert that she has no heart; but as
she is, after all, a woman, this assertion must be incorrect. She
is in love with an ideal, but that ideal has a title. So soon as
Mr. Briggs can dispose of his business, Miss Flora is to be
taken to Paris. Within two years afterwards she will be led
to the altar by a French duke, marquis, or count, who will fall
in love with her father's bank-book, and then she will figure as
an ornament of the French Court, or the *salons* of the Faubourg
Saint-Germain. This is her ambition, and she will certainly
accomplish it. The blood of the Van Duysens and the money
of Briggs can accomplish anything when united in Miss Flora.
With this end in view, the little lady is as inaccessible to ordinary admirers as a princess. She is a duchess by anticipation,
and feels the pride of station in advance. There is no danger
that she will falter in the race through any womanly weakness,
nor through any lack of knowledge of the wiles of men. With
the beauty of Venus and the chastity of Diana, she also possesses qualities derived directly from Mother Eve. An English

11

matron would blush to know, and a French *mère* would be astonished to learn, secrets which Miss Flora has at her pretty finger-ends. She has acquired her knowledge innocently, and she will use it judiciously. Nothing escapes her quick eyes and keen ears, and under that demure forehead is a faculty which enables her to 'put this and that together,' and arrive at conclusions which would amaze her less acute foreign sisters. You may not envy her this faculty, but do not accuse her of employing it improperly. She will never disgrace herself nor the coronet which she already feels pressing lightly upon her head. As she trips out of sight, it may give any man a heart-pang to think that there is at least one lovely woman who is impenetrable to love; but then, if she were like those dear, soft, fond, impressible, confiding beauties of a former age, she would not be herself—a Girl of the Period."

VI.

FASHIONABLE ENTERTAINMENTS.

NEW YORK has long been celebrated for its magnificent social entertainments. Its balls, dinner parties, receptions, private theatricals, pic-nics, croquet parties, and similar gatherings are unsurpassed in respect to show in any city in the world. Every year some new species of entertainment is devised by some leader in society, and repeated throughout the season by every one who can raise the money to pay for it. The variety, however, is chiefly in the name, for all parties, breakfasts, dinners, suppers, or receptions are alike.

Of late years it is becoming common not to give entertainments at one's residence, but to hire public rooms set apart for that purpose. There is a large house in the upper part of Fifth avenue, which is fitted up exclusively for the use of persons giving balls, suppers, or receptions. It is so large that several entertainments can be held at the same time on its different floors, without either annoying or inconveniencing the others.

The proprietor of the establishment provides everything down to the minutest detail, the wishes and tastes of the giver of the entertainment being scrupulously respected in everything. The host and hostess, in consequence, have no trouble, but have simply to be on hand at the proper time to receive their guests. This is a very expensive mode of entertaining, and costs from 5000 to 15,000 dollars, for the caterer expects a liberal profit on everything he provides; but to those who can afford it, it is a very sensible plan. It saves an immense amount of trouble at home, and preserves one's carpets and furniture from the damage invariably done to them on such occasions, and averts all possibility of robbery by the strange servants one is forced to employ. Still, many who possess large and elegant mansions of their own prefer to entertain at their own homes.

On such occasions, the lady giving the entertainment issues her invitations, and usually summons the famous Brown, the Sexton of Grace Church, to assist her in deciding who shall be asked beyond her immediate circle of friends. Mr. Brown is a very tyrant in such matters, and makes out the list to suit himself rather than to please the hostess. He has full authority from her to invite any distinguished strangers who may be in the city.

Upon the evening appointed a carpet is spread from the curbstone to the front door, and over this is placed a temporary awning. A policeman is engaged to keep off the crowd and regulate the movements of the carriages. About nine o'clock magnificent equipages, with drivers and footmen in livery, commence to arrive, and from these gorgeous vehicles richly dressed ladies and gentlemen alight, and pass up the carpeted steps to the entrance door. On such occasions gentlemen are excluded from the carriage if possible, as all the space within the vehicle is needed for the lady's skirts. The lady is accompanied by a maid whose business it is to adjust her *toilette* in the dressing room, and see that everything is in its proper place.

At the door stands some one, generally the inevitable Brown, to receive the cards of invitation. Once admitted, the ladies and gentlemen pass into the dressing rooms set apart for them.

Here they put the last touches to their dress and hair, and, the ladies having joined their escorts, enter the drawing room and pay their respects to the host and hostess. When from one to two thousand guests are to be received, the reader may imagine that the labors of the host and hostess are not slight.

Every arrangement is made for dancing. A fine orchestra is provided, and is placed so that it may consume as little space as possible. A row of chairs placed around the room, and tied in couples with pocket-handkerchiefs, denotes that "The German" is to be danced during the course of the evening. There is very little dancing, however, of any kind, before midnight, the intervening time being taken up with the arrivals of guests and promenading.

About midnight the supper room is thrown open, and there is a rush for the tables, which are loaded with every delicacy that money can buy. The New York physicians ought to be devoutly thankful for these suppers. They bring them many a fee. The servants are all French, and are clad in black swallow-tail coats and pants, with immaculate white vests, cravats and gloves. They are as active as a set of monkeys, and are capital hands at anticipating your wants. Sometimes the refreshments are served in the parlors, and are handed to the guests by the servants.

The richest and costliest of wines flow freely. At a certain entertainment given not long since, 500 bottles of champagne, worth over four dollars each, were drunk. Some young men make a habit of abstaining carefully during the day, in order to be the better prepared to drink at night. The ladies drink almost as heavily as the men, and some of them could easily drink their partners under the table.

After supper the dancing begins in earnest. If The German is danced it generally consumes the greater part of the evening. I shall not undertake to describe it here. It is a great mystery, and those who understand it appear to have exhausted in mastering it their capacity for understanding anything else. It is a dance in which the greatest freedom is permitted, and in which liberties are taken and encouraged, which would be re-

THE GERMAN.

sented under other circumstances. The figures really depend
upon the leader of the dance, who can set such as he choses, or
devise them, if he has wit enough.   All the rest are compelled
to follow his example. The dance is thoroughly suited to the

society we are considering, and owes its popularity to the liberties, to use no stronger term, it permits.

The *toilettes* of the persons present are magnificent. The ladies are very queens in their gorgeousness. They make their trails so long that half the men are in mortal dread of breaking their necks over them; and having gone to such expense for dry goods in this quarter, they display the greatest economy about the neck and bust. They may be in "full dress" as to the lower parts of their bodies, but they are fearfully undressed from the head to the waist.

Towards morning the ball breaks up. The guests, worn out with fatigue, and not unfrequently confused with liquor, take leave of their hosts and go home. Many of them repeat the same performance almost nightly during the season. No wonder that when the summer comes they are so much in need of recuperation.

VII.

MARRIAGE AND DEATH.

ONLY wealthy marriages are tolerated in New York society. For men or women to marry beneath them is a crime society cannot forgive. There must be fortune on one side at least. Marriages for money are directly encouraged. It is not uncommon for a man who has won a fortune to make the marriage of his daughter the means of getting his family into society. He will go to some young man within the pale of good society, and offer him the hand of his daughter and a fortune. The condition demanded of the aforesaid young man is that he shall do what may lie within his power to get the family of the bride within the charmed circle. If the girl is good looking, or agreeable, the offer is rarely refused.

When a marriage is decided upon, the engagement is announced through one of the "society newspapers," of which there are several. It is the bounden duty of the happy pair to be married in a fashionable church. To be married in or buried from

Grace or St. Thomas's Church, is the desire of every fashionable heart. Invitations are issued to the friends of the two families, and no one is admitted into the church without a card. Often " no cards " are issued, and the church is jammed by the outside throng, who profane the holy temple by their unmannerly struggles to secure places from which to view the ceremony. Two clergymen are usually engaged to tie the knot, in order that a Divorce Court may find it the easier to undo. A reporter is on hand, who furnishes the city papers with a full description of the grand affair. The dresses, the jewels, the appearance of the bride and groom, and the company generally, are described with all the eloquence Jenkins is master of.

If the wedding be at Grace Church, Brown, " the great sexton " is in charge. A wedding over which he presides is sure to be a great success. A wonderful man is Brown. No account of New York society would be complete without a few words about Brown. He has been sexton of Grace Church ever since the oldest inhabitant can remember, and those familiar with the matter are sorely puzzled to know what the church will do when Brown is gathered to his fathers. The congregation would sooner part with the best Rector they have ever had than give up Brown. A certain Rector did once try to compel him to resign his post because he, the Rector, did not fancy Brown's ways, which he said were hardly consistent with the reverence due the house of God. The congregation, however, were aghast at the prospect of losing Brown, and plainly gave the Rector to understand that he must not interfere with the sexton. Never mind about his want of reverence. The Rector's business was to look after the religious part of the congregation, while Brown superintended the secular affairs of that fashionable corporation. They had use for the Rector only on Sunday ; but Brown they looked up to every day in the week. The Rector meekly subsided, and Brown forgave him.

A very lucky man is Brown, and very far from being a fool. There is no sharper, shrewder man in New York, and no one who estimates his customers more correctly. He puts a high price on his services, and is said to have accumulated a handsome fortune, popularly estimated at about $300,000. Fat and sleek, and smooth of tongue, he can be a very despot when he chooses. He keeps a list of the fashionable young men of the city, who find it to their interest to be on good terms with him, since they are mainly dependent upon him for their invitations. Report says that, like a certain great statesman, Brown is not averse to receiving a small present now and then as a reminder of the gratitude of the recipients of his favors.

Brown is sixty years old, but time has dealt lightly with him, and he is still hale and hearty. He knows all the gossip of New York for thirty years back, but also knows how to hold his tongue. To see him in his glory, one should wait until the breaking up of some great party. Then he takes his stand on the steps of the mansion, and in the most pompous manner calls the carriages of the guests. There is no chance for sleep in the neighborhood when the great voice of the " great sexton" is roaring down the avenue. He takes care that the whole neighborhood shall know who have honored the entertainment with their presence.

He has a sharp tongue, too, this Brown, when he chooses to use it, and a good story is told of this quality of his. He was once calling the carriages at a brilliant party. Among the guests was Harry X——, a young gentleman of fortune, concerning whose morals some hard things were said. It was hinted that Mr. X—— was rather too fond of faro. The young gentleman and the great sexton were not on good terms, and when Brown, having summoned Mr. X——'s carriage, asked, as usual, " Where to, sir?" he received the short and sharp reply, " To where he brought me from." "All right, sir," said Brown, calmly, and turning to the driver he exclaimed in a loud tone, " Drive Mr. X—— to John Chamberlain's faro-bank." A roar of laughter greeted this sally, and Brown smiled serenely as his discomfited enemy was driven away.

Fashionable weddings are very costly affairs. The outfits of the bride and groom cost thousands of dollars, the extravagance of the man being fully equal to that of his bride. A wedding is attended with numerous entertainments, all of which are costly, and the expenses attendant upon the affair itself are enormous. The outlay is not confined to the parties immediately concerned, the friends of the happy pair must go to great expense to give to the bride elegant and appropriate presents. One, two, or three rooms, as may be required, are set apart at every fashionable wedding, for the display of the presents. These are visited and commented upon by the friends of the bride and groom, such being the prescribed custom. The presents are frequently worth a handsome fortune. At the marriage of the daughter of a notorious politician not long since, the wedding presents were valued at more than $250,000. Efforts have been repeatedly made to put a stop to the giving of such costly presents, but the custom still continues.

As it is the ambition of every one of the class we are discussing to live fashionably, so it is their chief wish to be laid in the grave in the same style. The undertaker at a fashionable funeral is generally the sexton of some fashionable church, perhaps of the church the deceased was in the habit of attending. This individual prescribes the manner in which the funeral ceremonies shall be conducted, and advises certain styles of mourning for the family. Sometimes the blinds of the house are closed, and the gas lighted in the hall and parlors. The lights in such cases are arranged in the most artistic manner, and everything is made to look as "interesting" as possible.

A certain fashionable sexton always refuses to allow the female members of the family to follow their dead to the grave. He will not let them be seen at the funeral, at all, as he says, "It's horribly vulgar to see a lot of women crying about a corpse; and, besides, they're always in the way."

The funeral over, the bereaved ones must remain in the house for a certain length of time, the period being regulated by a set decree. To be seen on the street within the prescribed time, would be to lose caste. Many of the days of their seclusion are passed in consultations with their *modiste*, in preparing the most fashionable mourning that can be thought of. They no doubt agree fully with a certain famous *modiste* of the city, who once declared to a widow, but recently bereaved, that "fashionable and becoming mourning is *so comforting* to persons in affliction."

Well, after all, only the rich can afford to die and be buried in style in the great city. A lot in Greenwood is worth more than many comfortable dwellings in Brooklyn. A fashionable funeral entails heavy expenses upon the family of the deceased. The coffin must be of rosewood, or some other costly material, and must be lined with satin. A profusion of white flowers must be had to cover it and to deck the room in which the corpse is laid out. The body must be dressed in a suit of the latest style and finest quality, and the cost of the hearse and carriages, the expenses at the church and cemetery, and the fees of the undertaker, are very heavy. The average expense of such an occasion may be set down at from $1500 to $2000.

VII.
THE MUNICIPAL POLICE.

UNTIL the passage of the new Charter in 1870, the Police Department was independent of the control of the city officials, and consequently independent of local political influences. There was a "Metropolitan Police District," embracing the cities of New York and Brooklyn, and the counties of New York, Kings, Richmond and Westchester, and a part of Queen's county, in all a circuit of about thirty miles. The control of this district was committed to a commission of five citizens, who were subject to the supervision of the Legislature of the State. The Mayors of New York and Brooklyn were ex-officio members of this board.

The Charter of 1870 changed all this. It broke up the Metropolitan District, and placed the police of New York and Brooklyn under the control of their respective municipal governments. To the credit of the force be it said, the police of New York were less under the influence of the Ring than any other portion of the municipality, and improved rather than depreciated in efficiency.

As at present constituted, the force is under the control and supervision of four Commissioners appointed by the Mayor. The force consists of a Superintendent, four Inspectors, thirty-two Captains, one hundred and twenty-eight Sergeants, sixty-four Roundsmen, and 2085 Patrolmen, Detectives, Doorkeepers, etc.

The present Superintendent of Police is Mr. James J. Kelso. He is the Commander-in-chief of the force, and it is through him that all orders are issued. His subordinates are responsible to him for the proper discharge of their duties, and he in his turn to the Commissioners. He was promoted to his present position on the death of Superintendent Jourdan, and has rendered himself popular with men of all parties by his conscientious discharge of his important duties. Mr. Kelso is eminently fitted for his position. His long service in the force, and great experience as a detective officer, have thoroughly familiarized him with the criminals with whom he has to deal, and the crimes against which he has to contend. He has maintained the discipline of the force at a high point, and has been rigorous in dealing with the offenders against the law. His sudden and sweeping descents upon the gambling hells, and other disreputable places of the city, have stricken terror to the frequenters thereof. They are constantly alarmed, for they know not at what moment they may be captured by Kelso in one of his characteristic raids.

In person Mr. Kelso is a fine-looking, and rather handsome man. He shows well at the head of the force. It is said that he was overwhelmed with mortification last July, when the Mayor compelled him to forbid the " Orange Parade," and thus make a cowardly surrender to the mob. When Governor Hoffman revoked Mayor Hall's order, at the demand of the indignant citizens, Kelso was perhaps the happiest man in New York. He had a chance to vindicate his own manhood and the honor of the force, and he and his men did nobly on that memorable day.

The city is divided into two Inspection Districts, each of which is in charge of two Inspectors. Each Inspector is held responsible for the general good conduct and order of his District. It is expected that he will visit portions of it at uncertain hours of the night, in order that the Patrolmen may be made more vigilant by their ignorance of the hour of his appearance on their "beats." The Inspectors keep a constant watch over the rank and file of the force. They examine the Police Stations, and everything connected with them, at pleasure, and receive and investigate complaints made by citizens against members of the force. The creation of this useful grade is due to John A. Kennedy, the first Superintendent of the Metropolitan Police.

The Inspection Districts are sub-divided into thirty-two pre-cincts, in each of which there is a Police Station. Each Station is in charge of a Captain, who is held to a strict accountability for the preservation of the peace and good order of his pre-cinct. He has authority to post the men under his command in such parts of his precinct, and to assign them to such duties as he deems expedient, under the supervision of the Superin-tendent. He is required to divide his force into two equal parts, called the First and Second Platoons. Each Platoon consists of two Sections. Each of the four Sections is in charge of a Sergeant.

In the illness or absence of the Captain, the Station and Pre-cinct are commanded by one of the Sergeants, who is named for that purpose by the Superintendent. The special duties of the Sergeants are to patrol their precincts, and see that the Roundsmen and Patrolmen are at their posts and performing their duties properly. They are severally responsible for the condition of their Sections. One of the Sergeants is required to remain at the Station House at all times.

Two Roundsmen are selected by the Commissioners from the Patrolmen of each precinct, and one of them is assigned to each platoon. They have the immediate supervision of the Patrol-men, and are required to exercise a vigilant watch over them at all times.

The Patrolmen are the privates of the force. They are assigned certain "beats" or districts to watch. Many of these beats are too large for the care of one man, and more is ex-pected of the Patrolman than he is capable of performing. He is required to exercise the utmost vigilance to prevent the occurrence of any crime within his beat, and to render the commission of it difficult, at the least. The occurrence of a crime on the streets is always regarded as presumptive evidence of negligence on his part, and he is obliged to show that he was strictly attending to his duties at the time. He is required to watch vigilantly every person passing him while on duty, to examine frequently the doors, lower windows, and gates of the houses on his beat, and warn the occupants if any are open or unlocked; to have a general knowledge of the persons residing in his beat; to report to his commanding officer "all persons known or suspected of being policy dealers, gamblers, receivers of stolen property, thieves, burglars, or offenders of any kind;" to watch all disorderly houses or houses of ill-fame, and observe "and report to his commanding officer *all persons by whom they are frequented;*" to do certain other things for the preservation of the public peace; and to arrest for certain offences, all of which are laid down in the volume of Regulations, of which each member of the force is obliged to have a copy. Patrolmen are not allowed to converse with each other, except to ask or impart information, upon meeting at the confines of their posts; "and they must not engage in conversation with any person on any part of their post, except in regard to matters concerning the immediate discharge of their duties."

The uniform of the force is a frock coat and pants of dark blue navy cloth, and a glazed cap. In the summer the dress is a sack and pants of dark blue navy flannel. The officers are distinguished by appropriate badges. Each member of the force is provided with a shield of a peculiar pattern, on which is his number. This is his badge of office, and he is obliged to show it when required. The men are armed with batons or short clubs of hard wood, and revolvers. The latter they are forbidden to use except in grave emergencies.

The general misdemeanors of which the police are bound to take notice, are: Attempts to pick a pocket, especially where the thief is a known pickpocket; cruel usage of animals in public places; interfering with the telegraph wires; selling or carrying a slungshot; aiding in any way in a prize fight, dog fight, or cock fight; destroying fences, trees, or lamps, or defacing property; aiding in theatrical entertainments on Sunday; disorderly conduct; participating in or inciting to riots; assaults; drunkenness on the streets; gambling; discharging fire-arms on the streets; and other stated offences. The officer must be careful to arrest the true offender, and not to interfere with any innocent person, and is forbidden to use violence unless the resistance of his prisoner is such as to render violence absolutely necessary, and even then he is held responsible for the particular degree of force exerted. If he is himself unable to make the arrest, or if he has good reason to fear an attempt at a rescue of the prisoner, it is his duty to call upon the bystanders for assistance; and any person who refuses him when so called on, is guilty of a misdemeanor, for which he may be arrested and punished.

Promotions are made in the force as follows: Inspectors are chosen from the Captains, Captains from Sergeants, Sergeants from Roundsmen, and Roundsmen from the most efficient Patrolmen.

The duties of a policeman are hard, and the salaries are moderate in every grade. The hours for duty of the Patrolmen are divided in the following manner: from six to eight o'clock in the morning; from eight o'clock in the morning to one in the afternoon; from one in the afternoon to six; from six to twelve midnight; from twelve midnight to six in the morning. These "tours" of duty are so distributed that no one man shall be called on duty at the same hour on two successive days. One-third of the entire force, about 700 in all, is on duty in the daytime, and two-thirds, about 1400 men, at night. Sickness and casualties bring down this estimate somewhat, but the men are such fine physical specimens that sick leaves are now comparatively rare.

Besides the Patrolmen there are several divisions of the force. Forty men, called the Court Squad, are on duty at the various Courts of Justice. Four have charge of the House of Detention for Witnesses, No. 203 Mulberry street. The Sanitary Squad consists of a captain, four sergeants, and fifty-seven patrolmen. Some of these are on duty at the ferries and steamboat landings. Others are detailed to examine the steam boilers in use in the city. Others execute the orders of the Board of Health. Another detachment, nine in number, look after truant children. Others are detailed for duty at banks and other places. The Detectives will be referred to hereafter.

The qualifications demanded of an applicant for admission into the force are thus set down in the book of Regulations:

FEMALE PRISONERS IN THE FOURTH POLICE STATION.

176

"No person will be appointed a Patrolman of the Metropolitan Police Force unless, he

"First, is able to read and write the English language understandingly.

"Second, is a citizen of the United States.

"Third, has been a resident of this State for a term of one year next prior to his application for the office.

"Fourth, has never been convicted of a crime.

"Fifth, is at least five feet eight inches in height.

"Sixth, is less than thirty-five years of age.

"Seventh, is in good health, and of sound body and mind.

"Eighth, is of good moral character and habits.

"Applicants for the office must present to the Board of Commissioners a petition signed by not less than five citizens of good character and habits, and verified by the affidavit of one of them."

As none but "sound" men are wanted, the applicant is then subjected to a rigid medical examination; and the writer is informed by one of the most efficient surgeons of the force, that scarcely one applicant in ten can stand this test. The applicant must also give, under oath, an exact statement as to his parentage, nationality, education, personal condition in every respect, business or employment, and physical condition.

The strictest discipline is maintained in the force, and offences are rigidly reported and punished. All members are required at once to communicate intelligence of importance to their superior officers. The men are regularly drilled in military exercises, to fit them for dealing efficiently with serious disturbances. The writer can testify, that during their parade in the Spring of 1871, they presented as fine an appearance, and executed their manœuvres as correctly as any body of regular troops.

The finest looking and largest men are detailed for service on Broadway. One of their principal duties is to keep the street free from obstructions, no slight task when one considers the usual jam in the great thoroughfare. It is a common habit to denounce the "Broadway Squad" as more ornamental

12

than useful, but the habitués of that street can testify to the
arduous labor performed by the "giants," and the amount of
protection afforded by them to the merchants and promenaders.
Scarcely a day passes that they do not prevent robberies and
cut short the operations of pickpockets.

The number of arrests made by the force is fair evidence of
their efficiency. Since 1862 the annual number has been as
follows:

1862.	Total arrests in New York				....	82,072
1863.	"	"	"	"	....	61,888
1864.	"	"	"	"	....	54,751
1865.	"	"	"	"	....	68,873
1866.	"	"	"	"	....	75,630
1867.	"	"	"	"	....	80,532
1868.	"	"	"	"	....	78,451
1869.	"	"	"	"	....	72,984

During the year 1869, the arrests were divided as follows:

Males............ 51,446
Females................................... 21,538

The principal causes for which these arrests were made were
as follows:

	Males.	Females.
Assault and battery..................	5.638	1,161
Disorderly conduct	9,376	5,559
Intoxication	15,918	8,105
Intoxication and disorderly conduct...	5,232	3,466
Petty larceny.......................	3,700	1,209
Grand larceny.......................	1,623	499
Malicious mischief...................	1,081	32
Vagrancy............................	1,065	701

During the past nine years over 73,000 lost children have
been restored to their parents by the police. More than 40,000
houses have been found open at night, owing to the carelessness
of the inmates, who have been warned of their danger by the
police in time to prevent robbery. There is scarcely a fire but
is marked by the individual heroism of some member of the
force, and the daily papers abound in instances of rescues from

drowning by the policemen stationed along the docks. In times of riot and other public danger, the police force have never been found lacking, and they have fairly won the "flag of honor" which the citizens of New York are about to present to them in recognition of their gallant and efficient services on the 12th of July, 1871. That there are individuals whose conduct reflects discredit upon the force is but natural; but as a whole, there does not exist a more devoted, gallant, and efficient body of men than those composing the police of New York.

The Station Houses of the city are so arranged as to be central to their respective precincts. The new buildings are models of their kind, and the old ones are being improved as rapidly as possible. Perhaps the best arranged, the handsomest, and most convenient, is that of the Fourth Precinct, located at No. 9 Oak street. The locality is one of the worst in the city, and it is necessary that the police accommodations should be perfect. The building is of red brick, with a fine white granite façade, with massive stone steps leading from the street to the main entrance. The entrance leads directly to the main room, or office. On the right of the entrance is the Sergeant's desk, of black walnut, massive and handsomely carved. Back of this is a fine book-case of the same material, for the record books and papers of the station. The telegraph instrument is at the side farthest from the windows—a precaution looking to its safety in case of a riot or attack on the station. Speaking-tubes, and boxes for papers, communicate with the other apartments. The walls are adorned with fine photographs of the late Superintendent Jourdan, the present Superintendent Kelso, and the Police Commissioners. Back of the office is the Surgeon's Room, with every convenience for the performance of the Surgeon's duties. The office of the Captain in command of the station is to the left of the entrance, and is fitted up with a Brussels carpet, and black walnut furniture. The walls are covered with fine engravings and photographs of prominent men. The Captain is also provided with a bed-room, bath-room, etc., which are elegantly furnished. The Sergeants' bed-

rooms are large, airy, and well furnished.   Bath-rooms for the
Sergeants and Patrolmen are located in the basement.   The
sleeping rooms of the Sergeants and Roundsmen, and four large
dormitories for the Patrolmen, are situated on the second and
third floors.   Each Patrolman has a private closet for his clothing, etc., and each bedstead is stamped with the occupant's
section number.   The fourth story is used for store-rooms.
On the first floor there is also a large sitting-room for the
Patrolmen.

Attached to the Station House, and connected with it by a
bridge, is the prison, a brick building three stories in height.
It is entered through the Patrolmen's sitting-room, and is the
largest in any city station house.   It contains fifty-two cells,
all of which are of a good size and are well ventilated.   Four
of these (Nos. 1, 16, 17, 32) are somewhat larger than the
others, and are humorously called by the force "Bridal chambers."   They are reserved for the more respectable prisoners.
Over the prison are two large rooms designed for the unfortunates who seek a night's shelter at the station—one for men and
the other for women.   They are provided with board platforms
to sleep on.   These platforms can be removed, and the whole
place drenched with water from hydrants conveniently located.

As a matter of course, this model station is in charge of one
of the most efficient, experienced, and reliable officers of the
force.   It is at present commanded by Captain A. J. Allaire,
whose personal and official record fairly entitles him to the high
and honorable position he holds in the force.

The station houses are kept scrupulously clean.   Neatness is
required in every department of the police service.   The Inspector may enter them at any hour, and he is almost sure to find
them in perfect order.

These stations afford a temporary shelter to the outdoor poor.
In all of them accommodations are provided for giving a night's
lodging to the poor wretches who seek it.   When the snow lies
white over the ground, or the frosts have driven them out of the
streets, these poor creatures come in crowds to the station houses,
and beg for a shelter for the night.   You may see them huddling

A WINTER NIGHT SCENE IN A POLICE STATION.

181

eagerly around the stove, spreading their thin hands to catch
the warmth, or holding some half-frozen child to be thawed by
the heat, silent, submissive, and grateful, yet even half afraid
that the kind-hearted Sergeant, who tries to hide his sympathy
for them by a show of gruffness, will turn them into the freezing streets again.   When the rooms devoted to their use are all
filled, others still come, begging, ah, so piteously, to be taken in
for the night.   I think there is no part of the Sergeant's duties
so hard, so painful to him, as to be forced to turn a deaf ear to
these appeals.   Let us thank God, however, he does not do so
often, and even at the risk of being "overhauled" for exceeding
his duty, the Sergeant finds, or makes, a place for those who
seek his assistance in this way.   Many of those who seek shelter
here are constant tramps, who have nowhere else to go.   Others
are strangers in the city—poor people who have come here in
search of employment.   Failing to find it, and what little money
they brought with them being exhausted, they have only the
alternative of the station house or the pavement.   Many who
are simply unfortunate, suffer almost to perishing before seeking
the station house, mistakenly supposing that in so doing they
place themselves on a par with those who are brought there for
offences against the law.   But at last the cold and the snow
drive them there, and they meet with kindness and consideration.   I could not here present a description of the quiet and
practical way in which the members of the "Force" relieve
such sufferers.   No record is kept of such good deeds by the
force, and the Sergeant's book is modestly silent on this subject;
but we may be sure it is written in letters of living light on the
great book that shall be opened at the last day.

The stations are connected with each other and with the
headquarters by telegraph.   The telegraph system has been so
perfected that by means of a set of numbers struck on a bell,
each of which refers to a corresponding number in the book of
signals, questions are asked and answered, and messages sent
from station to station with the greatest rapidity.

The Headquarters of the Police Force are located in a handsome building, five stories high, known as No. 300 Mulberry

street.   The building extends through to Mott street, in the rear.   It is situated on the easterly side of Mulberry street, between Bleecker and Houston streets.   It is ninety feet in width. The Mulberry street front is of white marble, and the Mott street front is of pressed brick, with white marble trimmings. It is fitted up with great taste, and every convenience and comfort is provided for the members of the force on duty here.   The greatest order is manifest.   Everything and every man has a place, and must be in it at the proper times.   There is no confusion.   Each department has its separate quarters.

The Superintendent's office is connected by telegraph with every precinct in the city.   By means of this wonderful invention, the Superintendent can communicate instantly with any point in the city.   The news of a robbery or burglary is flashed all over New York and the adjoining country before a man has fairly secured his plunder.   If a child is lost, all the precincts are furnished immediately with an accurate description of it, and the whole force is on the lookout for the little wanderer, and in a marvellously quick time it is restored to its mother's arms.   By means of his telegraph, the Superintendent can track a criminal, not only all over the city, but all over the civilized world, and that without leaving his office.   One of the most interesting rooms in the headquarters is that for the trial of complaints against members of the force.   Every charge must be sworn to.   It is then brought before the Commissioners, or rather before one who is appointed by the Board to hear such complaints.   He notifies the accused to appear before him to answer to the charge.   Except in very grave cases the men employ no counsel.   The charge is read, the Commissioner hears the statements of the accused, and the evidence on both sides, and renders his decision, which must be ratified by the full " Board."   The majority of the charges are for breaches of discipline.   A Patrolman leaves his beat for a cup of coffee on a cold morning, or night, or reads a newspaper, or smokes, or stops to converse while on duty.   The punishment for these offences is a stoppage of pay for a day or two.   First offences are usually forgiven.   Many well-meaning but officious citizens enter complaints against the men. They are generally frivolous, but are heard patiently, and are dismissed with a warning to the accused to avoid giving cause for complaint. Thieves and disreputable characters sometimes enter complaints against the men, with the hope of getting them into trouble. The Commissioner's experience enables him to settle these cases at once, generally to the dismay and grief of the accuser. Any real offence on the part of the men is punished promptly and severely, but the Commissioners endeavor by every means to protect them in the discharge of their duty, and against impositions of any kind.

Another room in the headquarters is called " The Property Room." This is a genuine "curiosity shop." It is filled with unclaimed property of every description, found by, or delivered to the police, by other parties finding the same, or taken from criminals at the time of their arrest. The room is in charge of the Property Clerk, who enters each article, and the facts connected with it, in a book kept for that purpose. Property once placed in this room is not allowed to be taken away except upon certain specified conditions. Unclaimed articles are sold, after being kept a certain time, and the proceeds are paid to the Police Life Insurance Fund.

The pay of a policeman is small, being only about $1200 per annum. In order to make some compensation for this deficiency, the Police Law contains the following provisions:

" If any member of the Municipal Police Force, whilst in the actual performance of duty, shall become permanently disabled, so as to render his dismissal from membership proper, or if any such member shall become superannuated after ten years of membership, a sum of not exceeding $150, as an annuity, to be paid such member, shall be chargeable upon the Municipal Police Life Insurance Fund. If any member of the Municipal Police Force, whilst in the actual discharge of his duty, shall be killed, or shall die from the immediate effect of any injury received by him, whilst in such discharge of duty, or shall die after ten years' service in the force, and shall leave a widow, and if no widow, any child or children under the age of sixteen years, a like sum by way of annuity shall become chargeable upon the said fund, to be paid to such widow so long only as she remains unmarried, or to such child or children so long as said child, or the youngest of said children, continues under the age of sixteen years.   In every case the Board of Municipal Police shall determine the circumstances thereof, and order payment of the annuity to be made by draft, signed by each trustee of the said fund.   But nothing herein contained shall render any payment of said annuity obligatory upon the said Board, or the said trustees, or chargeable as a matter of legal right.   The Board of Municipal Police, in its discretion, may at any time order such annuity to cease."

VIII.

THE BOWERY.

NEXT to Broadway, the most thoroughly characteristic street in the city is the Bowery. Passing out of Printing House Square, through Chatham street, one suddenly emerges from the dark, narrow lane, into a broad square, with streets radiating from it to all parts of the city. It is not over clean, and has an air of sharpness and repulsiveness that at once attracts attention. This is Chatham Square, the great promenade of the old time denizens of the Bowery, and still largely frequented by the class generally known as " the fancy."

At the upper end of the square begins a broad, flashy-looking street, stretching away to the northward, crowded with pedestrians, street cars, and wheeled vehicles of all kinds. This is *The Bowery*. It begins at Chatham Square, and extends as far as the Cooper Institute, on Eighth street, where the Third and Fourth avenues—the first on the east, and the other on the west side of the Institute—continue the thoroughfare to the Harlem River.

The Bowery first appears in the history of New York under the following circumstances. About the year 1642 or 1643, it was set apart by the Dutch for the residence of superannuated slaves, who, having served the Government faithfully from the earliest period of the settlement of the island, were at last allowed to devote their labors to the support of their dependent families, and were granted parcels of land embracing from eight to twenty acres each. The Dutch were influenced by other motives than charity in this matter. The district thus granted was well out of the limits of New Amsterdam, and they were anxious to make this negro settlement a sort of breakwater against the attacks of the Indians, who were beginning to be troublesome. At this time the Bowery was covered with a dense forest. A year or two later farms were laid out along its extent. These were called "Boweries," from which the street derives its present name. They were held by men of mark, in those simple and honest days. To the north of Chatham Square lay the broad lands of the De Lanceys, and above them the fine estates of the Dyckmans, and Brevoorts, all on the west of the present street. On the east side lay the lands of the Rutgers, Bayards, Minthornes, Van Cortlandts and others. Above all these lay the "Bouwerie" and other possessions of the strong-headed and hard-handed Governor Peter Stuyvesant, of whom many traces still exist in the city. His house stood about where St. Mark's (Episcopal) Church is now located. In 1660, or near about that year, a road or lane was laid off through what are now Chatham street, Chatham Square and the Bowery, from the Highway, as the portion of Broadway beyond the line of Wall street was called, to Governor Stuyvesant's farm. To this was given the distinctive name of the "Bowery lane." Some years later this lane was continued up the island under the name of the "Boston Road." In 1783 the Bowery again came into prominent notice. On the 25th of November of that year, the American army, under General Washington, marched into the Bowery early in the morning, and remained until noon, when the British troops evacuated the city and its defences. This done, the Americans marched down the Bowery, through Chatham and Pearl streets, to the Battery, where they lowered the British flag which had been left flying by the enemy, and hoisted in its place the "stars and stripes" of the new Republic.

After the city began to extend up the island, the Bowery commenced to lose caste. Decent people forsook it, and the poorer and more disreputable classes took possession. Finally, it become notorious. It was known all over the country for its roughs, or "Bowery B'hoys," as they were called, its rowdy firemen, and its doubtful women. In short, it was the paradise of the worst element of New York. On this street the Bowery boy was in his glory. You might see him "strutting along like

a king" with his breeches stuck in his boots, his coat on his arm,
his flaming red shirt tied at the collar with a cravat such as could
be seen nowhere else; with crape on his hat, the hat set deftly
on the side of his head, his hair evenly plastered down to his
skull, and a cigar in his mouth. If he condescended to adorn
his manly breast with any ornament it was generally a large
gold or brass figure representing the number of "der mersheen"
with which he ran. None so ready as he for a fight, none so
quick to resent the intrusion of a respectable man into his haunts.
So he had money enough to procure his peculiar garb, a "mersheen" to run with and fight for, a girl to console him, the "Old
Bowery Theatre" to beguile him from his ennui, and the Bowery
itself to disport his glory in, he was content. Rows were numerous in this quarter, and they afforded him all the other relaxation he desired. If there be any truth in the theories of Spirit-
ualism, let us be sure his ghost still haunts the Bowery.

And the Bowery girl—who shall describe her? She was a
"Bowery b'hoy" in petticoats; unlike him in this, however,
that she loved the greatest combination of bright colors, while
he clung religiously to red and black. Her bonnet was a perfect museum of ribbons and ornaments, and it sat jauntily on
the side of her head. Her skirts came to the shoe top and displayed her pretty feet and well-turned ankle, equipped with irreproachable gaiters and the most stunning of stockings. One arm
swung loosely to the motion of her body as she passed along with
a quick, lithe step, and the other held just over her nose her
parasol, which was sometimes swung over the right shoulder.
Even the Bowery boy was overcome by her stunning appearance,
and he forgot his own glory in his genuine admiration of his
girl.

Well! they have passed away. The street cars, the new police, and the rapid advance of trade up the island, have made
great changes here, but there are still left those who could tell
many a wondrous tale of the old time glories of the Bowery.

The street runs parallel with Broadway, is about double the
width of that thoroughfare, and is about one mile in length. It
is tolerably well built, and is improving in this respect every

THE BOWERY.

year. In connection with Chatham Square it is the great route
from the lower end of the island to Harlem Bridge.   Nearly all
of the east side street car lines touch it at some point, and the
Third avenue line traverses its entire length.   It lies within a
stone's throw of Broadway, but is entirely different from it in
every respect.   Were Broadway a street in another city the
difference could not be greater.

    The Bowery is devoted mainly to the cheap trade.   The chil-
dren of Israel abound here.   The display of goods in the shops
is flashy, and not often attractive.   Few persons who have the
means to buy elsewhere care to purchase an article in the Bowery,

as those familiar with it know there are but few reliable dealers in the street. If one were to believe the assertions of the Bowery merchants as set forth in their posters and hand bills, with which they cover the fronts of their shops, they are always on the verge of ruin, and are constantly throwing their goods away for the benefit of their customers. They always sell at a " ruinous sacrifice ; " yet snug fortunes are realized here, and many a Fifth avenue family can look back to days passed in the dingy back room of a Bowery shop, while papa "sacrificed" his wares in front. Sharp practice rules in the Bowery, and if beating an unwilling customer into buying what he does not want is the highest art of the merchant, then there are no such salesmen in the great city as those of this street. Strangers from the country, servant girls, and those who, for the want of means, are forced to put up with an inferior article, trade here. As a general rule, the goods sold here are of an inferior, and often worthless quality, and the prices asked are high, though seemingly cheap.

Pawnbrokers' shops, " Cheap Johns," third-class hotels, dance houses, fifth-rate lodging houses, low class theatres, and concert saloons, abound in the lower part of the street.

The Sunday law is a dead letter in the Bowery. Here, on the Sabbath, one may see shops of all kinds—the vilest especially—open for trade. Cheap clothing stores, concert saloons, and the most infamous dens of vice are in full blast. The street, and the cars traversing it, are thronged with the lower classes in search of what they call enjoyment. At night all the places of amusement are open, and are crowded to excess. Roughs, thieves, fallen women, and even little children throng them. Indeed it is sad to see how many children are to be found in these places. The price of admission is low, and strange as it may sound, almost any beggar can raise it. People have no idea how much of the charity they lavish on street beggars goes in this way. The amusement afforded at these places ranges from indelicate hints and allusions to the grossest indecency.

Along the line of almost the entire street are shooting galleries. Some of which open immediately upon the street. They are decorated in the most fanciful style, and the targets

represent nearly every variety of man and beast. Here is a
lion, who, if hit in the proper place, will utter a truly royal roar.
Here is a trumpeter. Strike his heart with your shot, and
he will raise his trumpet to his lips and send forth a blast
sufficient to wake every Bowery baby in existence. "Only five
cents a shot," cries the proprietor to the surrounding crowd
of barefoot, penniless boys, and half-grown lads, "and a knife
to be given to the man that hits the bull's eye." Many a penny
do these urchins spend here in the vain hope of winning the
knife, and many are the seeds of evil sown among them by
these "chances." In another gallery the proprietor offers
twenty dollars to any one who will hit a certain bull's eye three
times in succession. Here men contend for the prize, and as a
rule the proprietor wins all the money in their pockets before
the mark is struck as required.

The carnival of the Bowery is held on Saturday night. The
down-town stores, the factories, and other business places close
about five o'clock, and the street is thronged at an early hour.
Crowds are going to market, but the majority are bent on pleasure. As soon as the darkness falls over the city the street
blazes with light. Away up towards Prince street you may
see the flashy sign of Tony Pastor's Opera House, while from
below Canal street the Old Bowery Theatre stands white and
glittering in the glare of gas and transparencies. Just over the
way are the lights of the great German Stadt Theatre. The
Atlantic Garden stands by the side of the older theatre, rivalling it in brilliancy and attractiveness. Scores of restaurants,
with tempting bills of fare and prices astonishingly low, greet
you at every step. "*Lager Bier*," and "*Grosses Concert; Ein-
tritt frei*," are the signs which adorn nearly every other house.
The lamps of the street venders dot the side-walk at intervals,
and the many colored lights of the street cars stretch away as
far as the eye can reach. The scene is as interesting and as
brilliant as that to be witnessed in Broadway at the same hour;
but very different.

As different as the scene, is the crowd thronging this street
from that which is rushing along Broadway. Like that, it re-

presents all nationalities, but it is a crowd peculiar to the Bowery. The "rich Irish brogue" is well represented, it is true; but the "sweet German accent" predominates. The Germans are everywhere here. The street signs are more than one-half in German, and one might step fresh from the Fatherland into the Bowery and never know the difference, so far as the prevailing language is concerned. Every tongue is spoken here. You see the piratical looking Spaniard and Portuguese, the gypsy-like Italian, the chattering Frenchman with an irresistible smack of the Commune about him, the brutish looking Mexican, the sad and silent "Heathen Chinee," men from all quarters of the globe, nearly all retaining their native manner and habits, all very little Americanized. They are all "of the people." There is no aristocracy in the Bowery. The Latin Quarter itself is not more free from restraint.

Among the many signs which line the street the word "*Exchange*" is to be seen very often. The "Exchanges" are the lowest class lottery offices, and they are doing a good business to night, as you may see by the number of people passing in and out. The working people have just been paid off, and many of them are here now to squander their earnings in the swindles of the rascals who preside over the "Exchanges." These deluded creatures represent but a small part of the working class however. The Savings Banks are open to night, many of them the best and most respectable buildings on the Bowery, and thousands of dollars in very small sums are left here for safe keeping.

Many of the Bowery people, alas, have no money for either the banks or the lottery offices. You may see them coming and going if you will stand by one of the many doors adorned with the three gilt balls. The pawnbrokers are reaping a fine harvest to-night. The windows of these shops are full of unredeemed pledges, and are a sad commentary on the hope of the poor creature who feels so sure she will soon be able to redeem the treasure she has just pawned for a mere pittance.

Down in the cellars the Concert Saloons are in full blast, and the hot foul air comes rushing up the narrow openings as you pass them, laden with the sound of the fearful revelry that is going on below.   Occasionally a dog fight, or a struggle between some half drunken men, draws a crowd on the street and brings the police to the spot.   At other times there is a rush of human beings and a wild cry of " stop thief," and the throng sweeps rapidly down the side-walk overturning street stands, and knocking the unwary passer-by off his feet, in its mad chase after some unseen thief.   Beggars line the side-walk, many of them professing the most hopeless blindness, but with eyes keen enough to tell the difference between the coins tossed into their hats.   The "Bowery Bands," as the little street musicians are called, are out in force, and you can hear their discordant strains every few squares.

Until long after midnight the scene is the same, and even all through the night the street preserves its air of unrest.   Some hopeful vender of Lager Beer is almost always to be found at his post, seek him at what hour you will; and the cheap lodging houses and hotels seem never to close.

Respectable people avoid the Bowery as far as possible at night.   Every species of crime and vice is abroad at this time watching for its victims.   Those who do not wish to fall into trouble should keep out of the way.

13

IX.

PUBLIC SQUARES.

I.

THE BATTERY.

THE lowest and one of the largest of the pleasure grounds of the city, is the park lying at the extreme end of the island, at the junction of the Hudson and East rivers, and known as the Battery. At the first settlement of the Dutch, the fort, for the protection of the little colony, was built at some distance from the extreme edge of the island, which was then rocky and swampy, but near enough to it to sweep the point with a raking fire. This fort occupied the site of the present Bowling Green. In 1658 Governor Stuyvesant erected a fine mansion, afterwards known as "The Whitehall," in the street now called by that name, but "Capsey Rocks," as the southern point of the island was called, remained unoccupied. In 1693, the Kingdom of Great Britain being at war with France, the Governor ordered the erection of a battery " on the point of rocks under the fort," and after considerable trouble, succeeded in obtaining from the Common Council, who were very reluctant to pay out the public money for any purpose not specified in the charter—a virtue which seems to have died with them—the sum necessary for that purpose. 1734 a bill was passed by the General Assembly of the Province, ordering the erection of a battery on Capsey Rocks, and forbidding the erection of houses which would interfere with the fire of its guns, " on the river, or on parts which overflow with water, between the west part of the Battery, or Capsey Rocks, to Ells Corner on the Hudson River," (the present Marketfield street).

During the years preceding the Revolution, and throughout that struggle, the Battery was used exclusively for military purposes. About the year 1792 measures were taken for filling up, enclosing, and ornamenting the place as a public park, to which use it has since been devoted.

During the first half of the present century the Battery was the favorite park of the New Yorkers, and was indeed the handsomest. The march of trade, however, proved too much for it. The fashion and respectability of the city which had clustered near it were driven up town. Castle Garden, which had been a favorite Opera House, was converted into an emigrant depot, and the Battery was left to the emigrants and to the bummers. Dirt was carted and dumped here by the load, all sorts of trash was thrown here, and loafers and drunken wretches laid themselves out on the benches and on the grass to sleep in the sun, when the weather was mild enough. It became a plague spot, retaining as the only vestige of its former beauty, its grand old trees, which were once the pride of the city.

In 1869, however, the spot was redeemed. The sea-wall which the General Government had been building for the protection of the land was finished, and the Battery was extended out to meet it. The old rookeries and street-stands that had clustered about Castle Garden were removed, the rubbish which had accumulated here was carted away, and the Battery was again transformed into one of the handsomest of the city parks.

It now covers an area of about twelve acres, and is tastefully and regularly laid off. Broad stone paved walks traverse it in various directions, and the shrubbery and flowers are arranged with the best possible effect. A tall flag-staff rises from the centre of the park, and close by is a stand from which the city band give their concerts at stated times in the summer. A massive stone wall protects the harbor side from the washing of the waves, and at certain points granite stairs lead to the water.

The view from the Battery embraces a part of Brooklyn and

the East River, Governor's and Staten islands, the Inner Bay, the Jersey shore, North River and Jersey City. The eye ranges clear down to the Narrows, and almost out to sea, and commands a view which cannot be surpassed in beauty. Here the sea breeze is always pure and fresh, here one may come for a few moments' rest from the turmoil of the great city, and delight himself with the lovely picture spread out before him.

II.

THE BOWLING GREEN.

At the lower end of Broadway there is a small circular public square, enclosed with an iron railing, and ornamented with a fountain in the centre. This is known as the Bowling Green, and is the first public park ever laid out in the city.

The first fort built by the Dutch on Manhattan island covered a good part of the site of this square. In 1733 the Common Council passed a resolution ordering that "the piece of land lying at the lower end of Broadway fronting the fort, be leased to some of the inhabitants of Broadway, in order to be inclosed to make a Bowling Green, with walks therein, for the beauty and ornament of the said street, as well as for the recreation and delight of the inhabitants of this city, leaving the street on each side fifty feet wide." In October, 1734, the Bowling Green was leased to Frederick Philipse, John Chambers, and John Roosevelt, a trio of public spirited gentlemen, for ten years, for a Bowling Green only, and they agreed to keep it in repair at their own expense. In 1741 a fire swept away the fort, and afforded a chance of improving the park, which was done. A change for the better was brought about in the neighborhood by the establishment of the grounds, and substantial houses began to cluster about it.

A few years before the Revolution, the Colonial Assembly purchased in England a leaden statue of King George the Third, and set it up in the centre of the Bowling Green, in

May 1771. The grounds at this time had no fence around
them, as we learn from a resolution of the Common Council,
and were made the receptacle of filth and dirt, thrown there,
doubtless, by the patriots as an insult to the royalists. As the
troubles thickened, the people became more hostile to the statue
of King George, and heaped many indignities upon it, and
after the breaking out of the war, the unlucky monarch was
taken down and run into bullets for the guns of the Continental army.

After the close of the Revolution, Chancellor Livingston
enclosed the grounds with the iron fence which still surrounds
them, and subsequently a fountain was erected on the site of
the statue.

III.

THE PARK.

"THE PARK" is the title given by New Yorkers to the
enclosure containing the City Hall and County Buildings.
It originally embraced an area of eleven acres, but within the
past year and a half the lower end has been ceded to the General Government by the city, and upon this portion the Federal
authorities are erecting a magnificent edifice to be used as a
City Post Office. This building covers the extreme southern
end of the old Park, and the northern portion is occupied by
the City Hall, the new County Court-House and the Department of Finance of the city and county.

In the days of the Dutch in New Amsterdam, the site of the
Park, which was far outside the village limits, was set apart as
a common, and was known as the "Vlachte," or "Flat," and subsequently as the "Second Plains," "Commons," and "Fields."
It was the common grazing ground of the Knickerbocker cows,
and was by universal consent made public property—the first
ever owned by the city. It is believed that previous to this it
was the site of the village of the Manhattan Indians, a belief
which is strengthened by the frequent finding of Indian relics

THE CITY HALL PARK.

in digging up the soil on this spot.   It was connected with the
Dutch village by a road which ran through a beautiful valley
now known as Maiden lane.

Every morning the village cowherd, who was a most important personage, would walk the streets of New Amsterdam and
sound his horn at each burgher's door.   The cows were immediately turned out to him, and when he had collected his herd
he would drive them by the pretty valley road to the commons,
and there by his vigilance prevent them from straying into the
unsettled part beyond.   At a later period the mighty Dutch
warriors whose prowess the immortal Deiderich Knickerbocker
has celebrated, made the commons their training ground, and
here was also marshalled the force which wrested the city from
the Dutch.   Under the English it became a place of popular
resort, and was used for public celebrations, the town having

reached the lower limit of the commons.   Here were celebrated his Majesty's birth-day, the anniversary of the Gunpowder Plot, and other loyal holidays, and here were held the tumultuous assemblies, the meetings of the Liberty Boys, and other demonstrations which preceded the Revolution.

In 1736 the first building, a Poor-House, was erected on the site of the present City Hall.   In 1747 a powder-house was erected by the city within the limit of the commons, near the site of the present City Hall.   The gallows stood on the site of the new Post-office, and in 1756 was removed to the vicinity of the present Five Points.   In 1757 the new jail, more recently known as the Hall of Records, was erected.   In the same year, the old French war being in progress, wooden barracks were erected along the Chambers street front of the Park.

In 1757 a part of the site of the City Hall was laid out as a burying ground for the inmates of the Alms-House.   In 1764 a whipping-post, stocks, cage, and pillory were erected in front of the new jail.   In 1755 a Bridewell was built on that portion lying between the City Hall and Broadway.   After the Revolution, in 1785, the Park was first enclosed in its present form, by a post-and-rail fence, and a few years later this was replaced by wooden palings, and Broadway along the Park began to be noted as a fashionable place of residence.   In 1816, the wooden fence gave way to an iron railing, which was set with due ceremonies by the city authorities.   In 1795 a new Alms-House was built along the Chambers street front, but in 1812, Bellevue Hospital having been finished, the paupers were transferred thither, and the old building was refitted as a Museum. In 1802 the corner-stone of the present City Hall was laid. The building was finished in 1810.   Some years later the old buildings were removed or converted into offices for the city and county officials.

In 1870, the southern portion having been ceded to the Federal Government for the erection of a new Post-office thereon, the Park was laid out on a new plan, and handsomely adorned with walks, shrubbery, fountains, etc.   It is now an ornament to the city.

IV.

OTHER PARKS.

WASHINGTON SQUARE is located between Fourth and Seventh streets, at the lower end of Fifth avenue. The site was originally a Potter's Field, and it is said that over one hundred thousand persons were buried here in days gone by. The square contains a little over nine acres, and is handsomely laid out, and adorned with a fountain, around which passes the main carriage drive, flowers, shrubbery, etc. The trees are among the finest in the city, and are kept with great care. An iron railing formerly surrounded the grounds, but in 1870-71 this was removed, and Fifth avenue was extended through the square to Laurens street. This street was widened and called South Fifth avenue, thus practically extending the avenue to West Broadway at Canal street. The square is surrounded by handsome residences. On the east side are the University of New York and a Lutheran Church.

TOMPKINS SQUARE is one of the largest in the city, and is laid off without ornament, being designed for a drill ground for the police and military. It occupies the area formed by avenues A and B, and Seventh and Tenth streets.

UNION SQUARE, lying between Broadway and Fourth avenue, and Fourteenth and Seventeenth streets, was originally a portion of the estate of Elias Brevoort. In 1762 he sold twenty acres lying west of the "Bowery Road" to John Smith, whose executors sold it to Henry Spingler for the sum of £950, or about $4750. The original farm-house is believed to have stood within the limits of the present Union Square. About the year 1807 Broadway was laid off to the vicinity of Twenty-second street, and in 1815 Union Square was made a "public place," and in 1832 it was laid off as it now exists. The square is regular in shape, and the central portion is laid off as a park, and ornamented with shrubbery, flowers, walks, and a fountain. It is one of the prettiest parks in the city, and covers an area of several acres. It is oval in form, and is without an enclosure.

THE WASHINGTON STATUE IN UNION SQUARE.

Near the fountain is a thriving colony of English sparrows, imported and cared for by the city for the purpose of protecting the trees from the ravages of worms, etc. The birds have a regular village of quaint little houses built for them in the trees. They frequent all the parks of the city, but seem to regard this one as their headquarters. Some of the houses are quite extensive and are labelled with curious little signs, such as the following: "Sparrows' Chinese Pagoda," "Sparrows' Doctor Shop," "Sparrows' Restaurant," "Sparrows' Station House," etc. At the southeast angle of the square stands Hablot K. Browne's equestrian statue of Washington, a fine work in bronze, and at the southwest angle is his statue of Lincoln, of the same metal. The houses surrounding the square are large and handsome. They were once the most elegant residences in New York, but are now, with a few exceptions, used for business. Several hotels, the principal of which are the Everett and Spingler Houses, front on the Square. On the south side, east of Broadway, is the Union Square Theatre, and on the west side, at the corner of Fifteenth street, Tiffany's magnificent iron building. In a few years the square will doubtless be entirely surrounded with similar structures. It is here that the monster mass meetings are held.

STUYVESANT SQUARE lies to the east of Union Square, and is bisected by the line of the Second avenue. Its upper and lower boundaries are Fifteenth and Seventeenth streets. It consists of two beautiful parks of equal size, surrounded by a handsome iron railing, and filled with choice flowers and shrubbery. In the centre of each is a fountain. These parks are the property of St. George's Church (Episcopal), which stands on the west side of the square at the corner, and were given to the corporation of that church by the late Peter G. Stuyvesant, Esq.

GRAMMERCY PARK lies midway between the Fourth and Third avenues, and separates Lexington avenue on the north from Irving Place, really a part of the same avenue, on the south. Its northern and southern boundaries are Twentieth and Twenty-first streets. It is tastefully laid out, is enclosed with an iron fence, and is kept locked against the public, as it is the private property of the persons living around it. On the east side the entire block is taken up by the Grammercy Park Hotel —a first-class boarding house—the other three sides are occupied by the residences of some of the wealthiest capitalists in America. Here dwell Peter Cooper, Moses Taylor, Cyrus W. Field, James Harper (of Harper & Bros.), and others equally well known in the financial world.

MADISON SQUARE comprises about ten acres, and lies at the junction of Broadway and the Fifth avenue. The latter street bounds it on the west, Madison avenue on the east, Twenty-third street on the south, and Twenty-sixth street on the north. It is nearly square in form, and is beautifully laid off. It has no fence, and this adds to the appearance of space which the neighboring open area gives to it. The Fifth Avenue Hotel, the Hoffman, Albemarle, and Worth Houses face it on the west, the Hotel Brunswick is on the north side, and the Union League Club House and a handsome Presbyterian Church are on the east side along the line of Madison avenue. The land now included in Madison Square was owned by the city from a very early period, and was used as a Potter's Field. In 1806 it was ceded to the United States for the erection of an Arsenal, for which purpose it was occupied for several years. In 1824 the " Society for the Reformation of Juvenile Delinquents " obtained possession of the Arsenal grounds, on which they erected a House of Refuge, which was opened January 1st, 1825. This establishment consisted of two large stone buildings, and the grounds were enclosed with a stone wall seventeen feet high. In 1838 the House of Refuge was destroyed by fire, and a few years later Madison Square was laid out. It is now one of the most fashionable localities in the city, and the favorite promenade of the up-town people, who are drawn here in great numbers by the summer afternoon concerts of the Central Park Band.

RESERVOIR SQUARE occupies the site of the old Crystal Palace, and lies between Sixth avenue and the Croton Reservoir on Fifth avenue, and Fortieth and Forty-second streets. It has recently undergone great changes. It is a very pretty park, and is much frequented by the nurses and children of the adjacent neighborhoods.

X.

THE FIFTH AVENUE.

THE Fifth avenue, commencing at Washington Square, or Seventh street, and extending to the Harlem River, is said by the residents of New York to be the finest street in the world. It is about six miles in length, and is built up continuously from Washington Square to the Central Park, a distance of nearly three miles. From Fifty-ninth street to the upper end of the Central Park, One-hundred-and-tenth street, it is laid with the Nicholson or wooden pavement. It is being rapidly built up along its eastern side, the Park bounding the opposite side of the street, and this portion bids fair to be one of the most delightful and desirable neighborhoods in the city. In the vicinity of One-hundred-and-eighteenth street, the line of the avenue is broken by Mount Morris, an abrupt rocky height, which has been laid off as a pleasure ground. Around this the street sweeps in a half circle, and from here to the Harlem River, One-hundred-and-thirty-fifth street, it is lined with pretty villas, and paved with asphaltum.

From Madison Square to its lower end, the avenue is rapidly giving way to business, and its palatial residences are being converted into equally fine stores. Hotels and fashionable boarding-houses are thick in this quarter. Above Madison Square the street is devoted to private residences, and this part is *par excellence* " The Avenue."

The principal buildings, apart from the residences, are the Brevoort House, at the corner of Clinton Place, an ultra fashionable hostelrie. On the opposite side of the street, at the northwest corner of Tenth street, is the handsome brown stone Episcopal Church of the Ascension, and on the southwest corner

FIFTH AVENUE, NEAR TWENTY-FIRST STREET.

of Eleventh street is the equally handsome First Presbyterian Church, constructed of the same material.   At the northeast corner of Fourteenth street is Delmonico's famous restaurant, fronting on both streets; and diagonally opposite, on the southwest corner of Fifteenth street, the magnificent house of the Manhattan Club.   Not far from Delmonico's, and on the same side, is a brick mansion, adorned with a sign bearing a coat of arms, and the announcement that the ground floor is occupied by the eighth wonder of the world, "A Happy Tailor." At the southeast corner of Nineteenth street is the Fifth Avenue Presbyterian Church, in charge of the eloquent Dr. John Hall. Two blocks above, on the southwest corner of Twenty-first street, is the South Dutch Reformed Church, a handsome brown stone edifice, and diagonally opposite is the Glenham House. At the southwest corner of Twenty-second street, is the famous art gallery of Gonpil & Co., and immediately opposite the St. Germains Hotel. At Twenty-third street, Broadway crosses the avenue obliquely from northwest to southeast. On the left hand, going north, is the Fifth Avenue Hotel, and on the left Madison Square. The open space is very broad here, and is always thronged with a busy, lively crowd. At the northeast corner of Twenty-sixth street is the Hotel Brunswick, and on the southwest corner of Twenty-seventh street the Stevens House, both monster buildings rented in flats to families of wealth. At the northwest corner of Twenty-ninth street, is a handsome church of white granite, belonging to the Dutch Reformed faith, and familiarly known as the "Church of the Holy Rooster," from the large gilt cock on the spire. At the northwest corner of Thirty-fourth street is the new marble residence of Mr. A. T. Stewart, the most magnificent dwelling house in the land. Immediately opposite is a fine brown stone mansion, occupied at present by Mr. Stewart. On the southeast corner of Thirty-fifth street, is Christ Church (Episcopal), and on the northwest corner of Thirty-seventh street the Brick Church (Presbyterian), of which Dr. Gardiner Spring is the pastor. At Fortieth street, and extending to Forty-second, the west side of the avenue is taken up with the old distributing reservoir, a massive structure of stone, and immediately opposite is the Rutgers Female College. At the southeast corner of Forty-third street is the city residence of the notorious Boss Tweed, and at the northeast corner of the same street, the splendid Jewish synagogue known as the Temple E-manu-el. At the southwest corner of Forty-fifth street is the Church of the Divine Paternity (Universalist), of which Dr. Chapin is the pastor, and on the opposite side of the street in the block above, the Church of the Heavenly Rest (Episcopal). At the northwest corner of Forty-eighth street is the massive but unfinished structure of the Collegiate Dutch Reformed Church. On the east side of the avenue, and occupying the block between Fiftieth and Fifty-first streets, is the new St. Patrick's Cathedral, unfin-

ished, but destined to be the most elaborate church edifice in
America. The block above the Cathedral is occupied by the
Male Orphan Asylum of the same church, next door to which
is the mansion of Madame Restelle, one of the most noted abortionists of New York. On the northwest corner of Fifty-third
street is the new St. Thomas' Church (Episcopal), a fine edifice,
and owned by one of the wealthiest congregations in the city.
Between Fifty-fourth and Fifty-fifth streets, and on the same
side of the street, is St. Luke's Hospital, with its pretty grounds.
On the east side, between Fifty-eighth and Fifty-ninth streets,
and now in course of erection, will be located the Central Park
Hotel, which is to be one of the most imposing structures in
New York ; and just opposite is the main entrance to the Central Park.

From Seventh to Fifty-ninth streets, the avenue presents a
continuous line of magnificent mansions.   There are a few
marble, yellow stone, and brick buildings, but the prevailing
material is brown stone. The general appearance of the street
is magnificent, but sombre, owing to the dark color of the
stone. Nearly all the houses are built on the same design,
which gives to it an air of sameness and tameness that is not
pleasing. But it is a magnificent street, nevertheless, and has
not its equal in the great and unbroken extent of its splendor
in the world. It is a street of palaces. Madison and Park
avenues, and portions of Lexington avenue, are nearly as handsome, as are the cross streets connecting them with the Fifth
avenue, and many of the streets leading to the Sixth avenue are
similarly built. The great defect of the avenue is the poverty
of resource in the designs of the buildings, but this is the only
species of poverty present here.

If the houses are palatial without, they are even more so
within. Some of them are models of elegance and taste ; others
are miracles of flashy and reckless adornment. The walls and
ceilings are covered with exquisite frescoes. The floors are
rich in the finest and thickest of carpets, on whose luxurious
pile no footfall ever sounds. The light of the sun comes
struggling in through the richest of curtains, and at night the

brilliancy of the gas is softened by the warmest tinted porcelain shades, or heightened by the dazzling reflection of crystal chandeliers. The drawing rooms are filled with the costliest and the richest furniture which is the perfection of comfort, and with works of art worth a fortune in themselves. Back of these, or across the hall, through the half opened doors, you see the sumptuously furnished library, with its long rows of daintily bound books in their rosewood shelves. The library is a "feature" in most houses of the very wealthy, and in the majority of instances is more for ornament than for use. In the rear of all is the conservatory with its wealth of flowers and rare plants, which send their odors through the rooms beyond. The upper and lower stories are furnished on a corresponding scale of magnificence. Everything that money can procure for the comfort or luxury of the inmates is at hand. Nor are such residences few in number. They may be counted by the hundred, each with its contents worth a large fortune. The style of living is in keeping with the house, and, as a matter of course, only the very wealthy can afford such homes.

As for the occupants, they represent all classes—the good and the bad, the cultivated and the illiterate, the refined and the vulgar, the well-born and those who have risen from the gutters. If shoddy finds a home here, genuine merit is his neighbor. Those who have large and assured incomes can afford such a style of life ; but they do not comprise all the dwellers on the Avenue. Many are here who have strained every nerve to "get into the Avenue," and who would sell body and soul to stay there, yet who feel that the crash is coming before which they must give way. Others there are who would give half their possessions to move in the society in which their neighbors live. They reside on the Avenue, but they are ignored by one class of its occupants, because of their lack of refinement and cultivation, and by another because of their inferiority in wealth. Great wealth covers a multitude of defects in the Avenue.

Perhaps the most restless, care-worn faces in the city are to be seen on this street. Women clad in the richest attire pass you with unquiet face and wistful eyes, and men who are envied

JUNCTION OF THE FIFTH AVENUE AND THIRTY-FOURTH STREET,
SHOWING THE NEW RESIDENCE OF A. T. STEWART, ESQ.

by their fellows for their "good luck," startle you by the stern, hard set look their features wear. The first find little real happiness in the riches they have sold themselves for, and the latter find that the costly pleasures they courted have been gained at too dear a price.

Families are small in the Avenue, and Madame Restelle boasts, that her wealth has been earned in a large degree by keeping them so. Fashion has its requirements, and before them maternity must give way. Your fashionable lady has no time to give to children, but pets lap-dogs and parrots.

Well, the Avenue mansions have their skeletons, as well as the east side tenement houses. The sin of the fashionable lady

14

is covered up, however, and the poor girl must face the world. That is the difference. Madame married her husband for his money, and her love is given to one who has no right to claim it; and what between her loathing for her liege lord and her dread of detection, she leads a life not to be envied in spite of the luxury which surrounds her. The liege lord in his turn, never suspecting his wife, but disheartened by her coldness to him, seeks his "affinity" elsewhere; and, by and by, the divorce court tells some unpleasant truths about the Avenue.

Contemplating these things, I have thought that the most wretched quarter of the city hardly holds more unhappy hearts than dwell along the three miles of this grand street; and I have thanked God that the Avenue does not fairly represent the better and higher phases of social and domestic life in the great city.

XI.

STREET TRAVEL.

I.

THE STREET CARS.

THE peculiar shape of the island of Manhattan allows the city to grow in one direction only. The pressure of business is steadily bringing the mercantile district higher up the island, and compelling the residence sections to go farther to the north-ward. Persons in passing from their homes to their business go down town in the morning, and in returning come up town in the evening. Those who live in the better quarters of the city, or in the upper portion of the island, cannot think of walking between their homes and their business. To say nothing of the loss of time they would incur, the fatigue of such a walk would unfit nine out of ten for the duties of the day. In consequence of this, street railways and omnibuses are more necessary, and better patronized in New York than in any city in the Union.

The street cars are the most popular, as they constitute the quickest and most direct means of reaching the most of the city localities. There are about twenty-two lines in operation within the city limits. The majority of these run from north to south, and a few pass "across town" and connect points on the North and East Rivers. A number centre in Park Row at the new Post-office, and at the Astor House. The fare is usually five cents below Sixty-fifth street, and from six to eight cents to points above that street.

The Street Railway Companies are close corporations. Their

stock is very rarely in the market, and when it is offered at all sells readily at high prices. The actual dividends of these companies are large, often reaching as high as thirty-five per cent. This, however, is carefully concealed from the public, and the companies unite in declaring that the expenses of operating their roads are too heavy to admit of even a moderate profit. This they do, no doubt, to excuse in some degree the meanness with which they conduct their enterprises; for it is a striking fact that the heavier such a company's business grows, and the more its profits increase, the more parsimonious it becomes towards its employees and the public.

There is not a line in the city that has a sufficient number of cars to accommodate its patrons. More than one-half of those who ride on the cars are obliged to stand during their journey. As a rule, the cars are dirty and filled with vermin. The conductors and drivers are often appointed for political reasons alone, and are simply brutal ruffians. They treat the passengers with insolence, and often with brutality.

One meets all sorts of people on the street cars, and sometimes the contact is closer than is agreeable, and keeps sensitive people in constant dread of an attack of the itch or some kindred disease. Crowded cars are much frequented by pick-pockets, who are said to be frequently in league with the conductors, and many valuable articles and much money are annually stolen by the light-fingered in these vehicles.

If the drivers and conductors are often deserving of censure, they have their grievances also. Their employers are merciless in their treatment of them. They lead a hard life, working about fifteen hours out of every twenty-four, with no holidays. The conductors receive from $2.00 to $2.50 per day, and the drivers from $2.25 to $2.75. In order to make up the deficiency between their actual wages and their necessities, the conductors and drivers have fallen into the habit of appropriating a part of the money received from passengers to their own use. Many of them are very expert at this, but some are detected, discharged from the service of the company, and handed over to the police. The companies of course endeavor

NEW PALACE-CAR FOR CITY TRAVEL, IN USE ON THE THIRD
AVENUE LINE.

to put a stop to such practices, but thus far have not been successful, and plead as their excuse for the low wages they give, that this system of stealing prevents them from giving higher pay. Spies, or "spotters," as the conductors term them, are kept constantly travelling over the roads to watch the employees. They note the number of passengers carried during the trip, and when the conductors' reports are handed in, examine them and point out such inaccuracies as may exist. They soon become known to the men. They are cordially hated, and sometimes fare badly at the hands of those whose evil doings they have exposed. This practice of "knocking down," or appropriating money, begins with the conductor, as he alone receives the money paid for fares. Those interested in it defend it on various grounds. The President of the Third Avenue Railway Company, the principal horse-car line in the city, once said to a reporter for a morning paper :

"We try and get all honest men. We discharge a man immediately if he is found to be dishonest. You see, conductors are sometimes made more dishonest by the drivers, who demand so much a day from them. You have no idea how much a driver can worry a conductor if he wants to. For instance, he can drive a little past the corner every time when he ought to stop. He can be looking the other way when the conductor sees a passenger coming. He can run too fast, or let the car behind beat his, and so on, annoying the conductor continually. The only way the conductor can keep friends with him is to divide every night. . . . The conductors 'knock down' on an average about thirty-five or fifty cents per day. . . . I don't think the practice can be entirely stopped. We try all we can. Some will do it, and others think they have the same right. We can't stop it, but discharge a man mighty quick if he is detected." The Third Avenue line runs 200 cars, so that the loss of the company by the "knock-down" system is from $70 to $100 per day, or from $25,500 to $36,500 per annum.

A conductor gave his explanation of the system as follows:

"Well, I'll tell ye. When a conductor is put on a road he has to wait his turn before getting a car; it may be a month or six weeks before he is regularly on. He'll have to know the ropes or he'll be shelved before he knows it. He'll have to be a thief from the start or leave the road. His pay is $2 to $2.25 per day. Out of that sum he must pay the driver from $1 to $2 a day ; the starter he has to conciliate in various ways. A lump of stamps is better than drinks and cigars, though drinks and cigars have a good deal of influence on the roads ; and then the 'spotter' has to get $5 every week. "

" Why do the conductors allow themselves to be imposed on in this way ? "

" Why ? Because they can't help it. If they don't pay the driver, the driver will not stop for passengers, and the conductor is short in his returns ; if they don't have a 'deal' with the starter, the starter will fix him somehow. You see the driver. can stop behind time, or go beyond it if he likes. The latest car in the street, you understand, gets the most passsengers. So it is that the drivers who are feed by the conductors stay from two to five minutes behind time, to the inconvenience of passengers, but to the profit of the driver, the conductor, the starter, the spotter, and for all I know, the superintendent and president of the company. It is a fine system from beginning to end. The amount of drink disposed of by some of the fellows in authority is perfectly amazing. I know a starter to boast of taking fifteen cocktails (with any number of lagers between drinks) in a day, and all paid for by the 'road ;' for, of course, the conductors saved themselves from loss. Oh, yes, you bet they did! The conductor's actual expenses a day average $5 ; his pay is $2.25, which leaves a fine tail-end margin of profit. How the expenses are incurred I have told you. What ken a man do? Honesty? No man can be honest and remain a conductor. Conductors must help themselves, an' they do! Why, even the driver who profits by the conductor's operations, has to fee the stablemen, else how could he get good horses? Stablemen get from $1 to $2 per week from each driver."

" Then the system of horse railroad management is entirely corrupt ? "

"You bet. 'Knocking down' is a fine art, as they say : but it is not confined to the conductors. The worst thing about the car business though, and what disgusted me while I was in it, was the thieves."

"The thieves?"

"Ay, the thieves. The pick-pockets, a lot of roughs get on your car, refuse to pay their fares, insult ladies, and rob right and left. If you object you are likely to get knocked on the head; if you are armed and show fight you are attacked in another way. The thieves are (or rather they were until lately) influential politicians, and tell you to your face that they'll have you dismissed. Ten to one they do what they say. I tell ye a man ought to have leave to knock down lively to stand all this."

II.

THE STAGES.

THE stages of New York are a feature of the great city, which must be seen to be appreciated. They are the best to be found on this continent, but are far inferior to the elegant vehicles for the same purpose which are to be seen in London and Paris. The stages of New York are stiff, awkward look-ing affairs, very difficult to enter or leave, a fact which is some-times attended with considerable danger on the part of ladies. To ride in one is to incur considerable fatigue, for they are as rough as an old-fashioned country wagon. Unlike the Euro-pean omnibuses, they have no seats on top, but an adventurous passenger may, if he choses, clamber up over the side and seat himself by the Jehu in charge. From this lofty perch he can enjoy the best view of the streets along the route of the vehicle, and if the driver be inclined to loquacity, he may hear many a curious tale to repay him for his extra exertion.

The stages, however, as inconvenient as they are, constitute the favorite mode of conveyance for the better class of New Yorkers. The fare on these lines is ten cents, and is suffi-ciently high to exclude from them the rougher and dirtier portion of the community, and one meets with more courtesy and good breeding here than in the street cars. They are cleaner than the cars, and ladies are less liable to annoyance in them. Like the cars, however, they are well patronized by the pickpockets.

The driver also acts as conductor. The fares are passed up to him through a hole in the roof in the rear of his seat. The check-string passes from the door through this hole, and rests under the driver's foot. By pulling this string the passenger gives the signal to stop the stage, and in order to distinguish between this and a signal to receive the passenger's fare, a small gong, worked by means of a spring, is fastened at the side of the hole. By striking this the passenger attracts the driver's attention. A vigorous ringing of this gong by the driver is a signal for passengers to hand up their fares.

All the stage routes lie along Broadway below Twenty-third street. They begin at some of the various East River ferries, reach the great thoroughfare as directly as possible, and leave it to the right and left between Bleecker and Twenty-third streets, and pass thence to their destinations in the upper part of the city. The principal lines pass from Broadway into Madison, Fourth and Fifth avenues, and along their upper portions traverse the best quarter of the city. As the stages furnish the only conveyances on Broadway, they generally do well. The flow and ebb of the great tide down and up the island in the morning and evening crowd every vehicle, and during the remainder of the day, they manage by the exertions of the drivers to keep comfortably full.

The stage drivers constitute a distinct class in the metropolis, and though they lead a hard and laborious life, their lot, as a general thing, is much better than that of the car drivers. They suffer much from exposure to the weather. In the summer they frequently fall victims to sunstroke, and in the bitter winter weather they are sometimes terribly frozen before reaching the end of their route, as they cannot leave their boxes. In the summer they protect themselves from the rays of the sun by means of huge umbrellas fastened to the roof of

the coach, and in the winter they encase themselves in a multitude of wraps and comforters, and present a rather ludicrous
appearance. They are obliged to exercise considerable skill in
driving along Broadway, for the dense throng in the street
renders the occurrence of an accident always probable, and
Jehu has a holy horror of falling into the hands of the police.
Riding with one of them one day, I asked if he could tell me
why it was that the policemen on duty on the street were never
run over or injured in trying to clear the thoroughfare of its
frequent "blocks" of vehicles?

"There'll never be one of them hurt by a driver accustomed
to the street, sir," said he, dryly ; " I'd rather run over the richest man in New York. Why, the police would fix you quick
enough if you'd run a-foul of them. It would be a month or
two on the Island, and that's what none of us fancy."

It requires more skill to carry a stage safely through Broadway than to drive a horse car, and consequently good stage-
drivers are always in demand, and can command better wages
and more privileges than the latter. They are allowed the
greater part of Saturday, or some other day in the week, and as
the stages are not run on Sunday, that day is a season of rest
with them.

Like the street car conductors, they are given to the practice
of "knocking down," and it is said appropriate very much
more of their employers' money than the former. They defend
the practice with a variety of arguments, and assert that it is
really to their employers' interests for them to keep back a part
of the earnings of the day, since in order to cover up their
peculations, they must exert themselves to pick up as many
fares as possible. "It's a fact, sir," said one of them to the
writer, "that them as makes the most for themselves, makes the
biggest returns to the office."

"Many of the drivers are very communicative on the subjects of their profession, and not a few tell some good stories of
'slouches,' 'bums,' and 'beats,' the names given to those
gentlemen whose principal object in this world is to sponge
upon poor humanity to as great an extent as the latter will per-

mit.   One of the cheapest ways of 'getting a ride' is to present
a five or ten dollar bill ; very few drivers carry so much money,
as they hardly ever have that amount on their morning trips;
the bill cannot be changed, and the owner of it gets 'down
town' *free.*

"Apropos of this method, a talkative Jehu said to me one
morning, 'When I was a drivin' on the Knickerbocker,' a line
that ran some twenty years ago from South Ferry through
Broadway, Bleecker, and Eighth avenue, to Twenty-third
street, ' there was a middle-aged man that used to ride reg'lar ;
all the fellows got to knowin' him.   Well, he'd get in and hand
up a ten dollar note—you know the fare was only six cents
then—and we never had so much 'bout us, so, of course, he'd
ride for nothin' ; well, that fellow stuck me five mornin's
straight, and I sort o' got tired of it ; so on the six' day I went to
the office and says to the Boss, " There's a man ridin' free on this
line.   All the fellows knows him ; he gives 'em all a ten dollar
note and they can't break it.   He's rid with me these last five
mornin's, an' I'm goin' for him to-day, I want ten dollars in
pennies, an' six fares out.   If he rides I'll git square with him."
So the Boss he gives me nine dollars and sixty-four cents all in
pennies—you know they was all big ones then—an' they
weighed some, I tell you.   When I got down to Fourteenth
street he hailed me.   Then the fares used to pay when they got
out.   So he hands up his note ; I looked at it—it was on the
"Dry Dock "—an' I hands him down the pennies.   Well, how
he did blow about it an' said how he wouldn't take 'em.   Well,
says I, then I'll keep it all.   Well, he was the maddest fellow
you ever seen ; he was hoppin' !   But he got out an' some one
inside hollers out, " Put some one on the other side or you'll
capsize," an' he thought it was me.   He jumped on the sidewalk an' he called me everything he could lay his tongue to,
an' I a la'ffin' like blazes.   Says he, " I'll report you, you old
thief," an' I drove off.   Well, I told the Boss, an' he says, " Let
him come, I'll talk to him," but he never made no complaint
there.'

"Said another : 'A lady got in with me one day an' handed

up a fifty cent stamp. I put down forty cents. I don't never look gen'rally, but this time I see a man take the change an' put it in his pocket. Pretty soon a man rings the bell an' says, " Where's the lady's change?" Well, I thinks here's a go, an' I points to the man and says, " That there gentleman put it in his pocket." Well, that fellow looked like a sheet, an' a thunder-cloud an' all through the rainbow. He never said nothing but pulled out the change, gave it up, an' then he got out an' went 'round a corner like mad. Some don't wait like he did tho', but gits out right off. One day a chap got out an' another follered him, an they had it out on the street there, an' we all was a looking on.'

"Sometimes the drivers make 'a haul' in a curious way. Said one : 'A man handed me up a fifty dollar bill one night. I handed it back four times, and got mad because he wouldn't give me a small bill. He said he hadn't anything else, and I could take that or nothing, so, I gave him change for a dollar bill, and kept forty-nine dollars and ten cents for his fare. He didn't say anything, and after a while he got out. Why, the other day a lady gave me a hundred dollar note, and when I told her I thought she'd faint. " My goodness ! " said she, " I didn't know it was more than one." Such people ought to be beat; they'd be more careful when they lose a few thousand.'

" ' Some fellows,' said another driver, ' give you ten or fifteen cents, an' swear they give you a fifty cent stamp, an' you have to give them change for fifty cents, or they'll may be go to the office an' make a fuss, an' the bosses will sooner take their word than yours, an' you'll get sacked.'

"One of the most laborious ways of 'turning an honest penny ' was brought to my notice by one of these knights of the whip. Said he: ' Has you been a watchin' of my business this morning? P'r'aps you aint took notice of the money I'm takin' in? No, I guess not.' The latter remark was followed by a rough laugh, in which I thought there was distinguishable a little more than mere merriment, especially when I heard a mumbled imprecation. He continued aloud : ' I aint seen any yet myself.' Soon the bell rang, and a ticket was passed up.

' Well,' said he, ' he's goin' it strong, to be sure; this here's the fourteenth ticket I've had on this trip.'   An explanation being solicited, the fact was revealed that there was a man inside who made a practice of buying twelve tickets for a dollar, then seating himself near the bell, he would take the fares of every one and give the driver a ticket for each, that is, receive ten cents and give the driver the equivalent of eight and one-third cents, thereby making ten cents on every six passengers.   ' You see,' said the driver, ' what a blessin' those sort of fellers is.   Here I don't have no trouble whatsomever; he makes all the change for me, and 'spose my box should blow over, nothen's lost.' From time to time as the tickets were handed up he would cheer the toiler inside with such expressions as ' Go it boots,' ' How's the cash?'   ' How does the old thing work?' always loud enough to attract the attention of the ' insides.'

" This strange individual interested me so much that I made some inquiries about him, at first supposing him to be crazy or otherwise terribly afflicted ; but he is considered sound, is the third in a well-to-do firm, and is far beyond the need of having recourse to any such means for increasing his capital."

III.

STEAM RAILWAYS.

THE great necessity of New York is some sure means of rapid transit between the upper and lower parts of the island. The average New Yorker spends about an hour or an hour and a half each day in going to and from his business, and an immense amount of valuable time is thus lost, which loss is often increased by delays.   For the past few years the citizens of the metropolis have been seeking to procure the construction of a road from the Battery to Harlem to be operated by steam, and it seems probable now that a few years more will witness the completion of such a road.   Public opinion is divided between two plans, and it is probable that both will be tried, and that the city will soon contain a steam railway elevated above the street and a similar road under the ground.

The elevated railway has already been tried to a limited extent, but is not regarded with much favor by the citizens. This line extends along Greenwich street and Ninth avenue, from the Battery to Thirtieth street. The track of this road is laid on iron posts, at an elevation of about sixteen feet above the street. The cars are so constructed that it would be impossible for one of them to fall from the track. Dummy engines furnish the motive power. The running time from the present southern terminus at Courtlandt street to Thirtieth street, a distance of about three miles, is fifteen minutes. The road is pronounced perfectly safe by competent engineers, but the structure appears so light to the unscientific public that nine out of ten view it with distrust, and it is doubtful whether it will ever meet with the success the company hope for.

The only other elevated road at present contemplated, and for which a liberal charter has been obtained, is known as the *Viaduct Road.* It is proposed to build this on a series of arches of solid masonry, the streets to be spanned by light bridges. The line of the road is to be in the centre of the blocks along its route. The estimated cost of the road, including the sum to be paid for the right of way, is about $80,000,000 ; and it seems certain that this immense cost will necessitate radical changes in the original plan.

The underground plan has many supporters in the city, these basing their hopes upon the success achieved by the underground railway of London. There are several plans proposed for an underground road. The first is known as the *Arcade Railway.* It is proposed by the friends of this plan to excavate the streets along which it passes to a depth of about twenty feet, or in other words, to make a new street twenty feet below the level of those already in existence. This new street is to be provided with sidewalks, gas-lamps, telegraph lines, hydrants, etc., and upon the sidewalks the basements of the present buildings will open, thus adding an additional and valuable story to the existing edifices. The lower street is to be arched over with solid

TUNNEL UNDER BROADWAY.

223

masonry, rendered water-tight, and supported by heavy iron columns. Large glass plates, similar to those now used for lighting the cellars of stores, will be placed in the sidewalks of the street above, and will furnish light to the lower street during the day. The roadway of the lower street will be entirely devoted to the use of railway trains. The proposed route of the *Arcade* line is from the Battery, under Broadway, to Union Square. Thence the eastern branch is to extend along Fourth avenue to the Harlem River, while the western is to continue along Broadway to the junction of Ninth avenue, whence it will be prolonged to the northern end of the island.

The *Underground Railway* proper is to extend from the lower to the upper end of the island, and is to pass through one or more tunnels, after the manner of the Underground Railway of London.

The third plan for an underground road, is the only one that has yet been attempted. It is known as the "Beach Pneumatic Tunnel." A small section, several hundred yards in length, has been constructed under Broadway, and the company owning it claim that they have thus demonstrated their ability to construct and work successfully a road extending from the Battery to the upper end of the island.

The tunnel is eight feet in diameter. It commences in the cellar of the marble building of Messrs. Develin & Co., at the southwest corner of Broadway and Warren street, and extends under the great thoroughfare to a point a little below Murray street. It is dry and clean, is painted white, and is lighted with gas. It passes under all the gas and water pipes and sewers. The cars are made to fit the tunnel, and are propelled by means of atmospheric pressure. A strong blast of air, thrown out by means of an immense blowing machine, is forced against the rear end of a car, and sends it along the track like a sail-boat before the wind. This current of course secures perfect ventilation within the car. The company claim that they will be able, when their road is completed, to transport more than 20,000 passengers per hour, each way.

XII.

HORACE GREELEY.

THE best known man in New York, in one sense, and the least known in others, is Horace Greeley. If there is a man, woman, or child in all this broad land who has not heard of him, let that person apply to Barnum for an engagement as a natural curiosity. And yet how few know the man as he really is. The most absurd stories are told of him, and the likeness most familiar to the public is a ridiculous caricature.

He was born in Amherst, New Hampshire, on the 3d of February, 1811, and is consequently 61 years old. His parents were poor, and Horace received but a very plain education at the common schools of the vicinity. The natural talent of the boy made up for this, however, for he read everything he could lay his hands on. He was a rapid reader, too, and had the faculty of retaining the information thus acquired. He was kept too busy at work on his father's sterile farm to be able to read during the day, and he was too poor to afford to use candles at night, and so his early studies were carried on by the light of pine knots. He served a severe apprenticeship at the printing business, commencing it at a very early age, and finding employment first on one country paper, and then on another, working at his trade, and occasionally writing for the journals he put in type.

In 1831 he came to New York, convinced that the great city offered him a better opportunity for success than any other place, and resolved to win that success. He was very boyish in appearance, frail, delicate-looking, but hopeful and resolved. For ten years he worked hard in the various offices of the city, sometimes setting type and sometimes writing editorials. Sometimes he published his own journal, but generally found this a

15

"losing business." Failure did not discourage him, and he kept on, acquiring greater experience and becoming better known every year. He has himself told so well the story of his early struggles to so large an audience that I need not repeat it here.

In 1841, ten years from the time he wandered along Nassau street, without money or friends, and with all his wordly possessions tied up in a handkerchief, he began the publication of the *New York Tribune*, having succeeded in obtaining the necessary capital. It was a venture, and a bold one, but it proved a great success. He chose the name of the journal himself, and became its responsible editor. Though others have assisted him in his efforts, the success of the paper is his work. He has made it a great power in the land, and he is naturally proud of his work. Those who know him best say that the title dearest to his heart is that of "Founder of the New York Tribune."

Mr. Greeley's career has been one of incessant labor. His friends say he was never known to rest as other men do. When he goes to his farm in Westchester County for recreation, he rests by chopping wood and digging ditches. His editorial labors make up a daily average of about two columns of the *Tribune*, and he contributes the equivalent of about six *Tribune* columns per week to other journals. He writes from fifteen to twenty-five letters per day; he has published several large works; he goes thoroughly through his exchanges every day, and keeps himself well posted in the current literature of the times; he speaks or lectures about five or six times a month, and makes monthly visits to Albany and Washington, to see what is going on behind the scenes in the capitals of the State and Nation. He is constantly receiving people who come on business or from curiosity, and yet he never seems tired, though he is not always even-tempered.

He is somewhat peculiar in his personal appearance. Most people in thinking of him picture to themselves a slouchy looking man, with a white hat, a white overcoat, with one leg of his breeches caught over the top of his boot, his whole dress shabby and not overclean, and his pockets stuffed full of newspapers, and many have imagined that he " gets himself up " so, in order to attract attention on the streets. The true Horace Greeley, however, though careless as to outward appearances, is immaculately neat in his dress. No one ever saw him with dirty linen or soiled clothes except in muddy weather, when, in New York, even a Brummel must be content to be splashed with mud. Mr. Greeley's usual dress is a black frock coat, a white vest, and a pair of black pantaloons which come down to the ankle. His black cravat alone betrays his carelessness, and that only when it slips off the collar, and works its way around to the side. Mr. Greeley is five feet ten inches in height, and is stout in proportion. He is partly bald, and his hair is white. He has a light, pinkish complexion, and his eyes are blue, small, and sunken. His mouth is well-shaped, and his features are regular. His beard is worn around the throat and under the chin, and is perfectly white. His hands are small and soft; but his feet and legs are awkward and clumsy, and this gives to him a peculiar shuffling motion in walking. He is abstracted in manner, and when accosted suddenly replies abruptly, and as some think rudely.

One of his acquaintances thus describes him in his editorial office :

" We walk through the little gate in the counter, turn within the open doorway on our left, climb a short, narrow flight of stairs, and find ourselves in a small room, ten by fifteen, furnished with a green carpet, a bed lounge, an open book-rack, a high desk, a writing-desk, three arm-chairs, a short-legged table, and a small marble sink.

" Mr. Greeley's back is toward us. He is seated at his desk. His head is bent over his writing, and his round shoulders are quite prominent. He is scribbling rapidly. A quire of foolscap, occupying the only clear space on his desk, is melting rapidly beneath his pen. The desk itself is a heap of confusion. Here is Mr. Greeley's straw hat; there is his handkerchief. In front of him is a peck of newspaper clippings, not neatly rolled up, but loosely sprawled over the desk. At his left a rickety

pair of scissors catches a hurried nap, and at his right a paste-
pot and a half-broken box of wafers appear to have had a
rough-and-tumble fight. An odd-looking paper-holder is just
ready to tumble on the floor. An old-fashioned sand-box,
looking like a dilapidated hour-glass, is half-hidden under a
slashed copy of *The New York World*. Mr. Greeley still sticks
to wafers and sand, instead of using mucilage and blotting-paper.
A small drawer, filled with postage stamps and bright steel pens,
has crawled out on the desk. Packages of folded missives are
tucked in the pigeon-holes, winking at us from the back of the
desk, and scores of half-opened letters, mixed with seedy brown
envelopes, flop lazily about the table. Old papers lie gashed
and mangled about his chair, the *débris* of a literary battle field.
A clean towel hangs on a rack to his right. A bound copy of
The Tribune Almanac, from 1838 to 1868, swings from a small
chain fastened to a staple screwed in the side of his desk; two
other bound volumes stand on their feet in front of his nose, and
two more of the same kind are fast asleep on the book-rack in
the corner. Stray numbers of the almanac peep from every
nook. The man who would carry off Greeley's bound pile of
almanacs would deserve capital punishment. The Philosopher
could better afford to lose one of his legs than to lose his almanacs. The room is kept scrupulously clean and neat. A
waste paper basket squats between Mr. Greeley's legs, but one
half the torn envelopes and boshy communications flutter to the
floor instead of being tossed into the basket. The table at his
side is covered with a stray copy of *The New York Ledger*, and
a dozen magazines lie thereon. Here is an iron garden rake
wrapped up in an *Independent*. There hangs a pair of hand-
cuffs once worn by old John Brown, and sent Mr. Greeley by
an enthusiastic admirer of both Horace and John. A champagne
basket, filled with old scrap-books and pamphlets, occupies one
corner. A dirty bust of Lincoln, half hidden in dusty piles of
paper, struggles to be seen on the top of his desk. A pile of
election tables, dirty, ragged and torn, clipped from some unknown newspaper, looks as if they had half a mind to jump down
on the 'Old Man's' bald head. A certificate of life member-

ship in some tract or abolition society, and maps of the World, New York, and New Jersey hang on the wall. A rare geological specimen of quartz rock, weighing about ten pounds, is ready to roll down a high desk to the floor on the first alarm. Dirty pamphlets are as plentiful as cockroaches. His office library consists of 150 volumes.

"Pen, ink, paper, scissors, and envelopes are in unfailing demand. The cry, 'Mr. Greeley wants writing paper!' creates a commotion in the counting-room, and Mr. Greeley gets paper quicker than a hungry fisherman could skin an eel.

"Mr. Greeley can lay Virginia worm fences in ink faster than any other editor in New York City. He uses a fountain-pen, a present from some friend. He thinks a great deal of it, but during an experience of three years has failed to learn the simple principle of suction without getting his mouth full of ink, and he generally uses it with an empty receiver. He makes a dash at the ink-bottle every twenty seconds, places the third finger and thumb of his left hand on his paper, and scratches away at his worm fence like one possessed. He writes marvellously fast. Frequently the point of his pen pricks through his sheet, for he writes a heavy hand, and a snap follows, spreading inky spots over the paper, resembling a woodcut portraying the sparks from a blacksmith's hammer. Blots like mashed spiders, or crushed huckleberries, occasionally intervene, but the old veteran dashes them with sand, leaving a swearing compositor to scratch off the soil, and dig out the words underneath.

"Mr. Greeley's manuscript, when seen for the first time, resembles an intricate mass of lunatic hieroglyphics, or the tracks of a spider suffering from *delirium tremens*. But, by those accustomed to his writing, a remarkable exactness is observed. The spelling, punctuation, accented letters, and capitalizing are perfect. The old type-setters of the office prefer his manuscript above that of any other editor, for the simple reason that he writes his article as he wishes it to appear, and rarely, if ever, cuts or slashes a proof-sheet. And this punctuality is, in a great measure, a feature of his life. He is always in time, and never waits for anybody. He employs no private secretary, and when he receives a letter, answers it on the instant. No matter how trivial the request, the next outward-bound mail will carry away one of his autographs, if he thinks an answer necessary.

"He knows we have entered his room, yet he continues his writing. The only sound we hear within the sanctum is the scratch of his pen. He has the power of concentrating all the strength of his mind on the subject of his editorial, and will pay no attention to any question, however important, until he finishes his sentence. If the cry of 'Fire!' should resound through the building, Greeley would finish his sentence and ring his bell before he would leave his room. The sentence complete, he places the forefinger of his right hand at the end of the word last written, seizes the handle of his pen in his teeth, and looks his tormentor full in the face. It is a glance of inquiry, and the questioner, intuitively conscious of this fact, repeats his interrogation. Mr. Greeley divines the question before it is finished, and answers it pithily and quickly. The pen is then snatched from his mouth, dexterously dipped into his inkstand, and his fingers again travel across his transverse sheet of foolscap like a 'daddy-long-legs' caught in a storm. If his questioner is importunate, and insists on wasting his time, he continues his writing, never looking up, and either answers absent-mindedly, or in a low, impatient tone, tinged with a peculiar boyish nervousness. If his visitor is ungentlemanly enough to still continue his teasing importunities, a storm breaks forth, and the uncourteous person will trot out of the sanctum with an answer ringing in his ears that should bring a flush to his cheek.

"To Mr. Greeley time is more valuable than money or even friendship. When busy, he is no respecter of persons. President or hod-carrier, general or boot-black, clergyman or express-driver, authoress or apple-woman—all are treated alike. Eminent men have left his room under the impression that they have been deliberately slighted, while Horace still slashed away at his inky pickets, totally unconscious of any neglect."

Mr. Greeley's home is at Chappaqua, in Westchester County, New York, about thirty miles from the city. He owns a fine farm of about forty acres, which has cost him more money than he would care to tell.   Agriculture is one of his great hobbies, and he tests here all the theories that are presented to him.   His friends say that his turnips cost him about ten dollars apiece to produce, and bring about fifty cents per bushel in the market, and that all his farming operations are conducted on the same principle.

Mr. Greeley married when quite young, and has had three children.   Two daughters, aged about twenty and twelve, are living, but his son, a bright and unusually promising child, died some years ago.   Mr. Greeley is one of the principal stockholders in the *Tribune*, and is a rich man.   He is liberal and generous to those in need, and is a warm friend to benevolent enterprises of all kinds.

The chief reason of his popularity is the general confidence of the people in his personal integrity.   Not even his political enemies question his honesty—and surely in these days of corruption and crime in public life, an honest man is one that can not well be spared.

XIII.

THE TOMBS.

TURN out of Printing House Square, leaving the City Hall on your left, and pass up Centre street for about a quarter of a mile, and you will come to a massive granite edifice in the Egyptian style of architecture. It occupies an entire square, and is bounded by Centre and Elm, and Leonard and Franklin streets. The main entrance is on Centre street, and is approached by a broad flight of granite steps, which lead to a portico supported by massive Egyptian columns. The proper name of the edifice is *The Halls of Justice,* but it is popularly known all over the Union as *The Tombs,* which name was given to it in consequence of its gloomy appearance. It occupies the site of the old Collect Pond which once supplied the citizens of New York with drinking water, was begun in 1835 and completed in 1838.

The outer building occupies four sides of a hollow square, and is 253 by 200 feet in size. It was built at a time when New York contained scarcely half its present population, and has long since ceased to be equal to the necessities of the city. The site is low and damp, and the building is badly ventilated. The warden does all in his power to counteract these evils, and keeps the place remarkably neat, but it is still a terribly sickly and dreary abode. It was designed to accommodate about 200 prisoners, but for some years past the number of prisoners confined here at one time has averaged 400, and has sometimes exceeded that average. The Grand Jury of the County have recently condemned the place as a nuisance, and it is believed that the city will ere long possess a larger, cleaner, and more suitable prison.

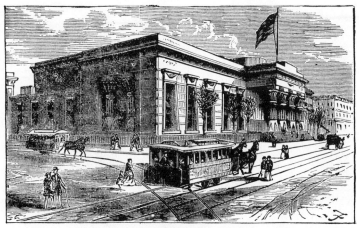

THE TOMBS.

When the prison was built the Five Points, on the western verge of which it lies, was a much worse section than it is now. It is bad enough at present, but then the Tombs constituted a solitary island in a sea of crime and suffering. A terrible island it was, too.

Entering through the gloomy portal upon which the sunlight never falls, the visitor is chilled with the dampness which greets him as soon as he passes into the shadow of the heavy columns. Upon reaching the inner side of the enclosure, he finds that the portion of the prison seen from the street encloses a large courtyard, in the centre of which stands a second prison, 142 feet long by 45 feet deep, and containing 148 cells. This is the male prison, and is connected with the outer building by a bridge known as the *Bridge of Sighs*, since it is by means of it that condemned criminals pass from their cells to the scaffold at the time of their execution.

The gallows is taken down and kept in the prison until there is need for it. Then it is set up in the courtyard near the Bridge of Sighs. All executions are conducted here in private, that is, they are witnessed only by such persons as the officers of the law may see fit to admit. But on such days the neighboring buildings are black with people, seeking to look down

THE BRIDGE OF SIGHS.

over the prison walls and witness the death agonies of the poor
wretch who is paying the penalty of the law.

The interior of the male prison consists of a narrow and
lofty hall, upon which open four tiers of cells, one above
another; those above the ground floor being reached by light
iron galleries. Each gallery is guarded by two keepers. The
cells are narrow, and each is lighted by a small iron-barred
window at the farther end. Light and air are also admitted by
the barred door of iron opening upon the corridor. There are
eleven cells of especial strength, in which convicts condemned
to death or to the State Prison are confined. There are six
other cells, which are used for the confinement of persons
charged with offences less grave, and six more, which are used
for sick prisoners. The cells are generally full of criminals.
Some of them are well furnished, and are provided with carpets, chairs, a table, and books and paper, which are bought at
the expense of the prisoner or his friends. Some of the
inmates shrink from the observation of visitors, but others are
hardened to crime and shame, and not unfrequently cause the
visitor's ears to tingle with the remarks they address to them.

INTERIOR OF MALE PRISON.

No lights are allowed in the cells, and the aspect of the place is very gloomy, the whole prison is kept scrupulously clean, the sanitary regulations being very strict, but the lack of room necessitates the crowding of the prisoners to a fearfully demoralizing extent.

The outer building contains the female prison, which lies along the Leonard street side, the boys' prison, and the halls of justice, or rooms occupied by the Tombs Police Court and the Court of Special Sessions. Over the main entrance on the Centre street side, are six comfortable cells. These are for the use of criminals of the wealthier class, who can afford to pay for such comforts. Forgers, fraudulent merchants, and the like, pass the hours of their detention in these rooms, while their humbler but not more guilty brothers in crime are shut in the close cells of the male prison. These rooms command a view of the street, so that their occupants are not entirely cut off from the outer world.

The female prison is in charge of an excellent matron, who has held her position for more than twenty years. Men are never confined here, and male visitors are subject to certain restrictions. In this portion is located the room used as a chapel. Religious services of some kind are held in the Tombs every day in the week except Saturday, and the effort is made to give all the denominations an opportunity of doing good. Sunday morning and Tuesday until noon are devoted to the Roman Catholics; Sunday and Tuesday afternoons to the Episcopalians; Monday to the Methodists, and Wednesday, Thursday and Friday to the other Protestant denominations. Some of the Protestant clergy sometimes attempt to hold religious services in the main hall of the male prison, so that the prisoners in their cells may hear what is going on. The latter pay little or no attention to the preacher, and frequently interrupt and annoy him by their shouts, jeers and imitations in their cells. The Sisters of Charity are in charge of the female and boys' prisons, and do a vast amount of good by their quiet ministrations. The boys are kept in a large room during the day, and are locked up in separate cells at night.

THE PRISON CHAPEL.

One of the principal rooms in the Tombs is "The Bummers' Cell." It is a large apartment, shut off from one of the main halls by an iron railing. It is always tolerably well filled, and on Saturday nights it is overflowing. Here are confined those against whom there is no serious charge; persons arrested for drunkenness, or for simple disorder on the streets. On Sunday morning the visitor will sometimes find a large crowd of men collected in it, not all of whom are unfortunates or criminals. Some are well-dressed, well-to-do persons, who have had the misfortune to be drunk and noisy on Saturday night. Some are strangers, residents of other cities, who have started out from their hotels to see the sights and have a merry time, and who have fallen at length—and fortunately for them—into the hands

238 LIGHTS AND SHADOWS OF NEW YORK LIFE; OR,

of the police. A few are persons who have been wrongfully or maliciously accused of crime.

From sunset until long after midnight on Saturday, the police are busy with ridding the streets of drunken and disorderly persons. As soon as a person is arrested, he is taken to the Tombs or to one of the station-houses. It is the duty of the officer in charge of the precinct to lock up every one against whom a definite charge is brought. Even though satisfied that the person is wrongfully accused, or is simply unfortunate, he has no discretion. He must hold for trial all charged with offences, and at the Tombs the officer is obliged to throw persons who command his sympathy into the company of the most abandoned wretches for an entire night. Drunkenness, disorderly conduct, and fighting, are the principal charges brought against the occupants of the Bummers' Cell. The noise, profanity, and obscenity are fearful. All classes and ages are represented there.

During the year 1870, 49,423 persons were confined for various periods of time in the Tombs.

The Tombs Police Court offers some interesting and instructive spectacles. It is opened at six o'clock on Sunday morning. It is presided over by Justice Joseph Dowling, a short, thickset man, with a handsome face, and a full, well-shaped head, indicating both ability and determination. Judge Dowling is still a young man, and is one of the most efficient magistrates in the city. His decisions are quickly rendered, and are usually just. His long experience with criminals has given him an intimate knowledge of the men with whom he has to deal, and their ways. This often helps him to a conclusion which is really true, although the evidence in the case does not confirm it, and he frequently startles criminals by boldly declaring that they did thus and so at such a time. The criminal overwhelmed with astonishment and confusion generally admits the charge, and is sentenced accordingly. A stranger is at once struck with the quick and penetrating power of Judge Dowling's glance. He seems to look right through a criminal, and persons brought before him generally find it impossible to deceive him. This has made him the terror of criminals, who have come to regard an arraignment before him as equivalent to a conviction, which is generally the case. At the same time he is kind and considerate to those who are simply unfortunate. As a man, he is kind-hearted, and inclined to lean toward the side of mercy.

As soon as the court is opened, the prisoners are called up in the order of their arrival during the previous night. Drunkenness and disorder, and first offences of a minor character, are punished with a reprimand, and the prisoner is dismissed. These cases constitute a majority of the charges, and the judge disposes of them with a rapidity which astonishes a stranger. The more serious cases are held for further examination, or are sent on for trial before the Court of Special Sessions.

All classes of people come to the Justice with complaints of every description. Women come to complain of their husbands, and men of their wives. Judge Dowling listens to them all, and if a remedy is needed, applies the proper one without delay. In most instances he dismisses the parties with good advice, as their cases are not provided for by the law.

The Court of Special Sessions sits in a large hall on the right of the main entrance to the prison. It is strictly a criminal court, and is for the trial of charges which are too serious to be disposed of in the Police Court. Two judges are supposed to sit during the sessions of this court, but Judge Dowling frequently conducts its business alone. The prisoner is allowed to employ counsel and introduce witnesses in his own behalf.

The following is an example of the way in which Judge Dowling transacts business in this court :

" The first case of importance was that of the People *vs.* James Day, *alias* ' Big-mouthed Scotty,' and William Jones, *alias* ' Billy Clews,' on the complaint of Captain Ira S. Garland, of the Twelfth precinct. Probably there are not two other men in this city who could fairly be compared with these. They are both of the most dissolute, desperate habits, and have been what they now are, thieves, since the date of their entry into this city. The first, who is truthfully styled ' big-mouthed '— that hole in his face being almost large enough to run in one of

COURT OF SPECIAL SESSIONS.

the cars on the elevated railroad in Greenwich street—was born in the Hielands o' Bonnie Scotland; but, be it said, he appears not to have become inoculated with the same spirit of honesty and perseverance that characterizes the greater portion of his countrymen. He arrived here nearly twenty years ago, and since that time he has been a lazy, contemptible thief, a shocking contrast with Caledonians in general. His companion, ' Billy Clews,' has been known in different circles of the same profession, and could usually be found in the neighborhood of Five Points. On Thursday there was what is usually termed a ' large' funeral, from a church at the corner of One-hundred-and-twenty-sixth street and Fourth avenue. Outside was a long line of coaches, and inside the church was full of mourners and the friends of the departed, whose remains were about to be consigned to that ' bourn whence no traveller returns.' The crowd inside was so great that the police were called in to put the people in the seats, as far as could be done, and remained there during the service to keep order. While Captain Garland was standing at the top of the centre aisle he saw ' Big-Mouth ' elbowing his way from the altar towards the door, and making various efforts to pick pockets as he came along. Presently he came close up behind a lady who was standing with her face to the altar, and, reaching his hands in the folds of her dress, quietly withdrew her pocket-book from its hiding place. The pocket-book vanished very quickly, however, so that the captain could not see which way it went or what, for the time, had become of it. At first the thieves did not observe the captain, but the instant Day caught a glance of him he turned quietly to his accomplice and said:—'Look out, Billy; there's a big cop.' Billy took the 'cue,' began to move off, and attempted to get out of the church. But as they were both in the doorway, and seeing the captain making for them, they made a rush out from the sacred edifice, passed the carriages and ran down the avenue as fast as 'shank's pony' could carry them. The captain gave chase, and, with the aid of an officer on duty at the church, succeeded in arresting the individuals who were thus trading on the mourners over a dead body. On returning to the church Garland was informed of the loss of the lady's pocket-book, but he failed to discover her among the crowd, and consequently could not produce her in evidence against the prisoners at the bar. He had seen them previously walking towards the church, and knowing Day to be a general thief, he gave orders to look out for them, but somehow for a long time the thieves escaped the vigilance of the officers. They allowed it was 'all wrong' to be in the church at the time, but they told the captain he ought to allow them to go, for he knew 'how it was' with them.

" ' What have you to say, Scotty ? ' asked the Judge.

" ' Oh, well,' replied Big-Mouth, ' I don't thenk a've got much to say, only to ask your Honor to deal mercifully with us. The captain at the police station didn't say he was to breng this prosecution agen us noo ; he only told us he wud tak us out o' harum's way, and didn't make no charge.'

" Judge Dowling.—' It is no use my saying anything to you, Day ; in fact, all that could be said is that you have never been anything else than what you are now, a thief, and that, too, of a most contemptible type. You go about to the various grave-yards and rob the poor persons who are too absorbed in interring

16

the dead and in grieving for their lost friends to notice that
you are there for the purpose of plunder; you also visit the
churches wherever there is a crowd of this sort paying their
last respects to the remains of a friend, and never leave without
robbing some poor persons of their money or jewelry. Scotchy,
you have done that business for the past eighteen years to my
own knowledge. I do not know so much about your accomplice,
or how long he has been travelling with you. I will, however,
rid the people of your presence, and do my best to stay your
heartless proceedings for some time to come. One year each in
the Penitentiary and a fine of $200 each, and both to stand com-
mitted until the amounts be paid.'

"'I told you how it 'oud be, Scotty,' yelled his partner, and
with a deplorable attitude the pair were marched over the
'Bridge of Sighs.'"

The Tombs is merely a prison of detention, and as soon as
prisoners are sentenced to the institutions on Blackwell's Island,
or the State Prison, they are conveyed to those establishments
with as little delay as possible. The vehicle used for transport-
ing them through the city is a close wagon, with wooden blinds
for light and ventilation, around the upper part of the sides.
This is known as "Black Maria," and may be daily seen
rumbling through the city on its way from the Police Courts
to the ferry to Blackwell's Island.

Closely connected with the penal system of the city is the
"Prison Association of New York." This society was organized in 1844. Its constitution declares that its objects are:
"I. A humane attention to persons arrested and held for examination or trial, including inquiry into the circumstances of
their arrest, and the crimes charged against them; securing to
the friendless an impartial trial, and protection from the depredations of unprincipled persons, whether professional sharpers or
fellow-prisoners. II. Encouragement and aid to discharged
convicts in their efforts to reform and earn an honest living.
This is done by assisting them to situations, providing them
with tools, and otherwise counselling them and helping them to
business. III. To study the question of prison discipline

"BLACK MARIA."

generally, the government of the State, County, and City prisons, to obtain statistics of crime, to disseminate information on this subject, to evolve the true principles of science, and impress a more reformatory character on our penitentiary system."

Between 1844 and 1869, the members and agents of the Association visited in the prisons of New York and Brooklyn 93,560 persons confined there. These were poor and friendless prisoners, and they received from the Association such advice and aid as their cases demanded. During the same period, 25,290 additional cases were examined by the officers of the Society. They succeeded in obtaining the withdrawal of 6148 complaints, as being trivial, or based upon prejudice or passion. Upon their recommendation, the courts discharged 7922 persons guilty of first offences, and who were penitent, or who had committed the offence under mitigating circumstances. They also provided 4130 discharged convicts with permanent situations, and furnished 18,307 other discharged convicts with board, money, railroad tickets, or clothing, to help them to better their condition. In the twenty-five years embraced in the above period, they thus extended their good offices to 156,368 persons. A noble record, truly.

XIV.

THE PRESS.

I.

THE DAILY JOURNALS.

THE Metropolitan Press is the model after which the journals of the entire country are shaped, and, taken as a whole, it is the best institution of its kind in existence. The leading New York journals have but one superior in the whole world—the London *Times*—and they frequently equal, though they do not surpass the "Thunderer" itself in the extent and importance of their news, and the ability and value of their editorials. They are the best managed, employ the greatest talent, and are the most influential upon the country at large of any American newspapers.

The leading journals are the morning papers. Five of these, the *Herald, Tribune, Times, World*, and *Staats Zeitung*, are huge eight-page sheets, and frequently issue supplements of from four to eight pages additional. The others consist of four large, old-fashioned pages.

The expense and labor of issuing a first-class morning journal are very great. The cost of publication ranges from $800,000 to $1,000,000 per annum; and the force employed, including editors, reporters, proof-readers, newsmen, pressmen, feeders, clerks and compositors, is over four hundred persons. The profits vary according to the paper and the times.

The *Herald* is private property, as are some of the others. The *Tribune, Times*, and *Sun*, are owned by stock companies. Under Mr. Raymond the *Times* was subject to his sole direction, but the *Tribune* has always suffered from the interference of the stockholders.

Each newspaper has its editor in chief, who controls the general tone and policy of the paper.   He decides all matters relating to its editorial conduct, and is known to the public as the responsible editor.   His principal assistant is the managing editor.   In the absence of the chief editor he is the controlling power of the journal.   His legitimate duties are to oversee the details of the paper, to see that its publication is not delayed, to engage and dismiss sub-editors and correspondents, to prescribe the character of the service required of these gentlemen, and to regulate the salaries paid to them.   All the writers on the paper are directly responsible to him, and he, in his turn, to the chief editor.   There is also a night editor, whose duties are heavy and responsible.   He is charged with the duty of "making up" the paper, and decides what shall and what shall not go in—a delicate duty sometimes.   He is at his post at 7 o'clock in the evening, and remains there until the paper goes to press in the morning, which is generally between 2 and 3 o'clock, though sometimes it is held back by important news until daylight. The foreign editor is usually a foreigner, and one well acquainted with the leading languages of Europe.   He controls the foreign correspondence, and writes editorials upon European topics. The financial editor writes the money article, and is quite an important personage.   He is obliged to be well informed concerning all the financial transactions of the day ; he is courted by bankers and capitalists, as he to a certain extent controls public opinion in money matters, and he has ample facilities for making money outside of his position.   The post is considered one of the most lucrative on the paper, and the salary is regarded as a minor consideration.   The city editor has charge of the city news, and is the chief of the reporters.   The leading dailies have from twelve to thirty reporters.   These are assigned to duty each day by the city editor, who enters his directions to them in a large book.   They are sometimes required to go to certain places to obtain news, and are expected to furnish so much matter concerning it.   Some of the reporters have special lines of

PRINTING HOUSE SQUARE.

duty, and report nothing but law cases, police matters, etc., and
some limit their operations to Brooklyn, Jersey City, and the
other suburban towns.   Some of the reporters are stenographers
also.   At times there will be scarcely any work to be done, and
again the powers of the whole staff of reporters will be severely
taxed.   There are also a literary editor, whose duties are to review and notice books and other publications; and art, dramatic
and musical critics. Some of these are, as they should be, gentlemen of the highest culture, and impartial in their opinions.
Others are quite the reverse.   The best of them, however, are
but men, though they too often assume to be something superior,
and their judgments are not infallible.   The leading journals
also employ translators, who put into English such extracts as
it may be necessary to use from the foreign papers.
    The amount of labor thus expended upon a morning news-

paper is immense.   It is followed by an almost equal outlay of
mechanical work in putting the paper in type and printing it.
The principal papers are stereotyped, and are printed from
plates.   Formerly the Eight and Ten Cylinder Hoe Presses
were used, but of late years the Bullock Press has become very
popular.   It works quite as rapidly as the Hoe press, prints on
both sides at once, and is said to spoil fewer sheets.   The paper
is put in in a large roll, and is cut by the machine into the
proper sizes and printed.   Only one feeder is necessary.

Nearly all the city newspapers are located in or around Printing House Square, immediately opposite and east of the City
Hall.   One of the greatest curiosities of this square is a huge
engine, which runs a large number of presses.   It is situated in
Spruce street, between William and Nassau streets, and occupies
the basement of the building in which it is located.   There are
two engines here—one of 150 horse power, which is used during
the day, and a smaller one of 75 horse power, which relieves it
at night.   Shafting and belting carry the power in every direction from the engine.   One hundred and twenty-five presses
are worked by these engines—each being estimated at so much
horse power, and charged accordingly.   They turn three-
quarters of a mile of main shafting, besides a mile or more of
connecting shafts, and as much belting.   One of these belts, an
India rubber one, 120 feet long, connects a fifth story press on
Nassau street with the main shafting on Spruce street, across
the intervening yards, and another of leather, on Beekman
street, 140 feet, perfectly perpendicular, connects the sub-cellar
and the attic.   Some of the shafting passes under and across the
streets.   Over fifty newspapers and literary papers, besides
magazines and books innumerable, are printed by this monster
engine.

The salaries paid by the newspapers are not large.   Those
who receive what is seemingly high pay do an amount of work
out of proportion to their compensation.   Mr. Greeley receives
$10,000 per annum.   Mr. Reid, the managing editor of the
Tribune, receives $5000.   Mr. Sinclair, the publisher, receives
$10,000.   These are considered good salaries.   Any one familiar

with the cost of living in New York will not think them very much in excess of the wants of their recipients, who are men with families.

As a newspaper, the *New York Herald* stands at the head of the city dailies. It aims to be a vehicle for imparting the latest news of the day, and as such it is a great success. Nobody cares for its opinions editorially expressed, for it is the general belief that the *Herald* has no fixed opinions. It is valued here simply as a newspaper. It is beyond a doubt the most energetic, and the best managed *newspaper* in the city. Mr. James Gordon Bennett, the elder, has no rival in the art of conducting a popular journal, but his son, Mr. J. G. Bennett, jr., does not seem to inherit his father's ability. Young Mr. Bennett is now the managing editor, and since his accession to that post there has been a marked decline in the ability of the paper, which, under the rule of Mr. Hudson, was unquestioned. Nobody expects consistency in the *Herald*, and its course to-day is no guarantee that it will hold the same tone to-morrow. Mr. Bennett aims to float with the popular current, to be always on the winning side, and he succeeds. The advertising patronage of the paper is immense.

The *Herald* office is one of the most conspicuous buildings in the city. It is located at the corner of Broadway and Ann street, and is built of white marble, in the modern French style. Below the sidewalk are two immense cellars or vaults, one below the other, in which are two steam engines of thirty-five horse power each. Three immense Hoe presses are kept running constantly from midnight until seven in the morning, printing the daily edition. The rooms and machinery are kept in the most perfect order. Nothing is allowed to be out of place, and the slightest speck of dirt visible in any part, calls forth a sharp rebuke from Mr. Bennett, who makes frequent visits to every department of the paper. On the street floor, the main room is the public office of the journal. Its entrances are on Broadway and Ann street. It is paved with marble tiles, and the desks, counters, racks, etc., are of solid black walnut, ornamented with plate glass. Every thing is scrupu-

THE HERALD OFFICE.

lously clean, and the room presents the appearance of some
wealthy banking office. On the third floor are the editorial
rooms. The principal apartment is the "Council Room," which
overlooks Broadway. Every other branch of the editorial department has its separate room, and all are furnished with every
convenience necessary for doing their work with the utmost
precision and dispatch. Each day, at noon, the editors of the
Herald, twelve in number, assemble in the "Council Room."
Mr. Bennett, if he is in the city, takes his seat at the head of
the table, and the others assume the places assigned. If Mr.
Bennett is not present, his son, James Gordon Bennett, jr., presides at the council, and in the absence of both father and son,

the managing editor takes the head of the table. The council is opened by Mr. Bennett, or his representative, who presents a list of subjects. These are taken up, *seriatim*, and discussed by all present. The topics to be presented in the editorial columns of the *Herald* the next day are determined upon, and each editor is assigned the subject he is to "write up." All this is determined in a short while. Then Mr. Bennett asks the gentlemen present for suggestions. He listens attentively to each one, and decides quickly whether they shall be presented in the *Herald*, and at what time; and if he desires any subject to be written upon, he states his wish, and "sketches," in his peculiar and decisive manner, the various headings and the style of treatment. There are twelve editors and thirty-five reporters employed on the *Herald*. They are liberally paid for their services. Any one bringing in news is well rewarded for his trouble. The composing rooms are located on the top floor, and are spacious, airy, and excellently lighted. A "dumb waiter," or vertical railway, communicates with the press room; and speaking tubes, and a smaller "railway," afford the means of conversation and transmitting small parcels between this room and the various parts of the building. Five hundred men are employed in the various departments of the paper.

The circulation of the daily edition of the *Herald* is estimated by competent judges at from 65,000 to 70,000 copies. In times of great public excitement, all the dailies overrun their usual number by many thousands.

The *Tribune* has a daily circulation of about 43,000 copies. It is, in point of ability, the best of the city dailies. It long ago surmounted its early difficulties, and has been for many years one of the most profitable enterprises in the city. It is owned by a joint stock company. It was begun by Mr. Greeley on $1000 of borrowed money. At the formation of the company the stock was divided into 100 shares at $1000 each. The number is still the same, but the shares could not now be bought for many times their original value. In 1870 the dividend declared amounted to $163,000; or, $1630 on each share. At present the shares are owned as follows:

Shares.

Samuel Sinclair, publisher	21
Horace Greeley, chief editor	12
Estate of Stephen Clark (formerly money editor)	14
Dr. J. C. Ayer (of Lowell)	16
Estate of A. D. Richardson	5
Bayard Taylor	5
T. N. Rooker, foreman in composing room	5
Mr. Runkle (husband of Mrs. L. G. Calhoun)	2
Oliver Johnson (of the *Independent*)	1
Mr. Cleveland (brother-in-law of Horace Greeley)	1
G. W. Smalley (London correspondent)	2
Solon Robinson (agricultural editor)	2
Two printers in the office	2
Solomon A. Cheeney	3
John Hooper	2
B. F. Camp	2

The *Tribune* property is valued at over $1,000,000, which includes nearly $300,000 in real estate. The stockholders, it is said, contemplate, at no distant day, erecting a large and handsome printing office on the site of the present unpretending building now occupied. The profits of the paper do not depend upon the daily edition. The semi-weekly circulates about 35,000 or 40,000 copies, and the weekly about 130,000 copies. The last is sent all over the United States, and has beyond a doubt the largest number of readers of any paper in the world.

The *Tribune* is the leading organ of the Republican party in the United States, and its influence is tremendous. It is a well written, well conducted paper, and is every year becoming more independent of party control. The chief editor is Horace Greeley, who imparts his strong personality to the whole journal. Many of the country people believe that the Philosopher writes every line on the editorial page. The managing editor is Whitelaw Reid, and the publisher Samuel Sinclair. Mr. Reid succeeded Mr. John Russell Young, and the paper has profited by the change. Mr. Sinclair is one of the most efficient publishers in the land, and the *Tribune* owes not a little of its success to his genius—for that is the only name to give it. The editorial staff comprises more ability than that of any other city journal, though some of the others make a better use of the talent at their disposal. Its correspondence, both domestic and foreign, is the best of all the city papers—perhaps the best in the Union—and the list of its correspondents contains some of the brightest names in literature.

The *Times* is also a Republican journal, and aims to represent the Administration of General Grant. Under the management of the late Henry J. Raymond, a born journalist, it was a power in the land. Since Mr. Raymond's death there has been a falling off in the ability, the manliness, and the influence of the paper. It is owned by a stock company, and is a profitable enterprise. The chief editor is Mr. Louis Jennings, an Englishman, and formerly the New York correspondent of the London *Times*. Mr. Jennings is a gentleman of ability and culture, and a journalist of considerable experience. His chief needs are a decided infusion of American ideas and sentiment, and a recognition of the dissimilarity between the London and New York mode of viewing matters. The publisher is Mr. George Jones.

The *Times*, under Mr. Raymond, was one of the freshest and most thoroughly up to the times journals on the continent. Its correspondence, especially that from Europe, was exceptionally good. There has been a falling off in this respect of late. The circulation of the paper is not known with certainty, but is believed to be about 30,000 or 35,000 copies.

The *World* is the principal Democratic journal of the city, and aspires to be the organ of the party throughout the country. It was begun about the year 1859 as a religious paper, and is said to have sunk about $300,000 for its projectors. It then became the organ of the Democracy of the city, and has for some time paid well. It is the property of its editor, Mr. Manton G. Marble. It is unquestionably one of the ablest journals in the country. Its editorials are well written, indicative of deep thought on the subjects treated of, and gentlemanly in tone. In literary excellence, it is not surpassed by any city journal. It aims to be in the front rank of the march of ideas, and makes a feature of discussions of the leading scientific and social questions of the day.   It is lightened by a brilliant display of wit, and the " Funny Man of the World " is well known in the city. The chief editor is Manton G. Marble.   He is the author of the majority of the leaders.   In this he is ably seconded by Mr. Chamberlain, one of the most forcible and successful writers on the city press.   Mr. Marble is not seen much in the office.   The *World* rooms are connected with his residence in the upper part of the city, by a private telegraph, by means of which he exercises a constant supervision over the paper.   The managing editor is Mr. David G. Croly (the husband of " Jennie June ").   He is a genius in his way.   He does not write much, but gives the greater part of the time to superintending the work of the office. He is said to be extremely fertile in suggesting themes for treatment to his brother editors.   The great faults of the *World* are its devotion to sensation journalism, its thick and thin Roman Catholic partizanism, and, strange to say, a little too much looseness in the tone of its Sunday edition.   Its circulation is variously estimated at from 15,000 to 30,000.   The exact number is known only to the publisher.

The *Sun* assumes to be the organ of the working classes, and claims a circulation of 85,000 copies.   It is a bright, sparkling journal, issued at a cost of two cents.   It is four pages in size, and has a fine list of advertisements.   It is owned by a stock company, who bought it from the late Moses Y. Beach, its founder.   The chief editor is Mr. Charles A. Dana, a journalist of long experience, and one of the most thoroughly cultivated men in the profession.   He has made it a great success.   It is piquant, forcible, and good-natured.   Mr. Dana is assisted by a corps of able editorial writers and reporters, who are thoroughly impressed with the wisdom of his policy.   He is very sanguine of making a still greater success of the *Sun*, and claims that he will yet run its circulation up to 200,000 copies.

The *Standard* is the property of Mr. John Russell Young, formerly the managing editor of the *Tribune*.   It is a Republican organ, and is struggling to reach an established and prosperous position. It is well managed, and is conducted with considerable editorial ability.

The *Journal of Commerce* is one of the few old-style papers left in New York. It is a ponderous four-page sheet, depending more upon its advertising than upon its circulation for its profits. It is edited with ability, and as it employs but few editors and reporters, and cares but little for general news, its publication is inexpensive. It is supplied by a regular carrier, and is not sold on the news-stands. It is taken by the leading hotels and by the down-town merchants, to whom it is valuable because of its commercial reports. The general reader would find it dull reading. It is one of the best paying papers in the city.

The *Star* is a two cent paper, and was started at the time of the sale of the *Sun* to Mr. Dana and his associates, with the hope of securing the patronage of the working classes. Its managing editor is Mr. Joseph Howard. It is a sprightly paper, intensely Democratic in tone, and is said to be prosperous.

The evening papers are much less influential than the morning journals, but the best of them are very successful.

The *Evening Post* heads the list. It is owned by William Cullen Bryant & Co., and Mr. Bryant is the principal editor. It is the ablest and the most influential of all the evening papers, and is one of the purest in its tone of any of the American journals. It is taken chiefly in the families of cultivated and professional men. Its book notices are considered the most reliable. Its circulation and advertising patronage are large, and it is a very profitable investment.

The *Commercial Advertiser* is now under the control of the venerable Thurlow Weed, and is a good paper.

The *Evening Express* is the property of the brothers James and Erastus Brooks. It is well manged, and well edited, and is regarded as ranking next to the *Post* in ability and general excellence. It is said to be worth $40,000 per annum above expenses to its proprietors.

The *Evening Mail* is younger than either of the others, but not far behind the best of them in ability and interest. It has a decided literary tone, and is one of the most enterprising *news* purveyors in the city.   It is now a thoroughly successful enterprise, and it deserves its good fortune.

The *Telegram* is little more than an evening edition of the *Herald*.   It is owned by James Gordon Bennett, jr., and is a lively sheet, full of news and gossip.   It sells for two cents, and has a large circulation.   Its first page always contains a rough, but sometimes spirited cartoon, caricaturing some notable event of the day.   It is a paying paper.

The *Evening News* is a penny paper.   It claims to have the largest circulation in the city, and is said to be very profitable. It is devoted almost exclusively to police news, and descriptions of crime, and finds its readers chiefly among the lower and rougher portion of the community.   It is owned and conducted by Mr. Benjamin Wood.

The evening papers are generally issued in four editions, at one, two, four and five o'clock in the afternoon.   On occasions of unusual interest, they often issue extras every hour until late in the night.   The evening papers contain the latest news and gossip, and a variety of light and entertaining reading matter, and are bought chiefly by persons who wish to read them at home after the cares and fatigues of the day are over, or to kill time in the cars on their way home.

There are three daily morning papers published in the German language, the *State Gazette*, the *Democrat*, and the *Journal*, and one evening paper, the *Times*. 'The *Courier of the United States*, and *Franco-American Messenger*, are issued in the French language.   They are also daily morning papers.   All are well supported by the citizens speaking the language they use.

II.

WEEKLY PRESS.

EXCLUSIVE of the weekly editions of the daily journals, there are about 133 weekly papers published in the city of New York.   Some of these are literary journals, some political, some the organs of the various religious bodies, and some devoted to the interests of trade and manufactures.

The best known weeklies are the literary, religious, and political papers, and of these the most noted are, *Harper's Weekly, Harper's Bazaar, Frank Leslie's Illustrated Newspaper*, the *Nation*, the *Chimney Corner*, the *Ledger*, *Home Journal*, *Weekly Review, Sunday Mercury, New York Weekly, Hearth and Home*, the *Sunday News*, the *Albion, Dispatch, Sunday Times, Citizen, Revolution, Spirit of the Times*, and *Police Gazette*, among the secular papers. The most prominent religious journals are the *Independent, Examiner, Evangelist, Methodist, Observer, Tablet, Liberal Christian, Christian Advocate, Christian Union, Christian Inquirer*, and *Church Journal*.

The *Ledger* has the largest circulation, having an actual sale of 300,000 copies per week. It is so well known throughout the country that it would be superfluous to describe it here. It is the property of Mr. Robert Bonner, who has reaped a large fortune from it. Next in popularity is the *New York Weekly*, which is much inferior to the *Ledger*, but which claims a circulation of over 200,000 copies. There are about a dozen illustrated papers of various degrees of merit, *Harper's Weekly*, the *Bazaar*, and *Frank Leslie's Illustrated Newspaper* head the list in popularity and worth. The first and second claim a circulation of over one hundred thousand, and Frank Leslie claims about seventy-five thousand for his paper. Some of the other illustrated journals are simply indecent sheets, and should be suppressed. The *Nation* is regarded as the highest critical authority in the country, and holds here very much the position of the *Saturday Review* in London.

The literary journals are well conducted, and one will often find articles of genuine merit in some of the most unpretending. The reason is that journalists are unable to live on their salaries, as a rule, if they be married men, and are forced to make up the deficiency by contributing to the magazines and weekly papers. As a matter of course, they must dispose of their wares wherever there is a market, and where they are sure of being paid, even at starvation rates, for their labors. From $2.50 to $5.00 per column is the rate of payment with the most of the weeklies, and many men and women with whose names and labors the literary world is familiar, are glad to write for them at this beggarly price as a means of increasing their legitimate incomes. The number of writers is very much in excess of the demand, and literature offers a thorny road to the majority of its followers in the metropolis.

The Sunday papers are generally high priced and nasty. They are entirely sensational in character, and are devoted to a class of news and literature which can hardly be termed healthy. They revel in detailed descriptions of subjects which are rigorously excluded from the daily papers, and abound in questionable advertisements. All of which they offer for Sabbath reading; and the reader would be startled to see into how many reputable households these dirty sheets find their way.

17

XV.

WALL STREET.

I.

THE STREET.

WALL STREET begins on the east side of Broadway, opposite Trinity Church, and terminates at the East River. It is about half a mile from the extreme southern end of the island, and about the same distance from the City Hall. It is a narrow street, about fifty feet in width, and slopes gradually from Broadway to the river. It is lined on both sides with handsome brown stone, yellow stone, granite, marble, iron, and brick buildings, and the Treasury and Custom-House rear their magnificent fronts about midway between the termini of the street. They are diagonally opposite each other. The buildings are covered with a multiplicity of signs, rivalling the edifices of Nassau street, in this respect. Scarcely a house has less than a score of offices within its walls, and some contain at least three times as many. Space is valuable, and rents are high in Wall street, and many of the leading firms in it have to content themselves with small, dark apartments, which a conscientious man would hesitate to call an "office." The rents paid for such quarters are enormous, and the buildings yield their owners large incomes ever year. The streets running into Wall street, on the right and left, are also occupied for several blocks with the offices of bankers and brokers, and are all included in the general term "Wall street," or "The Street."

Wall street first appears in the history of the city as a portion of a sheep pasture which was used in common by the inhabitants

WALL STREET.

of New Amsterdam. Its natural condition was partly rolling
upland and partly meadow of a swampy character. The name
of the street originated thus : About the middle of the seventeenth century, the English in the New England colonies began
to press heavily upon the Dutch in New Netherlands, and kept
the worthy burghers of New Amsterdam in a constant dread of
an invasion. Influenced by this feeling, the city authorities
resolved to fortify the place, and in 1653 constructed a wall or
stockade across the island, from river to river just beyond the
line of the village. This wall passed directly across the old
sheep pasture. Citizens were forbidden to build within 100 feet
of the stockade, this open space being reserved for the movements of troops. It soon became a prominent highway, and
the eastern portion has since remained so. The anticipated
attack on the city was not made, but the wall was kept in good

condition. Houses crept up close to the wall on the city side, and began to appear on the opposite side just under the wall. Thus a new street was formed, through which ran the old stockade. The open space along the wall was originally called *The Cingel*, signifying "the ramparts." Soon after the town reached the limit of the military reservation, persons residing here were spoken of as living "long de Wal," and from this the street came to be called "the Wall street," which name it has ever since borne. The wall having fallen into decay, was demolished about the year 1699, and its stones were used in the construction of the old City Hall, which stood at the intersection of Wall and Nassau streets, the site now occupied by the Sub-Treasury of the United States. The old building was used for the various purposes of the city government until the close of the Revolution. It contained, besides the council and court rooms, a jail for the detention and punishment of criminals, a debtors' prison, which was located in the attic, a fire-engine-room, a cage and a pillory. A pair of stocks was set up on the opposite side of the street, wherein criminals were exposed to the indignant gaze of the virtuous public.

At the close of the Revolution, the City Hall was enlarged and improved for the use of the General Government. It thus became the first capitol of the new Republic, and was known as Federal Hall. The first Congress of the United States assembled within its walls in the year 1789, and upon its spacious portico, in the presence of an immense multitude, George Washington took the oath to support and defend the constitution as first President of the United States.

Wall street was originally taken up with private residences, and the old views represent it as well shaded with trees. Even as late as 1830 it presented a very rural appearance between Broadway and William street. Prior to the Revolution, the lower part of the street had been built up with stores as far as Front street, and had become the centre of mercantile affairs in the city, the row of stores on Wall street being the first erected beyond Water street. About the year 1792, the old Tontine Coffee House was erected on the northwest corner of Wall and

UNITED STATES SUB-TREASURY.

Water streets, and this became the favorite rendezvous for the
city merchants, by whom, indeed, it was erected and controlled.
In 1791 the Bank of New York was located at the corner of
William street, and marked the first encroachment upon the
strictly private portion of the street.   It was also the first effort
to make this locality the centre of the financial operations of
the city.   Other institutions and private bankers soon followed,
and the character and architecture of the street began to undergo
a change.   The work of improvement went on steadily, and the
Wall street of to-day is the result.   Famous lawyers have also
had their offices in this street.   Alexander Hamilton's sign

might once have been seen here, not far from where his humble monument now stands in Trinity Churchyard, and the name of Caleb Cushing is still to be found near a doorway just below Broadway.

"In 1700 a house and lot on the southeast corner of Wall and Broad streets, 16 × 30, sold for £163. In 1706 a house and lot on the north of Wall street, 25 × 116, sold for £116. In 1737 a house and lot on the north of Wall street, 62 × 102, sold for £110. In 1793, the dwelling and lot of General Alexander Hamilton, on the south of Wall street, 42 × 108, sold for £2400. In 1794 a house and lot, 44 × 51, sold for £2510." At present the ground included in these sites is held at hundreds of thousands of dollars.

The street fairly began its present career in the days of Jacob Little, "the great bear of Wall street." He opened an office here in 1822, and by dint of such labor as few men are capable of performing, placed himself at the head of American operators. His credit was good for any amount, and his integrity was unimpeachable. He could sway the market as he pleased, and his contracts were met with a punctuality and fidelity which made "his word as good as his bond." Efforts were made to ruin him, but his genius and far-sightedness enabled him to defeat all his enemies with their own weapons. His gains were enormous, and so were his losses. The civil war brought upon him disasters which he could not surmount, and he died poor in the early part of 1861, leaving behind him one of the names of which New York is proud.

At the corner of Nassau street, and looking down into Broad street, is the Sub-Treasury of the United States, a handsome white marble edifice. It is built in the Doric style of architecture, and its massive flight of steps and imposing portico give to it a striking appearance. It is constructed in the most substantial manner, and has a rear entrance on Pine street. The interior is handsomely arranged, and tasteful but secure iron gratings protect the employees from surprise and robbery. The vaults are burglar proof. This is the principal depository of the Federal Government, and millions of dollars are always in its vaults.   The building was erected for, and was used for some years as, a Custom House.

From the steps of the Treasury one may enjoy a fine view of the entire street, and of Broad street also.   About the hour of noon the scene is busy and exciting.   The roadway in Wall street is full of struggling vehicles, and long rows of cabs stand in waiting in Broad street for the busy operators within the Exchanges.   The side walks are crowded with an eager, hurrying throng.   The steps and street around the Stock Exchange, in Broad street, are black with men who are shouting, pushing, and struggling in the effort to turn the transactions of the day to their advantage.   Overhead is an intricate maze of telegraph wires, along which flow the quick and feverish pulsations of the great financial heart of the country.   The sunlight falls brightly and cheerily over it all, and at intervals the clear, sweet chimes of old Trinity come floating down the street high above the noise and strife below them.

Diagonally opposite the Treasury, and at the corner of William street, is the Custom House, which occupies the irregular square bounded by Wall street, Exchange Place, William street, and Hanover street.   It is one of the finest and best arranged edifices in the city.

Just below the Custom House is the handsome marble building of Brown Brothers, one of the model houses of New York, as regards both the firm and the edifice.   The Messrs. Brown are regarded as the most reliable and accomplished operators in the street.   Across the way, in a dingy granite building, is the office of August Belmont & Co., the American agents of the Rothschilds, and bankers on their own account.   Jay Cooke & Co. occupy the fine marble building at the corner of Wall and Nassau streets, opposite the Treasury, and there conduct the New York branch of their enormous business.   Fisk & Hatch, the financial agents of the great Pacific Railway, are a few steps higher up Nassau street.   Henry Clews & Co. are in the building occupied by the United States Assay Office.   Other firms, of more or less eminence, fill the street.   Some have fine, showy offices, others operate in dark, dingy holes.

II.

THE STOCK EXCHANGE.

THE Stock Exchange is located on the west side of Broad street, just out of Wall street. It is a fine white marble edifice, with a portico of iron, painted flashily in black and gold. It extends back to New street, with an entrance on that street. There is also an entrance on Wall street. It contains the "New York Stock Exchange," "The Mining Board," and the "Government Board."

During the spring and summer of 1871 the internal arrangements of the building were very much improved. The refitting cost the brokers $60,000, but they now have the handsomest establishment of its kind in the world.

The main entrance is on Broad street, and from this the visitor passes into a room, the larger portion of which is separated from the Broad street end by an iron railing. This is "The Long Room," and during the day it is almost always filled with a noisy and not over-nice crowd. It is the scene of the irregular sales of stocks. Any one who can raise $50 can purchase a season ticket to this hall, and once admitted can sell and purchase stocks without being a member of the Regular Board. This arrangement has nearly put an end to the sales of stocks on the side walks, and has given a tinge of respectability to the class known as "Curb-stone Brokers." A dozen or more different stocks may be sold here at once, and the sale may be continued as long as the seller sees fit. There is no regular organization of the brokers operating here, though these men control the bulk of the sales made in the street. They are noisy and seem half demented in their frantic efforts to make sales.

The "Stock Exchange" occupies the main hall, which is on the floor above the Long Room. This hall is one of the most beautiful apartments in the city. It is seventy-four feet long, fifty-four feet wide, and fifty-two feet four inches high. Its lofty ceiling is arched and decorated with bright red and buff penciling upon a sky blue ground, while the walls are relieved by broad square pilasters, painted in brilliant bronze, with tall windows and arched tops rising between, and other spaces between the columns covered with drapery in more subdued colors. Up to a few feet from the floor the painting is in a dark-hued bronze. The coloring is in the Moorish style throughout, and the effect of the whole is very fine. At the north end is the platform for the desks of the Vice-President and Secretary, and on each side of this is a black board for recording the quotations of the session. On the same platform is the desk and instrument of the stock telegraph operator. At the south end of the hall is a light gallery capable of holding 200 persons, for the use of visitors. In connection with the hall are several committee, cloak and ante-rooms. In the centre of the ceiling is a huge ventilator, beneath which is suspended the lighting apparatus, containing 100 burners. A chamber five feet in depth underlies the hall and the adjoining

THE STOCK EXCHANGE.

lobby, and in it are laid pipes for conducting warm air. At the base of the walls is an open iron grating covering the apertures of a shaft leading from the engine-room. Through this shaft warm air is forced into the hall in winter, and cool air in summer, thus securing perfect ventilation.

The Stock Exchange Board is an incorporated company, and is the only lawful association in the city for the transaction of business connected with stocks. It consists of 1050 members, but the control of its affairs is vested in a council of forty members, together with the President, Secretary and Treasurer in their unofficial capacity. The admission fee is $5000, and a seat in the Board becomes the absolute personal property of the broker, who can sell or otherwise dispose of it as he would of his watch or his coat. Candidates are admitted by ballot and with great care, the object being to secure the exclusion of all but men of known integrity, for the Board requires the most scrupulous good faith in the transactions of all its members. Four black balls will prevent the admission of a candidate whether he wishes to enter by purchase or otherwise. Candidates must submit to a close scrutiny of their previous lives, and must show a clear record.

There are two daily sessions of the Board, one in the morning and the other in the afternoon. The securities offered at these meetings are divided into two classes, the Regular and the Free List. No stock or bond can be dealt in until it has been rigidly examined by a committee, and found to be a *bonâ fide* security.

At half-past ten o'clock in the morning, the Morning Board is called to order by the First Vice-President. The Regular List, which is made up in advance of the meeting, must always be called, and called first. The Free List may be called or not at the option of the Board. The Regular List consists of 1st. Miscellaneous Stocks. 2d. Railroad Stocks. 3d. State Bonds. 4th. City Stocks. 5th. Railroad Bonds.

The session opens with the reading of the minutes of the previous day. Then comes the call of the Regular List. The call of Miscellaneous Stocks awakens but little excitement. Bids follow quickly upon the announcement of the stocks, and the transactions, as they are announced by the

THE NEW YORK STOCK EXCHANGE BOARD IN SESSION.

267

cries of the brokers are repeated by the Vice-President to the Assistant Secretary, who records them in the journal, and they are also recorded by a clerk on a black board in full view of the members. Where there is a doubt respecting a sale or purchase the Vice-President decides, and his decision is final, unless reversed by the votes of a majority of the members present.

The call of railroad securities brings the brokers to their feet, and the real business of the day begins. Offers and bids, shouted in deep bass, high treble, or shrill falsetto, resound through the hall, and in a few minutes the jovial-looking brokers seem to be on the verge of madness. How they yell and shout, and stamp, and gesticulate. The roar and confusion are bewildering to a stranger, but the keen, practised ears of the Vice-President at once recognize the various transactions, and down they go in the Secretary's book, and on the black board, while the solemn-vizaged telegraph operator sends them clicking into every broker's office in the city. High over all rings the voice of Peter, the keeper of the gate, calling out members for whom telegrams or visitors have arrived.

The other stocks awaken more or less excitement, and when the 'Regular List is completed, the Free List is in order, and the Vice-President calls such stocks as the members express a desire to deal in. Then, unless there is a wish to call up some stock hastily passed over on the call of the Regular List, the session closes.

At one o'clock, the afternoon session is held, and the routine of the morning is gone over again. The transactions of both sessions are carefully recorded in the Secretary's books.

The Vice-President receives a salary of $7000 per annum for his services, which are not light. The Secretary and Assistant Secretary, and Roll-keeper do the rest of the work of the Board. The last named keeps a record of the fines, which yield an exceedingly large revenue to the Board. The brokers are not the most dignified of mortals in their meetings, but are very much given to disorderly conduct and practical jokes. The annual dues of the Exchange are but fifty dollars, but the aver-

age broker pays at least ten times as much in fines. To interrupt
the presiding officer during a call of the stocks subjects the
offender to a fine of not less than twenty-five cents for each
offence; to smoke a cigar within the Exchange costs five dollars; to be absent from special meetings is to incur a fine of
not more than five dollars; to stand on a table or chair is punishable with a fine of one dollar; to throw a paper dart or ball
at a member during the session of the Board costs ten dollars;
and other offences may be punished with fines assessed by the
Vice-President at any sum between twenty-five cents and five
dollars.

Each day a list of stocks to be put in the market is made out,
and no others can be sold during the sessions. The Board can
refuse to offer any particular stock for sale, and a guarantee is
required of the party making the sale. The members of the
Board are men of character, and their transactions are fair and
open. They are required to fulfil all contracts in good faith,
however great the loss to themselves, on pain of expulsion from
the Board, and it is very rare that an expelled member can be
reinstated.

III

THE GOVERNMENT BOARD.

THE room used by the Government Board, in which all
transactions in the bonds and securities of the United States
take place, is located on the second floor of the Exchange
building. It is handsomely frescoed and furnished in green
rep. The basement beneath this room is an immense vault,
containing 618 safes, arranged in three tiers, and guarded by
four policemen detailed for that purpose. These safes are a
foot and a half square, and are rented by the brokers who deposit in them overnight small tin boxes containing their bonds
and other securities. It is estimated that the value of the
securities nightly deposited here is over two hundred millions
of dollars.

The seats of the brokers in the Government Room are arranged in tiers, rising one above the other, from the floor to the wall. The officers occupy a platform at the head of the chamber. The order of business is very much like that of the Stock Board.

"The Vice-President begins :

"'6s '81 registered—'81 coupon. 5.20s '62 registered— coupon. What's bid?'

"Here and there from flanking chairs come sputtering bids or offers :

"'Ten thousand at $\frac{3}{8}$, buyer 3.'

"'I'll give an $\frac{1}{8}$, seller 3, for the lot.'

"'$\frac{1}{4}$, buyer 30, for fifty thousand.'

"'$\frac{1}{4}$, regular, for any part of five thousand.'

"*First Voice.* 'Sold,—five hundred.'

"The presiding officer repeats the sale and terms, the secretary makes his registry, and a new bond is started.

"Sometimes when 5.20s are called, there is at first only one voice which rings the changes on ' I'll give 115. I'll give '15 for a thousand,—'15 for a thousand.' Presently, however, before any response follows the offer, a member in a distant corner, either carelessly or maliciously, shouts out, ' I'll give '14 for a thousand,—'14 for a thousand.'

"The Vice-President plies his hammer : ' Fine Irving—fine Irving fifty cents.' The Roll keeper proceeds to make his little note of it, and Irving, who has violated the rule, founded on common sense, which forbids a member from making a bid below or an offer above the one which has the floor immediately subsides amid the laughter of his neighbors.

"Occasionally an interruption of a grosser character occurs, a member leaping from his seat on some slight provocation, and striking off the hat of the man who has offended. ' Fine Harrison, fine Harrison again, *fine*, FINE him again,—FINE Harrison,' cries the Vice-President, repeating the word without cessation until the broker's wrath has been appeased, and he returns to his chair with the disagreeable reflection that a heavy score is against him for the semi-annual settlement-day. Every repetition of that fatal monosyllable was a fresh mark of fifty cents or a dollar against his name.   Generally, however, the Government brokers are more orderly than their neighbors in the Regular Board.   Indeed, the whole proceedings are more decorous and respectful, the bidding, half the time, being carried on in a low conversational tone.   At second call there is a brief excitement, but when 'things are dull' throughout the street, this room peculiarly reflects the external influences.

"Very different it is, however, on days when some special cause provokes great fluctuations.   Then the members spring from their seats, arms, hands, excitable faces, rapid vociferations, all come in play, and the element of pantomime performs its part in assisting the human voice as naturally as among the Italians of Syracuse.   To the uninitiated the biddings here are as unintelligible as elsewhere, sounding to ordinary ears like the gibberish of Victor Hugo's Compachinos.   But the comparative quietude of this Board renders it easier to follow the course of the market, to detect the shades of difference in the running offers, and generally to get a clearer conception of this part of the machinery of stock brokerage."

In former times brokers were subjected to great expense in keeping a host of runners and messengers to bring them news of the transactions at the Exchanges.   The introduction of the Stock Telegraph has made a great and beneficial change in this respect.   In every broker's office, and in the principal hotels and restaurants of the city, there is an automatic recording instrument connected by telegraphic wires with an instrument in the Stock and Gold Exchanges.   The operator in these exchanges indicates the quotations of stocks and gold on his own instrument, and these quotations are repeated by the instruments in the offices throughout the city.   These office instruments print the quotations in plain Roman letters and figures on a ribbon of paper, so that any one can read and understand them.   Thus one man does the work formerly required of several hundred, and no time is lost in conveying the information.   The broker in his office is informed of the transactions at the Exchange at the very instant they are made.

IV.

THE GOLD EXCHANGE.

YOU pass from Broad street into the basement of a brown stone building just below the Stock Exchange, and find yourself in a long, dimly-lighted passage way, which leads into a small courtyard. Before you is a steep stairway leading to a narrow and dirty entry. At the end of this entry is a gloomy looking door. Pass through it, and you are in the famous Gold Exchange.

This is a showy apartment in the style of an amphitheatre, with an ugly fountain in the centre of the floor. An iron railing encloses the fountain. Against the New street end is the platform occupied by the President and Secretary, and on the right of this is the telegraph office. There are two galleries connected with the room, one for the use of visitors provided with tickets, and the other free to all comers. There is an indicator on the outer wall of the building on New street, from which the price of gold is announced to the crowd without. It is a common habit with sporting men of the lower class to frequent New street and bet on the indicator.

There are but few benches in the Gold Room. The members of the Board are too nervous and excitable to sit still, and seats would soon be broken to pieces in their wild rushing up and down the floor.

The business of the day begins about ten o'clock. The rap of the President's gavel opens the session, and as there is but one thing dealt in—gold—the bids follow the sound of the mallet. The noise and confusion are greater here than in the Stock Board or the Long Room, and it seems impossible to a stranger that the President should be able to follow the various transactions. When the excitement is at its height, the scene resembles "pandemonium broken loose." The members rush wildly about, without any apparent aim. They stamp, yell, shake their arms, heads, and bodies violently, and almost trample each other to death in their frenzied struggles. Men who in private life excite the admiration of their friends by the repose and dignity of their manner, here join in the furious whirl, and seem more like maniacs than sensible human beings. And yet every yell, every gesture, is fraught with the most momentous consequences. These seeming maniacs have a method in their madness, and are changing at every breath the value of the currency upon which the whole business of the country rests. When the fluctuations are very great, fortunes are made and lost here every hour.

Connected with the business of the Gold Room are the Gold Exchange Bank and the Clearing House. The method of settlement with these institutions, which are indispensable where gold passes so rapidly from hand to hand in the Exchange, is as follows: "On or before half past twelve o'clock, a statement of all the purchases or sales made by each broker on the preceding day must be rendered to the bank. If the gold bought be in excess of that sold, a check for the difference must accompany the statement. If deposits in gold or currency are not kept in the bank, the coin must be delivered at every deficiency. The Board adjourns at twelve, in order to enable tardy dealers to complete their accounts. Provided all contracts are honored, the bank must settle by two P. M. In case of default, the amount in abeyance is debited or credited to the broker who suffers by the failure."

The Clearing House Association was created in 1853, and represents the sum of the financial business of the city. "The Association is located in the third story of the building of the Bank of New York. The centre of the room is occupied by a bank counter, extending on four sides, with a passage inside and out. Fifty-nine desks are placed on the counter for the use of the fifty-nine banks represented in the Association. Each desk bears the name of the bank to which it belongs. Fitted up in each desk are fifty-nine pigeon holes for the checks of the various banks. Two clerks represent each bank. One remains at the desk and receives all the checks on his bank. He signs the name of the bank to the sheet which each outside clerk holds in his hand. These outside clerks go from desk to desk and

18

leave the checks received the day before, with the banks on which they are drawn. Banks do not begin public business till ten; but clerks have to be on hand at eight, when all checks are assorted and arranged for delivery at the Clearing House.

"At ten minutes before ten the bank messengers begin to assemble and take their places. As they enter they leave with the messenger a slip containing an exact account of the bank they represent. These statements are put on a sheet prepared for that purpose, and must conform precisely to the checks received inside, before the Clearing House closes its duties. If there is any error or discrepancy, the bank is immediately notified by telegraph, and the clerks kept until the matter is satisfactorily adjusted. At ten, promptly, business begins. Clerks come rushing in with small trunks, tin boxes, or with bundles in their arms, and take their seats at the desks. On the side of the room entered only from the manager's office is a desk, not unlike a pulpit. Precisely at ten the bell rings, the manager steps into his box, brings down his gavel, and the work of the day begins. Quiet prevails. No loud talking is allowed, and no confusion. A bank late is fined two dollars; a party violating the rules, or guilty of insubordination, is fined two dollars and reported to the bank. On repetition, he is expelled the Clearing House. The daily transactions of the Clearing House varies from ninety-eight to one hundred millions. The system is so nicely balanced that three millions daily settle the difference. Each bank indebted to the Clearing House must send in its check before half after one. Creditors get the Clearing House check at the same hour. Daily business is squared and all accounts closed at half after three. Every bank in the city is connected with the Clearing House by telegraph. The morning work of clearing one hundred millions, occupies ten minutes. Long before the clerks can reach the bank, its officers are acquainted with the exact state of their account, and know what loans to grant or refuse. Through the Clearing House each bank is connected with every other in the city. If a doubtful check is presented, if paper to be negotiated is not exactly clear, while the party offering the paper or check is entertained by some member of the bank, the telegraph is making minute inquiries about his financial standing. Before the conference closes, the bank knows the exact facts of the case."

V.

CURB–STONE BROKERS.

THE members of the Stock and Gold Exchange, as has been stated, are men of character. Their transactions are governed by certain fixed rules, and they are required, on pain of expulsion from the Exchange, to observe the strictest good faith in their dealings with each other and with their customers. If the operations of the street were entirely confined to them, business in Wall street might be regarded as in safe hands. But there is another class, even more numerous and quite as well skilled in the ways of the street, who transact a vast part of its business. They are not members of the Exchange, and in former times used to assemble around its doors in Broad and New streets, and carry on their operations on the sidewalk. Hence their designation, "Curb-stone brokers." They no longer assemble on the pavement, for the Exchange has thrown open to them its Long Room. Any one who can pay $50 a year for a ticket of admission, and who has brains and nerve enough to enter upon the struggle, can sell or buy in the Long Room. This is better than standing in the street, exposed to the weather, and moreover gives a certain respectability to the "operator," although he may carry his sole capital in his head, and his office in his breeches-pocket.

No rules or regulations apply to the Long Room. The honest man and the rogue mingle together here, and the broker must be sure of his man. Many of the members of the Exchange buy and sell here, either in person or through their representatives, and many good men who are unable to enter the Exchange conduct their business here. Others again prefer the freedom and the wider field of the Long Room. Still, there are many sharpers here, who would fleece a victim out of his last cent.

The daily transactions of the Long Room are said to average about $70,000,000, or ten times the business done in the Regular Board. Fortune is much more uncertain here than in the room up stairs. Men buy and sell here with the recklessness of gamblers. The noise and excitement are almost as great as in the Gold Room. The absence of the fixed laws of the Regular Boards puts every one on his own resources, and men are compelled to use all their ingenuity, all their determination to guard against a surprise or unfair dealing. It is every one for himself here. A dozen or more small or new operators are ruined and swept away daily, and in times of great financial excitement the Long Room shakes the foundations of even some of the strongest houses in the street.

VI.

THE BUSINESS OF THE STREET.

It is a common habit to speak of Wall street as the financial centre of the Republic; but only those who are acquainted with its transactions can know how true this is. Regarding Wall street and New York as synonymous terms, we find that the street is not only a great power in this country, but that it is one of the great controlling powers of the financial world. Indeed, if the prosperity of the country is as marked in the future as it has been in the past, there is good reason to believe that Wall street will control the whole world of finance. Its geographical location is in its favor. By noon the New York broker has full information of the same day's transactions in London, Frankfort, and Paris, and can shape his course in accordance with this knowledge, while the European broker cannot profit by his knowledge of matters in New York until the next day.

The Stock Exchange of New York numbers over 1000 members, and its aggregate wealth is greater than that of any similar association in the world. The par value of the annual sales made at the regular Boards and "over the counter" is estimated at over $22,000,000,000 annually. The par value of the authorized stocks, bonds, and Governments dealt in by the regular Boards is more than $3,000,000,000, and this vast sum is turned over and over many times durihg the year. The aggregate of the brokers' commissions on the sales and purchases made by them is estimated by competent authority at $43,750,000 annually. The bulk of this enormous business is in the hands of about 400 houses.

"Out of all the incorporated banks in the United States, there are thirty situated in Wall street and its neighborhood, whose office is not unlike that of the heart in the economy of animal life. Although less than half the full number of banks in the metropolis, these thirty have two-thirds of the capital, and quite two-thirds of the circulation. By a provision of statutory law, all outside National banks, numbering some 1600, are allowed to keep one-half, and many three-fifths, of their reserve balances in New York. In this way our great financial centre is rapidly acquiring the function of a National clearing-house. These temporary deposits bear a small interest, and are subject to be called for at a day's notice. They can only be used, therefore, by the employing banks on the same conditions. The stock market supplies these conditions. Bonds and shares bought to-day and sold to-morrow, endowed with all the properties of swift conversion, and held by men whose training has been one of incessant grappling with the new and unexpected, are the only class of property upon which money can safely be borrowed without a protection against sudden demands. On these securities, therefore, the down-town banks make call loans. The name implies the nature. The money which the thirty receive from without, together with their own reserves, is lent freely to stock-brokers, with the simple provision that it must be returned immediately upon notice, if financial exigencies require it. This vast volume of what may well be styled fluid wealth is difficult of estimate in figures. The published statements of loans made by city banks make no distinction between discounts of commercial paper and what is advanced on securities. In sum total, the thirty banks lend

THE PARK BANK, BROADWAY.

weekly about $165,000,000. Indeed, including all New York banks, the average is nearly $255,000,000. During the week ending September 18, 1868, these banks lent $266,496,024. The real meaning of these last figures will be better understood when it is known that they exceed the entire average loans and discounts of all the national banks of New England and New York State, with the exception, of course, of the city itself.

Or, to take a more sweeping view, they surpass the total weekly loans of national banks in Maryland, Virginia, North Carolina, South Carolina, West Virginia, Georgia, Alabama, Texas, Arkansas, Kentucky, Tennessee, Ohio, Nebraska, Kansas, Missouri, Minnesota, Iowa, Wisconsin, Illinois, Michigan, Indiana, Delaware, and New Jersey. Nigh $180,000,000 of the amount cited above were advanced by the down-town banks. What proportion of this was lent on stocks? Probably much over one-third. As many of the other banks also make call loans, we may, perhaps, estimate that from $70,000,000 to $100,000,000 are furnished daily to the brokers and operators of New York.

" This, however, is but one element in the lending force of the city. There are five Trust Companies, with capitals amounting in the aggregate to $5,500,000, which lend, at times, $60,000,000 a week. There are also a large number of private banking houses, of which Jay Cooke & Co. may be selected as representatives, that daily loan vast sums of money on security. The foreign houses alone, which, like Belmont & Co., Brown Brothers, Drexel, Winthrop & Co., operate in Wall street, employ not much less than $200,000,000 of capital."

VII.

STOCK GAMBLING.

IN the good old days gone by Wall street did business on principles very different from those which prevail there now. Then there was a holy horror in all hearts of speculation. Irresponsible men might indulge in it, and so incur the censure of the more respectable, but established houses confined themselves to a legitimate and regular business. They bought and sold on commission, and were satisfied with their earnings. Even now, indeed, the best houses profess to do simply a commission business, leaving the risk to the customer, but those who know the hidden ways of the street hint that there is not a house in it but has its secrets of large or small operations undertaken on account of the firm. The practice of buying and selling on commission is unquestionably the safest, but the mania for wealth leads many clear, cool-headed men into the feverish whirl of speculation, and keeps them there until they have realized their wildest hopes, or are ruined.

It has been remarked that the men who do business in Wall street have a prematurely old look, and that they die at a comparatively early age. This is not strange. They live too fast. Their bodies and brains are taxed too severely to last long. They pass their days in a state of great excitement. Every little fluctuation of the market elates or depresses them to an extent greater than they think. At night they are either planning the next day's campaign, or are hard at work at the hotels. On Sundays their minds are still on their business, and some are laboring in their offices, screened from public observation. Body and mind are worked too hard, and are given no rest.

The chief cause of this intense strain is the uncertainty attending the operations of Wall street. The chances there are not dependent upon the skill or the exertions of the operator. Some powerful clique may almost destroy the securities upon which he relies for success, or may make him wealthy by suddenly running up their value; so that no man who does not confine himself to a strictly legitimate or commission business —and but few do so—can say one week whether he will be a millionaire or a beggar the next. The chances are in favor of the latter result. Nine out of ten who speculate in gold or stocks, lose, especially persons unaccustomed to such operations. Like all gamblers, they are undismayed by their losses, and venture a second time, and a third, and so on. The fascination of stock gambling is equal to that of card gambling, and holds its victims with an iron hand. The only safe rule for those who wish to grow rich is to keep out of Wall street. While one man makes a fortune by a sudden rise in stocks or gold, hundreds lose by an equally sudden fall in the same commodities. Even old and established firms sometimes give way with a crash under these sudden changes.

The legimate operations of the street and the speculative ventures are becoming more and more concentrated every year in the hands of a few operators and capitalists. These move the market as they please, and fill their coffers, and sweep away younger or weaker men with a remorseless hand. It is useless to oppose them. They are masters of the field in every respect, and when they combine for a common object, their resources are inexhaustible and their power beyond computation. A dozen, or even half a dozen of the great capitalists could ruin the whole street were they so disposed, and once they came near doing so. This is the secret of the cordial hatred that is felt by the majority of Wall street men for Vanderbilt, Drew, and other great operators. They know and dread the power of these men, and would readily combine to destroy them singly.

The mania for stock gambling which now sways such masses of people, may be said to date from the war and the petroleum discoveries. Since then it has rolled over the country in a vast flood. The telegraph is kept busy all day and all night in sending orders for speculations from people in other States and cities to New York brokers. Everybody who can raise the funds, wishes to try his or her hand at a venture in stocks. Merchants, clergymen, women, professional men, clerks, come here to tempt fortune. Many win ; more lose.

Fortunes are made quicker and lost more easily in New York than in any place in the world. A sudden rise in stocks, or a lucky venture of some other kind, often places a comparatively poor man in possession of great wealth. Watch the carriages as they whirl through Fifth avenue, going and returning from the park. They are as elegant and sumptuous as wealth can make them. The owners, lying back amongst the soft cushions, are clad in the height of fashion. By their dresses they might be princes and princesses. This much is due to art. Now mark the coarse, rough features, the ill-bred stare, the haughty rudeness which they endeavor to palm off for dignity. Do you see any difference between them and the footman in livery on the carriage-box ? Both master and man belong to the same class—only one is wealthy and the other is not. But that footman may take the place of the master in a couple of years, or in less time. Such changes may seem remarkable, but they are very common in New York.

See that gentleman driving that splendid pair of sorrels. He is a fine specimen of mere animal beauty. How well he drives. The ease and carelessness with which he manages his splendid steeds, excites the admiration of every one on the road. He is used to it. Five years ago he was the driver of a public hack. He amassed a small sum of money, and being naturally a sharp, shrewd man, went into Wall street, and joined the "Curb-stone Brokers." His transactions were not always open to a rigid scrutiny, but they were profitable to him. He invested in oil stocks, and with his usual good luck made a fortune. Now he operates through his broker. His transactions are heavy, his speculations bold and daring, but he is usually successful. He lives in great splendor in one of the finest mansions in the city, and his carriages and horses are superb. His wife and daughters are completely carried away by their good fortune, and look with disdain upon all who are not their equals or superiors in wealth. They are vulgar and ill-bred, but they are wealthy, and society worships them. There will come a change some day. The husband and father will venture once too often in his speculations, and his magnificent fortune will go with a crash, and the family will return to their former state, or perhaps sink lower, for there are very few men who have the moral courage to try to rise again after such a fall, and this man is not one of them.

In watching the crowd on Broadway, one will frequently see, in some shabbily dressed individual, who, with his hat drawn down close over his eyes, is evidently shrinking from the possibility of being recognized, the man who but a few weeks ago was one of the wealthiest in the city. Then he was surrounded with splendor. Now he hardly knows where to get bread for his family. Then he lived in an elegant mansion. Now one or two rooms on the upper floor of some tenement house constitute his habitation. He shrinks from meeting his old friends, well knowing that not one of them will recognize him, except to insult him with a scornful stare. Families are constantly disappearing from the social circles in which they have shone for a greater or less time. They vanish almost in an instant, and are never seen again. You may meet them at some brilliant ball in the evening. Pass their residence the next day,

and you will see a bill announcing the early sale of the mansion and furniture. The worldly effects of the family are all in
the hands of the creditors of the " head," and the family themselves are either in a more modest home in the country, or in a
tenement house. You can scarcely walk twenty blocks on
Fifth avenue, without seeing one of these bills, telling its
mournful story of fallen greatness.

The best and safest way to be rich in New York, as elsewhere, is for a man to confine himself to his legitimate business.
Few men acquire wealth suddenly. Ninety-nine fail where one
succeeds. The bane of New York commercial life, however, is
that people have not the patience to wait for fortune. Every
one wants to be rich in a hurry, and as no regular business will
accomplish this, here or elsewhere, speculation is resorted to.
The sharpers and tricksters who infest Wall street know this
weakness of New York merchants. They take the pains to
inform themselves as to the character, means and credulity of
merchants, and then use every art to draw them into speculations, in which the tempter is enriched and the tempted ruined.
In nine cases out of ten a merchant is utterly ignorant of the
nature of the speculation he engages in. He is not capable of
forming a reasonable opinion as to its propriety or chance of
success, because the whole transaction is new to him, and is so
rapid that he has no time to study it. He leaves a business in
which he has acquired valuable knowledge and experience, and
trusts himself to the mercy of a man he knows little or nothing
of, and undertakes a transaction that he does not know how to
manage. Dabbling in speculations unfits men for their regular
pursuits. They come to like the excitement of such ventures,
and rush on in their mad course, hoping to make up their losses
by one lucky speculation, and at length utter ruin rouses them
from their dreams.

Not only do men squander their own money in this way, but
they risk and often lose the funds of others committed to their
charge. Bank officers, having the use of the deposits in their
institutions, take them for speculation, intending of course to
return them. Sometimes they are successful, and are able to

replace the money in the bank, so that no one hears of their dishonesty. Again, and most commonly, they fail, and they are ruined. Guardians thus misappropriate the funds of their wards. Even the funds of churches are thus used by their trustees. The amount of speculation engaged in by clergymen with their own money would astonish a novice. Some prominent divines in the city are well known in Wall street. Their brokers keep their secrets, but the habitués of the street are adepts at putting this and that together, and these reverend gentlemen, some of whom preach eloquently against the sins of speculation and gambling, become known as regular customers. The street is full of gossip concerning them, and if the stories told of them be true, some of them have made large fortunes in this way, while others have literally "gone to the bad."

It is not necessary that a person speculating in stocks should be master of the entire value of the stocks. If he be known to the broker operating for him as a responsible person, he may employ only ten per cent., or some other proportion, of the stock to be dealt in. By depositing $1000 with his broker, he can speculate to the extent of $10,000. This per centage is called a *margin*, and the deposit is designed to protect the broker from loss in case the stock should fall in value. As the stock depreciates, the customer must either sell out and bear the loss which is inevitable, or he must increase his margin to an extent sufficient to protect his broker. If he fails to increase his margin, the broker sells the stock and uses the money to save himself.

VIII.

THE WAYS OF THE STREET.

LIKE Brette Harte's Heathen Chinee,

> " For ways that are dark
> And tricks that are vain,
> Wall Street is peculiar."

It takes a clear, cool head, a large amount of brains, and unfaltering nerve, to thread one's way through the intricacies of the business of finance as carried on there.   It would be interesting to know how many come out of the ordeal untouched by the taint of corruption.   Members of the Exchanges are held by a rigid code of laws, but in questions of morality Wall street has a code of its own.   Expediency is a prominent consideration in the dealings of the street, and men have come to regard as honest and correct almost anything short of a regular breach of contract.   They do not spare their own flesh and blood.   Friendships are sacrificed, the ties of kinship are disregarded, if they stand in the way of some bold operation.   Every thing must give way to the desire for gain.   The great operators plunder and destroy their lesser rivals without a feeling of remorse, and by combinations which they know cannot be resisted blast the prospects and ruin the lives of scores whose greatest fault is an inability to oppose them successfully.   Tricks so mean and contemptible that their perpetrator would not be tolerated in social life, are resorted to, and if successful are applauded as evidences of smartness.   Every man's hand is against his neighbor.   Clerks are bribed to betray the secrets of their employers.   The baser their treachery, the larger their reward.   We do not propose, however, to discuss the morality of Wall street transactions, and so we drop the subject.

It is said by the gossips of the street that the great Railroad King, Commodore Vanderbilt, is not above using any means at hand to secure the success of his schemes.   It is said that he once tried to use his son William in this way.   He came to him one day, and advised him that he had better sell his Hudson River stock, as 110 was too high for it.   William thanked him, and made inquiries in the market, and found that his father was buying quietly all he could lay his hands upon.

William determined to follow suit.   Up jumped the stock to 137.   It was a clear twenty-six per cent. in pocket.

When the operation was concluded, the Commodore rode round to the son's office.

" Well, William, how much did you lose ? "

" I went in at 110 on 10,000 shares.   That ought to make me two hundred and sixty thousand dollars—"

"Very bad luck, William," quoth the father, trying to look extremely troubled,—"very bad luck, this time."

"But then I bought, and so made."

"Hey? What sent you doing that, sir?"

"O, I heard that was your line, and so concluded that you meant long instead of short."

"Ahem!" croaked Vanderbilt *père*, as he buttoned up his fur overcoat, and stalked out of the open door. He has always had a high opinion of William since that event!

Some years ago Vanderbilt wanted to consolidate the Hudson River and Harlem Railroads, and when the scheme was presented before the Legislature of New York, secured a sufficient number of votes in that body to insure the passage of the bill authorizing the consolidation. Before the bill was called upon its final passage, however, he learned from a trustworthy source that the members of the Legislature who had promised to vote for the bill, were determined to vote against it, with the hope of ruining him. The stock of the Harlem road was then selling very high, in consequence of the expected consolidation. The defeat of the bill would, of course, cause it to fall immediately. The unprincipled legislators at once began a shrewd game. They sold Harlem right and left, to be delivered at a future day, and found plenty of purchasers, every one but those in the plot expecting the consolidation of the roads and a consequent advance in the value of the stock. They let their friends into the secret, and there was soon a great deal of "selling short" in this stock. Commodore Vanderbilt managed to acquaint himself with the whole plot; but he held his peace, and resolved upon revenge. He went into the market quietly, with all the funds he could raise, and bought every certificate of Harlem stock that he could find. These certificates he locked up in his safe. When the bill came before the Legislature on its final passage, it was defeated.

The conspirators were jubilant. They were sure that the defeat of the bill would bring "Harlem" down with a rush. To their astonishment, however, "Harlem" did not fall. It remained stationary the first day, and then to their dismay rose steadily. Those to whom they had sold demanded the delivery of the stock, but the speculators found it impossible to buy it. There was none in the market at any price. In many of these instances Vanderbilt was the real claimant, the brokers acting in the transactions being merely his agents. Being unable to deliver the stock, the conspirators were forced to settle the demands against them in money, and the result was that they were ruined. One of the shrewdest operators in New York lost over $200,000. He refused to pay, and his name was stricken from the list of stockholders. This brought him to his senses, and he made good his contracts. Vanderbilt made money enough out of this transaction to pay for all the stock he owned in the Harlem Road.

Daniel Drew is a great operator. His gains are immense, as are also his losses. He is not popular in the street, and the brokers are fond of abusing him. He has handled too many of them mercilessly to have many friends. They say that he does not hesitate to sacrifice a friend to gain his ends, and that he is utterly without sympathy for those who go down before his heavy blows.

Bogus stock companies appear from time to time in Wall street. An office is rented and fitted up in magnificent style, a flaring programme is issued, and seemingly substantial evidences of the stability and prosperity of the company are exhibited to inquirers. The stock offered is readily taken up by the eager to be rich crowd. A dividend, most hopefully large, is declared and paid, to stimulate investments, and then, when the market has been drained dry, the bubble bursts, the directors disappear, the office is closed, and the shareholders lose their money.

On fine afternoons visitors to the Park do not fail to notice a handsome equipage driven by a stylish young man, with rosy cheeks and light curly hair. His face is the perfect picture of happy innocence. He is very wealthy, and owns a great deal of real estate in the city. The manner in which he made his money will show how other persons enrich themselves.

A few years ago, he, in company with several others, organized a scheme for working certain gold mines said to be located in a distant territory. A company was made up, the country was flooded with flaming descriptions of the valuable mine, and stock was issued which sold readily. The bonds were soon taken up, and in a month or two the so-called company commenced paying handsome dividends. A number of gold bars, bearing the stamp of the mint, were on exhibition in the company's office, and were triumphantly exhibited as amongst the first yields of the valuable mine. For several months the dividends were paid regularly, and the company's stock rose to a splendid premium. It could hardly be bought at any price. No one doubted for an instant the genuineness of the affair, and the lucky company was the envy of all Wall street.

In a few months, all the stock being disposed of, the company ceased paying dividends. This excited the suspicion of some of the shrewdest holders of the stock, and the affair was investigated. It was found that the wonderful mine had no real existence. The gold bars were simply gold coins melted into that form at the Mint, and stamped by the Government as so much bullion. The dividends had been paid out of money advanced by the company, who were simply half a dozen unprincipled sharpers. The stockholders were ruined, but the company made a profit of a clear half million of dollars out of the infamous transaction. Legal proceedings are expensive and tedious when instituted against such parties, and the stockholders, rather than increase their losses by the outlay necessary for a lawsuit, suffered the swindlers to go unmolested.

A certain stock broker, anxious to increase his wealth, purchased twenty acres of land a few years ago in one of the Western States, and commenced boring for oil. After a few weeks spent in this work, he discovered to his dismay that there was not the slightest trace of oil on his land. He kept his own counsel, however, and paid the workmen to hold their tongues. About the same time it became rumored throughout New York that he had struck oil. He at once organized a company, and had a committee appointed to go West and examine the well.

In a few weeks the committee returned in high glee, and re-ported that the well contained oil of the very best quality, and only needed capital and improved machinery to develop its capacity. In support of this assertion, they brought home numerous bottles containing specimens of the oil. This report settled the matter in Wall street, and the stock issued by the company was all sold at a handsome premium. When the sales ceased, it was rumored that the well had ceased to flow. This was true, for there was no oil anywhere on the land. That in the well had been bought in Pennsylvania, and poured into the well by the agents of the owner, and the examining committee had been paid large sums for their favorable report. The owner of the well was enriched, as were his confederates of the bogus company, and the holders of the stock were swindled, many of them being ruined.

Said the New York *Herald*, at a period when speculation was rampant:

" Within the past few days we have seen the most gigantic swindling operations carried on in Wall street that have as yet disgraced our financial centre. A great railway, one of the two that connect the West with the Atlantic seaboard, has been tossed about like a football, its real stockholders have seen their property abused by men to whom they have entrusted its interests, and who, in the betrayal of that trust, have committed crimes which in parallel cases on a smaller scale would have deservedly sent them to Sing Sing. If these parties go unwhipped of justice, then are we doing injustice in confining criminals in our State prisons for smaller crimes.

" To such a disgusting degree of depravity do we see these stock operations carried, that members of the church of high standing offer, when ' concerned,' to betray their brother ' pals,' and, in their forgetfulness of the morality to which they sanctimoniously listen every Sunday, state that ' all they care about is to look out for number one.' A manager of a great corporation is requested to issue bonds of his company without authority, offering ' to buy the bonds if you are caught, or buy the bonds with the understanding not to pay for them unless you are

19

caught.' This attempted fiscal operation, however, did not work, and resulted in a good proof of the old adage that it requires 'a rogue to catch a rogue.'

"A railroad treasurer boldy states that he has without authority over-issued stock of the company to a large amount. He offers it to a broker for sale, with the understanding that all received over a fixed value is to go into his (the treasurer's) pocket. From the fact that this man is not arrested for maladministration of the company's property, we judge this to be a legitimate operation, and that this may hereafter serve as a model or standard of morals to all presidents, directors, treasurers and managers of railway and other great corporations."

IX.

BLACK FRIDAY.

IN the month of September, 1869, one of the most gigantic attempts to run up the value of gold ever made was attempted by a powerful combination of Bulls, consisting of a set of unprincipled men whose only object was to make money. Their scheme came near attaining a success which would have broken the market utterly, have unsettled values of all kinds, and have precipitated upon the whole country a financial crisis of the most terrible proportions. Nothing but the interference of the Secretary of the Treasury at a critical moment averted this disaster. As it was, the losses were fearful. Men in Wall street were ruined by the score, and for several days the best houses in the street were uncertain as to their exact condition.

An account of this formidable transaction is interesting as revealing the method of conducting the great operations of the street.

"On the 22d of September, 1869, gold stood at $137\frac{1}{2}$ when Trinity bells rang out the hour of twelve. By two it was at 139. Before night its lowest quotation was 141. . . . . An advance of three and a half per cent. in five hours. At the same time the Stock Market exhibited tokens of excessive febril-

SCENE IN THE GOLD ROOM—BLACK FRIDAY.

ity, New York Central dropping twenty-three per cent. and
Harlem thirteen. Loans had become extremely difficult to ne-
gotiate. The most usurious prices for a twenty-four hours'
turn were freely paid. The storm was palpably reaching the
proportions of a tempest.

"Nevertheless, the brokers on the Bear side strove manfully
under their burden. The character and purposes of the clique
were fully known. Whatever of mystery had heretofore en-
folded them was now boldly thrown aside, and the men of Erie,
with the sublime Fisk in the forefront of the assailing column,
assured the shorts that they could not settle too quickly, since
it remained with the ring, now holding calls for one hundred
millions, either to kindly compromise at 150 or to carry the
metal to 200 and nail it there. This threat was accompanied
by consequences in which the mailed hand revealed itself under
the silken glove. The movement had intertwisted itself deep
into the affairs of every dealer in the street, and entangled in
its meshes vast numbers of outside speculators. In borrowing
or in margins the entire capital of the former had been nearly
absorbed, while some five millions had been deposited by the
latter with their brokers in answer to repeated calls. When
Thursday morning rose, gold started at 141⅝, and soon shot up
to 144. Then the clique began to tighten the screws. The
shorts received peremptory orders to increase their borrowing
margins. At the same moment the terms of loans overnight
were raised beyond the pitch of ordinary human endurance.
Stories were insidiously circulated exciting suspicion of the integrity of the Administration, and strengthening the belief that
the National Treasury would bring no help to the wounded
Bears. Whispers of an impending lock-up of money were pre-
valent; and the fact, then shrewdly suspected, and now known,
of certifications of checks to the amount of twenty-five millions
by one bank alone on that day, lent color to the rumor. Many
brokers lost courage, and settled instantly. The Gold Room
shook with the conflict, and the battle prolonged itself into a
midnight session at the Fifth Avenue Hotel. The din of the
tumult had penetrated to the upper chambers of journalism.

Reporters were on the alert. The great dailies magnified the struggle, and the Associated Press spread intelligence of the excitement to remote sections. When Friday opened clear and calm, the pavement of Broad and New streets soon filled up with unwonted visitors. All the idle population of the city and its neighborhood crowded into the financial quarter to witness the throes of the tortured shorts. Blended with the merely curious were hundreds of outside speculators who had ventured their all in the great stake, and trembled in doubt of the honor of their dealers. Long before 9 A. M. these men, intensely interested in the day's encounter, poured through the alley-way from Broad street, and between the narrow walls of New street, surging up around the doorways, and piling themselves densely and painfully within the cramped galleries of the Room itself. They had made good the fresh calls for margins up to 143, the closing figure of the night before. The paramount question now was, How would gold open? They had not many minutes to wait. Pressing up to the fountain, around which some fifty brokers had already congregated, a Bull operator with resonant voice bid 145 for twenty thousand. The shout startled the galleries. Their margins were once more in jeopardy. Would their brokers remain firm? It was a terrible moment. The Bears closed round the aggressors. Yells and shrieks filled the air. A confused and baffling whirl of sounds ensued, in which all sorts of fractional bids and offers mingled, till '46 emerged from the chaos. The crowd within the arena increased rapidly in numbers. The clique agents became vociferous. Gold steadily pushed forward in its perilous upward movement from '46 to '47, thence to '49, and, pausing for a brief twenty minutes, dashed on to 150½. It was now considerably past the hour of regular session. The President was in the chair. The Secretary's pen was bounding over his registry book. The floor of the Gold Room was covered with 300 agitated dealers and operators, shouting, heaving in masses against and around the iron railing of the fountain, falling back upon the approaches of the committee-rooms and the outer entrance, guarded with rigorous care by sturdy door-keepers. Many of the principal

brokers of the street were there,—Kimber, who had turned
traitor to the ring; Colgate, the Baptist; Clews, a veteran government broker; one of the Marvins; James Brown; Albert
Speyer, and dozens of others hardly less famous. Every individual of all that seething throng had a personal stake beyond,
and, in natural human estimate, a thousand-fold more dear than
that of any outside patron, no matter how deeply or ruinously
that patron might be involved. At 11 of the dial gold was $150\frac{1}{2}$;
in six minutes it jumped to 155. Then the pent-up tiger spirit
burst from control. The arena rocked as the Coliseum may
have rocked when the gates of the wild beasts were thrown
open, and with wails and shrieks the captives of the empire
sprang to merciless encounter with the ravenous demons of the
desert. The storm of voices lost human semblance. Clenched
hands, livid faces, pallid foreheads on which beads of cold sweat
told of the interior anguish, lurid, passion-fired eyes,—all the
symptoms of a fever which at any moment might become frenzy
were there. The shouts of golden millions upon millions hurtled
in all ears. The labor of years was disappearing and reappear-
ing in the wave line of advancing and receding prices. With
fortunes melting away in a second, with five hundred millions
of gold in process of sale or purchase, with the terror of yet
higher prices, and the exultation which came and went with
the whispers of fresh men entering from Broad street bearing
confused rumors of the probable interposition of the Government, it is not hard to understand how reason faltered on its
throne, and operators became reckless, buying or selling without
thought of the morrow or consciousness of the present. Then came
the terrific bid of Albert Speyer for any number of millions at
160. William Parks sold instantly two millions and a half in
one lot. Yet the bids so far from yielding rose to 161, 162, $162\frac{1}{2}$.
For five minutes the Board reeled under the ferocity of the attack. Seconds became hours. The agony of Wellington awaiting Blucher was in the souls of the Bears. Then a broker, reported to be acting for Baring & Brothers, at London, sold five
millions to the clique at the top price of the day. Hallgarten
followed; and as the shorts were gathering courage, the certain

news that the Secretary of the Treasury had come to the rescue swept through the chamber, gold fell from 160 to 140, and thence, with hardly the interval of one quotation, to 133.   The end had come, and the exhausted operators streamed out of the stifling hall into the fresh air of the street.   To them, however, came no peace.   In some offices customers by dozens, whose margins were irrevocably burnt away in the smelting-furnace of the Gold Board, confronted their dealers with taunts and threats of violence for their treachery.   In others the nucleus of mobs began to form, and, as the day wore off, Broad street had the aspect of a riot.   Huge masses of men gathered before the doorway of Smith, Gould, Martin & Co., and Heath & Co.   Fisk was assaulted, and his life threatened.   Deputy-sheriffs and police officers appeared on the scene.   In Brooklyn a company of troops were held in readiness to march upon Wall street.

"When night came, Broad street and its vicinity saw an unwonted sight.   The silence and the darkness which ever rests over the lower city after seven of the evening, was broken by the blaze of gas-light from a hundred windows, and the footfall of clerks hurrying from a hasty repast back to their desks. Until long after Trinity bells pealed out the dawn of a new day, men bent over their books, scrutinized the Clearing-House statement for the morrow, took what thought was possible for the future.   At the Gold Exchange Bank the weary accountants were making ineffective efforts to complete Thursday's business. That toilful midnight, at the close of the last great passion-day of the bullion-worshippers, will be ever memorable for its anxieties and unsatisfying anguish.

"Saturday brought no relief.   The Gold Board met only to adjourn, as the Clearing-House had been incapable of the task of settling its accounts, complicated as they were by ever fresh failures.   The small brokers had gone under by scores.   The rumors of the impending suspension of some of the largest houses of the street gave fresh grounds for fear.   The Stock Exchange was now the centre of attraction.   If that yielded, all was lost.   To sustain the market was vital.   But whence was the saving power to come?   All through yesterday shares

BROAD STREET ON BLACK FRIDAY.

had been falling headlong. New York Central careened to 148, and then recovered to 185¾. Hudson plunged from 173 to 145. Pittsburg fell to 68. Northwest reached 62½. The shrinkage throughout all securities had been not less than thirty millions. Would the impulse downward continue? The throngs which filled the corridors and overhung the stairway from which one can look down upon the Long Room saw only mad tumult, heard only the roar of the biddings. For any certain knowledge they might have been in Alaska. But the financial public in the quiet of their offices, and nervously scrutinizing the prices reeled off from the automaton telegraph, saw that Vanderbilt was supporting the New York stocks, and that the weakness in other shares was not sufficient to shadow forth panic.   It soon became known that the capitalists from Philadelphia, Boston, and the great Western cities had thrown themselves into the breach, and were earning fortunes for themselves as well as gratitude from the money-market, by the judicious daring of their purchases.   The consciousness of this new element was quieting, but Wall street was still too feverish to be reposed by any ordinary anodyne.   A run on the Tenth National Bank had commenced, and all day long a steady line of dealers filed up to the counter of the paying teller demanding their balances. The courage and the ability in withstanding the attack which were shown by the president and his associates deserve something more than praise.   The Gold Exchange Bank witnessed a similar scene, angry brokers assaulting the clerks and threatening all possible things unless instantaneous settlements were made. The freedom with which the press had given details of the explosion had been extremely hurtful to the credit of many of the best houses.   In a crisis like that of Black Friday the sluice-gates of passion open.   Cloaked in the masquerade of genuine distrust, came forth whispers whose only origin was in ancient enmities, long-treasured spites, the soundless depths of unquenchable malignities.   Firms of staunchest reputation felt the rapier-stroke of old angers.   The knowledge that certain houses were large holders of particular stocks was the signal of attacks upon the shares.   Despite of outside orders for vast amounts, these influences had their effect upon securities, and aided to tighten the loan market.   One, one and a half, two, and even four per cent. were the compulsory terms on which money could alone be borrowed to carry stocks over Sunday.

"On Monday the 27th the Gold Board met, but only to be informed that the Clearing-House was not yet ready to complete the work of Friday.   Important accounts had been kept back, and the dealings, swollen in sum-total to five hundred millions, were beyond the capacity of the clerical force of the Gold Bank to grapple with.   A resolution was brought forward proposing the resumption of operations Ex-Clearing-House. The measure took the members by surprise, for a moment quivered between acceptance and rejection, and then was swiftly tabled. It was an immense Bear scheme, for no exchange can transact business where its dealers are under suspicion. All outstanding accounts require immediate fulfilment. Failure to make good deliveries would have insured the instant selling out of defaulters 'under the rule.' As the majority of brokers were inextricably involved in the late difficulty, the only consequence would have been to throw them into bankruptcy, thus bringing some $60,000,000 under the hammer. The market could not have borne up under such an avalanche. It was decided that the Room should be kept open for borrowings and loans, but that all dealings should be suspended. One result of this complication was that gold had no fixed value. It could be bought at one house for 133 and at other offices sold for 139. The Board thus proved its utility at the very juncture when least in favor."

XVI.

THE FERRIES.

INCLUDING the Harlem, Staten Island, and Elizabethport routes, there are about twenty-five lines of ferries plying between New York and the adjacent shores. Ten of these lines are to Brooklyn, two to Hunter's Point, two to Green Point, one to Mott Haven, and one to Harlem, all in the East River; and five to Jersey City, one to Weehawken, one to Fort Lee, two to Staten Island, and one to Elizabethport, all in the North River. Thus there are sixteen lines in the East River, and ten in the North River. The boats are large side-wheel vessels, capable of carrying pedestrians, horses and vehicles. The fare to the Jersey shore is three cents, to Brooklyn two, and to Harlem and Staten Island ten cents. On some of the lines the boats ply every five minutes; on others the intervals are longer. The Staten Island and Harlem boats start every hour.

The boats are generally handsome, as well as large. Nearly all are lighted with gas, and at least a score of them are to be seen in the stream at any time. At night, with their many colored lamps, they give to the river quite a gala appearance. The Fulton, Barclay, and Courtlandt street lines run their boats all night. The others run from 4 A. M. until midnight. The travel on the various lines is immense. The aggregate is said, by reliable authority, to be upwards of 200,000 persons per day, or about 75,000,000 per annum. Many of the boats carry from 800 to 1000 passengers at a single trip.

During the summer it is pleasant enough to cross either of the rivers which encircle the island, but in the winter such travelling is very dangerous. Storms of snow, fogs, and floating ice interfere very greatly with the running of the boats, and render accidents imminent. Collisions are frequent during rough or thick weather, and the ice sometimes sweeps the boats for miles out of their course. The East River is always more or less crowded with vessels of all kinds, either in motion or at anchor, and even in fair weather it requires the greatest skill on the part of the pilot to avoid collisions.

Tens of thousands of people enter and leave the great city daily by means of the ferries. The country for twenty miles around the city is built up by persons who earn their bread in New York, and morning and evening they pass between their places of business and their homes. You may recognize them as they come into the city in the morning, or as they leave it at the close of the day. Towards five o'clock vast swarms of workingmen pour over the river, followed at six and seven by the factory and shop girls, the clerks and salesmen in the retail houses and offices, and from these the newsboys reap a harvest for the two-penny papers. Every one has his newspaper, and all who can find the necessary space on the ferry-boat economize their time by reading the news as they cross the river. Later still come the clerks in the wholesale houses, and later still the great merchants themselves. Between nine and ten the Wall street men put in an appearance, and later yet the great capitalists, residing out of the city, begin to show themselves. From eight o'clock the great dailies are in demand, and the newsboys have scarcely a call for the cheap papers. Towards noon the idlers and ladies bent on shopping expeditions cross over, and for a few hours the ferries are comparatively dull. Towards four o'clock in the afternoon, however, the tide flows back again, but in reverse order. The richest come first, for their working hours are short, and the poorest extend the crowd into the hours of darkness. Night brings another flow and ebb of pleasure-seekers, theatre-goers, etc., so that the midnight boats go almost as full as those of the early evening. Then a few stragglers avail themselves of the boats that ply between midnight and morning. They are mostly journalists, actors, or printers employed in the newspaper offices.

With the first light of dawn, and frequently long before the darkness has passed away, the market farmers and gardeners of Long Island and New Jersey crowd the boats with their huge wagons heavily loaded with vegetables and fruits for the city markets. They come in throngs, and the approaches to the ferries in Brooklyn and Jersey City are lined for blocks with their wagons. They are mostly Germans, but they show a decidedly American quality in the impatience they manifest at the delays to which they are subjected. On the lower Jersey ferries, they are often followed by droves of cattle, many of which have come from the Far West, all wending their way to the slaughter houses of New York.

The New York approaches to the ferries are always "jammed" with wagons and trucks. The luckless "foot-passenger" must take the chances of reaching the boat in time, and often must incur no little risk in making his way through the crowd of vehicles. The police try hard to keep these approaches free, but the throng is too great for them, and they have all they can do in seeing after the safety of the "foot-passengers." A man on foot has no rights that a New York driver is bound to respect, and Jehu thinks it no harm to run over any one who gets in his way.

The ferries are good places to study human nature, for all classes use them. You see here the poor, pale working girl, whom toil and poverty are making prematurely old, and the blooming lady of fashion; the beggar and the millionaire; the honest laborer and the thief; the virtuous mother and her children, and the brazen courtezan and her poodle dog. You can tell them all by their appearance and aspect, for here they enjoy a few moments of enforced idleness, and during that time they are natural in expression and attitude.

At night, the scene to be witnessed from these boats is very striking. The waters are dark and the current is strong, and the dash of the waves against the side of the boat is like the noise of the great ocean. Through the darkness you may dimly discern the stern outline of the cities on either side, with the forests of masts which line them rising from the dark hulls at the piers. The shadowy forms of vessels at anchor in the stream, each with its warning light, rise up and disappear as if by magic as you dart past them. On the shore the many colored lights mark the various ferry houses, and similar lights are flashing about the stream like fire-flies as the boats pass from shore to shore. Back of the ferry houses the long rows of lights in the cities stretch away into the distance, and high over all gleams the round white face of the illuminated clock on the City Hall in New York. The breeze is fresh and keen, and comes in laden with the sighing of the mighty ocean so near at hand.

The people standing out on the open deck are silent, impressed by the fascination of the scene. Hark! there is a splash at the side of the boat, a white figure gleams one moment on the crest of the waves, and then sinks under the dark waters. The bell strikes sharply, and the boat stops suddenly. Life-preservers are thrown overboard, and lights gleam along the side of the boat. There is no sign of the unfortunate girl who has so rashly sought peace, and the waters will hold her in their cold embrace till the sea gives up its dead. All search is hopeless, and the boat speeds on, a dumb horror holding its occupants mute.

In a fog, the scene is exciting beyond description. The passengers throng the forward end of the boat, and strive with eager eyes to pierce the dense mist which enshrouds the stream and hides the shore from view. From either side the hoarse clangor of the ferry bells, tolling their number, comes floating through the mist, to guide the pilot to his destination, and all around, on every hand, steamers are shrieking their shrill signals to each other. The boat moves slowly and with caution, and the pilot strains both eye and ear to keep her in the right course. One single error of judgment on his part, and the boat might go crashing into a similar steamer, or into one of the vessels lying in the stream. It is a moment of danger, and those who are used to the river know it. You could hear a pin drop in the silent crowd on the deck. If men speak at all, they do so in low, subdued tones. There is a sharp whistle on the right, and the boat suddenly stops. You hear the splashing of paddle wheels, and the next moment a huge steamer dashes past you in the mist. You can hear her, but the fog hides her. Then the boat goes ahead again, and gradually the fog bells on the shore grow louder and clearer, and in a little while the dock bursts suddenly upon you, so spectral and unearthly in its appearance that you hardly recognize it. The boat now glides swiftly into her "slip," and a sigh of relief breaks from the throng on board. The danger is over.

The boats carry such crowds that an accident to any of them is a terrible affair. The collision at the Fulton Ferry in 1868, and the terrible explosion of the Westfield in 1871, were attended with great loss of life. The injuries were none of them slight, and the disasters were of such magnitude as to throw a general gloom over the community.

XVII.

THE HOTELS.

NEW YORK is the paradise of hotels. In no other city do they flourish in such numbers, and nowhere else do they attain such a degree of excellence. The hotels of New York naturally take the lead of all others in America, and are regarded by all who have visited them as models of their kind.

It is said that there are from six to seven hundred hotels of all kinds in the City of New York. These afford accommodations for persons of every class, and are more or less expensive, according to the means of their guests. Of these, only about fifty are well known, even in the city, and only about twenty-five come under the head of "fashionable." The principal hotels are, beginning down town, the Astor, St. Nicholas, Metropolitan, Grand Central, Brevoort, New York, St. Denis, Spingler, Everett, Clarendon, Westminster, Glenham, Fifth Avenue, Hoffman, Albemarle, St. James, Coleman, Sturtevant, Gilsey, Grand, and St. Cloud. These are the largest, handsomest, and best kept houses in the city. Each has its characteristics and its special customers, and each in its way is worth studying.

The *Astor House* is one of the oldest hotels in the city. It is built of granite, and occupies an entire block on Broadway, from Vesey to Barclay streets. It is immediately opposite the *Herald* office, and the new Post-office. It was built by John Jacob Astor, and presented by him to his son William. It was opened for business in 1831, by Colonel Charles A. Stetson, the present proprietor, and for twenty years was the leading hotel of the country. In those days no one had seen New York unless he had "put up at the Astor." People talked of it all over

THE ASTOR HOUSE.

the country, and in all our leading cities monster hotels began
to appear, modelled upon the same general plan. Those were
the palmy days of the Astor, and if one could write their history
in full, it would be a record worth reading. The old registers
of the house would be valuable for the autographs they contain,
for there was scarcely a great or distinguished man of those days
but had written his name in Colonel Stetson's book.

   The house had from the first a strong flavor of politics about
it. The leading statesmen of the country were always there in
greater or less force, and their admirers kept up a continuous
throng of comers and goers. The house had a decided leaning
towards the Whig Party, and finally it became their New York
headquarters. For thirty years Thurlow Weed boarded here,
and the caucuses, committee meetings, and intrigues of various
kinds the old house has witnessed, would fill a volume with
their history. The Astor still keeps its political character, and

20

is one of the Republican strongholds of the city. It is safe to assert that very few Democrats now inscribe their names on its register, if they are free to seek quarters elsewhere.

The misfortune of the Astor is that it is too far down town to be a fashionable house. It is admirably located for merchants and others who have business in the lower part of the city, and to whom time is of value. A few old-time folks, who knew the house in its palmy days, still stop there, and many whose political faith is in sympathy with that of the proprietor, make it a matter of conscience to patronize the house, and Colonel Stetson's well-earned popularity brings him other guests. Although its glories have faded, the Astor is still a successful hotel, but in popularity with the general public, it has long since been eclipsed by the *up town* hotels.

The *St. Nicholas* is one of the best houses in the city. It shows a handsome marble front on Broadway, with a brown stone extension on the same thoroughfare to Prince street, and extends back to Mercer street. It is handsomely furnished, and is kept on a scale of comfort and magnificence worthy of its fame. Its spacious halls and sitting-rooms, on the street floor, furnish one of the most popular lounging places in the city. Towards nightfall they are full to overflowing. The table is said, by the lovers of good living, to be the best served of any house in the city. The hotel is always full, and is very profitable to its proprietors. It is said to pay better in proportion to its expenses than any of its rivals. It is much liked by the Western people, who come here in crowds. There is also a dashing element about its guests which gives to it its peculiar reputation in the city. It is popularly believed to be the head-quarters of "Shoddy," and certain it is that one sees among its habitués an immense number of flashily dressed, loud-voiced, self-asserting people.

The *Metropolitan* is a handsome brown stone edifice, situated at the northeast corner of Broadway and Prince street. It extends back to Crosby street, and has a frontage of about 300 feet on Broadway. It is one of the most elegant hotels in the city, in every respect. It contains about 400 rooms, and is

ST. NICHOLAS HOTEL.

always full.   It is very popular with army officers, with Cali-
fornians and the people of the mining States and Territories, as
well as with the New Englanders.   Capitalists and railroad
managers also have a fondness for it.   "Shoddy" is to be seen
here also in great force.

The *New York Hotel* is a plain red brick structure, occupying the entire block bounded by Broadway and Mercer street,
and East Washington and Waverley Places.   It has recently
been refitted and improved, and is one of the most comfortable
houses in the city.   In one respect, it may be regarded as the
counterpart of the Astor, since like that hotel, it is noted for
its political complexion.   It is the favorite stopping place of the
Democratic politicians visiting the city, and is mainly patronized
by members of that party.   It is very popular with the Southern
people, large numbers of whom come here to spend the summer,

to escape from the heat of their climate, or to pass the winter to enjoy the delights of the city. The guests of the New York generally stay a long time, and the house is said to do a good business.

The *Grand Central*, on Broadway, between Bleecker and Amity streets, and extending back to Mercer street, is a new house. It was opened in August, 1870, and is the largest hotel in America. It rises to a height of eight stories, or 127 feet, exclusive of the Mansard roof, above the street. Including the central dome, it is ten stories in height. The fitting up of the house is very handsome and elaborate, the furniture and decorations having cost over half a million of dollars. The dining-room will seat 600 persons at once.

The *Fifth Avenue Hotel*, at the junction of Broadway and Fifth avenue, and between Twenty-third and Twenty-fourth streets, is generally regarded as the best house in the city. It occupies the most conspicuous location in New York, and is one of the finest buildings of its kind in the world. It is constructed of white marble, is six stories in height, above ground, and fronts on Fifth avenue, Broadway, Twenty-third and Twenty-fourth streets. The land and building are valued at over $1,000,000, and are owned by Mr. Amos R. Eno, by whom the house was built. The proprietors are Messrs. Hitchcock, Darling & Co.

The hotel was begun in 1857, Mr. Eno having more faith in the rapid growth and prosperity of the city than most persons had at that day. The wise heads laughed him to scorn, and called his house "Eno's folly." They said it might make a popular summer resort, but would never take rank as a first class city hotel. It was too high up town. Undismayed by these criticisms, Mr. Eno went on with his work, and in 1860, the marble palace, to which he gave the name of the *Fifth Avenue Hotel*, was opened to the public. By this time the city had grown so fast as to make the need of this house imperative, but the first years of the war laid a burden upon it which only the most skilful financial management could overcome.

The hotel is the most perfectly appointed in the city. The

ground floor along Broadway and Fifth avenue is let out in
stores. The main entrance is on Fifth avenue, and is ornamented with a fine marble porch. From this, the visitor enters
into the spacious reception hall, tiled with marble and handsomely frescoed. A marble counter at the lower end encloses
the offices of the hotel, and on this counter is laid the Visitor's
Register, of which several fresh pages are filled daily with the
names of new-comers. Opposite the office are the stairs leading to the basement, in which are the billiard-rooms, store-
rooms, etc., of the house. The hall upon which the office
opens extends through to the rear of the building. On the
south side of this hall is the reading-room, in which are to be
found the daily papers of the leading cities of the Union. Opposite the reading-room is the bar-room, one of the most elegant
apartments of the house, and beyond this is the handsome and
well-appointed barber-shop. There is a private entrance on
Twenty-fourth street, used mainly by gentlemen, another on
Twenty-third street, and still another on Broadway. Each is
in charge of a door-keeper, whose duty it is to exclude improper
personages. Along the Twenty-third street side are suites of
private apartments on the ground floor, occupied by permanent
boarders.

The various floors are reached by means of an "elevator,"
the first ever used in this country. Similar arrangements are
now in use in all the large hotels. The main stairway commences immediately opposite the office. It is of white marble,
and massive in its design. Ascending it the visitor finds himself in a spacious hall, at one end of which is a corridor at right
angles to this hall. At the end nearest the stairs is the dining-
room, a magnificent apartment. When the tables are filled
with a handsomely dressed throng of guests at the dinner hour,
this room presents one of the most brilliant sights that can be
witnessed on the continent. The bill of fare comprises literally
everything that is in season. Back of the dining-room is the
kitchen, an immense establishment. Everything connected with
it goes on like clock-work, however, so perfect is the system
upon which it is managed. Beneath the kitchen are the ma-

FIFTH AVENUE HOTEL.

chines for warming and ventilating the hotel. By means of these a perfectly comfortable temperature is maintained in all parts of the house, and the smells of the kitchen are kept out of the halls and chambers.

At the end of the hall upon which the dining-room opens, are the parlors of the house. These are among the most magnificent rooms in the country. They are furnished with great taste and elegance, and their windows look out immediately upon Madison Square. There are also several private parlors adjoining the public rooms. Along the Twenty-third and Twenty-fourth street sides of the house are corridors, not quite so wide, but longer than the main corridor, and leading off from it. The three constitute one of the pleasantest promenades to be found. The floors are covered with the richest carpets, into which the feet sink noiselessly. In the day a half twilight prevails, and at night a rich flood of gaslight streams along their entire length.

The upper floors are occupied with private parlors, rooms for guests, etc. There are in this hotel pleasant quarters for 800 persons, and a greater number can be accommodated in case of necessity. There are 100 suites of rooms, besides the ordinary chambers. Each suite comprises a parlor, chamber, dressing-room, bath-room and water-closet. The number of permanent boarders is about 300. The transient arrivals average about 300 per day, sometimes amounting to about twice that number. The house is expensive, but its accommodations are unsurpassed, and if one can "get his money back" anywhere in the city he can at this hotel.

The house is mainly patronized by people from other parts of the State, from New England, and from the West. It is the most fashionable establishment in the city, and will doubtless hold its present rank as long as its energetic proprietors retain the control of it.

Towards eight o'clock in the evening, the hotel presents its most attractive features. It is full to overflowing. The lower halls, the reading and sitting-rooms are filled with well-dressed men, guests and citizens, who have sauntered here from all parts of the city. Four-fifths are smoking, and the air is hazy with the "vapor of the weed." The hum of conversation is incessant, but the general tone is well-bred and courteous. In the farther end of the great hall a group of stock brokers may be seen comparing notes, and making bargains for the sale and purchase of their fickle wares. The clink of glasses makes music in the bar-room, and beyond this you may see the barbers at work on their customers in the luxurious shaving saloon. Doors are opening and shutting continually, people are coming and going. Porters are pushing their way through the crowd bearing huge trunks on their shoulders. The office bell is sounding incessantly, from a dozen different chambers at once, and the servants are moving about in every direction to execute the orders of the guests.

On the floor above the scene is as animated, but of a different character. Every one here is in full dinner dress, and all are on their good behaviour. The grand dining-room is crowded with guests, who are doing ample justice to the sumptuous viands set before them. The parlors are thronged with ladies and gentlemen, and the corridors are filled with promenaders. The toilettes of the ladies are magnificent, and they can be seen here to better advantage than at any ball or evening party. You may see here some of the loveliest and most refined women, and some of the coarsest and vulgarest, some of the most courtly gentlemen, and some of the most insufferable snobs. If you will join the quiet-looking man moving through the throng as if seeking some one whom he cannot find, he can give you many an interesting bit of gossip about the various persons whom you will encounter in your walk. He is the detective of the house, and is on the watch for improper characters. Well-dressed thieves will make their way into hotels in spite of the precautions of the proprietors. Here a guest is comparatively safe. The detective is argus-eyed, and knows everybody. Let a pick-pocket or thief but show his face in this place, and his arrest is sure. All night the corridors are patrolled by watchmen to make sure of the safety of the sleeping guests. The house is absolutely fire-proof.

The cost of conducting such an establishment is immense, but the profits are in proportion. The average profit of this house is said to be about a quarter of a million of dollars per annum.

The hotels that have been mentioned are all conducted on the American plan of full board, or one charge for every expense. This enables a guest to calculate his expenses exactly, and has many other advantages.

Many of the most fashionable houses are conducted on what is called " the European plan," in which a separate charge is made for room, meals, and every service rendered. It is said that this is more economical than the other plan, and that it is less profitable to the proprietors. It is adopted by the Hoffman, St. Denis, Glenham, Brevoort, Coleman, St. James, Albemarle, Clarendon, Everett, Grand, Gilsey, and several other prominent houses.

The leading hotels of the city lie very close together, the majority of them being in the vicinity of Union and Madison Squares. This is found to be an advantage, as strangers find it pleasant to visit friends who are staying at other houses. The business of hotel keeping in New York is generally very profitable. A large outlay is required at the opening of the house, for furniture, etc., as much as from $200,000 to $500,000 being expended on the fitting up of a first-class house. The furniture, plate, etc., of the Fifth Avenue and Grand Central Hotels are valued at the latter sum for each establishment. If the house meet with success, a moderate sum will suffice to supply its current wants. The business is all cash, and large amounts of money are received daily. The annual profits of the Fifth Avenue Hotel are said to be about $250,000; those of the St. Nicholas about $200,000. Other leading houses, when well managed, are said to clear about twenty per cent. on the sum invested. Large fortunes have been made by not a few keepers of hotels in New York.

The large hotels depend entirely upon transient guests for their success. The city has, perhaps, the largest floating population in America. Thousands come and go daily, even in the summer months, and these are mostly persons who have money to spend. Bridal parties are constantly arriving, and these are not inclined to be the most economical in their expenditures. In the spring and fall, the Southern and Western merchants come to New York in great numbers to buy goods, and are among the best customers of the hotels. Thousands, on business, and for pleasure, come and go daily, and they all pour a constant stream of money into the coffers of the hotels.

The smaller houses, while they compete with their great rivals for transient custom, rely chiefly upon their permanent guests. These are filled with families who have come to them to avoid the trouble of keeping house, and who remain all through the fall, winter, and spring. In the summer they go to the watering places, so that they pass their whole lives in hotels. They are mostly persons of wealth and fashion. As may be supposed, the atmosphere of a hotel is not very favorable to domestic privacy, and such establishments are vast manufactories of scandal. People imagine that they are living privately, but their every action is subject to the inspection and comment of the other inmates of the house. The hotels are not the safest places for the growth of the domestic virtues. Indeed, it may be said that they furnish the best means of destroying them entirely. Neither are they the best place for the training of children. This last, however, may be a minor consideration, for the wives who live at the hotels seem, as a rule, to take care that there shall be no children to need training. Small families are a necessity at such places, and they remain small in that atmosphere. If another Asmodeus could look down into the hotels of New York, he would have some startling revelations to make, which would no doubt go far to corroborate the gossip one hears in the city concerning them.

The proprietors of the city hotels are very active in their efforts to exclude improper characters from their houses, but with all their vigilance do not always succeed in doing so. One is never certain as to the respectability of his neighbor at the table, and it is well to be over-cautious in forming acquaintanceships at such places. Impure women of the "higher," that is the more successful class, and gamblers, abound at the hotels. The proprietor cannot turn them out unless they are notorious, until they commit some overt act, for fear of getting himself into trouble. As soon, however, as his attention is called to any improper conduct on their part, they are turned into the street, no matter at what hour of the day or night.

Hotel proprietors are also the victims of adventurers of both sexes. These people live from house to house, often changing their names as fast as they change their quarters, and they are more numerous than is generally believed. One man who made himself known to the police in this way, used to take his family, consisting of a wife and three children, to the hotels, and engage the best rooms. When his bill was presented, he affected to be extremely busy, and promised to attend to it the next day. By the next day, however, he had disappeared with his family. His trunk, which had been left behind, was found to contain nothing but bricks and rags, or paper.

Another adventurer would put up at the most fashionable hotels, and when requested to pay his bills would feign madness. He would rave, and sing, and dance, call himself Nebuchadnezzar, or George Washington, or some such personage, and completely baffle the detectives, who were for a long time inclined to believe him a *bonâ fide* madman. In this way he ran up a bill of one hundred and seventy-one dollars at the Fifth Avenue Hotel, which he never paid.

Others do not seek to obtain lodgings at the hotels, but confine their efforts to securing meals without paying for them. They get into the dining-rooms along with the crowd at the meal hour, and once in and seated at the table are generally safe. Some two years ago as many as thirty-four of this class were detected at the Fifth Avenue Hotel in a single month. These men as they leave the dining-room generally manage to secure a better hat than that they deposited on the stand in entering. Under the regime of the Lelands, the Metropolitan Hotel had a colored man stationed at the door of its dining-room, who proved more than a match for the most expert thief.

All first class hotels keep private detectives and watchmen on duty at all hours. The business of these men is to keep guard over the upper part of the house, to prevent thieves from entering and robbing the rooms of the guests. Suspicious persons are at once apprehended, and required to give an account of themselves. Some queer mishaps often befall guests of the house who are not known to the detectives.

Bold robberies are often effected at the hotels of the city. Sometime ago a thief was captured at the St. Nicholas, and upon being searched a gold watch and chain, and five different parcels of money were found upon him, all of which were identified by guests as their property.

XVIII.

IMPOSTORS.

THERE is no city in the Union in which impostors of all kinds flourish so well as in New York. The immense size of the city, the heterogeneous character of its population, and the great variety of the interests and pursuits of the people, are all so many advantages to the cheat and swindler. It would require a volume to detail the tricks of these people, and some of their adventures would equal anything to be found in the annals of romance. All manner of tricks are practised upon the unsuspecting, and generally the perpetrator escapes without punishment. They come here from all parts of the country, and indeed from all parts of the world, in the hope of reaping a rich harvest, and the majority end by eking out a miserable existence in a manner which even the police who watch them so closely are sometimes unable to understand.

They find their way into all classes. One cannot mingle much in society here without meeting some bewhiskered, mysterious individual, who claims to be of noble birth. Sometimes he palms himself off as a political exile, sometimes he is travelling, and is so charmed with New York that he makes it his headquarters, and sometimes he lets a few friends into the secret of his rank, and begs that they will not reveal his true title, as a little unpleasant affair, a mere social scandal in his own country, made it necessary for him to absent himself for a while. He hopes the matter will blow over in a few months, and then he will go home. The fashionable New-Yorker, male or female, is powerless against the charms of aristocracy. The "foreign nobleman" is welcomed everywhere, fêted, petted, and allowed almost any privilege he chooses to claim—and he is far from being very modest in this respect; and by and by he is found out to be an impostor, probably the valet of some gentleman of rank in Europe. Then society holds up its hands in holy horror, and vows it always did suspect him. The men in society are weak enough in this respect; but the women are most frequently the victims.

Not long since, a handsome, well got up Englishman came to New York on a brief visit. He called himself Lord Richard X——. Society received him with open arms. Invitations were showered upon him. Brown's hands were always full of cards for his Lordship. The women went wild over him, especially since it was whispered that the young man was heir to a property worth ever so many millions of pounds. In short, his Lordship found himself so popular, and hints of his departure were received with such disfavor by his new found friends, that he concluded to extend his stay in New York indefinitely. He made a fine show, and his toilettes, turnouts, and presents were magnificent. The men did not fancy him. He was too haughty and uncivil, but the ladies found him intensely agreeable. It was whispered by his male acquaintances that he was a good hand at borrowing, and that he was remarkably lucky at cards and at the races. One or two of the large faro banks of the city were certainly the losers by his visits. The ladies, however, were indignant at such stories. His Lordship was divine. All the women were crazy after him, and any of them would have taken him at the first offer.

By and by the newspapers began to take notice of the young man, and boldly asserted that there was no such name as Lord Richard X—— in the British peerage. Society laughed at this, and declared that everybody but ignorant newspaper men was aware that the published lists of titled personages in England were notoriously incomplete.

Meanwhile, his Lordship played his cards well, and it was soon announced that he was " to be married shortly to a well-known belle of Fifth avenue." The women were green with jealousy, and the men, I think, were not a little relieved to find that the lion did not intend devouring all the Fifth avenue belles. The marriage came off in due season; the wedding-presents fairly poured in, and were magnificent. The new Lady X—— was at the summit of her felicity, and was the envied of all who knew her. The happy pair departed on their honey-moon, but his Lordship made no effort to return home to England.

During their absence, it leaked out that Lord X—— was an impostor. Creditors began to pour in upon his father-in-law with anxious inquiries after his Lordship, against whom they held heavy accounts. Proofs of the imposture were numerous and indisputable, and the newspapers declared that Lord X—— would not dare to show his face again in New York. Every-body was laughing at the result of the affair.

What passed between the father-in-law and the young couple is not known; but the bride decided to cling to her husband in spite of the imposture. Father-in-law was a prudent and a sensitive man, and very rich. For his daughter's sake, he ac-cepted the situation. He paid Lord X——'s debts, laughed at the charge of imposture, and spoke warmly to every one he met of the great happiness of his "dear children, Lord and Lady X——." On their return to the city, he received them with a grand party, at which all Fifth avenue was present, and, though he could not silence the comments of society, he succeeded in retaining for his children their places in the world of fashion. He was a nabob, and he knew the power of his wealth. He shook his purse in the face of society, and commanded it to con-tinue to recognize the impostor as Lord X——, and society meekly obeyed him.

Impostures of this kind do not always terminate so fortu-nately for the parties concerned. New York gossip has many a well-authenticated story of foreign counts and lords, who have set society in a flutter, and have married some foolish, trusting woman, only to be detected when it was too late to prevent the trouble. Some of these scoundrels have been proved to be married men already, and the consequences of their falsehood have, of course, been more serious to the bride. Others again do not enter the matrimonial market at all, but use their arts to secure loans from their new acquaintances. Not long since a foreigner, calling himself a Russian Count, and claiming to be sent here on a mission connected with the Russian navy, succeeded in borrowing from some credulous acquaintances, who were dazzled by his pretended rank, sums ranging from $500 to $2000, and amounting in the aggregate to $30,000. When the time of payment arrived, the Count had disappeared, and it was ascertained that he had escaped to Europe.

Impostors of other kinds are numerous. Men and women are always to be found in the city, seeking aid for some charitable institution, with which they claim to be connected. They carry memorandum books and pencils, in the former of which the donor is requested to inscribe his name and the amount of his gift, in order that it may be acknowledged in due form by the proper officers of the institution. Small favors are thankfully received, and they depart, assuring you in the most humble and sanctimonious manner that " the Lord loveth a cheerful giver." If you cannot give to-day, they are willing to call to-morrow— next week—any time that may suit your convenience. You cannot insult them by a sharp refusal, or in any way, for like Uriah Heep they are always "so 'umble." You find it hard to suspect them, but, in truth, they are the most genuine impostors to be met with in the city. They are soliciting money for themselves alone, and have no connection with any charitable institution whatever.

One-armed, or one-legged beggars, whose missing member, sound as your own, is strapped to their bodies so as to be safely out of sight, women wishing to bury their husbands or children, women with hired babies, and sundry other objects calculated to excite your pity, meet you at every step. They are vagabonds. God knows there is misery enough in this great city, but how to tell it from barefaced imposture, is perplexing and harassing to a charitably disposed person. Nine out of ten street beggars in New York are unworthy objects, and to give to them is simply to encourage vagrancy ; and yet to know how to discriminate. That would be valuable knowledge to many people in the great city.

In the fall of 1870, a middle aged woman committed suicide in New York. For some months she had pursued a singular career in the great city, and had literally lived by her wits. While her main object was to live comfortably at other people's expense, she also devoted herself to an attempt to acquire property without paying for it. She arrived in New York in the spring of 1868, and took lodgings at an up-town hotel. She brought no baggage, but assured the clerk that her trunks had been unjustly detained by a boarding house keeper in Boston with whom she had had a difficulty. She succeeded in winning the confidence of the clerk, and told him that she had just come into possession of a fortune of one million dollars, left her by a rich relative, and that she had come to New York to purchase a home. She completely deceived the clerk, who vouched for her respectability and responsibility, and thus satisfied the proprietor of the hotel. She made the acquaintance of nearly all the resident guests of the house, and so won their sympathy and confidence that she was able to borrow from them considerable sums of money. In this way she lived from house to house, making payments on account only when obliged to do so, and when she could no longer remain at the hotels, she took up her quarters at a private boarding house, passing thence to another, and so on. She spent two years in this way, borrowing money continually, and paying very little for her board.

In pursuance of her plan to acquire real estate without paying for it, she made her appearance in the market as a purchaser. In the summer of 1870, she obtained permits of one of the leading real estate agents of the city to examine property in his hands for sale, and finally selected a house on Madison avenue. The price asked was $100,000, but she coolly declared her readiness to pay the full amount in cash as soon as the necessary deeds could be prepared. The real estate dealer was completely deceived by her seeming frankness, and assured her that he would give his personal attention to the details of the transaction, so that her interests would not suffer, and a day was agreed upon for the completion of the purchase.

The woman then assumed a confidential tone, and told the

gentleman of her immense fortune. She was absolutely alone in the city, she said, without relatives or friends to whom she could apply for advice in the management of her property, and she urged him to become her trustee and manage the estate for her, offering him a liberal compensation for his services. Her object was to make him her trustee, induce him to act for her in the purchase of the house, and involve him so far as to secure the success of her scheme for getting possession of the property. The dealer, however, thanked her for her preference, but assured her that it was impossible for him to accept her proposition, as he had made it a rule never to act as trustee for any one. He did not in the least suspect her real design, and but for this previous and fixed determination would have acceded to her request. Finding that she could not shake his resolution, the lady took her departure, promising to return on the day appointed for the payment of the purchase money.

At the time designated, the deeds were ready, and the real estate agent and the owner of the Madison avenue mansion awaited the coming of the lady; but she did not appear, and, after a lapse of several days, the two gentlemen concluded they had been victimized, and then the true character of the trusteeship he had been asked to assume broke upon the real estate agent. The audacity and skill of the scheme fairly staggered him.

After the failure of this scheme, the woman tried several others of a similar character, with the same success. In October, 1870, a city newspaper, having obtained information respecting her transactions from some of her victims, published an account of her career. The next day she committed suicide, and was found dead in her bed.

Not long since a city lawyer, whom we shall call Smith, and who is much given to the procuring of patent divorces for dissatisfied husbands and wives, was visited by a richly dressed lady, who informed him that she was Mrs. P——, the wife of Mr. P——, of Fifth avenue, and that she wished to retain his services in procuring a divorce from her husband, on the ground of ill treatment. Mr. P—— was personally a stranger to the

21

lawyer, who knew him, however, as a man of great wealth. Visions of a heavy fee flashed before him, and he encouraged the lady to make a full statement of her grievances, promising to do his best to secure the desired divorce in the shortest possible time. He made full notes of her statement, and assured her that he felt confident that he would be able to obtain not only the divorce, but a very large sum as alimony. In reply to her question as to his charge for his services, he replied :

"Well, I ought to charge you $1000, but out of consideration for your sufferings, I will only take a retainer of $100, and when we have gained our suit, you will pay me $500 additional."

"That is very reasonable," said the lady, "and I accept the terms. Unfortunately, I have nothing with me but a check for $200, given me by my husband this morning to use in shopping. I shall only need half of it, and if you could get it cashed for me—but, no matter, I'll call to-morrow, and make the payment."

Smith, who had seen the millionaire's heavy signature at the bottom of the check, thought he had better make sure of his retainer, and offered to accept the check on the spot. He had just $100 in his pocket, and this he gave to the lady who handed him the check, with the urgent entreaty that he would not betray her to her husband.

"He shall know nothing of the matter until it is too late for him to harm you," said the lawyer, gallantly, as he bowed his fair client out of the office.

It was after three o'clock, and Smith was forced to wait until the next morning before presenting his check at the bank on which it was drawn. Then, to his astonishment, the teller informed him that the signature of Mr. P—— was a forgery. Thoroughly incensed, Smith hastened to the office of the millionaire, and, laying the check before him, informed him that his wife had been guilty of forging his name, and that he must make the check good, or the lady would be exposed and punished. The millionaire listened blandly, stroking his whiskers musingly, and when the lawyer paused, overcome with excitement, quietly informed him that he was sorry for him, but that he, Mr. P——, had the misfortune to be without a wife. He had been a widower for five years.

How Smith found his way into the street again, he could never tell, but he went back to his work a sadder and a wiser man, musing upon the trickiness of mankind in general, and of women in particular.

THE SOLDIER MINSTREL.

XIX.
STREET MUSICIANS.

It would be interesting to know the number of street musicians to be found in New York. Judging from outward appearances, it must be their most profitable field, for one cannot
walk two blocks in any part of the city without hearing one or
more musical instruments in full blast. A few are good and
in perfect tone, but the majority emit only the most horrible
discords.

Prominent among the street musicians are the organ grinders,
who in former days monopolized the business. They are mostly
Italians, though one sees among them Germans, Frenchmen,
Swiss, and even Englishmen and Irishmen. Against these people there seems to be an especial, and a not very reasonable prejudice. A lady, eminent for her good deeds among the poor of
the Five Points, once said, "There is no reason why an organ
grinder should be regarded as an altogether discreditable member of the community; his vocation is better than that of begging,
and he certainly works hard enough for the pennies thrown to
him, lugging his big box around the city from morning until
night." To this good word for the organ grinder it may be
added that he is generally an inoffensive person, who attends
closely to his business during the day, and rarely ever falls into
the hands of the police. Furthermore, however much grown
people with musical tastes may be annoyed, the organ grinders
furnish an immense amount of amusement and pleasure to the
children; and in some of the more wretched sections provide all
the music that the little ones ever hear.

Very few of them own their organs. There are several
firms in the city who manufacture or import hand organs, and

from these the majority of the grinders rent their instruments. The rent varies from two to twenty dollars per month, the last sum being paid for the French flute organs, which are the best. The owners of the instruments generally manage to inspire the grinders with a profound terror of them, so that few instruments are carried off unlawfully, and, after all, the organ grinders are more unfortunate than dishonest.

Organ grinding in New York was once a very profitable business, and even now pays well in some instances. Some of the grinding fraternity have made money. One of these was Francisco Ferrari, who came to this city ten years ago. He invested the money he brought with him in a hand organ and a monkey, and in about five years made money enough to return to Italy and purchase a small farm. He was not content in his native land, however, and soon returned to New York with his family and resumed his old trade. He is said to be worth about twenty thousand dollars.

At present, in fair weather, a man with a good flute organ can generally make from two to five dollars a day. Those who have the best and sweetest toned instruments seek the better neighborhoods, where they are always sure of an audience of children whose parents pay well. Some of these musicians earn as much as ten and fifteen dollars in a single day. In bad weather, however, they are forced to be idle, as a good organ cannot be exposed to the weather at such times without being injured.

A monkey is a great advantage to the grinder, as the animal, if clever, is sure to draw out a host of pennies from the crowd which never fails to gather around it. The monkey is generally the property of the grinder. It is his pet, and it is interesting to see the amount of affection which exists between the two. If the grinder is a married man, or has a daughter or sister, she generally accompanies him in his rounds. Sometimes girls and women make regular business engagements of this kind with the grinders, and receive for their services in beating the tamborine, or soliciting money from the bystanders, a certain fixed proportion of the earnings of the day,

If the organ grinder be successful in his business, he has every opportunity for saving his money. Apart from the rent of his organ, his expenses are slight. Few, however, save very much, as but few are able to earn the large sums we have mentioned. The grinders pay from five to eight dollars per month for their rooms, and they and their families live principally upon maccaroni. They use but a single room for all purposes, and, no matter how many are to be provided with sleeping accommodations, manage to get along in some way. As a general rule, they are better off here than they were in their own country, for poverty has been their lot in both. Their wants are simple, and they can live comfortably on an amazingly small sum. The better class of Italians keep their apartments as neat as possible. Children of a genial clime, they are fond of warmth, and the temperature of their rooms stands at a stage which would suffocate an American. They are very exclusive, and herd by themselves in a section of the Five Points. Baxter and Park and the adjoining streets are taken up to a great extent with Italians.

This is the life of the fortunate members of the class. There are many, however, who are not so lucky. These are the owners or renters of the majority of the street organs, the vile, discordant instruments which set all of one's nerves a tingling. They earn comparatively little, and are not tolerated by the irate householders whose tastes they offend. The police treat them with but small consideration. The poor wretches are nearly always in want, and soon fall into vagrancy, and some into vice and crime. Some of them are worthless vagabonds, and nearly all the Italians accused of crime in the city are included in their number. One of these men is to be seen on the Bowery at almost any time. He seats himself on the pavement, with his legs tucked under him, and turns the crank of an instrument which seems to be a doleful compromise between a music box and an accordeon. In front of this machine is a tin box for pennies, and by the side of it is a card on which is printed an appeal to the charitable. At night a flickering tallow dip sheds a dismal glare around. The man's head is tied up in a piece of white muslin, his eyes are closed, and his face and posture are expressive of the most intense misery. He turns the crank slowly, and the organ groans and moans in the most ludicrously mournful manner. At one side of the queer instrument sits a woman with a babe at her breast, on the other side sits a little boy, and a second boy squats on the ground in front. Not a sound is uttered by any of the group, who are arranged with genuine skill. Their whole attitude is expressive of the most fearful misery. The groans of the organ cannot fail to attract attention, and there are few kind-hearted persons who can resist the sight. Their pennies and ten-cent stamps are showered into the tin box, which is never allowed to contain more than two or three pennies. The man is an Italian, and is said by the police to be a worthless vagabond. Yet he is one of the most successful musicians of his class in the city.

The arrangements of a street organ being entirely automatic, any one who can turn a crank can manage one of these instruments. Another class of street musicians are required to possess a certain amount of musical skill in order to be successful. These are the strolling harpers and violinists. Like the organ grinders, they are Italians. Very few of them earn much money, and the majority live in want and misery.

Some of these strollers are men, or half-grown youths, and are excellent performers. The best of them frequent Broadway, Wall and Broad streets, and the up-town neighborhoods. At night they haunt the localities of the hotels. They constitute one of the pleasantest features of the street, for their music is good and well worth listening to. They generally reap a harvest of pennies and fractional currency. They form the aristocratic portion of the street minstrel class, and are the envy of their less fortunate rivals.

The vast majority of the strolling harpers and violinists are children; generally boys below the age of sixteen. They are chiefly Italians, though a few Swiss, French and Germans are to be found among them. They are commonly to be found in the streets in pairs; but sometimes three work together, and again only one is to be found. There are several hundreds of these children on the streets. Dirty, wan, shrunken, monkey-faced little creatures they are. Between them and other children lies a deep gulf, across which they gaze wistfully at the sports and joys that may not be theirs. All day long, and late into the night, they must ply their dreary trade.

Although natives of the land of song, they have little or no musical talent, as a class, and the majority of them are furnished with harps and violins from which not even Orpheus himself could bring harmony. Not a few of the little ones endeavor to make up in dancing what they lack in musical skill. They work energetically at their instruments, but they do no more than produce the vilest discord. At the best, their music is worthless, and their voices have a cracked, harsh, monotonous sound; but the sound of them is also very sad, and often brings a penny into the outstretched hand.

At all hours of the day, and until late at night you may hear their music along the street, and listen to their sad young voices going up to the ear that is always open to them. They are half clothed, half fed, and their filthiness is painful to behold. They sleep in fair weather under a door-step or in some passage way or cellar, or in a box or hogshead on the street, and in the winter huddle together in the cold and darkness of their sleeping places, for we cannot call them homes, and long for the morning to come. The cold weather is very hard upon them, they love the warm sunshine, and during the season of ice and snow are in a constant state of semi-torpor. You see them on the street, in their thin, ragged garments, so much overpowered by the cold that they can scarcely strike or utter a note. Sometimes a kind-hearted saloon-keeper will permit them to warm themselves at his stove for a moment or two. These are the bright periods in their dark lives, for as a general rule they are forced to remain on the street from early morning until late at night.

A recent writer, well informed on the subject, says: "It is a cruelty to encourage these children with a gift of money, for instead of such gifts inuring to their benefit, they are extracted for the support of cruel and selfish parents and taskmasters." This is true, but the gift is a benefit to the child, nevertheless.

These children have parents or relatives engaged in the same business, who require them to bring in a certain sum of money at the end of the day, and if they do not make up the amount they are received with blows and curses, and are refused the meagre suppers of which they are so much in need, or are turned into the streets to pass the night. The poor little wretches come crowding into the Five Points from nine o'clock until midnight, staggering under their heavy harps, those who have not made up the required sum sobbing bitterly in anticipation of the treatment in store for them. Give them a penny or two, should they ask it, reader. You will not miss it. It will go to the brutal parent or taskmaster, it is true, but it will give the little monkey-faced minstrel a supper, and save him from a beating. It is more to them than to you, and it will do you no harm for the recording angel to write opposite the follies and sins of your life, that you cast one gleam of sunshine into the heart of one of these children.

A number of Italian gentlemen resident in New York have generously devoted themselves to the task of bettering the lot of these little ones, and many of those who formerly lived on the streets are now in attendance upon the Italian schools of the city. Yet great is the suffering amongst those who have not been reached by these efforts. Only one or two years ago there were several wretches living in the city who carried on a regular business of importing children from Tuscany and Naples, and putting them on the streets here as beggars, musicians, and thieves. They half starved the little creatures, and forced them to steal as well as beg, and converted the girls into outcasts at the earliest possible age. The newspapers at length obtained information respecting these practices, and by exposing them, drew the attention of the civil authorities to them. One of the scoundrels, named Antonelli, was arrested, tried, and sentenced to the penitentiary, and the infamous business was broken up. The police authorities are possessed of information which justifies them in asserting that some Italian children fare quite as badly at the hands of their own parents. There have been several instances where Italian fathers have made a practice of hiring out their daughters for purposes of prostitution, while they were yet mere children.

As a rule, the future of these little folks is very sad. The Italian and the Mission schools in the Five Points and similar sections of the city are doing much for them, but the vast majority are growing up in ignorance. Without education, with an early and constant familiarity with want, misery, brutality and crime, the little minstrels rarely "come to any good." The girls grow up to lives of sin and shame, and many fortunately die young. The boys too often become thieves, vagrants, and assasssins. Everybody condemns them. They are forced onward in their sad career by all the machinery of modern civilization, and they are helpless to ward off their ruin.

During one of the heavy snows of a recent winter, a child harper trudged wearily down the Fifth avenue, on his way to the Five Points, where he was to pass the night. It was intensely cold, and the little fellow's strength was so exhausted by fatigue and the bleak night wind that he staggered under the weight of his harp. At length he sat down on the steps of a splendid mansion to rest himself. The house was brilliantly lighted, and he looked around timidly as he seated himself, expecting the usual command to move off. No one noticed him, however and he leaned wearily against the balustrade, and gazed at the handsome windows through which the rich, warm light streamed out into the wintry air. As he sat there, strains of exquisite music, and the sounds of dancing, floated out into the night. The little fellow clasped his hands in ecstasy and listened. He had never heard such melody, and it made his heart ache to think how poor and mean was his own minstrelsy compared with that with which his ears were now ravished. The wind blew fierce and keen down the grand street, whirling the snow about in blinding clouds, but the boy neither saw nor heard the strife of the elements. He heard only the exquisite melody that came floating out to him from the warm, luxurious mansion, and which grew sweeter and richer every moment. The cold, hard street became more and more indistinct to him, and he sat very still with his hands clasped and his eyes closed.

The ball ended towards the small hours of the morning, and the clatter of carriages dashing up to the door of the mansion gave the signal to the guests that it was time to depart. No one had seen the odd-looking bundle that lay on the street steps, half buried in the snow, and which might have lain there until the morning had not some one stumbled over it in descending to the carriages. With a half curse, one of the men stooped down to examine the strange object, and found that the bundle of rags and filth contained the unconscious form of a child. The harp, which lay beside him, told his story. He was one of the little outcasts of the streets. Scorning to handle such an object, the man touched him with his foot to arouse him, thinking he had fallen asleep. Alas! it was the eternal sleep.

XX.
THE CENTRAL PARK.

THOUGH of comparatively recent date, the Central Park, the chief pleasure ground of New York, has reached a degree of perfection in the beauty and variety of its attractions, that has made it an object of pride with the citizens of the metropolis.

For many years previous to its commencement, the want of a park was severely felt in New York. There was literally no place on the island where the people could obtain fresh air and pleasant exercise. Harlem lane and the Bloomingdale road were dusty and disagreeable, and moreover were open only to those who could afford the expense of keeping or hiring a conveyance. People of moderate means, and the laboring classes were obliged to leave the city to obtain such recreation. All classes agreed that a park was a necessity, and all were aware that such a place of resort would have to be constructed by artificial means.

The first step taken in the matter was by Mayor Kingsland, who, on the 5th of April 1851, submitted a message to the Common Council, setting forth the necessity of a park, and urging that measures be taken at once for securing a suitable site, before the island should be covered with streets and buildings. The message was referred to a select committee, who reported in favor of purchasing a tract of 150 acres, known as Jones's Woods, lying between Sixty-sixth and Seventy-fifth streets, and Third avenue and the East River. There was a strong pressure brought to bear upon the City Government to secure the purchase of this tract, although the citizens as a rule ridiculed the idea of providing a park of only 150 acres for a city whose population would soon be 1,000,000. Yet the Jones's Wood tract came very near being decided upon, and the pur-

VIEW FROM THE UPPER TERRACE.

chase was only prevented by a quarrel between two members of the Legislature from the City of New York, and the city was saved from a mistake which would have been fatal to its hopes. On the 5th of August, 1851, a committee was appointed by the Legislature to examine whether a more suitable location for a park could be found, and the result of the inquiry was the selection and purchase of the site now known as the Central Park, the bill for that purpose passing the Legislature on the 23d of July, 1853.

In November, 1853, Commissioners were appointed to assess the value of the land taken for the park, and on the 5th of February, 1856, their report was confirmed by the City Government. In May, 1856, the Common Council appointed the first Board of Commissioners, with power to select and carry

out a definite plan for the construction of the park. This
Board consisted of the Mayor and Street Commissioner, who
were *ex officio* members, Washington Irving, George Bancroft,
James E. Cooley, Charles F. Briggs, James Phalen, Charles A.
Dana, Stewart Brown and others. The designs submitted by
Messrs. Frederick L. Olmstead and C. Vaux were accepted,
and have since been substantially carried out. The surveys
had previously been made by a corps of engineers, at the head
of which was Mr., now General Egbert L. Viele.

The task before the architects and Commissioners was an
arduous one. With the exception of making a few hollows,
and throwing up a few rocks and bluffs, nature had done
nothing for this part of the island. It was bleak, dreary and
sickly. "The southern portion was already a part of the straggling suburbs of the city, and a suburb more filthy, squalid and
disgusting can hardly be imagined. A considerable number of
its inhabitants were engaged in occupations which are nuisances
in the eye of the law; and were consequently followed at night
in wretched hovels, half-hidden among the rocks, where also
heaps of cinders, brickbats, potsherds, and other rubbish were
deposited. The grading of streets through and across it had
been commenced, and the rude embankments and ragged rock-
excavations thus created added much to the natural irregularities of its surface. Large reaches of stagnant water made the
aspect yet more repulsive; and so ubiquitous were the rocks
that it is said, not a square rood could be found throughout
which a crowbar could be thrust its length into the ground
without encountering them. To complete the miseries of the
scene, the wretched squatters had, in the process of time, ruth-
lessly denuded it of all its vegetation except a miserable tan-
gled underbrush."

Looking around now upon the beautiful landscape, with its
exquisite lawns and shrubbery, its picturesque hills, and romantic walks and drives, its sparkling lakes, cascades and fountains,
it is hard to realize that so much loveliness was preceded by
such hideousness.

The Central Park, so called because it is situated almost in

FOOT-BRIDGE IN CENTRAL PARK.

the centre of the island of Manhattan, is a parallelogram in shape, and lies between Fifty-ninth street on the south, and One-hundred-and-tenth street on the north, the Fifth avenue on the east, and the Eighth avenue on the west. It covers an area of 843 acres, and is about two and a half miles long, by half a mile wide. There are nine miles of carriage drives, four miles of bridle roads, and twenty-five miles of walks within its limits. It is the second park in the Union in size; the Fairmount Park at Philadelphia being the largest. It is larger than any city park in Europe, with the exception of the Bois de Boulogne at Paris, the Prater at Vienna, and the Phœnix at Dublin. A rocky ridge, which traverses the whole island, passes through almost the exact centre of the grounds, and has afforded a means of rendering the scenery most beautiful and diversified. A part of the grounds forms a miniature Alpine region; another part is the perfection of water scenery; and still another stretches away in one of the loveliest lawns in the world. The soil will nurture almost any kind of tree, shrub, or plant; and more than one hundred and sixty thousand trees and shrubs of all kinds have been planted, and the work is still going on. Any of the principal walks will conduct the visitor all over the grounds, and afford him a fine view of the principal objects of interest.

The park is divided into two main sections, known as the Upper and Lower Parks, the two being separated by the immense Croton Reservoirs, which occupy the central portion of the grounds. Thus far the Lower Park has received the greatest amount of ornamentation. It is a miracle of exquisite landscape gardening. Its principal features are its lawns, the Pond, the Lake, the Mall, the Terrace, the Ramble, and the Museum of Natural History. The main entrances are on Fifty-ninth street, those at the Fifth and Eighth avenues being for vehicles, equestrians, and pedestrians, and those at the Sixth and Sventh avenues for pedestrians only. All these entrances will ultimately be ornamented with magnificent gateways. Paths leading from them converge at the handsome Marble Arch at the lower end of the Mall.

Near the Fifth avenue gate is a fine bronze colossal bust of Alexander Von Humboldt, the work of Professor Blaiser of Berlin, which was presented to the park by the German citizens of New York, and inaugurated on the 14th of September, 1869, the one-hundredth anniversary of the birth of the great man.

Near the Eighth avenue gate is a bronze statue of Commerce, the gift of Mr. Stephen B. Guion.

At the extreme southern end of the park, and between the Fifth and Sixth avenue gates, is a small, irregular sheet of water, lying in a deep hollow. The surrounding hills have been improved with great taste, and the pond and its surroundings constitute one of the prettiest features of the park. The water consists mainly of the natural drainage of the ground.

Along the Fifth avenue side of the park, near Sixty-fourth street, is a large and peculiar-looking building, not unlike the cadet barracks at West Point. This was formerly used by the State as an arsenal, but was purchased by the city, in 1856, for the sum of $275,000. It has been recently fitted up as a Museum of Natural History, and the first, second, and third floors contain the magnificent collection of the American Museum Association. This collection is in charge of Professor Bickmore, and includes 12,000 birds, 1000 mammals, 3000 reptiles and fishes, and a large number of insects and corals. It is the 'largest and most perfect collection in the country. The famous collection of the Archduke Maximilian forms the nucleus of this one.

In the top floor of the Museum building is the Meteorological Observatory of the Central Park, under charge of Professor Daniel Draper. Here are ingenious and interesting instruments for measuring the velocity and direction of the wind, the fall of rain and snow, and for ascertaining the variation of the temperature, etc. The establishment is very complete, and a portion of it is open to visitors. The basement floors of the building are occupied by the offices of the Central Park authorities, and a police station.

The open space surrounding the Museum edifice is taken up with buildings and cages containing the living animals, birds,

22

THE MARBLE ARCH.

and reptiles of the collection. They are admirably arranged, and the occupants are all fine specimens of their species. These accommodations are only temporary, as the Commissioners are now engaged in the construction of a Zoological Garden, on Eighth avenue, between Seventy-seventh and Eighty-first streets, immediately opposite the park, with which it will be connected by means of a tunnel under the Eighth avenue.

Just north of the pond, and on the high ground above it, is a pretty gothic structure of stone, known as *The Dairy*. It is contiguous to the South Transverse Road, and supplies may be taken to it without using the park thoroughfares. Pure milk and refreshments, especially such as are suited to children, may be obtained at a moderate cost.

A short distance from the Dairy is the children's summer house, near which is a cottage with toilette rooms, closets, etc., for the use of ladies and children. Near by are a number of self-acting swings, and a little to the north is the Carrousel, a circular building, containing a number of hobby-horses, which are made to gallop around in a circle by the turning of a crank in the centre of the machine. To the west of this building is the base-ball ground, covering some forty or fifty acres. A commodious brick cottage has been erected here for the accommodation of the ball players.

The paths from the Fifty-ninth street gates converge at the Marble Arch, which lies a little to the northeast of the Dairy. This is one of the most beautiful and costly structures in the park, and consists entirely of marble. Its purpose is to carry the main carriage drive over the foot-path without interrupting the level, and at the same time to furnish a pleasant access from the lower level of the Southwest Park to the Mall. A broad double stairway, to the right and left, leads from the Mall to the interior of the Arch. On either side runs a marble bench, on which, in the summer, the visitor may sit and enjoy the delightful coolness of the place; and opposite the upper end of the Arch, beyond the stairway, is a niche, around which is a marble bench. In the centre is a drinking fountain.

The Mall extends from the Marble Arch to the Terrace. It

constitutes the grand promenade of the park, and near its upper end is the handsome music stand, from which concerts are given by the Central Park Band, on Saturday afternoons during the mild season. The Mall is about 1200 feet long by 200 feet wide. In the centre is a promenade, thirty-five feet wide. The remainder is laid out in lawns, and is shaded by four rows of American elms. The Mall terminates on the north in a spacious square or plaza, which is ornamented with two pretty revolving fountains, and a number of bird cages mounted on pedestals. In the spring and summer, numerous vases of flowers are placed here. On concert days, the upper part of the Mall is covered with rustic seats shaded by canvass awnings, where the visitor may sit and listen to the music. At such times, a large programme of the performance is posted on a movable frame placed opposite the music stand. These concerts are very good, and draw large audiences.

To the west of the Mall is a beautiful lawn, called the Green, covering fifteen acres, and terminated on the northwest by a hill, on the summit of which is placed a gaudy building in which artificial mineral waters are sold.

Along the northeastern side of the Mall, and elevated about twenty feet above it, is a rustic bower of iron trellis work, over which are trained wistarias, honeysuckle, and rose vines. This is the Vine-covered Walk, and from it visitors may overlook the Terrace, Lake, Ramble, and Mall.

Adjoining it on the east is an open square, in which carriages only are allowed. Across this square is the Casino, a handsome brick cottage, used as a ladies' restaurant. The fare here is good, and the prices are moderate. The establishment is conducted by private parties under the supervision of the Commissioners.

In the grounds in the rear of the Casino, is a fine group of figures in sandstone, called "Auld Lang Syne," the work of Robert Thomson, the self-taught sculptor, and a little to the southeast of this is a bronze statue of Professor Morse, erected by the Telegraph Operators' Association, and executed by Byron M. Pickett.

VINE-COVERED WALK, OVERLOOKING THE MALL.

341

At the northern end of the Mall is the Terrace, and between the two is a magnificent screen work of Albert freestone, in which are two openings whereby persons can leave their carriages and enter the Mall, or from it can cross the drive and reach the stairs leading to the Lower Terrace. A flight of massive stairs leads directly from the Mall to the arcade or hall under the drive, through which the visitor may pass to the Lower Terrace, which is on the same level. This hall is paved, and the walls and ceiling are inlaid with beautiful designs in encaustic tiles. It is now used as a refreshment room. The Terrace is constructed almost entirely of Albert freestone, and is very massive and beautiful in design. It is elaborately and exquisitely carved with appropriate figures and emblems, some of which are very quaint. Our engraving will give the reader a fair idea of its appearance from the water. In the summer, the slope adjoining the Terrace is studded with flowers, which give to the scene a very brilliant effect.

In the centre of the Lower Terrace is a large basin from the midst of which rises a fine jet of water. This fountain is to be ornamented with magnificent bronze castings, now on their way from Munich, where they were made.

The Central Lake washes the northern end of the Lower Terrace, and stretches away from it to the east and west. It is without doubt the most beautiful feature of the park. It covers between twenty and thirty acres, and is as pretty a sheet of water as can be found in the country. Upon its upper side are the wooded heights of the Ramble, which in some places slope down gently to the water's edge, and in others jut out into the lake in bold, rocky headlands. The magnificent Terrace, with its fountain and flowers, and carvings, adorns the southeastern portion. To the west of the Terrace the lake narrows very greatly, and is spanned by a light iron structure, called the Bow Bridge, from its peculiar shape. It is used for pedestrians only. Heavy vases filled with trailing flowers adorn its abutments, and from this it is sometimes called the Flower Bridge. The western part of the lake is a lovely sheet of water, and comprises more than two-thirds of the whole lake. Its northwestern end is spanned by a handsome stone bridge, which carries the drive across that part of the lake, and close by is another, picturesquely constructed of wood, which conducts a foot-path across the head of the lake.

At the Terrace there is a boat-house, in which is to be found the manager of the fleet of pleasure boats which dot the surface of the water. The regular fare around the lake in the omnibus or public boats is ten cents. Persons may hire a boat for their private use on the payment of a moderate sum. They may either make the circuit of the lake in these boats, or may leave them at any of the six pretty boat-houses which are arranged at convenient points on the shore. The popularity of these boats may be judged from the fact that in 1869, 126,000 persons used them.

Whole fleets of snow-white swans are constantly sailing through the waters. They are among the finest specimens of their species in existence. At the opening of the park twelve of these birds were presented to the Commissioners by the city of Hamburg in Germany. Nine of these died, and twelve more were presented by the same city. Fifty others were given by some gentlemen in London. Of the original seventy-four, twenty-eight died, and the remaining forty-six with their progeny form one of the pleasantest attractions of the lake. A number of white ducks have been added to the collection. All the birds are quite tame, and come readily to the call.

On a bright moonlight night in the summer, the scene to be witnessed on the lake is brilliant. The clear waters gleam like polished steel in the moonlight, and are dotted in every direction with pleasure boats, each of which carries a red or blue light ; the swans sail majestically up and down in groups ; on every side is heard the dash of oars, and the sound of laughter and happy voices ; and the air is heavily laden with the perfume of the flowers along the shore. No sight or sound of the great city is at hand to disturb you, and you may lie back in your boat with half shut eyes, and think yourself in fairyland.

In the winter the scene is different. Huge houses are erected on the shores of all the sheets of water in the park, and are

THE TERRACE, AS SEEN FROM THE LAKE.

844

provided with sitting-rooms, fires, restaurants, and counters at which skates may be hired for a trifling sum. The water is lowered to a depth sufficient to prevent the occurrence of any serious accident in case the ice should break, and the ice itself is carefully watched, and is scraped smooth after the sports of the day are over. Rotten ice is quickly detected and marked with a sign bearing the word "Danger." When the ice is in suitable condition, a red ball is hoisted on the Arsenal, and little white flags, on which is printed a similar ball, are affixed to the cars running between the park and the lower part of the city. Then the pleasure seekers come out in throngs, and soon the ice is crowded. At night the lakes are lighted by numerous gas jets with powerful reflectors, placed along the shore. The Central Lake at such times is a sight worth seeing. The Commissioners prepare a code of liberal rules for the government of skaters, and post them at conspicuous points. All persons going on the ice are required to comply with them, on pain of exclusion from the sport.

To the east of the Central Lake, and along the Fifth avenue side, is a small pond, on the verge of which a large Conservatory, which is to be one of the principal ornaments of the park, is now in course of erection.

On the heights to the north of the lake lies the Ramble, which covers an area of about thirty-six acres, and is a labyrinth of wooded walks, abounding in the prettiest rustic nooks, with tiny bridges over little brooks, wild flowers and vines, and bits of lawn, and rock work, all so naturally and simply arranged that it is hard to believe it is not the work of nature. It is one of the most beautiful portions of the park.

At the northern end of the Ramble rises a fine gothic stone tower, which forms a prominent feature in almost any view of the park. This is the Belvedere, and is intended to serve as an observatory from which the entire park may be seen at a glance. The rock upon which it stands is the highest point in the park.

At the foot of this tower are the Croton Reservoirs. There are two of them. The old or lower one is a parallelogram in form, covering an area of thirty-one acres, and capable

VIEW ON THE CENTRAL LAKE.

346

of holding 150,000,000 gallons of water. The new reservoir lies to the north of the old, and is separated from it by a transverse road. It is a massive structure of granite, irregular in form, and extends almost entirely across the park. It covers an area of 106 acres, and will hold 1,000,000,000 gallons of water. Thus the two reservoirs take 136 acres from the park. The landscape gardeners have so arranged them that they constitute a very attractive feature of the landscape.

North of the new reservoir is the Upper Park. This has been less improved than the Lower Park, but is naturally very beautiful. A large part of it is taken up with the great ravine formerly known as McGowan's Pass. It was through this wild glen that the beaten and disheartened fragments of the American army escaped from the city of New York after their disastrous rout at the battle of Long Island. Close by they were rallied in time to make a stand at Harlem Plains. On the hills in the extreme northern part of the park are still to be seen the remains of a series of earthworks, which have been carefully turfed over, and on one of these heights, known as The Bluff, is an old stone structure said to have been used as a block-house or magazine during the war of 1812-15. A small part of the " old Boston Road " is still to be seen in this portion of the park, and in the distance a view is to be obtained of the High Bridge, the Heights of Westchester county, and the Palisades, on the New Jersey shore of the Hudson, while Washington Heights rise boldly to the northward. To the eastward one may see the white sails of the vessels in Long Island Sound, and get a faint glimpse of the town of Flushing, on Long Island, and New Rochelle, on the mainland, while nearer are Hell Gate, the picturesque East and Harlem rivers, with their islands and public buildings, and the lovely little village of Astoria.

The park occupies the centre of the island, from north to south, for a distance of two miles and a half. The cross streets do not extend through it, and all vehicles of a business nature are excluded from the pleasure drives. It was foreseen from the first that it would be necessary to provide means of communication between the eastern and western sides of the island, without compelling wagons and trucks to pass around the upper or lower ends of the enclosure. At the same time it was felt to be desirable to make these roads as private as possible, so that the beauty of the park should not be marred by them, or by the long trains of wagons, carts, and such other vehicles as would pass over them. The genius of the constructing engineers soon settled this difficulty. A system of *transverse roads* was adopted and carried out. There are four of them, and they cross the park at Sixty-fifth, Seventy-ninth, Eighty-fifth, and Ninety-seventh streets. They are sunken considerably below the general level of the park, and are securely walled in with masonry. Vines, trees, and shrubbery are planted and carefully trained along the edges of these walls, which conceal the roads from view. The visitors, by means of archways or bridges, pass over these roads, catching but a momentary glimpse of them in some places, and in utter ignorance of them in others.

Near the northeastern end of the park is an elevation known as Mount St. Vincent. It is crowned with a large rambling structure principally of wood, to which is attached a fine brick chapel. The building was originally used as a Roman Catholic Seminary for young men. It is now a restaurant, kept by private parties under the control of the Commissioners. The chapel is used as a gallery of sculpture, and contains the models of the works of the sculptor Thomas Crawford. They were presented to the city by his widow in 1860.

Just below this hill is the North Lake, into which flows a stream noted for its beauty.

At the Fifth and Eighth Avenue gates are the stations of the Park Omnibuses. These are controlled by the Commissioners, and transport passengers through the entire park for the sum of twenty-five cents. They are open, and afford every facility for seeing the beauties of the place.

The original cost of the land included within the park was $5,028,884, and up to the close of the year 1869, there had been expended upon it an additional sum of $5,775,387; making the total cost of the park, up to January 1st, 1870,

$10,804,271. Since that time it has cost about $1,000,000 additional.

The park is controlled by the Commissioners of the Department of Public Parks. The principal executive officer is the President. The discipline prescribed for the employés is very rigid. A force of special policemen, who may be recognized by their gray uniforms, has been placed on duty in the park, with the same powers and duties as the Metropolitan Police. One of these is always on duty at each gateway, to direct visitors and furnish information, as well as to prevent vehicles from entering the grounds at too rapid a rate. Others of the force are scattered through the grounds at such convenient distances that one of them is always within call. None of the employés are allowed to ask or to receive pay for their services. Their wages are liberal. When an article is found by any of the employés of the park, it is his duty to carry it to the property clerk at the Arsenal, where it can be identified and recovered by the rightful owner.

Improper conduct of all kinds is forbidden, and promptly checked. Visitors are requested not to walk on the grass, except in those places where the word "Common" is posted; not to pick flowers, leaves, or shrubs, or in any way deface the foliage; not to throw stones or other missiles, not to scratch or deface the masonry or carving; and not to harm or feed the birds.

No one is allowed to offer anything for sale within the limits of the enclosure, without a special licence from the Commissioners. There are several hotels, or restaurants, in the grounds. These are conducted in first-class style by persons of responsibility and character. Private closets for men, which may be distinguished by the sign, "For Gentlemen only," are located at convenient points throughout the park, and cottages for ladies and children are as numerous. These latter are each in charge of a female attendant, whose duty it is to wait upon visitors, and to care for them, in case of sudden illness, until medical aid can be procured.

The establishment of the park has been a great blessing to

all classes, but especially to the poor. It places within reach of the latter a great pleasure ground, where they may come and enjoy their holidays, and obtain the fresh air and bodily and mental enjoyment of which they are deprived in their quarters of the city. In mild weather they come here in throngs, with their families, and on Sundays the park is crowded with thousands who formerly passed the day in drunkenness or vice. The Commissioners have no trouble in enforcing their rules. All classes are proud of the park, and all observe the strictest decorum here. No crime or act of lawlessness has ever been committed within the limits of the Central Park since it was thrown open to the public. The popularity of the place is attested by the annual number of visitors. During the year 1870, 3,494,877 pedestrians, 75,511 equestrians, 1,616,935 vehicles, and 234 velocipedes, passed within the park gates. The total number of persons that entered the park during that year, including drivers and the occupants of carriages, was 8,421,427.

XXI.
THE DETECTIVES.

I.

THE REGULAR FORCE.

THE Detective Corps of New York consists of twenty-five
men, under the command of a Captain, or Chief. Though
they really constitute a part of the Municipal Police Force, and
are subject to the control of the Commissioners and higher
officers of that body, the detectives have a practically distinct
organization. The members of this corps are men of experience, intelligence, and energy. These qualities are indispensable to success in their profession. It requires an unusual
amount of intelligence to make a good Detective. The man
must be honest, determined, brave, and complete master over
every feeling of his nature. He must also be capable of great
endurance, of great fertility of resource, and possessed of no
little ingenuity. He has to adopt all kinds of disguises, incur
great personal risks, and is often subjected to temptations which
only an honest man can resist. It is said that the Detective's
familiarity with crime is in itself a great temptation, and often
leads him from the path of right. However this may be, it
is certain that a member of the New York force committing an
act savoring of dishonesty is punished by immediate expulsion
from his post.

The Detectives have a special department assigned them at
the Police Head-quarters in Mulberry street. There they may
be found when not on duty, and the Chief, when not in his
office, is always represented by some member of the corps.

They are kept quite busy. The strangers who visit the city throw an immense amount of work upon the Detectives. These people often get drunk over night, and frequent houses of bad repute, where they are robbed. They naturally invoke the aid of the police in seeking to recover their property. Frequently, by making a plain statement of their cases, they recover their money or valuables, through the assistance of the Detectives. Sometimes the stolen property cannot be regained at all. These people, as a rule, refuse to prosecute the thieves, and declare their determination to submit to the loss rather than endure the publicity which would attend a prosecution. Thus the Detectives are forced to compound felonies. The injured party refuses to prosecute, and the Detective knows that to make an arrest in the case would simply be to take trouble for nothing. Consequently, if the plunder is returned, the thief is allowed to escape without punishment.

None but those whose duty it is to search out and punish crime, can tell how much the administration of justice is embarrassed, how much the officers of the law are hampered, and how greatly their labors are increased by the refusal of respectable persons to prosecute criminals. These refusals are not confined to those who seek to avoid such an exposure as is mentioned above. Merchants and bankers who have been robbed by thieves, seem to care for nothing but the recovery of their money or property. They will even sacrifice a portion of this to regain the remainder. The Detective may fairly work up his case, and fasten the crime upon the perpetrator, but he is not sure of meeting with the cooperation upon the part of the injured person that he has a right to demand. The thief seeing that an arrest is inevitable, may offer to return a part or the whole of the property on condition of his being allowed to escape. In ninety-nine cases out of a hundred the proposal is accepted. The merchant recovers his property, and immediately exerts himself to secure the escape of the thief. He refuses to prosecute the wretch, or if the prosecution is carried on in spite of him, his evidence amounts to nothing. He has protected his own interests, and he cares nothing for society or justice. He throws his whole influence against both, and aids the thief, in going free, to commit the same crime in another quarter. The Detectives complain, and with justice, that it is of no use for them to arrest a burglar where the stolen property can be recovered. If persons who have been wronged in this way would refuse all proposals for a compromise, and would endeavor to secure the punishment of the offender, the criminal class would be wonderfully thinned out, and the Detectives would not, as now, be obliged to arrest the same person over and over again, only to see him go free every time.

In June, 1870, a gentleman, passing through Bleecker street, on his way home, at two o'clock in the morning, was knocked down and robbed of his watch and money. He was struck with such violence by the highwayman that his jaw was permanently injured. He was very eloquent in his complaints of the inefficiency of a police system which left one of the principal streets of the city so unguarded, and was loud in his demands for the punishment of his assailant, and the recovery of the property stolen from him. The best Detectives in the force were put in charge of the case, and the highwayman was tracked, discovered and arrested. The friends of the culprit at once returned the stolen property to its owner, and promised to reward him liberally if he would not press the prosecution of their comrade, who was one of the leading members of a notorious and dangerous gang of ruffians from whose depredations the city had been suffering for some time. The offer was accepted, and the gentleman flatly refused to prosecute, and when compelled by the authorities to state under oath, whether the prisoner was the man who had robbed him, became so doubtful and hesitating that his identification was worth nothing. This, too, in the face of his previous assertion that he could readily identify the criminal. In spite of his misconduct, however, there was evidence enough submitted to secure the conviction of the prisoner, who was sentenced to an imprisonment of ten years.

The Detectives are in constant telegraphic communication with other cities, and intelligence of crimes committed is being

23

constantly received and transmitted. Criminals arrested for serious offences are photographed, and their pictures placed in the collection known as the "Rogues' Gallery." These likenesses are shown to strangers only under certain restrictions, but they aid the force not a little in their efforts to discover criminals. The amount of crime annually brought to light by the Detectives is startling, but it does not exhibit all the evil doings of the great city. "The Police Commissioners of New York," says Mr. Edward Crapsey, "have never had the courage to inform the public of the number of burglaries and robberies annually committed in the metropolis; but enough is known in a general way for us to be certain that there are hundreds of these crimes committed of which the public is not told. The rule is to keep secret all such affairs when an arrest does not follow the offence, and hardly any police official will venture to claim that the arrest occurs in more than a moiety of the cases. There are hundreds of such crimes every year where the criminal is not detected, and hundreds of thousands of dollars worth of property stolen of which the police never find a trace."

The individuality of crime is remarkable. Each burglar has a distinct method of conducting his operations, and the experienced Detective can recognize these marks or characteristics as he would the features of the offender. Thanks to this experience, which comes only with long and patient study, he is rarely at a loss to name the perpetrator of a crime if that person be a "professional." Appearances which have no significance for the mere outsider are pregnant with meaning to him. He can determine with absolute certainty whether the mischief has been done by skilled or unskilled hands, and he can gather up and link together evidences which entirely escape the unpractised eye. He rejects nothing as unimportant until he has tested it, and is able to conduct his search in a systematic manner, which in the majority of cases is crowned with success.

A few years ago a man came into one of the police stations of the city, and complained that his house had been robbed. He had pursued the thief without success, but the latter had dropped a chisel, and had torn up and thrown away a piece of

paper in his flight. The captain commanding the station and
an experienced Detective were present when the complaint was
made. They carefully examined the owner of the house as to
the mode by which the entrance had been effected, the marks
left by the tools, the kind of property taken, and the action and
bearing of the thief while running away. When these facts
were laid before them, the two officers, without a moment's hesitation, concluded that the robbery had been committed by a
certain gang of thieves well known to them. This settled, it
became necessary to identify the individual or individuals
belonging to this gang, by whom the robbery had been committed. The chisel was examined, but it could give no clue.
The house-owner had fortunately secured the bits of paper which
the thief had thrown away. The officers spread a layer of
mucilage over a sheet of paper, and on this fitted the scraps
which were given them. This at once disclosed the name of the
robber, who was well known to the police as a member of the
gang to whom the officers attributed the robbery. Their suspicions were at once confirmed, and the next step was to make the
arrest. The Detective said that the thief would certainly be at
one of three places, which he named. Three policemen were
accordingly sent after him, one to each of the places named, and
in an hour or two the culprit was safely lodged in the station-
house.

It would require a volume to relate the incidents connected
with the exploits of the Detective Corps of New York. Sometimes the search for a criminal is swift and short, and the guilty
parties are utterly confounded by the suddenness of their detection and apprehension. Sometimes the search is long and toil-
some, involving the greatest personal danger, and abounding in
romance and adventure. Some of the best established incidents
of this kind would be regarded simply as Munchausen stories,
were they related without the authority upon which they rest.
Such adventures are well known to the reading public, and I
pass them by here.

But the Detectives are not always successful in their efforts.
If they are ingenious and full of resource, the criminals they

seek are equally so, and they find their best efforts foiled and brought to naught by the skill of this class in "covering up their tracks." To my mind the most interesting cases are not those in which the Detective's labors have been crowned with success, but those in which he has been baffled and perplexed at every step, and which to-day remain as deeply shrouded in mystery as at the time of their occurrence.

Inspector James Leonard, in the spring of 1869, related the following case to Mr. Edward Crapsey, in whose words it is presented here:

"One spring morning, during the first year of the war, a barrel of pitch was found to have disappeared from a Jersey City pier, and the porter in charge, when reporting the fact to his employers, took occasion to speak of the river-thieves in no very complimentary terms.

"On the same day, Ada Ricard, a woman of nomadic habits and dubious status, but of marvellous beauty, suddenly left her hotel in New York, without taking the trouble to announce her departure or state her destination. The clerks of the house only remarked that some women had queer ways.

"A few days after these simultaneous events, the same porter who had mourned the lost pitch, happening to look down from the end of his pier when the tide was out, saw a small and shapely human foot protruding above the waters of the North River. It was a singular circumstance, for the bodies of the drowned never float in such fashion; but the porter, not stopping to speculate upon it, procured the necessary assistance, and proceeded to land the body. It came up unusually heavy, and when at last brought to the surface, was found to be made fast by a rope around the waist to the missing barrel of pitch. There was a gag securely fastened in the mouth, and these two circumstances were positive evidence that murder had been done.

"When the body was landed upon the pier, it was found to be in a tolerable state of preservation, although there were conclusive signs that it had been in the water for some time. It was the body of a female, entirely nude, with the exception of an embroidered linen chemise and one lisle-thread stocking, two sizes larger than the foot, but exactly fitting the full-rounded limb. The face and contour of the form were, therefore, fully exposed to examination, and proved to be those of a woman who must have been very handsome. There was the cicatrice of an old wound on a lower limb, but otherwise there was no spot or blemish upon the body.

"In due time the body was buried; but the head was removed, and preserved in the office of the city physician, with the hope that it might be the means of establishing the identity of the dead, and leading to the detection of the murderer.

"The police on both sides of the river were intensely interested in the case; but they found themselves impotent before that head of a woman, who seemed to have never been seen upon earth in life. They could do nothing, therefore, but wait patiently for whatever developments time might bring.

"Chance finally led to the desired identification. A gentleman who had known her intimately for two years, happening to see the head, at once declared it to be that of Ada Ricard. The Detectives eagerly clutched at this thread, and were soon in possession of the coincidence in time of her disappearance and that of the barrel of pitch to which the body was lashed. They further found that, since that time, she had not been seen in the city, nor could any trace of her be discovered in other sections of the country, through correspondence with the police authorities of distant cities. They had thus a woman lost and a body found, and the case was considered to be in a most promising condition.

"The next step was to establish the identity by the testimony of those who had known the missing woman most intimately. The Detectives, therefore, instituted a search, which was finally successful, for Charles Ricard, her putative husband. He had not lived with her for some time, and had not even seen or heard of her for months; but his recollection was perfect, and he gave a very minute statement of her distinguishing marks. He remembered that she had persisted in wearing a pair of very heavy earrings, until their weight had slit one of her ears entirely, and the other nearly so, and that, as a consequence, both ears had been pierced a second time, and unusually high up. He regretted that her splendid array of teeth had been marred by the loss of one upon the left side of the mouth, and told how a wound had been received, whose cicatrice appeared upon one of her limbs, stating exactly its location. He dwelt with some pride upon the fact that she had been forced, by the unusual development, to wear stockings too large for her feet, and gave a general description of hair, cast of face, height, and weight that was valuable, because minute.

" When he gave this statement he was not aware of the death of his wife, or of the finding of her body, and without being informed of either fact he was taken to Jersey City, and suddenly confronted with the head. The instant he saw it he sank into a chair in horror.

" His statement having been compared with the head and the record of the body, the similitude was found to be exact, except as to the teeth. The head had one tooth missing on each side of the mouth, and this fact having been called to his attention, Ricard insisted that she had lost but one when he last saw her, but it was highly probable the other had been forced out in the struggle which robbed her of her life, and the physician, for the first time making a minute examination, found that the tooth upon the right side had been forced from its place, but was still adhering to the gum. He easily pushed it back to its proper position, and there was the head without a discrepancy between it and the description of Ada Ricard.

" The Detectives found other witnesses, and among them the hair-dresser who had acted in that capacity for Ada Ricard during many months, who, in common with all the others, fully confirmed the evidence of Charles Ricard. The identity of the murdered woman was therefore established beyond question.

" Naturally the next step was to solve the mystery of her death. The Detectives went to work with unusual caution, but persisted in the task they had assigned themselves, and were slowly gathering the shreds of her life, to weave from them a thread that would lead to the author of her tragical death, when they were suddenly 'floored,' to use their own energetic expression. Ada Ricard herself appeared at a down-town New York hotel, in perfect health and unscathed in person.

"The explanation was simple. The whim had suddenly seized her to go to New Orleans, and she had gone without leave-taking or warning. It was no unusual incident in her wandering life, and her speedy return was due only to the fact that she found the Southern city only a military camp under the iron rule of General Butler, and therefore an unprofitable field for her.

"The ghastly head became more of a mystery than before. The baffled Detectives could again only look at it helplessly, and send descriptions of it over the country. At last it was seen by a woman named Callahan, living in Boston, who was in search of a daughter who had gone astray. She instantly pronounced it to be that of her child, and she was corroborated by all the members of her family and several of her neighbors. The identification was no less specific than before, and the perplexed authorities, glad at last to know something certainly, gave Mrs. Callahan an order for the body. Before, however, she had completed her arrangements for its transfer to Boston, a message reached her from the daughter, who was lying sick in Bellevue Hospital, and so the head once more became a mystery. And such it has always remained. The body told that a female who had been delicately reared, who had fared sumptuously, and had been arrayed in costly fabrics, had been foully done to death, just as she was stepping into the dawn of womanhood— and that is all that is known. Her name, her station, her history, her virtues, or it may be, her frailties, all went down with her life, and were irrevocably lost. There is every probability that her case will always be classed as unfinished business."

On Friday, July 20th, 1870, Mr. Benjamin Nathan, a wealthy Jewish resident of New York, was foully and mysteriously murdered in his own dwelling by an unknown assassin. All the circumstances of the case were so mysterious, so horribly dramatic, that the public interest was wrought up to the highest pitch.

Mr. Nathan was a millionaire, a banker and citizen of irreproachable character, well known for his benevolence, and highly esteemed for his personal qualities. His residence stood on the south side of Twenty-third street, one door west of Fifth Avenue, and immediately opposite the Fifth Avenue Hotel, in one of the most desirable and fashionable neighborhoods of the city. The mansion itself was palatial, and its owner had not only surrounded himself with every luxury, but had taken every precaution to exclude housebreakers and thieves. But a short time before his death, he remarked to a friend that he believed that his house was as secure as a dwelling could be made.

On the night of the 28th of July, Mr. Nathan slept at his residence, his family, with the exception of two of his sons, being then at their country-seat in New Jersey, where they were passing the summer. One of these sons accompanied his father to his sleeping room towards eleven o'clock, but the other, coming in later, and finding his father asleep, passed to his chamber without saying " good-night," as was his custom.

On the morning of the 29th, at six o'clock, Mr. Washington Nathan descended from his chamber to call his father to a devotional duty of the day. Entering the chamber of the latter, a most appalling spectacle met his view. His father was lying on the floor in a pool of his own blood, dead, with five ghastly wounds upon his head. The young man at once summoned his brother Frederick, and the two together rushed to the street door and gave the alarm. The police were soon on the spot, and, taking possession of the house, they prepared to investigate the horrid affair. The newspapers spread the intelligence over the city, and the murder created the profoundest interest and uneasiness on the part of the citizens. All classes felt an interest in it, for it had been committed within the sacred precincts of the dead man's home, where he believed himself to be safe. If a murderer could reach him there, men asked, who could tell who would not be the next victim. This feeling of insecurity was widespread, and the whole community demanded of the police extraordinary efforts in tracking and securing the assassin.

The Superintendent of Police at that time was Captain John Jourdan, who was acknowledged to be the most accomplished detective on the Continent, and his principal assistant was Captain James Kelso (the present Superintendent), who was regarded as next to Jourdan in ability.   These two officers at once repaired to the Nathan mansion, and took personal charge of the case.

At the first glance Jourdan pronounced the murder to be the work of a thief.   The house was carefully searched.   The room bore evidences of a struggle between the dead man and his assassin, and three diamond studs, a sum of money, a Perregaux watch, No. 5657, and the key of a small safe, had been stolen from the clothing of the dead man which had been hung on a chair placed at some distance from the bed.   The safe stood in the library beside the door opening into the bed room.   Jourdan's theory was that the thief, having stolen the watch and other articles from the clothing, had gone to the safe to open it, and had aroused Mr. Nathan by the noise he made in opening it   Alarmed by this noise, Mr. Nathan had sprung from his bed, and at the same moment the thief had raised himself up from his kneeling posture, with his face toward Mr. Nathan, and lighted up by a small gas jet which was burning in the chamber.   The two men had met in the doorway between the rooms, and the thief, seeing himself identified, had struck Mr. Nathan a blow with a short iron bar curved at the ends, and known as a ship carpenter's " dog."   A struggle ensued, which resulted in the murder, the assassin striking his victim on the head nine times with terrible force.   Then, rifling the safe of its valuable contents, he had gone stealthily down the stairs, had unfastened the front door, which had been carefully secured at half an hour after midnight, and, laying the " dog " down on the hall floor, had passed out into the street.   His object in carrying the " dog " to the place where it was found by the police had been to be prepared to make sure of his escape by striking down any one whom he might chance to meet in the hall. Once in the street, the assassin had disappeared in safety.

Both Jourdan and Kelso were agreed that this theory of the

commission of the crime was correct, and this led to the inevitable conclusion that the murder was the work of an " outsider," that is, of some one not properly belonging to the criminal class. The weapon with which the murder had been committed was one which the Detectives had never before encountered in the annals of crime, and its appearance indicated long use in its legitimate sphere. No burglar or professional thief would have used it, and none of the inmates of the house recognized it as belonging to the mansion. Again, the professional thief would have despatched his victim with more speed and less brutality. There was not the slightest sign of the thief having forced an entrance into the mansion, and the most rigid search failed to reveal the mark of a burglar's tool on any of the doors or windows. This fact warranted the conclusion that the murderer had secreted himself in the house during the day. From the first Jourdan was convinced that the assassin was one of a class who pursue an honest trade during the day, and seek to fill their pockets more rapidly by committing robberies at night. From this conviction he never wavered.

As he stood by the side of the murdered man, Jourdan recognized the difficulty of the task of finding the assassin. The " dog " bewildered him. Had the weapon been any kind of a burglar's tool, or anything that any description of thief had ever been known to use, he would have been able to trace it to some one in the city; but the facts of the case plainly indicated that the assassin was an " outsider," and even Jourdan and Kelso were at a loss to know how to proceed to find him.

At the time of the murder, the only inmates of the house were Washington and Frederick Nathan, sons of the dead man, and Mrs. Kelly, the housekeeper, and her grown son, William Kelly. Had the murder been committed by any of these they must of necessity have stolen the missing articles, and as they had not left the house, must have destroyed or concealed them on the premises. Without the knowledge of these persons, Jourdan caused a rigid and thorough search of the house and lot to be made from cellar to garret. Every crack and crevice, every nook and corner was rigidly and minutely searched by

experienced persons.   Even the furniture and carpets were examined, the flooring of the stable was taken up, the water-
tank was emptied, the basins, closets, and waste-pipes of the
house were flushed, and the street-sewers were examined for a
long distance from the house, but no trace of the missing articles
could be found ; nor could any mark of the " dog" be discovered anywhere save on the body of the victim.   One by one, the
inmates of the house were subjected to the most searching cross-
examination, and within six hours after the discovery of the
deed, Captain Jourdan was satisfied that the inmates of the
mansion were entirely innocent of the crime.   The evidence
drawn out by the inquest subsequently confirmed the innocence
of these parties.

The only clew left by the assassin was the " dog."   At the
inquest, the policeman on the beat swore that when he passed
the house on his rounds at half-past four A. M., he tried both
front doors, and that they were fastened, and that when he passed
again a little before six o'clock, he noticed that the hall-door
was closed.   Another witness testified that about five o'clock, a
man in a laborer's dress, carrying a dinner-pail, ascended the
steps of the Nathan mansion, picked up a paper from the top-
most step, and passed on down the street.   The introduction of
this man in the laborer's dress but deepened the mystery and
increased the labors of the Detectives.

The entire police force of the city was set to work watching
the pawn-shops and jewelry stores where the thief might try to
dispose of the stolen property.   Every ship-yard and boat-
yard was searched for the identification of the " dog," but
without success, and almost every mechanical establishment in
the city where the instrument could have been used, was subjected to the same inspection, but without discovering anything.
A list of the missing property, and the marks by which it could
be identified, was given to the public and telegraphed all over
the Union.   Captain Jourdan declared that it was well to have as
many people as possible looking for these articles.   Every known
or suspected criminal in the city was waited on by the police,
and required to give an account of himself on the night of the

murder, and it is said that there was a general exodus of the professional thieves from New York. The ten days immediately succeeding the murder were singularly free from crime, so close was the espionage exercised over the criminals by the police.

It is safe to assert that the police never made such exertions in all their history, to secure a criminal, as in this case. Every sensible suggestion was acted upon, no matter by whom tendered. Neither labor nor expense was spared, and all with the same result. Captain Jourdan literally sank under his extraordinary exertions, his death, which occurred on the 10th of October, 1870, being the result of his severe and exhausting labors in this case. His successor, Superintendent Kelso, has been equally energetic, but thus far—nearly two years after the commission of the deed—no more is known concerning it than was presented to Jourdan and Kelso as they stood in the chamber of death, and nothing has occurred to destroy or shake their original theory respecting the murderer and his mode of committing the deed. The mystery which enshrouded it on that sad July morning still hangs over it unbroken.

II.

PRIVATE DETECTIVES.

THE Detectives, whose ways we have been considering, are sworn officers of the law, and it is their prime duty to secure the arrest and imprisonment of offenders. There is another class of men in the city who are sometimes confounded with the regular force, but who really make it their business to screen criminals from punishment. These men are called Private Detectives. Their task consists in tracing and recovering stolen property, watching suspected persons when hired to do so, and manufacturing such evidence in suits and private cases as they may be employed to furnish.

There are several "Private Detective Agencies" in the city, all of which are conducted on very much the same principles and plan, and for the same purpose—to make money for the proprietors. Mr. Edward Crapsey, to whom I am indebted for much of the information contained in this chapter, thus describes a well-known Agency of this kind :

" The visitor going up the broad stairs, finds himself in a large room, which is plainly the main office of the concern. There is a desk with the authoritative hedge of an iron railing, behind which sits a furrowed man, who looks an animated cork-screw, and who, the inquiring visitor soon discovers, can't speak above a whisper, or at least don't. This mysterious person is always mistaken for the chief of the establishment ; but, in fact, he is nothing but the ' Secretary,' and holds his place by reason of a marvellous capacity for drawing people out of themselves. A mystery, he is surrounded with mysteries. The doors upon his right and left—one of which is occasionally opened just far enough to permit a very diminutive call-boy to be squeezed through—seem to lead to unexplored regions. But stranger than even the clerk, or the undefined but yet perfectly tangible weirdness of the doors is the tinkling of a sepulchral bell, and the responsive tramp of a heavy-heeled boot. And strangest of all is a huge black board whereon are marked the figures from one to twenty, over some of which the word ' Out ' is written; and the visitor notices with ever-increasing wonder that the tinkling of the bell and the heavy-heeled tramp are usually followed by the mysterious secretary's scrawling ' Out ' over another number, being apparently incited thereto by a whisper of the ghostly call-boy who is squeezed through a crack in the door for that purpose. The door which the call-boy abjures is always slightly ajar, and at the aperture there is generally a wolfish eye glaring so steadily and rapaciously into the office as to raise a suspicion that beasts of prey are crouching behind that forbidding door.

" Nor is the resulting alarm entirely groundless, for that is the room where the ferrets of the house who assume the name of Detectives, but are more significantly called ' shadows,' are hidden from the prying eyes of the world. A ' shadow ' here is a mere numeral—No. 1, or something higher—and obeys cabalistic calls conveyed by bells or speaking-tubes, by which devices the stranger patron is convinced of the potency of the Detective Agency which moves in such mysterious ways to perform its wonders. If any doubt were left by all this para- phernalia of marvel, it would be dispelled from the average mind when it came in contact with the chief conjuror, who is seated in the dim seclusion of a retired room, fortified by bell-pulls, speaking-tubes, and an owlish expression in- tended to be considered as the mirror of taciturn wisdom. From his retreat he moves the outside puppets of secretary, shadows, and call-boys, as the requirements of his patrons, who are admitted singly to his presence, may demand. It is he whose hoarse whispers sound sepulchrally through the tubes, who rings the mysterious bell, and by such complex means despatches his 'shadows' upon their errands. It is he who permits the mildewed men in the other ante-room to be known only by numbers, and who guards them so carefully from the general view.

"By these assumptions of mystery the chief awes the patrons of his peculiar calling, of whom there are pretty sure to be several in waiting during the morning hours. These applicants for detective assistance always sit stolidly silent until their sepa- rate summons comes to join the chief, eyeing each other suspi- ciously and surveying their surroundings with unconcealed and fitting awe. One is of bluff and hearty appearance, but his full face is overcast for the moment with an expression half sad, half whimsical; it is plain that a conjunction of untoward circum- stances has raised doubts in his mind of the integrity of a business associate, and he has reluctantly determined to clear or confirm them by means of a 'shadow.' Next to him is a fidgety fur- rowed man, bristling with suspicion in every line of his face, and showing by his air of indifference to his surroundings that he is a frequenter of the place. He is in fact one of the best customers of the establishment, as he is constantly invoking its aid in the petty concerns of his corroded life. Sometimes it is a wife, daughter, sister, niece, or a mere female acquaintance he wishes watched; sometimes it is a business partner or a rival in trade he desires dogged; and he is never so miserable as when the reports of the agency show his suspicions, whatever they may have been, to be groundless.   It is but just, however, to the sagacity of the detectives to remark that he is seldom subjected to such disappointment.   Whatever other foolishness they may commit, these adroit operators never kill the goose that lays their golden eggs.   Beside this animated monument of distrust is a portly gentleman, his bearing in every way suggestive of plethoric pockets.   Paper and pencil in hand, he is nervously figuring.   He makes no secret of his figures because of his absorption, and a glance shows that he is correcting the numbers of bonds and making sure of the amounts they represent.

"It is plain that this last is a victim of a sneak robbery, and, the unerring scent of the chief selecting him as the most profitable customer of the morning, he is the first visitor called to an audience.   Large affairs are quickly despatched, and it is soon arranged how a part of the property can be recovered and justice cheated of its due.   Very soon a handbill will be publicly distributed, offering a reward for the return of the bonds, and it will be signed by the Agency.   The thief will know exactly what that means, and the affair being closed to mutual satisfaction, the thief will be at liberty to repeat the operation, which resulted in reasonable profit and was attended with no risk.

"There is also in the room a sallow, vinegary woman of uncertain years, and it seems so natural that a man should run away from her, we are not surprised that, being voluble in her grief, she declares her business to be the discovery of an absconding husband.   But near her is another and truer type of outraged womanhood, a wasted young wife, beautiful as ruins are beautiful, whom a rascal spendthrift has made a martyr to his selfishness until, patience and hope being exhausted, she is driven to the last extremity, and seeks by a means at which her nature revolts for a proof of but one of those numerous violations of the marriage vow which she feels certain he has committed.   It is a cruel resort, but the law which permits a man to outrage a woman in almost every other way frowns upon that one, and she is driven to it as the sole method of release from an intolerable and degrading bondage. In such cases as this might perhaps be found some justification for the existence of private detectives; but they themselves do not appear to know that they stand in need of extenuation, and so neglect the oportunity thus presented to vindicate their necessity by conducting this class of their business with, even for them, remarkable lack of conscience. Anxious always to furnish exactly what is desired, their reports are often lies, manufactured to suit the occasion, and once furnished they are stoutly adhered to, even to the last extremity. Frequently the same Agency is ready to and does serve both parties to a case with impartial wickedness, and earns its wages by giving to both precisely the sort of evidence each requires. Sometimes it is made to order, with no other foundation than previous experience in like affairs; but sometimes it has a more solid basis in fact. Two men from the same office are often detailed to 'shadow,' one the husband and the other the wife, and it occasionally happens that they have mastered the spirit of their calling so thoroughly that they do a little business on private account by 'giving away' each other. That is to say, the husband's man informs the wife she is watched, and gives her a minute description of her 'shadow,' for which information he of course gets an adequate reward, which the wife's man likewise earns and receives by doing the same kindly office for the husband. In such cases there are generally mutual recriminations between the watched, which end in a discovery of the double dealing of the Agency, and not unfrequently in a reconciliation of the estranged couple. But this rare result, which is not intended by the directing power, is the sole good purpose these agencies were ever known to serve. Lord Mansfield, it must be admitted, once seemed to justify the use of private detectives in divorce suits, but he was careful to cumber the faint praise with which he damned them by making honesty in the discharge of these delicate duties a first essential. Had he lived to see the iniquitous perfection the business has now attained, he would undoubtedly have withheld even that quasi-endorsement of a system naturally at war with the fundamental principles of justice.

" The waiters in the reception-room are never allowed to state their wants, or certainly not to leave the place, without being astonished by the charges made by the detective for attention to their business. Whatever differences there may be in minor matters, all these establishments are invariably true to the great purpose of their existence, and prepare the way for an exorbitant bill by a doleful explanation of the expenses and risks to be incurred in the special affair presented, dilating especially upon the rarity and cost of competent ' shadows.' Now the principal agencies estimate for them at $10 a day, whereas these disreputable fellows are found in multitudes, and are rarely paid more than $3 a day as wages; their expenses, paid in advance by the patron, are allowed them when assigned to duties, as they frequently are, involving outlay. The general truth is that these agencies, being conducted for the avowed purpose of making money, get as much as possible for doing work, and pay as little as possible for having it done. In their general business of espionage they may make perhaps only a moderate profit on each affair they take in hand; but in the more delicate branches of compounding felonies and manufacturing witnesses fancy prices obtain, and the profits are not computable. It is plain, knowing of these patrons and prices, that reasonable profit attends upon the practice of the convenient science of getting without giving, which, notwithstanding its prosperity and antiquity, is yet an infant in the perfection it has attained. Awkward, flimsy, transparent as they ever were, are yet the tricks and devices of the knaves who never want for a dollar, never earn an honest one, but never render themselves amenable to any statute ' in such case made and provided.' To say that the master-workmen in roguery who do this sort of thing are awkward and transparent seems to involve a paradox; but whoever so believes has not been fully informed as to the amazing gullibility of mankind. The average man of business now, as always before, seems to live only to be swindled by the same specious artifices that gulled his ancestors, and which will answer to pluck him again almost before the smart of his first depletion has ceased. Only by a thorough knowledge of this singular adaptation of the masses to

24

the purposes of the birds of prey, can we intelligently account for the vast bevies of the latter which exist, and are outwardly so sleek as to give evidence of a prosperous condition. When we know that the ' pocket-book dropper' yet decoys the money even of the city-bred by his stale device ; that the 'gift-enterprises,' 'envelope-game,' and similar thread-bare tricks yet serve to attain the ends of the sharpers, although the public has been warned scores and scores of times through the public press, and the swindlers thoroughly exposed, so that the veriest fool can understand the deception, we need not be amazed at the success which attends the practice of these arts. The truth is, that a large proportion of the victims are perfectly aware that fleecing is intended when they flutter round the bait of the rogues ; but they are allured by the glitter of sudden fortune which it offers, and bite eagerly with the hope that may be supposed to sustain any gudgeon of moderate experience of snapping the bait and escaping the barbed hook. Human greed is the reliance of the general sharper, and it has served him to excellent purpose for many years. But some of these operators must depend on actuating motives far different from the desire of gain in money ; and chief among them are these private detectives, who draw their sustenance from meaner and equally unfailing fountains.

"It is not upon record who bestowed a name which is more apt than designations usually are. The word detective, taken by itself, implies one who must descend to questionable shifts to attain justifiable ends ; but with the prefix of private, it means one using a machine permitted to the exigencies of justice for the purpose of surreptitious personal gain. Thus used, this agency, which even in honest hands and for lawful ends is one of doubtful propriety, becomes essentially dangerous and demoralizing. Originally an individual enterprise, the last resort of plausible rascals driven to desperation to evade honest labor, it has come to be one of associated effort, employing much capital in its establishment and some capacity in its direction. All the large commercial cities are now liberally provided with 'Detective Agencies,' as they are called, each thoroughly organized, and some of them employing a large number of 'shadows' to do the

business, which in large part they must first create before it can
be done.   The system being perfected and worked to its utmost
capacity, the details of the tasks assumed and the method of accomplishment are astonishing and alarming to the reflecting
citizen, who has the good name and well-being of the community at heart.   Employed in the mercantile world as supposed
guards against loss by unfaithful associates or employés, and in
social life as searchers for domestic laxness, these two items make
up the bulk of the business which the private detectives profess
to do, and through these their pernicious influence is felt in all
the relations of life.   Were they however only the instruments
of rapacious and unreasoning distrust, they might be suffered to
pass without rebuke as evils affecting only those who choose to
meddle with them; but as they go further, and the community
fares worse because they are ever ready to turn a dishonest penny
by recovering stolen property, which they can only do by compounding the crime by which it had been acquired, it is evident
that they are a peril to society in general no less than a pest to
particular classes."

XXII.

WILLIAM B. ASTOR.

MR. WILLIAM B. ASTOR would be unknown to fame were it not for two things. First, he is " the son of his father," the famous John Jacob Astor. Second, he is the richest citizen of the United States. In other respects, he is a plain, unpretending man, who attends closely to his own business, and cares nothing for notoriety.

Mr. Astor is the second son of John Jacob Astor, and is about seventy-three years old. He was born in New York, in an old-fashioned brick house which stood on the southern corner of Broadway and Vesey street, a site at present covered by the Astor House. He received a careful education, and upon leaving college was sent by his father to travel through Europe. Upon his return he went into business with his father, and it is said was even more thrifty and energetic in the management of their affairs than the old gentleman himself. The severe affliction of his elder brother made him the principal heir of his father's vast estate, but he lost no opportunity of bettering his own condition, and at the death of the elder Astor, he was worth about $6,000,000 of his own. About $500,000 of this he had inherited from his uncle Henry Astor, a wealthy butcher of New York. His father left him the bulk of his fortune, which made him the richest man in America, and since then he has devoted himself with great success to increasing the amount of his possessions. His wealth is variously estimated at from $60,000,000, to $100,000,000. No one but the fortunate possessor can tell the exact amount. The greater part of this is invested in real estate, much of which is very profitable. A large part, however, is unimproved, and brings in no immediate return. Mr. Astor, however, can afford to wait, and as there is no better judge of the prospective value of real estate in New York, he rarely makes a mistake in his purchases. He invests cautiously, allows others to improve the neighborhoods in which his property lies, and reaps the benefit of their labors.

In person Mr. Astor is tall and heavily built, with a decided German look, a dull, unintellectual face, and a cold, reserved manner. He is unlike his father in many of his personal traits. He lives very simply. His residence is a plain, but substantial-looking brick mansion in Lafayette Place, adjoining the Astor Library. He is not very sociable, but the entertainments given at his house are said to be among the pleasantest and most elaborate to be met with in the city. Those who know the family, however, give the credit of this to Mrs. Astor, an amiable and accomplished lady, and one eminent for her good deeds.

Mr. Astor attends to his own business. His office is in Prince street, just out of Broadway. It is a plain one-story building, very different from the offices of most of the rich men of the metropolis. At ten o'clock Mr. Astor makes his appearance here. It is no slight task to manage so vast an estate, and to direct all its affairs so that they shall be continually increasing the capital of the owner. There is scarcely a laborer in the city who works harder than the master of this office. He transacts all business connected with his estate, and is as cold and curt in his manner as can well be imagined. He wastes neither words nor time, and few persons find him an agreeable man to deal with. He is perfectly informed respecting every detail of his vast business, and it is impossible to deceive him. No tenant can make the slightest improvement, change, or repair in his property without Mr. Astor's consent, except at his own expense. He is accessible to all who have business with him, but he sees no one else during his working hours. At four o'clock he leaves his office, and sets out for home on foot. He rarely rides, this walk being his principal exercise. He is hale and hearty in constitution, looks much younger than he really is, and will doubtless live to be fully as old as his father was at the time of his death.

Mr. Astor is not regarded as a liberal man by his fellow-citizens, but this reputation is not altogether deserved. His friends say that he gives liberally when he gives at all. They add that he has a horror of subscription lists and solicitors of donations, and that he turns a deaf ear to common beggars. He makes it a rule never to give anything during business hours. If a case interests him, he investigates it thoroughly, and if it is found worthy of aid, he gives generously, but quietly. The truth is, that like all rich men, he is beset by a host of beggars of every class and description. Were he to grant every appeal addressed to him, his vast fortune would melt away in a few years. He must discriminate, and he has his own way of doing it.

Mr. Astor married a daughter of General Armstrong, the Secretary of War in Mr. Madison's cabinet. He has two sons, who are themselves fathers of families. They are John Jacob and William B. Astor, Jr. He has also several daughters, all married. The sons reside on Fifth avenue. They are in active business for themselves. John Jacob, the elder, is a large-framed, heavy-boned man, and resembles his father. William B. Astor, Jr., is a small, slim man, and resembles his mother. They are much more sociable than their father, inheriting much of the genial vivacity of their grandfather, who was very fond of the pleasures of society. They are shrewd, energetic business men, and it is said are very wealthy, independent of their father. Mr. John Jacob Astor entered the United States Army during the civil war, and saw considerable active service on the staff of General McClellan.

XXIII.

FASHIONABLE SHOPPING.

THE fashionable retail stores of New York lie chiefly along Broadway, between the St. Nicholas Hotel and Thirty-fourth street. A few are to be found in the cross streets leading from the great thoroughfare, and some are in the Sixth avenue, but Broadway almost monopolizes the fashionable retail trade of the city. All the large stores are conducted on the same general plan, the main object of which is to secure the greatest convenience and comfort for the purchaser, and the greatest dispatch and promptness on the part of the employés. The leading stores of the city have an established reputation with the citizens. They furnish a better class of goods than can be found elsewhere, and are the most reasonable in their prices. Furthermore, the purchaser may rely upon the assurances of the salesman concerning the goods. The salesmen in such houses are not allowed to represent anything as better than it really is. This certainty is worth a great deal to the purchaser, who is often incapable of judging intelligently of his purchase. The writer can assert, from actual experience, that for the same amount of money one can buy at the first-class stores a better article than is offered in the so-called "cheap stores."

Upon entering a first-class dry-goods store in New York, a stranger is impressed with the order and system which prevail throughout the whole establishment. The heavy plate glass door is opened for him by a small boy in entering and departing. If the weather be stormy and the visitor has a wet umbrella, he may leave it in charge of the aforesaid boy, who gives him a check for it. He can reclaim it at any time by presenting this check. As he enters he is met at the door by a well-

A FEMALE SHOPLIFTER.

376

dressed gentleman of easy address, who politely inquires what he wishes to purchase. Upon stating his business, he is promptly shown to the department in which the desired articles are kept, and the eye of the conductor is never removed from him until he has attracted the attention of the clerk from whom he makes his purchase. All this is done, however, without allowing him to see that he is watched. This espionage is necessary to guard against robbery. The city merchants are greatly annoyed, and are often subjected to heavy loss, by professional shoplifters, who throng their stores. The shoplifters do not constitute the only thieves, however. Women of respectable position, led on by their mad passion for dress, have been detected in taking small but costly articles, such as laces, handkerchiefs, etc., from some of the principal houses. Such matters have usually been "hushed up" through the influence of the friends of the offender. The opportunities for theft are very great in the city stores. Hundreds of small articles, many of them of considerable value, lie within easy reach of the customers, and all the employés are obliged to exert the greatest watchfulness. Private detectives are employed by the principal houses, and as soon as a professional shoplifter enters, he or she is warned off the premises by the detective, whose experience enables him to recognize such persons at a glance. A refusal to profit by this warning is followed by a summary arrest.

The salesmen are not allowed to receive the pay for their sales. They take the purchaser's money, make a memorandum in duplicate of the sale, and hand both the papers and the money to a small boy who takes it to the cashier. If any change is due the purchaser, the boy brings it back. The articles are also remeasured by the clerks who do them up in parcels, to see if the quantity is correct. The purchase is then delivered to the buyer, or sent to his residence. Thus the house is furnished with a check on all dishonest salesmen, and at the same time acquires accurate knowledge of their labors in their respective departments.

The small boys referred to are called "cash boys," and are now a necessity in a well regulated establishment. Good, steady cash boys are almost always in demand. Intelligence commands a premium in this department, and a bright, well recommended lad will generally be taken on trial. He starts out with a salary of $3 per week. If he shows capacity, he is promoted as rapidly as possible. The highest salary paid to a cash boy is $8 per week, but one who earns this amount does not stay long in this position. He is soon made a salesman, and may then go as high in the house as his abilities will carry him. These boys generally have a bright and lively appearance. Besides acting as cash boys, they are sometimes sent on errands, they attend the doors, and do sundry other useful acts. They are strictly watched, and any improper conduct is punished with an instantaneous dismissal. They generally belong to respectable families, and live at home with their parents. Many of them attend the night schools after business hours, and thus prepare for the great life struggle which is before them. Such boys are apt to do well in the world. Many, however, after being released from the stores, imitate the ways of the clerks and salesmen. They affect a fastness which is painful to see in boys so young. They sport an abundance of flashy jewelry, patronize the cheap places of amusement, and are seen in the low concert saloons, and other vile dens of the city. It is not difficult to predict the future of these boys.

The principal retail dry goods stores of New York are those of A. T. Stewart & Co., Lord & Taylor, Arnold, Constable & Co., and James McCreery & Co.

The house of A. T. Stewart & Co. is the best known to persons visiting the city. Indeed there are very few Americans who have not heard of and longed to visit "Stewart's." It is, besides, the largest and most complete establishment of its kind in the world. It occupies the entire block bounded by Broadway, Fourth avenue, Ninth and Tenth streets. The principal front is on Broadway, and the public entrances are on that street and on the Fourth avenue. The Ninth street entrances are reserved exclusively for the employés of the house. Many persons speak of the edifice as a "marble palace," but this is incorrect. It is constructed of iron, in the style of arcade upon arcade, and its fronts are so thickly studded with windows that they may be said to consist almost entirely of glass. It is five stories in height above the street, and above the fifth story there is an interior attic not visible from the sidewalk. Below the street there is a basement and a sub-cellar, so that the monster building is really eight stories in height. There is no attempt at outward display, the fine effect of the edifice being due to its vast size and its symmetry. The interior is as simple. The floors are uncarpeted, the shelves are plain, as are the counters and the customers' seats. The centre of the building is occupied by a large rotunda extending from the ground floor to the roof. All the upper floors are open around this rotunda. Two flights of massive stairs lead to the upper floors, and there are three handsome elevators for the use of customers who do not care to make the journey on foot. Three other elevators on the Ninth street side are used for carrying goods. Each of the floors covers an area of about two acres, so that the whole establishment, including the cellar, occupies sixteen acres of space.

The cellar contains coal bins with a capacity of 500 tons. Close by are eight Harrison boilers of fifty horse power each, used for operating the steam engines and warming the building with steam. There are in all ten steam engines located in this immense cellar. These are used for running the elevators, for working seven steam pumps, for feeding the boilers, and for forcing water up to the top floor, which is used as a laundry. In a certain part of the cellar is located the electrical battery, by means of which the gas jets in the building are lighted. Here are also rooms for the storage of goods.

The basement is occupied by the Carpet-making and Parcel departments. It is the largest room in the world, and is unbroken save by the light pillars which support the floors above. The Carpet-making department is interesting. The house deals largely in carpets, and one is surprised at the smallness of the force employed down here. The carpets purchased are cut, and the pieces matched as they lie on the floor by women. Then they are placed on a wide table, forty feet long, and are sewn together by a machine worked by steam. This machime moves along the edge of the table, and the man operating it rides on it. His only care is to hold the parts to be sewn perfectly even, and the machine sews a seam of forty feet in from three to five minutes.

In the centre of the basement floor is a space about thirty feet square, enclosed by counters. This is the Parcel department. All purchases to be sent to the buyer pass through this department, and these make up about ninety per cent. of the day's business. The purchases are sent here by the salesmen with a ticket affixed to each, stating the quantity and quality of the article bought, the amount paid, and the address of the buyer. The goods are then remeasured, and if an error has been made either in favor of or against the house, it is rectified. The goods are then made up in secure parcels, each of which is plainly marked with the address of the purchaser. These parcels are then turned over to the drivers of the wagons used by the house for delivering purchases. The drivers are furnished with bills for the amounts to be collected on the parcels, and they are held to a rigid accountability for the delivery of every parcel entrusted to them, and the collection of all moneys due on them.

The ground floor is the principal salesroom. It is a simple, but elegant apartment, and its chief ornaments are the goods for sale, which are displayed in the most attractive and tasteful manner. The room is 300 by 200 feet in size. It contains 100 counters, with an aggregate length of 5000 feet. Behind these counters are low shelves on which the goods are kept. In the centre is the immense rotunda, and at various points are the little wooden pens enclosed with lattice work used by the cashiers. Each article for sale has its separate department, and there are thirty ushers on duty to direct purchasers where to find the articles they seek. The display of goods is magnificent, and includes everything used for the clothing of ladies and children, either in the piece or ready made. There is also a department in which ladies and children may have all their clothing of every description made to order.

The second floor is used for the sale of ready-made clothing, suits, upholstery, etc., and the third floor is the carpet sales-room.   The other floors are closed to visitors, and are used as workshops, laundries, etc.

The convenience of having all these things, and in such great variety, under one roof is very great, and saves purchasers many a weary walk through the city.   The immense capital employed by Mr. Stewart, and his great facilities of all kinds, enable him to control the markets in which he makes his purchases and to buy on terms which render it easy for him to undersell all his competitors.   The smaller houses complain bitterly of this, and declare that he is ruining them.   In spite of its immense trade, " Stewart's " is not the most popular place in the city with resident purchasers.   The salesmen have the reputation of being rude and often insolent.   There can be no doubt that, were specific complaints made, Mr. Stewart would administer the necessary punishment to the offender without delay ; but as the offences complained of are chiefly a lack of civility, few care to complain.

The throng of visitors and purchasers is immense.   They have been known to reach the enormous number of 50,000 in a single day ; but the average is 15,000.   Looking down from one of the upper floors, through the rotunda, one can witness as busy and interesting a scene as New York affords.   All kinds of people come here, from the poor woman whose scanty garb tells too plainly the story of her poverty, to the wife of the millionaire whose purchases amount to a small fortune, and all classes can be suited.

The sales of the house average about $60,000 per day, and have been known to reach $87,000.   The bulk of the purchases is made between noon and five o'clock.   The average daily sales of the principal articles are as follows : Silks $15,000; dress goods, $6000 ; muslins, $3000 ; laces, $2000 ; shawls, $2500 ; suits, $1000 ; calicoes, $1500 ; velvets, $2000 ; gloves, $1000 ; furs, $1000 ; hosiery, $600 ; boys' clothing, $700 ; Yankee notions, $600 ; embroideries, $1000 ; carpets, $5500.

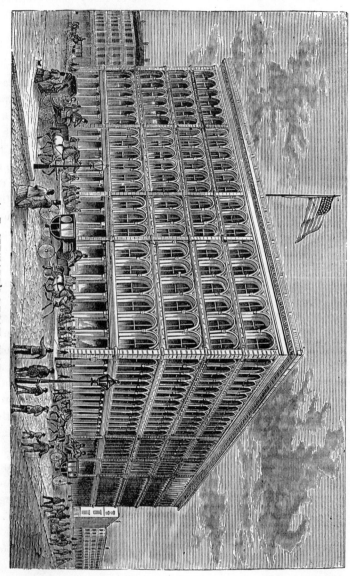

A. T. STEWART'S RETAIL STORE.

As may be supposed, the business of this great house requires an army of employés. The force consists of 1 general superintendent, 19 superintendents of departments, 9 cashiers, 25 book-keepers, 30 ushers, 55 porters, 200 cash boys, 900 seamstresses, working-women, laundresses, etc., 320 salesmen and saleswomen, and 150 salesmen and others in the carpet department, making a total of 1709 persons. There are other persons employed about the establishment in various capacities, and these, with the extra help often employed, make the aggregate frequently as much as 2200 persons. The business of the house opens at seven A. M., and closes at seven P. M. All the employés have thirty minutes allowed them for dinner. One half of all are alternately dismissed at six o'clock each evening. All the employés, when leaving, must pass through a private door on Ninth street. On each side of this door is a detective of great experience, whose business it is to see that none of the employés carry away with them any of the property of the house. The discipline of the establishment is very rigid, and is enforced by a system of fines and other penalties.

The general management of the house is entrusted to Mr. Tellur, the General Superintendent, but Mr. Stewart gives it his personal supervision as well. He comes to the store every morning at ten o'clock precisely, and consults with Mr. Tellur about the business of the previous day, and the wants of that just opening. He goes through the entire establishment, and personally acquaints himself with the exact condition of the business. He knows everything connected with the retail store, and every detail of its management receives his constant supervision, and is conducted in accordance with his instructions. He remains here about an hour and a half in the morning, and returns at five o'clock in the afternoon, and spends half an hour more. The rest of his working day is passed at his lower store.

Lord & Taylor rank next to Stewart, and are a more popular firm with residents than the latter. They occupy a magnificent iron building at the corner of Broadway and Twentieth street. It is one of the finest and most picturesque edifices in the city, and is filled with a stock of goods equal in costliness and supe-

LORD AND TAYLOR'S DRY GOODS STORE.

rior in taste to anything that can be bought at Stewart's. On "opening days," or days when the merchants set out their finest goods for the inspection of the public, Lord & Taylor generally carry off the palm for the handsomest and most tasteful display. The show windows of this house are among the sights of Broadway.

Two blocks below, on the same side of Broadway, is a row of magnificent white marble stores. The upper end, comprising about one-third of the entire block, is occupied by Messrs. Arnold, Constable & Co., a popular and wealthy house. They are noted for the taste and general excellence of their goods.

James McCreery & Co., at the corner of Broadway and Eleventh street, occupy a part of the ground floor of the magnificent edifice of the Methodist Book Concern. They do not make as extensive a display as their competitors, but are well known in the city for their rich and elegant goods. The ball and wedding dresses imported and made by this house are among the richest ever seen in New York.

25

XXIV.

BLEECKER STREET.

PERHAPS very few people out of the great city know Bleecker Street at all; perhaps they have passed it a dozen times or more without noticing it, or if they have marked it at all have regarded it only as a passably good-looking street going to decay. But he who does not know Bleecker street does not know New York. It is of all the localities of the metropolis one of the best worth studying.

It was once the abode of wealth and fashion, as its fine old time mansions testify. Then Broadway north of it was the very centre of the aristocracy of the island, and Bond street was a primitive Fifth avenue. Going west from the Bowery, nearly to Sixth avenue, you will find rows of stately mansions on either hand, which speak eloquently of greatness gone, and as eloquently of hard times present. They have a strange aspect too, and one may read their story at a glance. Twenty-five years ago they were homes of wealth and refinement. The most sumptuous hospitality was dispensed here, and the stately drawing rooms often welcomed brilliant assemblages. Now a profusion of signs announce that hospitality is to be had at a stated price, and the old mansions are put to the viler uses of third-rate boarding houses and restaurants.

In many respects Bleecker street is more characteristic of Paris than of New York. It reminds one strongly of the Latin Quarter, and one instinctively turns to look for the *Closerie des Lilas*. It is the headquarters of Bohemianism, and Mrs. Grundy now shivers with holy horror when she thinks it was once her home. The street has not entirely lost its reputation. No one is prepared to say it is a vile neighborhood; no one would care to class it with Houston, Mercer, Greene, or Water streets; but people shake their heads, look mysterious, and sigh ominously when you ask them about it. It is a suspicious neighborhood, to say the least, and he who frequents it must be prepared for the gossip and surmises of his friends. No one but its denizens, whose discretion can be absolutely trusted, knows anything with certainty about its doings or mode of life, but every one has his own opinion. Walk down it at almost any hour of the day or night, and you will see many things that are new to you. Strange characters meet you at every step; even the shops have a Bohemian aspect, for trade is nowhere so much the victim of chance as here. You see no breach of the public peace, no indecorous act offends you; but the people you meet have a certain air of independence, of scorn, of conventionality, a certain carelessness which mark them as very different from the throng you have just left on Broadway. They puzzle you, and set you to conjecturing who they are and what they are, and you find yourself weaving a romance about nearly every man or woman you meet.

That long-haired, queerly dressed young man, with a parcel under his arm, who passed you just then, is an artist, and his home is in the attic of that tall house from which you saw him pass out. It is a cheerless place, indeed, and hardly the home for a devotee of the Muse; but the artist is a philosopher, and he flatters himself that if the world has not given him a share of its good things, it has at least freed him from its restraints, and so long as he has the necessaries of life and a lot of jolly good fellows to smoke and drink and chat with him in that lofty dwelling place of his, he is content to take life as he finds it.

If you look up to the second floor, you may see a pretty, but not over fresh looking young woman, gazing down into the street. She meets your glance with composure, and with an expression which is a half invitation to "come up." She is used to looking at men, and to having them look at her, and she is not averse to their admiration. Her dress is a little flashy, and the traces of rouge are rather too strong on her face, but it is not a bad face. You may see her to-night at the —— Theatre, where she is the favorite. Not much of an actress, really, but very clever at winning over the dramatic critics of the great dailies who are but men, and not proof against feminine arts. This is her home, and an honest home, too. To be sure it would be better had she a mother or a brother, or husband— some recognized protector, who could save her from the "misfortune of living alone;" but this is Bleecker street, and she may live here according to her own fancy, "and no questions asked."

On the floor above her dwells Betty Mulligan, a pretty little butterfly well known to the lovers of the ballet as Mademoiselle Alexandrine. No one pretends to know her history. She pays her room rent, has hosts of friends, but beyond this no one knows anything. Surmises there are by the score, and people wonder how mademoiselle can live so well on her little salary ; but no charges are made. People shrug their shoulders, and hint that ballet girls have resources unknown to the uninitiated. The rule here is that every one must look after himself, and it requires such an effort to do this that there is no time left to watch a neighbor's shortcomings.

In the same house is a fine-looking woman, not young, but not old. Her " husband " has taken lodgings here for her, but he comes to see her only at intervals, and he is not counted in the landlady's bill. Business keeps him away, and he comes when he can. Bleecker street never asks madame for her marriage certificate, nor does it seek to know why her numerous friends are all gentlemen, or why they come only when the " husband " is away.

Honest, hard-working men come here with their families. Their earnings are regular, but small, and they prefer the life of this street to the misery of the tenement house. Others there are who live in the street, and occupy whole dwellings with their familes, who stay here from force of habit. They are " slow " people, dull of comprehension, and to them the mysteries of their neighborhood are a sealed book. Yet all are regarded as persons whose characters are " not proven," by the dwellers outside the street.

Money is a power in Bleecker street. It will purchase any-thing. Much is spent by those who do not dwell here, but come here to hide their secrets. Women come here to meet other men besides their husbands, and men bring women here who are not their wives. Bleecker street asks no questions, but it has come to suspect the men and women who are seen in it.

Indeed, so long as its tenants do not violate the written law of the land to an extent sufficient to warrant the interference of the police, they may do as they please. Thus it has come to pass that the various personages who are a law unto themselves have gradually drifted into Bleecker street, unless they can afford better quarters, and even then the freedom of the locality has for them a fascination hard to be resisted. No one loses caste here for any irregularity. You may dress as you please, live as you please, do as you please in all things, and no comments will be made. There is no " society " here to worry your life with its claims and laws. You are a law unto yourself. Your acts are exclusively your own business. No complaints will be made against you. You are absolutely your own master or mistress here. Life here is based on principles which differ from those which prevail in other parts of the city.

Yet, as I have said, no one dare call the street " bad." Let us say it is " irregular," " free," " above scandal," or " superior to criticism; " but let us not venture to term it " bad," as its neighbors Greene and Mercer are " bad." I cannot say it would be shocked by such a charge, for Bleecker street is never shocked at anything. It would, no doubt, laugh in our faces, and scorn-fully ask for our proofs of its badness, and proofs of this sort are hard to bring to light in this thoroughfare.

XXV.

CEMETERIES.

I.

GREENWOOD.

THE most beautiful cemetery of the city of New York, and the place where its people most long to sleep when "life's fitful fever" is over, is Greenwood. It is situated on Gowanus Heights, within the limits of the City of Brooklyn, and covers an area of 413 acres of land. It is two and a half miles distant from the South Ferry, and three from the Fulton Ferry, with lines of street cars from both ferries. A portion of the grounds is historic, for along the edge of the heights occurred the hardest fighting in the battle of Long Island, in 1776.

The cemetery is beautifully laid out. The heights have been graded at immense expense, and the grounds are provided with carriage roads built of stone, covered with gravel, and with foot-paths of concrete. The carriage drives are seventeen miles, and the foot-paths fifteen miles in extent. The sewerage is perfect, and the greatest care is exercised in keeping the grounds free from dirt and weeds. The cemetery was laid out under the supervision of a corps of accomplished landscape gardeners, and it abounds in the most exquisite scenery. From the higher portions the bay and the cities which border it, with the blue ocean in the distance, may all be seen. Everything that art could do to add to the attractions of a naturally beautiful spot has been done, and the place has come to be, next to the Central and Prospect Parks, one of the favorite resorts of the people of New York and Brooklyn. The entrances are all adorned with magnificent gateways of stone.   The northern gateway is adorned with sculptures representing the burial of the Saviour, and the raising of the widow's son and of Lazarus.   Above these are bas-relief figures, representing Faith, Hope, Memory, and Love.

The cemetery was opened for burials about twenty-seven years ago.   At the close of the year 1870 the interments had reached 150,000.   From fifteen to twenty interments are made here every day.   The deep-toned bell of the great gateway is forever tolling its knell, and some mournful train is forever wending its slow way under the beautiful trees.   Yet the sunlight falls brightly, the birds sing their sweetest over the new-made graves, the wind sighs its dirge through the tall trees, and the " sad sea waves " blend with it all their solemn undertone from afar.

The tombs and monuments to be seen at Greenwood are very beautiful.   Some of them are noted as works of art.   Many of them have cost from $10,000 to $100,000.   About 2000 of these tombs are scattered through the grounds.   In beauty of design and costliness they surpass any similar collection in the New World, but in one respect they are like all others, for they speak nothing but good of the dead.   Indeed, were one to believe their inscriptions, the conclusion would be inevitable that none but saints are buried in Greenwood.   All classes come here, but the cemetery is characteristic of the living city beyond.   Wealth governs everything here as there.

II.

CYPRESS HILLS.

NORTH of the Brooklyn and Jamaica Turnpike, is an elevated ridge known as the " backbone of Long Island," and on this ridge, partly in Kings and partly in Queens counties, about five miles from the Catharine Street Ferry, is the Cemetery of Cypress Hills.   It comprises an area of 400 acres, one-half of which is still covered with the native forest trees.   The other portion is handsomely adorned with shrubbery, and laid off tastefully. The entrance consists of a brick arch, surmounted by a statue of Faith. It rests on two beautiful lodges occupied by the gate-keeper and superintendent of the cemetery.

From the cemetery one may command an extensive view, embracing all the surrounding country, the cities of Brooklyn, New York, Jersey City, and Flushing, the Hudson as far as the Palisades, Long Island Sound, the distant hills of Connecticut, and the Atlantic.

Since the opening of the grounds, in 1848, upwards of 85,000 interments have been made here. Of these 4060 were officers and soldiers of the United States army, who were killed or who died during the Civil War. They are buried in a section set apart for them. The Sons of Temperance, the Odd-Fellows, the Masons, and the Police Forces of New York and Brooklyn have sections of their own here. When the old grave-yards of New York and Brooklyn were broken up, about 35,000 bodies were removed from them to these grounds.

III.

WOODLAWN.

WOODLAWN CEMETERY lies in Westchester County, eight miles north of Harlem Bridge, and along the line of the New York, Harlem and Albany Railway. It is easily reached by means of this road. It was incorporated in 1863, and laid out in 1865. It comprises about 325 acres, and is naturally one of the most beautiful cemeteries used by the city. It is easier of access than Greenwood, there being no ferry to cross, and the Harlem Railway Company having instituted a system of funeral trains which convey funeral corteges to the entrance to the grounds. This, together with its natural beauty, is making it a favorite place of burial with the New Yorkers. The grounds are being rapidly improved, and, it is believed, will eventually rival Greenwood. Since its opening, in 1865, there have been nearly 9000 interments in Woodlawn. Admiral Farragut was buried here in 1871. The main avenue or boulevard from the

Central Park to White Plains will pass through these grounds, and afford a broad and magnificent drive from the city to the cemetery.

IV.

CALVARY, AND THE EVERGREENS.

CALVARY CEMETERY is the property of the Roman Catholic Church, and contains only the graves of those who have died in that faith. It is situated in the town of Newtown, Long Island, about four miles from New York. It comprises about seventy-five acres, and was opened in August, 1848, since which time about 84,000 bodies have been buried in it.

The Cemetery of the Evergreens is situated about three miles and a half to the eastward of Williamsburg. It lies on the western end of a range of hills, and is one of the largest and most picturesque of all the cemeteries of New York. It is being steadily improved, and is growing in favor with the people of the great cities at its feet.

Another burial ground once used by the people of New York, but now abandoned by them, is the New York Bay Cemetery, situated on the shore of the bay in the State of New Jersey, about two and a half miles from the Courtlandt Street Ferry. It comprises about fifty acres of ground, and contains 50,000 graves.

No burials are now permitted on Manhattan Island, except in the Cemetery of Trinity Church, which lies at the intersection of Tenth avenue and One-hundred-and-fifty-fifth street. From Tenth avenue the grounds extend to the river. The new public drive passes through the cemetery, and has greatly injured it. The grounds comprise an area of thirty-six acres, are beautifully laid off, and are shaded by fine trees. Among the persons buried here are Philip Livingston, a signer of the Declaration of Independence, Bishops Wainright and Onderdonk, Madame Jumel, the last wife of Aaron Burr, Audubon, and John Jacob Astor. President Monroe was buried here, but his remains were removed to Richmond, Virginia, in 1859.

XXVI.
THE CLUBS.

WITH respect to the number and attractiveness of its clubs, New York bids fair to rival London. They embrace associations for almost every purpose, and are more or less successful according to their means and the object in view. Those for social enjoyment and intercourse are the most popular, and the best known. They are composed principally of men of fashion and wealth, and occupy some of the most elegant mansions in the city.

The best known are the Century, No. 109 East Fifteenth street; Manhattan, corner of Fifth avenue and Fifteenth street; Union League, corner of Madison avenue and Twenty-sixth street; Union, corner of Twenty-first street and Fifth avenue; Travellers', No. 222 Fifth avenue; Eclectic, corner of Twenty-sixth street and Fifth avenue; City, No. 31 East Seventeenth street; Harmonie, Forty-second street, west of Fifth avenue; Allemania, No. 18 East Sixteenth street; American Jockey Club, corner of Madison avenue and Twenty-seventh street; and New York Yacht Club, club-house on Staten Island.

The location of these clubs is very desirable. They are all in the most fashionable quarter of the city, and their houses are in keeping with their surroundings. They are elegantly furnished, and often contain valuable and beautiful works of art. Some are owned by the associations occupying them; others are rented at prices varying from $8000 to $20,000 per annum. The initiation fees range from $50 to $150, and the annual dues from $50 to $100. The number of members varies from 300 to 800, but in the best organizations the object is to avoid a large membership. Great care is taken in the investigation of the history of applicants for membership, and none but persons of good reputation are admitted. In the most exclusive, one adverse ballot in ten is sufficient to negative an application for membership.

By the payment of the sums named above, members have all the benefits of an elegant private hotel at a moderate cost, and are sure of enjoying the privacy which is so agreeable to cultivated tastes. They have constant opportunities of meeting with friends, and besides have a pleasant lounging place in which to pass their leisure hours.

The Century Club stands at the head of the list. It is considered the most desirable association in the city, and numerous applications for places made vacant in it, are always on file. It occupies a handsome red brick mansion just out of Union Square, on East Fifteenth street. It was organized more than thirty years ago, and was originally a sketch club, and its membership was rigidly confined to literary men and artists. Of late years, however, it has been thrown open to any gentleman who may be accepted by the members. Its President is William Cullen Bryant. Its roll of members includes men of all professions among them : Bayard Taylor, William Allan Butler, George William Curtis, and Parke Goodwin, authors; Rev. Dr. Bellows and Dr. Osgood, clergymen; John Brougham, Lester Wallack, and Edwin Booth, actors; Bierstadt, Gignoux, Cropsey, Church, and Kensett, artists; William H. Appleton, publisher; and A. T. Stewart, John Jacob Astor, and August Belmont, capitalists. This club has no restaurant, and is conducted inexpensively. Its Saturday night gatherings bring together the most talented men in the city, and its receptions are among the events of the season.

The Manhattan Club is a political as well as a social organization. It is the head-quarters of Democrats of the better class. It numbers 600 members, about 100 of these residing out of the city. It includes the leading Democratic politicians of the city and State, and when similar celebrities from other States are in the city they are generally entertained by the club, and have the freedom of the house. The club-house is a splendid brown stone edifice, built originally for a private residence by a man named Parker. It stands on leased ground, and the building only is owned by the club, which paid $110,000 for it. The annual dues are $50. Members are supplied with meals at cost prices. Wines are furnished at similar charges. The restaurant has for its chief cook a Frenchman, who is said to be the most accomplished "artist" in New York. He receives an annual salary of $1800. The house is palatial, but a trifle flashy in its appointments, and a more luxurious resort is not to be found on the island.

The Union League Club is domiciled in a magnificent brick and marble mansion. It is also a political organization, and is not so exclusive as the Manhattan as regards its membership. It is the headquarters of the Republican leaders, and has perhaps the largest membership of any of the city clubs. It possesses a fine restaurant, conducted on club principles, a collection of works of art, a private theatre, and lodging rooms which may be used by the members upon certain conditions.

The Union Club is emphatically a rich man's association. Its members are all men of great wealth, and its windows are always lined with idlers who seem to have nothing to do but to stare ladies passing by out of countenance. The club house is one of the handsomest buildings in the city, and its furniture and decorations are of the most costly description.

The Travellers' Club was originally designed for affording its members an opportunity of meeting with distinguished travellers visiting the city. This object is still kept in view, but the club is becoming more of a social organization than formerly. Travellers of note are invited to partake of its hospitalities upon arriving in the city, and frequently lecture before the club.

Many club members never see the interior of the club houses more than once or twice a year. They pay their dues, and remain on the rolls, but prefer their homes to the clubs. Others again pass a large part of their time in these elegant apartments in the society of congenial friends. Club life is not favorable to a fondness for home, and it is not surprising that the ladies are among the bitterest opponents of the system.

The ladies themselves, however, have their clubs. The most noted of these is the *Sorosis*, the object of which seems to be to bring together the strong-minded of the sex to enjoy a lunch at Delmonico's. Some of the most talented female writers of the country are members of the organization. It was stated in several of the city newspapers, about a year ago, that at one of the meetings of *Sorosis* the members became involved in a fierce dispute over some question concerning the management of the club, and that when the excitement became too intense for words, they relieved their overcharged feelings by "a good cry all around."

It is said that there is another club in the city, made up of females of nominal respectability, married and single, whose meetings have but one object—" to have a good time." It is said that the good time embraces not a little hard drinking, and a still greater amount of scandal-monging, and that many of the "leading ladies" of the club make a habit of getting "gloriously drunk" at these meetings. A faithfully written account of the transactions of this club would no doubt furnish a fine article for the *Day's Doings*.

The Yacht Club consists of a number of wealthy gentlemen who are devoted to salt-water sports. The club house is on Staten Island. The yachts of the members constitute one of the finest fleets of the kind in existence, and their annual regattas, which are held in the lower bay, are sights worth seeing.

XXVII.

THE FIVE POINTS.

I.

LIFE IN THE SHADOW.

JUST back of the City Hall, towards the East River, and within full sight of Broadway, is the terrible and wretched district known as the Five Points. You may stand in the open space at the intersection of Park and Worth streets, the true Five Points, in the midst of a wide sea of sin and suffering, and gaze right into Broadway with its marble palaces of trade, its busy, well-dressed throng, and its roar and bustle so indicative of wealth and prosperity. It is almost within pistol shot, but what a wide gulf lies between the two thoroughfares, a gulf that the wretched, shabby, dirty creatures who go slouching by you may never cross. There everything is bright and cheerful. Here every surrounding is dark and wretched. The streets are narrow and dirty, the dwellings are foul and gloomy, and the very air seems heavy with misery and crime. For many a block the scene is the same. This is the realm of Poverty. Here want and suffering, and vice hold their courts. It is a strange land to you who have known nothing but the upper and better quarters of the great city. It is a very terrible place to those who are forced to dwell in it. For many blocks to the north and south of where we stand in Worth street, and from Elm street back to East River, the Five Points presents a succession of similar scenes of wretchedness.

Yet, bad as it is, it was worse a few years ago. There was not more suffering, it is true, but crime was more frequent here.

A FIVE POINTS RUM SHOP.

A respectably dressed man could not pass through this section twelve years ago without risking his safety or his life. Murders, robberies, and crimes of all kinds were numerous. Fugitives from justice found a sure refuge here, and the officers of the law frequently did not dare to seek them in their hiding places. Now, thanks to the march of trade up the island, the work of the missionaries, and the vigilance of the new police, the Five Points quarter is safe enough during the day. But still, there are some sections of it in which it is not prudent to venture at night. The criminal class no longer herd here, but have scattered themselves over the island, so that the quarter now contains really more suffering than crime.

Twenty years ago there stood in Park street, near Worth, a large dilapidated building known as the "Old Brewery." It was almost in ruins, but it was the most densely populated building in the city. It is said to have contained at one time as many as 1200 people. Its passages were long and dark, and it abounded in rooms of all sizes and descriptions, in many of which were secure hiding places for men and stolen goods. The occupants were chiefly the most desperate characters in New York, and the "Old Brewery" was everywhere recognized as the headquarters of crime in the metropolis. The narrow thoroughfare extending around it was known as "Murderers' Alley" and "The Den of Thieves." No respectable person ever ventured near it, and even the officers of the law avoided it except when their duty compelled them to enter it. It was a terrible place.

Nor was the neighborhood in which this building was located any better. The ground was damp and marshy, the old Collect Pond having originally covered the site, and the streets were filthy beyond description. It is said that there were underground passages extending under the streets from some of the houses to others in different blocks, which were kept secret from all but professional criminals. These were used for facilitating the commission of crimes and the escape of criminals. Brothels and rum shops abounded, and from morning until night brawls were going on in a dozen or more of them at once.

The locality is better now.   In 1852, the Old Brewery was purchased by the *Ladies' Home Missionary Society* of the Methodist Episcopal Church, and was pulled down.   Its site is now occupied by the neat and comfortable buildings of the *Five Points Mission*.   Just across Worth street is the *Five Points House of Industry*, and business is creeping in slowly to change the character of this immediate locality forever.

In speaking of the Five Points, I include the Fourth and Sixth Wards, which are generally regarded as constituting that section—probably because they are the most wretched and criminal of all in the city.   This description will apply with almost equal force to a large part of the First Ward, lying along the North River side of the island.   The Fourth and Sixth Wards are also among the most densely populated, being the smallest wards in extent in the city.

The streets in this section are generally narrow and crooked. The gutters and the roadway are lined with filth, and from the dark, dingy houses comes up the most sickening stench.   Every house is packed to its utmost capacity.   In some are simply the poor, in others are those whose reputations make the policemen careful in entering them.   Some of these buildings are simply dens of thieves.   All the streets are wretched enough, but Baxter street has of late years succeeded to the reputation formerly enjoyed by its neighbor, Park street.   It is a narrow, crooked thoroughfare.   The sidewalk is almost gone in many places, and the street is full of holes.   Some of the buildings are of brick, and are lofty enough for a modern Tower of Babel. Others are one and two story wooden shanties.   All are hideously dirty.   From Canal to Chatham street there is not the slightest sign of cleanliness or comfort.   From Franklin to Chatham street there is scarcely a house without a bucket shop or "distillery," as the signs over the door read, on the ground floor.   Here the vilest and most poisonous compounds are sold as whiskey, gin, rum, and brandy.   Their effects are visible on every hand.   Some of these houses are brothels of the lowest description, and, ah, such terrible faces as look out upon you as you pass them by!   Surely no more hopeless, crime-stained

26

visages are to be seen this side of the home of the damned. The filth that is thrown into the street lies there and decays until the kindly heavens pour down a drenching shower and wash it away. As a natural consequence, the neighborhood is sickly, and sometimes the infection amounts almost to a plague.

Between Fourteenth street and the Battery, half a million of people are crowded into about one-fifth of the island of Manhattan. Within this section there are about 13,000 tenement houses, fully one-half of which are in bad condition, dirty and unhealthy. One small block of the Five Points district is said to contain 382 families. The most wretched tenement houses are to be found in the Five Points. The stairways are ricketty and groan and tremble beneath your tread. The entries are dark and foul. Some of these buildings have secret passages connecting them with others of a similar character. These passages are known only to criminals, and are used by them for their vile purposes. Offenders may safely hide from the police in these wretched abodes. Every room is crowded with people. Sometimes as many as a dozen are packed into a single apartment. Decency and morality soon fade away here. Drunkenness is the general rule. Some of the dwellers here never leave their abodes, but remain in them the year round stupefied with liquor, to procure which their wives, husbands or children will beg or steal. Thousands of children are born here every year, and thousands happily die in the first few months of infancy. Those who survive rarely see the sun until they are able to crawl out into the streets. Both old and young die at a fearful rate. They inhale disease with every breath.

The exact number of vagrant and destitute children to be found in the Five Points is not known. There are thousands, however. Some have placed the estimate as high as 15,000, and some higher. They are chiefly of foreign parentage. They do not attend the public schools, for they are too dirty and ragged. The poor little wretches have no friends but the attachés of the missions. The missionaries do much for them, but they cannot aid all. Indeed, they frequently have great difficulty in inducing the parents of the children to allow them to attend their schools. The parents are mostly of the Roman Catholic faith, and the clergy of that Church have from the first exerted their entire influence to destroy the missions, and put a stop to their work. They feared the effect of these establishments upon the minds of the children, and, strange as it may seem, preferred to let them starve in the street, or come to worse ending, rather than risk the effects of education and Protestant influence. To those who know what a great and blessed work these missions have done, this statement will no doubt be astounding. Yet it is true.

In spite of the missions, however, the lot of the majority of the Five Points children is very sad. Their parents are always poor, and unable to keep them in comfort. Too frequently they are drunken brutes, and then the life of the little one is simply miserable. In the morning the child is thrust out of its terrible home to pick rags, bones, cinders, or anything that can be used or sold, or to beg or steal, for many are carefully trained in dishonesty. They are disgustingly dirty, and all but the missionaries shrink from contact with them. The majority are old looking and ugly, but a few have bright, intelligent faces. From the time they are capable of receiving impressions, they are thrown into constant contact with vice and crime. They grow up to acquire surely and steadily the ways of their elders. The boys recruit the ranks of the pickpockets, thieves, and murderers of the city; the girls become waiters in the concert halls, or street walkers, and thence go down to ruin, greater misery and death.

In winter and summer suffering is the lot of the Five Points. In the summer the heat is intense, and the inmates of the houses pour out into the filthy streets to seek relief from the torture to which they are subjected indoors. In winter they are half frozen with cold. The missionaries and the police tell some dreary stories of this quarter. A writer in a city journal thus describes a visit made in company with the missionary of the Five Points House of Industry to one of these homes of sorrow :

" The next place visited was a perfect hovel. Mr. Shultz, in

passing along a narrow dark hall leading towards the head of
the stairs, knocked at an old door, through which the faintest
ray of light was struggling. 'Come in,' said a voice on the
opposite side of the room. The door being opened, a most
sickening scene appeared. The room was larger than the last
one, and filthier. The thin outside walls were patched with
pieces of pasteboard, the floor was covered with dirt, and what
straggling pieces of furniture they had were lying about as if
they had been shaken up by an earthquake. There was a
miserable fire, and the storm outside howled and rattled away
at the old roof, threatening to carry it off in every succeeding
gust. The tenants were a man, his wife, a boy, and a girl.
They had sold their table to pay their rent, and their wretched
meal of bones and crusts was set on an old packing box which
was drawn close up to the stove. When the visitors entered
the man and woman were standing, leaning over the stove.
The girl, aged about ten years, and a very bright looking child,
having just been off on some errand, had got both feet wet, and
now had her stockings off, holding them close to the coals to dry
them. The boy seemed to be overgrown for his age, and half
idiotic. He sat at one corner of the stove, his back to the
visitors, and his legs stretched out under the hearth. His big
coat collar was turned up around his neck, and his chin sunk
down, so that his face could not be seen. His long, straight
hair covered his ears and the sides of his face. He did not look
up until he was directly questioned by Mr. Shultz, and then he
simply raised his chin far enough to grunt. The girl, when
spoken to, looked up slyly and laughed.

" The man, on being asked if he was unable to work, said he
would be glad to work if he could get anything to do. He was
a painter, and belonged to a painters' protective union. But
there were so many out of employment, that it was useless trying
to get any help. He pointed to an old basket filled with coke,
and said he had just sold their last chair to buy it. He had
worked eighteen years at the Metropolitan Hotel, but got out
of work, and has been out ever since. Mr. Shultz offered to
take the little girl into the House of Industry, and give her

board, clothes, and education.   He asked the father if he would let her go, saying the place was only a few steps from them, and they could see her often.   The man replied that he did not like a separation from his child.   The missionary assured him that it would be no separation, and then asked the mother the same question.   She stood speechless for several moments, as if thinking over the matter, and when the missionary, after using his best arguments, again asked her whether she would allow him to take care of her child, she simply replied, ' No.'   She said they would all hang together as long as they could, and, if necessary, all would starve together.

" This family had evidently seen better times.   The man had an honest face, and talked as if he had once been able to earn a respectable living.   The woman had some features that would be called noble if they were worn in connection with costlier apparel.   The girl was unmistakably smart, and the only thing to mar their appearance as a family, so far as personal looks were concerned, was the thick-lipped, slovenly boy."

II.

THE CELLARS.

IF the people of whom I have written are sufferers, they at least exist upon the surface of the earth.   But what shall we say of those who pass their lives in the cellars of the wretched buildings I have described ?

A few of these cellars are dry, but all are dirty.   Some are occupied as dwelling-places, and some are divided into a sort of store or groggery and living and sleeping rooms.   Others still are kept as lodging-houses, where the poorest of the poor find shelter for the night.

In writing of these cellars, I wish it to be understood that I do not refer to the rooms partly above and partly below the level of the side-walk, with some chance of ventilation, and known to the Health Officers as " basements," but to the cellars pure and simple, all of which are sunk below the level of the street, and all of which are infinitely wretched. There were in April, 1869, about 12,000 of these cellars known to the Board of Health, and containing from 96,000 to 100,000 persons. With the exception of 211, all of these were such as were utterly forbidden, under the health ordinances of the city, to be used or rented as tenements. The Board of Health have frequently considered the advisability of removing this population, and have been prevented only by the magnitude of the task, and the certainty of rendering this large number of persons homeless for a time at least.

The larger portion of these cellars have but one entrance, and that furnishes the only means of ventilation. They have no outlet to the rear, and frequently the filth of the streets comes washing down the walls into the room within. In the brightest day they are dark and gloomy. The air is always foul. The drains of the houses above pass within a few feet of the floor, and as they are generally in bad condition the filth frequently comes oozing up and poisons the air with its foul odors. In some cases there has been found a direct opening from the drain into the cellar, affording a free passage for all the sewer gas into the room. The Board of Health do all they can to remedy this, but the owners and occupants of the cellars are hard to manage, and throw every obstacle in the way of the execution of the health ordinances.

The rents paid for these wretched abodes are exorbitant. Dr. Harris, the Superintendent of the Board of Health, states that as much as twenty dollars per month is often demanded of the occupants by the owners. Half of that sum would secure a clean and decent room in some of the up-town tenements. The poor creatures, in sheer despair, make no effort to better their condition, and live on here in misery, and often in vice, until death comes to their relief.

Many of the cellars are used as lodging-houses. These are known to the police as " Bed Houses." In company with Captain Allaire and Detective Finn, the writer once made a tour of inspection through these establishments. One of them shall serve as a specimen. Descending through a rickety

A FIVE POINTS LODGING CELLAR.

door-way, we passed into a room about sixteen feet square and eight feet high. At one end was a stove in which a fire burned feebly, and close by a small kerosene lamp on a table dimly lighted the room. An old hag, who had lost the greater part of her nose, and whose face was half hidden by the huge frill of the cap she wore, sat rocking herself in a rickety chair by the table. The room was more than half in the shadow, and the air was so dense and foul that I could scarcely breathe. By the dim light I could see that a number of filthy straw mattresses were ranged on the floor along the wall. Above these were wooden bunks, like those of a barracks, filled with dirty beds and screened by curtains. The room was capable of accommodating at least twenty persons, and I was told that the hag in the chair, who was the proprietress, was "a good hand at packing her lodgers well together." It was early, but several of the beds were occupied. The curtains were drawn in some cases, and we could not see the occupants. In one, however, was a child, but little more than a baby, as plump and ruddy, and as fair-skinned and pretty as though it had been the child of a lady of wealth. The little one was sleeping soundly, and, by a common instinct, we gathered about its bed, and watched it in silence.

"It is too pretty a child for such a place," said one of the party.

I glanced at Detective Finn. His face wore a troubled expression.

"A man becomes hardened to the sights I see," he said in answer to my glance, "but I can scarcely keep the tears from my eyes when I see a child like this in such a place ; for, you see, I know what a life it is growing up to."

This wretched place Mr. Finn told us was one of the best of all the bed houses. He proved his assertion by conducting us to one out of which we beat a hasty retreat. The night air never seemed so pure to me as it did as I came out of the vile den into the clear starlight. I could scarcely breathe in the fearful hole we had just been in, and yet it was rapidly filling up with people who were to pass the night there. There were men, wo-

men and children, but they were all huddled together in one
room.   There was no such thing as privacy.   Some of the
lodgers were simply unfortunate, some were vagrants, and others
were criminals.

I do not believe that all the sanitary measures in the world
could ever make these places clean or healthy.   The atmosphere
is always too foul and dense to be breathed by any but lungs
accustomed to it.   When the cellars are crowded with lodgers,
and the heat of the stove adds to the poison, it must be appalling.   The poor wretches who seek shelter here are more than
half stupefied by it, and pass the night in this condition instead
of in a healthful sleep.   They pay from ten to twenty-five cents
for their lodgings, and if they desire a supper or breakfast, are
given a cup of coffee and a piece of bread, or a bowl of soup for
a similar sum.

As a matter of course only vagrants and those who have gone
down into the depths of poverty come here.   They must choose
between the cellars and the streets, and the beds offered them
here are warmer and softer than the stones of the street.

"Have we seen the worst?" I asked Mr. Finn, as we came
out of the last place.

"No," he replied, "there are worse places yet.   But I'll not
take you there."

The reader will readily credit this assertion, after reading the
following account of a visit of the Health Officers to one of a
number of similar cellars in Washington Street, on the west side
of the city :

"The place next visited was No. 27 Washington street.   This
building is also owned by ' Butcher Burke,' and is one of the
most filthy and horrible places in the city.   We passed under an
old tumble-down doorway that seemed to have no earthly excuse
for standing there, and into a dismal, dark entry, with a zig-zag
wall covered with a leprous slime, our conductor crying out all
the time : 'Steady, gentlemen, steady, keep to your left; place
is full of holes.'

"Presently we emerged into a yard with a detestable pavement of broken bricks and mud, with high, towering houses

surmounting it all around, and a number of broken outhouses
and privies covering a large portion of the ground surface of the
yard. Turning around, we could see the back of the tenement
house from whose entry we had just emerged, with its number-
less and wretched windows, shutting out the sky, or the fog,
which was the only thing visible above us, and a cloud of
clothes-lines stretched hither and thither, like a spider's web.

"There were eight privies in the yard, and we entered them.
The night soil was within a *foot and a half* of the seats, and the
odor was terrible. From these privies a drain passed under the
surface of the muddy, sloppy yard, to the margin of the building,
where a descent of perhaps four feet was obtained, at the bottom
of which the basement floor was level with the windows, giving
a sickly light, but no air or ventilation whatever, to the inhabitants of the cellar. But the worst is yet to be told. The drain
from the privies connecting with the sewer in the street had a
man-hole, which was open, at the place where the yard was
broken for a descent into this infernal cellar. This man-hole
was about four feet wide and three feet deep, forming a small
table for a cataract of night soil and other fecal matter, which
poured over this artificial table in a miniature and loathsome
Niagara and into a cesspool at the bottom, and from thence was
conducted under the rotten boards of the cellar through a brick
drain, a few inches below the board flooring, to the main sewer
in the street. The bottom of the windows in this house are on
a dead level with this horrid cesspool, so that a man sitting on a
chair at the window would not have only the odor, but also the
view of this loathsome matter circulating at his feet in the pool
below. We entered the back cellar after knocking at the door
a few minutes, and a man, poverty-stricken and wretched in appearance, of the laboring class, came with a candle to let us in.
The room was in a filthy condition, ten by twenty-two and a
half feet, with a ceiling of six feet three inches elevation from
the floor. A woman, wretched and woe-begone as the man,
rose suddenly from a dirty bed at the back of the room, and
bade us welcome civilly enough, in her night clothing, which
was scanty.

"'And are yees the Boord of Helth, sure. Well it isn't much
we have to show thin, but yees can see it all without any charge
at all, at all.'

"'How much rent do you pay here?' asked the writer of
the man with the candle.

"'Is it rint ye mane? Nyah, its $6 a munth, shure, and
glad to get it, and if we don't pay it, it's the little time we'll get
from Burke, but out on the street wid us, like pigs, and the
divil resave the bit of sattysfaction we'll get from him than ye
would from the Lord Palmershtown, Nyah!'

"'How do you live?'

"'Shure, I put in coal now and thin, whin I can get it to put,
and that's not often, God knows, alanna!

"'How much do you earn?'

"'Is it earn d'ye say? Sometimes fifty cents a day, sometimes
two dollars a week; and thin it's good times wid me.'

"The Woman of the House.—'Don't mind him, man, what
he's saying Shure he niver earns two dollars a week at all.
That id be a good week faix for me. Two dollars indade!'

"'Have you any children?'

"'We have one dauther, a girl—a fine, big girl.'

"'How old is she?'

"'Well, I suppose she's twenty-two next Mikilmas.'

"Woman.—'Indade she's not, shure. She's only a slip of a
gerrul, fifteen or sixteen years of age, goin' on.'

"While the parents were arguing the age of their daughter,
who, it seems, worked as a servant girl in some private residence,
and only slept here when out of employment, the Health Officer
was testing the condition of the walls by poking his umbrella
at the base under the window and directly over the cess-pool.
The point of the umbrella, which was tipped with a thin sheet
of brass, made ready entrance into the walls, which were so soft
and damp that the point of the umbrella when drawn out left
each time a deep circular mark behind, as if it had been drawn
from a rotten or decomposed cheese in summer.

"'Take up a board from the floor,' said the Health Officer.
The man, who informed us that his name was William

McNamara, 'from Innis, in the County Clare, siventeen miles beyand Limerick,' readily complied, and taking an axe dug up a board without much trouble, as the boards were decayed, and right underneath we found the top of the brick drain, in a bad state of repair, the fecal matter oozing up with a rank stench. Every one stooped down to look at this proof of sanitary disregard, and while this entire party were on their knees, looking at the broken drain, two large rats ran across the floor, and nestling in a rather familiar manner between the legs of Mr. McNamara for an instant, frisked out of the dreary, dirty room into the luxurious cesspool.

" The physician asked, ' Are those rats ? ' of Mr. McNamara. " ' Rats is it ? endade they were. It's nothing out of the way here to see thim. Shure some of thim are as big as cats. And why wouldn't they—they have no wurrok or nothing else to do.' "

III.

THE MISSIONS.

THERE are now three thriving and much-needed Missions in the district, to which I have applied the general name of the Five Points. These are the *Five Points Mission*, the *Five Points House of Industry*, and the *Howard Mission, or Home for Little Wanderers*.

The *Five Points Mission* is the oldest. It is conducted by the " Ladies' Home Missionary Society of the Methodist Episcopal Church," and as has been stated, occupies the site of the " Old Brewery." I have already described the " Old Brewery " as it existed twenty years ago. Few decent people ever ventured near it at that time, and even the missionaries felt that they were incurring a risk in venturing into it.

A number of Christian women of position and means, who knew the locality only by reputation, determined, with a courage peculiar to their sex, to break up this den, and make it a stronghold of religion and virtue. Their plan was regarded by the public as chimerical, but they persevered in its execution,

THE LADIES' FIVE POINTS MISSION.

trusting in the help of Him in whose cause they were laboring.
A school was opened in Park street, immediately facing the
"Old Brewery," and was placed in charge of the Rev. L. M.
Pease, of the Methodist Church.   This school at once gathered
in the ragged and dirty children of the neighborhood, and at
first it seemed impossible to do anything with them.   Patience
and energy triumphed at last.   The school became a success, and
the ladies who had projected it resolved to enlarge it.   In 1852
the "Old Brewery" building was purchased and pulled down,
and in June, 1853, the present commodious and handsome Mission building was opened.   Since then constant success has
crowned the efforts of the Ladies' Society.   Their property is
now valued at $100,000.

The Mission is at present in charge of the Rev. James N.
Shaffer.   It receives a small appropriation from the State for
the support of its day-school, but is mainly dependent upon

voluntary contributions for its support. Food, clothing, money, in short, everything that can be useful in the establishment, are given it. Donations come to it from all parts of the country, for the Mission is widely known, and thousands of Christian people give it their assistance. The railroad and express companies forward, without charge, all packages designed for it.

Children are the chief care of the Mission. Those in charge of it believe that first impressions are the strongest and most lasting. They take young children away from the haunts of vice and crime, and clothe and care for them. They are regularly and carefully instructed in the rudiments of an English education, and are trained to serve the Lord. At a proper age they are provided with homes, or with respectable employment, and are placed in a way to become useful Christian men and women. Year after year the work goes on. Children are taken in every day, if there is room for them, and are trained in virtue and intelligence, and every year the "Home," as its inmates love to call it, sends out a band of brave, bright, useful young people into the world. But for its blessed aid they would have been so many more vagrants and criminals.

The school averages about 450 pupils. In the twenty years of the career of the Mission thousands have been educated by it. As I passed through the various class-rooms I found children of all ages. In the infant-class were little ones who were simply kept warm and amused. The amusement was instructive, as well, as they were taught to recognize various objects by the young lady in charge of them. They all bore evidences of the greatest poverty, but they were unquestionably happy and contented.

"Do you find harshness necessary?" I asked of the lady principal, who was my guide.

"No," was the reply. "We rely upon kindness. If they do not wish to stay with us, we let them go away in peace. They are mostly good children," she added, "and they really love the school."

A little curly-headed girl came up to her as she was speaking:

"What does Louisa want, now?" she asked, encouraging the child with a kind smile.

"Please, Mrs. Van Aiken," said the child, "Nelly Jackson wants another cake."

Nelly Jackson was one of the tiniest and plumpest of the infant class I had just inspected, and I had found her with a cake in hand at the time of my visit. Mrs. Van Aiken hesitated a moment, and then gave the desired permission.

"Cakes," she added, turning to me, "constitute one of our rewards of merit for the little ones. When they are very good we give them doll-babies at Christmas."

Says the Secretary in her last Report of the work of the Mission: "These children have quick perceptions and warm hearts, and they are not unworthy of the confidence placed in them by their teachers. All their happy moments come to them through the Mission School, and kind hearts and willing hands occasionally prepare for them a little festival or excursion, enjoyed with a zest unknown to more prosperous children. .... An excursion to Central Park was arranged for them one summer afternoon. The sight of the animals, the run over the soft green grass, so grateful to eye and touch, the sail on the lake, their sweet songs keeping time with the stroke of the oar—all this was a bit of fairy land to a childhood of so few pleasures. Then the evening of the Fourth of July spent on the roof of the Mission House, enjoying the display of fireworks, and singing patriotic songs. One kind friend makes a winter evening marvellous to childish eyes by the varied scenes, historic, scriptural, poetic, of the magic lantern."

If the Mission did no more than give these little ones a warm shelter during the day, and provide for them such pleasures as cakes, doll-babies, excursions, and magic lanterns, it would still be doing a noble work, for these children are dwellers in the Five Points, a locality where pleasure is almost unknown. The Mission does more, however, it educates the children; it provides them with the clothes they wear, and gives each child a lunch at midday. It also gives clothing, bedding and food to the parents of the children where they need it. It is provided with a tasteful chapel, in which religious services are held on Sunday and during the week. The Sunday-school is large, and provides religious instruction for the attendants. A "Free Library and Reading-room" has been opened in the basement, for the use of all who will avail themselves of it. It is open every night, and it is well patronized by the adult population of the vicinity. The homeless and friendless, who are simply unfortunate, are sheltered, as far as the accommodations will permit, and are provided with homes and employment. The work of the Mission, apart from its schools, for the year ending May 1st, 1871, is thus summed up by the Secretary: "The following statistics do not include coal nor medicine, which are very considerable items: 5197 pieces of clothing, including pairs of shoes and bed-quilts, have been distributed from the wardrobes, and 1293 through the office, making a total of 6490; 122,113 rations of food have been given to the needy; 4 infants have been adopted; 66 children have been provided with homes; and 119 adults have been sent to places of employment."

The Treasurer states that during the same period $3004 were given away in "direct charities."

The *Five Points House of Industry* is situated on Worth street, diagonally opposite the *Home Mission*. It consists of two large brick edifices, covering an area about 100 feet square. This Mission was begun by the Rev. L. M. Pease, the same gentleman who was in charge of the *Home Mission* at the time of the purchase of the "Old Brewery." He conceived a different plan for the management of the Home Mission from that determined upon by the ladies, and finding cooperation impossible, resigned his position, and began his labors afresh, according to his own plan, and trusting entirely to the generosity of the public for his support. He was ably assisted by his good wife in carrying out his plan. He began with one room, and in 1853 was able to hire five houses, which he filled with the occupants of the wretched hovels in the vicinity. He procured work for them, such as needle-work, basket-making, baking, straw-work, shoe-making, etc. He made himself personally responsible to the persons giving the work for its safe return. The expenses of the Mission were then, as now, paid from the profits of this work, and the donations of persons interested in the scheme. Five hundred persons were thus supported. Schools were opened, children were taught, clothed and fed, and religious services were regularly conducted.

In 1854, the health of Mr. Pease began to fail under his herculean labors. He had carried his enterprise to a successful issue, however. He had done good to thousands, and had won friends for the institution, who were resolved, and possessed of the means, to carry it on. A Society was incorporated for the conduct of the Mission, and, in 1856, the larger of the present buildings was erected. In 1869, the edifice was increased to its present size. Heavy donations were made to the institution by Mr. Sickles, who gave $20,000, and Mr. Chauncy Rose, who gave $10,000, and it was constantly in receipt of smaller sums, which made up an aggregate sufficient to provide for its wants. Its progress has been onward and upward, and it is a noble monument to the energy and Christian charity of Mr. Pease, its founder.

The main work of the Mission is with the children, but it also looks after the adults of the wretched quarter in which it is located. There are about two hundred children residing in the building. These have been taken from the cellars and garrets of the Five Points. Two hundred more, children of the very poor, are in attendance upon the schools. All are clothed and fed here. Besides being educated, they are taught useful trades. The House is supported partly by voluntary contributions and partly by the labor of its inmates.

Besides the children, there are always about forty destitute women, who would otherwise be homeless, residing in the building. The annual number thus sheltered is about six hundred. They are provided with situations as servants as rapidly as possible. Since its opening, sixteen years ago, the House has sheltered and provided for 20,000 persons. The number of lodgings furnished yearly is about 90,000, and the daily number of meals averages 1000. Since 1856, 4,135,218 meals have

27

been given to the poor. No one is ever turned away hungry, and sometimes as many as 150 persons, men and women, driven to the doors of the House by hunger, may be seen seated at its table at the dinner hour.

The Howard Mission and Home for Little Wanderers is situated in the heart of the Fourth Ward, in one of the most wretched quarters of the city. Here the inhabitants are packed into their dirty dwellings at the rate of 290,000 persons to the square mile. The dirt and the wretchedness of this part of the city are terrible to behold, the sufferings of the people are very great, and the mortality is heavy. Sailors' lodging houses of the lowest character, dance houses, rum shops, and thieves' cribs are numerous, and the moral condition of the Ward is worse than the sanitary.

In May, 1861, the Rev. W. C. Van Meter organized a Mission in the very heart of this locality, to which he gave the name of the *Howard Mission and Home for Little Wanderers.* For three years it was maintained by his individual exertions, but, in 1864, Mr. Van Meter having secured for it wealthy and powerful friends, it was regularly incorporated, and placed under the control of a Board of Managers, Mr. Van Meter still continuing to act as Superintendent. Since then, comfortable and tasteful brick buildings have been erected for the Mission, and it is succeeding now beyond the first hopes of its founder. Our engraving shows the New Bowery front as it will appear when completed.

The Mission is located in the New Bowery, just below its junction with Chatham Square. It extends back to Roosevelt street, upon which thoroughfare there is an entrance. The erection of the buildings on the New Bowery will about double the size of the Mission, and proportionately increase its capacity for doing good. It is entirely dependent upon voluntary contributions for its support.

"Our object," says Mr. Van Meter, "is to do all the good we can to the souls and bodies of all whom we can reach." It may be added, that the prime object of the Mission is to care for neglected and abused children, whether orphans or not, and

THE HOWARD MISSION (AS IT WILL APPEAR WHEN COMPLETED).

also for the children of honest and struggling poverty. It further undertakes to aid and comfort the sick, to furnish food, shelter, and clothing to the destitute, to procure work for the unemployed, and to impart intellectual, moral, and religious instruction to all who are willing to receive it.

"Our field," says Mr. Van Meter, "is the very concentration of all evil and the headquarters of the most desperate and degraded representatives of many nations. It swarms with poor little helpless victims, who are born in sin and shame, nursed in misery, want, and woe, and carefully trained to all manner of degradation, vice, and crime. The *packing* of these poor creatures is incredible. In this ward there are less than two dwelling houses for each low rum hole, gambling house, and den of infamy. Near us, on a small lot, but 150 by 240 feet, are twenty tenant houses, 111 families, 5 stables, a soap and candle factory, and a tan yard. On four blocks, close to the Mission, are 517 children, 318 Roman Catholic and 10 Protestant families, 35 rum holes, and 18 brothels. In No. 14 Baxter street, but three or four blocks from us, are 92 families, consisting of 92 men, 81 women, 54 boys and 53 girls. Of these, 151 are Italians, 92 Irish, 28 Chinese, 3 English, 2 Africans, 2 Jews, 1 German, and but 7 Americans.

"Our work," he says, "is chiefly with the children. These are divided into three classes, consisting of, I. Those placed under our care to be sent to homes and situations. II. Those whom we are not authorized to send to homes, but who need a temporary shelter until their friends can provide for them or surrender them to us. These two classes remain day and night in the Mission. III. Those who have homes or places in which to sleep. These enjoy the benefits of the wardrobe, dining and school rooms, but do not sleep in the Mission.

" Food, fuel and clothing are given to the poor, after a careful inspection of their condition. Mothers leave their small children in the day nursery during the day while they go out to work. The sick are visited, assisted, and comforted. Work is sought for the unemployed. We help the poor to help themselves.

"The children over whom we can get legal control are placed in carefully selected Christian families, chiefly in the country, either for adoption or as members of the families. . . They receive a good common school education, or are trained to some useful business, trade, or profession, and are thus fitted for the great duties of mature life. We know that our work prevents crime; keeps hundreds of children out of the streets, keeps boys out of bar-rooms, gambling houses, and prisons, and girls out of concert saloons, dance houses, and other avenues that lead down to death; and that it makes hundreds of cellar and attic homes more cleanly, more healthy, and more happy, and less wretched, wicked, and hopeless. We never turn a homeless child from our door. From past experience we are warranted in saying that one dollar a week will keep a well filled plate on our table for any little wanderer, and secure to it all the benefits of the Mission. Ten dollars will pay the average cost of placing a child in a good home."

During the ten years of its existence, the Mission has received more than 10,000 children into its day and Sunday schools. Hundreds of these have been provided with good homes. Thousands of poor women have left their little ones here while they were at their daily work, knowing that their babies are cared for with kindness and intelligence. The famous nurseries of Paris exact a fee of four cents, American money, per head for taking care of the children during the day, but at the Little Wanderers' Home, this service is rendered to the mother and child without charge.

Yet in spite of the great work which the Missions are carrying on, the wretchedness, the suffering, the vice and the crime of the Five Points are apalling. All these establishments need all the assistance and encouragement that can possibly be given them. More workers are needed, and more means to sustain them. "The harvest indeed is plenteous, but the laborers are few."

XXVIII.

THE MILITARY.

THE city is very proud of its military organization, and both the Municipal and State Governments contribute liberally to its support. This organization consists of the First Division of the National Guard of the State of New York. The law creating this division was passed in 1862, when the old volunteer system was entirely reorganized. Previous to this, the volunteers had borne their entire expenses, and had controlled their affairs in their own way. By the new law important changes were introduced.

The division consists of four brigades, and numbers about 13,000 men. The regiments comprising it are as follows: First, Second, Third, Fourth, Fifth, Sixth, Seventh, Eighth, Ninth, Eleventh, Twelfth, Twenty-second, Thirty-seventh, Fifty-fifth, Sixty-ninth, Seventy-first, Seventy-ninth, Ninety-sixth, Washington Grays (cavalry), First Cavalry, Second Cavalry, and First Artillery. The United States provides the arms and uniforms when required. These, when furnished by the General Government, are such as are prescribed by law for the Regular Army. The best regiments, however, prefer a handsomer dress, and provide their own uniforms. The city makes an appropriation of $500 per annum for each regiment, for an armory. The other expenses, such as parades, music, etc., are borne by the regiment itself. Each regiment has its armory, in which are deposited its arms and valuable property. An armorer is in charge of the building, and it is his duty to keep the guns in good order. A reading-room and library are attached to some of the armories, and are used as places of social reunion for the members of the command. Drills are held at stated times, and a rigid discipline is maintained. The men, as a general rule, are proud of their organizations, and are enthusiastic in military matters.   They are all well drilled, and will compare favorably with any troops in the world, in both appearance and efficiency.   Nearly all saw service during the late war, and there is not a regiment but treasures some smoke-begrimed, bullet-rent flag, as its most precious possession.   Out of the 13,000 men comprising the force, 9000 were in the field in active service, at one time during the war, and the division gave the country 3780 officers for the struggle.   The total force furnished by the city of New York during the war was 100,000 men.   Of these 9000 were killed or wounded, and 37,000 were officers at some period of the war.

The most popular and efficient regiments are the Seventh, Ninth, and Twenty-second.   The Seventh and Ninth are the best known.   The latter has the finest band in the city, and one of the best in the world.

The parade of the entire division is a sight worth seeing, and always brings a crowd upon the streets.   Every available place for viewing the march is eagerly sought.   The shop-keepers along the route of the procession find it an easy matter to rent their windows and balconies at large prices.   Even the house-tops are filled with spectators, and the sidewalks are "jammed."

Each regiment as it passes is greeted with greater or less applause, according to its popularity.   The day is a sort of holiday in the city, and the parade is one of the sights of the New World, for New York is the only city in the country which can put so large and splendid a force of troops in the field in a mere parade.

But the First Division is not a holiday force, and parades and receptions are not the only occasions which bring it upon the streets.   The city of New York contains a population hard to manage, and which can be controlled only by a strong, firm hand.   The police force, about 2000 in number, is utterly inadequate to the repression of an uprising of the criminal class of the city, and the scoundrels know it.   The police have never been lacking in emergencies, but their task is wonderfully lightened by the knowledge that behind them stand 13,000 disciplined and well-equipped troops to support them if the task of enforcing the law proves too great for them. The roughs of New York know that they are no match for such an army as this, and they are influenced greatly by this knowledge. The respectable class, the men of property, and the heads of families find no little comfort in this certainty of protection. They know they can trust to the troops, for the members of the National Guard represent the best part of the population of New York, and are to a man directly interested in preserving the peace and prosperity of the city.

The troops are always ready for duty. They are scattered all over the city, pursuing various useful callings, but at a certain signal sounded from the City Hall bell, they will rally at their armories, and in an hour there will be a strong body of trained troops ready to enforce the law in any emergency. No one can doubt that the summons will be obeyed, for the past history of the division proves that even the men who are careless about attending parades, etc., are very careful to be at their posts in the hour of danger.

The employment of this force is not open to the objections that are brought against the use of the military in a free country. These men are not mercenaries, but are useful and honorable citizens and members of society. They have a good record, and the history of the city contains several conspicuous instances of their gallantry and devotion. In 1837, when the banks suspended specie payments, they alone prevented a terrible and destructive riot. In 1849, they promptly suppressed the Astor Place Riot, which was brought about by a disgraceful attempt on the part of a band of ruffians to mob the English actor Macready, who was then playing at the Astor Place Opera House. They prevented a serious riot at the time of the creation of the Metropolitan Police Force, compelled Mayor Wood and his partisans to yield obedience to the laws they had sworn to disregard, and put down the disturbances which afterward occurred. In 1863, when the famous Draft Riots commenced, they were absent from the city, having been sent to meet Lee at Gettysburg. They were summoned back by telegraph, and returned in time to take up the battle which had been for two days so gallantly fought by the police. They made short work of the mob, and soon restored order. In July, 1871, they were called on by the City Authorities to protect the Orange Lodges in their right to parade. An ignorant, brutal mob declared that the parade should not take place because it was offensive to them, and made preparations to stop it by force. The Mayor of the city tamely yielded to the threats and demands of the mob, and forbade the parade. Fortunately for the credit of the city, fortunately for the moral power of the law, the Governor of the State revoked the order of the Mayor, and assured the Orangemen of full protection in their right to parade. The city, which had rung with indignant cries at the cowardly surrender of the Mayor to the mob, was now jubilant. The regiments ordered on duty by the Governor for the protection of the procession responded with alacrity, and came out with full ranks. The mob, still defiant, still thinking themselves masters of the situation, made an attack on the procession and its military escort. The troops submitted in silence, until some of their number were shot down in the ranks. Then wheeling suddenly, they poured a fatal volley into the midst of the rioters, who broke and fled in dismay. There was no further attempt at violence. The lesson was a useful one, and the effect fully worth the valuable lives that were laid down in the defence of the law.

XXIX.
NASSAU STREET.

IF you will go to the southern extremity of Printing House Square, on the east side of the City Hall Park, you will see the opening of a narrow street between the offices of the *Tribune* and *Times* newspapers. This is Nassau street. It runs parallel with Broadway, and terminates at Wall street. It is about half a mile in length, and is one of the narrowest and most inconvenient streets in the city, being less than fifty feet in width. The houses on each side are tall and sombre looking, and the street is almost always in the shadow. The roadway is hardly wide enough for two vehicles to pass abreast, and the sidewalks could never by any possible chance contain a crowd. Indeed, the street is seldom thronged, and the people you meet there seem to be possessed of but one desire—to get out of it as fast as possible. A stranger would, at the first glance, unhesitatingly pronounce it an inconvenient as well as a disagreeable thoroughfare, and yet the truth is that it is one of the most important streets in the city in respect of the amount and variety of the traffic carried on within its limits.

It would be hard to describe its architecture. Scarcely any two houses are built alike. At the lower end, in the vicinity of Wall street, iron, marble, and brown stone structures flourish, but above the Post-office the buildings are a study. The most of them are old, but all show signs of vigorous life, and from cellar to attic they are jammed full of busy, scheming, toiling men.

Along the street are some of the best known and most trusted banking houses of the city, and millions of dollars are represented in their daily transactions. The great Post-office receives

NASSAU STREET.

and sends out whole tons of matter every twenty-four hours.
The bulk of the periodical, and a large part of the book-trade
are carried on here through the agency of the great news companies. Real estate men flourish here. Struggling lawyers
seem to think this street the road to success, for here they cluster
by the score. You may buy here diamonds of the purest water,
and others that had better be kept out of water. The most
valuable of watches may be obtained here; also the most
genuine pinchbeck timepieces. If one is a judge of the article
he is buying, he may frequently purchase to advantage in

Nassau street, but as a rule he must examine his purchase closely
before paying for it, and be sure he receives what he has
selected. The variety of the pursuits carried on here may be
ascertained only by a diligent perusal of the signs that line the
street. Perhaps in no other thoroughfare is there to be seen
such a multitude of signs. The fronts of the houses are covered
with them. They appear in nearly every window, and the
walls of the halls of the buildings, and even the steps themselves are covered with them. Every device of the sign maker
has been exhausted here, and they tell their stories with more
or less emphasis, according to the ingenuity exercised upon them.
They tell you of "Counsellors at Law," Publishers, Artists,
Dealers in Foreign and American Engravings, Jewellers,
Engravers on Wood and Steel, Printers, Stock Brokers, Gold
Beaters, Restaurant Keepers, Dealers in Cheap Watches, Agents
of Literary Bureaux, Translators of Foreign Languages, Fruit
Sellers, Boarding House Brokers, Matrimonial Agents, Book
Sellers, Dealers in Indecent Publications, and a host of others
too numerous to mention.

Go into one of the numerous buildings, and a surprise awaits
you. You might spend half a day in exploring it. It rivals
the Tower of Babel in height, and is alive with little closets
called "offices." How people doing business here are ever
found by those having dealings with them is a mystery. Many,
indeed, come here to avoid being found, for Nassau street is the
headquarters of those who carry on their business by circulars,
and under assumed names. It is a good hiding place, and one
in which a culprit might safely defy the far-reaching arm of
Justice.

Along the street, and mostly in the cellars, cluster the "Old
Book Stores" of New York, of which I shall have more to say
hereafter, and they add not a little to the singular character of
the street. The proprietors are generally men who have been
here for years, and who know the locality well. Many curious
tales could they tell of their cramped and dingy thoroughfare,
tales that in vivid interest and dramatic force would set up half
a dozen novelists.

The Post-office draws all sorts of people into the street, and it is interesting to watch them as they come and go. But, as has been said, no one stays here long ; no one thinks of lounging in Nassau street. Every one goes at the top of his speed, and bumps and thumps are given and taken with a coolness and patience known only to the New Yorker. You may even knock a man off his legs, and send him rolling into the gutter, and he will smile, pick himself up again, and think no more of the matter. On Broadway the same man would not fail to resent such an assault as an intentional insult. Every one here is full of unrest; every one seems pre-occupied with his own affairs, and totally oblivious to all that is passing around him. In no part of the great city are you so fully impressed with the shortness and value of time. Even in the eating houses, where the denizens of the street seek their noontide meal, you see the same haste that is manifest on the street. The waiters seem terribly agitated and excited, they fairly fly to do your bidding, pushing and bumping each other with a force that often sends their loads of dishes clattering to the floor. The man at the desk can hardly count your change fast enough. The guests bolt their food, gulp their liquors, and dart through the green baize doors as if their lives depended upon their speed.

So all day long they pour in and out of the marble banks, in and out of the great Post-office, in and out of the dingy offices— the good and the bad, the rich and the poor, the honest dealer and the sharper. Few know their neighbors here, fewer care for them ; and gigantic successes and dreary failures find their way into the street, adding year by year to its romance and to its mystery. At night the street is dark and deserted. Yet away up in some of the lofty buildings, the lights shining through the dingy windows tell you that some busy brain is still scheming and struggling—whether honestly or dishonestly, who can tell ?

XXX.

THE METROPOLITAN FIRE DEPARTMENT.

THE history of New York has been marked by a series of terrible fires, which have destroyed many lives and swept away millions of dollars worth of property. In 1741 the first of these conflagrations swept over the lower part of the city, consuming many houses, among them the old Dutch fort and church. On the 21st of September, 1776, during the occupation of the city by the British, 493 houses were burned, and great distress entailed in consequence upon the people. On the 9th of August, 1778, a third fire destroyed nearly 300 buildings east of Broadway and below Pearl street. In May, 1811, a fourth fire broke out in Chatham street and consumed nearly 100 houses. In 1828 a fifth fire destroyed about a million of dollars worth of property. On the 16th of December, 1835, began the sixth and most disastrous of these conflagrations. It raged for three days and nights continuously, swept over an area of 45 acres, destroyed 648 buildings, and entailed upon the citizens a loss of $18,000,000. In the face of this great disaster the insurance companies unanimously suspended. On the 19th of July, 1845, the seventh and last fire broke out in New street, near Wall street, and swept in a southerly direction, destroying 345 buildings. The loss was $5,000,000.

As a matter of course, a city that has suffered so much from fires is in especial need of the best known means of preventing and suppressing them. Since the year 1653 there has been a Fire Department in New York, and it would be an interesting task to review its history had we the space to do so. In its early days it was considered an honor to be a member of a fire company, and some of the best of the old-time citizens were to be found in the ranks of the various organizations. The city took care to keep the force provided with the most improved machines, and every effort was made to render it as efficient as possible. As the city increased in wealth and population the character of the firemen changed. The respectable men left the organization, and their places were filled with men who were drawn into it by the excitement which was to be found in such a life. Soon the department passed entirely into the hands of the Bowery boys and other disreputable characters. The engine houses were rallying places for the worst characters of the vicinity, who amused themselves in their leisure hours by fighting among themselves, or by assaulting respectable passers-by. A fire was the dread of the city, not only for the damage the conflagration was sure to do, but for the disturbance it brought about on the streets. As soon as an alarm was sounded the streets were filled with a yelling, reckless crowd, through which the engines and hose-carriages dashed, regardless of those who were run over. Pandemonium seemed to have broken loose and taken possession of the great thoroughfares. If two rival companies met on the streets they would leave the fire to work its will and fight their battle then and there. There was scarcely a fire without its accompanying riot. The fires themselves were disastrous. Very little good was accomplished by the firemen, and the losses were tremendous. Adjoining buildings were often broken open and robbed under pretence of saving them from the flames. In short, the whole department was a nuisance, and thinking men saw that it was a great nursery of criminals and blackguards. Efforts were made to remedy the evil, but without success. The members of the department were volunteers, and were particularly impatient of control. Many of the companies owned their own engines and other apparatus, and refused to submit to any sort of restraint. There was but one way to bring good out of this evil, and at length the best men of the city determined upon abolishing the old system entirely. The demand for a change grew stronger every day, and at last the Legislature of the State set on foot measures for the abolition of the volunteer system and the substitution of a paid force.

In March, 1865, the Legislature passed the bill creating the Metropolitan Fire Department, and it at once received the Executive signature. The friends of the old system resolved to resist the attempt to overthrow it. A case involving the constitutionality of the bill was brought before the Court of Appeals, which body sustained the law. Efforts were made by the newly-appointed Commissioners to get the new system at work as soon as possible; but in the meanwhile the partizans of the old system endeavored to be revenged by disbanding the old force and leaving the city without any means of extinguishing fires. The danger was great, but it was averted by detailing a force from the police to act as firemen in case of necessity. By November, 1865, the new system was thoroughly organized and fairly at work. Each succeeding year has witnessed some fresh improvement, and at present New York has the best appointed and most efficient Fire Department in the Union.

The force, as at present organized, is under the control of five commissioners, appointed by the Mayor of the city. They make rules and regulations for the government of the force, exercise a general supervision over its affairs, and are responsible to the municipal government for their acts. The force consists of a chief engineer, an assistant engineer, ten district engineers, and 587 officers and men. Each company consists of twelve persons, viz. : a foreman, assistant foreman, engineer of steamer, a stoker, a driver, and seven firemen. Each company is provided with a house, with engine room, stables, quarters for the men, and rooms for study, drill, etc. The basement contains a furnace, by means of which the building is warmed and the water in the engine kept hot. Everything is kept in perfect order. The houses are clean and neat, and the engines and hose-carriages shine like gold and silver.

The men are all paid by the city. The firemen receive $1000 dollars per annum, and the officers a higher sum, according to their duties and responsibilities. The men undergo a rigid physical examination, and are required to present proofs of their good moral character before they are admitted to the force. The object is to have none but men perfectly sound and free from habits tending to impair their usefulness in the force. They are generally fine specimens of manhood, are noticeably neat in their dress and habits, and are just the opposite of the old-time volunteer firemen. Furthermore, they may be relied upon in any emergency.

There are thirty-seven steam-engines in the department. They are of the second class or size, and perfect in all their appointments. They were built by the Amoskeag Manufacturing Company, of Manchester, New Hampshire, and cost $4000 a-piece. There is also a powerful floating engine located on a steamboat, and used for extinguishing fires on the piers or on vessels in the harbor. It is kept near the Battery, so as to be convenient to points in either river. There are four hand engines, located in the upper part of the island, and twelve hook and ladder companies in the department. Several engines are kept in reserve, and are not counted in the active force.

The horses of the department are 156 in number. They are large and powerful animals, and are kept with the greatest care. They are groomed every day, and are fed punctually at six o'clock morning and evening. If not used on duty, they are exercised every day by being led to and fro in the streets adjoining the engine-house. They are thoroughly trained, and will stand with perfect steadiness under the most exciting circumstances. They know the sound of the alarm-bell as well as their driver, and the moment it strikes they exhibit an impatience to be off which is remarkable. They are kept harnessed constantly, and it takes but a few seconds to attach them to the engines.

The men are not allowed to have any other employment. The department claims their whole duty. A certain number are required to be always at the engine-house. In case of an alarm being sounded during the absence of a fireman from the engine-house he runs directly to the fire, where he is sure to find his company. A watch is always kept in the engine-room day and night. After ten at night the men are allowed to go to bed, but must so arrange matters beforehand that they shall lose no time in dressing. The horses stand har-

28

nessed in their stalls, the boiler is filled with hot water, and the furnaces are supplied with wood which burns at the touch of a match.   It requires but fifteen seconds in the day and but one minute at night to be ready for action and on the way to the fire.

Scattered through the city are lofty towers, from which men keep a constant watch for fires.   They are thoroughly acquainted with the various localities of New York, and can tell at a glance the exact neighborhood of the fire.   From their lofty elevation they see the first cloud of smoke if it be day, or the first red glare if at night, and the next instant the alarm is sent over the city on the wings of electricity.

All signals and messages connected with the Fire Department are transmitted by telegraph, and for this purpose there is a distinct line through the city for the use of the department.   By means of this line the various engine-houses are brought into communication with each other and with the central station and police headquarters.   As the station-houses alone, however, would not suffice for the prompt communication of alarms, signal-boxes are scattered through the city at the most convenient points.   These boxes are so situated that they may be reached from any point in a few minutes.   They are several hundred in number, and are being multipled as rapidly as possible.   The engraving accompanying this chapter shows the appearance and mechanism of the signal box.

The box is attached to the telegraph pole, and is about twenty-four inches high, by twelve inches wide, and five inches deep. Every officer and member of the Fire Department, every officer and member of the Police Force, and every officer of the Fire Insurance Patrol is furnished with a key which will open all the boxes.   A key is also deposited with the occupant of a building near the box, and a notice showing the location of this key is always placed in a glass case at the top of the box.   Key-holders are cautioned not to open the box except in case of fire ; not to give an alarm unless sure of a fire ; not to give an alarm for a fire seen at a distance ; not to pull down the hook more than once in giving an alarm ; to be sure, after giving an alarm,

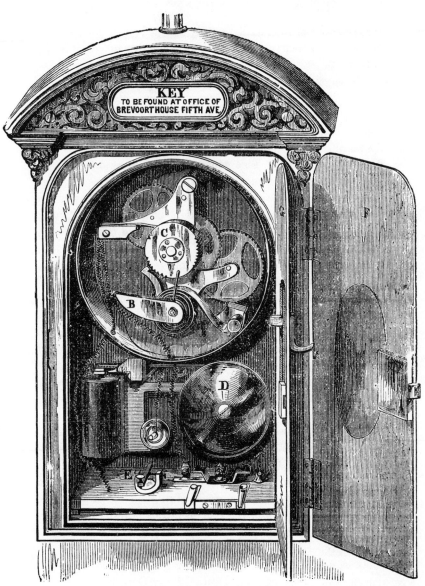

FIRE ALARM SIGNAL-BOX.

that the door of the box is securely fastened; and not to let the key go out of their possession except when demanded by proper authority.

The engraving referred to will show the manner of giving an alarm. There are two doors to each box, an outer and an inner door, lettered respectively F and G in the engraving. The door G is to be kept closed unless it becomes necessary to repeat the alarm. The outer door, F, is opened, and the catch A is drawn down firmly. This winds up a spring, by means of the lever B, which sets in motion the wheel C, and strikes the number of the box on the gong D and on the instrument at the Fire Department headquarters. Should it be necessary to give a second or third alarm, the door G is opened and the Morse key E is struck ten times.

In this way all alarms are sent, first to the central office, and thence to the various engine-houses. The alarm from the central office is struck on a large gong placed in a conspicuous part of the engine-room of every engine or hook and ladder company. The locality, and often the precise site of the fire can be ascertained by means of these signals. For instance, the bell strikes 157 thus: *one*—a pause—*five*—another pause—*seven*. The indicator will show that this alarm-box is at the corner of the Bowery and Grand street. The fire is either at this point or within its immediate neighborhood. The signals are repeated on all the bells in the fire-towers of the city, and the citizens, by consulting their printed indicators, can inform themselves of the location of the fire. On an alarm of fire about one-sixth of the whole force goes to the place of danger. If the alarm be repeated the number is increased by another sixth, and so on until the necessary force is obtained. Each company is restricted to certain portions of the city, so that there is no confusion in sending out the proper force.

As soon as the sharp strokes of the gong give the signal of danger, and point out the locality, every man springs to his post. The horses are attached in a few seconds, the fire is lighted in the furnace, and the steamer and hose carriage start for the scene of action. The foreman runs on foot, ahead of his steamer, to clear the way, and the driver may keep up with him, but is not allowed to pass him.   Only the engineer, his assistant, and the stoker are allowed to ride on the engine.   The rest of the company go on foot.   Fast driving is severely punished, and racing is absolutely prohibited.   The men are required to be quiet and orderly in their deportment in going to and returning from fires.   The engines have the right of way in all the streets.   This is well understood, and it is astonishing to see the rapidity with which a route is cleared for them through the most crowded streets.

Upon reaching the fire, communication is made between the plug or hydrant and the engine, and the work begins.   The chief engineer is required to attend all fires, and all orders proceed from him.   The most rigid discipline is preserved, and the work goes on with a rapidity and precision which are in striking contrast to the noise and inefficiency of the old system.

A force of policemen is at once sent to a fire.   They stretch ropes across the streets at proper distances from the burning buildings, and no one but the members of the Fire Department is allowed to pass these barriers.   In this way the firemen have room for the performance of their duties, lookers-on are kept at a safe distance, and the movable property in the burning house is saved from thieves.   Merchants and others have frequently given grateful testimony to the protection afforded their property by the firemen.   Upon one occasion the members of the department had complete possession for several hours of every part of the building containing the immense and valuable stock of jewelry of Messrs. Tiffany & Co.   This firm made a public declaration that after a rigid investigation they had not missed a penny's worth of their property, and gratefully acknowledged the protection afforded them.   Under the old system Messrs. Tiffany & Co. would have been ruined.

The life of a fireman is very arduous and dangerous, but the applicants for vacancies in the department are numerous.   The men are often called upon not only to face great personal danger, but they are also subjected to a severe physical strain from the

A FIRE IN NEW YORK.

438

loss of rest, and fatigue. Sometimes they will be called out and worked hard every night in the week, and all the while they are required to be as prompt and active as though they had never lost a night's rest. They are constantly performing deeds of heroism, which pass unnoticed in the bustle and whirl of the busy life around them, but which are treasured up in the grateful heart of some mother, wife, or parent, whose loved ones owe their lives to the fireman's gallantry.

During the recent visit to New York of the Prince Alexis of Russia, a pleasing instance of the efficiency of the department was given. The Prince had just reviewed a detachment of the department, and had returned to his hotel (the Clarendon), in Fourth avenue, just out of Union Square. One of the Fire Commissioners proposed to him to test the efficiency of the force he had just inspected, and accompanied him to the alarm box at the corner of Fourth avenue and Seventeenth street, about half a block from the hotel. The box being opened, the Prince gave the signal, and immediately returned to his hotel. Before he had reached the balcony, the sharp clatter of wheels was heard in the distance, and in a few seconds several steamers dashed up, "breathing fire and smoke," followed by a hook and ladder detachment and the Insurance Patrol. Within three minutes after the alarm had been sounded, two streams were thrown on the Everett House, and within five minutes ladders were raised to the hotel windows, and the men were on the roofs of the adjoining buildings.

Thanks to the model department, New York feels a security from fires unknown until now. The hopes of the friends of the new system have been more than realized. The fire statistics speak more eloquently than words could, and they show a steady decrease of the loss by fire. In 1866, there were 796 fires, involving a loss of $6,428,000; in 1867, the number of fires was 873, and the loss $5,711,000; in 1868, the fires were 740 in number, and the loss was $4,342,371; and in 1869 there were 850 fires, with a loss of $2,626,393. In the last mentioned year, only 43 out of the 850 fires were communicated to the adjoining buildings, a fact which speaks volumes for the exertions of the department.

The Headquarters of the department are located at 127 Mercer street, in a handsome building known as Fireman's Hall. Here are the offices of the Commissioners, the Chief Engineer, Secretary, Medical officer, Telegraph Bureau, Bureau of Combustible materials, and Fireman's Lyceum. The Lyceum contains a library of over 4000 volumes, and a collection of engravings, documents, and relics relating to the old Fire Department. All fines exacted of firemen, and those imposed on citizens for violating the ordinances relating to hatchways and kerosene lamps, are paid into the treasury of the " Fire Department Relief Fund," for the maintenance of the widows and orphans of firemen.

XXXI.

THE BUSINESS OF NEW YORK.

NEW York is the commercial metropolis of the Union. Its local trade is immense, but its foreign trade and its trade with the rest of the country are much greater. The port is the American terminus of nearly all the steamship lines plying between the United States and foreign countries. About two-thirds of all the imports of the United States arrive in New York, and about forty per cent. of all the exports of the country are shipped from the same point. In 1870, the total imports amounted to $315,200,022. The Customs duties on these amounted to $135,310,995. The imports are given at their foreign cost in gold, and freight and duty are not included in this estimate. The exports for the same year (including $58,191,475 in specie) were worth $254,137,208. The total of imports and exports for that year was $569,337,230, the value of the foreign trade of New York.

The domestic trade is also immense. During the year 1864 some of the receipts of the port were as follows:

Barrels of wheat flour	3,967,717
Bushels of wheat	13,453,135
" " oats	12,952,238
" " corn	7,164,895
Packages of pork	332,454
" " beef	209,664
" " cut meats	268,417
" " butter	551,153
" " cheese	756,872
Tierces and barrels of lard	186,000
Kegs of lard	16,104
Barrels of whiskey	289,481
" " petroleum	775,587

New York has many advantages over its rivals. Merchants find a better and a more extensive and varied market, and as they like to combine pleasure with business, find more attractions here than elsewhere. New York is emphatically a great city, and it is entirely free from provincialisms of any kind. The narrow notions of smaller places are quickly replaced here with metropolitan and cosmopolitan ideas, tastes and habits. Moreover, the city is the chief centre of wealth, of art, of talent, and of luxury. These things are too firmly secured to be taken away, and strangers must come here to enjoy them. Merchants from other States and cities like the liberal and enterprising spirit which characterizes the dealings of the New York merchants. They can buy here on better terms than elsewhere, and their relations with the merchants of this city are generally satisfactory and pleasant. Besides this, they find their visits here of real benefit to them in their own callings. The energy, or to use an American term, "the push" of New York exhilarates them, and shows them how easily difficulties, which in less enterprising places seem insurmountable, may be overcome. They go back home braced up to their work, and filled with new and larger ideas.

Between ten and fifteen millions of strangers annually visit New York for business and pleasure. All spend large sums of money during their stay, and a very large part of this finds its way into the pockets of the retail dealers of the city. The hotels, boarding houses, restaurants, livery stables, and places of amusement reap large profits from these visitors. Indeed, the whole city is benefited to a very great extent by them, and it thus enjoys a decided advantage over all its rivals.

Everything here gives way to business. The changes in the city are, perhaps, more strictly due to this than to the increase of the population. It is a common saying that "business is rapidly coming up town." Private neighborhoods disappear every year, and long lines of substantial and elegant warehouses take the places of the comfortable mansions of other days. The lower part of the city is taken up almost exclusively by wholesale and commission houses, and manufactories. The retail men and small dealers are being constantly forced higher up town. A few years ago the section of the city lying between Fourth and Twenty-third streets was almost exclusively a private quarter. Now it is being rapidly invaded by business houses. Broadway has scarcely a residence below the Park. The lower part of Fifth avenue is being swiftly converted into a region of stores and hotels, and residents are being steadily driven out of Washington and Union Squares. Even Madison Square is beginning to feel the change. But a few years ago it was regarded as the highest point that New York would ever reach in its upward growth.

Enterprise, talent, and energy are indispensable to any one who wishes to succeed in business in New York. Fortunes can be made legitimately here quicker than in many other places, but the worker must have patience. Fortune comes slowly everywhere if honestly sought. There is also another quality indispensable to a genuine success. It is honesty and integrity. Sharp practices abound in the city, but those who use them find their road a hard one. No man can acquire a good and steady credit—which credit is of more service to him here than in almost any other place in the world—without establishing a reputation for rigid integrity. The merchants of the city are keen judges of character, and they have no patience with sharpers. They will deal with them only on a strictly cash basis.

The city abounds in instances of the success which has attended honest, patient, and intelligent efforts. John Jacob Astor was a poor butcher's son. Cornelius Vanderbilt was a boatman. Daniel Drew was a drover. The Harpers and Appletons were printers' apprentices. A. T. Stewart was an humble, struggling shopkeeper. A well-known financier began by blacking a pair of boots. Opportunities as good as these men ever had are occurring every day. Those who are competent to seize them may do so, and rise to fortune and position.

Many of the colossal fortunes of the city have been created by the rise in the value of real estate. The rapid growth of the city during the past twelve years has greatly increased the value of property in the upper sections. Many persons who but a few years ago were owners of tracts which were simply burdensome by reason of the numerous and heavy assessments upon them, and for which no purchasers could be found, have become very wealthy by the rapid increase in the value of their property. Many persons owning property of this kind sold at a heavy advance during the real estate speculations that succeeded the war. Others leased their lands to parties wishing to build on them. Others still hold on for further improvement. The Astors, A. T. Stewart, Vanderbilt and others have made a large share of their money by their investments in real estate.

A farm near the Central Park, which could not find a purchaser in 1862, when it was offered at a few thousand dollars, sold in 1868 in building lots for almost as many millions.

In 1860 a gentleman purchased a handsome house in a fashionable neighborhood. It was a corner house and fronted on Fifth avenue. He paid $50,000 for it, and spent $25,000 more in fitting up and furnishing it. His friends shook their heads at his extravagance. Since then he has resided in the house, and each year his property has increased in value. In 1869 he was offered nearly $300,000 dollars for the house and furniture, but refused to sell at this price, believing that he would be able in a few years to command a still larger sum.

XXXII.

THE SABBATH IN NEW YORK.

ON Sunday morning New York puts on its holiday dress. The stores are closed, the streets have a deserted aspect, for the crowds of vehicles, animals and human beings that fill them on other days are absent.   There are no signs of trade anywhere except in the Bowery and Chatham street.   The city has an appearance of cleanliness and quietness pleasant to behold.   The wharves are hushed and still, and the river and bay lie calm and bright in the light of the Sabbath sun.   One misses the stages from Broadway, and a stranger at once credits the coach-men with a greater regard for the day than their brothers of the street cars.   The fact is, however, that Jehu of the stage-coach rests on the Sabbath because his business would be unprofitable on that day.   The people who patronize him in the week have no use for him on Sunday.   The horse-cars make their trips as in the week.   They are a necessity in so large a city. The distances one is compelled to pass over here, even on Sunday, are too great to be traversed on foot.

Towards ten o'clock the streets begin to fill up with church-goers.   The cars are crowded, and handsome carriages dash by conveying their owners to their places of worship.   The up-town churches are the most fashionable, and are the best attended, but all the sacred edifices are well filled on Sunday morning.   New York compromises with its conscience by a scrupulous attendance upon morning worship, and reserves the rest of the day for its own convenience.   The up-town churches all strive to get in, or as near as possible to, the Fifth avenue. One reason for this is, doubtless, the desire that all well-to-do New Yorkers have to participate in the after-church promenade.

The churches close their services near about the same hour, and then each pours its throng of fashionably dressed people into the avenue. The congregations of distant churches all find their way to the avenue, and for about an hour after church the splendid street presents a very attractive spectacle. The toilettes of the ladies show well here, and it is a pleasant place to meet one's acquaintances.

The majority of New Yorkers dine at one o'clock on Sunday, the object being to allow the servants the afternoon for themselves. After dinner your New Yorker, male or female, thinks of enjoyment. If the weather is fair the fashionables promenade the Fifth and Madison avenues, or drive in the park. The working classes fill the street-cars, and throng the Central Park. In the summer whole families of laboring people go to the park early in the morning, taking a lunch with them, and there spend the entire day. In the skating season the lakes are thronged with skaters. The church bells ring out mournfully towards three o'clock, but few persons answer the call. The afternoon congregations are wofully thin.

In the mild season, the adjacent rivers and the harbor are thronged with pleasure boats filled with excursionists, and the various horse and steam railway lines leading from the city to the sea-shore are well patronized.

Broadway wears a silent and deserted aspect all day long, but towards sunset the Bowery brightens up wonderfully, and after nightfall the street is ablaze with a thousand gaslights. The low class theatres and places of amusement in that thorough-fare are opened towards dark, and then vice reigns triumphant in the Bowery. The Bowery beer-gardens do a good business. The most of them are provided with orchestras or huge orches-trions, and these play music from the ritual of the Roman Catholic Church.

Until very recently the bar-rooms were closed from midnight on Saturday until midnight on Sunday, and during that period the sale of intoxicating liquors was prohibited. Now all this is changed. The bar-rooms do a good business on Sunday, and especially on Sunday night. The Monday morning papers tell a fearful tale of crimes committed on the holy day. Assaults, fights, murders, robberies, and minor offences are reported in considerable numbers. Drunkenness is very common, and the Monday Police Courts have plenty of work to do.

At night the churches are better attended than in the afternoon, but not as well as in the morning.

Sunday concerts, given at first-class places of amusement, are now quite common. The music consists of masses, and other sacred airs, varied with selections from popular operas. The performers are famous throughout the country for their musical skill, and the audiences are large and fashionable. No one seems to think it sinful thus to desecrate the Lord's Day; and it must be confessed that these concerts are the least objectionable Sunday amusements known to our people.

It must not be supposed that the dissipation of which we have spoken is confined exclusively to the rougher class. Old and young men of respectable position participate in it as well. Some are never called on to answer for it, others get into trouble with the police authorities. One reason for this dissipation is plain. People are so much engrossed in the pursuit of wealth that they really have no leisure time in the week. They must take Sunday for relaxation and recreation, and they grudge the few hours in the morning that decency requires them to pass in church.

XXXIII.

THE POST-OFFICE.

I.

INTERNAL ARRANGEMENTS.

STRANGE to say, the great metropolis, in which the largest postal business in the country is transacted, has never had a building for a Post-office, which was erected for that purpose. It has been compelled to put up with any temporary accommodation that could be obtained, and for many years past its Post-office has been simply a disgrace to the nation.

In the days of the Dutch, letters were brought over from Europe by the shipmasters and delivered to some coffee house keeper, who took charge of them until the persons to whom they were addressed could call for them. This custom was continued under the English until 1686, when the authorities required that all ship letters should be placed in charge of the Collector of the Port. In 1692, the city authorities established a Post-office, and in 1710, the Postmaster-General of Great Britain removed the headquarters of the postal service of the Colonies from Philadelphia to New York. The first city Post-office was located in Broadway opposite Beaver street. About the year 1804, the Post-office was removed to No. 29 William street, corner of Garden street, now Exchange Place, where it remained until 1825, when the Government leased the "Academy building" in Garden street, now Exchange Place, and opened it as a Post-office. In 1827, the office was transferred to the basement of the Merchants' Exchange, the site now occupied by the Custom House. Wall street was then just undergoing the

THE OLD POST-OFFICE.

change from private residences to bankers' and brokers' offices.
The Merchants' Exchange was destroyed in the great fire of
1835, and the next day a Post-office was extemporized in a
brick building in Pine, near Nassau street, and shortly after
was transferred to the Rotunda, in the City Hall Park, which
had been offered to the Government by the municipal authorities.   The Rotunda, however, proved too small for the business
of the department, which had been greatly increased by the establishment of lines of railways and steamboats between New
York and the various parts of the country, and in 1845 the
Post-office was removed to the Middle Dutch Church, in Nassau
street, between Pine and Cedar streets, its present location, which
was purchased by the Government for the sum of $350,000.

This building has always been entirely unsuited to the needs
of a Post-office for such a city as New York.   It was dedicated
in 1732, and was used for worship by one of the Dutch congregations of the city.   In 1776, the British having occupied the

29

city, it was converted into a prison by the conquerors for the incarceration of their rebellious captives. It was subsequently used by them as a riding school for the instruction of cavalry. After the British evacuated the city, the congregation reoccupied it, and refitted it for religious worship. After paying for it the large sum mentioned above, the Government was compelled to make a further expenditure of $80,000, to fit it up for its new uses. Since then many changes, some involving a heavy outlay, have been made in the building, but even now it is not capable of meeting the demands upon it, and the Government is now engaged in the erection of a new building expressly designed for a Post-office.

The Pine street front is devoted to the reception and departure of the mails. The street is generally filled with wagons bearing the mystic words, " U. S. Mail." Some are single-horse vehicles, used for carrying the bags between the main office and the numerous stations scattered through the city; others are immense wagons, drawn by four and six horses, and carrying several tons of matter at a time. These are used for the great Eastern, Western, and Southern, and the Foreign Mails. The Pine street doors present a busy sight at all hours, and the duties of the men employed there are not light. Huge sacks from all parts of the world are arriving nearly every hour, and immense piles of similar sacks are dispatched with the regularity of clockwork.

The body of the building, by which is meant the old church room itself, is used for opening and making up the mails. This work is carried on on the main floor, and in the heavy, old-fashioned gallery which runs around three of the sides. Huge semi-circular forms are scattered about the floor, each divided into a number of open squares. From each of these squares hangs a mail bag, each square being marked with the name of the city or town to which the bag is to be sent. A clerk stands within the curve of the form, before a table filled with letters and papers, and tosses them one by one into the squares to which they belong. This is done with the utmost rapidity, and long practice has made the clerk so proficient that he never misses the proper square. The stamping of the office mark and cancelling of the postage stamps on letters to be sent away is incessant, and the room resounds with the heavy thud of the stamp. This is no slight work, as the clerks who perform it can testify. The upper floor is devoted to the use of the Postmaster and his Assistants, the Superintendent of the City Delivery, and the Money Order and Registered Letter Offices. A wooden corridor has been built along the side of the church along Nassau and Cedar streets, and here, on the street floor, are the box and general deliveries, and the stamp windows. This is the public portion of the office, and is always thronged.

The visitor will notice, in various parts of this corridor, the slides for the depositing of letters and papers intended for the mails. The accumulation of mail matter here is so great that it is necessary that letters designed for a certain part of the country should be deposited in one particular place. Letters for New England must be placed in a certain box, those for the Middle States in another, those for the Southern States in another, those for the West in another. The names of the States are painted conspicuously above each box, so that there may be no mistake on the part of strangers. Letters for the principal countries of Europe and Asia are posted in the same way. Newspapers and periodicals have a separate department. The mails of these journals are made up in the office of publication, according to certain instructions furnished by the Postmaster, and go to the Post-office properly assorted for distribution. This system of depositing mail matter saves an immense amount of labor on the part of the clerks, and also hastens the departure of the mails from the office.

The Box Delivery contains nearly seven thousand boxes, on each of which the enormous rent of $16 per annum is charged. Considering that the box system is quite as advantageous to the Government as to the box holder, this rent is simply extortionate.

The daily business of the New York Post-office is enormous, and is rapidly increasing. The letters received by mail steamers from foreign countries, partly for delivery in the city, and partly to be forwarded to other places, average about fifteen thousand daily. The number dispatched from this office by steamer to foreign countries is about seventeen thousand daily. The number of letters sent from New York to other offices in the United States is about one hundred and fifty-five thousand daily. The number received from domestic offices for delivery in the city is about one hundred and twenty-six thousand daily; in addition to about seventy-two thousand per day, which are to be forwarded to other offices. About one hundred thousand letters, and about twenty thousand printed circulars, are mailed every day in the city, for city delivery. The carriers deliver daily, to persons who do not hire boxes at the general office, about fifty-three thousand letters; and collect from the street boxes about one hundred and one thousand letters every twenty-four hours. About five hundred registered letters, of which about four hundred are for delivery in the city, are received, and about two hundred and fifty are dispatched, daily. About one thousand dollars are paid out daily on money orders, and a much larger amount is received for orders granted to applicants. The sales of postage stamps amount to about forty-four thousand dollars per week. About two hundred unstamped letters are deposited in the office daily, and about one hundred letters on which the name of the town or State is written improperly, or on which the address is illegible. These are all sent to the Dead Letter Office, in Washington.

The number of persons employed as clerks, porters, etc., in the general office and the various stations, is 715.

The city is too large to admit of the transaction of all its business by the general office. To meet the necessities of the town, and to insure the rapid dispatch of the postal business, about 700 "lamp-post boxes," or iron boxes attached to the posts of the street lamps, are scattered through the city. Letters for the mails and for delivery in the city are deposited in these boxes, from which they are collected by the letter-carriers nine times each day, except Sunday, between the hours of seven A. M. and seven P. M. The Sunday collection is made once, at seven in the evening.

There are fourteen branch or Sub-Post-offices, designated as "Stations," located in convenient parts of the city, north of the general office.   They are named from the letters of the alphabet, and are known as "Stations A, B, C, D, E, F, G, H, J, K, L, M, N, and O."   They are designed to serve as distributing centres for certain sections of the city.   They receive from the general office all letters and papers for delivery in their sections, and to them the carriers bring all the matter collected from the lamp-boxes.   There is no delivery from them except through the carriers.   They dispatch to the general office, at stated times throughout the day, all matter deposited in their boxes or collected from the lamp-boxes by the carriers.

A recent writer thus relates some of the gossip connected with the office :

"People who come to the Post-office and make complaints of being robbed, when they discover that they were mistaken never call and make reparation, or relieve the department of the charge made against its employés.   A merchant, much excited, complained that a letter sent to him 'by a most responsible house,' containing $500, had not been received.   This charge was fortified by showing a letter from the postmaster who mailed the missing letter, certifying that it was forwarded, and contained the $500.   Detectives were at once set to work to unravel the iniquity, but all efforts proved unavailing.   Finally the Post-office authorities, after weeks of hard work, called on the complaining merchant and asked if he had heard anything about the missing money.   'Oh,' replied the gentleman, with great vivacity, 'that's all right ; by mistake that letter was thrown into the safe, and remained unopened nearly four weeks.   Funny, wasn't it ?'   Not even an apology was made for charging the Post-office with purloining the money, or for giving its officers so much unnecessary trouble.

"Charges of dishonesty against the Post-office are made where nobody but 'extraordinary circumstances' are to blame.   A letter containing two $1000 bills in it was delivered by the carrier, who, according to custom (ignorant of its contents, of course), at the house of its owner, shoved it into the hallway, under the door. The letter was missing. Complaint was made at the Post-office; evidence was produced that the money had been forwarded. The detectives were set to work to trace out the robbery. The poor carrier, and the clerks in the office who handled the letter were placed under surveillance. The clerks where the letter was mailed were 'shadowed.' Every dollar they expended after the probable robbery was secretly inquired into, to see if any of them had been at any given time, after the letter was lost, unusually 'flush;' but all signs failed. After a long time the floor covering of the hall was taken up, and there was the letter, 'safe and sound;' the unfortunate carrier had thrust it *under*, instead of over, the oilcloth.

" The misdirection of letters is the cause of serious charges against the Post-office. A letter containing $700 was mailed from Albany to New York. It was sent from a well-known person, and the package which was supposed to contain the letter, made up in Albany, was not opened until it reached New York. Both ends of the line were under suspicion. It was stated that the letter was addressed to Mr. —— ——, Broadway, New York. After a long search it was found that the letter had never left Albany at all, being directed by mistake, Mr. —— ——, Broadway, Albany, and the faithful clerks had thrown it into their own city delivery box instead of forwarding it to New York. The confusion in the mind of the writer grew out of the fact that there is a Broadway in both cities, and from force of habit he wrote the wrong address.

" Miserable chirography is one of the most prolific causes of Post-office inefficiency. It is safe to say that unmistakably written directions would remove nine-tenths of the complaints. What is a non-plussed clerk to do with letters addressed to ' Mahara Seney,' ' Old Cort,' or ' Cow House,' when Morrisonia, Olcott, and Cohoes were really intended ?

" One day, possibly four years ago, Mr. Kelly was sitting in his private office opening his *personal* letters, and enjoying the delusion that everything was working satisfactorily, when, to his surprise, he found one letter from Washington calling his especial attention to the ' inclosed editorial,' cut from the *Tri-*

bune, in which the carelessness of his clerks, and the generally
unsatisfactory manner with which he carried on his business,
were dilated upon, ending with the startling announcement that,
under the present management of the department, it took *four
days* to get a letter from New York to Chappaqua, distance
about thirty miles, and made literally no distance by a fast railway!   Consternation ensued, and Mr. Kelly, to commence
examination into these serious charges, sent a special agent to
Chappaqua for the envelope of said delayed letter.   At the
place named the official fortunately not only found what he went
after (the envelope), but also Mr. Greeley and ' Miles O'Reilly.'
After due explanations, the envelope was handed to Miles
O'Reilly, with the query of what he thought was the meaning
of the superscription.

" ' Why,' said that genial wit, who had once been a deputy
postmaster, ' the devil himself couldn't make it out.'

" The envelope was then brought to the attention of the
berated clerks, who looked at it with glazed eyes, the hieroglyphics suggesting somewhat the same intellectual speculation
that would result from studying the footprints of a gigantic
spider that had, after wading knee-deep in ink, retreated hastily
across the paper.

"At the Post-office, when they distribute letters, those on
which the direction is not instantly made out, to save time, are
thrown in a pile for especial examination; if a second and more
careful study fails, they are consigned to an especial clerk, who
is denominated the chief of the bureau of ' hards.'   To this
important functionary the envelope of Chappaqua was at last
referred.   He examined it a moment, and his eye flashed with
the expression of recognizing an old acquaintance.   ' This
thing,' said he, holding up the envelope with the tip ends of his
fingers, ' came to me some days ago along with the other
" hards."   I studied the superscription at my leisure a whole
day, but couldn't make it out.   I then showed it to the best
experts in handwriting attached to the office, and called on outsiders to test their skill; but what the writing meant, *if it was
writing,* was a conundrum that we all gave up.   Finally, in

desperation, it was suggested, as a last resort, to send it to Chappaqua, which happened to be its place of destination.' Such is the *literal* history of the reason of an earnestly written denunciation of the inefficiency of the city post."

II.

THE NEW POST-OFFICE.

In 1869, the General Government decided to depart from the niggardly policy it had hitherto pursued towards the City of New York, and to take steps toward the erection of a Post-office adequate to the needs of the great and growing community which demanded this act of justice at its hands. It was decided to erect an edifice which should be an ornament to the city, and capable of accommodating the City Postal service for generations to come. The Municipal Authorities, in order to secure the erection of the building in the most convenient part of the city, offered to sell to the General Government the lower end of the City Hall Park. The offer was accepted, and the land was purchased by the Government. The corner stone was laid in June, 1869. At the present writing (January, 1872,) the first story has been finished. It will probably require several years to complete the edifice. The price paid for the land was $500,000, a merely nominal sum. It is expected that the building will cost about $4,000,000.

"The exterior walls are to be of Dix Island granite, and the dimensions of the four fronts are severally as follows: the northerly side (toward the City Hall) is about 300 feet; the Broadway and Park Row fronts, respectively, 270 feet; and the southerly part, 130 feet.

"The difficulty of laying the foundations may be judged from the following facts: The depth of excavation over the entire plot was over thirty feet, and the material to be removed was entirely loose sand, while the traffic in Broadway and Park Row, including railroad cars and omnibuses, was enormous, involving the danger of a caving-in of both streets! The trenches

THE NEW POST-OFFICE.

457

in which the retaining walls and pier foundations were to be laid had to be completely incased in sheet-piling, shored across with timbers, under the protection of which the excavation was carried on and the masonry laid. The excavation was done mostly at night, the ground being illuminated by magnesium light. The outer walls, and those of the court, and the foundations of the interior columns are based on huge granite blocks, the granite being laid on massive beds of concrete. One hundred and fifty-nine iron columns in the basement, and 117 in the first story, support the walls and floors. The piers of the cellar are of granite, or arcaded brick and iron; the stairs are of stone and iron; the chimneys, of stone; the roof and its ornaments, of iron, covered with slate and copper. Four large low-pressure boilers supply the steam for heating the entire building. The roofs of the corner pavilions rise 107 feet above the sidewalk. The cellar is a little more than seven feet in the clear; the basement, sixteen feet; the first corridor, fourteen feet; and the half-story above it—both completing the first story—also fourteen feet. The entire circuit of the building is over one-fifth of a mile.

" The style of architecture is the classical Italian Renaissance, with some modifications to harmonize with the treatment of the roofs, which are to be French, as best suited to such architecture on a large scale. The Mansard roof will be covered with an ironclad cornice and metallic cresting.

" The irregular angles imposed by the shape of the lot are marked by semi-hexagonal pavilions. The main building line is withdrawn from the lower, or southerly front, to extend the façade on that side. The roof, square-domed, rests on three arms of a Greek cross, out of the centre of which rises a heavily buttressed.cupola, carrying projecting pediments, with detached columns on its four faces. The foot of the flagstaff, which is to surmount the cupola, will be 160 feet above the sidewalk.

" The fronts on Broadway and Park Row, respectively, are broken by square central pavilions, with pyramidal roofs, of which the first and second stories are faced with detached colonnades of coupled columns. Below are the main lateral entrances

to the Post-office corridor. The centre of the largest and northerly front is relieved by a broad pavilion with a two-story
colonnade, roofed with a dome, the balustrade of which is 150
feet above the sidewalk. The dome is lighted by a range of
round windows, and surmounted by an attic, ornamented by a
sculptured pediment and a crown with the national arms. The
form of the building is, substantially, a trapezoid, with an open
triangular court in the centre, below the main story ; it includes a
sub-basement, basement, three stories in the walls, and a roof story.

"A drive-way, or street, forty feet in width, reserved from
the northerly side of the ground purchased by the Government,
serves as an approach to that front, and secures the perfect iso-
lation of the building, with perpetual access of light and air on
that side, as well as on the other sides, whatever changes may
hereafter be made in the adjoining ground.

"The principal entrances are at the southwest front under a
portico, which gives access to the Post-office corridor, and by a
broad double staircase to the upper stories ; and at the northerly
corner pavilions on Broadway and Park Row, where two great
elliptical stairways lead again to the higher stories, but do not
communicate with the ground-floor, being reserved for the United
States Courts, and their dependencies. Besides these, there are
lateral entrances to the Post-office corridor on Broadway and
Park Row, and to the Post-office proper on those two sides, and
also on the northerly front.

"The sub-basement, or cellar, and the basement, cover the
whole area of the lot, and are extended under the sidewalks,
the central court and the drive-way on the northerly side. The
cellar will be used for the boilers, engines and heating apparatus,
and for the storage of coal and other bulky material. The basements and the first story are reserved for the use of the Post-office.

"The first story occupies the entire space of the building, including the central court, which is here roofed with glass ; the
walls of which, with all the interior partitions of the stories
above, are, in this story and the basement, carried on columns,
leaving the whole area of the Post-office roof open to light and
free use and communication.

" The corridor for the use of the public occupies the exterior belt of the ground-floor on the southerly front, and on the Broadway and Park Row fronts far enough to include the central pavilions, and it is separated from the Post-office room by a Box and Delivery screen. This corridor is half the height of the first story, and the space above it is occupied by a half-story, which, being entirely open on the inside, forms a gallery encompassing the Post-office room on three sides. The high windows of the first story, running through both the corridor and the half-story, give an uninterrupted communication of light and air to the interior, while the supply of light is increased by the whole breadth of the glass roof over the court. The floor under this floor is also of glass, giving light to the sub-basement, which is also lighted by means of illuminating tile in the sidewalks.

" In the upper stories, corridors fourteen feet wide make the circuit of the whole building ; and from those corridors, rooms open on either hand toward the streets and the inner court. The rooms over the principal entrance, and which look down Broadway, are reserved for the Postmaster ; and those for the Assistant Postmaster and Cashier are close at hand.

" The whole of the northerly front is given to the United States Courts. There are three court-rooms, of which the two largest are continued up through two stories in height. Adjoining these, are special rooms for the Judges, near which private stairways furnish the only access to the jury-rooms in the third story. The remainder of the second story is occupied by rooms for Marshals, United States Attorney, Clerks of the Courts, record-rooms, etc., etc. Other United States officers are to be accommodated with rooms in the upper story."

III.

THE LETTER CARRIERS.

For the purpose of distributing the letters received at the New York Post-office, the Government has organized a force

of Letter Carriers, or, as they are sometimes called, "Postmen."
All letters that are addressed to the places of business or the
residences of citizens, unless such persons are renters of boxes in
the General Post-office, are turned over to the Carriers for
delivery.

The force is organized under the direction of a Superintendent,
who is appointed by and responsible to the Postmaster of the
city. Applicants for positions in the force of Letter Carriers
must, as a prime necessity, be able to command a sufficient degree of political influence to secure their appointments. Possessing this, they make their applications in duplicate, on blank
forms supplied by the Department. The applicant must state
his age, general condition, former occupation, experience in
business, his reason for leaving his last place, and whether he
has served in the army or navy. One of these applications is
laid before the Postmaster of the city, and the other is sent to
the Post-office Department at Washington. If the applicant is
successful, he is subjected to a physical examination by the surgeon of the Department, in order to make sure of his bodily
soundness. Good eye-sight is imperatively required of every
applicant. If "passed" by the surgeon, the applicant must then
furnish two bonds in five hundred dollars each, for the faithful
performance of his duties. This done, he is enrolled as a member of the corps of Letter Carriers, and is assigned by the Superintendent of the force to a station.

Together with his certificate of appointment, the Superintendent hands him an order on a certain firm of tailors for an
"outfit," or uniform, which consists of a coat, pants, vest, and
cap of gray cloth, trimmed with black braid, and with gilt
buttons. The cost of this uniform is in winter twenty-four
dollars, and in summer twenty dollars. It is paid for by the
Post-office Department, and the amount deducted from the first
two months' pay of the carrier.

Upon being assigned to a station, the Carrier is required to
commit to memory the rules laid down for his guidance. His
route is then marked out for him, and he is frequently accompanied over it several times by an older member of the force to

familiarize him with it.   The Superintendent of the Station is his immediate superior.   From him the Carrier receives his orders, and to him submits his reports.

There is a "time-book" kept in each station, in which the employés are required to enter the time of their arrival at the station in the morning.   The Carriers are also required to enter the time of their departure on their routes, and the time of their return to the station.   Once a month this book is submitted to the inspection of the Superintendent of the force, and any delays or other negligences that are noted are reprimanded by him.

The Station-clerk, whose duty it is to assort the mail, is required to be at his post at ten minutes after six o'clock in the morning.   He places each Carrier's mail in a separate box, leaving to him the arrangement of it.   The Carriers must be at the station at half-past six.   They at once proceed to arrange their mail in such a manner as will facilitate its prompt delivery, and at half-past seven A. M., they start out on their routes.   If any of the postage on the letters to be delivered is unpaid, it is charged by the clerk to the Carrier, who is held responsible for its collection.   Once a week the Superintendent of the Station goes over the accounts of the Carriers, and requires them to pay over to him all the sums charged against them.

There are nine deliveries from the stations every day.   The first at half-past seven A. M., and the last at five P. M.   This entails an immense amount of labor upon the Carriers.   They are obliged to perform their duties regardless of the weather, and are subjected to an exposure which is very trying to them. They are very efficient, and perform their task faithfully and promptly.

The pay of a carrier is small.   By law he is entitled to $800 per annum for the first six months.   After this he is to receive $900 per annum, and at the expiration of one year, he may, upon the recommendation of the Superintendent of the Station, receive an additional $100 per annum ; but $1000 is the limit. It is said, however, that it is very rare for a carrier to receive an increase of salary before the expiration of one year.   Why he is subjected to this loss, in defiance of the law, the writer has been unable to ascertain.

Although the pay is so small, the Carrier is not allowed to enjoy it in peace. The party in power, or rather its managers, tax him unmercifully. From one to two per cent. of his salary is deducted for party expenses, and he is required to contribute at least five dollars to the expenses of every City and State election. The Postmaster of the city does not trouble himself about this robbery of his employés, but allows it to go on with his indirect approval, at least. General Dix has the honor of being the only Postmaster who ever had the moral courage to protect his subordinates from this extortion.

The Carriers have organized a benevolent association among themselves. Upon the death of a member, each surviving member of the association makes a contribution of two dollars to the relief fund. From this fund the funeral expenses are paid, and the surplus is handed over to the widow and children of the dead man.

The tenure by which the Carriers hold their positions is very uncertain. A new Postmaster may remove any or all of them, to make way for his political friends, and any refusal on their part to submit to the orders or extortions of their party-managers is sure to result in a dismissal.

XXXIV.
A. T. STEWART.

ALEXANDER T. STEWART was born in Belfast, in Ireland, in 1802. He is of Scotch-Irish parentage. At the age of three years he lost his father, and was adopted by his grandfather, who gave him a good common school and collegiate education, intending him for the ministry. His grandfather died during his collegiate course, and this threw him upon his own resources. He at once abandoned all hope of a professional career, and set sail for America. He reached New York in 1818, and began his career here as assistant teacher in a commercial school. His first salary was $300. In a year or two he went into business for himself, carrying on a modest little store, and manifesting no especial talent for business.

At the age of twenty-one, he went back to Ireland to take possession of a legacy of nearly one thousand pounds, left him by his grandfather. He invested the greater part of this sum in "insertions" and "scollop trimmings," and returned to New York. He rented a little store at 283 Broadway, and there displayed his stock, which he sold readily at a fair profit. His store was next door to the then popular Bonafanti, who kept the largest and best patronized variety store of the day. Stewart's little room was twenty-two feet wide by twenty feet deep.

Without mercantile experience, and possessing no advantage but his determination to succeed, Mr. Stewart started boldly on what proved the road to fortune. He gave from fourteen to eighteen hours per day to his business. He could not afford to employ any help, and he did all his own work. He was almost a total stranger to the business community of New York, and he had no credit. He kept a small stock of goods on hand, which he bought for cash and sold in the same way for a small profit. His purchases were made chiefly at auctions, and consisted of "sample lots"—that is, miscellaneous collections of small articles thrown together in heaps and sold for what they would bring. He spent several hours after business each day in assorting and dressing these goods. They were sold at a low price, but his profit was fair, as he had paid but a trifle for them. Little by little his trade increased, and he was soon obliged to employ an assistant. About this time he inaugurated the system of "selling off below cost." He had a note to pay, and no money to meet it. His store was full of goods, but he was short of ready money. No man could then afford to let his note go to protest. Such a step in those days meant financial ruin to a young man. Stewart proved himself the man for the crisis. He marked every article in his store down far below the wholesale price, and scattered over the city a cloud of handbills announcing that he would dispose of his entire stock of goods below cost within a given time. His announcement drew crowds of purchasers to his store, and before the period he had fixed for the duration of the sale, Mr. Stewart found his shelves empty and his treasury full. He paid his note with a part of the money thus obtained, and with the rest laid in a fresh stock of goods. He made his purchases at a time when the market was very dull, and, as he paid cash, secured his goods at very low prices.

The energy and business tact displayed by Mr. Stewart at length brought him their reward. In 1828, he found his little room too small for his trade. He leased a small store, thirty feet deep, on Broadway, between Chambers and Warren streets. Here he remained four years, his trade increasing rapidly all the while. In 1832, he removed to a two-story building in Broadway, between Murray and Warren streets, and in a short time was obliged by the growth of his business to add twenty feet to the depth of his store, and to put an additional story on the building. A year or two later he added a fourth story, and in 1837 a fifth story, so rapidly did he prosper. He had now a large and fashionable trade, had fairly surmounted all his early

30

difficulties, and had laid the foundation of the immense fortune he has since acquired.

The great commercial crisis of 1837 was not unexpected by him. It had always been his habit to watch the market closely, in order to profit by any sudden change in it, and his keen sagacity enabled him to foresee the approach of the storm and to prepare for it. He marked his goods down at an early day and began to "sell for cost," conducting his operations on a strictly cash basis. The prices were very low, the goods of the best quality, and he found no difficulty in obtaining purchasers. People were glad to save money by availing themselves of his low prices. In the midst of the most terrible crisis the country had ever seen, when old and established houses were breaking all around him, he was carrying on a thriving business. His cash sales averaged five thousand dollars per day. Other houses, to save themselves, were obliged to sell their goods at auction. Thither went Stewart regularly. He bought these goods for cash, and sold them over his counters at an average profit of forty per cent. On a lot of silks for which he paid fifty thousand dollars he cleared twenty thousand dollars in a few days. He came out of the crisis a rich man and the leading dry-goods dealer of New York.

A few years later he purchased the property lying on the east side of Broadway, between Chambers and Reade streets, on which he built a magnificent marble store. He moved into it in 1846. His friends declared that he had made a mistake in erecting such a costly edifice, and that he had located it on the wrong side of Broadway. Besides, he was too far up town. He listened to them patiently, and told them that in a short time they would see his new store the centre of the fashionable retail trade of the city. His prediction was speedily fulfilled.

A few years ago, finding that the retail trade was deserting its old haunts, below Canal street, and going up town, he began the erection of his present retail store, into which he moved as soon as it was completed, retaining his lower store for his wholesale business.

During the war, he made large profits from his sales to the

Government, though he exhibited genuine patriotism in these dealings by charging only the most liberal prices for his goods. The gains thus realized by him more than counterbalanced the losses he sustained by the sudden cessation of his trade with the South.

Fifty-four years have now elapsed since he first set foot in New York, poor and unknown, and to-day Mr. Stewart is the possessor of a fortune variously estimated at from thirty to fifty millions of dollars, and which is growing larger every year. The greater portion of his wealth is invested in real estate. He owns his two stores, the Metropolitan Hotel, and the Globe Theatre, on Broadway, and nearly all of Bleecker street from Broadway to Depau Row, several churches, and other valuable property. He owns more real estate than any man in America except William B. Astor, and is the most successful merchant in the world. He has acquired all this by his own unaided efforts, and without ever tarnishing his good name by one single dishonest act. Any man may be proud of such a record.

Mr. Stewart is one of the hardest workers in his vast establishment. Though he has partners to assist him, he keeps the whole of his extensive operations well in hand, and is really the directing power of them. He goes to his business between nine and ten in the morning, and works until five, and is never absent from his post unless compelled to be away.

His time is valuable, and he is not willing to waste it; therefore access to him is difficult. Many persons endeavor to see him merely to gratify their impertinent curiosity, and others wish to "interview" him for purposes which simply consume his time. To protect himself, he has been compelled to resort to the following expedient: A gentleman is kept on guard near the main door of the store, whose duty it is to inquire the business of visitors. If the visitor replies that his business is private, he is told that Mr. Stewart has no private business. If he states his business to the satisfaction of the "sentinel," he is allowed to go up stairs, where he is met by the confidential agent of the great merchant, to whom he must repeat the object of his visit. If this gentleman is satisfied, or cannot get rid of the visitor, he enters the private office of his employer, and lays the case before him. If the business of the visitor is urgent, he is admitted, otherwise an interview is denied him. If admitted, the interview is brief and to the point. There is no time lost. Matters are dispatched with a method and promptitude which astonish strangers. If the visitor attempts to draw the merchant into a conversation, or indulges in complimentary phrases, after his business is arranged, Mr. Stewart's manner instantly becomes cold and repelling, and troublesome persons are not unfrequently given a hint to leave the room. This is his working time, and he cannot afford to waste it. In social life, he is said to be a cultivated and agreeable man.

Mr. Stewart resides in a handsome brown stone mansion at the northeast corner of Fifth avenue and Thirty-fourth street. Immediately across the avenue, he has erected a residence of white marble, the handsomest and costliest dwelling in the Union, and one of the handsomest private residences in the world. It is said to have cost upwards of two millions of dollars. "The marble work, which forms the most distinguishing characteristic of this palatial abode, receives its entire shape and finish in the basement and first floor of the building. The fluted columns (purely Corinthian, and with capitals elaborately and delicately carved), which are the most striking feature of the main hall, are alone worth between three thousand five hundred and four thousand dollars each. On the right of this noble passage, as you proceed north from the side entrance, are the reception and drawing rooms, and the breakfast and dining rooms, all with marble finish, and with open doors, affording space for as splendid a promenade or ball as could be furnished probably by any private residence in Europe. To the left of the grand hall are the marble staircase and the picture-gallery— the latter about seventy-two by thirty-six feet, lofty and elegant, and singularly well designed. The sleeping apartments above are executed upon a scale equally luxurious and regardless of expense. Externally, the building must ever remain a monument of the splendor which, as far as opulence is concerned, places some of our merchants on a footing almost with royalty itself, and a glance at the interior will be a privilege eagerly sought by the visiting stranger."

Mr. Stewart is not generally regarded as a liberal man in the metropolis, probably because he refuses to give indiscriminately to those who ask his assistance.   Yet he has made munificent donations to objects which have enlisted his sympathy, and has on hand now several schemes for bettering the condition of the working classes, which will continue to exert a beneficent influence upon them long after he has passed away.   His friends— and he has many—speak of him as a very kind and liberal man, and seem much attached to him.

Mr. Stewart is now seventy years old, but looks twenty years younger.   He is of the medium height, has light brown hair and beard, which are closely trimmed.   His features are sharp, well cut, his eye bright, and his general expression calm, thoughtful, and self-reliant.   His manner is courteous to all, but reserved and cold except to his intimate friends.   He dresses quietly in the style of the day, his habits are simple, and he shuns publicity.

XXXV.
PLACES OF AMUSEMENT.

I.

THE THEATRES.

THERE are sixteen theatres in New York usually in full operation. Taking them in their order of location from south to north, they are the Stadt, the Bowery, Niblo's, Theatre Comique, the Olympic, Lina Edwin's, the Globe, Wallack's, Union Square, the Academy of Music, the Fourteenth Street, Booth's, the Grand Opera House, the Fifth Avenue, the St. James, and Wood's.

They are open throughout the fall and winter season, are well patronized, and with one or two exceptions are successful in a pecuniary sense. There are usually from 50,000 to 100,000 strangers in the city, and the majority of these find the evenings dull without some amusement to enliven them. Many of them are persons who come for pleasure, and who regard the theatres as one of the most enjoyable of all the sights of the city; but a very large portion are merchants, who are wearied with buying stock, and who really need some pleasant relaxation after the fatigues of the day. To these must be added a large class of citizens who are fond of the drama, and who patronize the theatres liberally. All these, it is stated, expend upon the various amusements of the place about $30,000 per night; and of this sum the larger part goes into the treasury of the theatres. The sum annually expended on amusements is said to be from $7,000,000 to $8,000,000.

The New York theatres richly deserve the liberal patronage

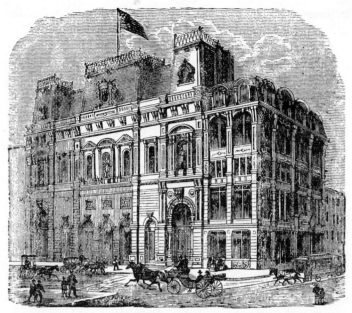

BOOTH'S THEATRE.

they enjoy.   In no other city are such establishments as elegant
and commodious, and nowhere else in America are the companies as proficient in their art, or the plays as admirably put
upon the stage.

The most beautiful theatre in the city is *Booth's*, at the southeast corner of the Sixth avenue and Twenty-third street.   It
was begun in the summer of 1867, and opened to the public in
January, 1869.   It is in the Renaissance style of architecture,
and stands seventy feet high from the sidewalk to the main
cornice, crowning which is a Mansard roof of twenty-four feet.
" The theatre proper fronts one hundred and forty-nine feet on
Twenty-third street, and is divided into three parts, so combined as to form an almost perfect whole, with arched entrances
at either extremity on the side, for the admission of the public,
and on the other for another entrance, and the use of actors and
those employed in the house.   There are three doors on the
frontage, devised for securing the most rapid egress of a crowded

audience in case of fire, and, in connection with other facilities, said to permit the building to be vacated in five minutes. On either side of these main entrances are broad and lofty windows; and above them, forming a part of the second story, are niches for statues surrounded by coupled columns resting on finely sculptured pedestals. The central or main niche is flanked on either side by quaintly contrived blank windows; and between the columns, at the depth of the recesses, are simple pilasters sustaining the elliptic arches, which serve to top and span the niches, the latter to be occupied by statues of the great creators and interpreters of the drama in every age and country. The finest Concord granite, from the best quarries in New Hampshire, is the material used in the entire façade, as well as in the Sixth avenue side. The glittering granite mass, exquisitely poised, adorned with rich and appropriate carving, statuary, columns, pilasters, and arches, and capped by the springing French roof, fringed with its shapely balustrades, offers an imposing and majestic aspect, and forms one of the architectural jewels of the city."

In its internal arragements the theatre is in keeping with its external magnificence. Entering through a sumptuous vestibule, the visitor passes into the magnificent auditorium, which is, in itself, a rare specimen of decorative art. The seats are admirably arranged, each one commanding a view of the stage. They are luxuriously upholstered, and harmonize with the rich carpets which cover the floor. Three elegant light galleries rise above the parquet. The walls and ceiling are exquisitely frescoed, and ornamented with bas reliefs in plaster. The proscenium is beautifully carved and frescoed, and is adorned with busts of the elder Booth and the proprietor of the theatre; and in the sides before the curtain are arranged six sumptuous private boxes. The curtain is an exquisite landscape. The decoration of the house is not done in the rough scenic style so common in the theatres of the country, but is the perfection of frescoe painting, and will bear the closest inspection. It is impossible, even with a strong glass, to distinguish between some of the frescoes and the bas reliefs. The stage is very large, and rises gradually from the footlights to the rear. The orchestra pen is sunk below the level of the stage, so that the heads of the musicians do not interfere with the view of the audience. The dressing of the stage is novel. The side scenes, or wings, instead of being placed at right angles to the audience, as in most theatres, are so arranged that the scene appears to extend to the right and left as well as to the rear. In this way the spectator is saved the annoyance of often looking through the wings, a defect which in most theatres completely dispels the illusion of the play. The scenery here is not set by hand, but is moved by machinery, by means of immense hydraulic rams beneath the stage, and the changes are made with such regularity and precision that they have very much the effect of "dissolving views." The scenes themselves are the work of gifted and highly educated artists, and never degenerate into the rough daubs with which most playgoers are familiar. The building is fireproof, and is warmed and ventilated by machinery. The great central chandelier and the jets around the cornice of the auditorium are lighted by electricity.

The plays presented here are superbly put on the stage. The scenery is strictly accurate when meant to represent some historic locality, and is the finest to be found in America. Perhaps the grandest stage picture ever given to an audience was the graveyard scene in "Hamlet," which drama, in the winter of 1869–70, "held the boards" for over one hundred nights. The dresses, the equipments, and general "make up" of the actors are in keeping with the scenery. Even the minutest detail is carefully attended to. Nothing is so unimportant as to be overlooked in this establishment.

With a few exceptions, the company is unworthy of the place and the fame of the proprietor. Mr. Booth, himself, is the great attraction. It is his custom to open the season with engagements of other distinguished "stars," and to follow them himself about the beginning of the winter, and to continue his performances until the spring, when he again gives way to others. When he is performing it is impossible to procure a seat after the rising of the curtain.

GRAND OPERA HOUSE.

The Grand Opera House is next to Booth's in beauty. It is much larger than that theatre. But for its unfortunate location, nearly a mile from Broadway, it would be one of the most successful establishments in the city. The theatre is divided into two buildings, one fronting on the Eighth avenue and Twenty-third street, and containing the offices and entrances, and the theatre proper, which is in the rear of the former. The former building is a magnificent structure of white marble, in the Italian style of architecture. It fronts 113 feet on Eighth avenue, and 98 feet on Twenty-third street. It is adorned with statuary and carvings, and is far too handsome for the part of the city in which it is located. The greater portion of this building is taken up with the offices of the Erie Railway Company.

The theatre proper is connected with the front building by means of a superb vestibule, into which open the doors of the auditorium. It is one of the most beautiful halls in America, and one of the pleasantest lounging places. The auditorium is finished in light blue, white, and gold, and when lighted up is magnificent. Every appointment and decoration is tasteful and beautiful, and there are many persons who consider it the finest interior in America. The stage is large and convenient, and the scenery good. The performances are passable.

The house was built by Mr. Samuel N. Pike for an Opera House. It was not successful, and was sold by him to the late Colonel James Fisk, Jr., for $1,000,000, a slight advance upon its cost.

Wallack's Theatre, at the northeast corner of Broadway and Thirteenth street, is, *par eminence, the theatre* of New York. Its audiences are more exclusively composed of citizens than those of any other house. New Yorkers are proud of it, and on Thursday evenings, or the first night of some new play, the audience will consist almost entirely of city people. The theatre itself is very plain, and there are many things about it that might be bettered. In other respects it is unqualifiedly the best theatre in which the English language is spoken. It is devoted almost entirely to comedy, and the plays presented on its stage are always of a high character. The Star system is not adopted here, but the company consists of the best and most carefully trained actors and actresses to be found here or in England. It is emphatically a company of gentlemen and ladies. At present it includes Lester Wallack, the proprietor, John Brougham, Charles Mathews, John Gilbert, Charles Fisher, and J. H. Stoddart, and Mrs. Jennings, Miss Plessy Mordaunt, Miss Effie Germon, and Mrs. John Sefton. Mr. Wallack is very proud of his theatre, and with good reason. He has made it the best in the country, and a model for the best establishments in other cities. The greatest care is taken in the production of plays, and every detail is presented to the audience with a degree of perfection which other managers vainly strive to attain. The scenery is exquisite and natural, the dresses are perfect—the toilettes of the ladies being famed for their elegance, and the acting is true to nature. There is no ranting, no straining for effect here. The members of the company talk and act like men and women of the world, and faithfully "hold the mirror up to nature." It is a common saying in New York that even a mean play will be a success at Wallack's. It will be so well put on the stage, and so perfectly performed by the company, that the most critical audience will be disarmed.

The Fifth Avenue Theatre, on Twenty-fourth street, in the rear of the Fifth Avenue Hotel, is next to Wallack's in popular favor. It is very much such an establishment in the character and excellence of its performances. It possesses a first-class company of ladies and gentlemen, some of whom have achieved national reputations, and all of whom are worthy of the highest praise. The theatre itself is a handsome marble edifice, not very large, but of very attractive appearance. The interior is bright and cheerful. The ceiling is finely frescoed, the walls are panelled with large plate-glass mirrors, and the general effect is very brilliant. The building was owned by the late Col. James Fisk, Jr. The manager is Mr. Augustin Daly, a well-known writer of successful plays. To his literary gifts Mr. Daly adds a high order of managerial talent, and it is to his efforts exclusively that the very marked success of the theatre is due.

The Academy of Music is, as its name indicates, the Opera House of New York. It is a gloomy-looking structure without, but possesses a magnificent auditorium, fitted up in the style of the European Opera Houses. Its decorations are in crimson and gold, and are magnificent and tasteful. It is the largest theatre in the city, and one of the largest in the world. It is opened occasionally during the winter for operatic performances. The audiences to be seen here are always in full dress, and the toilettes of the ladies, to say nothing of the beauty of many of the fair ones, offer a great attraction to sight-seers.

Niblo's Theatre, or as it is generally called, " Niblo's Garden,"

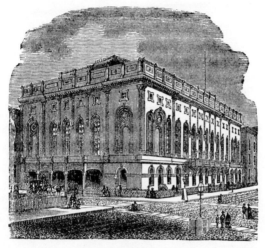

ACADEMY OF MUSIC.

is situated in the rear of the Metropolitan Hotel, with an entrance on Broadway. It is one of the largest and handsomest theatres in the city, and by far the coolest in warm weather. It is devoted principally to the spectacular drama. It was here that the famous spectacle of the Black Crook was produced. Its revival is to take plack before these pages are in print, and it will probably be continued throughout the remainder of the season.

The Olympic is a large, old-fashioned theatre, on Broadway, between Houston and Bleecker streets. It is devoted to pantomime, and is famous as the headquarters of the erratic genius who calls himself Humpty Dumpty.

The Old Bowery Theatre, situated on the thoroughfare from which it takes its name, below Canal street, is the only old theatre left standing in the city. Three theatres have preceded it on this site, and all have been destroyed by fire. Within the last few years, the interior of the present theatre has been greatly modernized. The plays presented here are of a character peculiarly suited to that order of genius which despises Shakspeare, and hopes to be one day capable of appreciating the Black

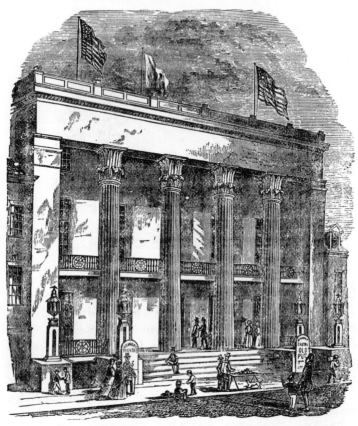

THE OLD BOWERY THEATRE.

Crook. " Blood and thunder dramas," they are called in the city. The titles are stunning—the plays themselves even more so. A writer in one of the current publications of the day gives the following truthful picture of a " Saturday night at the Bowery :"

" I had not loitered long at the entrance after the gas blazed up, when from up the street, and from down the street, and from across the street, there came little squads of dirty, ragged urchins—the true gamin of New York. These at once made a gymnasium of the stone steps—stood on their heads upon the

pavements or climbed, like locusts, the neighboring lamp-posts ;
itching for mischief ; poking fun furiously ; they were the mer-
riest gang of young dare-devils I have seen in a long day.   It
was not long before they were recruited by a fresh lot of young
'sardines' from somewhere else—then they went in for more
monkey-shines until the door should be unbarred.   They
seemed to know each other very well, as· if they were some
young club of genial spirits that had been organized outside of
the barriers of society for a long while.   What funny habili-
ments they sported.   It had never been my experience to see
old clothes thrown upon young limbs so grotesquely.   The coat
·that would have been a fit for a corpulent youth nearly buried a
skinny form the height of your cane.

"And on the other hand, 'young dropsy's' legs and arms
were like links of dried ' bolonas ' in the garments which misfortune's raffle had drawn for him.   Hats without rims—hats
of fur, dreadfully plucked, with free ventilation for the scalp—
caps with big tips like little porches of leather—caps without
tips, or, if a tip still clung to it, it was by a single thread and
dangled on the wearer's cheek like the husk of a banana.   The
majority seemed to have a weakness for the costumes of the
army and the navy.   Where a domestic tailor had clipped the
skirts of a long blue military coat he had spared the two buttons of the waist-band, and they rested on the bare heels like a
set of veritable spurs.   Shoes and boots (and remember it's a
December night) are rather scarce—and those by which these
savoyards could have sworn by grinned fearfully with sets of
naked toes.   One ' young sport,' he had seen scarcely ten such
winters, rejoiced in a pair of odd-mated rubber over-shoes,
about the dimensions of snow-shoes.   They saluted him as
'Gums.'   A youngster, with a childish face and clear blue eyes,
now shuffled upon the scene.

" ' O Lordy, here's Horace, jist see his get up.'   A shout of
laughter went up, and Horace was swallowed in the ragged mob.

" ' Horace ' sported a big army cap like a huge blue extin-
guisher.   He wrapped his wiry form in a cut-down, long-napped
white beaver coat, the lappels of which were a foot square, and

shingled his ankles as if he stood between a couple of placards. I had seen the latest caricature on the philosopher of the *Tribune*, but this second edition of H. G. swamped it. I knew that that young rogue had counted upon the effect of his white coat, and he enjoyed his christening with a gleeful face and a sparkle in his blue eyes. O, for the pencil of a Beard or a Bellew, to portray those saucy pug-noses, those dirty and begrimed faces! Faces with bars of blacking, like the shadows of small gridirons—faces with woful bruised peepers—faces with fun-flashing eyes—faces of striplings, yet so old and haggard—faces full of evil and deceit.

"Every mother's son of them had his fists anchored in his breeches pockets, and swaggered about, nudging each other's ribs with their sharp little elbows. They were not many minutes together before a battle took place. Some one had tripped 'Gums,' and one of his old shoes flew into the air. I think he of the white coat was the rascal, but being dubbed a philosopher, he did his best to look very wise, but a slap on the side of the ridge of his white collar upset his dignity, and 'Horace' 'went in,' and his bony fists rattled away on the close-shaven pate of 'Gums.'

"The doors are now unbarred, and this ragged 'pent up little Utica' rends itself, but not without much more scratching and much swearing. O, the cold-blooded oaths that rang from those young lips! As the passage to the pit is by a sort of cellar door, I lost sight of the young scamps as the last one pitched down its gloomy passage.

"In the human stream—in a whirlpool of fellow-beings—nudging their way to the boxes and the upper tiers, I now found myself. It was a terrible struggle; females screaming, were eddied around and around until their very faces were in a wire cage of their own 'skeletons.'

"'Look out for pickpockets,' shouted a Metropolitan. Every body then tried to button his coat over his breast, and every body gave it up as a bad job. In at last, but with the heat of that exertion—the smell of the hot gas—the fetid breath of two thousand souls, not particular, many, as to the quality of their gin—what a sweltering bath follows! The usher sees a ticket clutched before him, and a breathless individual saying wildly, 'where!' He points to a distant part of the house, and the way to it is through a sea of humanity. A sort of a Dead Sea, for one can walk on it easier than he can dive through it. I shall never know how I got there at last; all I remember now are the low curses, the angry growls and a road over corns and bunions.

"The prompter's bell tingles and then tingles again. The bearded Germans of the orchestra hush their music, and the big field of green baize shoots to the cob-web arch.

"Now is the time to scan the scene—that teeming house— that instant when all faces are turned eagerly to the foot-lights, waiting breathlessly the first sound of the actor's voice. The restlessness of that tossing sea of humanity is at a dead calm now. Every nook and cranny is occupied—none too young— none too old to be there at the rise of the curtain. The suckling infant 'mewing and puking in its mother's arms.' The youngster rubbing his sleepy eyes. The timid Miss, half frightened with the great mob and longing for the fairy world to be created. Elder boys and elder sisters. Mothers, fathers, and the wrinkled old grand-sire. Many of these men sit in their shirt-sleeves, sweating in the humid atmosphere. Women are giving suck to fat infants. Blue-shirted sailors encircle their black-eyed Susans, with brawny arms (they make no 'bones' of showing their honest love in this democratic temple of Thespis). Division street milliners, black-eyed, rosy-cheeked, and flashy dressed sit close to their jealous-eyed lovers. Little Jew boys, with glossy ringlets and beady black eyes, with teeth and noses like their fat mammas and avaricious-looking papas, are yawning everywhere. Then there is a great crowd of roughs, prentice boys and pale, German tailors—the latter with their legs uncrossed for a relaxation. Emaciated German and Italian barbers, you know them from their dirty linen, their clean-shaven cheeks and their locks redolent with bear's grease.

"Through this mass, wandering from pit to gallery, go the red-shirted peanut-venders, and almost every jaw in the vast concern is crushing nut-shells. You fancy you hear it in the lulls of the play like a low unbroken growl.

31

" In the boxes sit some very handsome females—rather loudly dressed,—but beauty will beam and flash from any setting.

" Lean over the balcony, and behold in the depths below the famous pit, now crowded by that gang of little outlaws we parted with a short time ago.

" Of old times—of a bygone age—is this institution. In no other theatre in the whole town is that choice spot yielded to the unwashed. But this is the ' Bowery,' and those squally little spectators so busy scratching their close-mown polls, so vigorously pummeling each other, so unmercifully rattaned by despotic ushers—they are its best patrons.

" And are they not, in their light, great critics, too ? Don't they know when to laugh, when to blubber, and when to applaud, and don't they know when to *hiss*, though ! What a *fiat* is their withering hiss ! What poor actor dare brave it ? It has gone deep, deep into many a poor player's heart and crushed him forever.

" The royal road to a news-boy's heart is to rant in style.

" Versatile Eddy and vigorous Boniface are the lads, in our day, for the news-boys' stamps.

" Ranting is out of the female line, but Bowery actresses have a substitute for it.

" At the proper moment, they draw themselves up in a rigid statue, they flash their big eyes, they dash about wildly their dishevelled hair, with out-stretched arms and protruding chins they then shriek out, V-i-l-l-a-i-n !

" O, Fannie Herring ! what a tumult you have stirred up in the roused pit ! No help for it, my dear lady. See, there's ' Horace,' standing on his seat and swinging his big blue cap in a cloud of other caps—encore ! encore ! And the pretty actress bows to the pit, and there is more joy in her heart from the yells of those skinny little throats than from all the flowers that ladies and gents from above may pelt her with.

" The bill of fare for an evening's entertainment at the Old Bowery is as long as your cane, and the last piece takes us far into the night—yet the big house sits it out, and the little ones sleep it out, and the tired actor well earns his pay.

"I'll not criticise the acting—a great part of the community thinks it's beyond the pale of criticism—this peculiarity of tearing things to pieces, and tossing around 'supes' promiscuously.

"And another thing, those little ungodly imps down there have a great appreciation of virtue and pathos. They dash their dirty fists into their peepers at the childish treble of a little Eva—and they cheer, O, so lustily, when Chastity sets her heavy foot upon the villain's heart and points her sharp sword at his rascal throat. They are very fickle in their bestowal of approbation, and their little fires die out or swell into a hot volcano according to the vehemence of the actor. 'Wake me up when Kirby dies,' said a veteran little denizen of the pit to his companions, and he laid down on the bench to snooze.

"'Mind yer eye, Porgie,' said his companion, before Porgie had got a dozen winks. 'I think ther's somthen goen to bust now.' Porgie's friend had a keen scent for sensation.

"As I came out, at the end of the performance, I again saw 'Horace.' He had just rescued a 'butt' from a watery grave in the gutter. 'Jeminy! don't chaps about town smoke 'em awful short now'days!' was the observation of the young philosopher.

"The theatre is almost the only amusement that the ragged newsboy has, apart from those of the senses. The Newsboys' Lodging House, which has been the agent of so much good among this neglected class of our population, find the late hours of the theatre a serious obstacle to their usefulness. It is safe to say that if the managers of the two Bowery Theatres would close at an earlier hour, say eleven o'clock, they would prosper as greatly as at present, and the boys who patronize their establishments would be much better off in body and mind. An effort is about to be made to obtain this reform from the managers voluntarily—instead of seeking legislative aid. We are quite sure it will be for the interest of all to close the theatres early."

The Stadt Theatre, just across the street from the Old Bowery, is exclusively a German establishment. It is a plain old-fashioned building, without and within, but is worth a fortune to its proprietors. The performances are given in the German language, and the company is usually good. The prices are high and the audiences are large. Occasionally a season of German opera is given. I doubt that a more appreciative audience is to be found than that which assembles within the walls of the Stadt on opera nights. They are to a man good judges and dear lovers of music, and their applause, when it breaks forth, is a spontaneous outburst which shakes the house to its foundations. It is generously given, too, and must be particularly grateful to the performers.

It is said that the members of the dramatic profession and the various attachés of the theatres number 5000 persons. They constitute a class, or rather a world of their own. We shall have more to say of some portions of them in other chapters, and can only speak of them in a general way here. As a rule they are poor, and are compelled to work hard. Wallack's and a few other establishments pay good salaries and have many "off nights," but of the majority of performers constant labor is required, at poor pay. It is said that Forrest and Booth have received as much as $500 per night, and that Jefferson and Owens are paid at very near the same rate. The "stars," however, can make their own terms, but the rank and file of the profession have to take what they can get. The pay of these ranges from $15 to $50 per week. Some of the leading ladies and gentlemen receive from $100 to $200 per week, but these can be counted on the fingers of one hand. Considering the work, the pay is poor, for an actor's life requires an immense amount of study and preparation, and is terribly trying to the nervous system. At some of the theatres three performances are sometimes given in a single day, the same members of the company appearing each time.

"Ballet girls," says Olive Logan, "get from $8 to $15 per week; the prompter $25 to $30; the call boy $15; the property man's salary ranges from $15 to $30. Then there are men up in the rigging loft, who attend to the flies and the curtain wheel, and various assistants, at salaries of $20 and $10. There are from two to three scene painters at salaries of from $60 to $100. The back door keeper has $10, and two women to clean the theatre every day at $6 each. The orchestra consists of a leader, at $100, and from twelve to sixteen musicians, whose salaries range from $30 to $18 a week. The gasman and fireman get from $6 to $25 a week ; costumer or wardrobe keeper $20 to $40; dressers $5 to $6 ; ushers $4 to $6 ; doorkeepers $12 ; policeman $5 ; treasurer $25 to $40."

One of the most important positions in the establishment is the ticket clerk. The receipts of the house pass through his hands, and as a constant effort is made to pass off bad money in this way, it is necessary to have some one in this position who is a good judge of money. In some of the theatres a broker's clerk or bank clerk is employed in this capacity.

With the exception of Wallack's, the Fifth Avenue, and perhaps Booth's, the theatres generally change their companies every season. The houses named retain the favorites, and there are among these companies many whose loss would be loudly deplored by the theatre-going people of the city. Many of the best actors, having distinguished themselves here, assume the rank of stars, and play engagements throughout the States. A metropolitan reputation will carry them successfully over the whole Union.

II.

MINOR AMUSEMENTS.

NEXT in popularity to the theatres are the performances of the Negro Minstrels. Some of these companies have permanent halls which they occupy during the winter. The summer and early autumn are spent in travelling through the country. The principal companies are Bryant's and the San Francisco Minstrels.

Dan Bryant is now the proprietor of a beautiful little theatre in Twenty-third street, just west of the Sixth avenue. It is one of the cosiest and most comfortable places in the city, and is usually filled with an audience of city people of the better class. The music is good, the singing excellent, and the mirth unrestrained and hearty. Dan Bryant, himself one of the most irresistibly humorous delineators of the " burnt cork opera," has collected a band of genuine artists, and has fairly won his success. He has raised Negro Minstrelsy to the dignity of a fashionable amusement, and has banished from it all that is coarse and offensive. Men worn out with business cares go there to laugh, and they do laugh most heartily. I think that even the king who " never smiled again," would have been forced to hold his sides here. Families come by the score to laugh at the vagaries of the sable minstrels, and the mirth of the little folks is one of the heartiest and healthiest sounds to be heard in the great city.

Next in order are the concerts. These are well patronized when the performers are well known. There are several fine halls used for concerts and lectures. The principal are Steinway Hall, in Fourteenth street, and Irving Hall, in Irving Place.

Lectures also draw largely. The principal halls used for this purpose are Steinway Hall, and the Halls of the Young Men's Christian Association and the Cooper Institute.

Last, but not least in the estimation of New Yorkers, is the Circus. This is a permanent entertainment during the fall and winter. The performances are given in a handsome iron building located on Fourteenth street, opposite Irving Place. The building is in the form of a circus tent, and is lighted with gas, and warmed by steam coils. The audiences are large, and consist to a great extent of children. The little folks are very fond of the sports of the ring, and are among Mr. Lent's best patrons.

XXXVI.
THE MARKETS.

THE principal markets of New York are the Fulton, Washington, Jefferson, Catharine, Union, Clinton, Franklin, Centre, and Tompkins Markets. With the exception of Tompkins Market, they are, as far as the houses are concerned, unmitigated nuisances to the city. They are in the last stages of dilapidation, and from without present the most ungainly spectacles to be witnessed in New York. The streets around them are always dirty and crowded, and in the hot days of the summer the air is loaded with foul smells which arise from them.

Within, however, the scene is very different. The ricketty old buildings are crammed to repletion with everything edible the season affords. In the summer the display of fruit is often magnificent. The products of every section of the Union are piled up here in the greatest profusion. The country for miles around the city has been stripped of its choicest luxuries, and even the distant West, and the far-off South have sent their contributions to the bountiful store. Meats, fish, and fowl also abound, of every species and description. Indeed, one who has the means can purchase here almost everything the heart can desire. The demand is great, and the prices are high. The stock seems immense, but it disappears rapidly. Fruits command high prices in New York, but sell readily. The market is very rarely overstocked. The same may be said of vegetables. Good vegetables are always in demand. Those who furnish pure, fresh vegetables and meats are sure of a prosperous trade, but the amount of tainted wares of this kind disposed of daily is surprising. Nothing is lost here. Everything finds a purchaser.

WASHINGTON MARKET.

498

Two-thirds of the people of the city, to save time and trouble, deal with the " corner groceries," and " provision stores," and never see the markets, but still the number of persons patronizing these establishments is very large. The sales begin between four and five o'clock in the morning. The first comers are the caterers for the hotels, the restaurants, the fashionable boarding houses and the mansions of the rich, and the proprietors of the aforesaid " corner groceries " and " provision stores." These latter charge their own customers an advance of from twenty-five to fifty per cent. on the market rates. Prices are high at this hour, and the best the market affords is quickly disposed of. The hotels and restaurants leave standing orders with the dealers, but always send their caterers to see that these orders are faithfully executed. " Market-men have to be watched," say the caterers.

As the morning advances, prices decline. The dealers have reaped their harvest, and can afford to " fall " on what is left. Now come those whose means compel them to be content with indifferent fare. With them is seen a perfect torrent of boarding-house keepers, who are too smart to come when the prices are high and the articles good and fresh. Others, too, the dealers will tell you, are independently wealthy, some are said to be millionaires. They are niggardly as to their tables, though they make great show in other respects, and they will haggle over the last penny. Last of all, towards ten o'clock, and later, come the poor, to purchase what is left. God help them! It is no wonder the death rate is large in this class.

The best known markets are the Fulton, at the end of Fulton street, on East River, and the Washington, at the western end of the same street, on North River. Almost anything can be found in the Fulton market. There are all kinds of provisions here; eating stands abound; bar rooms are located in the cellars; cheap finery is offered by the bushel in some of the stalls; books, newspapers, and periodicals are to be found in others, at prices lower than those of the regular stores; and ice creams, confections, and even hardware and dry goods are sold here. The oysters of this market have a worldwide reputation.

Dorlan's oyster house is the best known. It is a plain, rough-looking room, but it is patronized by the best people in the city, for nowhere else on the island are such delicious oysters to be had. Ladies in full street dress, young bloods in all their finery, statesmen, distinguished soldiers, those whom you will meet in the most exclusive drawing rooms of the avenue, come here to partake of the proprietor's splendid "stews."

It is more than thirty years since Dorlan began business here, and he has amassed a handsome fortune. He has done so by providing the best oysters in the market. He is well known throughout the city, and is deservedly popular. He is conscientious, upright in the minutest particular, and gives his personal attention to every detail of his business. Although very wealthy, he may still be seen at his stand, in his shirt sleeves, as of old, superintending the operations of his establishment, and setting an excellent example to younger men who are seeking to rise in the world.

The Washington market is more of a wholesale than a retail establishment. Supplies of meat, fish, vegetables, etc., are usually sent to the wholesale dealers here, to be sold on commission. These dealers will frequently go into the country, and engage a truckman's entire crop of vegetables and fruits, and then retail them to city dealers at their own prices.

XXXVII.

THE CHURCHES.

I.

THE SACRED EDIFICES.

IN some respects New York may be called "the City of
Churches." It contains 430 Protestant churches and chapels,
with "sittings" for nearly 400,000 persons. Exclusive of
endowments, the church property of the Protestant denominations is estimated at over $30,000,000. The annual expenses
of these churches make an aggregate of about $1,500,000, and
they pay out in charities about $5,000,000 more. The Roman
Catholics have forty churches, each with a large and rapidly
increasing congregation. Their church property is estimated at
about $4,000,000, and their other property used for religious
and educational purposes is exceedingly valuable. The Greek
Church has one congregation, now worshipping in a temporary
chapel. The Jews have twenty-seven synagogues, some of
which are very handsome. In all, there are nearly 500 edifices
in New York used for the public worship of God.

The first churches built in the city were those of the Dutch.
Their church records are uninterrupted as far back as the year
1639. Their successors are now known as the Reformed Dutch,
and are now in possession of twenty-five churches and chapels
in the city. Some of these are very handsome. The new Collegiate Church, at the northwest corner of the Fifth avenue and
Forty-eighth street, is to be built of brown stone, with light stone
trimmings. It is nearly completed, and when finished will be
one of the most massive and imposing church edifices in America,

The Protestant Episcopal Church was introduced into the city at the advent of the English. The conquerors seized and appropriated to their own use the old Dutch Church in the fort, and introduced the service of the Church of England, which was continued there until the completion of the first Trinity Church in 1697. This denomination now possesses ninety-four churches and chapels in the city, and a number of benevolent and charitable institutions. Its churches outnumber those of any other denomination, and its membership is the wealthiest. The General Theological Seminary of the Protestant Episcopal Church is located in New York. Trinity, mentioned elsewhere in this work, is the principal church. Grace, St. Thomas's, St. George's, Ascension, Calvary, the new St. Bartholomew's, St. John's, Trinity Chapel, St. Paul's, St. Peter's, the Transfiguration, and the Heavenly Rest, are among the most beautiful in the city.

The Lutherans were the third in the order of their appearance in New York. They were to be found here before the capture of the city by the English, but their first church was not erected until 1702. It was a small stone edifice, and was located at the corner of Broadway and Rector street. They have now fifteen flourishing churches, and are very strong in members and wealth.

The Presbyterians now constitute one of the largest and most flourishing denominations of the city. Owing to the intolerance of the Established Church and the Civil Government, they had considerable difficulty in introducing their faith here. They at first met in private houses. In 1707, one of their ministers was heavily fined, and condemned to pay the costs of the suit for preaching and baptizing a child in a private house. In 1716 they organized their first society, and connected it with the Philadelphia Presbytery. The city authorities now granted them toleration, and allowed them to worship in the City Hall until 1719. In the latter year they opened their first church in Wall street, near Broadway. The Presbyterian churches and mission chapels of New York are now as follows: Presbyterian proper, 70; United Presbyterian, 8; Reformed Presbyterian, 7 ; Congregationalists, 9 ; making a total of 94.   The denomination is extremely wealthy, and many of its churches are noted for their beauty and magnificence.   The Presbyterians also support a number of noble benevolent and charitable enterprises.

The Baptists, like the Presbyterians, had considerable difficulty in establishing themselves here.   In 1709, a Baptist minister was sentenced to three months' imprisonment for preaching in New York without the permission of the city authorities.   For some time the Baptists were subjected to considerable hostility, and were often obliged to immerse their proselytes by night to avoid interruption.   Their first church was erected on Golden Hill, now known as Gold street, about 1725.   The various branches of this denomination have now about fifty churches and chapels in the city.   The First and the Fifth Avenue Churches are among the wealthiest corporations in the city, and their sacred edifices are noted for their beauty and elegance.

The Methodists appeared here soon after their church had become strong in Great Britain.   In 1766, Philip Embury, an Irishman, and a local preacher in the Wesleyan Church, began to hold religious services in his own house, in Barrack Row, now Park Place, to a congregation of half a dozen persons. The church growing greatly in numbers, a large room was rented for public worship on what is now William street, between Fulton and John streets, and was used by them until the completion of their first church in John street, in 1768.   The Methodists now have sixty churches and chapels in the city. They claim a membership of 13,000, and estimate the value of their church property at over $2,000,000.   Some of their churches are very handsome.   St. Paul's, at the northeast corner of Fourth avenue and Twenty-second street, is a beautiful structure.   It is built of white marble, in the Romanesque style.   The Rectory, adjoining it, is of the same material.   It is the gift of Daniel Drew to the congregation.   The spire is 210 feet high, and the church will seat 1300 persons.

The Jews are said to have come into New York with its

early settlers, and there seems to be good authority for this statement. Finding tolerance and protection here, they have increased and multiplied rapidly, and are now very numerous. They are immensely wealthy as a class, and make a liberal provision for the unfortunate of their own creed. They have twenty-seven synagogues, several of which are among the most prominent buildings in the city. The Temple Emanuel, Fifth avenue and Forty-third street, is one of the costliest and most beautiful religious edifices in America. It is built of a light colored stone, with an elaborately carved front, and from the north and south ends rise slender and graceful towers, which give an air of lightness to the whole structure. The Temple is said to have cost, including the site, about one million of dollars.

The Roman Catholics are, in point of numbers, one of the strongest, if not the strongest denomination in the city. In the early history of the colony a law was enacted which required that every Roman Catholic priest who should come into the city of his own free will, should be hanged forthwith. This barbarous statute was never put in force, and one cannot help smiling to think how times have changed since then for the people of the Roman faith. Their first church occupied the site of the present St. Peter's, in Barclay street, and was built in 1786. In 1815, they were strong enough to erect St. Patrick's Cathedral, on the corner of Mott and Prince streets. They have now forty churches in the city, and own a vast amount of real estate. The city authorities, being frequently of this faith, have made liberal grants to their church, and in this way have excited no little hostility on the part of the Protestant churches, who are, as a rule, opposed to secular grants to religious denominations.

The Roman Catholics of New York consist principally of the poorer classes, though the church contains a large body of cultivated and wealthy people. Still its strength is among the poor. Consequently the majority of its churches are located in the meaner quarters of the city, so that they may be convenient to those to whose spiritual wants they minister. The attendance upon these churches is immense. The pastor of a church in the

Fourth Ward once said to the writer that he had 25,000 persons of all ages and both sexes under his pastoral care, and that nearly all of them were very poor.   His labors were arduous, and they were well performed.

Some of the Roman Catholic churches, on the other hand, are located in the most desirable portions of the city, and are extremely handsome within, even if plain without. St. Stephen's, on Twenty-eighth street, between Third and Lexington avenues, is an unattractive brick structure extending through to Twenty-ninth street. The interior is very large and very beautiful. The altar is of pure white marble, and its adornments are of the richest description. The church is decorated with a series of excellent fresco paintings of a devotional character. The altar piece, representing The Crucifixion, is a magnificent work. The music is perhaps the best in the city. The church will seat nearly 4000 people, and is usually crowded.

The new St. Patrick's Cathedral, now in course of erection, will be the most elaborate church edifice in the Union. It covers the entire block bounded by Fifth and Madison avenues, and Fiftieth and Fifty-first streets, fronting on Fifth avenue. The corner stone was laid by Archbishop Hughes in 1858, and the work has been in progress, with some interruptions, ever since. Archbishop McCloskey has for several years past been pushing the work forward with steadfastness, and it is believed that a few years more will witness its completion.

The site of the church is very fine. It is the most elevated spot on Fifth avenue. The length of the building will be 332 feet; breadth of the nave and choir, 132 feet; breadth at the transepts, 174 feet. The foundations rest upon a stratum of solid rock. The first course is of Maine granite, the material used in the Treasury Building at Washington. The upper portions of this course are neatly dressed with the chisel. The remainder of the church is to be constructed of white marble, from the Pleasantville quarries, in Westchester county. The crystalline character of this stone produces very beautiful effects in those portions which are most elaborately worked. The style of the edifice is the "decorated Gothic," which was most

THE NEW ST. PATRICK'S CATHEDRAL.

popular in Europe between the ninth and fifteenth centuries. The design would seem to be modelled after the famous Cathedral of Cologne, the most beautiful specimen of this order of architecture. The Fifth avenue front will be exceedingly beautiful. The carvings and statuary for its ornament are genuine works of art, and this portion of the building will be equal to anything in the world. The central gable will be 156 feet high. On each side of it will rise towers which are to reach a height of 328 feet from the ground, counting from the summit of the cross on each. These towers are to be square in form to a point 136 feet above the ground. They are then to rise in octagonal lanterns 54 feet high, above which are to soar magnificent spires to a further elevation of 138 feet. The towers and spires are to be adorned with buttresses, niches filled with statues, and pinnacles, which will have the effect of concealing the change from the square to the octagon. The cost of the church is estimated at over two millions of dollars.

The Unitarians made their appearance in the city in 1819, and have now five churches. One of these, the Church of the Messiah, Park avenue and Thirty-fourth street, is very handsome.

The Friends, or Quakers, opened their first meeting-house in 1703, and now have five places of worship, and own considerable property in the city.

All the denominations are actively engaged in missionary work. They have mission houses and chapels and schools in the worst quarters of the city, which are doing a noble work, and support them liberally.

The majority of the city churches are above Canal street. In some localities, especially on the fashionable streets, they crowd each other too greatly. A few are very wealthy, but the majority are compelled to struggle to get along. Pew rent is very high in New York, and only persons in good circumstances can have pews in a thriving church. In a fashionable church large sums are paid for pews.

The New Yorkers can hardly be said to be a church-going people. The morning services are usually well attended, but the afternoon and evening services show a " beggarly array of empty benches." It is astonishing to see the widespread carelessness which prevails here on the subject of church-going. There are thousands of respectable people in the great city who never see the inside of a church, unless drawn there by some special attraction. The support of the churches, therefore, falls on comparatively a few. These give liberally, and it may be

32

doubted whether any other band of Christians are more munificent in their offerings.

The distinctions which govern the world prevail in the city churches. Fashion and wealth rule here with an iron hand. The fashionable churches, with the exception of Grace Church, are now located high up town. They are large and handsome, and the congregations are wealthy and exclusive. Forms are rigidly insisted upon, and the reputation of the church for exclusiveness is so well known that those in the humbler walks of life shrink from entering its doors. They feel that they would not be welcome, that the congregation would consider them hardly fit to address their prayers to the Great White Throne from so exclusive a place. The widow's mite would cause the warden's face to wear a well-bred look of pitying amazement if laid in the midst of the crisp bank notes of the collection; and Lazarus would lie a long time at the doors of some of these churches, unless the police should remove him.

Riches and magnificence are seen on every side. The music is divine, and is rendered by a select choir of professional singers. The service is performed to perfection. The sermon is short and very pretty, and the congregation roll away in their carriages, or stroll along the avenue, well satisfied that they are in the "narrow way," which the Master once declared to be so difficult to the feet of the rich man. But that was eighteen hundred years ago, and the world has grown wiser in its own estimation.

II.

THE CLERGY.

TALENT, backed by experience and industry, will succeed in the long run in New York, but talent is not essential to success in the ministry here. We have often wondered what does make the success of some clergymen in this city. They have done well, and are popular, but they are not pulpit orators. In other cities a good pastor need not always be a good preacher. He may endear himself to his people in many different ways, so that his other good qualities atone for his oratorical deficiencies.   In New York, however, pastoral duties are almost entirely confined to the ministrations in the church, visitation of the sick, marriages, and attendance upon funerals.   The city is so immense, the flock so widely scattered, that very few clergymen can visit all their people.   The result is that pastoral visiting is but little practised here.   The clergyman is generally " at home " to all who choose to call, on a certain evening in each week.   A few civil, common-place words pass between the shepherd and the sheep, but that is all.   The mass of the people of this city are neglected by the clergy.   Possibly the fault is with the people. Indeed, it is highly probable, considering the carelessness which New Yorkers manifest on the subject of church going.   During the summer months a large part of New York is left to do without the Gospel.   Very many of the churches are closed. The ministers are, many of them, delicate men, and they cannot bear the strain of an unbroken year of preaching.   So they shut up their churches during the warm season, go off to Long Branch, Saratoga, or the mountains, or cross the ocean.   With the fall of the leaves, they come back to town by the score, and their churches are again opened " for preaching."   Don't be deceived by their robust appearance.   It is only temporary.   By the approach of the next summer they will grow thin and weak-voiced again, and nothing will restore them but a season at some fashionable resort, or a run over the ocean.

A man of real talent will always, if he has a church conveniently and fashionably located, draw a large congregation to hear him ; but the location and prestige of the church often do more than the minister, for some of our poorer churches have men of genius in their pulpits, while some of the wealthiest and most fashionable congregations are called on every Sunday to listen to the merest platitudes.

Let us not be misunderstood.   There are able men in the New York pulpit—such men as Vinton, Hall, Chapin, Spring, Osgood, John Cotton Smith, Adams, and others—but we have some weak-headed brethren also.

A few clergymen grow rich in this city, the wealthy members

of their flock no doubt aiding them. Some marry fortunes. As a general rule, however, they have no chance of saving any money. Salaries are large here, but expenses are in proportion; and it requires a large income for a minister to live respectably. One in charge of a prosperous congregation cannot maintain his social position, or uphold the dignity of his parish, on less than from eight to ten thousand dollars per annum, if he has even a moderate family. Very little, if any, of this will go in extravagance. Many clergymen are obliged to live here on smaller salaries, but they do it "by the skin of their teeth."

As a rule, the clergymen of New York are like those of other places. Whether weak-headed, or strong-minded, they are, as a class, honest, God-fearing, self-denying men. There are, however, some black sheep in the fold; but, let us thank Heaven, they are few, and all the more conspicuous for that reason.

The speculative mania (in financial, not theological matters) invades even the ranks of the clergy, and there are several well-known gentlemen of the cloth who operate boldly and skilfully in the stock markets through their brokers. One of these was once sharply rebuked by his broker for his unclerical conduct, and was advised, if he wished to carry on his speculations further, to go into the market himself, as the broker declined to be any longer the representative of a man who was ashamed of his business. There are others still who are not ashamed to mingle openly with the throng of curb-stone brokers, and carry on their operations behind the sanctity of their white cravats. These last, however, may be termed "Independents," as they have no standing in their churches, and are roundly censured by them.

Others there are who, on small salaries, support large families. These are the heroes of the profession, but the world knows little of their heroism. With their slender means, they provide homes that are models for all. They do their duty bravely, and with an amount of self-denial which is sometimes amazing. They have happy homes, too, even if it is hard to make both ends meet at the end of the year. They are often men of taste and culture, to whom such trials are particularly hard. They carry their culture into their homes, and the fruits of it blossom all around them. Wealth could not give them these pleasures, nor can poverty deprive them of them. They bring up their children in the fear and admonition of the Lord, and, thanks to the free schools and their own efforts, give them a good education. They send them out into the world well equipped for the battle of life, and reap the reward of their efforts in the honorable and useful lives of those children. They go down into the grave without knowing any of the comforts of wealth, without having ever preached to a fashionable congregation, and the world comes at last to find that their places cannot easily be filled. Let us be sure " their works do follow them."

XXXVIII.
BOARDING-HOUSE LIFE.

NEW YORK is a vast boarding-house. Let him who doubts this assertion turn to the columns of the *Herald*, and there read its confirmation in the long columns of advertisements of " Boarders wanted," which adorn that sheet. Or, better still, let him insert an advertisement in the aforesaid *Herald*, applying for board, and he will find himself in receipt of a mail next morning that will tax the postman's utmost capacity. The boarding-houses of New York are a feature, and not the pleasantest one, of the great city. How many there are, is not known, but in some localities they cover both sides of the street for several blocks. Those which are termed fashionable, and which imitate the expensiveness of the hotels without furnishing a tithe of their comforts, are located in the Fifth avenue, Broadway, and the Fourth avenue, or near those streets. Some are showily furnished as to the public rooms, and are conducted in seemingly elegant style, but the proprietress, for it is generally a woman who is at the head of these establishments, pays for all this show by economizing in the table and other things essential to comfort. The really " elegant establishments," where magnificence of display is combined with a good table and substantial comfort in other respects, may be almost named in a breath.

Whether fashionable or unfashionable, all boarding-houses ar · alike. They are supremely uncomfortable. The boarder is never really satisfied, and lives in a state of perpetual warfare with his landlady. The landlady, on her part, takes care that her guests shall not be too comfortable. People generally become accustomed to this feverish mode of life; so accustomed to it indeed that they cannot exist without it. They find a sort of positive pleasure in boarding-house quarrels, and would not be able to exist without the excitement of them.

The majority of boarders in the city are persons who have not the means to live in their own houses. Others there are, who fancy they have less trouble in boarding than in keeping their own establishments. This is a singular but common delusion, and its victims endure with what patience they can the wretched fare, the constant changes, and the uninterrupted inconvenience and strife of a boarding-house, and imagine all the while that they are experiencing less trouble and annoyance than they would undergo in keeping house. The truth is, living is so expensive in New York, that all modes of life are troublesome to those who are not wealthy enough to disregard expense. But, here, as elsewhere, the privacy of one's own home is better than the publicity of a boarding-house, and a fuss with Bridget in one's own kitchen preferable to a row with a landlady, who may turn you out of doors at the very moment you are congratulating yourself that you are settled for the season. To persons with families, boarding-house life ought to be intolerable. Those who have children find that they cannot rear them as properly as they could within their own homes, that they cannot as surely shield them from unfavorable outside influences. Indeed, the troubles which these "incumbrances" cause are so great that the wife and mother comes to the conclusion that more children will simply add to her difficulties of this kind, and so she commences to "regulate" her family, and the little ones cease coming. Some boarding-houses will not receive children at any price. Year by year the number of such establishments is increasing. What will be the result? The question is not hard to answer.

The boarding-house is generally a cast-off mansion of gentility. There are a score of things about it to remind you that it was once a home, and to set you to speculating on the ways of the grim fate that has changed it into a place of torment. Whole volumes have been written on the subject, and all agree that it is simply what I have described it to be. From the fashionable Fifth avenue establishment down to the cellar lodging-houses of the Five Points, all boarding-houses are alike in this respect. Their success in tormenting their victims depends upon the susceptibility and refinement of feeling and taste on the part of the latter.

Landladies and boarders are mutually suspicious of each other. The landlady constantly suspects her guest of a desire to escape from her clutches with unpaid bills. The latter is always on the look-out for some omission on the part of the hostess to comply with the letter of her contract. Landladies are frequently swindled by adventurers of both sexes, and guests most commonly find that the hostess does not comply very strictly with her bargain. Furthermore, the boarder has not only to endure his own troubles, but those of the landlady as well. Her sorrows are unending, and she pours them out to him at every opportunity. He dare not refuse to listen, for his experience teaches him that his hostess will find a way to punish him for his unfeeling conduct. It is of no use to change his quarters, for he may fare worse in this respect at the next place. And so he submits, and grows peevish and fretful, and even bald and gray over the woes of his tormentor. He consoles himself with one thought—in the next world landladies cease from troubling and boarding-houses do not exist.

All boarding-houses begin to fill up for the winter about the first of October. Few of the proprietors have any trouble in filling their establishments, as there is generally a rush of strangers to the city at that time. The majority of boarders change their quarters every fall, if they do not do so oftener. At first, the table is well supplied with good fare, the attendance is excellent, and the proprietress as obliging as one can wish. This continues until the house is full, and the guests have made arrangements which would render a removal inconvenient. Then a change comes over the establishment. The attendance becomes inferior. The landlady cannot afford to keep so many servants, and the best in the house are discharged. The fare becomes poor and scanty, and there begin to appear dishes upon which the landlady has exercised an amount of ingenuity which is astounding. They are fearfully

UNION SQUARE.

and wonderfully compounded, and it is best to ask no questions about them. The landlady keeps a keen watch over the table at such times; and woe to him who slights or turns up his nose at these dishes. She is sorry Mr. X——'s appetite is so delicate; but really her prices of board do not permit her to rival Delmonico or the Fifth Avenue Hotel in her table. Mr. P——, who was worth his millions, and who boarded with her for ten years, was very fond of that dish, and Mr. P—— was a regular *bon vivant*, if there ever was one. Hang your head, friend X——, mutter some incoherent excuse, gulp down your fair share of the dish in question—and fast the next time it makes its appearance at the table.

The landlady has shrewdly calculated the chances of retain-

ing her boarders. She knows that few care to or can change in
the middle of the season, when all the other houses are full; and
that they will hang on to her establishment until the spring.
If they do not come back the next fall, others will, and as the
population is large, she can play the same game upon a fresh
set of victims for many years to come. It is of no use to complain. She knows human nature better than you do, and she
adheres rigidly to her programme, grimly replying to your tale
of woes, that, if you do not like her establishment, you can go
elsewhere. You would go if you could find a better place; but
you know they are all alike. So you make up your mind to
endure your discomforts until May, with her smiling face, calls
you into the country.

Boarding-houses allow their guests a brief respite in the summer. The city is then comparatively deserted, and the most
of these "highly respectable" establishments are very much in
want of inmates. Expenses are heavy and receipts light then,
and the landladies offer an unusual degree of comfort to those
who will help them to tide over this dull season.

As regards the ferreting out of impropriety on the part of her
guests, the New York landlady is unequalled by the most skilful detective in the city. She doubts the character of every
woman beneath her roof, but in spite of her acuteness she is
often deceived, and it may be safely asserted that the boarding-
houses into which improper characters do not sometimes find
their way are very few. It is simply impossible to keep them
out. The average boarding-house contains a goodly number of
men who are so many objects of the designs of the adventurers.
Again, if the adventuress wishes to maintain the guise of respectability, she must have a respectable home, and this the
boarding-house affords her. One is struck with the great number of handsome young widows who are to be found in these
establishments. Sometimes they do not assume the character
of a widow, but claim to be the wives of men absent in the distant Territories, or in Europe, and pretend to receive letters
and remittances from them. The majority of these women are
adventuresses, and they make their living in a way they do not

care to have known. They conduct themselves with the utmost outward propriety in the house, and disarm even the suspicious landlady by their ladylike deportment. They are ripe for an intrigue with any man in the house, and as their object is simply to make money, they care little for an exposure if that object be attained.

XXXIX.
THE RESTAURANTS.

NEW YORK is said to contain between five and six thousand restaurants. These are of every kind and description known to man, from Delmonico's down to the Fulton Market stands. A very large number of persons live altogether at these places. They are those who cannot afford the expense of a hotel, and who will not endure a boarding-house. They rent rooms in convenient or inconvenient locations, and take their meals at the restaurants. At many nominally reputable establishments the fare is infamous, but as a rule New York is far ahead of any American city with respect to the character and capabilities of its eating-houses.

The better class restaurants lie along Broadway and Fifth avenue. The other longitudinal streets are well supplied with establishments of all kinds, and in the Bowery are to be found houses in which the fare is prepared and served entirely in accordance with German ideas. In other parts of the city are to be found Italian, French, and Spanish restaurants, and English chop houses.

The fashionable restaurants lie chiefly above Fourteenth, and entirely above Canal street. Delmonico's, at the northeast corner of Fourteenth street and the Fifth avenue, is the best known. It is a very extensive establishment, is fitted up in elegant style, and is equal to any eating-house in the world. The prices are very high. A modest dinner, without wine, for two persons, will cost here from four to five dollars. The fare is good, however. The house enjoys a large custom, and every visitor to New York who can afford it, takes a meal here before leaving the city. Delmonico is said to be very rich.

A young man, to whom the ways of the house were unknown, once took his sweetheart to lunch at this famous place. His purse was light, and when he came to scan the bill of fare, and note the large sums affixed to each item, his heart sank within him, and he waited in silent agony to hear his fair companion make her selection. After due consideration, she ordered a woodcock. Now woodcocks are expensive luxuries at Delmonico's, and the cost of one such bird represented more than the total contents of the lover's purse. He was in despair, but a lucky thought occurred to him. Turning to the lady, he asked with an air of profound astonishment:

" Do you think you can eat a whole woodcock ? "

" How large is it ? " asked the fair one, timidly.

" About as large as a full grown turkey " was the grave reply.

" O, I'll take an oyster stew," said the lady, quickly.

The fashionable restaurants make large profits on their sales. Their customers are chiefly ladies, and men who have nothing to do. Their busiest hours are the early afternoon, and during the evening. After the theatres are closed, they are thronged with parties of ladies and gentlemen who come in for supper.

Some of the best restaurants in the city are those in which a lady is never seen. It must not be supposed that they are disreputable places. They are entirely the opposite. They are located in the lower part of the city, often in some by-street of the heavy business section, and are patronized chiefly by merchants and clerks, who come here to get lunch and dinner. The fare is excellent, and the prices are reasonable. The eating houses of Henry Bodé, in Water street, near Wall street, Rudolph in Broadway, near Courtlandt street, and Nash & Fuller (late Crook, Fox & Nash), in Park Row, are the best of this kind. In the last there is a department for ladies.

Between the hours of noon and three o'clock, the down-town restaurants are generally crowded with a hungry throng. In some of them every seat at the long counters and at the tables is filled, and the floor is crowded with men standing and eating from plates which they hold in their hands. The noise, the bustle, the clatter of knives and dishes, the slamming of doors, and the cries of the waiters as they shout out the orders of the guests, are deafening. The waiters move about with a celerity that is astonishing; food is served and eaten with a dispatch peculiar to these places. A constant stream of men is pouring out of the doors, and as steady a stream flowing in to take their places. At some of the largest of these establishments as many as fifteen hundred people are supplied with food during the course of the day. A well patronized restaurant is very profitable in New York, even if its prices are moderate, and the higher priced establishments make their proprietors rich in a comparatively short time. The proprietor of a Broadway oyster saloon made a fortune of $150,000 by his legitimate business in five years. A large part of the income of the restaurants is derived from the sale of liquors at the bar.

The principal up-town restaurants are largely patronized by disreputable people. Impure women go there to pick up custom, and men to find such companions. Women whose social position is good, do not hesitate to meet their lovers at such places, for there is a great deal of truth in the old adage which tells us that "there's no place so private as a crowded hall." A quiet but close observer will frequently see a nod, or a smile, or a meaning glance pass between the most respectable looking persons of opposite sexes, who are seemingly strangers to each other, and will sometimes see a note slyly sent by a waiter, or dropped adroitly into the hand of the woman as the man passes out, while her face wears the demurest and most rigidly virtuous expression. Such women frequent some of the best known up-town establishments to so great an extent that a lady entering one of them is apt to be insulted in this way by the male habitués of the place. These wretches hold all women to be alike, and act upon this belief.

XL.

THE CHEAP LODGING-HOUSES.

THE Bowery and the eastern section of the city are full of cheap lodging-houses, which are a grade lower than the lowest hotels, and several grades above the cellars. One or two of these are immense establishments, five and six stories in height. Some of them provide their lodgers with beds and covering, others supply pallets laid down on the floor of a cheerless room, and others again give merely the pallets and no sheets or coverings. The rooms, the beds, and the bedding in all these establishments are horribly dirty, and are badly ventilated. Bed bugs abound in the summer, and in the winter the lodger is nearly frozen, the covering, when furnished, being utterly inadequate to the task of keeping out the cold. From six to ten persons are put in a room together. The price varies from ten to twenty-five cents, according to the accommodations furnished. Each of these houses is provided with a bar, at which the vilest liquors are sold at ten cents a drink. The profits of the business are very great, not counting the receipts of the bar, which are in proportion. The expense of fitting up and conducting such an establishment is trifling. One of them accommodates nearly two hundred lodgers per night, which at ten cents per head, would be a net receipt of twenty dollars.

The persons who patronize these establishments are mainly vagrants, men who live from hand to mouth, and who will not be received by the humblest boarding-house. Some are doubtless unfortunate, but the majority are vagrants from choice. Some have irregular occupations, others get the price of their lodgings by begging.

The business of a lodging-house seldom commences before

ten o'clock, and its greatest rush is just after the closing of the theatres; but all through the night, till three o'clock in the morning, they are receiving such of the outcast population as can offer the price of a bed. To any one interested in the misery of the city, the array presented on such an occasion is very striking. One sees every variety of character, runaway boys, truant apprentices, drunken mechanics, and broken-down mankind generally. Among these are men who have seen better days. They are decayed gentlemen who appear regularly in Wall street, and eke out the day by such petty business as they may get hold of, and are lucky if they can make enough to carry them through the night. In all lodging-houses the rule holds good, "First come, first served," and the last man in the room gets the worst spot. Each one sleeps with his clothes on, and his hat under his head, to keep it from being stolen. At eight o'clock in the morning all oversleepers are awakened, and the rooms got ready for the coming night. No one is allowed to take anything away, and if the lodger has a parcel, he is required to leave it at the bar. This prevents the theft of bed-clothes.

XLI.

THE LIBRARIES.

THE Libraries of New York are large and well patronized. The various collections, including those of the institutions of learning, number over 500,000 volumes.

The oldest collection is the "Society Library," which is contained in a handsome brick edifice in University Place. In 1729, the Rev. John Wellington, Rector of Newington, in England, generously bequeathed his library, consisting of 1622 volumes, to the "Society for the Propagation of the Gospel in Foreign Parts." To this was added a collection of books presented by the Rev. John Sharp, Chaplain to Lord Bellamont. The whole collection was sent to New York, and opened for public use in 1731, under the name of the "Corporation Library." The death of the librarian occurred soon after, and the library was suffered to fall into disuse. In 1754, a number of citizens of means and literary taste, founded the "Society Library," to which, with the consent of the city, they added the old "Corporation Library." In 1772, the Society received a charter from King George III. It is one of the wealthiest and most flourishing institutions in the city. The annual subscription is $10. The collection of books is very valuable and interesting, and comprises over 50,000 volumes.

The "Astor Library" is the best known outside of the city. The library building is a massive structure of brick with brown stone trimmings, situated in Lafayette Place, next door to the residence of William B. Astor, Esq. It was founded by John Jacob Astor, and enlarged by his son William. The books are contained in two large and elegant halls, occupying the entire building above the first floor. The collection numbers about

33

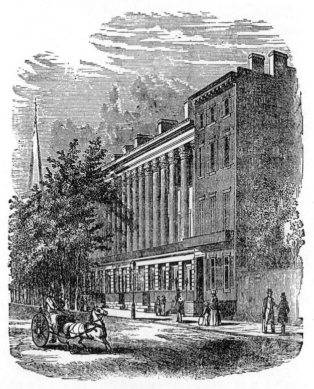

LAFAYETTE PLACE.

150,000 volumes, and was made by the late Dr. Coggeswell, the first Librarian, whose judgment, taste, and learning were highly appreciated by the elder Astor. The library is mainly one of reference, and is very complete in most of the subjects it comprises. In the departments of science, history, biography, and philology, it is especially fine. It also contains many rare and valuable illustrated works, a number of original editions of the earliest books, and some valuable manuscripts. The collection is free to the public, and is open daily except on Sundays and holidays, and during the month of August, from 10 A. M. until 4 P. M. The books cannot be taken from the reading-room, nor are visitors allowed to use pen and ink in making notes from them. It is said that the classes Mr. Astor desired most to benefit by this library were the working people, who are unable to buy books of their own. If this be true, his wishes have been entirely defeated, as the hall is open only during the hours when it is impossible for working people to attend. In the facilities which it affords to those who wish to use it, the Astor is very much behind the great libraries of Europe, or even the Public Library of Boston.

The most popular, and the most thoroughly representative library of the city, is the Mercantile Library, located in Clinton Hall, in Astor Place. It owns this building, and its property is valued at $500,000. It was founded in 1820, by William Wood, a native of Boston, and a gentleman eminent for his efforts in behalf of the spread of education and liberal ideas. It began as a subscription library with a collection of 700 volumes, and was located in a small room at No. 49 Fulton street. The collection now numbers 120,000 volumes, and increases at the rate of 13,000 volumes a year. It is the fourth library in size in the Union. Those which are larger are the Library of Congress, the Public Library of Boston, and the Astor Library. The library is the property of the clerks of New York, and though it does not compare with the Astor in the solidity or value of its contents, is a creditable monument to the good sense and taste of the young men of our mercantile community. No one but a clerk can hold an office in it. The term " clerk " is made to include all men who live on a salary. These members pay an initiation fee of $1, and an annual subscription of $4. To all other persons the privileges of the library are offered at an annual subscription of $5. In April, 1870, the books of the institution showed a roll of 12,867 persons entitled to the use of the library and reading-room, the latter of which contains 400 newspapers and periodicals.

A large part of the collection consists of works of fiction. It is a lending library, and its books are sent to readers in Yonkers, Norwalk, Stamford, Elizabeth, and Jersey City, as well as in New York, in each of which it has branches. There are also branch offices in Yorkville and in Cedar street. Every morning a canvass bag, containing the books returned and applications for others wanted, is sent from each branch to the library, and is returned in the afternoon full. The directors offer to establish a branch in any of the suburban towns in which one hundred subscribers can be obtained in advance. The average daily delivery of books is 760, of which about three-quarters are taken from the library proper, the rest from the branches. On Saturday evening the demand for books is very great.

The system of delivery is as follows :

" Each member on joining the library has a folio assigned him in the ledger, and its number is written on the ticket which is given him as a certificate of membership. Let us suppose you have received one of these tickets, and have made your selection of the book you want. You fill up a blank application card, with the name of the book desired. You hand that to one of the attendants. When he has found a book for you, he hands it, with your application card, to the delivery clerk. This gentleman occupies a large desk at the central counter, and has before him two immense drawers, divided into partitions for the reception of the cards. Each member's name has a place in one or the other of these drawers, and the number of the folio shows where that place is. The clerk instantly turns to your name, and finds the card you handed in when you last borrowed a book. If the date, stamped at the time of delivery, shows that you have kept it longer than the rules allow, he levies a small fine, and you must pay it before you can borrow again. All formalities transacted, the old card is destroyed, the new one put in its place, and you are sent away in peace.

" The system of checking books, as we have described it, enables the librarian to ascertain in a moment just what any particular member has borrowed ; but it does not show what has become of any particular book. Many attempts have been made to devise a system of double accounts, so that a check could be kept upon the members and the books at the same time, but without success. A partial record book, however, is now kept. Whenever a standard book is borrowed, the delivery clerk marks upon a little yellow ticket simply the folio number

CLINTON HALL.

of the borrower.   Every day the yellow tickets are examined, and if it appear, say, that folio 10,029 has had a book more than three weeks, the clerk turns to the drawer and finds out who folio 10,029 is, and what book is charged against. him, and sends him a notice that his time is up.   It is found impracticable to apply this system to novels, which form the greater part of the circulation of the library; but it is useful as far as it goes, and prevents the loss of many valuable books.

"Of late years a postal order scheme has been perfected, and for convenience and simplicity it could hardly be improved. Its design is to enable members to draw books without visiting the library.   Blank forms are obtained from the Post-office Department, about the size and shape of a newspaper wrapper, bearing on one side a two-cent postage stamp, and the printed address, 'Mercantile Library, Astor Place, City,' and on the other a blank application, with a five-cent 'Mercantile Library delivery stamp,' and some printed directions. You fill up the application in the usual way, fold the wrapper like a note (it is already gummed), and drop it in the nearest Post-office box.   In a few hours at furthest a messenger brings to your house the book you have asked for, and takes away the volume you want to return. The system is fast increasing in popularity. A horse and wagon are constantly employed in the collection and delivery, and the number of volumes sent out in this way is about 12,000 annually. The delivery blanks are sold at the rate of seven cents each— two cents representing the postage and five the cost of the delivery."

The other collections are the Library of the New York Historical Society, embracing over 30,000 volumes, besides many interesting manuscripts, papers, coins and antiquities; the Apprentices' Library, 18,000 volumes; the Library of the American Institute, 10,000 volumes; the City Library, 5000 volumes, the Law Institute Library, about 5000 volumes; the Library of the Young Men's Christian Association, about 15,000 volumes; the Library of the Protestant Episcopal General Theological Seminary, 18,000 volumes; the Library of the Union Theological Seminary, 26,000 volumes; the Library of the Cooper Institute; and the libraries of the various institutions of learning.

Mr. James Lenox, a wealthy and prominent citizen, is now erecting on the Fifth avenue, near Seventieth street, and immediately opposite the Central Park, a massive building of granite, which is to be one of the most imposing structures in the city. In this, at its completion, he intends placing his magnificent collection of books and works of art, which constitute the most superb private collection in America. The whole will be opened to the public under certain restrictions.

XLII.

PROFESSIONAL MEN.

NEW YORK is full of professional men, that is, of men who earn their living by brain work. One class—the clergy—has already been mentioned.

The Bar is next in numbers. There are about three thousand lawyers practising at the New York bar. A few of these have large incomes, two or three making as much as fifty thousand dollars per annum ; but the average income of the majority is limited. An income of ten or fifteen thousand dollars is considered large in the profession, and the number of those earning such a sum is small.

In most cities the members of the legal profession form a clique, and are very clannish. Each one knows everybody else, and if one member of the bar is assailed, the rest are prompt to defend him. In New York, however, there is no such thing as a legal "fraternity." Each man is wrapped in his own affairs, and knows little and cares less about other members of the profession. We have been surprised to find how little these men know about each other. Some have never even heard of others who are really prosperous and talented.

The courts of the city are very numerous; and each man, in entering upon his practice, makes a specialty of some one or more of them, and confines himself to them. His chances of success are better for doing this, than they would be by adopting a general practice. Indeed, it would be simply impossible for one man to practise in all.

Many of the best lawyers rarely go into the courts. They prefer chamber practice, and will not try a case in court if they can help it. The process in the courts is slow and vexatious, and consumes too much of their time.   Their chamber practice is profitable to them, and beneficial to the community, as it prevents much tedious litigation.

Many lawyers with fair prospects and comfortable incomes, who are succeeding in their profession in other places, come to New York, expecting to rise to fame and fortune more rapidly here. They are mistaken.   The most accomplished city barrister finds success a slow and uncertain thing.   It requires some unusually fortunate circumstance to introduce a new lawyer favorably to a New York public.

The profession in this city can boast some of the most eminent names in the legal world, such men as Charles O'Connor, William M. Evarts, and others of a similar reputation.

The Medical Profession is also well represented.   It is said that there are about as many physicians and surgeons as lawyers practising in the city.   New York offers a fine field for a man of genuine skill.   Its hospitals and medical establishments are the best conducted of any in the country, and afford ample opportunity for study and observation.   The opportunity for studying human nature is all that one can desire.   The most eminent medical men in the country either reside here or are constantly visiting the city.

Some of the city practitioners are very fortunate in a pecuniary sense.   It is said that some of them receive very large sums every year.   Dr. Willard Parker was once called out of town to see a patient, to whom he sent a bill of $300.   The amount was objected to, and Dr. Parker proved by his books that his daily receipts were over that sum.   He is said to be an exception to the general rule, however, which rule is that but very few of the best paid medical men receive over $20,000 per annum.   Surgeons are paid much better than physicians.   Dr. Carnochan is said to have received as much as $2000 for a single operation.   As a rule, however, the city physicians do little more than pay expenses, especially if they have families.   From $5000 to $10,000 is a good income, and a man of family has but little chance of saving out of this if he lives in any degree of comfort.

Literary men and women are even more numerous in the metropolis than lawyers or doctors. They are of all classes, from the great author of world-wide fame to the veriest scribbler. The supply is very largely in advance of the demand, and as a consequence, all have to exert themselves to get along. A writer in the *World* estimates the annual receipts of New York authors at about one million of dollars, and the number of writers at 2000, which would give an average income to each of about $500. As a matter of course, it is impossible to make any reliable estimate, and there can be little doubt that the writer referred to has been too generous in his average. Authorship in New York offers few inducements of a pecuniary nature. Men of undoubted genius often narrowly escape starvation, and to make a bare living by the pen requires, in the majority of instances, an amount of mental and manual labor and application which in any mercantile pursuit would ensure a fortune.

XLIII.

PROFESSIONAL CRIMINALS.

I.

THE THIEVES.

THE criminal class of New York is very large, but it is not so large as is commonly supposed. In the spring of 1871, the Rev. Dr. Bellows stated that the City of New York contained 30,000 professional thieves, 20,000 lewd women and harlots, 3000 rum shops, and 2000 gambling houses, and this statement was accepted without question by a large portion of the newspapers of other parts of the country. New York is a very wicked place, but it is not as bad as the above statement would indicate. The personal character of the gentleman who made it compels the conviction that he believed in the truth of his figures; but a closer examination of the case makes it plain that he was singularly deceived by the sources from which he derived his information.

It is very hard to obtain accurate information as to the criminal statistics of this city. The reports and estimates of the Police Commissioners are notoriously incomplete and unreliable. They show a large number of arrests, but they deal mainly with the class known as "casuals," persons who merely dabble in crime, and who do not make it a profession, and the larger proportion of the arrests reported are for such trifling offences as drunkenness. Indeed many of the arrests reported ought not to be counted in the records of crime at all, as the persons apprehended are released upon the instant by the officer in charge of the station, the arrests being the result of the ignorant zeal or malice of the patrolmen, and the prisoners being guiltless of any offence.

The population of New York is unlike that of any other American city. It is made up of every nationality known to man. The majority of the people are very poor. Life with them is one long unbroken struggle, and to exist at all is simply to be wretched. They are packed together at a fearful rate in dirt and wretchedness, and they have every incentive to commit crimes which will bring them the means of supplying their wants. It is a common habit of some European governments to ship their criminals to this port, where they have a new field opened to them. The political system of the city teaches the lower class to disregard all rights, either of property or person, and, indeed, clothes some of the most infamous criminals with an amount of influence which is more than dangerous in their hands, and shields them from punishment when detected in the commission of crime. All these things considered, the wonder is not that the criminal class of the city is as large as it is; but that it is not larger and more dangerous.

The truth is, that the class generally known as Professional Criminals number about 3000. Besides these, there are about 5000 women of ill-fame, known as such, living in 600 houses of prostitution, and frequenting assignation and bed-houses, about 7000 rum shops, 92 faro banks, and about 500 other gambling houses, and lottery and policy offices, within the limits of the City of New York.

The professional criminals are those who live by thieving, and who occasionally vary their career by the commission of a murder or some other desperate crime. They rarely resort to violence, however, unless it becomes necessary to ensure their own safety. Then they make their work as simple and as brief as possible. They form a distinct community, frequent certain parts of the city, where they can easily and rapidly communicate with each other, and where they can also hide from the police without fear of detection. They have signs by which they may recognize each other, and a language, or *argot*, peculiar to themselves. Those who have been raised to the business use this argot to such an extent that to one not accustomed to it they speak in an unknown tongue. The following specimens, taken from the "Detective's Manual," under the head of the letter B, will illustrate this:

Badger.—A panel-thief.
Bagged.—Imprisoned.
Bag of nails.—All in confusion.
Balram.—Money.
Bandog.—A civil officer.
Barking irons.—Pistols.
Bene.—Good, first-rate.
Benjamin.—A coat.
Bilk.—To cheat.
Bill of sale.—A widow's weeds.
Bingo.—Liquor.
Bingo boy.—A drunken man.
Bingo mort.—A drunken woman.
Blue-billy.—A strange handkerchief.
Blue ruin.—Bad gin.
Boarding-school.—The penitentiary.
Bone box.—The mouth.
Bowsprit in parenthesis.—A pulled nose.
Brother of the blade.—A soldier.
Brother of the bolus.—A doctor.
Brush.—To flatter, to humbug.
Bug.—A breast-pin.
Bugger.—A pickpocket.
Bull.—A locomotive.
Bull-traps.—Rogues who personate officials to extort money.

As a rule, the professional thief of every grade is a very respectable looking individual outwardly. He dresses well, but flashily, and is generally plentifully supplied with money. In a "crib," or rendezvous, which he once visited in company with a detective, the writer could not select a single individual whose outward appearance indicated his calling. The New York thief generally has money, which he squanders with great recklessness. It comes to him easily, and it goes in the same way. There are many instances on record which go to show that the "members of the profession" are frequently most generous to each other in money matters. The thief is usually a man of

THE OCCASIONAL FATE OF NEW YORK THIEVES.

steady habits.   He rarely drinks to excess, for that would unfit
him for his work, and he is not usually given to licentiousness,
for a similar reason.   If he be found living with a woman, she
is generally a thief also, and plies her trade with equal activity.

Altogether, there are about three thousand thieves of various
kinds, known to the officers of justice in New York, who live
by the practice of their trade.   They are divided into various
classes, each known by a distinctive title, and to each of which
its respective members cling tenaciously.   These are known as
Burglars, Bank Sneaks, Damper Sneaks, Safe-blowers, Safe-
bursters, Safe-breakers, and Sneak Thieves.   The last constitute the most numerous class.

The Burglar is the aristocrat of crime, and you cannot offend him more than by calling him a thief. He scorns the small game of the sneak thief, and conducts his operations on a large scale, in which the risk is very great, and the plunder in proportion. His peculiar "racket" is to break open some first-class business house, a bonded warehouse, or the vaults of a bank. The burglar class has three divisions, known to the police as Safe-blowers, Safe-bursters, and Safe-breakers. They are said to be less than 250 in number, those of the first and second class comprising about seventy-five members each. The safe-blowers are accounted the most skilful. They rarely force an entrance into a building, but admit themselves by means of false keys made from wax impressions of the genuine keys. Once inside, their mode of operation is rapid and systematic. They lower the windows from the top about an inch. This is usually sufficient to prevent the breaking of the glass by the concussion of the air in the room, and not enough to attract attention from without. The safe is then wrapped in wet blankets, to smother the noise of the explosion. Holes are then drilled in the door of the safe near the lock, these are filled with powder, which is fired by a fuse, and the safe is blown open. The securing of the contents requires but a few minutes, and the false keys enable the thieves to escape with ease. This method of robbery is very dangerous, as, in spite of the precautions taken, the explosion may produce sufficient noise to bring the watchman or the police to the spot. Experienced burglars only engage in it, and these never undertake it without being sure that the plunder to be secured will fully repay them for the danger to be encountered. This knowledge they acquire in various ways.

The Safe-bursters are the silent workers of the "profession." Like the class just mentioned, they enter buildings by means of false keys. They adopt a thoroughly systematic course, which requires the combined efforts of several persons, and consequently they operate in parties of three and four. They first make the safe so fast to the floor, by means of clamps, that it will resist any degree of pressure. Then they drill holes in the door, and into these fit jack-screws worked by means of levers.

The tremendous force thus exerted soon cuts the safe literally to pieces, and its contents are at the mercy of the thieves. The whole process is noiseless and rapid, and so complete has been the destruction of some safes that even the most experienced detectives have been astounded at the sight of the wreck. Such an operation is never undertaken without a knowledge on the part of the thieves of the contents of the safe, and the chances of conducting the enterprise in safety. The Safe-blowers and bursters do nothing by chance, and their plans are so well arranged beforehand that they rarely fail.

The Safe-breakers, though really a part of the burglar class, are looked upon with contempt and disowned by their more scientific associates in crime. They do nothing by calculation, and trust everything to chance. They enter buildings by force, and trust to the same method to get into the safes. Their favorite instrument is a "jimmy," or short iron bar with a sharp end. With this they pry open the safe, and then knock it to pieces with a hammer. In order to deaden the sound of the blows, the hammer is wrapped with cloth. They are not as successful as the others in their operations, and are most frequently arrested. Indeed the arrests for burglary reported by the Police Commissioners occur almost exclusively in this class. A really first-class burglar in a prison cell would be a curiosity in New York.

Closely allied with the Safe-blowers and bursters is a class known as Bed-chamber Sneaks. These men are employed by the burglars to enter dwellings and obtain impressions in wax of keys of the places to be robbed. They adopt an infinite number of ways of effecting such an entrance, often operating through the servant girls. They never disturb or carry off anything, but confine their efforts to obtaining impressions in wax of the keys of the store or office to be robbed. The keys of business houses are mainly kept by the porters, into whose humble dwellings it is easy to enter. When they wish to obtain the keys of a dwelling, they come as visitors to the servant girls, and while they stand chatting with them manage to slip the key from the lock, take its impression in wax, and return it

to the lock, unobserved by the girl.   They are generally on the
watch for chances for robberies, and report them promptly to
their burglar confederates.

The Bank Sneak is better known as the Bond Robber.   He
is of necessity a man of intelligence and of great fertility of resource.   He steals United States Bonds almost entirely, and
prefers coupons to registered, as the former can always be disposed of without detection.   He manages, by means best known
to himself, to gain information of the places in which these
bonds are kept by the banks, of the times at which it is easiest
to gain access to them, and the hours at which the theft is most
likely to be successful.   All this requires an immense amount
of patient study and of personal observation of the premises,
which must be conducted in such a way as not to attract attention or excite suspicion.   When everything is ready for the
commission of the deed, the thief proceeds to the place where
the bonds are kept, seizes them and makes off.   If a package
of bank notes is at hand, he adds that to his other plunder.
Usually his operations are so well planned and conducted that
he is not observed by the bank officers, and he escapes with his
plunder.   Once at large, he proceeds to sell the bonds, if they
are coupons, or to use the bank notes, if he has secured any.
Registered bonds require more care in their disposition.   Generally the bank offers a reward for the arrest of the robber and
the recovery of the goods, and calls in a detective to work up
the case.   The thief at once manages to communicate with the
detective, and offers to compromise with the bank, that is, to
restore a part of the plunder upon condition that he is allowed
the rest and escape punishment.   Ninety-nine times out of a
hundred his offer is accepted, the bank preferring the recovery
of a part of its loss to the punishment of the thief.   In this way
the thief secures a large part of the amount stolen, sometimes
one-half.   Should the thief be caught with his plunder upon
him, and the bank be thus saved from loss, which is rare, the
offender is turned over to the police, and the bank joins heartily
in the effort to send him to the penitentiary.

The Damper Sneak confines his attentions to the safes of the business men of the city. Wall street has suffered heavily from this class. The thief enters a broker's office, in which the safe is generally left open during business hours, and asks permission to look at the directory, or to write a note. If this permission be accorded him, he manages to get inside the railing, in close proximity to the safe, if its doors are open. A confederate (or sometimes more) now enters and attracts the attention of the broker or the clerk, by making fictitious arrangements for the purchase of gold or some security. The thief who first entered watches his opportunity, and then, with the greatest rapidity, darts to the safe, abstracts whatever he can lay his hands on, and passes out, always thanking the broker for his courtesy. The confederates leave soon after, and then the robbery is discovered. The Damper Sneak has to steal at random, taking the first thing within his reach, but he often secures a rich prize. He takes his peculiar name from the safe, which, in the thief language, is called a "Damper." One of the boldest of these robberies occurred a year or more ago, in Wall street. A broker employing a number of clerks, and doing a heavy business, was standing one day in front of his safe, during business hours, talking to a gentleman. A man, without a hat, with a pen behind his ear, and a piece of paper in his hand, entered the office, passed around the counter to where the broker stood, and said to him quietly, "Will you please to move, sir, so that I can get at the safe?" Being very much interested in his conversation, the broker scarcely noticed the man, supposing from his general appearance and manner that he was one of the clerks, and accordingly stepped aside without giving him a second glance. The man went up to the safe, took out a package of United States Bonds, and coolly walked out of the office. The bonds amounted to one hundred thousand dollars. The loss was discovered in the afternoon, but no trace of the thief or of his plunder was ever found. Strange as it may seem, the city is constantly suffering from similar robberies, and the rogues almost invariably escape.

The Sneak Thieves are the last and lowest on the list. As has been stated, they constitute the bulk of the light-fingered

34

fraternity. These confine their attentions principally to private dwellings, are adroit and successful, but incur constant danger of detection and punishment. A sneak thief will pass along the street with that rapid, rolling glance of the eyes which distinguishes the tribe; now he checks himself in his career; it is but for an instant; no unprofessional eye directed towards him would notice it; but the sudden pause would speak volumes to an experienced police officer. He knows that the thief's eye has caught the sight of silver lying exposed in the basement. In an hour after he hears that the basement has been entered, and the silver in it carried off. He knows who has taken it, as well as if he had seen the man take it with his own eyes; but if the thief has had time to run to the nearest receiver's den, the silver is already in the melting-pot, beyond the reach of identification.

Somtimes the sneak thieves work in pairs. Upon discovering the basement door of a residence ajar, one of them takes position at it, while the other ascends the front steps and rings the bell. As soon as the servant has gone up from the basement to answer the bell, the thief at the lower door slips in, and gathers up the silver or such other articles as he can lay his hands upon. Again, selecting the dinner hour, which is usually between six and seven o'clock, and operating in the winter season when the streets are dark at that hour, one of the thieves will remain on the side-walk, on the lookout for the police, while the other climbs up a pillar of the stoop and reaches the level of the second story window. The window fastenings offer but a feeble resistance, and he is soon in the room. The family being all at dinner in the lower part of the house, the entire mansion is open to him. Securing his plunder, he leaves the house as he entered it, and makes off with his confederate. Some of the wealthiest mansions in the city have been robbed in this way, and heavy losses in jewelry, furs, and clothing have been entailed upon householders in all localities. Sometimes the thief has a confederate in the servant girl, but professionals do not often trust this class, who are always ready to betray them at the slightest indication of danger.

II.

THE PICK-POCKETS.

THE activity of the pick-pockets of New York is very great, and they oftentimes make large "hauls" in the practice of their trade. It is said that there are about 300 of them in the city, though the detectives state their belief that the number is really larger and increasing. Scarcely a day passes without the police authorities receiving numerous complaints from respectable persons of losses by pick-pockets.

On all the street cars, you will see the sign, "*Beware of Pick-pockets !*" posted conspicuously, for the purpose of warning passengers. These wretches work in gangs of two, or three or four. They make their way into crowded cars, and rarely leave them without bringing away something of value. An officer will recognize them at once. He sees a well-known pick-pocket obstructing the car entrance; another pickpocket is abusing him in the sharpest terms for doing so, while, at the same time, he is eagerly assisting a respectable gentleman, or a well-dressed lady, to pass the obstruction. One or two other pick-pockets stand near. All this is as intelligible to a police officer as the letters on a street sign. He knows that the man, who is assisting the gentleman or lady, is picking his or her pocket; he knows that the man who obstructs the entrance is his confederate; he knows that the others, who are hanging about, will receive the contents of the pocket-book as soon as their principal has abstracted the same. He cannot arrest them, however, unless he, or some one else, sees the act committed; but they will not remain long after they see him—they will take the alarm, as they know his eye is on them, and leave the car as soon as possible.

A lady, riding in an omnibus, discovers that she has lost her purse, which she knows was in her possession when she entered the stage. A well-dressed gentleman sits by her, whose arms are quietly crossed before him, and his fingers, encased in spotless kid gloves, are entwined in his lap, in plain sight of all the passengers, who are sure that he has not moved them since he entered the stage. Several persons have entered and left the vehicle, and the lady, naturally supposing one of them to be the thief, gets out to consult a policeman as to her best course. The officer could tell her, after a glance at the faultless gentleman who was her neighbor, that the arms so conspicuously crossed in his lap, are false, his real arms all the time being free to operate under the folds of his talma. The officer would rightly point him out as the thief.

The ferry-boats which go and come crowded with passengers, the theatres, and even the churches, are all frequented by pick-pockets, who reap rich harvests from them. Persons wearing prominent shirt pins or other articles of jewelry frequently lose them in this way, and these wretches will often boldly take a purse out of a lady's hand or a bracelet from her arm, and make off. If the robbery be done in the midst of a crowd, the chance of escape is all the better.

The street car conductors complain that they can do nothing to check the depredations of the pick-pockets. If they are put off the cars, they exert themselves to have the conductors discharged, and are generally possessed of influence enough to accomplish their ends. Strange as this may seem, it is true, for the pick-pocket is generally employed by the city politicians to manage the rougher class at the elections. In return for the influence which they thus exert the pick-pockets receive payment in money, and are shielded from punishment if unlucky enough to be arrested. Both parties are responsible for this infamous course, the party in power usually making the greatest use of these scoundrels. This is the cause of the confidence with which thieves of this kind carry on their trade. Those who desire the city's welfare will find food for reflection in this fact.

Many of the pick-pockets are women, whose lightness and delicacy of touch make them dangerous operators. Others are boys. These are usually termed " kids," and are very dangerous, as people are not inclined to suspect them. They work in gangs of three or four, and, pushing against their victim, seize what they can, and make off. Sometimes one of this gang is arrested, but as he has transferred the plunder to his confederates, who have escaped, there is no evidence against him.

III.

THE FEMALE THIEVES.

In the collection of photographs at the Police Headquarters, to which the authorities have given the name of "The Rogues' Gallery," there are but seventy-three portraits of females. The best informed detectives, however, estimate the actual number of professional female thieves in the city at about 350.

Women do not often succeed in effecting large robberies, but the total of their stealings makes up a large sum each year. They are not as liable to suspicion as men, and most persons hesitate before accusing a woman of theft. Yet, if successful, the woman's chances of escaping arrest and punishment are better than those of a man. Her sex compels her to lead a quieter and more retired life, and she does not as a rule frequent places in which she is brought under a detective's observation.

Some of the female thieves are the children of thief parents, and are trained to their lives, others come to such a mode of existence by degrees. All, as a rule, are loose women, and were so before they became professional thieves. A few of them are well educated, and some of these state that they adopted thieving only when all other means failed them, and that they hoped it would keep them from sacrificing their virtue. This hope proved vain, and imperceptibly they glided into the latter sin. Some of these women live in handsomely furnished private rooms in such localities as Bleecker street. Others herd together in the lower quarters of the city. The female thief, even the most abandoned, generally has a husband, who is himself a thief or something worse. She takes great pride in being a married woman, and whenever she gets into trouble invariably seeks to establish a good character by producing her marriage certificate. Even the lowest panel thieves will do this.

The Female Thieves are divided into Pick-pockets, Shop-lifters, and Panel Thieves.

" A short while ago a private detective happened to drop into a large dry-goods store in Grand street, and observed a hand-some-looking girl, about eighteen years old, dressed with the best taste, pricing laces at a counter.   An indefinable expression about her eyes was suspicious, and as she left the store without purchasing, the spectator followed her to the corner of Essex Market, where, walking beside her, he noticed something of a square form under her cloak.   At once suspecting it to be a stolen card of lace, he jostled against her, and, as he suspected, the card of lace fell from under her arm to the sidewalk.   She colored, and was walking away without picking it up when the detective stopped her, said he knew the lace was stolen, and that she must return to the shop.   She begged of him not to arrest her but restore the lace, which he did.   After thanking him for not taking her into custody, she invited him to call on her and learn the story of her life.   She has two rooms in a very re-spectable locality, furnished in the best manner, several of Prang's chromos are hung on the walls, and a piano, on which she plays well, is in her sitting-room.   She is very well edu-cated, and was driven into her way of life by being left without friends or help, and one day stole a shawl without being dis-covered.   Emboldened by the success of her first theft, she chose shop-lifting as her way of life, has followed it ever since, and was never in prison.   Some few call her Sarah Wright ; but those who know her best style her ' Anonyma,' as she dis-likes the former title."

IV.

THE RIVER THIEVES.

THE Harbor Thieves constitute one of the most dangerous and active portions of the criminal class.   There are only about fifty professional thieves of this class, but they give the police a vast amount of trouble, and inflict great loss in the aggregate upon the mercantile community. Twenty years ago the harbor was infested with a gang of pirates, who not only committed the most daring robberies, but also added nightly murders to their misdeeds. Their victims were thrown into the deep waters of the river or bay, and all trace of the foul work was removed. At length, however, the leaders of the gang, Saul and Howlett by name, mere lads both, were arrested, convicted, and executed, and for a while a stop was put to the robberies in the harbor; but in course of time the infamous trade was resumed, but without its old accompaniment of murder. It is at present carried on with great activity in spite of the efforts of the police to put a stop to it. The North River front of the city is troubled with but one gang of these ruffians, which has its headquarters at the foot of Charlton street. This front is lined with piers which are well built, well lighted, and well guarded, being occupied chiefly by steamboats plying on the river, and by the foreign and coasting steamships. The East River is not so well guarded, the piers are dark, and the vessels, mostly sailing ships, are left to the protection of their crews. It is in this river, therefore, and in the harbor, that the principal depredations of the river thieves are carried on. "Slaughter House Point," the intersection of James and South streets, and so called by the police because of the many murders which have occurred there, is the principal rendezvous of the East River thieves. Hook Dock, at the foot of Cherry street, is also one of their favorite gathering places.

The life of a river thief is a very hard one, and his gains, as a rule, are small. He is subjected to a great deal of manual labor in the effort to secure his plunder, and is exposed to all sorts of weather. Night work in an open boat in New York harbor is not favorable to longevity, and in eight or ten years the most robust constitution will give way before the constant attacks of rheumatism and neuralgia. There would be some compensation to society in this but for the fact that the police, whose duty it is to watch the river thieves, suffer in a similar way.

The river thieves generally work in gangs of three and four. Each gang has its rowboat, which is constructed with reference to carrying off as much plunder as possible, and making the best attainable time when chased by the harbor police. The thieves will not go out on a moonlight or even a bright starlight night. Nights when the darkness is so thick that it hides everything, or when the harbor is covered with a dense fog, are most favorable to them. Then, emerging from their starting point, they pull to the middle of the stream, where they lie-to long enough to ascertain if they are observed or followed. Then they pull swiftly to the point where the vessel they mean to rob is lying. Their oars are muffled, and their boat glides along noiselessly through the darkness. Frequently they pause for a moment, and listen to catch the sound of the oars of the police-boats, if any are on their track. Upon reaching the vessel, they generally manage to board her by means of her chains, or some rope which is hanging down her side. The crew are asleep, and the watch is similarly overcome. The thieves are cautious and silent in their movements, and succeed in securing their spoil without awakening any one. They will steal anything they can get their hands on, but deal principally in articles which cannot be identified, such as sugar, coffee, tea, rice, cotton, etc. They go provided with their own bags, and fill these from the original bags, barrels, or cases in which these articles are found on the ship. They are very careful to take away with them nothing which has a distinctive mark by which it may be identified. Having filled their boat, they slip over the side of the ship into it, and pull back to a point on shore designated beforehand, and, landing, convey their plunder to the shop of a junkman with whom they have already arranged matters, where they dispose of it for ready money. They do not confine their operations to vessels lying at the East River piers of New York, but rob those discharging cargo at the Brooklyn stores, or lying at anchor in the East or North rivers, even going as far as to assail those lying at quarantine.

In order to check their operations as far as possible, a force of about thirty policemen, under Captain James Todd, is assigned to duty in the harbor. The headquarters of this force are on a steamer, which boat was expected to accomplish wonders, but

THE RIVER THIEVES

which is too large and clumsy to be of any real service. In consequence of this, Captain Todd is obliged to patrol the harbor with row-boats, of which there are several. These boats visit all the piers on the two rivers, and search for thieves or their boats. Sometimes the thieves are encountered just as they are approaching a pier with their boat filled with stolen property, and again the chase will be kept up clear across the harbor. If they once get sight of them, the police rarely fail to overhaul the thieves. Generally the latter submit without a struggle, but sometimes a fight ensues.

The thieves, however, prefer to submit where they have such goods as rice, sugar, coffee, or tea in their possession. They know that it will be impossible to convict them, and they prefer a slight detention to the consequences of a struggle with their captors. The merchant or master of the ship, from whom the goods are stolen, may feel sure in his own mind that the articles found in the possession of the thieves are his property, but he cannot swear that they are his, it being simply impossible to identify such goods. And so the magistrate, though satisfied of the theft, must discharge the prisoner and return him the stolen goods. The only charge against him is that he was found under suspicious circumstances with these articles in his possession. From three to four river thieves are arrested every week, but, for the reason given, but few are punished. Sometimes, in order to secure their conviction, the police turn over the thieves to the United States authorities, by whom they are charged with smuggling, this charge being based upon their being found in possession of goods on which they can show no payment of duties. Sometimes they are prosecuted, not for larceny, but for violating the quarantine laws in boarding vessels detained at quarantine.

Several times the most daring of the river thieves have robbed the piers of the European steamship lines. In one instance, they passed under the pier of the Cunard steamers at Jersey City, cut out a portion of the flooring, and removed several valuable packages through the opening thus made. They then replaced the flooring, and secured it in its place by means of lifting-jacks, and decamped with their plunder. The next night they returned and removed other packages, and for several nights the performance was repeated. The company's agent, upon the discovery of the loss, exerted himself actively to discover the thieves, but without success. The watchmen on shore were positive that the warehouse, which is built on the pier, had not been entered from the land, and there were no signs to be discovered of its having been forced from the water side. Matters began to look bad for the watchmen, when, one night, the harbor police unexpectedly made a dash under the pier and caught the thieves at their work.

The North River gang are said to own a fine schooner, in which they cruise along the Hudson almost to Albany, and carry on a system of piracy at the river towns. Farmers and country merchants suffer greatly from their depredations. A year or so ago, it was rumored that they were commanded by a beautiful and dashing woman, but this story is now believed to be a mere fiction.

"Another gang is called the 'Daybreak Boys,' from the fact that none of them are a dozen years of age, and that they always select the hour of dawn for their depredations, which are exclusively confined to the small craft moored in the East River just below Hell Gate. They find the men on these vessels locked in the deep sleep of exhaustion, the result of their severe labors of the day; and as there are no watchmen, they meet little difficulty in rifling not only the vessels, but the persons of those on board. If there is any such thing as a watch or money, it is sure to disappear; and it has often happened that one of these vessels has been robbed of every portable article on board, including every article of clothing."

V.

THE FENCES.

In the thief language, a person who buys stolen goods is called a "Fence." Without his fence, the thief could do nothing, for he could not dispose of his plunder without a serious risk of detection. The Fence, however, is not known as a thief, and can buy and sell with a freedom which renders it easy for him to dispose of all stolen property which comes into his hands. A noted thief once declared that a man in his business was powerless to accomplish anything unless he knew the names and characters of all the Fences in the city.

The professional Fences of New York are as well known to the police as they are to the thieves. Their stores are located in Chatham street, in the Bowery, and other public thoroughfares, and even Broadway itself has one or more of these establishments within its limits. Some of the Fences are dirty, wretched-looking creatures, but one at least—the Broadway dealer—is a fine-looking, well-dressed man, with the manners and bearing of a gentleman. All are alike in one respect, however. They all buy and sell that which has been stolen. They drive hard bargains with the thieves who offer them goods, paying them but a small portion of the actual value of the prize. If the article is advertised, and a reward sufficiently in excess of what he paid for it is offered, the Fence frequently returns it to its rightful owner, upon condition that no questions shall be asked, and claims the reward. Vigorous efforts have been made by the police authorities to bring the Fences to justice, but without success. The necessary legal evidence can rarely be obtained, and though numerous arrests have been made, scarcely a conviction has followed.

The Fences are well skilled in the art of baffling justice. The study of the means of rapidly and effectually removing the marks by which the property in their hands can be identified, is the main business of their lives, and they acquire a degree of skill and dexterity in altering or effacing these marks which is truly surprising. A melting-pot is always over the fire, to which all silverware is consigned the instant it is received. The marks on linen, towels, and handkerchiefs are removed, sometimes by chemicals, sometimes by fine scissors made expressly for the purpose. Jewelry is at once removed from its settings, and the gold is either melted or the engraving is burnished out,

A FENCE STORE IN CHATHAM STREET.

so as in either case to make identification impossible. Rich velvet and silk garments are transmogrified by the removal and re-arrangement of the buttons and trimmings. Pointed edges are rounded, and rounded edges are pointed, entirely changing the whole aspect of the garment, with such celerity that the lady who had worn the dress in the morning would not have the slightest suspicion that it was the same in the evening. Cotton, wool, rags, and old ropes require no manipulation. When once thrown upon the heap, they defy the closest scrutiny of the owners. There is scarcely an article which can be the subject of theft, which the resources of these men do not enable them, in a very short time, to disguise beyond the power of recognition. Their premises are skilfully arranged for concealment. They are abundantly provided with secret doors and sliding panels, communicating with dark recesses. Apertures are cut in the partitions, so that a person coming in from the front can be distinctly seen before he enters the apartment. The Fence is as well skilled as any lawyer in the nature of evidence. He knows the difference between probability and proof as well as Sir William Hamilton himself. He does not trouble himself about any amount of probabilities that the detectives may accumulate against him ; but the said detectives must be remarkably expert if they are ever able to get anything against him which will amount to strictly legal proof.

The Fences not only deal with thieves, but carry on a large business with clerks, salesmen, and porters, who steal goods from their employers, and bring them to the Fences for sale.

VI.

THE ROUGHS.

ANOTHER class of those who live in open defiance of the law consists of the "Roughs." The New York Rough is simply a ruffian. He is usually of foreign parentage, though born in America, and in personal appearance is as near like a huge English bull-dog as it is possible for a human being to resemble

THE ROUGH'S PARADISE.

a brute. Of the two, the dog is the nobler animal. The Rough is not usually a professional thief, though he will steal if he has a chance, and often does steal in order to procure the means of raising money. He is familiar with crime of all kinds, for he was born in the slums and has never known anything better. In some cases he can read, in others he cannot. Those who can read never make use of their talent for any purpose of improvement. Their staple literature consists of the flash papers and obscene books. They are thoroughly versed in the history of crime, and nothing pleases them so much as a sensational account of an execution, a prize fight, or a murder. They are the patrons and supporters of dog and rat pits, and every brutal sport. Their boon companions are the keepers of the low-class bar rooms and dance houses, prize fighters, thieves, and fallen women. There is scarcely a Rough in the city but has a mistress among the lost sisterhood. The redeeming feature of the lives of some of these women is the devotion with which they cling to their " man." The Rough, on his part, beats and robs the woman, but protects her from violence or wrong at the hands of others. A large majority of these scoundrels have no other means of support than the infamous earnings of their mistresses.

Unlike the brute, the Rough is insensible to kindness. Civility is thrown away upon him. Usually he resents it. His delight is to fall upon some unoffending and helpless person, and beat him to a jelly. Sometimes—indeed commonly—he adds robbery to these assaults. Often gangs of Roughs will enter the pleasure grounds in the upper part of the city, in which a pic-nic or social gathering is going on, for the sole purpose of breaking up the meeting. They fall upon the unoffending pleasure-seekers, beat the men unmercifully, maltreat, insult, and sometimes outrage the women, rob all parties who have valuables to be taken, and then make their escape. Pleasure parties of this kind are usually unprovided with the means of resistance, while their assailants are well armed. It sometimes happens, however, that the pleasure seekers are more than a match for the Roughs, who, in such cases, are driven out after very severe handling.

The Rough does not hesitate to commit murder, or to outrage a woman. He is capable of any crime. He is a sort of human hyena who lives only to prey upon the better portions of the community. Sometimes he degenerates into a burglar or common thief, sometimes he becomes the proprietor of a panel house or a policy office. Crime-stained and worthy of punishment as he is, he walks the streets with a sense of security equal to that of the most innocent man.

This feeling of security is caused by the conviction on his part that he will not be punished for his misdeeds. The reason is simple: He is a voter, and he has influence with others of his class. He is necessary to the performance of the dirty work of the city politicians, and as soon as he gets into trouble, the politicians exert themselves to secure his discharge. They are usually successful, and consequently but few Roughs are ever punished in New York, no matter how revolting their crime. This is not all, however. There are well authenticated instances in which men of this class have been carried by their fellows, oftentimes by ballot-box stuffing and fraudulent voting, into high and responsible offices under the city. The recent state of affairs under the Ring illustrates the results of this system.

In the year 1871, 179 persons were "found drowned" in the waters of the city. Of these, many are supposed, with good reason, to have been the victims of foul play at the hands of the Roughs. In the same year, 42 persons were murdered in New York, and one man was hanged by the officers of the law.

35

XLIV.
THE PAWNBROKERS.

THE sign of the Lombards is very common in the great city. In the Bowery, East Broadway, Chatham, Catharine, Division, Oliver, Canal, and Grand streets, the three gilt balls are thickest, but they may also be seen in every portion of the city in which there is poverty and suffering. The law recognizes the fact that in all large communities these dealers are a necessary evil, and, while tolerating them as such, endeavors to interpose a safeguard in behalf of the community, by requiring that none but persons of good character and integrity shall exercise the calling. They must have been dreamers who framed this law, or they must have known but little of the class who carry on this business. The truth is, that there is not a pawnbroker of " good character and integrity " in the city. In New York the Mayor alone has the power of licensing them, and revoking their licence, and none but those so licensed can conduct their business in the city. " But," says the Report of the New York Prison Association, " Mayors of all cliques and parties have exercised this power with, apparently, little sense of the responsibility which rests upon them. They have not, ordinarily at least, required clear proof of the integrity of the applicants; but have usually licensed every applicant possessed of political influence. There is scarcely an instance where they have revoked a licence thus granted, even when they have been furnished with proofs of the dishonesty of the holders."

The pawnbrokers are, with scarcely an exception, the most rascally set to be found in the city. They are not generally receivers of goods which they know to be stolen, for there is too much risk to them in carrying on such a business. Their shops are overhauled almost every week by the detectives in searching for stolen property, and the pawnbrokers, as a class, prefer to turn over this business entirely to the Fences. Some of the most reckless, however, will receive pledges which they know to have been stolen, and the police occasionally find stolen goods on their hands. Upon one occasion, a whole basket of watches was found in one of these establishments. Another was found in possession of a diamond which was identified by its owner. It had been stolen by a servant girl. It was worth over seven hundred dollars, and had been pawned for two dollars and a half.

The pawnbrokers, though not receivers of stolen goods, are not a whit better. They are the meanest of thieves and swindlers. Section eight of the statute, under which they hold their licences, requires that, " No pawnbroker shall ask, demand, or receive any greater rate of interest than twenty-five per cent. per annum upon any loan not exceeding the sum of twenty-five dollars, or than seven per cent. per annum upon any loan exceeding the sum .of twenty-five dollars, under the penalty of one hundred dollars for every such offence." This law is invariably violated by the pawnbroker, who trades upon the ignorance of his customers. The rate habitually charged for loaning money is three per cent. a month, or any fractional part of a month, or thirty-six per cent. a year, regardless of the amount. Many laboring men and women pawn the same articles regularly on the first of the week, and redeem them on Saturday when their wages are paid them.

" The following is a schedule of charges made on articles irrespective of interest: On diamonds, watches, jewelry, silverware, opera-glasses, articles of *vertu*, ten per cent. on the amount loaned, over and above the interest, for what is called putting them away in the safes. On coats, vests, pants, dresses, cloaks, skirts, basques, from twenty cents to one dollar is charged for hanging up. On laces, silks, velvets, shawls, etc., from twenty-five cents to one dollar for putting away in bureau, wardrobe or drawer. For wrappers from fifteen to fifty cents is charged. Persons offering goods done up in papers are compelled to hire a wrapper, or the pawnbroker refuses to advance. The wrapper is simply a dirty piece of old muslin. The hire of one of these wrappers has been known to have amounted to over five dollars in one year. Upon trunks, valises, beds, pillows, carpets, tool-chests, musical instruments, sewing machines, clocks, pictures, etc., etc., in proportion to their bulk, from one dollar to five dollars is charged for storage. A still greater profit to the pawnbrokers is the penny fraud. They buy pennies, getting from 104 to 108 for one dollar. These they pay out, and on every $100 thus paid out an average gain of six dollars is made. This amounts to something with the prominent ones, who often pay out many hundred dollars in a day. Another source of profit is the sur-plus over the amount loaned which the pawnbroker receives from the sales of unredeemed pledges. This surplus, although belonging to the depositor, according to law, is never paid. In fact, not one in a thousand who have dealings with pawnbrokers is aware of his rights."

As a rule, these wretches grow rich very fast. They are prin-cipally Jews of the lowest class. They allow their wives and children to wear the jewelry, ornaments, and finer clothing placed in their keeping, and in this way save much of the ordi-nary expense of the head of a family. In the case of clothing, the articles are frequently worn out by their families. They are either returned in this condition when demanded, or the owner is told that they cannot be found. Payment for them is always refused. As has been stated, they refuse to pay to the owner the amount received in excess of the loan for an article which has been sold. This, added to their excessive rate of interest, is said to make their gains amount to nearly five hundred per cent. on the capital invested in their business—"the Jews' five per cent."

The principal customers are the poor. Persons of former respectability or wealth, widows and orphans, are always sure to carry with them into their poverty some of the trinkets that were theirs in the heyday of prosperity. These articles go one by one to buy bread. The pawnbroker advances not more than a twentieth part of their value, and haggles over that. He knows full well that the pledges will never be redeemed, that these unhappy creatures must grow less able every day to recover them. Jewelry, clothing, ornaments of all kinds, and even the wedding ring of the wife and mother, come to him one by one, never to be regained by their owners. He takes them at a mere pittance, and sells them at a profit of several hundred per cent.

You may see the poor pass into the doors of these shops every day. The saddest faces we ever saw were those of women coming away from them. Want leaves its victims no choice, but drives them mercilessly into the clutches of the pawnbroker.

The majority of the articles pawned are forced there by want, undoubtedly, but very many of them go to buy drink. Women are driven by brutal husbands to this course, and there are wretches who will absolutely steal the clothing from their shivering wives and little ones, and with them procure the means of buying gin.

Of late years another class of pawnbrokers, calling themselves "Diamond Brokers," has appeared in the city. They make advances on the jewels of persons—mostly women—in need of money. The extravagance of fashionable life brings them many customers. They drive as hard bargains as the others of their class, and their transactions being larger, they grow rich quicker. They are very discreet, and all dealings with them are carried on in the strictest secrecy, but, were they disposed, they could tell many a strange tale by which the peace of some "highly respectable families" in the Avenue would be rudely disturbed.

XLV.
THE BEER-GARDENS.

In some respects, New York is as much German as American. A large part of it is a genuine reproduction of the Fatherland as regards the manners, customs, people, and language spoken. In the thickly settled sections east of the Bowery the Germans predominate, and one might live there for a year without ever hearing an English word spoken.   The Germans of New York are a very steady, hard-working people, and withal very sociable. During the day they confine themselves closely to business, and at night they insist upon enjoying themselves.   The huge Stadt Theatre draws several thousand within its walls whenever its doors are opened, and concerts and festivals of various kinds attract others.   But the most popular of all places with this class of citizens is the beer-garden. Here one can sit and smoke, and drink beer by the gallon, listen to music, move about, meet his friends, and enjoy himself in his own way—all at a moderate cost.

From one end of the Bowery to the other, beer-gardens abound, and their brilliantly illuminated signs and transparencies form one of the most remarkable features of that curious street.   Not all of them are reputable.   In some there is a species of theatrical performance which is often broadly indecent.   These are patronized by but few Germans, although they are mainly carried on by men of that nationality.   The Rough and servant girl elements predominate in the audiences, and there is an unmistakably Irish stamp on most of the faces present.

The true beer-garden finds its highest development in the monster Atlantic Garden, which is located in the Bowery, next

door to the Old Bowery Theatre.   It is an immense room, with
a lofty curved ceiling, handsomely frescoed, and lighted by
numerous chandeliers and by brackets along the walls.   It is
lighted during the day from the roof.   At one side is an open
space planted with trees and flowers, the only mark of a garden
visible.   A large gallery rises above the floor at each end.   That
at the eastern or upper end is used as a restaurant for those who
desire regular meals.   The lower gallery is, like the rest of the
place, for beer-drinkers only.   Under the latter gallery is a
shooting hall, which is usually filled with marksmen trying
their skill.   On the right hand side of the room is a huge
orchestrion or monster music-box, and by its side is a raised
platform, occupied by the orchestra employed at the place.   The
floor is sanded, and is lined with plain tables, six feet by two
in size, to each of which is a couple of benches.   The only
ornaments of the immense hall are the frescoes and the chandeliers.   Everything else is plain and substantial.   Between
the hall and the Bowery is the bar room, with its lunch
counters.   The fare provided at the latter is strictly German,
but the former retails drinks of every description.

During the day the Atlantic does a good business through its
bar and restaurant, many persons taking their meals here regularly.   As night comes on, the great hall begins to fill up, and
by eight o'clock the place is in its glory.   From three to four
thousand people, mainly Germans, may be seen here at one
time, eating, drinking, smoking.   Strong liquors are not sold,
the drinks being beer and the lighter Rhine wines.   The German capacity for holding beer is immense.   An amount sufficient to burst an American makes him only comfortable and
good humored.   The consumption of the article here nightly is
tremendous, but there is no drunkenness.   The audience is well
behaved, and the noise is simply the hearty merriment of a
large crowd.   There is no disorder, no indecency.   The place is
thoroughly respectable, and the audience are interested in keeping it so.   They come here with their families, spend a social,
pleasant evening, meet their friends, hear the news, enjoy the
music and the beer, and go home refreshed and happy.   The

THE ATLANTIC GARDEN.

Germans are very proud of this resort, and they would not tolerate the introduction of any feature that would make it an unfit place for their wives and daughters. It is a decided advantage to the people who frequent this place, whatever the Temperance advocates may say, that men have here a resort where they can enjoy themselves with their families, instead of seeking their pleasure away from the society of their wives and children.

The buzz and the hum of the conversation, and the laughter, are overpowering, and you wander through the vast crowd with your ears deafened by the sound. Suddenly the leader of the orchestra raps sharply on his desk, and there is a profound silence all over the hall. In an instant the orchestra breaks forth into some wonderful German melody, or some deep-voiced, strong-lunged singer sends his rich notes rolling through the hall. The auditors have suddenly lost their merriment, and are now listening pensively to the music, which is good. They sip their beer absently, and are thinking no doubt of the far-off Fatherland, for you see their features grow softer and their eyes glisten. Then, when it is all over, they burst into an enthusiastic encore, or resume their suspended conversations.

On the night of the reception of the news of Napoleon's capitulation at Sedan, the Atlantic Garden was a sight worth seeing. The orchestra was doubled, and the music and the songs were all patriotic. The hall was packed with excited people, and the huge building fairly rocked with the cheers which went up from it. The "German's Fatherland" and Luther's Hymn were sung by five thousand voices, hoarse or shrill with excitement. Oceans of beer were drunk, men and women shook hands and embraced, and the excitement was kept up until long after midnight. Yet nobody was drunk, save with the excitement of the moment.

The Central Park Garden, at the corner of Seventh avenue and Fifty-ninth street, is more of an American institution than the Atlantic. It consists of a handsome hall surrounded on three sides by a gallery, and opening at the back upon grounds of moderate size, tastefully laid out, and adorned with rustic stalls and arbors for the use of guests. At the Atlantic the admission is free. Here one pays fifty cents for the privilege of entering the grounds and building. During the summer months nightly concerts, with Saturday matinées, are given here by Theodore Thomas and his famous orchestra—the finest organization of its kind in America. The music is of a high order, and is rendered in a masterly manner. Many lovers of music come to New York in the summer simply to hear these concerts.

The place is the fashionable resort of the city in the summer. The audience is equal to anything to be seen in the city. One can meet here all the celebrities who happen to be in town, and as every one is free to do as he pleases, there is no restraint to hamper one's enjoyment. You may sit and smoke and drink, or stroll through the place the whole evening, merely greeting your acquaintances with a nod, or you may join them, and chat to your heart's content. Refreshments and liquors of all kinds are sold to guests; but the prices are high. The Central Park Garden, or, as it is called by strangers, "Thomas's Garden," is the most thoroughly enjoyable place in the city in the summer.

XLVI.

JAMES FISK, JR.

JAMES FISK, JR., was born at Bennington, Vermont, on the 1st of April, 1834. His father was a pedlar, and the early life of the boy was passed in hard work. What little education he received was obtained at the public schools. At the age of seventeen he obtained his first employment, being engaged by Van Amburgh to clean out the cages of the animals in his menagerie and to assist in the erection of the tents. He made himself so useful to his employer that he was soon promoted to the position of ticket receiver. He remained with Van Amburgh for eight years, travelling with him through the United States, Canada, and Europe, and, at the age of twenty-five, left him to begin life for himself in the calling of his father. He went back to Vermont, and began peddling such small articles as steel pens and lead pencils through the towns of the State. He succeeded in acquiring and saving a small sum of money, and was able to borrow a little more. He then purchased a horse and wagon, and began a series of more extended operations as a pedlar of dry goods. He visited all the principal towns and villages of Vermont, and met with a ready sale for his goods. His energy and business tact were eminently successful, and his business soon grew to such an extent that his one-horse wagon was too small for it. He accordingly sold this vehicle, and purchased a handsome "four in hand," with which he travelled through Massachusetts and Connecticut, as well as Vermont. He was very popular with his customers, and established a reputation for fair dealing, selling good articles at a moderate profit.

His energy and success attracted the attention of the Boston wholesale house from which he bought his goods, and they thinking that he would prove a useful acquisition to them, offered him an interest in their business. Their offer was accepted, and, in 1860, he became a partner in the house of Jordan, Marsh & Co., of Boston. He was sent South by the firm, and though he succeeded in conducting for them several large and profitable transactions during the early part of the war, and though they remained his friends to the close of his life, the connection was not altogether satisfactory to them, and, in 1862, they purchased his interest in the business for the sum of $64,000.

About this time, some capitalists in Boston were desirous of purchasing the Stonington line of steamboats, then owned by Daniel Drew. Fisk became aware of their desire, and, coming to New York, in 1863, obtained an introduction to Daniel Drew, and so won the favor and confidence of that gentleman that he was employed by him to manage the negotiation for the sale of the steamers, which he did to Mr. Drew's entire satisfaction. From that time, Drew became his friend, and soon gained him a position in Wall street.

Upon entering the street, Fisk began a series of speculations on his own account, and, in the short space of two years, he lost all his money. It is said that he swore a mighty oath that as Wall street had ruined him, Wall street should pay for it. Daniel Drew now came to his aid, and, in 1865, helped him to form the firm of Fisk, Belden & Co., stock-brokers, and assisted the new house by employing them as his brokers in many of his heaviest transactions.

In 1867 occurred the great struggle between Drew and Vanderbilt for the possession of the Erie Railway. James Fisk and Jay Gould now made their appearance as Directors in the Erie Railway. The following is the New York *Tribune's* account of this affair:

"When the crisis came, on the eve of the election for Directors, in October, 1867, there were three contestants in the field. Fisk was serving under the Drew party, who wanted to be retained in office. Vanderbilt, master of Harlem, Hudson River, and Central, seemed to be on the point of securing Erie also. Eldridge was the leader of the Boston, Hartford, and Erie

JAMES FISK, JR.

party, which wanted to get into the Erie Directory for the purpose of making that Company guarantee the bonds of their own
worthless road. Eldridge was assisted by Gould. As a result
of the compromise by which the three opposing interests coal-
esced, Fisk and Gould were both chosen Directors of Erie, and
from the month of October, 1867, dates the memorable association of these two choice spirits since so famous in the money
markets of the world. They were not the counterparts, but the
complements of each other. Fisk was bold, unscrupulous,
dashing, enterprising, ready in execution, powerful in his influence over the lower and more sensual order of men. Gould
was artful, reticent, long-headed, clear of brain, fertile of invention, tenacious of purpose, and no more burdened with unnecessary scruples than his more noisy and flashy companion. They
were not long in joining fortunes. At the time of the famous
Erie corner, the next March, they were ostensibly working on
opposite sides, Gould acting for Vanderbilt, and Fisk being the
man to whom Drew intrusted 50,000 shares of new stock,
secretly issued, to be used when Vanderbilt's brokers began to
buy. The mysteries of that transaction are fully known only
to a few of the principal actors. An injunction of Judge Barnard's had forbidden Drew or anybody connected with the road
to manufacture any more stock by the issue of convertible bonds.
But Drew was 'short' of Erie; the Vanderbilt pool threatened
ruin; and stock must be had. The new certificates had already
been made out in the name of James Fisk, jr., and were in the
hands of the Secretary who was enjoined from issuing them.
Mr. Fisk saw a way out of the difficulty. The Secretary gave
the certificate books to an employé of the road, with directions
to carry them carefully to the transfer office. The messenger
returned in a moment empty-handed, and told the astonished
Secretary that Mr. Fisk had met him at the door, taken the
books, and 'run away with them!' On the same day the convertible bonds corresponding to these certificates were placed on
the Secretary's desk, and as soon as Vanderbilt had forced up
the price of Erie, Fisk's new shares were thrown upon the
market, and bought by Vanderbilt's agents before their origin

was suspected.   Mr. Fisk unfortunately had not yet cultivated the intimate relations with Judge Barnard which he subsequently sustained.   When the Drew party applied for an order from Judge Gilbert in Brooklyn, enjoining Barnard's injunctions, the petitioner who accused that ornament of the New York bench of a corrupt conspiracy to speculate in Erie stock, was none other than Fisk's partner, Mr. Belden.   The next morning Barnard issued an order of arrest for contempt, and Fisk, with the whole Erie Directory, fled to Jersey City, carrying $7,000,000 of money and the books and papers of the Company.   Among the most valuable of the assets transferred on that occasion to Taylor's Hotel was Miss Helen Josephine Mansfield.   'I went to Jersey,' testified this fair creature some weeks ago, in the suit which has just come to so tragical a termination, 'with the officers of the Erie Company, and the railroad paid all the expense.'   Mr. Fisk could afford to amuse himself.   He had made fifty or sixty thousand dollars by his day's work in Broad street, and he had the satisfaction of knowing that he had not only beaten Vanderbilt and Barnard, but outwitted even his particular friend and patron, Mr. Drew.   He had now practically the greater share of the management on his shoulders, though in name he was only Controller.   He softened public indignation by subsidizing a gang of ruffians, ostensibly in the Vanderbilt interest, to besiege 'Fort Taylor,' as if for the purpose of kidnapping the Directors, and organizing a band of railway hands to mount guard about the hotel.   He dogged the steps of Mr. Drew, who was stealing over to New York by night to make a secret compromise for himself alone with Mr. Vanderbilt, and when Drew carried off the funds of the Company, Fisk compelled him to bring them back by putting an attachment on his money in bank.   A bill was now introduced at Albany to legalize Drew's overissue of stock.   It was defeated.   Mr. Gould visited the capital with half a million dollars, and came back without a cent, and the bill which three weeks before had been rejected by a vote of 83 to 32 was carried by a vote of 101 to 6.   This was followed by a general suspension of hostilities.   The scandalous network of injunctions had

JAY GOULD.

become so intricate that one general order was obtained sweeping it all away.   Judge Barnard was placated in some manner not made public.   Mr. Peter B. Sweeny, who, as the representative of Tammany, had been appointed 'Receiver' of the property of the railway company after it had been carried out of reach, was allowed $150,000 for his trouble of taking care of nothing; and the exiles returned to New York.   In one of his characteristic fits of frankness, James Fisk afterward on the witness stand described the settlement which ensued as an 'almighty robbery.'   The Directors of Erie took 50,000 shares of stock off Vanderbilt's shoulders at 70, and gave him $1,000,000 besides.   Eldridge got $4,000,000 of Erie acceptances in exchange for $5,000,000 of Boston, Hartford, and Erie, which became bankrupt very soon afterward.   Drew kept all he had made, but was to pay $540,000 into the Erie treasury and stand acquitted of all claims the corporation might have against him.   Nearly half a million more was required to pay the lawyers and discontinue the suits.   Fisk, getting nothing personally, stood out against the arrangement until the conspirators consented to give him—the Erie Railroad!   Drew and some others were to resign, and Fisk and Gould to take possession of the property."

Out of his first operations in Erie stock, Fisk is said to have made $1,300,000.   The Legislature of New York legalized his acts, through the influence, it is said, of Mr. William M. Tweed. It is certain that this act was followed by the entrance of Tweed and Sweeny into the Board of Directors.

Once in possession of the Erie road, Fisk and his colleagues managed it in their own interests.   It was commonly believed in the city that Fisk was but the executor of the designs which were conceived by an abler brain than his own.

He figured largely in the infamous Black Friday transactions of Wall street, and is credited by the public with being one of the originators of that vast conspiracy to destroy the business of the street.   How near he came to success has already been shown.

Soon after coming into possession of the Erie road, he pur-

36

chased Pike's Opera House for $1,000,000 in the name of the Erie Railway Company. The Directors, however, refused to approve the transaction, and he refunded to them the amount of the purchase, taking the building on his private account, and repaying the road in some of its stock owned by him. Subsequently he leased the front building to the road at an enormous rent, and opened for it a suite of the most gorgeous railway offices in the world. He subsequently bought the Fifth Avenue Theatre, and the Central Park Garden, and the Bristol line of steamers, and the steamers plying in connection with the Long Branch Railway. He made himself "Admiral" of this magnificent fleet, and dressed himself in a gorgeous naval uniform. When President Grant visited the Coliseum Concert at Boston, Fisk accompanied him in this dress, having previously played the part of host to the President during the voyage down the Sound on one of his boats. A year or two previous to his death, he was elected Colonel of the Ninth Regiment of the National Guard.

Previous to his purchase of the Grand Opera House, Mr. Fisk was an unknown man, but the ownership of this palatial establishment gave him an opportunity of enjoying the notoriety he coveted. His career in connection with this establishment, and his unscrupulous management of the Erie Railway, soon made him notorious in all parts of America and Europe. His monogram was placed on everything he owned or was connected with, and he literally lived in the gaze of the public. He can scarcely be said to have had any private life, for the whole town was talking of his theatres, his dashing four in hand, his railway and steamboats, his regiment, his toilettes, his magnificence, his reckless generosity, and his love affairs. He had little regard for morality or public sentiment, and hesitated at nothing necessary to the success of his schemes. His great passion was for notoriety, and he cared not what he did so it made people talk about him. He surrounded himself with a kind of barbaric splendor, which won him the name of the "Prince of Erie." Some of his acts were utterly ludicrous, and he had the wit to perceive it, but he cared not so it made James Fisk, jr., the talk of the day. His influence upon the community was bad. He had not only his admirers, but his imitators, and these sought to reproduce his bad qualities rather than his virtues.

In some respects he was a strange compound of good and evil. He was utterly unprincipled, yet he was generous to a fault. No one ever came to him in distress without meeting with assistance, and it adds to the virtue of these good deeds that he never proclaimed them to the world. Says one of his intimate friends: " His personal expenses were, at a liberal esti- mate, not one-fifth as large as the amount which he spent in providing for persons in whose affairs he took a kindly interest, who had seen misfortune in life, and whom he felt to be de- pendent upon him for assistance. He gave away constantly enormous amounts in still more direct charities, concerning which he rarely spoke to any one, and it was only by accident that even his most intimate friends found out what he was doing. He supported for some years an entire family of blind persons without ever saying a word about it to his nearest friends. He was particularly generous towards actors and ac- tresses, who, whenever they suffered from misfortune, would always appeal to him ; and one lady, herself an actress of con- siderable repute and of very generous nature, was in the habit of coming constantly to Mr. Fisk to appeal to him for assistance to aged or unfortunate members of their profession, assistance which he never refused. Very recently a lady, who was for- merly a New York favorite, but who made an unhappy mar- riage, and to escape from a drunken husband had carried her child to England, where, after struggling in provincial theatres for more than a year, she came to almost her last penny and had hardly the means to return to this country, without a change of clothing and without being able to bring away her child, made her case known to the lady before-mentioned, who imme- diately, after helping to the extent of her own scanty means, sent her with a note to Mr. Fisk. Mr. Fisk listened to her story, advanced her $250 on the spot, procured her an engage- ment in a theatre at $75 a week, and interested the captain of one of our finest sea-going vessels in the case so far as to provide a free passage for the child to this country, the captain, in order to please Mr. Fisk, taking great pains to discover the whereabouts of the child and restore her to its mother. These are but incidental illustrations of what Mr. Fisk was daily doing, and always doing with the utmost privacy and with the greatest reluctance to allow it to become known. He would rarely subscribe to any public charity, because he disliked to make any pretence of liberality before the public."

In the fall of 1867, Fisk made the acquaintance of Mrs. Helen Josephine Mansfield, an actress, who had just been divorced from her husband, Frank Lawler. He became deeply enamored of her, and she became his mistress and lived with him several years, her main object being, it would seem, to obtain from him all the money he was willing to expend upon her. Fisk subsequently introduced one of his friends, Edward S. Stokes, to Mrs. Mansfield, and the woman was not long in transferring her affections from her protector to Stokes. This aroused Fisk's jealousy, and led to constant trouble between his mistress and himself. His quarrel with Stokes was complicated by business disputes, which were carried into the courts, where Fisk was all powerful. The matter went from bad to worse, until at length Stokes and Mrs. Mansfield instituted a libel suit against Fisk, which was commonly regarded in the city as simply an attempt on their part to extort money from him. The suit dragged its slow way through the court in which it was instituted, and every day diminished the chances of the success of the plaintiffs.

For reasons which he has not yet made public, Stokes now resolved to take matters into his own hands, and on the afternoon of the 6th of January, 1872, waylaid Fisk, as the latter was ascending the private stairway of the Grand Central Hotel, and, firing upon him twice from his hiding place, inflicted on him severe wounds from which he died the next day. The assassination was most cowardly and brutal, and awakened a feeling of horror and indignation on the part of all classes.

XLVII.

TRINITY CHURCH.

ON the west side of Broadway, facing Wall street, stands Trinity Church, or, as it is commonly called, "Old Trinity," the handsomest ecclesiastical structure in the city. It is the third edifice which has occupied the site. The first church was built in 1697, at the organization of the parish, and was a plain square edifice with an ugly steeple. In 1776, this building was destroyed in the great fire of that year. A second church was built on the site of the old one, in 1790. In 1839, this was pulled down, and the present noble edifice was erected. It was finished and consecrated in 1846.

The present church is a beautiful structure of brown-stone, built as nearly in the pure Gothic style as modern churches ever are. The walls are fifty feet in height, and the apex of the roof is sixty feet from the floor of the church. The interior is finished in brown-stone, with massive columns of the same material supporting the roof. There are no transepts, but it is proposed to enlarge the church by the addition of transepts, and to extend the choir back to the end of the churchyard. The nave and the aisles make up the public portion of the church. The choir is occupied by the clergy. The windows are of stained glass. Those at the sides are very simple, but the oriel over the altar is a grand work. There are two organs, a monster instrument over the main entrance, and a smaller organ in the choir. Both are remarkably fine instruments. The vestry rooms, which lie on each side of the chancel, contain a number of handsome memorial tablets, and in the north room there is a fine tomb in memory of Bishop Onderdonk, with a full-length effigy of the deceased prelate in his episcopal robes.

Service is held twice a day in the church. On Sundays and high feast days there is full service and a sermon. The choral service is used altogether on such occasions. Trinity has long been famous for its excellent music. The choir consists of men and boys, who are trained with great care by the musical director. The service is very beautiful and impressive, and is thoroughly in keeping with the grand and cathedral-like edifice in which it is conducted. The two organs, the voices of the choristers, and often the chime of bells, all combine to send a flood of melody rolling through the beautiful arches such as is never heard elsewhere in the city.

The spire is 284 feet in height, and is built of solid brownstone from the base to the summit of the cross. It contains a clock, with three faces, just above the roof of the church, and a chime of bells. About 110 feet from the ground the square form of the tower terminates, and a massive but graceful octagonal spire rises to a height of 174 feet. At the base of this spire is a narrow gallery enclosed with a stone balustrade, from which a fine view of the city and the surrounding country is obtained. The visitor may, however, climb within the spire to a point nearly two hundred and fifty feet from the street. Here is a small wooden platform, and about four feet above it are four small windows through which one may look out upon the magnificent view spread out below him. The eye can range over the entire city, and take in Brooklyn and its suburban towns as well. To the eastward are Long Island Sound and the distant hills of Connecticut. To the southward stretches away the glorious bay, and beyond it is the dark blue line of the Atlantic. Sandy Hook, the Highlands, the Narrows, and Staten Island are all in full view. To the westward is the New Jersey shore, and back of Jersey city rise the blue Orange Mountains, with Newark, Elizabeth, Orange and Patterson in full sight. To the northward, the Hudson stretches away until it seems to disappear in the dark shadow of the Palisades. From where you stand, you look down on the habitations of nearly three millions of people. The bay, the rivers, and the distant Sound are crowded with vessels of all kinds. If the day be clear, you may see the railway trains dashing across the meadows back of Jersey City. The roar of the great city comes up to you from below, and beneath you is a perfect maze of telegraph wires. The people in the streets seem like pigmies, and the vehicles are like so many toys. You know they are moving rapidly, but they seem from this lofty height to be crawling. It is a long way to these upper windows, but the view which they command is worth the exertion. The tower is open to visitors during the week, on payment of a trifling fee to the sexton.

The chimes are hung in the square tower, just above the roof of the church. The bells are nine in number. The smallest weighs several hundred pounds, while the largest weighs several thousand. The musical range is an octave and a quarter, rather a limited scale, it is true, but the ringer is a thorough musician, and has managed to ring out many an air within this compass, which but for his ingenuity would have been unsuited to these bells. The largest bell, the "Big Ben," and several others, are connected with the clock, and the former strikes the hours, while the rest of this set chime the quarters. Five of the bells, the large one and the four smaller ones, were brought here from England, in 1846. The other four were made in West Troy, by Meneely & Son, a few years later, and are fully equal to their English mates in tone and compass. The entire chime is very rich and sweet in tone, and, in this respect, is surpassed by very few bells in the world. The bells are hung on swinging frames, but are lashed, so as to stand motionless during the chiming, the notes being struck by the tongues, which are movable. The tongue always strikes in the same place, and thus the notes are full and regular. From the tongue of each bell there is a cord which is attached to a wooden lever in the ringer's room, about thirty feet below. These nine levers are arranged side by side, and are so arranged as to work as easy as possible. Each is as large as a handspike, and it requires no little strength to sustain the exertion of working them. The ringer places his music before him, and strikes each note as it occurs by suddenly pushing down the proper lever. At the end of his work, he is thoroughly tired. The ringer now in charge of the bells is Mr. James Ayliffe, an accomplished musician.

In favorable weather, the chimes can be heard for a distance of from five to ten miles. There are few strangers who leave the city without hearing the sweet bells of the old church. The city people would count it a great misfortune to be deprived of their music. For nearly thirty years they have heard them, in in seasons of joy and in hours of sadness. On Christmas eve, at midnight, the chimes ring in the blessed morning of our Lord's nativity, thus continuing an old and beautiful custom now observed only in parts of Europe.

The church is kept open from early morning until sunset. In the winter season it is always well heated, and hundreds of the poor find warmth and shelter within its holy walls. It is the only church in New York in which there is no distinction made between the rich and the poor. The writer has frequently seen beggars in tatters conducted, by the sexton, to the best seats in the church.

The rector and his assistants are alive to the fact that this is one of the few churches now left to the lower part of the city, and they strive to make it a great missionary centre. Their best efforts are for the poor. Those who sneer at the wealth of the parish, would do well to trouble themselves to see what a good use is made of it.

The ultra fashionable element of the congregation attend Trinity Chapel, or " Up-town Trinity," in Twenty-fifth street, near Broadway. This is a handsome church, and has a large and wealthy congregation.

Trinity Parish embraces a large part of the city. It includes the following churches, or chapels, as they are called : St. Paul's, St. John's, Trinity Chapel, and Trinity Church. It is in charge of a rector, who is a sort of small bishop in this little diocese. He has eight assistants. Each church or chapel has its pastor, who is subject to the supervision of the rector. The Rev. Morgan Dix, D.D., a son of General John A. Dix, is the present rector.

Trinity takes good care of its clergy. The salaries are amply sufficient to insure a comfortable support, and a well-furnished house is provided for each one who has a family. Should a clergy-

TRINITY CHURCH.

man become superannuated in the service of the parish, he is liberally maintained during his life; and should he die in his ministry, provision is made for his family.

The wealth of the parish is very great. It is variously stated at from sixty to one hundred millions of dollars. It is chiefly in real estate, the leases of which yield an immense revenue.

The churchyard of Old Trinity covers about two acres of ground. A handsome iron railing separates it from Broadway, and the thick rows of gravestones, all crumbling and stained with age, present a strange contrast to the bustle, vitality, and splendor with which they are surrounded. They stare solemnly down into Wall street, and offer a bitter commentary upon the struggles and anxiety of the money kings.

The place has an air of peace that is pleasant in the midst of so much noise and confusion, and is well worth visiting.

In the churchyard, near the south door of the church, you will see a plain brown-stone slab, bearing this inscription: " *The vault of Walter and Robert C. Livingston, sons of Robert Livingston, of the Manor of Livingston.*" This is one of the Meccas of the world of science, for the mortal part of *Robert Fulton* sleeps in the vault below, in sight of the mighty steam fleets which his genius has called into existence. A plain obelisk, near the centre of the southern extremity of the yard, marks the grave of Alexander Hamilton. At the west end of the south side of the church is the sarcophagus of Albert Gallatin, and James Lawrence, the heroic but ill-fated commander of the Chesapeake sleeps close by the south door of the church, his handsome tomb being the most prominent object in that portion of the yard. At the northern extremity of the churchyard, and within a few feet of Broadway, is the splendid "Martyrs' Monument," erected to the memory of the patriots of the American Revolution, who died from the effects of British cruelty in the "Old Sugar House" and in the prison ships in Wallabout Bay, the site of the present Brooklyn Navy Yard.

Close to the Broadway railing, and so close that one can almost touch it from the street, is a worn brown-stone slab, bearing but two words, "Charlotte Temple." It is difficult to find, and but few strangers ever see it, but for years it has been the most prominent spot in the enclosure to the lovers of romance. Charlotte Temple's history is a very sad one, and unhappily not a rare one. She lived and died nearly a century ago. She was young and surpassingly lovely, and she attracted the attention of a British officer of high rank, who carried her off from her boarding school, seduced her, and deserted her. Her friends discarded her, and she sank under her heavy load of sorrow. She was found by her father in a wretched garret, with her child. Both were at the point of death. The father came just in time to close their eyes forever. They were laid to rest in the same grave in the old churchyard, and, some years after, the seducer, stung with remorse for his brutality, placed over them the slab which still marks the spot. The sad story was written out in book form, and was dramatized and played in every part of the country, so that there are few old time people in all the land who are ignorant of it.

XLVIII.

THE HOLIDAYS.

I.

NEW YEAR'S DAY.

ALL the holidays are observed in New York with more or less heartiness, but those which claim especial attention are New Year's Day and Christmas.

The observance of New Year's Day dates from the earliest times. The Dutch settlers brought the custom from their old homes across the sea, and made the day an occasion for renewing old friendships and wishing each other well. All feuds were forgotten, family breaches were repaired, and every one made it a matter of conscience to enter upon the opening year with kind feelings towards his neighbor. Subsequent generations have continued to observe the custom, though differently from the primitive but hearty style of their fathers.

For weeks before the New Year dawns, nearly every house in the city is in a state of confusion. The whole establishment is thoroughly overhauled and cleaned, and neither mistress nor maid has any rest from her labors. The men folks are nuisances at such times, and gradually keep themselves out of the way, lest they should interfere with the cleaning. Persons who contemplate refurnishing their houses, generally wait until near the close of the year before doing so, in order that everything may be new on the great day. Those who cannot refurnish, endeavor to make their establishments look as fresh and new as possible. A general baking, brewing, stewing, broiling, and frying is begun, and the pantries are loaded with good things to eat and to drink.

All the family must have new outfits for the occasion, and tailors and *modistes* find this a profitable season.   To be seen in a dress that has ever been worn before, is considered the height of vulgarity.

The table is set in magnificent style.   Elegant china and glassware, and splendid plate, adorn it.   It is loaded down with dainties of every description.   Wines, lemonades, coffee, brandy, whiskey and punch are in abundance.   Punch is seen in all its glory on this day, and each householder strives to have the best of this article.   There are regular punch-makers in the city, who reap a harvest at this time.   Their services are engaged long before-hand, and they are kept busy all the morning going from house to house, to make this beverage, which is nowhere so palatable as in this city.

Hairdressers, or " *artistes* in hair," as they call themselves, are also in demand at New Year, for each lady then wishes to have her *coiffure* as magnificent as possible.   This is a day of hard work to these *artistes*, and in order to meet all their engagements, they begin their rounds at midnight.   They are punctual to the moment, and from that time until noon on New Year's Day are busily engaged.   Of course those whose heads are dressed at such unseasonable hours cannot think of lying down to sleep, as their " head-gear " would be ruined by such a procedure.   They are compelled to rest sitting bolt upright, or with their heads resting on a table or the back of a chair.

All New York is stirring by eight o'clock in the morning. By nine the streets are filled with gayly-dressed persons on their way to make their annual calls.   Private carriages, hacks, and other vehicles soon appear, filled with persons bent upon similar expeditions.   Business is entirely suspended in the city. The day is a legal holiday, and is faithfully observed by all classes.   Hack hire is enormous—forty or fifty dollars being sometimes paid for a carriage for the day.   The cars and omnibuses are crowded, and every one is in the highest spirits.   The crowds consist entirely of men.   Scarcely a female is seen on the

streets. It is not considered respectable for a lady to venture
out, and the truth is, it is not prudent for her to do so.

Callers begin their rounds at ten o'clock. The ultra fashionables do not receive until twelve. At the proper time, the lady
of the house, attended by her daughters, if there be any, takes
her stand in the drawing-room by the hospitable board. In a
little while the door-bell rings, and the first visitor is ushered in
by the pompous domestic in charge of the door. The first
callers are generally young men, who are ambitious to make as
many visits as possible. The old hands know where the best
tables are set, and confine their attentions principally to them.
The caller salutes the hostess and the ladies present, says it's a
fine or a bad day, as the case may be, offers the compliments
of the season, and accepts with alacrity the invitation of the
hostess to partake of the refreshments. A few eatables are
swallowed in haste—the vistor managing to get out a word or
two between each mouthful—a glass of wine or punch is gulped
down, the visitor bows himself out, and the ladies avenge
themselves for the infliction by ridiculing him after he has gone.
This is the routine, and it goes on all day, and until long after
dark.

Sometimes a family, not wishing to receive callers, will hang
a card-basket on the front-door knob and close the front of the
house. The callers deposit their cards in the basket, and go
their way rejoicing. Perhaps the mansion is one that is famed
for the excellence of its wines and eatables on such occasions.
The veteran caller has promised himself a genuine treat here,
and he views the basket with dismay. There is no help for it,
however, so he deposits his card, and departs, wondering at " the
manners of some people who refuse to observe a time-honored
custom."

A gentleman in starting out, provides himself with a written
memorandum of the places he intends visiting, and " checks,"
each one off with his pencil, when the call is made. This list is
necessary, as few sober men can remember all their friends
without it, and with the majority the list is a necessity before
the day is half over. The driver takes charge of it often, and

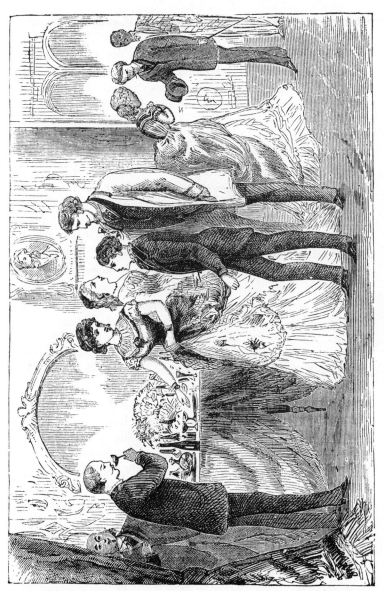

NEW YEAR'S CALLS.

575

when the caller is too hazy to act for himself, carries him sometimes to the door of the house, and rings the bell for him.
Each man tries to make as many calls as possible, so that he
may boast of the feat afterwards. At the outset, of course,
everything is conducted with the utmost propriety, but, as the
day wears on, the generous liquors they have imbibed begin to
"tell" upon the callers, and many eccentricities, to use no
harsher term, are the result. Towards the close of the day,
everything is in confusion—the door-bell is never silent.
Crowds of young men, in various stages of intoxication, rush
into the lighted parlors, leer at the hostess in the vain effort to
offer their respects, call for liquor, drink it, and stagger out,
to repeat the scene at some other house. Frequently, they
are unable to recognize the residences of their friends, and
stagger into the wrong house. Some fall early in the day, and
are put to bed by their friends; others sink down helpless at
the feet of their hostess, and are sent home; and a few
manage to get through the day. Strange as it may seem, it is
no disgrace to get drunk on New Year's Day. These indiscretions are expected at such times; and it has happened
that some of the ladies themselves have succumbed to the se-
ductive influences of "punch," and have been carried to bed by
the servants.

The Kitchen, as well as the parlor, observes the day. During
the Christmas week housekeepers become impressed with the
fact that the usual amount of provisions utterly fails to meet
the wants of the family. They attribute it to the increased ap-
petites of the establishment. Biddy could tell a different tale,
however, and on New Year's Day sets a fine table for her
"Cousins" and friends, at the expense of the master of the
house. "Shure, she must say her friends, as well as the missus;
and bedad, it's a free counthry, and a poor ghirl has to look out
for hersilf."

The next day one half of New York has a headache, and the
other half is "used up" with fatigue. The doctors are kept
busy, and so are the police courts. This day is commonly
called "The Ladies' Day," and is devoted by those who feel

inclined, to making calls on each other and comparing notes as
to the work of the previous day.

II.

CHRISTMAS.

For weeks before the high festival of Christendom, New York
puts on its holiday attire.   The stores are filled with the richest
and most attractive goods, toys of every description fill up
every available space in the great thoroughfares, the markets
and provision stores abound in good things in the eatable line,
and the whole city looks brighter and more cheerful than it has
done since the last Christmas season. Broadway and the Bowery
are ablaze with gaslight at night, and shops that usually close
their doors at dark, remain open until nine or ten o'clock.   All
are crowded, and millions of dollars are spent in providing for
the happy day.   On Christmas Eve, or perhaps a day or two
later, many of the churches provide Christmas trees for their
Sunday schools.

When the bell of "Old Trinity " rings out the last stroke
of the midnight hour of Christmas Eve, there is a pause.   The
city is dark and still, and there is not a sound in all the vast
edifice which towers so majestically in the gloom of the night.
The heavy clangor of the clock bell dies away in the stillness,
when suddenly there bursts out from the dark tower of the old
church a perfect flood of melody.   The bells seem beside
themselves with joy, and they send their merry tones rolling
through the silent streets below, and out upon the blue waters
of the bay, bidding all men rejoice, for Christ is born.

On Christmas Day the festivities are much the same as those
in other places.   They are hearty and merry here, as elsewhere, and the season is one of happiness.   The poor are not
forgotten.   Those who give nothing at other times, will subscribe for dinners or clothing for the unfortunate at Christmas.
The various charitable institutions are kept busy receiving
and delivering the presents sent them.   Their inmates are

37

provided with plentiful, substantial dinners, and have abundant means of sharing in the happiness which seems to pervade the whole city.

Thanksgiving Day, Evacuation Day (November 25th), the Fourth of July, and the Birthday of Washington, all receive appropriate honors, but they do not compare with the two great festivals of the Metropolis.

XLIX.

THE SOCIAL EVIL.

THE LOST SISTERHOOD.

In January, 1866, Bishop Simpson, of the Methodist Episcopal Church, at a public meeting at the Cooper Institute, made the astounding declaration that there were as many prostitutes in the city of New York as there were members of the Methodist Church, the membership of which at that time was estimated at between eleven and twelve thousand. In the spring of 1871, the Rev. Dr. Bellows estimated the number of these women at 20,000. These declarations were repeated all over the country by the press, and New York was held up to public rebuke as a second Sodom. The estimate of Dr. Bellows would brand one female in every twenty-four, of all ages, as notoriously impure, and taking away from the actual population those too old and too young to be included in this class, the per centage would be, according to that gentleman, very much larger—something like one in every eighteen or twenty. New York is bad enough in this respect, but not so bad as the gentlemen we have named suppose. The real facts are somewhat difficult to ascertain. The police authorities boast that they have full information as to the inmates of every house of ill-fame in the city, but their published statistics are notoriously inaccurate. As near as can be ascertained, there are about 600 houses of ill-fame in the city. The number of women living in them, and those frequenting the bed-houses and lower class assignation houses, is about 5000. In this estimate is included about 700 waiter-girls in the concert saloons.

This is the number of professional women of the town, but it does not include those who, while nominally virtuous, really live upon the wages of their shame, or the nominally respectable married and single women who occasionally visit assignation houses. It is impossible to estimate these, but it is believed that the number is proportionately small. Their sin is known only to themselves and their lovers, and they do not figure in the police records as abandoned women.

The fallen women of New York include every grade of their class, from those who are living in luxury, to the poor wretches who are dying by inches in the slums. Every stage of the road to ruin is represented.

There are not many first-class houses of ill-fame in the city— probably not over fifty in all—but they are located in the best neighborhoods, and it is said that Fifth avenue itself is not free from the taint of their presence. As a rule, they are hired fully furnished, the owners being respectable and often wealthy people. The finest of these houses command from ten to twelve thousand dollars rent. The neighbors do not suspect the true character of the place, unless some of them happen to be among its visitors. The police soon discover the truth, however. The establishment is palatial in its character, and is conducted with the most rigid outward propriety.

The proprietress is generally a middle-aged woman, of fine personal appearance. She has a man living with her, who passes as her husband, in order that she may be able to show a legal protector in case of trouble with the authorities. This couple usually assume some foreign name, and pass themselves off upon the unsuspecting as persons of the highest respectability.

The inmates are usually young women, or women in the prime of life. They are carefully chosen for their beauty and charms, and are frequently persons of education and refinement. They are required to observe the utmost decorum in the parlors of the house, and their toilettes are exquisite and modest. They never make acquaintances on the street, and, indeed, have no need to do so. The women who fill these houses are generally of respectable origin. They are the daughters, often the wives or widows, of persons of the best social position. Some have been drawn astray by villains; some have been drugged and ruined, and have fled to these places to hide their shame from their friends; some have adopted the life in order to avoid poverty, their means having been suddenly swept away; some have entered upon it from motives of extravagance and vanity; some are married women, who have been unfaithful to their husbands, and who have been deserted in consequence; some have been ruined by the cruelty and neglect of their husbands; some, horrible as it may seem, have been forced into such a life by their parents; and others have adopted the life from motives of pure licentiousness. The proprietress takes care to keep her house full, and has agents whose business it is to provide her with fresh women as fast as they are needed. Whatever may be the cause of their fall, these houses are always full of women competent to grace the best circles of social life.

The visitors to these establishments are men of means. No one can afford to visit them who has not money to spend on them. Besides the money paid to the inmates, the visitors expend large sums for wines. The liquors furnished are of an inferior quality, and the price is nearly double that of the best retail houses in the city. It is not pleasant to contemplate, but it is nevertheless a fact, that the visitors include some of the leading men of the country, men high in public life, and eminent for their professional abilities. Even ministers of the gospel visiting the city have been seen at these houses. The proportion of married men is frightfully large. There is scarcely a night that does not witness the visits of numbers of husbands and fathers to these infamous palaces of sin. These same men would be merciless in their resentment of any lapse of virtue on the part of their wives. New York is not alone to blame for this. The city is full of strangers, and they contribute largely to the support of these places, and the city is called upon to bear the odium of their conduct. Men coming to New York from other parts of the country seem to think themselves freed from all the restraints of morality and religion, and while here commit acts of dissipation and sin, such as they would not dream of indulging in in their own communities, and they go home and denounce New York as the worst place in the world.

The proprietress takes care that the visitors shall enjoy all the privacy they desire. If one wishes to avoid the other visitors, he is shown into a private room. Should the visitor desire an interview with any particular person he is quickly admitted to her presence. If his visit is "general," he awaits in the parlor the entrance of the inmates of the house, who drop in at intervals.

The earnings of the inmates of these houses are very large, but their expenses are in proportion. They are charged the most exorbitant board by the proprietress, whose only object is to get all the money out of them she can. They are obliged to dress handsomely, and their wants are numerous, so that they save nothing. The proprietress cares for them faithfully as long as they are of use to her, but she is not disinterested, as a rule, and turns them out of doors without mercy in case of sickness or loss of beauty.

The inmates of these first-class houses remain in them about one year. Many go from them sooner. In entering upon their sin, and tasting the sweets of wealth and luxury, they form false estimates of the life that lies before them, and imagine that though others have failed, they will always be able to retain their places in the aristocracy of shame. They are mistaken. The exceptions to the rule are very rare, so that we are warranted in asserting that these first-class houses change their inmates every year. A life of shame soon makes havoc with a woman's freshness, if not with her beauty, and the proprietress has no use for faded women. She knows the attraction of "strange women," and she makes frequent changes as a matter of policy. Furthermore, the privacy of these places demands that the women shall be as little known to the general public as possible.

Whatever may be the reason, the change is inevitable. One year of luxury and pleasure, and then the woman begins her downward course. The next step is to a second-class house, where the proprietress is more cruel and exacting, and where

the visitors are rougher and ruder than those who frequented
the place in which the lost one began her career.   Two or
three years in these houses is the average, and by this time
the woman has become a thorough prostitute.   She has lost
her refinement, and, it may be, has added drunkenness to her
other sin, and has become full-mouthed and reckless.   She has
sunk too low to be fit for even such a place as this, and she
is turned out without pity to take the next step in her ruin.
Greene street, with its horrible bagnios, claims her next.   She
becomes the companion of thieves—perhaps a thief herself—
and passes her days in misery.   She is a slave to her employer,
and is robbed of her wretched earnings.   Disease and sickness
are her lot, and from them she cannot escape.   She is never
by any chance the companion of a "respectable" man, but her
associates are as degraded as herself.   She may fall into the
hands of the police, and be sent to the Island, where the seal
is set to her damnation.   A year or two in a Greene street house
is all that a human being can stand.   The next descent is
to Water street or some kindred thoroughfare.   Almost immediately she falls a victim to the terrible scourge of these
places.   Disease of the most loathsome kind fastens itself upon
her, and she literally rots to death.   Such faces as look out upon
you from those Water street dens!   Foul, bloated with gin and
disease, distorted with suffering and despair, the poor creatures
do what they can to hasten their sure doom.   It all happens
in a few years, seven or eight at the longest.   Ninety-nine
women out of every hundred go down the fearful road I have
marked out.   I care not how beautiful, how attractive, how
sanguine may be the woman who is to-day the acknowledged
belle of a fashionable house of ill-fame, her doom is sure.   Would
you see her seven years hence, should she live that long, you
must seek her among the living corpses of the Water street
dens.

"The wages of sin is death!"   Never were truer words written.   Ask any one whose duties have called him into constant
contact with the shadowy side of city life, and he will tell you
that there is no escape from the doom of the fallen women.   Let

no woman deceive herself.   Once entered upon a life of shame, however brilliant the opening may be, the end is certain, unless she anticipates it by suicide.   The longer her life, the greater her suffering.   It is very hard for a woman to reform from such a life.   Not one in a hundred feels the desire to reform. Everything is against her.   Her mode of life is utterly destructive of her better nature, her higher impulses.   There is but one means of safety.   Avoid the first step.   There is no turning back, when once a woman enters upon the downward path. "The wages of sin is death!"—death in its most awful form.

It is generally very hard to learn the true history of these unfortunates.   As a rule, they have lively imaginations, and rarely confine themselves to facts.   All wish to excite the sympathy of those to whom they speak, and make themselves as irresponsible for their fall as possible.   It is safe to assert that the truly unfortunate are the exceptions.   Women of cultivation and refinement are exceptionally rare in this grade of life.   The majority were of humble position originally, and either deliberately adopted or allowed themselves to be led into the life as a means of escaping poverty and gratifying a love for fine clothes and display.   The greater part of these women begin their careers at second and third class houses, and, as a matter of course, their descent into the depths is all the more rapid.   Very many are led astray through their ignorance, and by the persuasions of their acquaintances engaged in the same wretched business.   The proprietors of these houses, of every class, spare no pains to draw into their nets all the victims that can be ensnared.   They have their agents scattered all over the country, who use every means to tempt young girls to come to the great city to engage in this life of shame.   They promise them money, fine clothes, ease, and an elegant home.   The seminaries and rural districts of the land furnish a large proportion of this class.   The hotels in this city are closely watched by the agents of these infamous establishments, especially hotels of the plainer and less expensive kind.   These harpies watch their chance, and when they lay siege to a blooming young girl, surround her with every species of enticement.   She is taken to church, to places of amusement, or to the park, and, in returning, a visit is paid to the house of a friend of the harpy. Refreshments are offered, and a glass of drugged wine plunges the victim into a stupor, from which she awakes a ruined woman.

A large number of the fallen women of this city are from New England. The excess of the female population in that overcrowded section of the country makes it impossible for all to find husbands, and throws many upon their own resources for their support. There is not room for all at home, and hundreds come every year to this city. They are ignorant of the difficulty of finding employment here, but soon learn it by experience. The runners of the houses of ill-fame are always on the watch for them, and from various causes many of these girls fall victims to them and join the lost sisterhood. They are generally the daughters of farmers, or working men, and when they come are fresh in constitution and blooming in their young beauty. God pity them ! These blessings soon vanish. They dare not escape from their slavery, for they have no means of earning a living in the great city, and they know they would not be received at home, were their story known. Their very mothers would turn from them with loathing. Without hope, they cling to their shame, and sink lower and lower, until death mercifully ends their human sufferings. As long as they are prosperous, they represent in their letters home that they are engaged in a steady, honest business, and the parents' fears are lulled. After awhile these letters are rarer. Finally they cease altogether. Would a father find his child after this, he must seek her in the foulest hells of the city.

When other arts fail, the wretches who lie in wait for women here seek to ruin them by foul means. They are drugged, or are forced into ruin. A woman in New York cannot be too careful. There are many scoundrels in the city who make it their business to annoy and insult respectable ladies in the hope of luring them to lives of shame. Young girls have been frequently enticed into low class brothels and forced to submit to outrage. Very few of the perpetrators of these crimes are punished as they deserve. Even if the victim complains to the police, it amounts to nothing. The same species of crime is practised every year.

The police are frequently called upon by persons from other parts of the country, for aid in seeking a lost daughter, or a sister, or some female relative. Sometimes these searches, which are always promptly made, are rewarded with success. Some unfortunates are, in this way, saved before they have fallen so low as to make efforts in their behalf vain. Others, overwhelmed with despair, will refuse to leave their shame. They cannot bear the pity or silent scorn of their former relatives and friends, and prefer to cling to their present homes. It is very hard for a fallen woman to retrace her steps, even if her friends or relatives are willing to help her do so.

Last winter an old gray-haired man came to the city from his farm in New England, accompanied by his son, a manly youth, in search of his lost daughter. His description enabled the police to recognize the girl as one who had but recently appeared in the city, and they at once led the father and brother to the house of which she was an inmate. As they entered the parlor, the girl recognized her father, and with a cry of joy sprang into his arms. She readily consented to go back with him, and that night all three left the city for their distant home.

A gentleman once found his daughter in one of the first-class houses of the city, to which she had been tracked by the police. He sought her there, and she received him with every demonstration of joy and affection. He urged her to return home with him, promising that all should be forgiven and forgotten, but she refused to do so, and was deaf to all his entreaties. He brought her mother to see her, and though the girl clung to her and wept bitterly in parting, she would not go home. She felt that it was too late. She was lost.

Many of these poor creatures treasure sacredly the memories of their childhood and home. They will speak of them with a calmness which shows how deep and real is their despair. They would flee from their horrible lives if they could, but they are so enslaved that they are not able to do so. Their sin crushes them to the earth, and they cannot rise above it.

Drunkenness is very common among women of this class. Generally the liquors used are of an inferior quality, and do their dreadful work on the health and beauty of their victim very quickly. The use of narcotics is also very common. All the drug stores in the vicinity of these houses sell large quantities of opium, chloroform, and morphia. Absinthe is a popular drink. This liquor is a slow but deadly poison, and destroys the nervous system and brain, and produces insanity. Suicides are frequent, and many of the poor creatures fall victims to the brutality of the men who seek their society.

II.

HOUSES OF ASSIGNATION.

THERE are over one hundred houses of assignation of all kinds in the city known to the police. This estimate includes the bed-houses, of which we shall speak further on. Besides these, there are places used for assignations which the officials of the law do not and cannot include in their returns. These are the smaller hotels, and sometimes the larger ones. Sometimes women take rooms in some of the cheap hotels, and there receive the visits of men whose acquaintance they have made on the street or at some place of amusement. Very often the proprietor of the house is simply victimized by such people, and several respectable houses have been so far overrun by them that decent persons have avoided them altogether. One or two of the smaller hotels of the city bear a most unenviable reputation of this kind. Even the first-class hotels cannot keep themselves entirely free from the presence of courtezans of the better class. Rich men keep their mistresses at them in elegant style, and the guests, and sometimes the proprietors, are in utter ignorance of the woman's true character. Again, women will live at the fashionable hotels in the strictest propriety, and live by the proceeds of their meetings with men at houses of assignation.

The best houses are located in respectable, and a few in

fashionable neighborhoods.   In various ways they soon acquire
a notoriety amongst persons having use for them.   In the
majority of them, the proprietress resides alone.   Her visitors
are persons of all classes in society.   Married women meet their
lovers here, and young girls pass in these polluted chambers the
hours their parents suppose them to be devoting to healthful
and innocent amusements.   There are many nominally virtuous
women in the city who visit these places one or more times
each week.   They come in the day, if necessary, but generally
at night.   A visit to the theatre, the opera, or a concert is too
often followed by a visit to one of these places.   It is said by
those who claim to know, that sometimes women of good social
position even possess pass keys to such houses.   The hot-house
fashionable society, to which we have referred elsewhere, sends
many visitors here.   Some married women visit these places
because they love other men better than their lawful husbands.
Others sin from mercenary motives.   Their limited means do
not allow them to gratify their taste for dress and display, and
they acquire the desired ability in this infamous manner.

The majority of the houses are well known, and are scarcely
conducted with secresy, which is the chief requisite.   The better
class houses are handsomely furnished, and everything is conducted in the most secret manner.   The police have often discovered assignation houses in residences which they believed to
be simply the homes of private families.   All these houses bring
high rents.   Men of "respectable" position have been known
to furnish houses for this use, and have either engaged women
to manage them, or have let them at enormous rents, supporting their own families in style on the proceeds of these dens of
infamy.

The prices paid by visitors for the use of the rooms are
large, and the receipts of the keeper make her fully able to pay
the large rent demanded of her.

The city papers contain numerous advertisements, which reveal to the initiated the locality of these houses.   They are
represented as "Rooms to let to quiet persons," or "Rooms in
a strictly private family, where boarders are not annoyed with

impertinent questions," or "A handsome room to let, with board for the lady only," or " Handsome apartments to gentlemen, by a widow lady living alone." These advertisements are at once recognized by those in search of them. Families from the country frequently stumble across these places by accident. If the female members are young and handsome, they are received, and the mistake is not found out, perhaps, until it is too late.

Public houses of prostitution are bad enough, but houses of assignation are worse. The former are frequented only by the notoriously impure. The latter draw to them women who, while sinning, retain their positions in society. The more secret the place, the more dangerous it is. The secresy is but an encouragement to sin. Were the chance of detection greater, women, at least, would hesitate longer before visiting them, but they know that they can frequent them habitually, without fear of discovery. Their outward appearance of respectability is a great assistance to the scoundrels who seek to entrap an innocent female within their walls. They form the worst feature of the Social Evil, and something should be done to suppress them.

III.

THE STREET WALKERS.

STRANGERS visiting the city are struck with the number of women who are to be found on Broadway and the streets running parallel with it, without male escorts, after dark. They pass up and down the great thoroughfares at a rapid pace peculiar to them, glancing sharply at all the men they meet, and sometimes speaking to them in a low, quick undertone. One accustomed to the city can recognize them at a glance, and no man of common sense could fail to distinguish them from the respectable women who are forced to be out on the streets alone. They are known as Street Walkers, and constitute one of the lowest orders of prostitutes to be found in New York. They seem to be on the increase during the present winter; and in Broadway especially are more numerous and bolder than they have been for several years. The best looking and the best dressed are seen on Broadway, and in parts of the Fifth and Fourth avenues. The others correspond to the localities they frequent. They are chiefly young girls, seventeen being the average age, but you will see children of twelve and thirteen among them. Very few promenade Broadway below Canal street. The neighborhoods of the hotels and places of amusement are the most frequented. Some of the girls are quite pretty and affect a modest deportment, but the majority are hideous and brazen. New faces are constantly appearing on Broadway, to take the places of those who have gone down into the depths.

Many of these girls have some regular employment, at which they work during the day. Their regular earnings are small, and they take this means of increasing them. The majority, however, depend upon their infamous trade for their support. There have been rare cases in which girls have been driven upon the streets by their parents, who either wish to rid themselves of the support of the girl, or profit by her earnings. We have known cases where the girls have voluntarily supported their parents by the wages of their shame. There were once two sisters, well known on Broadway, who devoted their earnings to paying off a heavy debt of their father, which he was unable to meet. Such instances, however, are very rare.

As a rule the girls seek the streets from mercenary motives. They begin their wretched lives in the society of the most depraved, and are not long in becoming criminals themselves. They are nearly all thieves, and a very large proportion of them are but the decoys of the most desperate male garroters and thieves. The majority of them are the confederates of panel thieves. They are coarse, ugly, and disgusting, and medical men who are called on to treat them professionally, state that as a class they are terribly diseased. A healthy Street Walker is almost a myth.

Were these women dependent for their custom upon the city people, who know them for what they are, they would starve. They know this, and they exert their arts principally upon strangers. Strangers are more easily deceived, and, as a rule, have money to lose. Hundreds of strangers, coming to the city, follow them to their rooms, only to find themselves in the power of thieves, who compel them on pain of instant death to surrender all their valuables. The room taken by the decoy is vacated immediately after the robbery, the girl and her confederate disappear, and it is impossible to find them.

I know that this whole subject is unsavory, and I have not introduced it from choice. The Social Evil is a terrible fact here, and it is impossible to ignore it, and I believe that some good may be done by speaking of it plainly and stripping it of any romantic features. It is simply a disgusting and appalling feature of city life, and as such it is presented here. I know that these pages will find their way into the hands of those who contemplate visiting the city, and who will be assailed by the street girls. To them I would say that to accompany these women to their homes is simply to invite robbery and disease. New York has an abundance of attractions of the better kind, and those who desire amusement may find it in innocent enjoyment. Those who deliberately seek to indulge in sensuality and dissipation in a city to which they are strangers, deserve all the misfortunes which come to them in consequence.

The police do not allow the girls to stop and converse with men on Broadway. If a girl succeeds in finding a companion, she beckons him into one of the side streets, where the police will not interfere with her. If he is willing to go with her, she conducts him to her room, which is in one of the numerous Bed Houses of the city. These bed houses are simply large or small dwellings containing many furnished rooms, which are let to street walkers by the week, or which are hired to applicants of any class by the night. They are very profitable, and are frequently owned by men of good social position, who rent them out to others, or who retain the ownership, and employ a manager. The rent, whether weekly or nightly, is invariably paid in advance, so that the landlord loses nothing.

The girl leads her companion to one of these houses, and if she has a room already engaged, proceeds directly to it; if not,

THE RESULT OF FOLLOWING A STREET WALKER.

one is engaged from a domestic on the spot, the price is paid, and the parties are shown up stairs. The place is kept dark and quiet, in order to avoid the attention of the police. The houses are more or less comfortable and handsome, according to the class by which they are patronized. They are sometimes preferred by guilty parties in high life, as the risk of being seen and recognized is less there than in more aristocratic houses. These houses have a constant run of visitors from about eight o'clock until long after midnight.

The Street Walkers not only infest the city itself, but literally overrun the various night lines of steamers plying between New York and the neighboring towns. The Albany and Bos-

ton lines are so thronged by these women that ladies are subjected to the greatest annoyance.

We have referred once or twice to panel thieving. This
method of robbery is closely connected with street walking.
The girl in this case acts in concert with a confederate, who is
generally a man. She takes her victim to her room, and directs
him to deposit his clothing on a chair, which is placed but a
few inches from the wall at the end of the room. This wall is
false, and generally of wood. It is built some three or four feet
from the real wall of the room, thus forming a closet. As the
whole room is papered and but dimly lighted, a visitor cannot
detect the fact that it is a sham. A panel, which slides noiselessly and rapidly, is arranged in the false wall, and the chair
with the visitor's clothing upon it is placed just in front of it.
While the visitor's attention is engaged in another quarter, the
girl's confederate, who is concealed in the closet, slides back the
panel, and rifles the pockets of the clothes on the chair. The
panel is then noiselessly closed. When the visitor is about to
depart, or sometimes not until long after his departure, he discovers his loss. He is sure the girl did not rob him, and he is
completely bewildered in his efforts to account for the robbery.
Of course the police could tell him how his money was taken,
and could recover it, too, but in nine cases out of ten the man is
ashamed to seek their assistance, as he does not wish his visit
to such a place to be known. The thieves know this, and this
knowledge gives them a feeling of security which emboldens
them to commit still further depredations. The panel houses
are generally conducted by men, who employ the women to
work for them. The woman is sometimes the wife of the proprietor of the house. The robberies nightly perpetrated foot up
an immense aggregate. The visitors are mainly strangers, and
many of these go into these dens with large sums of money on
their persons. The police have been notified of losses occuring
in this way, amounting in a single instance to thousands of dollars. The majority of the sums stolen are small, however, and the
victims bear the loss in silence. The police authorities are thoroughly informed concerning the locality and operations of these

38

establishments, but they suffer them to go on without any effort to break them up.

IV.

THE CONCERT SALOONS.

THERE are about seventy-five or eighty concert saloons in New York, employing abandoned women as waitresses. The flashiest of these are located on Broadway, there being nearly twenty of these infamous places on the great thoroughfare between Spring and Fourth streets. During the day they are closed, but one of the most prominent sets out before its doors a large frame containing twenty or thirty exquisite card photographs, and bearing these words, "Portraits of the young ladies employed in this saloon." It is needless to say that the pictures are taken at random from the stock of some photograph dealer, and have no connection whatever with the hags employed in the saloon. The Bowery, Chatham street, and some of the streets leading from Broadway, contain the greater number of these concert saloons. The majority are located in the basements of the buildings, but one or two of the Broadway establishments use second story rooms. These places may be recognized by their numerous gaudy transparencies and lamps, and by the discordant strains of music which float up into the street from them. The Broadway saloons are owned by a few scoundrels, many of them being conducted by the same proprietor. A writer in the New York *World* was recently favored with the following truthful description of these places by one of the best known proprietors :

"A concert saloon is a gin-mill on an improved plan—that's all, my friend. I don't pay the girls any wages. They get a percentage on the drinks they sell. Some saloon-keepers pays their girls regular wages and a small percentage besides, but it don't work. The girls wont work unless they have to. Now, my girls gets a third of whatever they sell. The consequence is, they sell twice as much as they would if they was on wages. You never can get people to work faithfully for you unless they

can make money by it.   The liquor is cheap, and I don't mind
telling you its d——d nasty, then we charge double prices for
it.   Now, I charge twenty cents for drinks that a regular gin-
mill would sell for ten.   Then there are a lot of drinks that the
girls takes themselves, which we charges fifty cents for.   They
don't cost us more than four or five, but after a girl has said
what she'll take, and a man has ordered it, he can't go back on
the price.   Then hardly any man stops at less than two or three
drinks here, when he would take only one at a bar.   The lights
are the same as they would be anywheres else, and the music
don't cost much.   Then there's other ways to make in this
business.   But you don't want to know all about the speculations.   There's keno, for instance.   The keno business is attached to lots of saloons.   You see the girls manages to get
young fellows that come here—like those hounds yonder—pretty
full, and then they says : ' Why don't you try your luck in the
next room, and go shares with me?'   So the fool he bites at
once, and goes in for keno.   Of course luck goes against him,
for he's too drunk to play—O, the game's a square one—and
he finally comes back for another drink.   The girls then takes
care that he doesn't go away till he's too drunk to remember
where he lost his money.   Even if he goes away sober, he seldom splits.   I'll give the fellows that much credit.   Bad as
they are, they seldom splits."

The concert saloons derive their names from the fact that a
low order of music is provided by the proprietor as a cover to
the real character of the place.   It may be an old cracked
piano, with a single, half-drunken performer, or a couple or more
musicians who cannot by any possible means draw melody from
their wheezy instruments.

Persons entering these places assume a considerable risk.
They voluntarily place themselves in the midst of a number of
abandoned wretches, who are ready for any deed of violence or
crime.   They care for nothing but money, and will rob or kill
for it.   Respectable people have no business in such places.
They are very apt to have their pockets picked, and are in
danger of violence.   Many men, who leave their happy homes

in the morning, visit these places, for amusement or through curiosity, at night. They are drugged, robbed, murdered, and then the harbor police may find their lifeless forms floating in the river at daybreak.

The women known outside of the city as "pretty waiter girls," are simply a collection of poor wretches who have gone down almost to the end of their fatal career. They may retain faint vestiges of their former beauty, but that is all. They are beastly, foul-mouthed, brutal wretches. Very many of them are half dead with consumption and disease. They are in every respect disgusting. Yet young and old men, strangers and citizens, come here to talk with them and spend their money on them. Says the writer we have quoted, after describing a characteristic scene in one of these places:

"The only noticeable thing about this exhibition of beastliness is the utter unconcern of the other occupants of the room. They are accustomed to it. One wonders, too, at the attraction this has for strangers. There is really nothing in the people, the place, or the onlookers worthy of a decent man's curiosity. The girls are, without exception, the nastiest, most besotted drabs that ever walked the streets. They havn't even the pride that clings to certain of their sisters who are in prison. The whole assemblage, with the exception of such stragglers as myself, who have a motive in studying it, is a mess of the meanest human rubbish that a great city exudes. In the company there is a large preponderance of the cub of seventeen and eighteen. Some of these boys are the sons of merchants and lawyers, and are 'seeing life.' If they were told to go into their kitchens at home and talk with the cook and the chambermaid, they would consider themselves insulted. Yet they come here and talk with other Irish girls every whit as ignorant and unattractive as the servants at home—only the latter are virtuous and these are infamous. Thus does one touch of vileness make the whole world kin."

V.

THE DANCE HOUSES.

THE dance houses differ from the concert saloons in this respect, that they are one grade lower both as regards the inmates and the visitors, and that dancing as well as drinking is carried on in them.   They are owned chiefly by men, though there are some which are the property of and are managed by women.   They are located in the worst quarters of the city, generally in the streets near the East and North rivers, in order to be easy of access to the sailors.

The buildings are greatly out of repair, and have a rickety, dirty appearance.   The main entrance leads to a long, narrow hall, the floor of which is well sanded.   The walls are ornamented with flashy prints, and the ceiling with colored tissue paper cut in various fantastic shapes.   There is a bar at the farther end of the room, which is well stocked with the meanest liquors, and chairs and benches are scattered about.

From five to a dozen women, so bloated and horrible to look upon, that a decent man shudders with disgust as he beholds them, are lounging about the room.   They have reached the last step in the downward career of fallen women, and will never leave this place until they are carried from it to their graves, which are not far distant.   They are miserably clad, and are nearly always half crazy with liquor.   They are cursed and kicked about by the brutal owner of the place, and suffer still greater violence, at times, in the drunken brawls for which these houses are famous.   Their sleeping rooms are above. They are sought by sailors and by the lowest and most degraded of the city population.   They are the slaves of their masters. They have no money of their own.   He claims a part of their infamous earnings, and demands the rest for board and clothes. Few have the courage to fly from these hells, and if they make the attempt, they are forced back by the proprietor, who is frequently aided in this unholy act by the law of the land.   They cannot go into the streets naked, and he claims the clothes on their backs as his property. If they leave the premises with these clothes on, he charges them with theft.

Let no one suppose that these women entered upon this grade of their wretched life voluntarily. Many were drugged and forced into it, but the majority are lost women who have come regularly down the ladder to this depth. You can find in these hells women who, but a few years ago, were ornaments of society. No woman who enters upon a life of shame can hope to avoid coming to these places in the end. As sure as she takes the first step in sin, she will take this last one also, struggle against it as she may. This is the last depth. It has but one bright ray in all its darkness—it does not last over a few months, for death soon ends it. But, O, the horrors of such a death! No human being who has not looked on such a death-bed can imagine the horrible form in which the Great Destroyer comes. There is no hope. The poor wretch passes from untold misery in this life to the doom which awaits those who die in their sins.

The keepers of these wretched places use every art to entice young and innocent women into their dens, 'where they are ruined by force. The police frequently rescue women from them who have been enticed into them or carried there by force. Emigrant girls, who have strolled from the depot at Castle Garden into the lower part of the city, are decoyed into these places by being promised employment. Men and women are sent into the country districts to ensnare young girls to these city hells. Advertisements for employment are answered by these wretches, and every art is exhausted in the effort to draw pure women within the walls of the dance house. Let such a woman once cross the threshold, and she will be drugged or forced to submit to her ruin. This accomplished, she will not be allowed to leave the place until she has lost all hope of giving up the life into which she has been driven.

The Missionaries are constant visitors to these dens. They go with hope that they may succeed in rescuing some poor creature from her terrible life. As a rule, they meet with the vilest abuse, and are driven away with curses, but sometimes

NOONDAY PRAYER MEETING AT WATER STREET HOME.

they are successful. During the present winter they have succeeded in effecting a change for the better in one of the most
notorious women in Water street.

VI.

HARRY HILL'S.

HARRY HILL is a well-known man among the disreputable
classes of New York. He is the proprietor of the largest and
best known dance house in the city. His establishment is in
Houston street, a few doors west of Mulberry street, and almost
under the shadow of the Police Headquarters. It is in full sight
from Broadway, and at night a huge red and blue lantern marks
the entrance door. Near the main entrance there is a private door
for women. They are admitted free, as they constitute the chief
attraction to the men who visit the place. Entering through
the main door, the visitor finds himself in a low bar-room, very
much like the other establishments of the kind in the neighborhood. Passing between the counters he reaches a door in the
rear of them which opens into the dance hall, which is above
the level of the bar-room. Visitors to this hall are charged an
entrance fee of twenty-five cents, and are expected to call for
refreshments as soon as they enter.

Harry Hill is generally present during the evening, moving
about among his guests. He is a short, thick-set man, with a
self-possessed, resolute air, and a face indicative of his calling,
and is about fifty-four years old. He is sharp and decided in
his manner, and exerts himself to maintain order among his
guests. He is enough of a politician to be very sure that the
authorities will not be severe with him in case of trouble,
but he has a horror of having his place entered by the police in
their official capacity. He enforces his orders with his fists if
necessary, and hustles refractory guests from his premises without hesitating. The " fancy " generally submit to his commands,
as they know he is a formidable man when aroused. He keeps
his eye on everything, and though he has a business manager,

conducts the whole establishment himself. He has been in his
wretched business fifteen years, and is said to be wealthy. His
profits have been estimated as high as fifty thousand dollars per
annum.

Harry Hill boasts that he keeps a "respectable house," but
his establishment is nothing more than one of the many gates to
hell with which the city abounds. There are no girls attached
to the establishment. All the guests of both sexes are merely
outsiders who come here to spend the evening. The rules of
the house are printed in rhyme, and are hung in the most conspicuous parts of the hall. They are rigid, and prohibit any
indecent or boisterous conduct or profane swearing. The most
disreputable characters are seen in the audience, but no thieving
or violence ever occurs within the hall. Whatever happens
after persons leave the place, the proprietor allows no violation
of the law within his doors.

The hall itself consists simply of a series of rooms which have
been "knocked into one" by the removal of the partition walls.
As all these rooms were not of the same height, the ceiling presents a curious patchwork appearance. A long counter occupies
one end of the hall, at which refreshments and liquors are
served. There is a stage at the other side, on which low farces
are performed, and a tall Punch and Judy box occupies a conspicuous position. Benches and chairs are scattered about, and
a raised platform is provided for the "orchestra," which consists of a piano, violin, and a bass viol. The centre of the room
is a clear space, and is used for dancing. If you do not dance
you must leave, unless you atone for your deficiency by a liberal
expenditure of money. The amusements are coarse and low.
The songs are broad, and are full of blasphemous outbursts,
which are received with shouts of delight.

You will see all sorts of people at Harry Hill's. The women
are, of course, women of the town; but they are either just en
tering upon their career, or still in its most prosperous phase.
They are all handsomely dressed, and some of them are very
pretty. Some of them have come from the better classes of
society, and have an elegance and refinement of manner and

HARRY HILL'S DANCE HOUSE.

conversation which win them many admirers in the crowd.
They drink deep and constantly during the evening.   Indeed,
one is surprised to see how much liquor they imbibe.   The majority come here early in the evening alone, but few go away
without company for the night.   You do not see the same face
here very long.   The women cannot escape the inevitable doom
of the lost sisterhood.   They go down the ladder; and Harry
Hill keeps his place clear of them after the first flush of their
beauty and success is past.   You will then find them in the
Five Points and Water street hells.

As for the men, they represent all kinds of people and professions.   You may see here men high in public life, side by
side with the Five Points ruffian.   Judges, lawyers, policemen
off duty and in plain clothes, officers of the army and navy, merchants, bankers, editors, soldiers, sailors, clerks, and even boys,
mingle here in friendly confusion.   As the profits of the establishment are derived from the bar, drinking is, of course, encouraged, and the majority of the men are more or less drunk
all the time.   They spend their money freely in such a condition.   Harry Hill watches the course of affairs closely during
the evening.   If he knows a guest and likes him, he will take
care that he is not exposed to danger, after he is too far gone
in liquor to protect himself.   He will either send him home, or
send for his friends.   If the man is a stranger, he does not interfere—only, no crime must be committed in his house.
Thieves, pickpockets, burglars, roughs, and pugilists are plentifully scattered through the audience.   These men are constantly on the watch for victims.   It is easy for them to drug
the liquor of a man they are endeavoring to secure, without the
knowledge of the proprietor of the house; or, if they do not
tamper with his liquor, they can persuade him to drink to excess.   In either case, they lead him from the hall, under pretence
of taking him home.   He never sees home until they have
stripped him of all his valuables.   Sometimes he finds his long
home, in less than an hour after leaving the hall; and the harbor police find his body floating on the tide at sunrise.   Women frequently decoy men to places where they are robbed.   No

crime is committed in the dance hall, but plans are laid there, victims are marked, and tracked to loss or death, and, frequently, an idle, thoughtless visit there, has been the beginning of a life of ruin. The company to be met with is that which ought to be shunned. Visits from curiosity are dangerous. Stay away. To be found on the Devil's ground is voluntarily to surrender yourself a willing captive to him. Stay away. It is a place in which no virtuous woman is ever seen, and in which an honest man ought to be ashamed to show his face.

VII.

MASKED BALLS.

THE masked balls, which are held in the city every winter, are largely attended by impure women and their male friends. Even those which assume to be the most select are invaded by these people in spite of the precautions of the managers. Some of them are notoriously indecent, and it may be safely asserted that all are favorable to the growth of immorality. On the 22d of December, 1869, one of the most infamous affairs of this kind was held in the French Theatre, on Fourteenth street. I give the account of it published in the *World* of December 24th, of that year :

" The '*Société des Bals d'Artistes*,' an organization which has no other excuse for existing than the profits of an annual dance, and which last year combined debauchery with dancing in a manner entirely new to this city, on Wednesday night had possession of the *Théâtre Français*, in which was to be given what was extensively advertised as the 'First *Bal d'Opéra*.' The only conspicuous name in this society (which is composed of Frenchmen) is that attached to the circular published below, but it is reasonable to suppose that the men who got up the ball were animated by a purely French desire to make a little money and have a good deal of Parisian carousing, which should end, as those things do only in Paris, in high and comparatively harmless exhilaration. But they mistake the locality. This is

not Paris. The peculiar success of the ball given under their
auspices last year was not forgotten by the class of roughs in-
digenous to New York. Under the name of *Bal d'Opéra,*
licence, it was found, could be had for actions that would be no
where else tolerated in a civilized community. It was found,
moreover, that this description of ball would bring together,
with its promise of licence, that class of reckless women who
find opportunities to exhibit themselves in their full harlotry to
the world, too much restricted and narrowed by enactment and
public opinion not to take advantage of this one. The scenes
which took place about the entrancé of the French Theatre,
when the '*artistes*' commenced to arrive, were sufficiently indicative of the character of the entertainment. At 11 o'clock
there were about a thousand men and boys there congregated,
forming an impenetrable jam, through which the police kept
open a narrow avenue for the masqueraders to pass from the
coaches to the door. This crowd was manifestly made up of
the two *sui generis* types of character which in this city have
received the appellation of 'loafers' and 'counter-jumpers.'
Wide apart as they ordinarily may be, on such an occasion as
this they are animated by common desires and common misfortunes. The inability to · buy a ticket of admission, and the
overpowering desire to see women disporting themselves in
semi-nude attire and unprotected by any of the doubts which
attach to their characters in ordinary street life, brought these
moon-calves together, on a wet and chilly night, to stand for
hours in the street to catch a passing glimpse of a stockinged
leg or a bare arm, and to shout their ribald criticisms in the full
immunity of fellowship. It was enough for them that the
women came unattended. Every mask that stepped from her
coach was beset by hoots and yells and the vile wit of shallow-
brained ruffians, or the criticism of the staring counter-jumpers.
There was also the chance open to the rougher members of this
assemblage of ultimately getting into the ball without paying.
They had no well-defined plan, but they felt instinctively that
when their own passions had been sufficiently aroused, and
when the later scenes inside had grown tumultuous, they could

knock the door-keeper's hat over his face, and go brawling in like wolves. There were knots of half-grown men on the corners of the street and about the adjacent pot-houses who were driving a good traffic in tickets, and other knots of creatures, neither men nor boys, but that New York intermedium, who has lost the honesty of the boy without gaining the manliness of the man, were speculating upon the probabilities of a fight, and expressing very decided opinions as to the possibility of licking the Frenchmen who would endeavor to keep them out or keep them orderly after they got in.

"The attendants upon the ball, on entering the vestibule, were handed the following circular, printed neatly in blue ink :

"'The purpose of the President and Committee of the Société des Bals d'Artistes is to preserve the most stringent order, and to prevent any infraction of the laws of decency.   Any attempt at disturbance or lewd-ness will be repressed with the most extreme severity, and sufficient force is provided to warrant quietness and obedience to laws.

'The President,   L. MERCIER.'

"That such was the purpose of the committee we have no reason to doubt.   But it was no wiser than the purpose of the man who invited a smoking party to his powder magazine, and told them his object was to prevent explosion.   The dancing commenced at 11 o'clock.   At that time the floor, extending from the edge of the dress-circle to the extreme limit of the stage, presented a curious spectacle.   Probably there were a hundred masked women present, among five hundred masked and un-masked men.   These women were dressed in fancy costumes, nearly all selected with a view to expose as much of the person as possible.   By far the greater number wore trunk hose and fleshings; but many were attired in the short skirts of the ballet, with some attempt at bayadere and daughter of the regiment in the bodices and trimmings.   Here and there a woman wore trailing skirts of rich material, and flashed her diamonds in the gaslight as she swung the train about.   There was no attempt on the part of the men to assume imposing or elegant disguises.   The cheapest dominoes, and generally nothing more than a mask, afforded them all they wanted—the opportunity to carry on a bravado and promiscuous flirtation with these women. That part of the family circle tier which faces the stage was given up to the musicians. The rest of the gallery was crowded with spectators. The boxes below were all taken up, the occupants being mainly maskers overlooking the dance. But the proscenium boxes, and notably the two lower ones on either side, were filled with a crew of coarse-featured, semi-officious looking roughs, who might be politicians, or gamblers, or deputy-sheriffs, or cut-throats, or all, but who, at all events, had no intention of dancing, and had hired these boxes with the one view of having a good time at the expense of the women, the managers, and, if necessary, the public peace itself. They were crowded in; some of them stood up and smoked cigars; all of them kept their hats on; one or two were burly beasts, who glared upon the half-exposed women on the floor with a stolid interest that could only be heightened and intensified by some outrageous departure from the seemliness of simple enjoyment. They have their fellows on the floor, to whom they shout and telegraph. They have liquor in the boxes, and they use it with a show of conviviality to increase their recklessness.

"At twelve o'clock there is a jam; most of the crowd outside has got in by some means; the floor is a mass of people. Suddenly there is a fight in the boxes. Exultant cries issue from the proscenium. At once turn up all the masked faces in the whirling mass. It is a Frenchman beset by two, aye three, Americans. Blows are given and taken; then they all go down out of sight—only to appear again; the three are on him; they are screeching with that fierce animal sound that comes through set teeth, and in men and bull-dogs is pitched upon the same note. The maskers rather like it; they applaud and cheer on—not the parties, but the fight—and when the police get into the boxes and drag out the assaulted man, and leave the assailants behind, the proscenium bellows a moment with ironical laughter, the music breaks out afresh, and the dancers resume their antics as though nothing had happened.

"Enough liquor has now been swallowed to float recklessness

up to the high-water mark.   There is another fight going on in the vestibule.   One of the women has been caught up by the crowd and tossed bodily into the proscenium box, where she is caught and dragged by half a dozen brutes in over the sill and furniture in such a manner as to disarrange as much as possible what small vestige of raiment there is on her.   The feat awakens general enjoyment.   Men and women below vent their coarse laughter at the sorry figure she cuts and at the exposure of her person.   Presently the trick is repeated on the other side. A young woman, rather pretty and dressed in long skirts, is thrown up, and falls back into the arms of the crowd, who turn her over, envelop her head in her own skirts, and again toss her up temporarily denuded.   The more exactly this proceeding outrages decency, the better it is liked.   One or two repetitions of it occurred which exceeded the limits of proper recital.   The women were bundled into the boxes, and there they were fallen upon by the crew of half drunken ruffians, and mauled, and pulled, and exhibited in the worst possible aspects, amid the jeers and laughter of the other drunken wretches upon the floor. One, a heavier woman than the rest, is thrown out of the box and falls heavily upon the floor.   She is picked up insensible by the police and carried out.   There is not a whisper of shame in the crowd.   It is now drunken with liquor and its own beastliness.   It whirls in mad eddies round and round.   The panting women in the delirium of excitement; their eyes, flashing with the sudden abnormal light of physical elation, bound and leap like tigresses; they have lost the last sense of prudence and safety.   Some of them are unmasked, and reveal the faces of brazen and notorious she-devils, who elsewhere are cut off by edict from this contact with the public; a few of them are young, and would be pretty but for the lascivious glare now lighting their faces and the smears of paint which overlay their skins; all of them are poisonous, pitiable creatures, suffering now with the only kind of delirium which their lives afford, rancorous, obscene, filthy beauties, out of the gutter of civilization, gone mad with the licence of music and the contact of men, and beset by crowds of libidinous and unscrupulous ninnies who, anywhere else, would be ashamed of their intimacy, or roughs to whom this kind of a ball affords the only opportunity to exercise the few animal faculties that are left to them.

"M. Mercier stands in the middle of the floor, and shouts to the musicians to go on. For it isn't safe for them to stop. Whenever they do, there is a fight. One stalwart beauty, in bare arms, has knocked down a young man in the entrance way, and left the marks of her high heels on his face. She would have kicked the life out of him while her bully held him down, if a still stronger policeman had not flung her like a mass of offal into a corner. There she is picked up, and, backed by a half dozen of her associates, pushes and strikes promiscuously, and the dense crowd about her push also and strike, and sway here and there, and yell, and hiss, and curse, until the entire police force in the place drag out a score of them, and then the rest go on with the dancing, between which and the fighting there is so little difference.

"In one of the boxes sits —— ——, with a masked woman. But it is getting too warm for him. The few French women who came as spectators, and occupied the seats in the family circle, went away long ago. They were probably respectable. On the floor one sees at intervals well known men, who either were deceived by the announcement of a *Bal d'Opéra*, or were too smart to be deceived by anything of this sort. A few newspaper reporters, looking on with stoical eye; here a prize-fighter, and there a knot of gamblers; here an adolescent alderman, dancing with a notorious inmate of the police courts; there a deputy sheriff, too drunk to be anything but sick and sensual. Now the can-can commences. But it comes without any zest, for all of its peculiarities have been indulged in long before. It is no longer a dance at all, but a wild series of indecent exposures, a tumultuous orgie, in which one man is struck by an unknown assailant; and his cheek laid open with a sharp ring, and his white vest and tie splashed with blood, give a horrible color to the figure that is led out.

"There is an evident fear on the part of the ball officials that

39

matters will proceed too far. They endeavor to prevent the women from being pulled up into the boxes by laying hold of them and pulling them back, in which struggle the women are curiously wrenched and disordered, and the men in the boxes curse, and laugh, and shout, and the dancers, now accustomed to the spectacle, give it no heed whatever.

" If there is anything in the behaviour of the women that is at all peculiar to the eye of an observer who is not familiar with the impulses and the manifestations of them in this class, it is the feverish abandonment into which drink and other excitements have driven them. It is not often that a common bawd, without brains or beauty enough to attract a passing glance, thus has the opportunity to elicit volleys of applause from crowds of men; and, without stopping to question the value of it, she makes herself doubly drunken with it. If to kick up her skirts is to attract attention—hoop la! If indecency is then the distinguishing feature of the evening, she is the woman for your money. So she jumps rather than dances. She has a whole set of lascivious motions, fashioned quickly, which outdo the worst imaginings of the dirty-minded men who applaud her. She springs upon the backs of the men, she swaggers, she kicks off hats. She is a small sensation in herself, and feels it, and goes about with a defiant and pitiless recklessness, reigning for the few brief hours over the besotted men who feel a fiend's satisfaction in the unnatural exhibition.

" To particularize to any greater extent would be to make public the habits and manners of the vilest prostitutes in their proper haunts, where, out of the glare of publicity, they may, and probably do, perfect themselves in the indecencies most likely to catch the eyes of men little better than themselves, but which thus brought together under the gaslight of the public chandelier is, to the healthy man, like the application of the microscope to some common article of food then found to be a feculent and writhing mass of living nastiness. That respectable foreigners were induced to attend this ball by the representations made by the managers is certain. That they were outraged by what took place there, is beyond all doubt. To suppose a man deceived as to the character of the entertainment, and to go there and mingle with masked ladies, who for a while ape the deportment of their betters, is to suppose a sensation for him at once startling; for when the richly dressed ladies doff their masks, he finds himself surrounded by a ghastly assemblage of all the most virulent social corruption in our civilization; dowagers turn out to be the fluffy and painted keepers of brothels; the misses sink into grinning hussies, who are branded on the cheeks and forehead with the ineradicable mark of shame; and the warm and coy pages, whom at the worst he might have supposed to be imprudent or improvident girls, stare at him with the deathly-cold implacability of the commonest street-walkers—those in fact who glory in their shame, and whose very contact is vile to anything with a spark of healthy moral or physical life in it. If, indeed, they had lain off their sickly flesh with their masks, and gone grinning and rattling round the brilliant hall in their skeletons, the transformation could not have chilled your unsuspecting man with a keener horror. But it is safe to say the unsuspecting were few indeed.

"At two o'clock this curious spectacle was at its height. All about the Institute, and on the stairs, and in the cloak-rooms, and through the narrow, tortuous passages leading to the stage dressing-rooms were vile tableaus of inflamed women and tipsy men, bandying brutality and obscenity. The animal was now in full possession of its faculties. But, just as the orgie is bursting into the last stage—a free fight—when the poor creatures in their hired costumes are ready to grovel in the last half-oblivious scenes, the musicians rattle off 'Home, Sweet Home,' with a strange, hurried irony, and the managers, with the same haste, turn off the gas of the main chandelier, and the *Bal d'Opéra* is at an end."

VIII.

PERSONALS.

THE first column of one of the most prominent daily newspapers, which is taken in many respectable families of the city, and which claims to be at the head of American journalism, bears the above heading, and there is also a personal column in a prominent Sunday paper, which is also read by many respectable people.   Very many persons are inclined to smile at these communications, and are far from supposing that these journals are making themselves the mediums through which assignations and burglaries, and almost every disreputable enterprise are arranged and carried on.   Yet such is the fact.   Many of these advertisements are inserted by notorious roués, and others are from women of the town.   Women wishing to meet their lovers, or men their mistresses, use these personal columns.

Respectable women have much to annoy them in the street conveyances, and at the places of amusement.   If a lady allows her face to wear a pleasant expression while glancing by the merest chance at a man, she is very apt to find some such personal as the following addressed to her in the next morning's issue of the paper referred to:

> THIRD AVENUE CAR, DOWN TOWN YESTER-
> day morning; young lady in black, who noticed gent opposite, who endeavored to draw her attention to Personal column of —— in his hand, will oblige admirer by sending address to B., Box 102, —— office.

If she is a vile woman, undoubtedly she will do so, and that establishment will deliver her letter, and do its part in helping on the assignation.

A gentleman will bow to a lady, and she, thinking it may be a friend, returns the bow.   The next day appears the following:

> TALL LADY DRESSED IN BLACK, WHO AC-
> knowledged gentleman's salute, Broadway and Tenth street, please address D., box 119, —— office, if she wishes to form his acquaintance.

Sometimes a man will whisper the word "personal" to the lady whom he dares not insult further, and the next day the following appears:

TUESDAY, DECEMBER 7, 4 P. M.—"CAN YOU answer a personal?" Fifth avenue stage from Grand to Twenty-third street. Please address BEN. VAN DYKE, —— office, appointing interview. To prevent mistake, mention some particulars.

Others more modest:

WILL THE LADY THAT WAS LEFT WAITING by her companion on Monday evening, near the door of an up-town theatre, grant an interview to the gentleman that would have spoken if he had thought the place appropriate? Address ROMANO, —— office.

It is really dangerous to notice a patron of the paper mentioned, for he immediately considers it ground for a personal, such as the following:

LADY IN GRAND STREET CAR, SATURDAY evening 7.30.—Had on plaid shawl, black silk dress; noticed gentleman in front; both got out at Bowery; will oblige by sending her address to C. L., box 199, —— office.

Young ladies with attendants are not more free from this public insult, as shown by the following:

WILL THE YOUNG LADY THAT GOT OUT OF a Fifth avenue stage, with a gentleman with a cap on, at 10 yesterday, at Forty-sixth street, address E. ROBERTS, New York Post-office.

This public notice must be pleasing to the young lady and to "the gentleman with the cap on." It is a notice that the gentleman believes the lady to be willing to have an intrigue with him. If it goes as far as that, this newspapers will lend its columns to the assignation as follows:

LOUISE K.—DEAR, I HAVE RECEIVED YOUR letter, last Saturday, but not in time to meet you. Next Tuesday, Dec. 7, I will meet you at the same time and place. East. Write to me again, and give your address. Your old acquaintance.

Or as follows:

L. HATTIE B.—FRIDAY, AT 2.30 P. M.

The personal column is also used to publicly advertise the residences of women of the town.   The following are specimens:

MISS GERTIE DAVIS, FORMERLY OF LEXING-
ton avenue, will be pleased to see her friends at
106 Clinton place.

ERASTUS—CALL ON JENNIE HOWARD at 123
West Twenty-seventh street.   I have left Heath's.
132.   ALBANY.

The *World* very justly remarks: "The cards of courtesans
and the advertisements of houses of ill-fame might as well be
put up in the panels of the street cars.   If the public permits a
newspaper to do it for the consideration of a few dollars, why
make the pretence that there is anything wrong in the thing
itself?   If the advertisement is legitimate, then the business
must be."

IX.

THE MIDNIGHT MISSION.

WITH the hope of checking the terrible evil of immorality
which is doing such harm in the city, several associations for
the reformation of fallen women have been organized by benevolent citizens.

One of the most interesting of these is "*The Midnight Mission*," which is located at No. 260 Greene street, in the very
midst of the worst houses of prostitution in the city.   It was
organized about four years ago, and from its organization to
the latter part of the year 1870, had sheltered about 600 women.
In 1870, 202 women and girls sought refuge in the Mission.
Twenty-eight of these were sent to other institutions, forty-seven
were placed in good situations, fifteen were restored to their
friends, and forty-nine went back to their old ways.   The building is capable of accommodating from forty-five to fifty inmates.
The members of the Society go out on the streets every Friday
night, and as they encounter the Street Walkers, accost them,
detain them a few moments in conversation, and hand each of
them a card bearing the following in print:

THE COMMITTEE OF THE MIDNIGHT MISSION

WILL BE HAPPY TO SEE YOU AT TEA,

ON FRIDAY EVENING, AT 10 O'CLOCK,

AT NO. 260 GREENE STREET.

————

*Rooms open every day from 2 to 4 P. M., for private
conversation and friendly advice.*

This invitation is sometimes tossed into the gutter or flung
in the face of the giver, but it is often accepted.   More than
this, it is a reminder to the girl that there is a place of refuge
open to her, where she may find friends willing and able to
help her to escape from her life of sin.   Even those who at first
receive the card with insults to the giver, are won over by this
thought, and they come to the Mission and ask to be received.
Many of them, it is true, seek to make it a mere lodging-house,
and deceive the officers by their false penitence, but many are
saved from sin every year.   The inmates come voluntarily, and
leave when they please.   There is no force used, but every
moral influence that can be brought to bear upon them is exerted to induce them to remain.   The preference is given to applicants who are very young.   Those seeking the Mission are
provided with refreshments, and are drawn into conversation.
They are given such advice as they seem to need, and are induced to remain until the hour for prayers.   Those who remain
and show a genuine desire to reform are provided with work,
and are given one-half of their earnings for their own use.

The Midnight Mission is a noble institution, and is doing a
noble work, but it is sorely in need of funds.

The other institutions for the reformation of fallen women
are the "House of the Good Shepherd," on the East River, at
Ninetieth street, the "House of Mercy," on the North River,
at Eighty-sixth street, and the "New York Magdalen and
Benevolent Society," at the intersection of the Fifth avenue

SCENE IN THE MAGDALEN ASYLUM.

and Eighty-eighth street. These are all correctional establishments, and more or less force is employed in the treatment of
those who are refractory. Many of the inmates are sent here
by the courts of the city. The "House of the Good Shepherd"
is a Roman Catholic institution, and is in charge of the Sisters
of the order of "Our Lady of Charity of the Good Shepherd."
The other two are Protestant institutions. The "House of
Mercy" is conducted by the Protestant Episcopal Church. The
Magdalen Society is not sectarian. All are doing a good work.
The statistics of the "House of the Good Shepherd" give a total
of about 2900 inmates in twenty-two years. How many of
these were reformed, it is impossible to say. The statistics of

tne " House of Mercy " are not available, but its inmates are
said to number about one hundred annually.   The " Magdalen
Society " has a noble record of its thirty-five years of usefulness.
It is as follows: Total number of inmates, 2000; placed in
private families, 600; restored to relatives, 400; left the Asylum
at their own request, 400; left without permission, 300; expelled,
100; transferred temporarily to the hospital, 300; died, 41; received into evangelical churches, 24; legally married, 20.

L.

CHILD MURDER.

ON the 26th of August, 1871, at three o'clock in the afternoon, a truck drove up to the baggage-room of the Hudson River Railway depot, in Thirtieth street, and deposited on the sidewalk a large, common-looking travelling trunk. The driver, with the assistance of a boy hanging about the depot, carried the trunk into the baggage-room, and at this instant a woman of middle age, and poorly attired, entered the room, presented a ticket to Chicago, which she had just purchased, and asked to have the trunk checked to that place. The check was given her, and she took her departure. The baggage-master, half an hour later, in attempting to remove the trunk to the platform from which it was to be transferred to the baggage-car, discovered a very offensive odor arising from it. His suspicions were at once aroused, and he communicated them to the superintendent of the baggage-room, who caused the trunk to be removed to an old shed close by and opened. As the lid was raised a terrible sight was revealed. The trunk contained the dead body of a young woman, fully grown, and the limbs were compressed into its narrow space in the most appalling manner. The discovery was at once communicated to the police, and the body was soon after removed to the Morgue, where an inquest was held upon it.

The woman had been young and beautiful, and evidently a person of refinement, and the post mortem examination, which was made as speedily as possible, revealed the fact that she had been murdered in the effort to produce an abortion upon her. The case was at once placed in the hands of the detectives, and full details of the horrible affair were laid before the pub-

lic in the daily press.   The efforts to discover the murderer
were unusually successful.   Little by little the truth came out.
The cartman who had taken the trunk to the depot came forward, after reading the account of the affair in the newspapers,
and conducted the police to the house where he had received it.
This was none other than the residence of Dr. Jacob Rosenzweig (No. 687 Second avenue), a notorious abortionist, who
carried on his infamous business at No. 3 Amity Place, as Dr.
Ascher. Suspecting his danger, Rosenzweig endeavored to avoid
the police, but they soon succeeded in securing him.   His residence was taken possession of and searched, and papers were
found which completely established the fact that Rosenzweig
and Ascher were one and the same person.   Rosenzweig was
arrested on suspicion, and committed to the Tombs to await the
result of the inquest.   The body was subsequently identified by
an acquaintance of the dead woman, as that of Miss Alice
Bowlsby, of Patterson, New Jersey. A further search of Rosenzweig's premises resulted in the finding of a handkerchief marked
with the dead woman's name, and other evidence was brought
to light all making it too plain for doubt that Alice Bowlsby
had died from the effects of an abortion produced upon her by
Jacob Rosenzweig.   The wretch was tried for his offence, convicted, and sentenced to seven years of hard labor in the penitentiary.

This affair produced a profound impression not only upon
the city, but upon the whole country, and drew the attention of
the public so strongly to the subject of abortion as a trade, that
there is reason to believe that some steps will be taken to check
the horrible traffic.

Bad as Rosenzweig was, he was but one of a set who are so
numerous in the city that they constitute one of the many distinct classes of vile men and women who infest it.

The readers of certain of the city newspapers are familiar
with the advertisements of these people, such as the following :

A LADIES' PHYSICIAN, DR. ——, PROFES-
sor of Midwifery, over 20 years' successful practice in this city, guarantees certain relief to ladies, with or

without medicine, at one interview. Unfortunates please call. Relief certain. Residence, ———. Elegant rooms for ladies requiring nursing.

IMPORTANT TO FEMALES. DR. AND MADAME ———, (25 years' practice,) guarantee certain relief to married ladies, with or without medicine, at one interview. Patients from a distance provided with nursing, board, etc. Electricity scientifically applied.

A CURE FOR LADIES IMMEDIATELY. MADame ———'s Female Antidote. The only reliable medicine that can be procured; certain to have the desired effect in twenty-four hours, without any injurious results.

SURE CURE FOR LADIES IN TROUBLE. NO injurious medicines or instruments used. Consultation and advice free.

These are genuine advertisements, taken from a daily journal of great wealth and influence, which every morning finds its way into hundreds of families. The persons thus advertising are all of them members of the most dangerous and disreputable portion of the community. They do not, indeed, attack citizens on the streets, but, what is worse and more cowardly, exert their skill for the purpose of destroying human life which is too helpless to resist, and which has no protector. These persons impudently assert that they do not violate the law in their infamous trade, but it needs scarcely a physician's endorsement to make plain to sensible persons the fact that successful abortions are extremely rare. Indeed, the secrecy with which the infamous business is carried on, shows that its practitioners are conscious of its criminality. The laws of all the States punish the procuring of an abortion with severe penalties. That of the State of New York declares, " The wilful killing of an unborn quick child by any injury to the mother of the child, which would be murder if it resulted in the death of such mother, shall be deemed manslaughter in the first degree." The punishment for this crime is an imprisonment in the penitentiary for *not less* than seven years. The law further declares : " Every person who shall administer to any woman pregnant with a quick child, or prescribe for any such woman, or advise and procure for any such woman, any medicine, drugs, or substance whatever, or shall use or employ any instrument or other means, with intent thereby to destroy such child, unless the same shall have been necessary to preserve the life of such mother, shall, in case the death of such child or such mother be thereby produced, be deemed guilty of manslaughter in the second degree." The law prescribes as the punishment for this crime an imprisonment of not less than four years', nor more than seven years' duration.

This is seemingly very severe, but in reality it is not. Now that science has established the fact that to expel the fœtus at any period of pregnancy is to take life, or, in other words, to commit murder, the law should make the selling of drugs or medicines for such purpose a felony, and should punish with great severity any person publicly exposing or privately offering them for sale. Such a statute, so far from embarrassing any reputable member of the medical profession, would be hailed with joy by all; for science has progressed so far, that the cases in which it is necessary to produce an abortion for the sake of saving the mother's life are extremely rare. Further than this, it may be added that the drugs used by these Professors of Infanticide, are, as a rule, unused by the Medical Faculty.

Being well aware then of the penalties to which they are exposed, the Professors of Infanticide conduct their business with extreme caution. They have a great advantage under our present legal system. It has been found by experience that the only evidence, by which they can generally be convicted of their crime, is that of the patient herself. Their knowledge of human nature teaches them that she is the last person in the world to ruin her own reputation by exposing them; and their knowledge of their devilish business teaches them that, if the case does terminate fatally, death will occur in all probability before an *ante-mortem* statement implicating them can be made by their victim. A recent writer thus describes these wretches and their mode of operations :

"Under the head of abortionists, it must be understood there are different classes. First, there is the one whose advertisements, under the head of 'Dr.,' are conspicuous in almost every paper which will print them. Next comes the female abortionists, the richer classes of whom also advertise largely; and lastly, the midwives, who, when it pays them to do so, will in some cases consent to earn money by the commission of this fearful crime.

"First in order, then, the doctor, who styles himself the 'ladies' friend,' which appellation would be more truthful if the second letter were omitted from that word of endearment. He is, as a rule, either a man who has studied for a diploma and failed to pass his examination, or one who, though he is really an M. D., because it pays better, devotes his time to this particular branch of his profession, and advertises largely to that effect; while, in nine cases out of ten, if he attended to a legitimate branch of his vocation, he would prove worthless and inefficient. There are many abortionists in New York to-day who live in first-class style, attend to nothing but 'first-class' cases, receive nothing but first-class fees.

"These men, some of them at least, are received into fashionable society, not because of their gentlemanly or engaging manners, nor even yet on account of their money, but from the fact that they exercise a certain amount of influence and are possessed of a vast deal of audacity. They are cognizant of many a family secret that comes under the jurisdiction of their peculiar vocation; and this fact enables them successfully, if they like, to dare these parties to treat them any other than respectfully. There is a skeleton in every house, a secret in every family; and too often the doctor, midwife, and accoucheur have to be treated publicly, socially, and pecuniarily in accordance with this fact. It is such men as these who, by their nefarious practices, have been enabled to accumulate a large amount of money, that are the proprietors of private hospitals or lying-in asylums, where the better class of women who have fallen from the path of virtue may, under a pretence of a prolonged visit to some distant friends, become inmates, and, after all traces of their guilt have been successfully hidden, can unblushingly return to their friends, and be regarded in their social circles as models of chastity and perfections of virtue.

"Next come the female abortionists, who in some cases transact a larger and more profitable business than the doctors. There are several reasons for this, the principal of which is, that a female would, under the peculiar circumstances in which she is placed, reveal her condition to one of her own sex rather than to a man. The number of female abortionists in New York City is a disgrace and a ridicule upon the laws for the prevention of such inhuman proceedings. True, the majority of them are of the poorer class, but there are many who are literally rolling in wealth, the result of their illegal and unnatural pursuits. The names of many could be mentioned. One, however, will be sufficient, and, although she has been the most successful of her contemporaries, yet her card is a good criterion for the rest of her class. Her name, Madame ——, is well known, and needs no comment. Most of the better and most successful of her kind are in the habit of receiving no less than one hundred or one hundred and fifty dollars for each case, and often as much as five hundred or one thousand dollars. The less successful of the female abortionists, whose practice or business is limited, to some extent, through lack of funds to advertise the same, are content with considerably less sums for their services. Cases have been known where as low as five dollars have been received, and very rarely do they get a chance to make more than fifty or sixty dollars, which is considered a first-rate fee.

"The female abortionists in New York are mostly of foreign birth or extraction, and have generally risen to their present position from being first-class nurses—in Germany, especially, there being medicine schools or colleges in which they graduate after a course of probably six or nine months' study as nurses. The object for which these colleges were established is entirely ignored by the woman, who, from the smattering of medical knowledge she obtains there, seeks to perfect herself as an abortionist."

The principal, and indeed the only object of these wretches is to extort money from their victims. They have no interest in their "patients," either scientific or humane, as is shown by the readiness with which they consent to risk the lives of the poor creatures in their hands, and the rapacity with which they drain their money from them.

Perhaps the reader may ask, " Why, then, do women seek these wretches, instead of applying to educated physicians?" The answer is plain. Educated physicians are, as a rule, men of honor and humanity as well as skill. They know that to produce an abortion at any stage of pregnancy is to commit murder by destroying the child, and they also know that such an act, if it does not endanger the mother's life at the time, will doom her to great future suffering and disease, and probably to a painful death at the " turn of life." Therefore, as men of honor and good citizens, as well as lovers of science, they refuse to prostitute their profession and stain their souls with crime.

The medicines used by the Professors of Infanticide are in most cases such as they know will not produce the relief the patient desires. The object of this is to drain the poor woman's purse, first by causing her to purchase these medicines, and then to force her to submit to an operation; for the " doctor " well knows that the " pills " will " do her no good," and that when she finds there is no escape from an operation, she will come to him, as he is already in possession of her secret. Yet occasionally we find powerful and active medicines administered by these wretches; and it may be said here that all the medicines possessing sufficient power to expel the fœtus prematurely, are also sufficiently powerful to, and invariably do, shatter a woman's system to an extent from which she rarely recovers. The majority of abortionists, however, prefer to use instruments for this purpose, although this is with them the most dangerous of all means of procuring abortion, many of their victims dying from such use of instruments. The most skilful surgeon would be very cautious in using an instrument, well knowing that the most practised hand may in a few minutes fatally injure a woman; yet these ignorant wretches employ this means without hesitation. They plead that it is the quickest and surest means of accomplishing their object.

It is not flattering to our pride to be told that this crime is

one peculiar to our own country; yet so it is.   European communities provide asylums in which pregnant women may seek
refuge, and, secure from the curiosity or censure of their acquaintances, may be safely delivered of their offspring at the
completion of their natural period.   Should they desire to retain the child, they may do so; but should they be unwilling
to claim the proof of their shame, the little innocent may be
placed where it will be cared for and protected by the good
Sisters of the foundling hospitals, and the mother's hands are
thus kept free from the blood of her child.   One does not see
in the Old World the journals crowded with such advertisements as we have referred to, or find such wretches, either
openly or secretly, practising their infamous trade there.   No
European Government would tolerate such a state of affairs, for
if it cannot prevent adultery, it can protect the lives of its
people.   Furthermore, there is in that part of the world a
public sentiment sufficiently pure in this respect, however it
may be in others, to prevent such practices.   It is only in this
land of boasted intelligence and freedom that such wretches can
thrive, that such practices can be carried on with the full
knowledge of the community, and no effectual step be taken to
put a stop to them.

That we have presented no over-drawn picture every candid
reader will confess.   If proof is needed the reader has only to
turn to the advertising columns of the newspapers referred to,
and he will find one or more of the advertisements we have
spoken of.   In this city there are over twenty of these wretches
plying their trade, and advertising it in the public prints.   How
well they succeed we have already shown, and in order to make
it evident how great are their profits, we quote the following
description of one of the most notorious female abortionists:

"By common consent, as well as by reason of her peculiar
calling, Madam ——, of Fifth avenue, is styled 'The wickedest
woman in New York.'   According to her advertisement in the
papers and the City Directory, she calls herself a 'female physician and professor of midwifery.'

"Madam —— is about fifty-five years of age, is a short,

40

plump, vulgar-looking woman, with dark, piercing eyes and jet-black hair.   Once she was handsome, but possesses now no traces of her former beauty.   She looks like an upstart or 'shoddy' female, but not particularly wicked or heartless.   She commenced business about twenty years ago.   Her establishment at that time was in C—— street, and for some time she was but little known.   About four years after she had begun business an event occurred which rendered her one of the most notorious women of the city.   A young woman died who had been under her treatment, and Madam —— was arrested. She was tried before one of the courts, and her trial became a sensation for many days.   The papers were filled with the testimony in the case, and the arguments of the leading counsel were given in full.   All sorts of accounts, too, were furnished as to the history of the accused, the evil of abortion, and the necessity of adopting stricter laws in regard to it.   There was ample testimony offered on which Madam —— could be convicted, but justice at that time, as at the present, was open to pecuniary inducements.   Madam —— had already made considerable money from her improper trade, and it was rumored at the time that she purchased a verdict of 'Not Guilty' for one hundred thousand dollars.   It was a big price to pay, but she regained her liberty, and, what was more, made money by the large investment.   Her trial proved to be an immense advertisement for her, and shortly afterward she removed from C—— street, purchasing a large mansion on Fifth avenue, not far from the Central Park.   In that house she has lived from that time to the present, and says she intends to remain there until her death.   The building is of brown stone, and is one of the finest on the avenue.   It is a corner house, five stories high, the windows of which command from below a fine view of the Fifth avenue, and the Central Park from above.   Shades of a most gaudy, though very vulgar, pattern, are at the windows. No other house in Fifth avenue or in New York possesses such shades, or, indeed, would any one else in the city want to.

"Madam —— purchased this house, it is stated, through an agent in real estate.   She could not have procured it otherwise, as the owner would have refused to sell it to her on account of her business.   Property in the neighborhood in which she lives cannot be sold for any reasonable figure.   The vacant lots on the side of her mansion have been offered for several years at reduced prices, but no one will take them.   Efforts have been made to buy her out, but without success; she has been offered many thousand dollars in advance of the price she paid for her mansion, but she refuses to sell, saying that she bought the house not for speculation, but for a home, and she intends to remain there as long as she lives.

"Her residence is the most magnificently furnished of any establishment on Fifth avenue.   It is finished and furnished like a palace.   Each window consists of but two enormous panes of plate glass.   There are fifty-two windows, hung with satin and French lace curtains.   Her office is in the basement, where she receives her callers.   On the first floor are the grand hall of tessellated marble, lined with mirrors; the three immense dining-rooms, furnished in bronze and gold, with yellow satin hangings, an enormous French mirror in mosaic gilding at every panel; ceilings in medallions and cornices; more parlors and reception-rooms; butler's pantry, lined with solid silver services; dining-room with all imported furniture.   Other parlors on the floor above; a guest-chamber in blue brocade satin, with gold-and-ebony bedstead elegantly covered; boudoir for dressing in every room; madam and husband's own room, granddaughter's room, news-room, study.   Fourth floor—servants' rooms in mahogany and Brussels carpet, and circular picture-gallery; the fifth floor contains a magnificent billiard-room, dancing-hall, with pictures, piano, etc., and commands a fine view of Fifth avenue.   The whole house is filled with statuettes, paintings, rare bronzes, ornamental and valuable clocks, candelabras, silver globes and articles of *vertu*, chosen with unexceptionable taste.

"Madam —— is a married woman, her husband being Mr. ——, a Frenchman.   He is in the same business as herself, practising it under an assumed name, having an office in the lower part of the city, and his advertisements are next to madam's in the daily papers. The interesting couple have a daughter, aged about fifteen, a blonde and beautiful girl, who looks too pure and good to live in such a magnificent den of infamy which is called her home.

"Madam —— keeps seven servants and four fast horses. In winter she drives in tandem, with large ermine sleigh-robes. On every afternoon in the summer she may be seen out alone driving in the Central Park. Her carriage is noted for its extraordinary showiness. There are various statements given as to how she came to adopt her profession. One is, that she was once a servant-girl in a large boarding-house. A couple left one day, and in cleaning up their room the girl, who was afterward to take the name of Madam ——, found a written receipt for a certain purpose. That she preserved, afterward recommending its use to a female friend, and finding it worked well, opened her C—— street office, and sold the medicine at a high figure. Another story is, that she was once a pretty bar-maid in a tavern in the suburbs of London, came to this country when about twenty years of age, made the acquaintance of a physician, and acquired some medical knowledge; was an astrologer and clairvoyant for a time, and afterward adopted her present profession. She is said to have considerable knowledge as to her specialty, which is probably the fact.

"She is said to be worth fully a million of dollars. She has practised her peculiar branch of medicine for many years, and with uniform success. Every one knows it, yet none can bring her to justice. She is too careful and too rich for that. Her immunity from punishment has been entirely owing to the fact that she only takes safe cases, never practising on a woman who has been pregnant more than four months. Her charge is $500 a case. Need there be any better confirmation of the assertion that the rich are greater votaries of the crime of abortion than the poor? Yet every crime has its punishment. Madame ——'s is her loneliness. She has made frantic efforts to get into some part of society better than the lowest. But the rich women who resort to her for 'relief' (this is the word used), turn their backs upon her in public. Madame —— has a daughter, and she offered a quarter of a million to any man laying claim to respectability who would marry her.   But her daughter is yet unmarried.   Her eldest daughter ran away and married a policeman, and is now happy in being disowned by her own mother. Madame —— has her mansion, and carriages and horses, and every luxury riches can bring.   All but position."

Yet this woman and her associates continue to ply their fearful trade, and day after day in this great city this terrible slaughter of innocent beings goes on, and it will go on until the law makes the publication of the advertisements of these wretches, and the practice of their arts and the sale of their drugs, criminal offences.

It must not be supposed, however, that the best customers of the vendors of medicines for producing miscarriage and abortion are those who seek to hide their shame.   It is a terrible fact that here, as in many other parts of the country, the crime of destroying their unborn offspring is repeatedly practised by married women in the secresy of domestic life.   These buy largely of the drugs and pills sold by the professional abortionists. New York is bad enough in this respect, but the crime is not confined to it.   It is an appalling truth that so many American wives are practicers of the horrible sin of " prevention " that in certain sections of our country, the native population is either stationary or is dying out.   So common is the practice, that the Roman Catholic Archbishop of Baltimore and the Episcopal Bishop of Western New York, felt themselves called upon, a year or two ago, to publicly warn their people of the awful nature of it.

It is fashionable here, as elsewhere, not to have more than one, two, or three children.   Men and women tell their friends every day that they do not mean to increase their families. They do mean, however, to enjoy the blessings of the married state, and to avoid its responsibilities.   There is scarcely a physician in the city who is not applied to almost daily by persons of good position for advice as to the best means of preventing conception.   The physicians of New York are men of honor, and they not only refuse to comply with the request, but warn the applicants for advice as to the true moral and physical nature of the course they are seeking to adopt. Yet this warning does not turn them from their purpose. Failing to secure the assistance of scientific men, they seek the advice, and purchase the drugs, of the wretches whose trade is child murder. The evil grows greater every year. These wretches send their drugs all over the country, and "the American race is dying out." In 1865, there were 780,931 families in the State of New York. Of these, 196,802 families had no children, 148,208 families had but one child each, 140,572 families had but two children each, and 107,342 families had but three children each. In nearly one-fourth of all the families there was not a child, and in 592,924 families, or more than three-fourths of all in the State, there was only a small fraction over one child to each family. Only about one child to each mother in the State reaches maturity. The New England States show even a worse state of affairs.

Is it a wonder, then, that Madame —— and her associates grow rich?

LI.

THE EAST RIVER ISLANDS AND THEIR INSTITUTIONS.

I.

BLACKWELL'S ISLAND.

THE three islands lying in the East River are among the most noticeable features of New York, and offer many attractions to the visitor to the city. They are Blackwell's, Ward's, and Randall's islands. Of these, Blackwell's Island is the most southern. It is about a mile and three-quarters in length, extending from Fifty-first to Eighty-eighth street, and comprises an area of about 120 acres. It takes its name from the Blackwell family, who once owned it, and whose ancestral residence, a tasteful wooden cottage, over a hundred years old, stands near the centre of the island, and is occupied by the Keeper of the Almshouse. The island was purchased by the city, in 1828, for the sum of $30,000. A further outlay of $20,000 was made in 1843 to perfect the title. The land alone is now worth over $600,000. The island is surrounded by a granite sea-wall, and has been made to slope gradually towards the water on each side by a thorough system of grading. This labor was performed by the convicts of the Penitentiary, and the inmates of the Workhouse. There is an excellent dock near the Penitentiary for boats, but no vessels are allowed to land here but the boats of the Department of Charities and Corrections. Visitors must obtain a permit from this department or they will not be allowed to set foot upon the island. The institutions on this and the other islands are supplied with

RESIDENCE OF THE KEEPER OF THE ALMSHOUSE.

the Croton water, a large main being carried across under the river.

On the extreme southern end of the island is a stone building of moderate size and handsome design. This is the Small-pox Hospital. It was erected in 1854, at a cost of $38,000, and will accommodate one hundred patients. It is the only hospital in New York devoted to small-pox cases, and receives them from all the public and private institutions, and from private families. The accommodations are excellent, the attention the best. Those who are able to pay are required to do so. At the water's edge, on the eastern side of this hospital, are several wooden buildings designed for the treatment of patients suffering from typhus and ship fever. These will accommodate one hundred patients, though the number is often greater.

Immediately in the rear of the Small-pox Hospital, though far enough from it to be removed from danger, is the Charity Hospital, a magnificent structure of gray granite, said to be the largest hospital in America. It consists of a central building with two wings, each three and a half stories in height, with a

SMALL-POX HOSPITAL.

Mansard roof. The entire building is 354 feet long, and 122 feet wide. The eastern wing is occupied by males, and the western by females. The hospital is divided into 29 wards, the smallest of which contains 13 beds, and the largest 39. Twelve hundred patients can be accommodated with comfort. There are separate wards for the treatment of different diseases, and the medical attendance is the best that New York can afford. The whole establishment is a model of neatness, and is conducted in the most systematic and skilful manner. About seven thousand patients are annually treated here, the majority being charity patients. The average number of deaths is about four hundred and fifty.

Back of the Charity Hospital, and extending north and south, or parallel with the course of the island and river, is the New York Penitentiary, the first public institution erected on the island. It is a gloomy and massive edifice, constructed of hewn stone and rubble masonry. It is four stories in height, and consists of a central building and wings. The central building is 65 by 75 feet, and the wings each 200 by 50 feet in size.

CHARITY HOSPITAL.

The entire building is exceedingly strong. The floors are of stone, and the stairways and doors of iron. It contains 500 cells for men, and 256 for women, but the number of convicts is generally in excess of the number of cells, and still greater accommodations are needed. It is probable that a new and larger Penitentiary will be erected on Hart's Island, in Long Island Sound, about twelve miles from Blackwell's Island. The prisoners at this institution are sent here by the city courts, for terms of from one to six months. Some, however, are sentenced to imprisonment for several years. The convicts are all required to labor. Formerly the men were required to engage in excavating stone from the rich quarries with which the island abounded, but which have now been exhausted. The erection of the new buildings on Randall's, Ward's, and Hart's islands, furnishes constant employment to the convicts, who are daily conveyed between the prison and these institutions. Those who are able to work at the ordinary trades are allowed to do so in the workshops of the Penitentiary. The women are required to do sewing, housework, and the like.

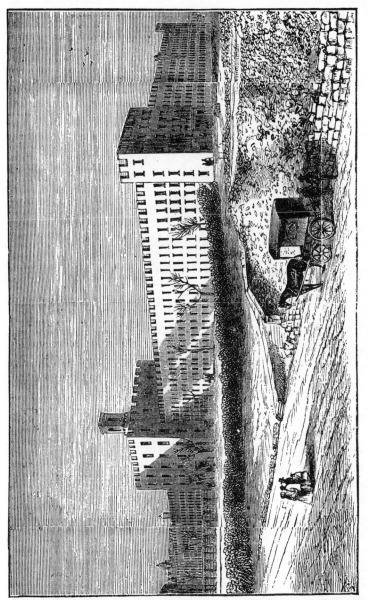

NEW YORK PENITENTIARY.

635

GUARD-BOATS.

No visitors are allowed on the Penitentiary grounds without a permit from the Commissioners. Sentinels are stationed along the water fronts, and guard-boats patrol the river to prevent the escape of the convicts. In spite of these precautions, however, men have succeeded in making their escape to the opposite shore.

The convicts are clothed in a uniform of striped woollen garments, and are supplied with a sufficient amount of bedding and with an abundance of excellent but plain food. The allowance is about one pound of beef, and a quart of vegetable soup at dinner, ten ounces of bread at each meal, and one quart of coffee at breakfast and supper, to each man. In 1869, the total number of prisoners confined here during the year was 2005. A very large number of those sentenced to the Penitentiary are under the age of twenty-five. The proportion of females is about one-fifth. The foreigners are a little more than one-half of the whole number. A system of evening schools, at which the attendance is voluntary, has been instituted. The commutation system is also practised, by which the prisoner by good

ALMSHOUSE.

conduct may receive a proportionate abridgment of his term of
confinement.   Such conduct is reported every month by the
Warden to the Commissioners, who report it to the Governor
of the State, who alone has the power to shorten the terms in
the manner mentioned.   Religious services are conducted every
Sabbath by Protestant and Roman Catholic clergymen.

To the north of the Penitentiary are two handsome and similar
structures of stone, separated by a distance of 650 feet.   These
are the Almshouses.   Each consists of a central story, fifty feet
square and fifty-seven feet high, with a cupola thirty feet in
height, and two wings, each ninety feet long, sixty feet wide,
and forty feet high.   Each is three stories in height.   Each
floor is provided with an outside iron verandah, with stairways
of iron, and each building will furnish comfortable quarters for
600 people, adults only being admitted.   One of these buildings is devoted exclusively to men, the other to women.   Both
are kept scrupulously clean, and it is said that they are kept
by a daily brushing of the beds, which are taken to pieces every
morning, entirely free from vermin.   The grounds are well laid

off, and are in admirable order. In short, the whole place is a model of neatness and careful administration. None but the aged and infirm, who are destitute, are admitted. Each new-comer is bathed immediately upon his or her arrival, and clad in the plain but comfortable garments provided by the estab-lishment. He is then taken to the Warden's office, where his name, age, and bodily condition are registered. At the same time, he is given a card inscribed with the number of the ward and the class to which he is assigned, this allotment being based upon an examination by the House Physician. The inmates are divided into four classes, as follows : I. Able-bodied men. II. Those who are able to do light labor and to act as inspec-tors or orderlies of the different wards. III. Those who are able to sweep the walks or break stones. IV. Those who are too old or infirm for any labor. Those assigned to the first three classes are compelled to perform the duties required of them on pain of dismissal. In the female house, the infirm are more numerous than among the males. Those able to work are employed in sewing and knitting, in keeping the wards in order, and in nursing the feeble and cripples. In 1870, there were 1114 persons in the Almshouses, from fifteen years of age up-wards. A special provision is made in each house for blind inmates.

Attached to the Almshouse are the Hospitals for Incurables, which consist of two one-story buildings, 175 feet long, and 25 feet wide. One is devoted to men and the other to wo-men. In these buildings are quartered those who are afflicted with incurable diseases, but who require no medical attention.

The Bureau for the Relief of the Outdoor Poor is connected with the Almshouse, though it conducts its operations in the city. The city is divided into eleven districts, each of which is in charge of a visitor, subject to the orders of the Superin-tendent of the Bureau. It is the duty of these visitors to ex-amine into the causes of sickness, crime, and pauperism in their respective districts, and to report their observations to the Superintendent, who communicates them to the Department of Charities and Corrections. Temporary shelter is given to

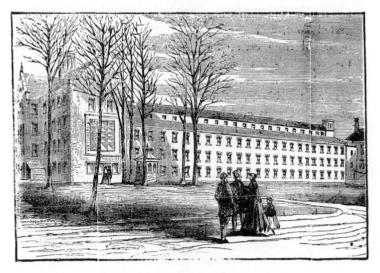

THE WORKHOUSE.

needy persons in the winter, and money, fuel, food, clothing, etc., distributed to deserving persons. In 1869, 5275 families were given money, and 7555 fuel by this Bureau; $128,000 being expended for these charities.

In the rear of the Almshouse is the Workhouse, one of the handsomest buildings on the island. It is constructed of hewn stone, and consists of a central building four stories in height, with a northern and a southern wing, with a traverse section across the extreme end of each wing. In these traverse sections are located the workshops. The entire length of the building is 680 feet. Not counting the convict labor, the cost of its construction was over $100,000. The stone of which it was built was obtained on the island.

In the central building are located the kitchens, and storerooms, the private quarters of the Superintendent and the other officials, and a large and handsome chapel. The wings contain each a broad hall, on each side of which are three tiers of cells, one above the other. Iron galleries, with stairways, extend along the fronts of these cells, and afford access to them. There

are 150 cells in each wing.   Each cell is provided with an iron
grated door, and contains four single berths.   The cells are
separated from each other by brick walls.   In the workshops,
the carpenter's, blacksmith's, wheelwright's, tinner's, tailor's, and
other trades are carried on.   The men are also kept at work
grading the island, building the seawall, and cultivating the
gardens.   Gangs of laborers are sent daily to engage in the
works on Ward's and Randall's islands.   The women are made
to do the housework and cleaning of the various institutions on
the island, and are employed in washing, mending, sewing,
knitting, etc.   All the inmates are obliged to labor.

The number of persons annually sent to the Workhouse is
from 15,000 to 20,000.   The vagrant, dissipated, and disorderly classes are sent here by the city police courts, ten
days being the average term of commitment.   Drunkenness is
the principal cause of their detention here.   Very few are
Americans.   Of the foreigners, the Irish are the most numerous, the Germans next.

Back of the Workhouse, and occupying the extreme upper
portion of the island, is the New York City Lunatic Asylum.
It is a large and commodious building, with several out-build-
ings, with accommodations for 576 patients.   A new Lunatic
Asylum is now in course of erection on Ward's Island.   It is
to accommodate 500 patients.   It is one of the most complete
establishments in the country, and is built of brick and Ohio
freestone.   It is a very handsome building, with an imposing
front of 475 feet.   The two asylums will accommodate 1076
patients, but they are not adequate to the accommodation of all
the afflicted for whom the city is required to provide.   Still
further accommodations are needed.   In 1870, the number of
patients committed to the care of the Commissioners was
over 1300.

II.

WARD'S ISLAND.

WARD'S ISLAND takes its name from Jasper and Bartholomew
Ward, who formerly owned it.   It comprises an area of about

two hundred acres, and is owned in about equal portions by the Commissioners of Emigration and the Department of Charities and Corrections.   It is separated from New York by the Harlem River, from Blackwell's and Long islands by that portion of the East River known as Hell Gate, and from Randall's Island by a narrow strait called Little Hell Gate.   It lies a little to the northeast of Blackwell's Island, about half a mile from it, and is the widest of the three islands in the East River.

The Emigrant Hospital is described in another chapter.

The new Lunatic Asylum is located on the extreme eastern portion of the island.

Between the Emigrant Hospital and the Lunatic Asylum is the New York Inebriate Asylum, a handsome brick edifice, three stories in height, with a frontage of 474 feet, and a depth of 50 feet.   It is provided with every convenience, is supplied with the Croton water, and has accommodations for 400 patients.   The patients consist of those who either seek the Asylum voluntarily or are placed there by their friends, and who pay for their accommodations, and those who are sent to the institution by the police authorities for reformation.   The treatment is moral as well as physical.   The physician's efforts to repair the ravages of dissipation in the physical system are supplemented by the labors of the chaplain and the other officers of the institution, who seek to revive in the patient a sound, healthy morality, which they strive to make the basis of his reformation.

III.

RANDALL'S ISLAND.

RANDALL'S ISLAND is so called from Jonathan Randall, a former owner.   It lies about one hundred yards to the north of Ward's Island, from which it is separated by Little Hell Gate. The Harlem Kills separate it from Westchester county, and the Harlem River from New York.   About thirty acres of the southern portion are owned by the "Society for the Reformation

41

HOUSE OF REFUGE: RANDALL'S ISLAND.

of Juvenile Delinquents." The remainder is the property of the "Commissioners of Charities and Corrections."

The southern portion is occupied by the "House of Refuge," which is under the control of the "Society for the Reformation of Juvenile Delinquents." The buildings are of brick, and are constructed in the Italian style. They have a frontage of nearly 1000 feet, and were constructed at a cost of about $500,000. They constitute one of the handsomest public institutions in the city. The main buildings contain 886 dormitories, several spacious and fully furnished school rooms, a handsome chapel, which will seat 1000 persons, the kitchens, hospital, and officers' quarters. The average number of inmates is about 700 boys and 150 girls. Every child is compelled to labor from six to eight hours every day in the week, and to attend school from four to five hours. The inmates consist of such juvenile offenders against the law as the courts commit to the Refuge in preference to sending them to prison. Some of them are young people, whose parents, unable to manage them, and wishing to save them from lives of sin and crime, have placed them in the hands of the Society for reformation. The discipline is mainly reformatory, though the inmates are subjected to the restraints, but not the degradation of a prison.

"The boys' building is divided into two compartments; the first division, in the one, is thus entirely separated from the second division in the other compartment. The second division is composed of those whose characters are decidedly bad, or whose offence was great. A boy may, by good conduct, however, get promoted from the second into the first division. As a rule, the second division is much older than the first. Each division is divided into four grades. Every boy on entering the Reformatory is placed in the third grade; if he behaves well, he is placed in the second in a week, and a month after in the first grade; if he continues in a satisfactory course for three months, he is placed in the grade of honor, and wears a badge on his breast. Every boy in the first division must remain six months, in the second division twelve months in the first grade, before he can be indentured to any trade. These two divisions are under the charge of twenty-five teachers and twenty-five guards. At half-past six o'clock the cells are all unlocked, every one reports himself to the overseer, and then goes to the lavatories; at seven, after parading, they are marched to the school rooms to join in the religious exercises for half an hour; at half-past seven, they have breakfast, and at eight are told off to the workshops, where they remain till twelve, when they again parade, previous to going to dinner. For dinner they have a large plate of soup, a small portion of meat, a small loaf of bread, and a mug of water. At one o'clock, they return to their work. When they have completed their allotted task, they are allowed to play till four, when they have supper. At half-past four they go to school, where they remain till eight o'clock, the time for going to bed. Each boy has a separate cell, which is locked and barred at night. The cells are in long, lofty, well ventilated corridors, each corridor containing one hundred cells. The doors of the cells are all grated, in order that the boys may have light and air, and also be under the direct super-vision of the officers, who, though very strict, apparently know well how to temper strictness with kindness. Before going to bed, half an hour is again devoted to religious exercises, singing hymns, reading the Bible, etc.

"One of the most interesting, and at the same time, one of the most important features of the Refuge, is the workshop. On entering the shop, the visitor is amused by finding a lot of little urchins occupied in making ladies' hoopskirts of the la-test fashionable design; nearly 100 are engaged in the crinoline department. In the same long room, about fifty are weaving wire for sifting cotton, making wire sieves, rat-traps, gridirons, flower baskets, cattle noses, etc. The principal work, however, is carried on in the boot and shoe department. The labor of the boys is let out to contractors, who supply their own foremen to teach the boys and superintend the work, but the society have their own men to keep order and correct the boys when necessary, the contractors' men not being allowed to interfere with them in any way whatever. There are 590 boys in this department. They manage on an average to turn out about

2500 pairs of boots and shoes daily, which are mostly shipped
to the Southern States.   Each one has a certain amount of work
allotted to him in the morning, which he is bound to complete
before four o'clock in the afternoon.   Some are quicker and
more industrious than others, and will get their work done by
two o'clock; this gives two hours' play to those in the first
division, the second division have to go to school when they
have finished, till three o'clock, they only being allowed one
hour for recreation.   The authorities are very anxious to make
arrangements to have a Government vessel stationed off the
island, to be used as a training-ship for the most adventurous
spirits.   If this design is carried out it will be a very valuable
adjunct to the working of the institution, and will enable the
Directors to take in many more boys, without incurring the expense of extending the present buildings.   The girls are also
employed in making hoopskirts, in making clothes for themselves and the boys, in all sorts of repairing, in washing linen,
and in general housework.   The girls are generally less tracta-
ble than the boys; perhaps this is accounted for by their being
older, some of them being as much as five or six and twenty.
The boys average about thirteen or fourteen, the girls seventeen
or eighteen years of age.   Nearly two-thirds of the boys have
been bootblacks, the remainder mostly 'wharf rats.'

"The Directors of the House of Refuge, while having a due
regard for the well-being of its inmates, very properly take care
that they are not so comfortable or so well-fed as to lead them
to remain longer in the reformatory than necessary.   As soon as
the boys appear to be really reformed, they are indentured out
to farmers and different trades.   In the year 1867, no less than
633 boys and 146 girls were started in life in this way.   Any
person wishing to have a child indentured to him, has to make
a formal application to the Committee to that effect, at the same
time giving references as to character, etc.   Inquiries are made,
and if satisfactorily answered, the child is handed over to his
custody, the applicant engaging to feed, clothe, and educate his
young apprentice.   The boy's new master has to forward a
written report to the officer, as to his health and general be-

haviour from time to time. If the boy does not do well, he is sent back to the Refuge, and remains there till he is twenty-one years of age. Most of the children, however, get on, and many of them have made for themselves respectable positions in society. The annals of the Society in this respect are very gratifying and interesting. Many young men never lose sight of a Refuge which rescued them in time from a criminal life, and to which they owe almost their very existence. Instead of alternating between the purlieus of Water street and Sing Sing, they are many of them in a fair way to make a fortune. One young man who was brought up there, and is now thriving, lately called at the office to make arrangements for placing his two younger brothers in the House, they having got into bad company since their father's death. A very remarkable occurence took place at the institution not long ago. A gentleman and his wife, apparently occupying a good position in society, called at the Refuge and asked to be allowed to go over it. Having inspected the various departments, just before leaving, the gentleman said to his wife, ' Now I will tell you a great secret. I was brought up in this place.' The lady seemed much surprised, and astounded all by quietly observing, ' And so was I.' So strange are the coincidences of human life."

The institutions on this island controlled by the Department of Public Charities and Corrections, are the " Nurseries," the " Infant Hospital," and the " Idiot Asylum."

The Nurseries consist of six large brick buildings, each three-stories in height, arranged without reference to any special plan, and separated from each other by a distance of several hundred feet. Each is in charge of an assistant matron, the whole being under the supervision of a Warden and matron. These nurseries are devoted to the care of children over four years old, abandoned by their parents, and found in the streets by the police, and children whose parents are unable to care for them. Wherever the parent is known the Commissioners afford only temporary shelter to the children, requiring the parents to resume their care of them at the earliest possible moment. Three months is the limit for gratuitous shelter in such cases. Where the parent is unknown, the child is cared for until it is of an age to be apprenticed, or until some respectable persons take it for adoption. Only healthy children are received into the nurseries, and none may remain in them after reaching the age of sixteen years. The average number of inmates is about 2400 per annum.

The Infant Hospital is for the reception of children under the age of four years, for foundlings, for children whose parents are too poor to take care of them, and for the sick of the Nurseries proper. The children are divided into three classes: I. The "Wet nursed:" II. The "Bottle fed:" III. The "Walking Children." They are retained here unless claimed by their parents until they attain the age of three or four years, when they are transferred to the Nurseries mentioned above. The Hospital is a large and handsome brick building, and will accommodate several hundred children and their nurses.

The Idiot Asylum is a large brick building, with accommodations for several hundred patients. It contains at present about 150 of these, whose ages vary from six to thirty years. They represent nearly all the different phases of idiocy, and are well cared for. Some of them have been greatly improved in mind by the treatment and discipline pursued.

LII.

BENEVOLENT AND CHARITABLE INSTITUTIONS.

IT would be simply impossible to present within the limits of a single chapter, or indeed in half a dozen chapters of the size of this, a description of the Benevolent and Charitable Institutions of New York. We can do no more than glance at them. Besides the institutions already mentioned, there are twenty-one hospitals, twenty-three asylums, seventeen homes, five missions, industrial schools, and miscellaneous societies, making a total of sixty-six institutions, or with those already noticed, a total of nearly one hundred benevolent, charitable, penal, and reformatory institutions supported by the city and people of New York.

Among the hospitals the largest and oldest is the New York Hospital, formerly located on Broadway opposite Pearl street. The Hospital is in charge of the medical faculty of the University of New York. At present the operations of this institution are entirely suspended, and will not be resumed until the completion of new buildings, the old ones having been sold and pulled down.

The Bloomingdale Asylum for the Insane, is a branch of the New York Hospital. It is situated on One-hundred-and-seventeenth street, between Tenth and Eleventh avenues. It is one of the most complete establishments in the world, and is admirably conducted.

Bellevue Hospital, on the East River, at the foot of Twenty-sixth street, is one of the largest in the city. It will accommodate 1200 patients, and is conducted by the Commissioners of Charities and Corrections. There is no charge for treatment and attendance, everything being free. The hospital is in charge

BLOOMINGDALE ASYLUM FOR THE INSANE.

of the most distinguished physicians of the city, and as a school of clinical instruction ranks among the first in the world.   The course is open to the students of all the medical schools in the city.

St. Luke's Hospital, on Fifty-fourth street and Fifth avenue, is a noble institution, and one of the prettiest places on the great thoroughfare of fashion.   Its erection is due to the labors of the Rev. Dr. W. A. Muhlenberg.   It is the property of the Episcopal Church, by which body it is conducted.   The sick are nursed here by the "Sisters of the Holy Communion," a voluntary association of unmarried Protestant ladies.   The hospital has accommodations for over one hundred patients, and is said to be the best conducted of any denominational charity in the city.   Patients who are able to pay are required to do so, but the poor are received without charge.

The Roosevelt Hospital, a magnificent structure, is situated on West Fifty-ninth street, between Ninth and Tenth avenues, and is to furnish, when completed, accommodations for 600 patients.   It is the gift of the late Jas. H. Roosevelt of New York to the suffering.

ST. LUKE'S HOSPITAL.

The Presbyterian Hospital, on Seventy-first street, between Fourth and Madison avenues, is not yet completed. It is a beautiful structure, and is to have accommodations for several hundred patients. It is the property of the Presbyterian Church of New York. The site, valued at $250,000, and a further sum of $250,000 in cash, were the gift of Mr. James Lenox.

The Roman Catholic Church conducts the Hospitals of St. Francis and St. Vincent, the former on East Fifth street, and the latter on the corner of Eleventh street and Seventh avenue. These two institutions contain about 250 beds.

The German Hospital, Seventy-seventh street and Fourth avenue, is, as yet, incomplete. It was erected by the German citizens of New York, but receives patients of every nationality and color. The poor are received without charge under certain restrictions. There are accommodations for about seventy-five patients in the present buildings. Connected with the hospital is a dispensary from which medical advice and medicines are given to the poor.

The Jews of New York have just completed a magnificent edifice, known as the Mount Sinai Hospital, on Lexington avenue, between Sixty-sixth and Sixty-seventh streets.   It will contain 200 beds.   The present Hebrew Hospital, in Twenty-eighth street, near Eighth avenue, contains about sixty-five beds. The Jews also have a burial ground, in which those of their faith who die in the Hospital are buried without expense to their friends.

The Child's Hospital, Lexington avenue and Fiftieth street, embraces four distinct charities: A Foundling Asylum, a Nursery for the children of laboring women, a Child's Hospital, and a Lying-in Asylum.   The buildings are very extensive. The annual Charity Ball is given in behalf of this institution.

The Woman's Hospital of the State of New York, Fourth avenue and Fiftieth street, is a handsome building, and the only institution of its kind in the country.   It owes its existence to the exertions of Dr. J. Marion Sims, who is, together with Dr. Emmett, still in charge of it.   It is devoted exclusively to the treatment of female diseases.   It is attended by physicians from all parts of the country, who come to receive clinical instruction in this branch of their profession.

The other prominent hospitals are, Dr. Knight's Institution for the Relief of the Ruptured and Crippled; the New York Eye and Ear Infirmary; the House of Rest for Consumptives; the New York Infirmary for Women and Children; the New York Medical College and Hospital for Women; the Hahneman Hospital; the Stranger's Hospital (a private charity); the New York Ophthalmic Hospital; the New York Aural Institute; and the Manhattan Eye and Ear Hospital.

Among the asylums are the Institution for the Blind, on Ninth avenue and Thirty-fourth street; the New York Institution for the Instruction of the Deaf and Dumb, on Washington Heights, overlooking the Hudson; the Institution for the Improved Instruction of Deaf Mutes, Broadway, near Forty-fifth street; the New York Orphan Asylum, Seventy-third street, west of Broadway; the Colored Orphan Asylum, One-hundred-and-tenth street and Tenth avenue; the Orphan Home

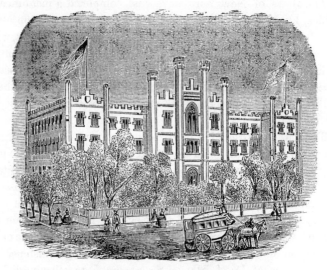

INSTITUTION FOR THE BLIND.

and Asylum of the Protestant Episcopal Church, Forty-ninth
street and Lexington avenue; the Sheltering Arms, an Episcopal institution for the Protection and Care of Orphans and
half Orphans, especially those whose bodily infirmities would
exclude them from other institutions; three Roman Catholic
Orphan Asylums, one at the corner of Mott and Prince streets,
one on Fifth avenue (for boys), on the block above the new
Cathedral, and one in Madison avenue (for girls), immediately
in the rear of that just mentioned; the New York Asylum for
Lying-in Women, 83 Marion street; the Society for the Relief
of Half Orphans and Destitute Children, 67 West Tenth street;
the Leake and Watts Orphan House, West One-hundred-and-
tenth street, near the Central Park; the New York Juvenile
Asylum, One-hundred-and-seventy-sixth street, devoted to the
reformation of juvenile vagrants; the Hebrew Benevolent and
Orphan Asylum, Third avenue and Seventy-seventh street;
St. Barnabas House, 304 Mulberry street, an Episcopal "Home
for Homeless Women and Children;" the Institution of Mercy,
33 Houston street, a Roman Catholic institution for the visita-

tion of the sick and prisoners, the instruction of poor children, and the protection of virtuous women in distress; the Roman Catholic Orphan Asylum of St. Vincent de Paul, Thirty-ninth street, near Seventh avenue; the Society for the Protection of Destitute Roman Catholic Children, the Protectory of which is located at West Farms, in Westchester County; the New York Foundling Asylum, in Washington Square; the Shepherd's Fold, Eighty-sixth street and Second avenue, an establishment similar to the "Sheltering Arms," and conducted by the Episcopal Church; the Woman's Aid Society and Home for Training Young Girls, Seventh avenue and Thirteenth street; and St. Joseph's Orphan Asylum (Roman Catholic), Avenue A and Eighty-ninth street.

Among the Homes and Missions are, the Association for the Relief of Respectable Aged Indigent Females, in East Twentieth street; the Ladies' Union Aid Society of the Methodist Episcopal Church, Forty-second street, near Eighth avenue; the American Female Guardian Society and Home for the Friendless, 29 East Twenty-ninth, and 32 East Thirtieth streets; the Home for Incurables, an Episcopal institution, with its buildings at West Farms; the Samaritan Home for the Aged, Ninth avenue and Fourteenth street; the Colored Home, First avenue and Sixty-fifth street; St. Luke's (Episcopal) Home for Indigent Christian Females, Madison avenue and Eighty-ninth street; the Presbyterian Home for Aged Women, Seventy-third street, between Fourth and Madison avenues; the Union Home School, for the Orphans of Soldiers and Sailors, on the Boulevard at One-hundred-and-fifty-first street; the Female Christian Home for Women, 314 East Fifteenth street; the Home for Friendless Women, 86 West Fourth street; the Women's Prison Association, 213 Tenth avenue; the Roman Catholic Home for the Aged Poor, 447 West Thirty-second street; the Chapin Home for the Aged and Infirm (Universalist), now in course of erection; the Baptist Home for Aged and Infirm Persons, 41 Grove street; the Home for Aged Hebrews, 215 West Seventeenth street; the Ladies Christian Union or Young Women's Home, 27 and 28 Washington Square; the Water street Home for Women, 273 Water street, devoted to the reformation of fallen women, and occupying the building formerly used by John Allen, "the wickedest man in New York," as a dance house; Wilson's Industrial School for Girls, Avenue A and St. Mark's place; the New York House and School of Industry, 120 West Sixteenth street; and the Society for the Employment and Relief of Poor Women (Unitarian).

The city conducts five large and excellent dispensaries, at which the poor may receive medical advice, treatment and medicines free of charge. There are also a number of dispensaries devoted to the gratuitous treatment of special diseases.

LIII.

HENRY WARD BEECHER.

ALTHOUGH Mr. Beecher is a resident of Brooklyn, and although Plymouth Church is located in that city, yet the great preacher is sufficiently bound to New York by business and socialities to make him a part of the great metropolis.

He was born in Litchfield, Connecticut, on the 24th of June, 1813, and is now in his fifty-ninth year, though he looks very much younger. He was the eighth child of Dr. Lyman Beecher, and was regarded as the dunce of the family, and, according to his own account, had the usual unpleasant experience of ministers' children. Being of a naturally strong, vigorous constitution, his body far outran his mind, and the little fellow lagged behind until nature asserted her rights. The forcing process accomplished very little with him. He was quick-witted, however, and fond of fun. The gloomy doctrines of his learned father made him shudder, and he came to the conclusion that Sunday was a day of penance, and the Catechism a species of torture invented for the punishment of dull boys. At the age of ten, he was sent to a boarding-school in Bethlehem, where he studied by shouldering his gun and going after partridges. Then his sister, Catharine, took him in hand, but he spent his time in teazing the girls of her school, and she was compelled to give him up as a hopeless case. The boy of ten could not be made a mental prodigy, do what they would. The result is that the man of fifty-nine is as fresh and vigorous in body and mind as most others are at thirty-five.

When he was twelve years old, his father removed to Boston, and there Henry began to show his true powers. He learned rapidly, and was soon sent to the Mount Pleasant Institute, at

Amherst, from which he passed to Amherst College, where he graduated with distinction in 1834. While at Mount Pleasant, he formed the resolution of entering the ministry, and all his studies were thenceforward shaped to that end. In 1832, his father had removed to Cincinnati, to assume the presidency of the Lane Theological Seminary, and, after leaving Amherst, Henry followed him to the West, and completed his theological course at the Lane Seminary in 1836. In that year he was admitted to the ministry of the Presbyterian Church.

Immediately after his ordination, Mr. Beecher married, and accepted a call to Lawrenceburg, Indiana, on the Ohio River, twenty miles below Cincinnati. He did not stay there long, but passed to the charge of a church in Indianapolis, where he spent eight years—eight valuable years to him, for he says he learned how to preach there. In the summer of 1847, he received and accepted a call to the pastorate of Plymouth Church, in Brooklyn, which had just been founded, and on the 11th of November, 1847, he was publicly installed in the position which he has since held.

Few persons of education and taste ever come to New York without hearing the great preacher. Plymouth Church is a familiar place to them. It is located in Orange street, between Hicks and Henry streets, Brooklyn. It is a plain structure of red brick. The interior is as simple as the exterior. It is a plain, square room, with a large gallery extending entirely around it. At the upper end is a platform on which stands the pulpit—an exquisitely carved little stand of wood from the Garden of Gethsemane. In the gallery, back of the pulpit, is the organ, one of the grandest instruments in the country. The seats are arranged in semicircles. By placing chairs in the aisles, the house will seat with comfort twenty-five hundred people. The congregation usually numbers about three thousand, every available place being crowded. The upholstering is in crimson, and contrasts well with the prevailing white color of the interior.

The singing is congregational, and is magnificent. One never hears such singing outside of Plymouth Church.

The gem of the whole service, however, is the sermon ; and these sermons are characteristic of the man. They come warm and fresh from his heart, and they go home to the hearer, giving him food for thought for days afterward. Mr. Beecher talks to his people of what they have been thinking of during the week, of trials that have perplexed them, and of joys which have blessed them. He takes the merchant and the clerk to task for their conduct in the walks of business, and warns them of the snares and pitfalls which lie along their paths. He strips the thin guise of honesty from the questionable trans-actions of Wall street, and holds them up to public scorn. His dramatic power is extraordinary. He can hardly be respon-sible for it, since it breaks forth almost without his will. He moves his audience to tears, or brings a mirthful smile to their lips, with a power that is irresistible. His illustrations and figures are drawn chiefly from nature, and are fresh and striking. He can startle his hearers with the terrors of the law, but he prefers to preach the gospel of love. His sermons are printed weekly in the *Plymouth Pulpit,* and are read by thousands.

His literary labors, apart from his ministerial duties, have been constant. He has published several books, has edited *The Independent* and *The Christian Union,* and has contributed regularly to the *New York Ledger* and other papers. He has been almost constantly in the lecture field, and has spoken fre-quently before public assemblies on the various questions of the day.

Mr. Beecher is young-looking and vigorous. He has the face of a great orator, and one that is well worth studying. He dresses plainly, with something of the farmer in his air, and lives simply. He is blessed with robust health, and, like his father, is fond of vigorous exercise. He has a fine farm on the Hudson, to which he repairs in the summer. Here he can in-dulge his love of nature without restraint. He is said to be a capital farmer, though he complains that he does not find the pursuit any more remunerative than does his friend, Mr. Greeley.

42

LIV.

BLACK-MAILING.

To live at the expense of other people, and to procure the means of living in comfort without working for it, is an art in which there are many proficients in New York. Certain of those who practise this art are known in city parlance as "Black-mailers," and they constitute one of the most dangerous portions of the community. The Blackmailer is generally a woman, though she is frequently sustained or urged on by a rough, professional thief, or pick-pocket. The indiscretions of men of nominally spotless character are constantly becoming known through the instrumentality of the gossips, and as soon as these reach the ears of the Blackmailers, who are ever on the watch for them, they proceed to take advantage of them to extort money from the person implicated. They are not content, however, with making victims of those who are really guilty of indiscretions, but boldly assail the innocent and virtuous, well-knowing that nine persons out of ten, though guiltless of wrong-doing, will sooner comply with their demands than incur the annoyance of a public scandal. Such persons think the wretch will never dare to charge them with the same offence or endeavor to extort money from them a second time, and make the first payment merely to rid themselves of the annoyance. They ought never to yield, whether innocent or guilty, for the Black-mailer is sure to repeat her demand. The law makes it a crime for any one to endeavor to extort money in this way, and no person so threatened should hesitate to apply to the police for protection.

As a rule, the Blackmailer is easily driven off with the aid of the police, but sometimes her plans are so skilfully laid that it requires all the ingenuity of the most experienced detectives to ferret out the plot.   These women act upon the well-established fact that respectable people dread scandal, and that a man guilty of an indiscretion will make many sacrifices to conceal it. They rarely assail women, as there is not much money to be made out of them, but they know that almost any story about a man will be believed, and they fasten themselves like leeches upon men. Young men about to make rich marriages are their favorite victims.   These generally yield to them, not caring to risk a scandal which might break off the whole affair.   If a young man refuses one of them on such occasions, she goes boldly to the lady he is to marry, and declares herself the innocent and wronged victim of the aforesaid young man.   This is her revenge, and the majority of young men, knowing them to be capable of such a course, comply with their demands on the spot.   There is nothing these wretches will not do, no place they will not invade, in order to extort money from their victims.

Persons from the country, stopping at the hotels of the city, are frequently the objects of the attacks of the Blackmailers. A man's name is learned from the hotel register, and he is boldly approached and charged with conduct he never dreamed of being guilty of.   The scoundrel professes to know him and his whole family, and names the price of his silence.   Too often the demand is complied with, and the money paid. The proper course to pursue when accosted in such a manner, is to call upon the nearest policeman for assistance in shaking off the wretch.

A few years ago a minister, in charge of a prominent and wealthy city church abruptly left the city.   There had never been a whisper of any kind of scandal connected with his name, and his friends were at a loss to account for his strange action. He refused, at first, when his retreat was discovered, to give any reason for his conduct, and begged that his hiding-place should be kept secret.   At length, however, he confessed that he was the innocent victim of a female Blackmailer.   He was a weak man, proud of his reputation, and more than usually timid in such matters.   The woman had approached him, and had boldly charged him with a crime of which he was innocent, and had demanded a sum of money as the price of her silence. Finding it impossible to get rid of her, and dreading a scandal, the minister had paid the money. The demand was repeated again and again for two years, until the woman had wrung from her victim a sum of several thousand dollars, and had driven him to such a state of despair that he had abandoned his home and his prospects, and had fled to escape from her clutches. His friends came to his aid, and by securing the interposition of the police, compelled the woman to relinquish her hold upon her victim.

Many of the female Blackmailers are very young, mere girls. A couple of years ago, Police Captain Thorne discovered a regularly organized band of them. They are mostly flower girls, from twelve to sixteen years of age. They are generally modest in demeanor, and some of them are attractive in appearance. They gain admittance to the offices and counting rooms of professional men and merchants, under the pretext of selling their flowers, and then, if the gentleman is alone, close the door, and threaten to scream and accuse him of taking improper liberties with them, unless he consents to pay them the sum they demand.

A merchant of great wealth, high position, and irreproachable character, called upon Captain Thorne, about two years ago, and "frankly stated that he was the victim of one of these flower girls, who had already despoiled him of large sums of money, and whose persecutions were actually killing him. It appears that she always came to his counting-house on particular days, and, watching until he was alone, went boldly into his private office. In police parlance, they 'put up a job on her.' Captain Thorne was secreted in the office the next time she called, and the gentleman talked to her as previously arranged. He began by asking her why she persisted in her demands upon him, for, said he, 'you know I never had anything to do with you, never said an improper word to you.' The young analyst of human nature answered, unabashed, 'I know that; but who'll believe you if I say you did?' Captain Thorne, dressed in full police

uniform, stepped from the closet with, ' I will for one, Mary.'
The girl, young as she was, had experience enough in devious
ways to see that her game had escaped, and readily, although
sullenly, promised to cease exacting tribute in that particular
quarter.   The gentleman would go no further, and to the earnest entreaties of Captain Thorne to prosecute the girl, both for
her own good and that of society, returned an absolute refusal.
Captain Thorne was, therefore, obliged to let her go with a
warning not to attempt her operations again anywhere.   He
also remonstrated with her upon her way of living, and asked
her why she did such things.   The hardened girl morosely answered that all the other girls did them, and thus gave a clue
which was followed until it developed a gang of feminine
blackmailers of tender years, working in concert.   Although
the band was then dispersed, the method of robbery it employed
survived, and is yet extensively used by scores of girls, under
the cover of selling not only flowers, but apples and other
fruits."

LV.

FEMALE SHARPERS.

I.

FORTUNE-TELLERS AND CLAIRVOYANTS.

THE city journals frequently contain such advertisements as the following:

A TEST MEDIUM.—THE ORIGINAL MADAME F—— tells everything, traces absent friends, losses, causes speedy marriages, gives lucky numbers. Ladies, fifty cents; gentlemen, one dollar. 464 —— th Avenue.

A FACT—NO IMPOSITION. THE GREAT EUROpean Clairvoyant. She consults you on all affairs of life. Born with a natural gift, she tells past, present, and future; she brings together those long separated; causes speedy marriages; shows you a correct likeness of your future husband or friends in love affairs. She was never known to fail. She tells his name; also lucky numbers free of charge. She succeeds when all others fail. Two thousand dollars reward for any one that can equal her in professional skill. Ladies, fifty cents to one dollar. Positively no gents admitted. No 40 —— Avenue.

It seems strange that, in this boasted age of enlightenment, the persons who make such announcements as the above can find any one simple enough to believe them. Yet, it is a fact, that these persons, who are generally women, frequently make large sums of money out of the credulity of their fellow creatures. Every mail brings them letters from persons in various parts of the country. These letters are generally answered, and the contents have disgusted more than one simpleton. The information furnished is such as any casual acquaintance could give, and just as trustworthy as the reports of the "reliable gentleman just from the front," used to prove during the late war.   The city custom of these impostors is about equal to that brought to them from the country by means of their advertisements.   Some of them make as much as one hundred dollars per day, all of which is a clear profit.   The majority earn from three to six dollars per day.   Servant girls are profitable customers.   Indeed, but for female credulity the business would go down.

Still, there are many male visitors.   Speculators, victims of the gaming table and the lottery, come to ask for advice, which is given at random.   The woman knows but little of her visitors, and has no means of learning anything about them. Sometimes her statements are found to be true, but it is by the merest accident.

The clairvoyants do not hesitate to confess to their friends, in a confidential way, of course, that their pretensions are mere humbuggery, and they laugh at the credulity of their victims, whilst they encourage it.   It seems absurd to discuss this subject seriously.   We can only say to those who shall read this chapter, that there is not in the City of New York an honest fortune-teller or clairvoyant.   They knowingly deceive persons as to their powers.   It is not given to human beings to read the future—certainly not to such wretched specimens as the persons who compose the class of which we are writing.   The only sensible plan is to keep your money, dear reader.   You know more than these impostors can possibly tell you.

Many of these fortune-tellers and clairvoyants are simply procuresses.   They draw women into their houses, and ply them so with temptations, that they frequently ruin them. This is the real business of most of them.   They are leagued with the keepers of houses of ill-fame.   No woman is safe who enters their doors.

The women also offer for sale "amulets," "charms," or "recipes," which they declare will enable a person to win the love of any one of the opposite sex, and excite the admiration of friends; or which will "give you an influence over your enemies or rivals, moulding them to your own will or purpose;" or which will "enable you to discover lost, stolen, or hidden treasures," etc., etc. For each or any of these charms, from three to five dollars is asked, "with return postage," when sent by mail. All these, as well as "love powders," "love elixirs," and the like, are either worthless, or are composed of dangerous chemical substances. Strange to say, the sale of these things is large. The world is full of fools, and the best proof of it is that two of the most noted women of New York, who practise the arts we have described, are worth respectively one hundred thousand dollars and eighty thousand dollars.

II.

MATRIMONIAL BROKERS.

THERE are several women in the city who advertise to intro-duce strangers into the best society, and to procure wives and husbands from the same element for their customers. As a general rule, these women are simply procuresses. If, however, a man desiring to marry a woman in this city, seeks their aid, they will always find some means of assisting him. The charge for their services is either a percentage on the lady's fortune, or a certain specified sum. The woman, or broker, will devise some means of making the acquaintance of the lady against whom her arts are to be directed, and will proceed cautiously, step by step, until she has caused her victim to meet the man for whom she is working. The arts used vary according to circumstances, but they rarely fail of success. Men who wish to accomplish the ruin of some innocent girl, also seek the aid of these brokers, and frequently, through their assistance, effect their purpose. If it is necessary, the victim, after being allured to the broker's house, is drugged. These women are the vam-pires of society. It is very difficult for the authorities to make a case against them, and they generally go unpunished.

The offers of these wretches to procure wives for men wish-ing to be married, are often accepted by simpletons living in country districts.   The fool is induced to come to the city, where he is introduced to a woman who is perhaps a prostitute, or a servant girl, or one who is willing to marry any man who will support her.   She readily enters into the arrangement proposed by the broker, and marries the silly fellow, who goes back to his rural home with her, thinking he has married a lady.

LVI.

EDUCATIONAL ESTABLISHMENTS.

I.

THE FREE SCHOOLS.

THE provision made by the city and the people of New York for the education of the young is in keeping with their metropolitan character. The public and private schools are numerous, and are well supported.

The first in importance are the Public or Free Schools, which are acknowledged to be the best in the Union. The Free School system is under the control of a Board of Education, whose offices are located in a handsome brown stone building at the northwest corner of Grand and Elm streets. The Board consists of twelve Commissioners, who have the general supervision of the schools, the disbursement of the moneys appropriated for the cause of education, the purchase of sites and the erection of new buildings, the purchase and distribution of books, stationery, fuel, lights, and all supplies needed by the schools. There are also five Trustees for each ward, or 110 in all, who were, until recently, chosen by the people. Besides these, are twenty-one Inspectors of Schools, who were, until recently, appointed by the Mayor and confirmed by the people. The charter of 1870, however, changed the whole system, and gave to the Mayor the power of appointing all the officers named above, taking the control of the school system entirely out of the hands of the people. It is needless to add this was the work of the Ring, and was done to secure to them additional power and plunder.

A NEW YORK FREE SCHOOL.

There are about one hundred buildings in the city used by the public schools. About eighty-five of these are owned by the city; the others are rented. The property under the charge of the Board of Education is valued at more than $10,000,000. The annual expenditure for the support of the schools averages $3,000,000. In 1869 it was $3,136,136. Of this sum, $1,-759,634, represented teachers' salaries; $41,908, was for the support of the colored schools; and $164,717, was for the purchase of school apparatus, maps, globes, blackboards, books, etc. The teachers employed in the public schools number 2500, a large proportion being women. The average annual attendance of pupils is 225,000.

The school buildings are generally of brick, tastefully trimmed with brown stone, though some of those more recently erected are entirely of brown or Ohio stone. They are among

the most handsome edifices in the city. They are generally
four stories in height, with a frontage of 100 or 150 feet. All
that were erected for the purpose are commodious and comfortable, though the more recent structures are the best arranged.
They are provided with every convenience for teaching, and
for the comfort of both teacher and pupil. Some of them cover
two city lots, while others occupy as many as six of these lots.
Some will accommodate as many as 2000 pupils, and these large
buildings have been found to be more economical than small
ones. Each is provided with several fire-proof stairways, and
each is in charge of a janitor, who resides in the building. The
entrances for pupils are at the sides of the building. Visitors
enter through the large door in the centre.

The public schools are divided into Primary, Grammar,
Evening, and Normal Schools. There are about 200 of these
schools in the city, a Primary and a Grammar School often
occupying the same building. Some of the Primaries are for
boys or girls only, while in others both sexes are admitted. The
course in the Primaries is very simple, as very young children
are taught here. The pupils are divided, according to qualifi-
cation, into six grades. The lowest grade receives the simplest
instruction, such as conversational lessons about common objects, or "object teaching," which is designed to form habits
of accurate observation ; simple instruction in regard to morals
and manners ; reading and spelling easy words from the black-
board or chart ; counting ; and simple addition by the aid of
the numerical frame. From this simple, but substantial basis,
the pupil is advanced as rapidly as his capabilities will permit,
from grade to grade ; until the first, or highest, is reached. In
this the instruction embraces the four ground rules of arithme-
tic, geography, writing, drawing on the slate, and advanced
object lessons. When the pupil is proficient in these studies,
he is transferred to the Grammar School.

The Grammar School takes up the course where it is dropped by the Primary, and gives to the pupil a sound and practical "common school education." It embraces in its various
grades, such studies as English grammar, history, astronomy

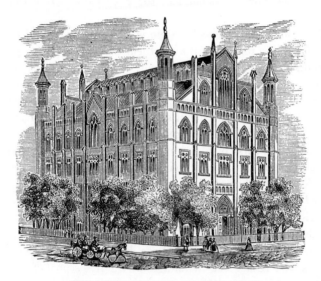

THE FREE COLLEGE OF NEW YORK.

(in its simpler form), physical geography, composition, drawing, and book keeping, besides the simpler studies of the lower grades which were begun in the Primary School.

Girls who are found proficient in the Grammar School course, are advanced to the Normal School, which is temporarily located at the corner of Broadway and Fourth street. Here they may enjoy the benefits of a course as thorough and extended as that afforded by the Free College.

Boys who have attended the Grammar Schools for a certain period, and are found proficient in the course taught there, are promoted to the Free College of the city of New York. This noble institution is located at the southeast corner of Lexington avenue and Twenty-third street. It is a handsome edifice of brick, stuccoed in imitation of brown stone, and was founded in 1848. The President is Horace Webster, LL.D., and the faculty includes some of the ablest men in the country. The course taught here is full and thorough, and is about the same as that of the best colleges in the land. The entire expense of the Female Normal School, and the Free College is borne by the city.

The whole public school system is free to all the children of the city, whose parents will avail themselves of it. Books, and everything needed, are furnished without charge. The pupil is put to no expense whatever, but is required to maintain habits of order and personal neatness. The cost to the city is gladly borne by the tax payers, for it saves the metropolis from an increase of the great army of ignorant and idle men and women, which are the curse of all great cities. The very poorest men or women can thus give to their children the priceless boon of knowledge, of which their youth was deprived. Profiting by the advantage thus acquired, these little ones, in after years, may rise to fame and fortune. Thus not only the metropolis but the whole country reaps the blessings of this magnificent system of free education. The poor, however, are not the only persons who secure the advantages of the free schools for their children. Many wealthy, or moderately comfortable parents send their children to these schools, because they are the best in the city.

Connected with the day schools, there are twenty-seven evening schools, with an average annual attendance of 20,000 pupils. These are designed for the instruction of those whose avocations or age prevent them from attending the day schools. Only simple studies are taught in these schools. The pupils consist of cash boys, clerks, porters, and laboring men and women. Many of them are foreigners, who come to learn the English language. The adults show as much eagerness to learn as the younger pupils. All are generally neat in person, though their clothing may be rough and worn. Sometime ago, a member of the Board of Education, in addressing one of these evening classes, dwelt especially upon the necessity of cultivating habits of personal neatness. It happened that there were several men present, whose appearance indicated that they had come directly from their work to the school. One of them arose, and offered the following excuse for their appearance. He said, " We don't always come to school in this way, but we were at work in the yard pretty late, and had no time to go home for supper even, as we didn't want to be late at school ; and not expecting any visitors, we made up our minds to come as we were. The Principal knows us, and we knew he would excuse us for coming so."

An Evening High School, for males only, has been established, at which working men, and others unable to attend the day schools, may pursue a more extended course of study. English grammar, mathematics, natural science, drawing, navigation, municipal and constitutional law, phonography, declamation, book-keeping, Latin, French, German, and Spanish are embraced in the course. The students may pursue one or more studies, as they may desire.

The Mission Schools have been mentioned already.

II.

THE COLLEGES.

THE higher institutions of learning are numerous, but we can mention only the principal here.

The University of the City of New York was established in 1831, and is regarded as one of the best institutions of its kind in the country. It has a chancellor and a full corps of professors in its several schools. It includes a preparatory department, a grammar school, a school of art, a school of civil engineering, a school of analytical and practical chemistry, a school of medicine, and a school of law. The medical school has been especially famous, and has numbered among its professors, at various times, such men as Valentine Mott, John W. Draper, and William H. Van Buren.

The University building is a showy edifice of white marble, in the English collegiate style of architecture, and is situated on the east side of Washington Square, between Waverley and East Washington Places, fronting on University Place. It has a frontage of 200 feet and a depth of 100 feet. The principal entrance is by the central door. From this a flight of marble

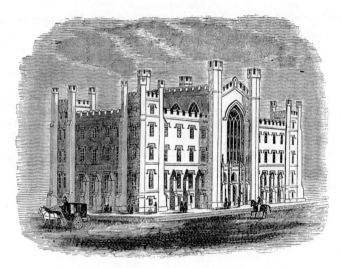

UNIVERSITY OF NEW YORK.

steps leads to the main floor. Besides the rooms used for the various purposes of the University, there is a handsome chapel, and a hall containing a valuable library. Many of the rooms of the building are occupied by physicians, artists, and various societies, and as chambers by single men.

Columbia College, occupying the block bounded by Madison and Fourth avenues, and Forty-ninth and Fiftieth streets, is the oldest institution of learning in the State, and ranks among the leading institutions of the country. It was founded by George II., in 1754, under the title of King's College. The college was originally located in the lower part of the city, but, in 1849, the trustees purchased the present buildings, which were formerly used by the State Institution for Deaf Mutes. Attached to the college is a school of mines, in which full instruction is given in all the branches required to make a perfect scientific as well as a practical mining engineer. Large and extensive laboratories are attached to the school. There is also a law school, which forms a portion of the college, and which is located in Lafayette Place, opposite the Astor Library. The College of Physicians and Surgeons, at the corner of Twenty-third street

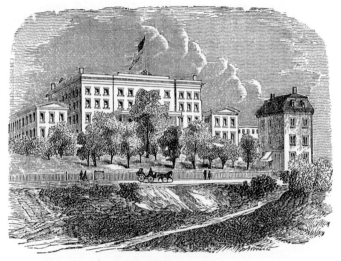

COLUMBIA COLLEGE.

and Fourth avenue, constitutes the medical school of Columbia College. The college is very wealthy, and its property is valued at several millions of dollars.

The other colleges are, the College of St. Francis Xavier, in West Fifteenth street, the Union Theological Seminary, conducted by the Presbyterian Church, the College of Pharmacy, the New York Medical College for Women, the New York College of Veterinary Surgeons, the General Theological Seminary of the Protestant Episcopal Church, the Rutgers Female College, the New York Homœopathic College, several other medical colleges, and several business colleges.

There are about 325 private and sectarian schools and academies in New York, with an average annual attendance of about 15,000 or 20,000 pupils, and employing more than 1500 teachers.

The Cooper Institute is an imposing edifice of brown stone, occupying the block bounded by Third and Fourth avenues, and Seventh and Eighth streets. It was erected at a cost of nearly half a million dollars, by Peter Cooper, Esq., an emi-

43

THE COOPER INSTITUTE.

nent merchant of New York. The basement is occupied by an immense lecture room, capable of seating several thousand persons. The street floor is taken up with stores. The floor above this contains a number of offices, and the remainder of the building is occupied by a free library and reading room, and halls for lectures and for study.

The Institute is designed for the gratuitous instruction of the working classes in science, art, telegraphy, English literature, and the foreign languages. One of its departments is a School of Design for women. The course is thorough and the standard of proficiency is high. The examinations are very searching, and it may be safely asserted, that the graduates of this institution are thoroughly grounded in the practical arts and sciences. The institution is a noble monument to the wisdom and benevolence of its founder, and is doing an immense amount of good to the class he designed to benefit. It is liberally endowed, and is managed by a Board of Directors. The stores and offices yield an annual income of nearly $30,000. The annual attendance upon the schools is about 1800.

LVII.

JEROME PARK.

"THE opening of the Central Park saved horseflesh in New York," said an old jockey. Few who know the truth will gainsay this assertion. The opening of Jerome Park did as much for "horseflesh" by rescuing the sport of horse racing from the blackguards and thieves, into whose hands it had fallen, and placing it upon a respectable footing.

The Jerome Park Race Course owes its existence to Mr. Leonard W. Jerome, after whom it was named. The way in which it came into existence at all, was as follows: "The trains of the New York and New Haven Railroad enter the Metropolis upon the Harlem track. Justified by highly satisfactory reasons, the management of the Company decided to secure a different means of ingress to the city, and a tacit agreement was made with Leonard W. Jerome to the effect that if he would secure the right of way from the proper terminus of the New Haven Road clear through to New York, they would change their route. The firm at once bought all the land they could find along a strip of nine miles through Westchester County, up what is known as the Saw-Mill River Valley. Some portion of their purchase cost them at the rate of $300 an acre. Meanwhile Commodore Vanderbilt got news of the movement, bought largely of the New Haven stock, and at the succeeding election of directors was able to make such changes in the board as effectually estopped the change of base from the Harlem Line. The contract on which Jerome had acted was not in such a form as admitted of litigation. He had acquired an immense amount of real estate with no prospect of immediate realizations. Then came the idea of the race-course. Not less than $100,000 was cleared as net profit from that expedient. Another portion of the land was sold as a cemetery. But Jerome has the greater part of the property still on his hands."

The race-course is the property of the American Jockey Club, and the Spring and Fall Meetings of that association are held there, and are attended by large and fashionable crowds. The Club House and Club Stand occupy the most retired and elevated portion of the grounds, but the best point of view is the Grand Stand, in front of which is the usual starting point and winning post. The price of admission is high, but the grounds are thronged with vehicles and persons on foot. As many as ten or fifteen thousand persons may be seen within the enclosure, while the favorable positions outside of the grounds are black with more economical spectators. The crowd is orderly and good-humored, and the occasion is rarely marred by any act of rowdyism or lawlessness.

A great deal of money changes hands at the races. Bets are freely offered and taken on the various horses. The pools sell rapidly, and the genial auctioneer finds his post no sinecure. The struggles of the noble animals are watched with the deepest interest. The greatest excitement prevails amongst the *élite* in the private stands, as well as throughout the common herd below. Every eye is strained to watch the swift coursers as they whirl down the track, and when the quarter stretch is gained the excitement is beyond control. The victor steed flashes with lightning speed by the winning post amidst a storm of cheers and yells of delight.

The course is still new, but the system which it has inaugurated is becoming more thorough every year. The management is in the hands of gentlemen of character, who are seeking to make at least one place in the country where the blackguards and reckless gamblers who disgrace the American turf shall be powerless to control affairs. The benefits of this management will be very great. The stock of the State will be vastly improved, and the metropolis, especially, will be able to boast some of the finest blooded racers in the world.

LVIII.

COMMODORE VANDERBILT.

VISITORS to the Central Park on pleasant afternoons, rarely fail to notice a light buggy, generally with a single occupant, drawn by a pair of fine horses, whose whole appearance is indicative of their high breeding and great speed. The animals would command attention anywhere, and the driver would excite equal notice, for all are physically among the finest specimens of their kind to be met with in the country. The man is almost seventy-eight years of age, but he looks twenty years younger. He is large of frame, tall, erect, and with a face as handsome and as cold as a statue. He is one of the best known men in the country, and he is called Cornelius Vanderbilt.

He was born on Staten Island, May 27th, 1794. His father was a boatman, who had acquired money enough by attention to his business to purchase and stock a farm, on which the subject of this sketch passed his boyhood. Many interesting stories are told of Vanderbilt's boyhood, showing an early development of the vigorous traits which have marked his maturer life. His passion for horses seems to have been born with him. In his seventeenth year he became a boatman in New York harbor, devoting himself to the task of rowing passengers about or across the harbor in his own boat. He displayed great energy and determination, and not a little genius, in this calling, and earned money rapidly and steadily. At the age of nineteen he married. In 1815, having saved money enough, he built a fine schooner, and in the winter embarked in the coasting trade, going as far south as Charleston, S. C., but continuing to ply his boat in the harbor during the summer. By the time he was twenty-four years old, he had saved nine thousand dollars, and had built several small vessels.

In 1818, he suddenly abandoned his flourishing business, and accepted the command of a steamboat, with a salary of one thousand dollars. His friends were greatly astonished at this step, and remonstrated with him warmly, but without shaking his resolution. He had the sagacity to perceive that the steamboats were about to revolutionize the whole system of water transportation, and he meant to secure a foothold in the new order of affairs without delay. The result vindicated his wisdom.

The steamer which he commanded was one of a line plying between New York and New Brunswick—the old route to Philadelphia. This line was conducted by Mr. Thomas Gibbons, and was warmly opposed by the representatives of Fulton and Livingston, who claimed a monopoly of the right to navigate the waters of New York by steam. Gibbons was effectively supported by Vanderbilt, who ran his boat regularly in spite of all efforts made to stop him, until the courts sustained him in his rights. Then Vanderbilt was allowed to control the line in his own way, and conducted it with such success that it paid Gibbons an annual profit of forty thousand dollars.

In 1829, at the age of thirty-five, he left the service of Mr. Gibbons, and for the second time began life on his own account. He built a small steamer, called the " Caroline," and commanded her himself. In a few years he was the owner of several small steamers plying between New York and the neighboring towns. Thus began his remarkable career as a steamboat owner, which was one unbroken round of prosperity. He eventually became the most important man in the steamboat interest of the country. He has owned or has had an interest in one hundred steam vessels—hence his title of Commodore—and has been instrumental in a greater degree than any other man, in bringing down the tariff of steamboat fares. He has never lost a vessel by fire, by explosion, or a wreck. His " North Star " and " Vanderbilt " were famous steamships in their day, and in the latter he made an extended tour to the various ports of Europe.

A year or two before the Civil War, Mr. Vanderbilt began to invest largely in railroad stocks and iron works. He at length secured the control of the Hudson River, Harlem and New York Central Roads, and their dependencies, which made him as important a personage in this branch of our industry as he had been in the steamboat interest. His control of these roads also gave him a commanding influence in the stock market of Wall street, and brought within his reach numerous opportunities for enriching himself by speculations, of which he was not slow to avail himself. Wall street is full of stories concerning him, and it is evident from many of these that he has dealt the dealers there too many hard blows to be popular amongst them.

Mr. Vanderbilt resides in a handsome old-fashioned brick mansion in East Washington Place. His business office is in Fourth street, near Broadway. His wealth is very great, and is generally estimated in the city at over forty millions of dollars. He is said to have a greater command of large sums of ready money than almost any other American capitalist.

Mr. Vanderbilt has been twice married, and is the father of thirteen children—nine daughters and four sons, all the children of his first wife. His grandchildren are numerous.

LIX.

THE BUMMERS.

THE Bummer is simply one who detests work, and who manages to live in some degree of comfort without earning the means of doing so. There are many such in the city. The genuine Bummer is more of a beggar than a thief, though he will steal if he has an opportunity. Nothing will induce him to go to work, not even the prospect of starvation. He has a sublime confidence in his ability to get through life easily and lazily, and his greatest horror is the probability of falling into the hands of the police, and being sent to Blackwell's Island as a vagrant. All that he desires is money enough to gratify a few actual wants, food enough to eat, clothing to cover his nakedness, and a place where he can enjoy the warmth of a fire in the winter. He has great faith in the charitableness of New York, and thinks that any of the necessities of life may be had here for the asking, and he does not hesitate to ask for them. You would wound him deeply by calling him a beggar. He never begs, he only *asks*. He asks bread of the baker, or from the housekeepers of the city, and obtains his clothing in the same way. If he wants a little pocket money, he does not hesitate to ask for it from the passers-by on the streets. He never spends money on food. Such a use of " the needful " is a deadly sin in his eyes. Money was made to furnish him with cheap whiskey and bad tobacco. It is too easy to obtain food by asking for it to think of buying it. If he does not receive enough to satisfy his hunger at one house, he goes to another, and repeats his efforts until he is satisfied. One hates to refuse food to any human being who claims to have need of it, and the Bummer knows this. Some of these people keep lists of various householders, with a memorandum attached to each name, showing the best hours for calling, and the nature of the articles that will probably be given.   They assist each other by information as to the charitably disposed, and should any householder display any degree of liberality toward them, he is sure to be overrun by a host of seedy and hungry Bummers.

A few years ago, the City Hall Park, which was then shaded by noble old trees, and the Battery, were the favorite resorts of this class in fair weather.   They would sit on the benches of the park, and doze, or, when very sleepy, would lie at full length upon them, until aroused by a blow from a policeman's club upon the soles of their shoes.   They were not allowed to sleep in the park, and when caught in the act were compelled to join the throng of promenaders in Broadway, and "move on." At the Battery they were rarely disturbed.   That locality was then a mere receptacle for trash, and the Bummer was at home there.   The dirt heaps were softer than the stones, and the breeze that came in from the bay was highly favorable to slumber.   Now, all has been changed.   The massive edifice of the New Post-office covers the old resort of the Bummer, and the Battery has been made so spruce and trim that it needs not the gruff voice of the gray-coated guardian of the place to make the Bummer feel that it is lost to him forever.

During the day, the Bummer roams about the city, resting where he can, and occasionally dropping into a bar-room to fill himself with five-cent whiskey.   He is not averse to receiving a treat, and it should be mentioned to his credit that he is always ready to treat his friends to his favorite drink when he is in funds.   When hungry, he "asks" for food.   He is fond of visiting the second-rate theatres at the expense of somebody else, and hangs around them, hoping some one will give him a check before the performance is over.   In mild weather, he will sleep almost anywhere, in or around a market house, or in an empty wagon.   The hay-barges in North River afford comfortable beds, and many Bummers occupy them.   In wet or cold weather, the Bummer patronizes the cheap lodging-houses, or the cellars, and as a last resort applies for shelter at the station house.   He is diffident about asking assistance at the last place, however, for he has a vague idea that the police would be only too glad to get him safely lodged on the Island.   One of his favorite amusements is attendance upon the police courts.   This affords him a few hours of rest in a comfortable place, and furnishes him with material for thought.

In begging, the Bummer never asks boldly for aid.   He always prefaces his request with a pitiful story of misfortune, and expresses his sense of shame at being an able-bodied man and yet compelled to "ask" for assistance.   He is an adept at deceiving good-hearted people, and very clever at assuming the air of innocent misfortune.   Thus he supplies his wants.

In his confidential moments, he readily admits that "Bumming" is a hard life, but he is confident that it is better than working for a living.   You cannot induce him to accept any species of employment, however light.   Vagrancy has a strange fascination for him, and he will be nothing but what he is until five-cent whiskey sinks him to a grade still lower.   Sometimes he sees his doom afar off, and anticipates it by seeking the cold waters of the East River.   At the best, suicide is the happiest end he can hope for, and it does not require much exertion to drown oneself.   Should he allow events to take their natural course, there is but one prospect before him—a pauper's death and the dissecting-table.

Some of these men have had fair starts in life.   Some of them are well educated, and could have risen to eminence in some useful calling.   A fondness for liquor and a disinclination to work have been their ruin.

LX.

TENEMENT HOUSE LIFE.

THE peculiar formation of the island of Manhattan renders it impossible for the city to expand save in one direction.   On the south, east, and west its growth is checked by the waters of the rivers and bay, so that it can increase only to the north-ward.   The lower part of the island is being occupied for busi-ness purposes more and more exclusively every year, and the people are being forced higher up town.   Those who remain in the extreme lower portion for purposes of residence are simply the very poor.   Those who can afford to do so, seek locations removed as far as is convenient to them from the business sec-tion.   The laboring class, by which I mean all who are forced to pursue some regular occupation for their support, are not able to go far from their work, and are obliged to remain in locations which will enable them to reach their places of busi-ness with as little delay as possible.

Consequently the bulk of the population is packed into that portion of the city which lies between the City Hall and Four-teenth street.   By the United States Census of 1870, the popu-lation of the wards in this district was reported as follows:

Wards.	Natives.	Foreigners.	Total.
4	10,456	13,292	23,748
5	9,245	7,905	17,150
6	9,444	11,709	21,153
7	24,130	20,688	44,818
8	20,285	14,628	34,913
9	33,020	14,589	47,609
10	18,851	22,580	41.431
11	34,805	29,425	64,230
13	19,288	14,076	33,364
14	13,379	13,057	26,436
15	16,821	10,766	27,587
17	46,033	49,332	95,365
Total	255,757	222,047	477,804

A NEW YORK TENEMENT HOUSE.

By the same census, the total population of the city in 1870 was 942,292.   The district included in the above wards is about two miles square, which would give for this portion of New York an average population of 238,902 to the mile square. The Seventeenth ward covers less than one-fortieth of the whole area of the island, and contains more than one-tenth of the whole population.

The total area of the city is twenty-two square miles, and we find that one-half of its population is cramped within an area of about four square miles.   It is evident, therefore, that they must be housed in a very small number of buildings, and such indeed is the case.

The section of the city embraced in the wards we have named is filled with a class of buildings called tenement houses.   The law classes all dwellings containing three or more families as tenement houses, but the true tenement house is an institution peculiar to New York.   There are about 70,000 buildings in the city used for purposes of business and as dwellings, and of these, 20,000 are tenement houses, containing about 160,000 families, or about 500,000 people.   This would give an average population of eight families or twenty persons to each tenement house in the city.   In 1867 the number of tenement houses was 18,582.   The following table will show their distribution among the wards at that time, and their sanitary condition:

Wards.	Tenement Houses, No. of.	In Bad Sanitary Condition from Any Cause.	Wards.	Tenement Houses, No. of.	In Bad Sanitary Condition from Any Cause.
1	275	175	13	550	275
2	—	—	14	550	346
3	40	24	15	200	132
4	500	300	16	1300	433
5	300	180	17	2395	1138
6	600	360	18 and 21	2276	1516
7	1847	890	19	761	380
8	850	546	20	1250	417
9	650	434	22	1200	800
10	430	196			
11	2400	1200	Total	18,582	9846
12	208	104			

The reader will no doubt suppose that the inmates of these houses are compelled to remain in them because of extreme poverty. This is not the case. The tenement houses are occupied mainly by the honest laboring population of New York, who receive fair wages for their work. They herd here because the rents of single houses are either out of proportion to, or beyond their means, and because they are convenient to their work. They are not paupers, but they cannot afford the fearful cost of a separate home, and they are forced to resort to this mode of life in order to live with any degree of comfort. Many of the most skilled mechanics, many of the best paid operatives of both sexes, who are earning comfortable wages, are forced to live in these vast barracks, simply because the bare rent of an empty house in a moderately decent neighbórhood, is from $1000 upward. Did the city possess some means of rapid transit between its upper and lower extremities, which would prevent the loss of the time now wasted in traversing the length of the island, there can be no doubt that the tenement sections would soon be thinned out.

There are two classes of tenement houses in the city. Those occupied by the well-to-do working people, and those which are simply the homes of the poor. The first are immense, but spruce looking structures, and are kept cleaner than the latter, but all suffer from the evils incident to and inseparable from such close packing. Those of the second class are simply dens of vice and misery. In the older quarters of the city, many of the old time residences are now occupied as tenement houses. The old Walton mansion in Pearl street, opposite the vast establishment of Harper & Brothers, was once the most elegant and hospitable mansion in New York. It is now one of the most wretched tenement houses in the city. The tenement houses of the upper wards, however, were constructed for the uses to which they are put. As pecuniary investments they pay well, the rents sometimes yielding as much as thirty per cent. on the investment. One of them shall serve as a description of the average tenement house. The building stands on a lot with a front of 50 feet, and a depth of 250 feet. It has an alley running the whole depth on each side of it. These alley-ways are excavated to the depth of the cellars, arched over, and covered with flag stones, in which, at intervals, are open gratings to give light below; the whole length of which space is occupied by water closets, without doors, and under which are open drains communicating with the street sewers. The building is five stories high, and has a flat roof. The only ventilation is by a window, which opens against a dead wall eight feet distant, and to which rises the vapor from the vault below. There is water on each floor, and gas pipes are laid through the building, so that those who desire it can use gas. The building contains 126 families, or about 700 inhabitants. Each family has a narrow sitting-room, which is used also for working and eating, and a closet called a bed room. But few of the rooms are properly ventilated. The sun never shines in at the windows, and if the sky is overcast the rooms are so dark as to need artificial light. The whole house is dirty, and is filled with the mingled odors from the cooking-stoves and the sinks. In the winter the rooms are kept too close by the stoves, and in the summer the natural heat is made tenfold greater by the fires for cooking and washing. Pass these houses on a hot night, and you will see the streets in front of them filled with the occupants, and every window choked up with human heads, all panting and praying for relief and fresh air. Sometimes the families living in the close rooms we have described, take " boarders," who pay a part of the expenses of the " establishment." Formerly the occupants of these buildings emptied their filth and refuse matter into the public streets, which in these quarters were simply horrible to behold ; but of late years, the police, by compelling a rigid observance of the sanitary laws, have greatly improved the condition of the houses and streets, and consequently the health of the people. During the past winter, however, many of the East side streets have become horribly filthy.

The reader must not suppose that the house just described is an exceptional establishment. In the Eleventh and Seventeenth wards whole streets, for many blocks, are lined with similar houses. There are many single blocks of dwellings containing

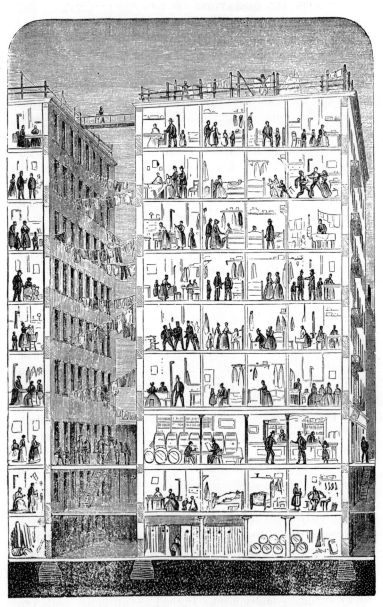

AN INSIDE VIEW OF A TENEMENT HOUSE.

twice the number of families residing on Fifth avenue, on both sides of that street, from Washington Square to the Park, or than a continuous row of dwellings similar to those on Fifth avenue, three or four miles in length. The Fourth ward, covering an area of 83 acres, contains 23,748 inhabitants.   The city of Springfield (Massachusetts), contains 26,703 inhabitants.   The Eleventh ward, comprising 196 acres, contains more people than the cities of Mobile (Alabama), and Salem (Massachusetts), combined.   The Seventh ward, covering 110 acres, contains more inhabitants than the city of Syracuse (New York).   The Seventeenth ward, covering 331 acres, contains more inhabitants than the city of Cleveland (Ohio), which is the fifteenth city in the Union in respect of population.

The best of the tenement houses are uncomfortable.   Where so large a number of people are gathered under the same roof to live as they please, it is impossible to keep the premises clean. A very large portion of them are in bad repair and in equally bad sanitary condition.   In 1867 these houses made up fifty-two per cent. of the whole number, and there is no reason to believe that there has been any improvement since then.   Many of them are simply appalling.   They become more wretched and squalid as the East River and Five Points sections are reached.   Cherry, Water, and the neighboring streets, are little better than charnel houses.

About three months ago one of the most wretched rookeries in the city was cleared out and cleansed by order of the Board of Health.   This was known as "Sweeney's," and stood in Gotham Court.   The immediate cause of its overhauling was the discovery of its actual condition made by Detective Finn and Mr. Edward Crapsey of the New York *Times*, during a visit to it.   Mr. Crapsey gives the following interesting account of his visit:

"As we stopped in Cherry street at the entrance to Gotham Court, and Detective Finn dug a tunnel of light with his bulls-eye lantern into the foulness and blackness of that smirch on civilization, a score or more of boys who had been congregated at the edge of the court suddenly plunged back into the ob-

44

scurity, and we heard the splash of their feet in the foul collections of the pavements.

" 'This bullseye is an old acquaintance here,' said the detective, 'and as its coming most always means "somebody wanted," you see how they hide. Though why they should object to go to jail is more than I know; I'd rather stay in the worst dungeon in town than here. Come this way and I'll show you why.'

" Carefully keeping in the little track of light cut into the darkness by the lantern, I followed the speaker, who turned into the first door on the right, and I found myself in an entry about four feet by six, with steep, rough, rickety stairs leading upward in the foreground, and their counterparts at the rear giving access to as successful a manufactory of disease and death as any city on earth can show. Coming to the first of these stairs, I was peremptorily halted by the foul stenches rising from below; but Finn, who had reached the bottom, threw back the relentless light upon the descending way and urged me on. Every step oozed with moisture and was covered sole deep with unmentionable filth; but I ventured on, and reaching my conductor, stood in a vault some twelve feet wide and two hundred long, which extended under the whole of West Gotham Court. The walls of rough stone dripped with slimy exudations, while the pavements yielded to the slightest pressure of the feet a suffocating odor compounded of bilge-water and sulphuretted hydrogen. Upon one side of this elongated cave of horrors were ranged a hundred closets, every one of which reeked with this filth, mixed with that slimy moisture which was everywhere as a proof that the waters of the neighboring East River penetrated, and lingered here to foul instead of purify.

" 'What do you think of this?' said Finn, throwing the light of his lantern hither and thither so that every horror might be dragged from the darkness that all seemed to covet. ' All the thousands living in the barracks must come here, and just think of all the young ones above that never did any harm having to take in this stuff;' and the detective struck out spitefully at the noxious air. As he did so, the gurgling of water at the Cherry street end of the vault caught his ear, and penetrating thither, he peered curiously about.

"'I say, Tom,' he called back to his companion, who had remained with me in the darkness, 'here's a big break in the Croton main.' But a moment later, in an affrighted voice: 'No, it ain't. Its the sewer! I never knew of this opening into it before. Paugh! how it smells. That's nothing up where you are. I'll bet on the undertaker having more jobs in the house than ever.'

"By this time I began to feel sick and faint in that tainted air, and would have rushed up the stairs if I could have seen them. But Finn was exploring that sewer horror with his lantern. As I came down I had seen a pool of stagnant, green-coated water somewhere near the foot of the stairs, and, being afraid to stir in the thick darkness, was forced to call my guide, and, frankly state the urgent necessity for an immediate return above. The matter-of-fact policeman came up, and cast the liberating light upon the stairs, but rebuked me as I eagerly took in the comparatively purer atmosphere from above. 'You can't stand it five minutes; how do you suppose they do, year in and year out?' 'Even they don't stand it many years, I should think,' was my involuntary reply.

"As we stepped out into the court again, the glare of the bullseye dragged a strange face out of the darkness. It was that of a youth of eighteen or twenty years, ruddy, puffed, with the corners of the mouth grotesquely twisted. The detective greeted the person owning this face with the fervor of old acquaintanceship: 'Eh, Buster! What's up?' 'Hello, Jimmy Finn! What yez doin' here?' 'Never mind, Buster. What's up?' 'Why, Jimmy, didn't yez know I lodges here now?' 'No, I didn't. Where? Who with?' 'Beyant, wid the Pensioner.' 'Go on. Show me where you lodge.' 'Sure, Jimmy, it isn't me as would lie to yez.'

"But I had expressed a desire to penetrate into some of these kennels for crushed humanity; and Finn, with the happy acumen of his tribe, seizing the first plausible pretext, was relentless, and insisted on doubting the word of the Buster.

That unfortunate with the puffy face, who seemed to know his man too well to protract resistance, puffed ahead of us up the black, oozy court, with myriads of windows made ghastly by the pale flicker of kerosene lamps in tiers above us, until he came to the last door but one upon the left side of the court, over which the letter S was sprawled upon the coping stone. The bullseye had been darkened, and when the Buster plunged through the doorway he was lost to sight in the impenetrable darkness beyond. We heard him though, stumbling against stairs that creaked dismally, and the slide being drawn back, the friendly light made clear the way for him and us. There was an entry pecisely like the one we had entered before, with a flight of narrow, almost perpendicular stairs, with so sharp a twist in them that we could see only half up. The banisters in sight had precisely three uprights, and looked as if the whole thing would crumble at a touch; while the stairs were so smooth and thin with the treading of innumerable feet that they almost refused a foothold. Following the Buster, who grappled with the steep and dangerous ascent with the daring born of habit, I somehow got up stairs, wondering how any one ever got down in the dark without breaking his neck. Thinking it possible there might be a light sometimes to guide the pauper hosts from their hazardous heights to the stability of the street, I inquired as to the fact, only to meet the contempt of the Buster for the gross ignorance that could dictate such a question. ' A light for the stairs! Who'd give it? Sweeney? Not much! Or the tenants? Skasely! Them's too poor!' While he mut- tered, the Buster had pawed his way up stairs with sur- prising agility, until he reached a door on the third land- ing. Turning triumphantly to the detective, he announced: ' Here's where I lodges, Jimmy! You knows I wouldn't lie to yez.'

" ' We'll see whether you would or no,' said Finn, tapping on the door. Being told to come in, he opened it; and on this trivial but dexterous pretext we invaded the sanctity of a home.

" No tale is so good as one plainly told, and I tell precisely what I saw.   This home was composed, in the parlance of the place, of a ' room and bedroom.'   The room was about twelve feet square, and eight feet from floor to ceiling.   It had two windows opening upon the court, and a large fireplace filled with a cooking stove.   In the way of additional furniture, it had a common deal table, three broken wooden chairs, a few dishes and cooking utensils, and two ' shakedowns,' as the piles of straw stuffed into bed-ticks are called ; but it had nothing whatever beyond these articles.   There was not even the remnant of a bedstead ; not a cheap print, so common in the hovels of the poor, to relieve the blankness of the rough, whitewashed walls. The bedroom, which was little more than half the size of the other, was that outrage of capital upon poverty known as a ' dark room,' by which is meant that it had no window opening to the outer air ; and this closet had no furniture whatever except two ' shakedowns.'

" In the contracted space of these two rooms, and supplied with these scanty appliances for comfort, nine human beings were stowed.   First there was the ' Pensioner,' a man of about thirty-five years, next his wife, then their three children, a woman lodger with two children, and the ' Buster,' the latter paying fifteen cents per night for his shelter ; but I did not learn the amount paid by the woman for the accommodation of herself and children.   The Buster, having been indignant at my inquiry as to the light upon the stairs, was now made merry by Finn supposing he had a regular bed and bedstead for the money.   ' Indade, he has not, but a " shakedown " like the rest of us,' said the woman ; but the Buster rebuked this assumption of an impossible prosperity by promptly exclaiming, ' Whist! ye knows I stretch on the boords without any shakedown whatsumdever.'

" Finn was of opinion the bed was hard but healthy, and fixing his eyes on the Buster's flabby face thought it possible he had any desirable number of ' square meals ' per day ; but that individual limited his acquirements in that way for the day then closed to four.   Finn then touching on the number of drinks, the Buster, being driven into conjecture and a corner by the problem, was thrust out of the foreground of our investigations.

"By various wily tricks of his trade, Detective Finn managed to get a deal of information out of the Pensioner without seeming to be either inquisitive or intrusive, or even without rubbing the coat of his poverty the wrong way.   From this source I learned that five dollars per month was paid as rent for these two third-floor rooms, and that everybody concerned deemed them dirt cheap at the price.   Light was obtained from kerosene lamps at the expense of the tenant, and water had to be carried from the court below, while all refuse matter not emptied into the court itself, had to be taken to the foul vaults beneath it.   The rooms, having all these drawbacks, and being destitute of the commonest appliances for comfort or decency, did not appear to be in the highest degree eligible; yet the Pensioner considered himself fortunate in having secured them. His experience in living must have been very doleful, for he declared that he had seen worse places.   In itself, and so far as the landlord was concerned, I doubted him; but I had myself seen fouler places than these two rooms, which had been made so by the tenants.   All that cleanliness could do to make the kennel of the Pensioner habitable had been done, and I looked with more respect upon the uncouth woman who had scoured the rough floor white, than I ever had upon a gaudily attired dame sweeping Broadway with her silken trail.   The thrift that had so little for its nourishment had not been expended wholly upon the floor, for I noticed that the two children asleep on the shakedown were clean, while the little fellow four years of age, who was apparently prepared for bed as he was entirely naked, but sat as yet upon one of the three chairs, had no speck of dirt upon his fair white skin.   A painter should have seen him as he gazed wonderingly upon us, and my respect deepened for the woman who could, spite the hard lines of her rugged life, bring forth and preserve so much of childish symmetry and beauty.

"Having absorbed these general facts, I turned to the master of this household.   He was a man of small stature but rugged frame, and his left shirt sleeve dangled empty at his side. That adroit Finn, noticing my inquiring look, blurted out: ' That arm went in a street accident, I suppose?'

"' No, sir; it wint at the battle of Spottsylvania.'

"Here was a hero!   The narrow limits of his humble home expanded to embrace the brown and kneaded Virginian glades as I saw them just seven years ago, pictured with the lurid pageantry of that stubborn fight when Sedgwick fell. This man, crammed with his family into twelve feet square at the top of Sweeney's Shambles, was once part of that glorious scene.   In answer to my test questions he said he belonged to the Thirty-ninth New York, which was attached to the Second Corps, and that he received a pension of $15 per month from the grateful country he had served as payment in full for an arm.   It was enough to keep body and soul together, and he could not complain.   Nor could I; but I could and did signify to my guide by a nod that I had seen and heard enough, and we went down again into the slimy, reeking court."

There is a square on the East side bounded by Houston, Stanton, Pitt, and Willett streets.   It contains a group of three front and seven rear houses, and is known as "Rag-pickers' Row."   These ten houses contain a total of 106 families, or 452 persons.   All these persons are rag-pickers, or more properly chiffonniers, for their business is to pick up every thing saleable they can find in the streets.   Formerly they brought their gatherings to this place and assorted them here before taking them to the junk stores to sell them.   Now, however, they assort them elsewhere, and their wretched dwellings are as clean as it is possible to keep them.   They are generally peaceable and quiet, and their quarrels are commonly referred to the agent in charge of the row, who decides them to their satisfaction.   They are very industrious in their callings, and some of them have money in the Savings banks.   Nearly all who have children send them to the Mission Schools.

The Board of Health, in one of their recent publications, express themselves as follows:

"The worst class of tenement houses was those where a landlord had accommodations for ten families, and these buildings comprise more than half of the tenement houses of the city, and accommodate fully two-thirds of the entire tenement-house population. When the number of families living under one owner exceeded ten, it was found that such owner was engaged in the keeping of a tenement-house as a business, and generally as a speculator. It is among this class of owners that nearly all the evils of the tenement-house system are found. The little colony exhibit in their rooms, and in the little areas around their dwellings, extreme want of care. The street in front of the place was reeking with slops and garbage; the alleys and passage ways were foul with excrements; the court was imperfectly paved, wet, and covered with domestic refuse; the privies, located in a close court between the rear and front houses, were dilapidated, and gave out volumes of noisome odors, which filled the whole area, and were diffused through all the rooms opening upon it; and the halls and apartments of the wretched occupants were close, unventilated, and unclean. The complaint was universal among the tenants that they are entirely uncared for, and that the only answer to their request to have the place put in order, by repairs and necessary improvements, was, that they must pay their rent or leave. Inquiry often disclosed the fact that the owner of the property was a wealthy gentleman or lady, either living in an aristocratic part of the city or in a neighboring city, or, as was occasionally found to be the case, in Europe. The property is usually managed entirely by an agent, whose instructions are simple, but emphatic, viz., 'collect the rent in advance, or, failing, eject the occupants.' The profits on this sort of property, so administered, are rarely less than fifteen per cent., and more generally thirty per cent. upon the investment."

The evils of the tenement house system are almost incalculable. It is the experience of all nations that barrack life is demoralizing, and the tenement house is but a barrack without the rigid discipline of a military establishment. Its inmates know no such thing as privacy. Home is but a word with them. They have habitations, but not homes. Within the same walls are gathered the virtuous and the depraved, the honest laborer and the thief. There can be no such thing as shielding the young from improper outside influences. They have every opportunity to become thoroughly corrupted without leaving the house. Decency is impossible. Families exist in the greatest amount of personal discomfort, and the children take every opportunity to escape from the house into the streets. The tenement houses every year send many girls into the ranks of the street walkers, and a greater number of young men into the ranks of the roughs and thieves.

Drunkenness is very common among the inhabitants of these houses. Men and women are literally driven into intemperance by the discomfort in which they live. Nearly all the domestic murders occuring in the city are perpetrated in the tenement houses. Immorality is very common. Indeed, the latter crime is the logical result of such dense packing of the sexes. It is a terrible thing to contemplate, but it is a fact that one half of the population of this great city is subjected to the demoralizing influences of these vast barracks. The laboring class, who should constitute the backbone and sinew of the community, are thus degraded to a level with paupers, forced to herd among them, and to adopt a mode of life which is utterly destructive of the characteristics which should distinguish them. It is no wonder that crime is so common in the Metropolis. The real wonder is that it does not defy all restraint.

The tenement houses are afflicted with a terrible mortality. Says Dr. Harris, " Consumption and all the inflammatory diseases of the lungs vie with the infectious and other zymotic disorders, in wasting the health and destroying the life of the tenement population." Of late years a new disease, the relapsing fever, which, though rarely fatal, destroys the health and vigor of its victims, has made havoc among the tenement population. The mortality among children is very great, and perhaps this is fortunate for them, for it would seem that death in

their first flush of innocence is far better than a life of wretchedness and perhaps of infamy. Small pox and all the contagious
and infectious diseases would make short work with the tenement-house population, were any of them to become epidemic in
the city.   There would be nothing to check them, and the unfortunate people living in these sections would find no means
of escaping from them.

LXI.

CHATHAM STREET.

THE oldest inhabitant cannot remember when Chatham
street did not exist.   It still contains many half decayed houses
which bear witness to its antiquity.   It begins at City Hall
Place, and ends at Chatham Square.   It is not over a quarter
of a mile in length, and is narrow and dirty.   The inhabitants
are principally Jews and low class foreigners.   Near the lower
end are one or two good restaurants, and several cheap hotels,
but the remainder of the street is taken up with establishments
into which respectable buyers do not care to venture.   Cheap
lodging houses abound, pawnbrokers are numerous, several
fence stores are to be found here, and some twenty or twenty-
five cellars are occupied as dance houses and concert saloons.
These are among the lowest and vilest of their kind in New
York.

Chatham street is the paradise of dealers in mock jewelry
and old clothes.   Some of the shops sell new clothing of an
inferior quality, but old clothes do most abound.   Here you
may find the cast-off finery of the wife of a millionaire—the
most of it stolen—or the discarded rags of a pauper.   It seems
as if all New York had placed its cast-off clothing here for sale,
and that the stock had accumulated for generations.   Who the
dealers sell to is a mystery.   You see them constantly inviting
trade, but you rarely see a customer within their doors.

Honesty is a stranger in Chatham street, and any one making
a purchase here must expect to be cheated.   The streets running
off to the right and left lead to the Five Points and similar
sections, and it is this wretched portion of the city that supports
trade in Chatham street.   The horse car lines of the east side

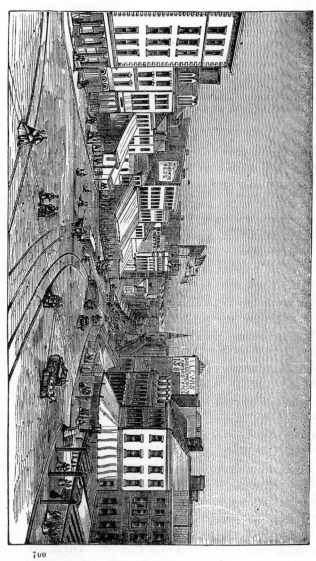

CHATHAM SQUARE.

palace or mansion to the rear. There are pla...

ed to the rear and put up in the Five Points and othe...

sections of our city, in their smaller section of blocks that wou...

to the Chatham Street. The figures (710) of the...

pass through the entire length of the street, and the heaviest portion of the city travel flows through it, but respectable people rarely leave the cars in this dirty thoroughfare, and are heartily glad when they are well out of it. The buildings are generally old and dilapidated. The shops are low and dark. They are rank with foul odors, and are suggestive of disease. The men and women who conduct them look like convicts, and as they sit in their doorways watching for custom, they seem more like wild beasts waiting for their prey, than like human beings. Even the children have a keener, more disreputable appearance here than elsewhere. The lowest class Jews abound in this vile quarter, and filthy creatures they are.

The Chatham street merchants are shrewd dealers, and never suffer an opportunity to make a penny to pass by unimproved. They are not particular as to the character of the transaction. They know they are never expected to sell honestly, and they make it a rule not to disappoint their customers. One of their favorite expedients to create trade in dull times is called a "forced sale." They practise this only on those whom they recognize as strangers, for long experience has enabled them to tell a city man at a glance. A stranger walking along the street will be accosted by the proprietor of a shop and his clerks with offers of "sheap" clothing. If he pauses to listen, he is lost. He is seized by the harpies, who pretend to assist him, and is literally forced into the shop. He may protest that he does not wish to buy anything, but the "merchant" and his clerks will insist that he does, and before he can well help himself, they will haul off his coat, clap one of the store coats on his back, and declare it a "perfect fit." The new coat will then be removed and replaced by the old one, and the victim will be allowed to leave the shop. As he passes out of the door, the new coat is thrust under his arm, and he is seized by the proprietor and his assistants, who shout "stop thief!" and charge him with stealing the coat. Their noise, and the dread of being arrested upon a charge of theft, will frequently so confuse and frighten the victim that he will comply with their demand, which is that he shall buy the coat. This done he is suffered to depart. A refusal to yield would not injure him, for the scoundrels would seldom dare to call in the police, for fear of getting themselves into trouble with the officials. They have reckoned with certainty, however, upon the stranger's timidity and bewilderment, and know they are safe.

LXII.

JAMES GORDON BENNETT.

JAMES GORDON BENNETT was born at New Mill, Keith, in Banffshire, on the northeastern coast of Scotland, about the year 1800. His relatives were Roman Catholics, and he was destined for the priesthood of that church. He entered the Roman Catholic Seminary at Aberdeen, in 1814, and remained there two years, acquiring the basis of an excellent education. Chance having thrown in his way a copy of Benjamin Franklin's Autobiograpy, he was so much impressed by it that he abandoned all thought of a clerical life, and resolved to emigrate to America, which he did in 1819, arriving in Halifax in May of that year, being then nearly twenty years old. He had not an acquaintance on this side of the Atlantic, had no profession save that of a bookkeeper, and had but twenty-five dollars in his pocket.

He began by giving lessons in bookkeeping, in Halifax, but his success was so poor that he came to the United States, landing at Portland, where he took passage for Boston. Arriving in Boston he found great difficulty in procuring employment, and was reduced to the verge of starvation, but at length obtained a place as a proof-reader. He held this position for two years, and, having lost it by the failure of his employers, came to New York in 1822. Soon after this, he accepted an engagement on the *Charleston* (S. C.) *Courier*, but held it for a short time only. Returning to New York he attempted to organize a Commercial School, but was unsuccessful. He next tried lecturing, with equally bad luck, and was obliged to renew his connection with the press. He held various positions on the New York newspapers, in each and all of which he proved himself a journalist of large ideas and great originality and power.

In 1828, he became the Washington correspondent of the *New York Enquirer,* and in this position inaugurated the style of newspaper correspondence which is now adopted by all the leading journals of the country. He was poorly paid for his services, and was obliged to do an immense amount of miscellaneous literary work in order to earn a bare support. In the autumn of 1829 he became assistant editor of the *Courier and Enquirer,* with James Watson Webb as his chief. In this position he did great service, and really made the success of the paper. He found his position unpleasant, however, and abandoned it in 1832.

He tried several other expedients, all of which were unsuccessful, and even tried to induce Horace Greeley, then a struggling printer, to join him in the establishment of a newspaper. Horace refused, but recommended him to another printer who accepted his proposition. His next step was to rent a cellar in Wall street, and in this cellar, on the 6th of May, 1835, the *New York Herald* was born. The coal vaults of the present *Herald* office are an improvement upon the original office, which was sanctum and counting-house all in one. Mr. Bennett performed all the work on the paper, except setting it up and printing it. He collected the news, wrote the contents, sold the paper, and received advertisements. He worked manfully, but his difficulties were enormous. He made his little journal spicy, attractive, and even impudent—though not indecent, as some have wrongly asserted—in the hope of making it popular. He worked from sixteen to eighteen hours a day, but in spite of all his efforts he lost money until the end of the third month, after which he contrived to pay the actual expense of publication for some time longer. Then a fire destroyed the printing office, and his partners refused to continue their connection with the paper. By almost superhuman efforts he succeeded in securing the means of going on with the *Herald,* and in a short while the "great fire" occurred just in time to save him. It was the most terrible catastrophe that had ever occurred in America, and Bennett resolved to profit by it. He went himself among the ruins, note-book in hand, and the result of his labors was a series of graphic and accurate reports in

the *Herald* of the disaster, that at once created a large demand
for the paper.   This demand did not fall off, but it was not sufficient to place the *Herald* on a successful footing.   At this time,
Mr. Bennett was fortunate enough to secure a large contract
from Dr. Brandreth for advertising his pills in the *Herald*.
The sum received was very large, and was conscientiously expended in the purchase of news, and in improving and increasing the attractions of the paper.   At the end of the fifteenth
month of its career, Mr. Bennett ventured to increase the size
of the *Herald*, and to raise its price from one to two cents.
Since then the paper has prospered steadily, and is now one of
the wealthiest and most powerful journals in the land, and the
best purveyor of news in the world.   Its success is due almost
exclusively to the proprietor.   Mr. Bennett has not only built
up his own paper, but has revolutionized the press of the world.
This is his chief claim to distinction.

He rarely writes for the paper now, though he maintains a
close supervision over all parts of it, as well as over the mechanical department of his enterprise.

He is married, and has two children, a son, James Gordon
Bennett, jr., who will succeed his father in the ownership of the
Herald, and a daughter.   He resides on the Fifth avenue.   He
is said to be a courtly and agreeable host, and his long and extensive experience as a journalist has made him one of the best
informed men of the day.

In person he is tall and firmly built, and walks with a dig-
nified carriage.   His head is large and his features are prominent
and irregular.   He is cross-eyed, and has a thoroughly Scotch
face.   His expression is firm and somewhat cold—that of a man
who has had a hard fight with fortune, and has conquered it.
He is reserved in his manner to strangers, but is always courteous
and approachable.

45

LXIII.

DRUNKENNESS.

DURING the year 1869, there were 15,918 men, and 8105 women arrested for intoxication, and 5222 men and 3466 women for intoxication and disorderly conduct, making a total of 21,140 men and 11,571 women, or 32,711 persons in all arrested for drunkenness. Now if to this we add the 21,734 men and women arrested during the same year for assault and battery, and for disorderly conduct, and regard these offences as caused, as they undoubtedly were, by liquor, we shall have a total of 54,445 persons brought to grief by the use of intoxicating liquors.

But it does not require this estimate to convince a New Yorker that drunkenness is very common in the city. One has but to walk through the streets, and especially those in the poorer sections, and notice the liquor shops of various kinds, from the Broadway rum palace to the "Gin Mill" of the Bowery, or the "Bucket Shop" of the Five Points. There are 7071 licensed places for the sale of liquor in the city, and they all enjoy a greater or less degree of prosperity. Very few liquor sellers, confining themselves to their legitimate business, fail in this city. The majority grow rich, and their children not unfrequently take their places in the fashionable society of the city. The liquors sold at these places are simply abominable. Whiskey commands the largest sale, and it is in the majority of instances a vile compound. About three years ago, the *New York World* published a list of the principal bar-rooms of the city, with a report of chemical analyses of the liquors obtained at each, and proved conclusively that pure liquors were not sold over the bar at any establishment in the city. A few months ago a *World* reporter published the following estimate of the business of the bar-rooms in the vicinity of Wall street, patronized principally by the brokers:

	Hot spiced rums.	Hot whiskeys.	Whiskeys straight.	Brandies.	Wines.	Mixed liquors.	Ale, beer, etc.	Bottles Champagne.
L. Dardy..........	56	59	62	15	23	30	105	6
Mike's............	65	110	70	20	28	23	90	10
V. B. Carpenter....	43	62	112	30	35	27	110	5
Young............	35	40	52	10	12	15	65	2
P. Murphy........	34	49	63	12	15	25	45	2
Schedler..........	51	48	112	35	52	45	315	18
Delmonico.........	213	205	315	90	135	180	210	35
Riley	105	123	180	25	30	62	80	6
Sammis & Sharp..	23	31	30	8	10	15	35	1
Van Riper........	27	22	19	10	13	18	40	1
Ed. Schultze......	18	29	38	12	15	20	60	2
Delatour's.........	15	20	45	27	30	12	25	2
Gault's	28	32	125	23	35	28	85	5
Total..........	713	830	1223	317	433	500	1265	94

" This makes a total of 5281 drinks and 94 bottles of champagne consumed in thirteen of the largest saloons, supported by the brokers; and including the dozen or more of small places, the number of drinks taken in and about Wall street per day is over 7500, while over 125 bottles of champagne are disposed of. The amount of money expended for fuel to feed the flagging energies of the speculators is, therefore, over $2000 per day, and it is not at all strange that the brokers occasionally cut up queer antics in the boards, and stocks take twists and turns that unsettle the street for weeks."

The brokers, however, are not the only generous patrons of the bar-rooms. The vice of drunkenness pervades all classes. Every day men are being ruined by it, and the most promising careers totally destroyed. Day after day, you see men and women reeling along the streets, or falling helpless. The police soon secure them, and at night they are kept quite busy attend-

A FEMALE DRINKER.

ing to them. But the arrests, numerous as they are, do not represent the sum total of the drunkenness of the city. The
drinking in private life, which oftentimes does not result in actual intoxication, but which kills by slowly poisoning body and
mind, is very great, but there is no means of estimating it.

Respectable men patronize the better class bar-rooms, and
respectable women the ladies' restaurants. At the latter places
a very large amount of money is spent by women for drink.

Wives and mothers, and even young girls, who are ashamed to drink at home, go to these fashionable restaurants for their liquor. Some will drink it openly, others will disguise it as much as possible. Absinthe has been introduced at these places of late years, and it is said to be very popular with the gentler sex. Those who know its effects will shudder at this. We have seen many drunken women in New York, and the majority have been well dressed and of respectable appearance. Not long since, a lady making purchases in a city store, fell helpless to the floor. The salesman, thinking she had fainted, hastened to her assistance, and found her dead drunk.

We have already written of the Bucket Shops. They represent the lowest grade of this vice. They sell nothing but poisons.

Is it strange then that crime flourishes? Is it a wonder that Saturday night and Sunday, the chosen periods for drinking heavily, are productive of more murders and assaults than any other portion of the week?

LXIV.

WHAT IT COSTS TO LIVE IN NEW YORK.

THE question is very frequently asked, "Is living in New York very expensive?" An emphatic affirmative may be safely returned to every such interrogatory. Let one's idea of comfort be what it may, it is impossible to live cheaply in this city with any degree of decency. One can go to a cellar lodging-house, and live for from twenty to forty cents a day, but he will find himself overcharged for the accommodation given him. He may live in a tenement house, and his expenses will still be disproportioned to the return received. The discomforts of life in New York, however, fall chiefly upon educated and refined people of moderate means. The very rich have an abundance for their wants, and are able to make their arrangements to suit themselves. The very poor expect nothing but misery.

To begin at the beginning, the expenses of a family in fashionable life are something appalling. Fifty thousand dollars per annum may be set down as the average outlay of a family of five or six persons residing in a fashionable street, and owning their residence. Some persons spend more, some less, but this amount may be taken as a fair average, and it will not admit of much of what would be called extravagance in such a station.

For those who own their houses, keep a carriage, and do not "live fashionably," or give many entertainments, the average is from fifteen to twenty thousand dollars.

For those who aspire to live in comfort and in a respectable neighborhood, and to occupy a whole house, the average is from five to six thousand dollars. With six thousand dollars a year, a family of five persons, living in a rented house, will be compelled to economise. Those who have smaller incomes are obliged to board, to occupy a part of a house, or to leave the city.

The average rent of a moderate sized house in New York is $1800 per annum. This amount may or may not include the use of the gas fixtures, and the house may or may not have a furnace in it. There will be a dining-room and kitchen, with hall or passage in the basement. The first floor will contain two parlors and the front hall. The second floor will contain a bath-room, water closet, and two, or perhaps three, chambers. The third floor usually contains two large and two small rooms, and several closets. The chambers in the more modern houses contain marble basins, with hot and cold water laid on. Where the tenant is unknown to the landlord, he is required to pay his rent monthly, in advance, or to give security for its quarterly payment. Such a house will require the services of at least two women, and if there be children to be cared for, a nurse is necessary. The wages of these, per month, are as follows: cook, $16 to $20; chambermaid, $12 to $15; nurse, $12 to $16. In many of the wealthier families a higher rate of wages is paid. At the rate given, however, from $480 to $582 is the annual outlay for servants, to which must be added a considerable sum for "changing help." Instances are known to the writer in which this "changing help," in the case of discharging an old cook and securing a new one, has cost a housekeeper as much as $30 in a single change. This will be easily understood when I state that ladies who go to look after "girls," in the places from which they advertise for situations, are obliged to go to the expense of hiring a carriage, it being unsafe for them to venture into these sections on foot. Without counting the changes, however, and taking the lower estimate of wages, we have a total of $2280 for house rent and servants' hire. This leaves, from $6000, the sum of $3720 for food, clothing, sickness, education, and all the incidentals of a family. The General Government secures a large slice of this through its iniquitous income tax, and State and county taxes take up several hundred more. Those who have had experience in keeping house in any portion of the country can easily understand how the rest goes, when one has to pay fifty cents per pound for butter, fifty cents a dozen for eggs, sixteen cents a pound for crushed sugar, twenty-five cents a pound for fowls, and thirty-five cents a pound for the choice cuts of beef. All this, too, with the certainty of getting light weights from your butcher and grocer.

Many persons seek refuge in boarding. Those who have no children, or but one or two, may live cheaper in this way, but not in the same degree of comfort that their outlay would bring them in their own homes. A couple with two or three children and a nurse, cannot live in any respectable boarding-house in New York, except in instances so rare that they do not deserve to be mentioned, for less than sixty dollars per week for board and lodging alone. Such persons must pay extra for washing, and there are many "incidentals" which add to the landlady's receipts.

For such a family, giving them two chambers and a parlor, the Fifth Avenue Hotel charges $30 per day, or $10,950 per annum. The figures are high, but "the Fifth Avenue" gives a fair return for the money. The charges of the other hotels are in proportion. None of them will receive such a family for less than $6000 or $7000 per annum.

Of late years, a new style of living has been introduced. The city now contains a number of houses located in unexceptionable neighborhoods, and built in first-class style, which are rented in flats, or suites of apartments, as in the Parisian houses. The largest of these are the monster "Stevens House," on Twenty-seventh street, fronting on Broadway and Fifth avenue, Dr. Haight's House, on the corner of Fifth avenue and Fifteenth street, and Mr. Stuyvesant's House, in East Eighteenth street, the last of which was the pioneer house of its kind in this city. The "Stevens House" was built and is owned by Paran Stevens, Esq., and is one of the largest buildings in the city. It is constructed of red brick, with marble and light stone trimmings, and is eight stories in height above the street, with a large cellar below the sidewalk. The cost of this edifice is to be one million of dollars. "The woodwork of the interior is of black walnut; the walls are finely frescoed and harmoniously tinted.

There are, in all, eight floors, including the servants' attics. Five stores occupy the lower tier. There are eighteen suites of rooms, to which access is had by a steam elevator. The building is heated upon the principle of indirect radiation, by forcing steam-heated air through pipes into the different rooms. The main staircase is of iron, with marble steps, and the main halls to each story are tiled. The chief suites comprise parlor, dining-room, boudoir, dressing-rooms, and butler's pantry; each principal suite comprehending five commodious chambers on the first floor, and two at the top of the house. Each kitchen is furnished with improved ranges. The roof is supplied with water tanks, and, as a further protection against fire, the second floor is supported by iron arched beams, filled in with concrete."

The Haight House is said to be the most thoroughly comfortable establishment of the kind in New York. "It consists of five floors, having twenty suites of apartments for families, and fifteen for bachelors, at a yearly rental of from three thousand to two thousand dollars for the former, and from one thousand four hundred to six hundred and fifty dollars for the latter. These suites are entered from the hallways, each suite having a separate entrance of its own, and at the entrance to the principal suites there is a small antechamber, from which a servant may announce the names of visitors. The family suites embrace a commodious parlor, a large dining-room, with butler's pantry attached, a kitchen, three bed rooms, and a bath room. Each suite has its own dumb-waiter; a dump for coal and refuse, and the proper provision for ventilation; while the suites intended for single occupants are furnished with every appliance necessary to the securing of perfect comfort and ease. Although every accommodation is furnished by the house, some of the tenants have chosen to go to the expense of decorating their own apartments, and have had their rooms elegantly frescoed and painted by some of the first artists in the city. The mantels are either of walnut or the finest marble, of elegant design and workmanship. The supposition is that a majority of the guests will cook for themselves, but arrangements may be effected by which the cooking may be done in a general kitchen for the purpose.

There is a steam elevator, and a general system of kitchens, sculleries, pantries, store and ice rooms, with the engines, and a well-devised workshop for the engineer. There is a steam laundry, capable of washing one thousand pieces per day, where guests may have their washing done at a cheaper rate than could be possible under any of the ordinary methods; and also a drying room—all of the principal work of the establishment being effected by steam. Each apartment has its bell and whistle, communicating with the basement. A janitor, or porter, has a lodge in the main hall, within which there is also a ' post-office.' In the basement is another porter's lodge for the facilitation of business with the butcher, the baker, and the expressman."

These houses, however, are accessible only to people of ample means. The apartments rent for sums which will secure comfortable dwellings, and the other expenses are about the same one would incur in his own house. The great need of the city is a system of such houses in respectable neighborhoods, in which apartments may be had at moderate rents.

LXV.

GAMBLING.

I.

FARO BANKS.

IN spite of the fact that games of chance for money are prohibited by the laws of the State of New York, there is no city in the Union in which they are carried on to a greater extent than in the Metropolis.   There are about 200 gambling houses proper in the city, and from 350 to 400 lottery offices, policy shops, and places where gambling is carried on with more or less regularity.   About 2500 persons are known to the police as professional gamblers.   Some of the establishments are conducted with great secrecy.   Others are carried on with perfect openness, and are as well known as any place of legitimate business in the city.   The police, for reasons best known to themselves, decline to execute the laws against them, and they continue their career from year to year without molestation.   There are about twenty of these houses in Broadway, occupying locations which make them conspicuous to every passer-by.   In the cross streets, within a block of Broadway, there are from twenty-five to thirty more, and the Bowery and East side streets are full of them.

Ninety-five of the gambling houses of the city are classed as "Faro Banks."   Faro is the principal game, but there are appliances for others.   Faro is emphatically an American game, and is preferred by amateurs because of its supposed fairness. An experienced gambler, however, does not need to be told that the game offers as many chances for cheating as any others that are played. It has attained its highest development in New York.

The gambling houses of New York are usually divided into three classes : First and Second Class, and Day Houses. The First-Class Houses are few in number. There are probably not more than half a dozen in all, if as many. In these houses the playing is fair—that is, cheating is never resorted to. The Bank relies upon the chances in its favor, the " splits," and the superior skill and experience of the dealer. The first-class houses are located in fashionable side streets leading from Broadway, and are easy of access. Outwardly they differ in nothing from the elegant mansions on either side of them, except that the blinds are closed all day long, and the house has a silent, deserted air. In its internal arrangements the house is magnificent. The furniture, carpets, and all its appointments are superb. Choice paintings and works of art are scattered through the rooms in truly regal profusion. All that money can do to make the place attractive and luxurious has been done, and as money can always command taste, the work has been well done.

The servants attached to the place are generally negroes of the better class. They are well trained, many of them having been brought up as the *valets*, or butlers of the Southern gentry, and answer better for such places than 'whites, inasmuch as they are quiet, uncommunicative, attentive and respectful. One of these men is always in charge of the front door, and visitors are admitted with caution, it being highly desirable to admit only the nominally respectable. The best known houses are those of Morrissey, in Twenty-fourth street, and Ransom's and Chamberlain's, in Twenty-fifth street. Chamberlain's is, perhaps, the most palatial and the best conducted establishment in the country.

The house is a magnificent brown-stone mansion, not far from Broadway. Ascending the broad stone steps, and ringing the bell, the visitor is ushered into the hall by the man in charge of the door, who is selected with great care. An attentive colored servant takes his hat and overcoat, and throws open the door of the drawing rooms. These apartments are furnished with

A FIRST-CLASS GAMBLING HOUSE.

717

taste as well as with magnificence. The carpet is of velvet, and the foot sinks noiselessly into it. The walls are tinted with delicate shades of lavender, and the ceiling is exquisitely frescoed. The furniture is of a beautiful design, and is upholstered in colors which harmonize with the prevailing tint of the walls and ceiling. The mantels are of Vermont marble, and over each is a large wall mirror. At each end of the room is a long pier glass, placed between richly curtained windows. Fine bronzes are scattered about the room, and in the front parlor are large and well-executed copies of Doré's "Dante and Virgil in the Frozen Regions of Hell," and "Jephthah's Daughter." The front parlor is entirely devoted to the reception and entertainment of guests. The gaming is carried on in the back parlor.

In the rear of the back parlor is the supper room, one of the richest and most tasteful apartments in the city. A long table, capable of seating fifty guests, is spread every evening with the finest of linen, plate, and table-ware. The best the market can afford is spread here every night. The steward of the establishment is an accomplished member of his profession, and is invaluable to his employer, who gives him free scope for the exercise of his talents. There is not a better table in all New York. The wines and cigars are of the finest brands, and are served in the greatest profusion. Chamberlain well understands that a good table is an important adjunct to his business, and he makes the attraction as strong as possible. There is no charge for the supper, or for liquors or cigars, but the guests are men above the petty meanness of enjoying all these luxuries without making some return for them. This return is made through the medium of the card table.

The proprietor of the house, John Chamberlain, is one of the handsomest men in the city. He is of middle height, compactly built, with a fine head, with black hair and eyes, and small features. His expression is pleasant and winning, and he is said to be invariably good natured, even under the most trying circumstances. In manner he is a thorough-bred gentleman, and exceedingly attractive. He is of middle age, and is finely educated. His selfpossession is remarkable, and never deserts him, and he has the quality of putting his guests thoroughly at their ease. In short, he is a man fitted to adorn any position in life, and capable of reaching a very high one, but who has chosen to place himself in a position which both the law and popular sentiment have branded as infamous. Indeed, his very attractions and amiable qualities make him a very dangerous member of the community. He draws to the card table many who would be repelled from it by the ordinary gambler, and the fairness with which he conducts his house renders it all the more dangerous to society.

The guests consist of the most distinguished men in the city and country. Chamberlain says frankly that he does not care to receive visitors who are possessed of limited incomes and to whom losses would bring misfortune. He says it hurts him more to win the money of a man on a salary, especially if he has a family, than to lose his own, and as he does not care to be a loser he keeps these people away as far as possible. In plain English, he wishes to demoralize only the higher classes of society. His visitors are chiefly men who are wealthy and who can afford to lose, or whose high social or political stations make them welcome guests. You may see at his table Governors, Senators, members of Congress and of Legislatures, generals, judges, lawyers, bankers, merchants, great operators in Wall street, famous actors and authors, journalists, artists—in short, all grades of men who have attained eminence or won wealth in their callings. Consequently, the company is brilliant, and the conversations are such as are seldom heard in the most aristocratic private mansions of the city. The early part of the evening is almost exclusively devoted to social enjoyment, and there is very little gambling until after supper, which is served about half-past eleven, after the theatres have closed.

Then the back parlor is the centre of attraction. There is a roulette table on the eastern side of this apartment, said to be the handsomest piece of furniture in the Union. At the opposite side is a large side-board bountifully provided with liquor and cigars. The faro table stands across the room at the southern end, and is the most popular resort of the guests, though some of the other games find their votaries in other parts of the room.

"The table upon which faro is played is not unlike an ordinary dining-table with rounded corners. At the middle of one side, the place generally occupied by the head of a family, the dealer sits in a space of about three square feet, which has been fashioned in from the table. The surface is covered with tightly drawn green ladies' cloth. The thirteen suit cards of a whist pack are inlaid upon the surface in two rows, with the odd card placed as at the round of the letter U. The dealer has a full pack, which he shuffles, then inserts in a silver box with an open face. This box is laid upon the table directly to his front.

"The cards are confined within it by a stiff spring, and the top card is visible to all, save a narrow strip running about its edge, which is necessarily covered by the rim of the box to hold it securely in position.

"The game now begins. The dealer pushes out the top card, and the second card acted upon by the spring rises and fills its place. The second card is pushed off likewise laterally through the narrow slit constructed for the exit of all the cards. This pair thus drawn out constitutes a 'turn,' the first one being the winning and the second the losing card; so that the first, third, fifth, and in the same progression throughout the fifty-two are winning cards, and the second, fourth and sixth, etc., are the losing cards. The betting is done this way: The player buys ivory checks and never uses money openly. The checks are white, red, blue, and purple. The white checks are one dollar each, the red five dollars, the blue twenty-five and the purple one hundred dollars.

"Having provided himself with the number of checks (which in size resemble an old-fashioned cent), he lays down any amount to suit his fancy on any one card upon the table—one of the thirteen described. Suppose the deal is about to begin. He puts $100 in checks on the ace. The dealer throws off the cards till finally an ace appears. If it be the third, fifth, seventh, etc., card the player wins, and the dealer pays him $100 in checks—the 'bank's' loss. If, however, it were the second, fourth, sixth, etc., card the dealer takes the checks and the bank is $100 winner. Should a player desire to bet on a card to lose, he expresses this intention by putting a 'copper' in his checks, and then if the card is thrown off from the pack by the dealer as a losing card the player wins. This is practically all there is in faro.

"It should be remembered that the losing cards fall on one pile and the winning cards on another. When only four cards remain in the box there is generally lively betting as to how the three under cards will come out in precise order, the top one being visible. In this instance alone the player can treble his stake if fortunate in his prediction. This evolution is a 'call.'

"A tally board is kept, showing what cards remain in the box after each turn. This provision is to guard the player. Of course four of each kind are thrown from the box—four aces, etc.

"Some one will inquire how does the bank make it pay while taking such even chances? In this way. If two of a kind should come out in one 'turn,' as, for instance, two aces, half of the money bet on the ace, either to win or lose, goes to the bank. This is known as a 'split." They are very frequent, and large sums pass to the dealer through this channel. That is where the bank makes the money.

"Chamberlain says that if men were to study and labor ten thousand years they could never beat the bank, or rather the game. It is something which no one understands. When only one of a kind remains in the box, as an ace, for instance, to bet then that the card will come to win or to lose is just like throwing up a copper and awaiting the result, head or tail. So it will be seen that the bank is in a position where it has everything to risk.

"The playing is conducted largely by means of checks on the National banks of the city, men seldom carrying money about their persons. Here Mr. Chamberlain has to use his wits. A check given for gaming purposes is not valid in law. Therefore it is necessary to know his man—to be sure of his wealth, to be certain of his credit. It requires instantaneous

46

decision. If the check is refused the drawer is mortally offended. But a few evenings since a city millionnaire offered his check; it was declined. This was Chamberlain's mistake. It is said that if a merchant repudiates his gambling check at the bank it will destroy his credit in commercial circles. This is the only safeguard upon which the faro bank relies. It shows, however, to what a dangerous extent gambling has laid hold of the mercantile community, how rottenness is at this hour the inward germ of apparent soundness, and how heads of heavy concerns fritter away their capital at faro.

" The largest number of business men who play at Chamberlain's are stock brokers, and these persons say openly that it is a fairer game than the cunning and unscrupulous gambling of Wall street. The brokers, as well as other patrons, go in the night time to try and regain what they lost by day in speculation. Thus they alternate between one gaming resort and the other throughout the year. At the faro table they may lose several thousand dollars; but this they consider equivalent pay for rich suppers, costly wines, fine cigars and a merry time, and they are willing to pay for fun.

" Besides the opportunities which Chamberlain affords to his patrons to lose or win, as luck may direct, he keeps a sort of midnight national bank, where he will cash a check for any man he knows as a reliable party, and many who never think of gambling take advantage of his accommodating spirit. This is why he is reputed a good and valuable neighbor.

" How skilfully contrived are all these minutiæ of a gambling palace! They seduce even those who would gladly have never seen a game of chance, and before one is aware of his danger he is past redemption."

Next to the first-class houses come the Second-Class Houses, or " Hells," as they are called in the city. These lie principally along Broadway and the side streets leading from it, and in the Bowery. They are numerous, and are the most frequented by strangers. They are neither as elegantly furnished, nor as exclusive as to their guests, as the first-class houses. Any one may visit them, and they keep a regular force of runners, or " ropers

THE SKIN GAME.

in," for the purpose of enticing strangers within their walls. They are located over stores, as a general rule, and the Broadway establishments usually have a number of flashily-dressed, vulgar-looking men about their doors in the day time, who are insufferably rude to ladies passing by.

Faro is the usual game played at these houses, but it is a very different game from that which goes on under the supervision of John Chamberlain. In gambler's parlance, it is called a "skin game." In plain English it means that the bank sets out to win the player's money by deliberate and premeditated fraud. In first-class houses a visitor is never urged to play. Here every guest must stake his money at the risk of encountering personal violence from the proprietor or his associates. The dealer is well skilled in manipulating the cards so as to make them win for the bank always, and every effort is made to render the victim hazy with liquor, so that he shall not be able to keep a clear record in his mind of the progress of the game. A common trick is to use sanded cards, or cards with their surfaces roughened, so that two, by being handled in a certain way, will adhere and fall as one card. Again, the dealer will so arrange his cards as to be sure of the exact order in which they will come out. He can thus pull out one card, or two at a time, as the "necessities of the bank" may require. Frequently no tally is kept of the game, and the player is unable to tell how many turns have been made—whether the full number or less. Even if the fraud is discovered, the visitor will find it a serious matter to attempt to expose it. The majority of the persons present are in the pay of the bank, and all are operating with but one object—to get possession of the money of visitors. The slightest effort at resistance will ensure an assault, and the guest is either beaten and thrown into the street, or he is robbed and murdered, and his body thrown into the river. There are always men hanging around these places who are on the watch for an opportunity to commit a robbery. The most notorious burglars and criminals of the city visit these hells. They keep a close watch over visitors who stay until the small hours of the morning, especially upon those who are under the influence of liquor. They follow them down into the dark and silent streets, and, at a favorable moment, spring upon them, knock them senseless and rob them. If necessary to ensure their own safety, they do not hesitate to murder their victims.

Many persons coming to the city yield to the temptation to visit these places, merely to see them. They intend to lose only a dollar or two as the price of the exhibition. Such men voluntarily seek the danger which threatens them. Nine out of ten who go there merely through curiosity, lose all their money.

The men who conduct the "hell" understand how to deal with such cases, and are rarely unsuccessful.

It is in these places that clerks and other young men are ruined. They lose, and play again, hoping to make good their losses. In this way they squander their own means; and too frequently commence to steal from their employers, in the vain hope of regaining all they have lost.

There is only one means of safety for all classes—*Keep away from the gaming table altogether*.

At first gambling was carried on only at night. The fascination of the game, however, has now become so great, that day gambling houses have been opened in the lower part of the city. These are located in Broadway, below Fulton street, and in one or two other streets within the immediate neighborhood of Wall street.

These "houses," as they are called, are really nothing more than rooms. They are located on the top floor of a building, the rest of which is taken up with stores, offices, etc. They are managed on a plan similar to the night gambling houses, and the windows are all carefully closed with wooden shutters, to prevent any sound being heard without. The rooms are elegantly furnished, brilliantly lighted with gas, and liquors and refreshments are in abundance. As the stairway is thronged with persons passing up and down, at all hours of the day, no one is noticed in entering the building for the purpose of play. The establishment has its "runners" and "ropers in," like the night houses, who are paid a percentage on the winnings from their victims, and the proprietor of the day house is generally the owner of a night house higher up town.

Square games are rarely played in these houses. The victim is generally fleeced. Men who gamble in stocks, curbstone brokers, and others, vainly endeavor to make good a part of their losses at these places. They are simply unsuccessful. Clerks, office-boys, and others, who can spend but a few minutes and lose only a few dollars at a time, are constantly seen in these hells. The aggregate of these slight winnings by the bank is very great in the course of the day. Pickpockets and thieves are also seen here in considerable numbers. They do not come to practise their arts, for they would be shown no mercy if they should do so, but come to gamble away their plunder, or its proceeds.

It is not necessary to speak of the evils of gambling, of the effect of the vice upon society. I have merely to describe the practice as it prevails here. New York is full of the wrecks it has made. Respectable and wealthy families there are by the score whose means have been squandered on the green cloth. There are widows and orphans here whose husbands and fathers have been driven into suicide by gambling losses. The State Prisons hold men whose good names have been blasted, and whose souls have been stained with crime in consequence of this vice. Yet the evil is suffered to grow, and no honest effort is made to check it.

II.

LOTTERIES.

THE lottery business of New York is extensive, and, though conducted in violation of the law, those who carry it on make scarcely a show of secrecy.

The principal lottery office of the city is located on Broadway, near St. Paul's church. It is ostensibly a broker's office, and the windows display the usual collection of gold and silver coins, bills, drafts, etc. At the rear end of the front room is a door which leads into the office in which lottery tickets are sold. It is a long, narrow apartment, lighted from the ceiling, and so dark that the gas is usually kept burning. A high counter extends along two sides of the room, and the walls back of this are lined with handbills setting forth the schemes of the various lotteries. Two large black-boards are affixed to the wall back of the main counter, and on these are written the numbers as soon as the drawings have been made. There is always a crowd of anxious faces in this room at the hour when the drawings are received.

The regular lotteries for which tickets are sold here, are the

Havana Lottery, which is conducted by the Government of the Island of Cuba, the Kentucky State Lottery, drawn at Covington, Kentucky, and the Missouri State Lottery, drawn at St. Louis, Mo.

The Havana Lottery is managed on the single number plan. There are 26,000 tickets and 739 prizes. The 26,000 tickets are put in the wheel, and are drawn out one at a time. At the same time another ticket inscribed with the amount of a prize is drawn from another wheel, and this prize is accorded to the number drawn from the ticket wheel. This is continued until the 739 prizes have been disposed of.

The Kentucky and Missouri lotteries are drawn every day at noon, and every night. The prizes are neither as large nor as numerous as in the Havana lottery. The drawings are made in public, and the numbers so drawn are telegraphed all over the country to the agents of the lottery.

" The lottery schemes are what is known as the ternary combination of seventy-eight numbers, being one to seventy-eight, inclusive; or in other words, 'three number' schemes. The numbers vary with the day. To-day seventy-eight numbers may be placed in the wheel and fourteen of them drawn out. Any ticket having on it three of the drawn numbers takes a prize, ranging from fifty thousand dollars to three hundred dollars, as the scheme may indicate for the day. Tickets with two of the drawn numbers on them pay an advance of about a hundred per cent. of their cost. Tickets with only one of the drawn numbers on them get back first cost. On another day only seventy-five numbers will be put in the wheel, and only twelve or thirteen drawn out. And so it goes.

" The owners or managers of these concerns are prominent sporting men and gamblers of New York and elsewhere. Considerable capital is invested. It is said that it takes nearly two million dollars to work this business, and that the profits average five hundred thousand dollars or more a year. The ticket sellers get a commission of twelve per cent. on all sales. The tickets are issued to them in lots, one set of combinations going to one section of the country this week, another next; and all tickets unsold up to the hour for the drawing at Covington, are sent back to headquarters. In this way many prizes are drawn by tickets which remain unsold in dealers' hands after they have reported to the agents; and the lottery makes it clear."

It is argued that lotteries, if managed by honest men, are of necessity fair. This is true; but there is a vast amount of questionable honesty in the whole management. The numbers may be so manipulated as to be entirely in favor of the proprietors, and in the fairest lottery the chances are always very slim in favor of the exact combination expressed on any given ticket being drawn from the wheel. The vast majority of ticket buyers never receive a cent on their outlay. They simply throw their money away. Yet all continue their ventures in the hope that they may at some time draw a lucky number. The amount annually expended in this city in the purchase of lottery tickets is princely. The amount received in prizes is beggarly. The effect upon the lottery gamblers is appalling. Men and women of all ages are simply demoralized by it. They neglect their legitimate pursuits, stint themselves and their families, commit thefts and forgeries, and are even driven into madness and suicide by the hope of growing rich in a day.

III.

POLICY DEALING.

POLICY dealing is closely allied with the lottery business, and is carried on by the agents for their own benefit. It is one of the most dangerous forms of gambling practised in the city. It consists of betting on certain numbers, within the range of the lottery schemes, being drawn at the noon or evening drawings. You can take any three numbers of the seventy-eight, and bet, or "policy" on them. You may bet on single numbers, or on combinations. The single number may come out anywhere in the drawing. It is called a "Day Number," and the player deposits one dollar in making his bet. If the number is drawn, he wins five dollars. The stake is always one dollar, unless a number of bets of the same description are taken. Two numbers constitute a "Saddle," and both being drawn, the player wins from twenty-four dollars to thirty-two dollars. Three numbers constitute a "Gig," and win $150 to $225. Four numbers make a "Horse," and win $640. A "Capital Saddle" is a bet that two numbers will be among the first three drawn, and wins $500. A "Station Number" is a bet that a given number will come out in a certain place—for instance, that twenty-four will be the tenth number drawn,—and this wins sixty dollars. Any number of "Saddles," "Gigs," or "Horses," may be taken by a single player.

All this seems very simple, and indeed it is so simple that the merest child ought to understand it. The policy dealers know that the chances are always against a single number being drawn, and still greater against the drawing of a combination. Therefore they offer an enormous advance upon the amount staked, knowing that they are as sure of winning as they could desire to be. A man might play policy for a year, and never see his numbers drawn. Yet thousands annually throw away large sums in this wretched game. A large share of the earnings of the poor go in policy playing. It seems to exercise a terrible fascination over its victims. They concentrate all their efforts on devising systems and lucky numbers, and continue betting in the vain hope that fortune will yet reward them with a lucky "gig" or "saddle." All the while they grow poorer, and the policy dealers richer. The negroes are most inveterate policy players. They are firm believers in dreams and dream books. Every dream has its corresponding number set down in the books. To dream of a man, is one; of a woman, five; of both, fifteen; of a colored man, fourteen; of a "*genteel* colored man," eleven; and so on. A publishing firm in Ann street sells several thousand copies of these dream books every month. The negroes are not the only purchasers. Even men accounted "shrewd" in Wall street are among the number. Indeed Wall street furnishes some of the most noted policy players in the city.

The policy offices are generally dingy little holes, and may be recognized by the invariable sign, "Exchange," over the door or in the window. They are located principally in the most wretched quarters of the city.

Vistors to the Lunatic Asylum and the Almshouse may see a number of instances of the fatal results of policy playing.

LXVI.

PETER COOPER.

PETER COOPER was born in New York, on the 12th of February, 1791. His maternal grandfather, John Campbell, was Mayor of New York and Deputy Quartermaster General during the Revolution, and his father was a lieutenant in the Continental army. After the return of peace, Lieutenant Cooper resumed his avocation as a hatter, in which he continued until his death. It required close attention to business and hard work to make a living in those days, and as soon as young Peter was old enough to pick the fur from the rabbit skins which were used in making hats, he was set to work. He had no opportunity to go to school. " I have never had any time to get an education," he once said, " and all that I know I have had to pick up as I went along." He continued in the hat trade until he had thoroughly mastered it, and afterwards became a brewer, pursuing this trade for two years, at the end of which time he apprenticed himself to a coachmaker. Upon completing his term at this trade, he engaged with his brother in the cloth-shearing business, and continued in it until the general introduction of foreign cloths, after the War of 1812, made it unprofitable. He then became a cabinet maker, but soon after opened a small grocery store on the present site of the Cooper Institute.

With his savings he purchased a woollen factory, which he conducted successfully, and some time after this, enlarged his operations by manufacturing glue. In 1830 he erected large iron works at Canton, one of the suburbs of Baltimore, and he subsequently carried on extensive iron and wire works at Trenton, New Jersey. The greater part of his fortune has been gained by the manufacture of iron and glue. He was the first person to roll wrought iron beams for fire-proof buildings, and soon after opening his Baltimore works, he manufactured there, from his own designs, the first locomotive ever made in America. He has been interested in various enterprises, the majority of which have proved successful, and has shown a remarkable capacity for conducting a number of entirely different undertakings at the same time. He is now very wealthy, and has made every dollar of his fortune by his own unaided exertions. He resides in a handsome mansion in Grammercy Park, but lives simply and without ostentation.

He does not enjoy the marked respect and popularity of which he never fails to receive hearty evidences when he appears in public, because of his success alone. He is one of the principal benefactors of the city, and has placed the whole community under heavy obligations to him by his noble gift to the public of the Cooper Institute, which institution has been described in another chapter.

He conceived the idea of this institution more than forty years ago, and long before he was able to carry it out. Having been much impressed with a description of the *Écoles d'Industrie* of Paris, he was resolved that his native city should have at least one similar institution. As soon as he felt able to do so, he began the erection of the Cooper Institute. The entire cost was borne by him, and the actual outlay exceeded the estimate upon which he had begun the work by nearly thirty thousand dollars. He had many obstacles, mechanical, as well as pecuniary, to overcome, and when the building was completed and paid for, he found himself comparatively a poor man. Almost every dollar of his fortune had been expended upon his great gift to the working men and women of New York. He persevered, however, and his Institute began the career of usefulness which it has since pursued.

Since then he has prospered to a greater extent than ever, and has acquired a large fortune. He has taken an active part in the extension of the telegraph interests of the country, and is now a stockholder and an officer in the Atlantic Cable Companies.   He is very popular among all classes of citizens, and his appearance at public meetings is always greeted with applause.

Mr. Cooper is of medium height, and is rather thin in person.   He has a profusion of silvery white hair, and wears his beard under his chin, with the lip and chin clean shaven.   His large gold spectacles give a peculiar expression to his eyes, which are small and gray.   His face is sharp and thin, and very intelligent, and one of the most thoroughly amiable and benevolent countenances to be met with in New York.   It is emphatically the face of a good man.

LXVII.
THE "HEATHEN CHINEE."

ACCORDING to the Census of 1870, there were twenty-three Chinese inhabitants of New York, but the actual number of Celestials in the city at present is believed to be about seventy-five. The most of these are very poor, and nearly all reside in the Five Points district, generally in Baxter street. Some of them are wretched and depraved, but the majority are industrious and well behaved.

The Chinese candy and cigar sellers are well known. They stand on the street corners, by little wooden tables covered with broken bits of candy, which they sell at a penny a piece. They are dirty, dull, and hopeless looking. No one ever sees them smile, and they rarely pay any attention to what is passing on the street. Of all the dwellers in the great city they seem the most utterly forlorn. The patience with which they remain at their posts, day after day, and in all weathers, is touching, and one cannot help pitying them. Their earnings must be very small, but they manage to live on them.

The cigar makers are more fortunate. They buy cheap remnants of tobacco from the dealers in that article, and at night make these lots up into cigars, averaging from 150 to 180 cigars per night. They dispose of these the next day at three cents apiece, and some of them earn as much as $30 or $35 per week. The cigar maker has a peculiar song which he sings or chants while rolling out his cigars, and varies this chant by occasionally puffing a cigar.

There are scarcely any Chinese women in the city, but nearly all the Chinamen are married. They have a great fondness for Irish wives, and nearly all have two, and some of them three wives apiece.   Families of this size are very expensive luxuries, and it takes all John's industry to provide for them.   A gentleman not long since asked one of these much married individuals how he managed to keep his wives from fighting.   He was answered that they got along very peaceably together.   Upon being pressed, however, John admitted that they did fight sometimes.

"Then how do you manage them?"

"When he fightee," said John, dryly, "me turnee him out in the yardee.   Me lockee the door, and let him fightee out.   He git tired soon, and me let him in.   Me—what you call him?—boss here."

The children by these queer unions seem to be healthy, and nearly all of them speak Chinese in talking to their fathers, and their English has a decided brogue.   Many of the Chinese decorate their houses with the letters they have received from home.   These letters are curious collections of hieroglyphics, some of which are executed in brilliant colors.

There is a Chinese boarding house for sailors of that nationality in Baxter street, kept by a Chinaman and his wife, who is also an Oriental.   These Chinese sailors are simply cooks or stewards of vessels arriving here from China or California, and not ablebodied seamen.   They do not frequent the ordinary sailor's boarding houses, and are never seen in the dance houses or hells of Water street.   They pass their time on shore quietly in their countryman's establishment, and some of them use this season of leisure in trying to acquaint themselves with the English language.   All are opium smokers.

The main room of the boarding house in Baxter street is fitted up with a series of beds or berths, one above another, extending around it.   At almost any time one may find several Chinese lying in these berths smoking opium.   The opium pipe is a large piece of wood pierced down the centre with a fine hole.   The stem is very thick, and is about eighteen inches long.   The smoker has before him a box of soft gum opium and a small lamp.   He takes a little steel rod, picks off a small piece of opium with it, holds it in the flame of the lamp for a few

CHINESE CANDY DEALER.

minutes, and when it has become thoroughly ignited, places it in the bowl of his pipe and puffs away, repeating the operation until he is satisfied, or is insensible.

They are very fond of cards. Those used by them are brought from China, and are curiosities. They are about one inch in width and five inches long, and are gorgeously painted with old time Chinese men and women. To each card there is attached a certain value. The cards are divided into six lots of equal size. Each of the two players chooses one of these packs alternately. The first player places a card on the table, and his opponent places another immediately across it. The others are placed obliquely to these, in the form of a star, and each player scores the value of his card as he lays it down. The game is won by the player who has the largest score.

Altogether, in spite of the misconduct of a few, the Chinese of New York are, barring their bigamous affection for the Irish women, a very innocent and well-behaved class.

47

LXVIII.

STREET CHILDREN.

In spite of the labors of the Missions and the Reformatory Institutions, there are ten thousand children living on the streets of New York, gaining their bread by blacking boots, by selling newspapers, watches, pins, etc., and by stealing. Some are thrust into the streets by dissolute parents, some are orphans, some are voluntary outcasts, and others drift here from the surrounding country. Wherever they may come from, or however they may get here, they are here, and they are nearly all leading a vagrant life which will ripen into crime or pauperism.

The newsboys constitute an important division of this army of homeless children. You see them everywhere, in all parts of the city, but they are most numerous in and about Printing House Square, near the offices of the great dailies. They rend the air and deafen you with their shrill cries. They surround you on the sidewalk, and almost force you to buy their papers. They climb up the steps of the stage, thrust their grim little faces into the windows, and bring nervous passengers to their feet with their shrill yells; or, scrambling into a street car, at the risk of being kicked into the street by a brutal conductor, they will offer you their papers in such an earnest, appealing way, that, nine times out of ten, you buy from sheer pity for the child.

The boys who sell the morning papers are very few in number. The newspaper stands seem to have the whole monopoly of this branch of the trade, and the efforts of the newsboys are confined to the afternoon journals—especially the cheap ones—some of which, however, are dear bargains at a penny. They swarm around the City Hall, and in the eastern section of the

THE NEWSBOYS.

city, below Canal street; and in the former locality, half a dozen will sometimes surround a luckless pedestrian, thrusting their wares in his face, and literally forcing him to buy one to get rid of them. The moment he shows the least disposition to yield, they commence fighting among themselves for the "honor" of serving him. They are ragged and dirty. Some have no coats, no shoes, and no hat. Some are simply stupid, others are bright, intelligent little fellows, who would make good and useful men if they could have a chance.

The majority of these boys live at home, but many of them are wanderers in the streets, selling papers at times, and begging at others. Some pay their earnings, which rarely amount to more than thirty cents per day, to their mothers—others spend them in tobacco, strong drink, and in visiting the low-class theatres and concert halls.

Formerly, these little fellows suffered very much from exposure and hunger. In the cold nights of winter, they slept on the stairways of the newspaper offices, in old boxes or barrels, under door steps, and sometimes sought a "warm bed" on the street gratings of the printing offices, where the warm steam from the vaults below could pass over them.

740 LIGHTS AND SHADOWS OF NEW YORK LIFE; OR,

The Bootblacks rank next to the newsboys. They are generally older, being from ten to sixteen years of age. Some are both newsboys and bootblacks, carrying on these pursuits at different hours of the day.

They provide themselves with the usual bootblack's "kit," of box and brushes. They are sharp, quick-witted boys, with any number of bad habits, and are always ready to fall into criminal practices when enticed into them by older hands. Burglars make constant use of them to enter dwellings and stores and open the doors from the inside. Sometimes these little fellows undertake burglaries on their own account, but they are generally caught by the police.

The bootblacks are said to form a regular confraternity, with fixed laws. They are said to have a " captain," who is the chief of the order, and to pay an initiation fee of from two dollars downwards. This money is said to find its way to the pockets of the captain, whose duty it is to " punch the head " of any member violating the rules of the society. The society fixes the price of blacking a pair of boots or shoes at ten cents, and severely punishes those who work for a less sum. They are at liberty, however, to receive any sum that may be given them in excess of this price. They surround their calling with a great deal of mystery, and those who profess to be members of the society flatly refuse to communicate anything concerning its place of meeting, or its transactions.

A large part of the earnings of the bootblacks is spent for tobacco and liquors. These children are regular patrons of the Bowery Theatre and the low-class concert halls. Their course of life leads to miserable results. Upon reaching the age of seventeen or eighteen the bootblack generally abandons his calling, and as he is unfit for any other employment by reason of his laziness and want of skill, he becomes a loafer, a bummer, or a criminal.

For the purpose of helping these and other outcasts, the Children's Aid Society was organized nineteen years ago. Since then it has labored actively among them, and has saved many from their wretched lives, and has enabled them to become respectable and useful members of society.

The Children's Aid Society extends its labors to every class of poor and needy children that can be reached, but makes the street children the especial objects of its care.   It conducts five lodging houses, in which shelter and food are furnished at nominal prices to boys and girls, and carries on nineteen day and eleven evening Industrial Schools in various parts of the city. The success of the society is greatly, if not chiefly, due to the labors and management of Charles Loring Brace, its secretary, who has been the good genius of the New York street children for nearly twenty years.

The best known, and one of the most interesting establishments of the Children's Aid Society, is the *Newsboys' Lodging House*, in Park Place, near Broadway.   It was organized in March, 1854, and, after many hard struggles, has now reached a position of assured success.   It is not a charity in any sense that could offend the selfrespect and independence of its inmates. Indeed, it relies for its success mainly in cultivating these qualities in them.   It is in charge of Mr. Charles O'Connor, who is assisted in its management by his wife.   Its hospitality is not confined to newsboys.   Bootblacks, street venders, and juvenile vagrants of all kinds are welcomed, and every effort is made to induce them to come regularly that they may profit by the influences and instruction of the house.   Boys pay five cents for supper (and they get an excellent meal), five cents for lodging, and five cents for breakfast.   Those who are found unable to pay are given shelter and food without charge, and if they are willing to work for themselves are assisted in doing so.

The boys come in toward nightfall, in time for supper, which is served between six and seven o'clock.   Many, however, do not come until after the theatres close.   If they are strangers, their names and a description of them are recorded in the register.   "Boys have come in," says Mr. Brace, "who did not know their own names.   They are generally known to one another by slang names, such as the following: 'Mickety,' 'Round Hearts,' 'Horace Greeley,' 'Wandering Jew,' 'Fat Jack,' 'Pickle Nose,' 'Cranky Jim,' 'Dodge-me-John,' 'Tickle-me-foot,' 'Know-Nothing Mike,' 'O'Neill the Great,' 'Professor,' and innumerable others. They have also a slang dialect."

Upon being registered, the boy deposits his cap, overcoat, if he has one, comforter, boots, "kit," or other impedimenta, in a closet, of which there are a number, for safe keeping. He passes then to the bath tub, where he receives a good scrubbing. His hair is combed, and if he is in need of clothing, he receives it from a stock of second hand garments given by charitable individuals for the use of the society. Supper is then served, after which the boys assemble in the class room, which is also the chapel. Here they engage in study, or are entertained by lectures or addresses from visitors. They also sing hymns and familiar songs, and the sitting usually terminates about nine o'clock with the recitation of the Lord's Prayer and the singing of the Doxology. After this they may go to bed, or play dominoes for an hour or two longer, or repair to the gymnasium.

On Sunday evening divine service is held in the chapel. Says Mr. Brace: "There is something unspeakably solemn and affecting in the crowded and attentive meetings of these boys, of a Sunday evening, and in the thought that you speak for a few minutes on the high themes of eternity to a young audience who to-morrow will be battling with misery, temptation, and sin in every shape and form, and to whom your words may be the last they ever hear of either friendly sympathy or warning."

"The effect on the boys," he adds, "of this constant, patient, religious instruction, we know to have been most happy. Some have acknowledged it, living, and have shown better lives. Others have spoken of it in the hospitals and on their death-beds, or have written their gratitude from the battle field."

The officers of the Lodging House use their influence to induce the boys, who are the most notoriously improvident creatures in the city, to save their earnings. They have met with considerable success. There is now a Newsboys' Savings Bank, which began in this way: A former superintendent, Mr. Tracy, caused a large table to be provided and placed in the Lodging House. This table contained "a drawer divided into

separate compartments, each with a slit in the lid, into which
the boys dropped their pennies, each box being numbered and
reserved for a depositor.   The drawer was carefully locked, and,
after an experience of one or two forays on it from petty thieves
who crept in with the others, it was fastened to the floor, and
the under part lined with tin.   The Superintendent called the
lads together, told them the object of the Bank, which was to
make them save their money, and put it to vote how long it
should be kept locked.   They voted for two months, and thus,
for all this time, the depositors could not get at their savings.
Some repented, and wanted their money, but the rule was rigid.
At the end of the period, the Bank was opened in the presence
of all the lodgers, with much ceremony, and the separate deposits were made known, amid an immense deal of 'chaffing'
from one another.   The depositors were amazed at the amount
of their savings; the increase seemed to awaken in them the
instinct of property, and they at once determined to deposit the
amounts in the city savings banks, or to buy clothes with them.
Very little was spent foolishly.   This simple contrivance has
done more to break up the gambling and extravagant habits of
the class than any other one influence.   The Superintendent
now pays a large interest on deposits, and the Trustees have
offered prizes to the lads who save the most."   The deposits of
the boys now foot up an aggregate of about $1800.

The boys are assisted to earn their own support.   Says Mr.
Brace, writing in 1870:

"Through the liberality of one of our warmest friends, and
generous trustee, B. J. Howland, Esq., a fund, which we call
the 'Howland Fund,' was established.   He contributed $10, to
which other patrons added their contributions subsequently.
The object of this fund is to aid poor and needy boys, and
supply them with the means to start in business.   We have
loaned from this fund during the year $155.66, on which the
borrowers have realized a profit of $381.42.   It will be seen
that they made a profit of 246 per cent.   We loan it in sums
of 5 cents and upward; in many cases it has been returned in a
few hours.   At the date of our last report there was due and

outstanding of this fund $11.05, of which $5 has since been paid, leaving $6.05 unpaid.".

The work of the Lodging House for seventeen years is thus summed up by the same authority :

"The Lodging House has existed seventeen years. During that time we have lodged 82,519 different boys, restored 6178 lost and missing boys to their friends, provided 6008 with homes and employment, furnished 523,488 lodgings, and 373,366 meals.   The expense of all this has been $109,325.26, of which amount the boys have contributed $28,956.67, leaving actual expenses over and above the receipts from the boys $80,368.59, being about $1 to each boy."

The other institutions of the Children's Aid Society are conducted with similar liberality and success. We have not the space to devote to them here, and pass them by with regret.

It is not claimed that the Society has revolutionized the character of the street children of New York.   It will never do that.   But it has saved many of them from sin and vagrancy, and has put them in paths of respectability and virtue.   It has done a great work among them, and it deserves to be encouraged by all.   It is sadly in need of funds during the present winter, and will at all times make the best use of moneys contributed towards its support.

It employs an agent to conduct its children to homes in other parts of the country, principally in the West, as soon as it is deemed expedient to send them away from its institutions.   It takes care that all so placed in homes are also placed under proper Christian influences.

LXIX.

SWINDLERS.

THERE are a large number of persons in New York who make considerable sums of money by conducting "Gift Enterprises," and similar schemes. These usually open an office in some prominent part of the city, and flood the country with circulars and handbills of their schemes. They sometimes advertise that the affair is for the benefit of some school, or library, or charitable association. In a few instances they announce that the scheme is merely a means of disposing quickly of an extensive estate, or a building. Whatever may be the pretext, the object is always to wring money out of the credulous, and the plan is substantially the same. Generally, in order to evade the law against lotteries, a concert is announced, and the tickets are sold ostensibly as admissions to that amusement. Buyers are told that the result will be announced at this concert. The tickets are sold at prices varying from one to five dollars. Directories of other cities are obtained, and the mailing clerks of the city newspapers are paid for copies of the subscription lists of those journals. Circulars are mailed to parties in other parts of the country, whose names are thus obtained. There is scarcely a town or village in the United States but is reached in this way, and as there are many simpletons in every community, responses of the character desired by the swindlers come in rapidly. Each person to whom a circular is sent is requested to act as an agent for the scheme, and is promised a prize in the distribution if he will use his influence to sell tickets, and he is requested to say nothing of the inducements offered to him, as such knowledge would make others dissatisfied. The prize is represented as of great value. The person receiving the circular is usually flat-

ATTACK ON A SWINDLER.

tered by being selected as the agent of a New York house, and is also tempted by the liberal offer made to him. He sets to work at once, sells a number of tickets, and forwards the proceeds to his principals in New York. The money is simply thrown away. No concert is ever held, no drawing is ever made. The scoundrels in charge of the swindle continue the sale as long as there is a demand for the tickets, and pocket all the receipts. When there is danger of interference by the police, they close their office and disappear. In a short while, they resume operations under a new name with an entirely new scheme, and repeat the same trick from year to year.

The police are constantly called upon to break up these affairs. Not long ago, a well-known Gift Enterprise manager was brought before the Tombs Police Court upon the complaint of several of his victims.   The plaintiffs were unable, however, to make out a successful case against him, and he was discharged. His victims—the court room was crowded with them—then resolved to be their own avengers, and as he came out into the street radiant with triumph, they fell upon him, and but for the interference of the police would have beaten him severely.

A few months ago, a Gift Enterprise establishment was opened in Broadway, not far from the Grand Central Hotel.   The plan was as follows: A large stock of jewelry, pianos, fancy articles, musical instruments, etc., all of which were subsequently proved to have been hired for the purpose, was displayed in a large store in Broadway.   Purchasers, attracted by the handsome stock, and the announcement that it would be disposed of by a "grand drawing," were induced to purchase sealed envelopes from the clerks, at one dollar each.   Each envelope contained a check on which was a printed number.   Purchasers, after buying these checks and ascertaining the numbers, were requested to pass down into the basement.   Here a large wheel, turned by a man, was constantly revolving.   The purchaser presented his check, and a clerk thrust his hand into the wheel and drew out a small slip of pasteboard.   If the number thus drawn corresponded with the number of the check held by the purchaser, the purchaser was entitled to the article the name of which was affixed to the said number, on a printed list of the contents of the store.   The scheme was seemingly fair enough, but the majority of the tickets drew blanks.   Occasionally, however, when the sales began to show signs of slackening, a lucky number would draw a watch, a diamond pin, or a piano, and the article would be formally delivered to the holder of the ticket.   Immediately the crowd which filled the store would invest anew in tickets, but nothing but blanks would reward them.

The captain of police, commanding the precinct in which the affair was conducted, became interested in the scheme.   His quick eye detected many irregularities in the transaction, and he saw that the holders of the lucky numbers were always the same men, and that they at once passed into a back room of the establishment.   Convinced that the purchasers were being swindled, he attired himself in plain clothes, purchased a ticket, went down to the basement, and drew a blank.   Taking his stand by the wheel, he watched the drawing of sixty-five tickets in succession.   Each drew a blank.   Thoroughly satisfied of the fraud, he procured a warrant for the arrest of the manager of the scheme, and seized the establishment.   The wheel was found to contain about a bushel of bits of pasteboard, every one of which was blank.   Efforts were made to punish the parties connected with the swindle, but without success.

Another trick of the New York swindlers is to send a circular to some one in a distant town, notifying him that he has drawn a prize in their lottery, say a watch worth two hundred dollars.   They state that he must forward five per cent. (ten dollars) on the valuation of the watch within ten days.   The person receiving this circular well knows that he has purchased no ticket in the above concern, and at once supposes that he has received through mistake the notification intended for some other man.   Still, as the parties offer to send him, for ten dollars, a watch worth two hundred dollars, he cannot resist the temptation to close with the bargain at once.   He sends his ten dollars, and never hears of it again.   These circulars are sent out by the thousand to all parts of the country, and, strange as it may seem, the trick is successful in the majority of instances.

The scoundrels who carry on these enterprises feel perfectly safe.   They know that their victims dare not prosecute them, as by purchasing a ticket a man becomes a party to the transaction, and violates the laws of the State of New York.   No one cares to avow himself a party to any such transaction, and consequently the swindlers are safe from prosecution.

The Post-office authorities of the city state that over five hundred letters per day are received in this city from various parts of the country, addressed to the principal gift establishments of the city.   Nearly all of these letters contain various sums of money.   Last winter these mails were seized and opened by the Post-office Department, and some of the letters were found to contain as much as three hundred dollars.

The profits of these swindlers are enormous. Those which are well conducted realize half a million of dollars in three or four months. Instead of resting satisfied with this amount, the rogues close up their business, and start a fresh enterprise.

From this description the reader will see how the various gift enterprises, under whatever name they are presented, are managed, and how certain he is to lose every cent he invests in them. The description applies also to the various Manufacturing and Co-operative Jewelry Associations, and all schemes of a kindred nature.

A little common sense ought to teach persons that no man can afford to sell a watch worth one hundred dollars for five dollars, or a diamond pin worth two hundred dollars for one dollar. And yet thousands innocently believe the assertions of the swindlers, and part with their money never to see it again. The gold pens, jewelry, watches, etc., sold by these advertising swindlers are not worth a twentieth of the cost of the tickets.

The Dollar stores reap enormous profits from the sale of their bogus jewelry, etc. They ask a dollar for an article which is dear at twenty-five cents.

"Situation Agencies" are common in the city. There are always a number of people here out of employment and anxious to obtain it. These are attracted by advertisements such as the following:

WANTED, CLERKS, COPYISTS, COLLECTORS, timekeepers, watchmen, porters, bartenders, coachmen, grooms, two valets to travel. Immediate employment.

They call at the "Agency," which is usually in one of the upper stories of a Nassau street building. The agent, a flashy young man, personates his clerk on such occasions. He informs the applicant that the proprietor is not in, but will be soon, and that in order to secure the very first chance of employment, he must register his name and make a deposit of two dollars. He overcomes the objections of the applicant by stating that the office is overrun with persons needing assistants, and that there are a dozen openings ready for the applicant. The proprietor, however, manages all these things himself. He is sure to be in in the afternoon. The name is registered, the money is paid, but the proprietor is never to be found. The "clerk," if pressed for the return of the money, utterly denies the whole transaction, destroys the register, if necessary, and as there is no evidence to convict him, he escapes the punishment of his crime.

Another "circular swindle" is practised as follows: Circulars are sent to persons in other parts of the Union, offering one hundred dollars in perfect counterfeits of United States Treasury notes and fractional currency for five dollars. One of the most ingenious of these circulars, all of which are lithographed, reads as follows:

"When Congress authorized the present issue of greenbacks, the Treasury Department executed plates of enormous cost and wonderful workmanship, from which the whole amount of currency-authorized by Congress was to be printed, and it was ordered at the time, that, as soon as the whole amount had been printed, the plates, some one hundred ·in number, should be taken from the Treasury Department, conveyed to the Navy Yard, and melted. Now, it so happened that the plates from which the one, two, and five dollar bills had been printed, were not destroyed. How it was brought about, we, as a matter of prudence, do not state. It is enough to know that the plates are still preserved uninjured, and we trust their whereabouts will never be known, except to us."

Formerly this business was carried on through the Postoffice, the rascals sending their victims the photographic cards of the currency of the United States, which sell on the streets for a penny or two apiece. The Government, however, suddenly put a stop to this by seizing the letters addressed to the swindlers, and returning them, with the money enclosed, to the writers. Now the knaves are careful to caution their correspondents to send money by express, and to prepay the charges. Very many of these circulars are successful. The money is sent in advance, or the "queer" is shipped C. O. D. In the latter case, the box is delivered on payment of the charges, and the money thus secured to the swindler, as it is the plain duty of the express company to forward it to the sender of the C. O. D. The box, upon being opened by the victim, is found to contain old paper, or bits of iron or stone.

As a matter of course, only dishonest men will answer these circulars, or consent to buy money known to be counterfeit. The world is full of such, however, and large sums are annually received by the New York swindlers in answer to their circulars. The victim, in the majority of instances, is afraid to expose the trick. The police of the city are fully informed as to the names, appearance, and residence of each of these swindlers, but are powerless to interfere with them. They do not issue counterfeit money, and are not, therefore, liable to the charge of counterfeiting. They screen themselves from the charge of obtaining money under false pretences by never transacting their business in person. Everything is done by letter, and even the C. O. D. part of the business is managed in such a way as to make identification impossible.

The country newspapers are filled with advertisements of cheap sewing machines, which range in price from one to ten dollars. The men who insert these advertisements are among the most unprincipled swindlers in New York. Sometimes they pocket the money and send nothing in return, but when they do send a "machine" it is worthless. The actual cost of it never exceeds twenty-five cents. One scoundrel, some time ago, sent a lady who had remitted him three dollars a large needle, and wrote that it was "the best sewing machine in the world."

Another swindler advertises a music box for $2.50, "warranted to play six airs." In return for the money, he sends a child's harmonicon, the retail price of which is fifty cents.

Another advertises a "Pocket Time-keeper," at one dollar. It is usually a wretched pasteboard, tin or brass imitation of a sun dial. Sometimes it is a child's toy watch.

The day of mock auctions has gone by, but there are still one or two of these establishments lingering in the city. These are managed in various ways.

A STRANGER'S EXIT FROM A "CHEAP JOHN SHOP."

At some of these establishments a lot of pencil cases, watches, or other goods, is offered for sale. The lot generally contains a dozen or a gross of articles. Bids are started by the "decoys" of the proprietor, who are scattered through the crowd, and strangers are thus induced to make offers for them. Each man supposes he is bidding for a single lot, and is greatly astonished to find the whole lot knocked down to him. He is told he must take the entire lot, that his bid was for all. Some are weak enough to comply with the demand, but others resist it.

A well-known Broadway auctioneer was brought before the Mayor, some time ago, on the following complaint. A gentleman, who appeared against the auctioneer, stated that he had attended his last sale.   The auctioneer put up a box containing twelve silver pencil-cases, and the gentleman, supposing from his manner and language, that he was selling them fairly, bid two dollars and fifty cents for the lot. To his surprise, he was told that he had bid two dollars and fifty cents for *each* pencil-case, and that he must pay thirty dollars for the whole lot. The money had been paid and the auctioneer refused to return it, insisting that the gentleman should take one pencil-case or nothing.   The Mayor compelled the scamp to refund the money, and warned him that he would revoke his licence if a similar complaint were again made against him.

In some of these establishments, a stranger who attempts to remonstrate against the swindle fares badly.   He is hustled out by the confederates of the proprietor, and if he attempts to defend himself, is handed over to the police on a charge of attempting to create a disturbance.

Other establishments sell watches and cheap jewelry. A really good article is put up, and passed around through the crowd as a sample. It draws bids rapidly, and is knocked down to the highest bidder. It has by this time been handed back to the auctioneer, and when the purchaser demands it, he is given some worthless article, which the dealer and his assistants swear was the one exhibited to the crowd. Remonstrances are useless. The bogus article must be taken or the money lost, unless the victim calls in the police. The city authorities have recently stationed a policeman at the door of one of these establishments, to warn strangers of its true character.

The pocket-book dropping game is of common occurrence, but is rarely practised on residents of the city. A man suddenly darts from a crowd on the street and appears to pick up something at the feet of his intended victim. This, of course, attracts

48

THE POCKET-BOOK GAME.

the attention of the latter. The former displays a well-filled pocket-book, and asks the stranger if he dropped it, as it was found at his feet. He is answered in the negative.

"Strange," remarks the swindler, "it was lying right at your feet, and I felt sure it was yours. However, it is a rich prize."

He then inquires if the stranger intends staying in town. If answered affirmatively, he says:

"Then I will turn over the pocket-book to you. You can advertise it. Give me ten dollars and take the wallet. You can advertise it, or the owner will no doubt advertise it himself. Then you can claim the reward, which will certainly not be less than fifty dollars."

The other party reasons that he is sure of his money, with the wallet in his possession, and he sometimes dishonestly purposes appropriating the entire contents to his own use. He pays the ten dollars to the finder of the book, who hurries off, saying that he has just time to catch the train by which he intends leaving the city. Upon examining the wallet, the victim finds that its contents consist of a wad of paper wrapped in a wretched counterfeit note. He has given his ten dollars for a collection of worthless paper.

It would require a volume to describe all the swindles and rogueries carried on in this city. The instances we have presented will be sufficient to give the reader an insight into the subject, and to warn him against the wiles of the sharpers which assail him even in his own home.

LXX.

ROBERT BONNER.

THE circulation of the *New York Ledger* is over 300,000 copies, and its readers cannot be far short of one million of people.   To all these the name of ROBERT BONNER is as familiar as that of his paper.

He was born in the north of Ireland, near Londonderry, in 1824.   He came to this country when a mere child, and was brought up in the State of Connecticut, where he received a good common school education.   He was apprenticed to the printer's trade at an early age, and began his apprenticeship in the office of the Hartford *Courant*.   He came to New York at the age of twenty, and obtained employment in the office of a political journal, which soon suspended publication.   He then secured a position in the office of the *Evening Mirror*, from which he passed to the post of foreman in the office of a small, struggling, commercial paper, called the *Merchants' Ledger*.   In a year or two after forming this connection, he purchased the *Ledger*, and determined to change both its character and form, and convert it into a literary journal.   He had the good sense to perceive that there was a great need of a cheap literary journal, suited to the comprehension and tastes of the masses, who cared nothing for the higher class periodicals.   He proceeded very cautiously, however, and it was not until some time after that he made the *Ledger* entirely a literary paper, and issued it in its present form.   He induced Fanny Fern, who was then in the flush of the reputation gained for her by her "Ruth Hall," to write him a story, ten columns long, and paid her one thousand dollars in cash for it.   He double-leaded the story, and made it twenty columns in length, and advertised in nearly

every newspaper of prominence in the country that he was publishing a story for which he had paid one hundred dollars per
column. His mode of advertising was entirely new, and was
sneered at at the time as "sensational." It accomplished its
object, however. It attracted the attention of the readers of the
papers, and they bought the *Ledger* "to see what it was."
They liked the paper, and since then there has been no abate-
ment in the demand for it. The venture was entirely successful.
Mr. Bonner's energy and genius, and Fanny Fern's popularity,
placed the *Ledger* on a substantial footing from the start, and
out of the profits of the story for which he had paid such an
unusually large price, Mr. Bonner purchased a handsome city
residence.

He did not content himself with Fanny Fern, though she
became a regular contributor to his paper. He secured the
services of Edward Everett, offering him ten thousand dollars
for a series of papers, the money to be devoted to the purchase
of Mount Vernon, an object very dear to the heart of the great
orator. Mr. Bonner not only secured a valuable contributor,
but won a warm personal friend in Mr. Everett. The latter
continued his connection with the *Ledger* until the close of his
life. Mr. Bonner also secured as regular contributors to his
paper George Bancroft, the historian, James Parton (Fanny
Fern's husband), Henry Ward Beecher, and many of the leading men of the country, and a number of brilliant and popular
female writers.

The *Ledger* is steadily growing in the public favor. From
the profits of his paper, Mr. Bonner has erected a splendid
marble publishing house, at the corner of William and Spruce
streets, in New York, from which the *Ledger* is now issued. It
is one of the most complete establishments in the country, and
is fitted up with every convenience necessary to the performance
of the work upon the paper in the most complete and expe-
ditious manner.

Mr. Bonner is married, and has a family. He owns a country
seat in Westchester county, to which he repairs in the summer.
His city residence is on the south side of Fifty-sixth street, a

few doors west of the Fifth avenue. It is a handsome brown stone mansion. In the rear of it, on Fifty-fifth street, is his stable, a large and tasteful edifice of brick. It is the most perfect establishment of its kind in the country. Everything is at hand that is necessary for the comfort and care of the horses, and the men in charge of the place are thoroughly skilled in their business. Mr. Bonner owns seven of the finest horses in the world. First on the list is " Dexter," the fastest horse " on the planet." He has made his mile in 2.17$\frac{1}{4}$ in harness, and 2.18 under the saddle. " Lantern," a splendid bay, 15$\frac{1}{2}$ hands high, has made his mile in 2.20. " Pocahontas " has made her mile in 2.23, and " Peerless," a fine gray mare, has followed close on to her in 2.23$\frac{1}{4}$. The former is said to be the most perfectly formed horse in the world. " Lady Palmer" has made 2 miles, with a 350 pound wagon and driver, in 4.59, while her companion, " Flatbush Mare," has made a 2 mile heat to a road wagon in 5.01$\frac{1}{4}$. The "Auburn Horse," a large sorrel, 16$\frac{1}{2}$ hands high, with four white feet and a white face, was declared by Hiram Woodruff to be the fastest horse he ever drove. These horses cost their owner over two hundred thousand dollars, and he would not part with them for double that sum. He will not race them, though almost every inducement has been offered him to do so, as he is opposed to racing for money. He bought them for his own enjoyment, and drives them himself.

Mr. Bonner is now very wealthy. He lives simply, however, and detests and shuns personal notoriety or ostentation. He has the reputation of being a warm-hearted, generous man, and has many friends. He is short, thick-set, and solidly made. His hair is sandy, his complexion florid, his forehead large and thoughtful, his eye bright and pleasant, and his manner frank, genial, and winning.

LXXI.

PUBLIC BUILDINGS.

THE Public Buildings of New York are not numerous. Some of them are handsome, and others are models of ugliness. We shall mention here only those which are not described elsewhere in this volume.

The most prominent is the City Hall, which is located in the City Hall Park. It faces the south, and the ground line is perpendicular to Broadway. It is a handsome edifice, and is surmounted by the best clock tower in the Union, above which is a marble image of Justice. The front and ends of the City Hall are constructed of white marble, but the rear face is of brown stone. The building was erected between the years 1803 and 1810, and the city fathers, sagely premising that New York would never extend above the Park, decided to save the difference between marble and brown stone at this side, "as this portion would face the country." The building contains the offices of the Mayor and city officials. Some of its rooms are very handsome, and are elegantly decorated.

The clock tower and the upper portions of the building were set on fire by the pyrotechnical display in honor of the Atlantic Telegraph of 1859. They were rebuilt soon afterwards, in much better style.

"Previous to the completion of the new cupola, our city fathers contracted with Messrs. Sperry & Co., the celebrated tower-clock makers of Broadway, to build a clock for it, at a cost not exceeding four thousand dollars, that our citizens might place the utmost reliance upon, as a time-keeper of unvarying correctness. During the month of April the clock was completed, and the busy thousands who were daily wont to look up

THE CITY HALL.

to the silent monitor, above which the figure of Justice was enthroned, hailed its appearance with the utmost satisfaction. It is undoubtedly the finest specimen of a tower-clock on this side of the Atlantic, and, as an accurate time-keeper, competent judges pronounce it to be unsurpassed in the world. The main wheels are thirty inches in diameter, the escapement is jewelled, and the pendulum, which is in itself a curiosity, is over fourteen feet in length. It is a curious fact that the pendulum bob weighs over three hundred pounds; but so finely finished is every wheel, pinion, and pivot in the clock, and so little power is required to drive them, that a weight of only one hundred pounds is all that is necessary to keep this ponderous mass of metal vibrating, and turn four pairs of hands on the dials of the cupola. The clock does not stand, as many suppose, directly behind the dials, but in the story below, and a perpendicular iron rod, twenty-five feet in length, connects it with the dial-works above."

To the east of the City Hall, and within the limits of the Park, is the Hall of Records, a stone building, covered with stucco. It was erected in 1757, as a city prison. It is now occupied by the Registrar of the city and his clerks.

In the rear of the City Hall, and fronting on Chambers street, is the New County Court House, which, when completed, will be one of the finest edifices in the New World. It was begun more than eight years ago, and is constructed of "East Chester and Massachusetts white marble, with iron beams and supports, iron staircases, outside iron doors, solid black-walnut doors (on the inside), and marble tiling on every hall-floor of the building, laid upon iron beams, concreted over, and bricked up. With a basis of concrete, Georgia-pine, over yellow-pine, is used for the flooring of the apartments. The iron supports and beams are of immense strength—some of the girders crossing the rooms weighing over fifty thousand pounds. The pervading order of architecture is Corinthian, but, although excellent, the building cannot be said to be purely Corinthian. An additional depth of, say, thirty feet, would have prevented a cramping of the windows on the sides, which now necessarily exists, and have added power and comprehension to the structure as an entirety; but the general effect is grand and striking in the extreme. The building is two hundred and fifty feet long, and one hundred and fifty feet wide. From the base-course to the top of the pediment the height is ninety-seven feet, and to the top of the dome, not yet erected, two hundred and twenty-five feet. From the sidewalk to the top of the pediment measures eighty-two feet; to the top of the dome two hundred and ten feet. When completed, the building will be surmounted by a large dome, giving a general resemblance to the main portion of the Capitol at Washington. The dome, viewed from the rear, appears something heavy and cumbrous for the general character of the structure which it crowns; but a front view, from Chambers street, when the eye, in its upward sweep, takes in the broad flight of steps, the grand columns, and the general robustness of the main entrance, dissipates this idea, and attaches grace and integrity to the whole. One of the most novel features of the dome will be the arrangement of the tower, crowning its apex, into a light-house, which, from its extreme power and height, it is supposed, will furnish guidance to vessels as far out at sea as that afforded by any beacon on the

neighboring coast. This is the suggestion of the architect, Mr.
Kellum, but, whether or not it will be carried out in the execution of the design, Mr. Tucker, the superintendent of the work,
is unable to say. The interior of the edifice is equally elaborate
and complete, and several of the apartments are now occupied
by the County Clerk, the Supreme Court, and as other offices.
The portico and stoop, now being completed, on Chambers
street, will, it is said, be the finest piece of work of the kind in
America."

It was this building which furnished the Ring with their
favorite pretext for stealing the public money. The manner in
which this was done has been described in another chapter.

The Bible House is a massive structure of red brick, with
brown stone trimmings, and covers the block bounded by Third
and Fourth avenues and Eighth and Ninth streets. It covers
three-quarters of an acre, its four fronts measuring a total of
710 feet. It was completed in 1853, at a cost, including the
ground, of $303,000, and is to-day worth nearly double that
sum. It contains fifty stores and offices, which yield an aggregate annual rent of nearly $40,000. These rooms are occupied
chiefly by benevolent and charitable societies, so that the Bible
House has become the great centre from which radiate the principal labors of charity and benevolence in the City and State.

The Bible House is owned by, and forms the headquarters
of the American Bible Society. The Bibles of this Society are
printed here, every portion of their publication being carried on
under this vast roof. The receipts of the Society since its organization in 1816 have amounted to nearly $6,000,000. Thou-
sands of copies are annually printed and distributed from here.
The entire Union has been canvassed three times by the agents
of the Society, and hundreds of thousands of destitute families
have been furnished each with a copy of the Blessed Book.
The Bible has been printed here in twenty-nine different languages, and parts of it have been issued in other languages.

About 625 persons find employment in this gigantic establishment. Of these about three hundred are girls, and twenty or
thirty boys. The girls feed the presses, sew the books, apply

TAMMANY HALL.

gold-leaf to the covers ready for tooling, etc.   About a dozen
little girls are employed in the press-room in laying the sheets,
of the best description of Bibles, between glazed boards, and so
preparing them for being placed in the hydraulic presses.
Every day there are six thousand Bibles printed in this establishment, and three hundred and fifty turned out of hand completely bound and finished.

Tammany Hall, in East Fourteenth street, between Irving
Place and Third avenue, is a handsome edifice of red brick,
with white marble trimmings.   It contains several fine halls,
and a number of committee rooms.   The main hall is one of
the handsomest in the city, and was formerly used as a theatre.
It was in this hall that the National Democratic Convention of
1868 was held.   The building is the property of the "Tammany Society."   This Society was organized in 1789 as a

NATIONAL ACADEMY OF DESIGN.

benevolent association, but subsequently became a political organization and the ruling power in the Democratic politics of
the City and State.

The Academy of Design is located at the northwest corner of
Fourth avenue and Twenty-third street. It is one of the most
beautiful edifices in the city. It is built in the pure Gothic
style of the thirteenth century, and the external walls are composed of variegated marble. It has an air of lightness and
elegance, that at once elicit the admiration of the gazer. The
interior is finished with white pine, ash, mahogany, oak, and
black walnut in their natural colors; no paint being used in
the building. Schools of art, a library, reading room, lecture
room, and the necessary rooms for the business of the institution,
occupy the first and second stories. The third floor is devoted

STEINWAY & SONS' PIANO FACTORY.

to the gallery of paintings and the sculpture room. At certain seasons of the year exhibitions of paintings and statuary are held here. None but works of living artists are exhibited.

One of the most imposing buildings in the city is the new Grand Central Depot, on Forty-second street and Fourth avenue. It is constructed of red brick, with iron trimmings painted white, in imitation of marble. The south front is adorned with three and the west front with two massive pavilions. The central pavilion of each front contains an illuminated clock. The entire building is 696 feet long and 240 feet wide. The space for the accommodation of the trains is 610 feet long and 200 feet wide. The remainder of the edifice is devoted to the offices of the various railways using it. Waiting-rooms, baggage-rooms, etc. The car-shed is covered with an immense circular roof of iron and glass. The remainder of the building is of brick and iron. The principal front is on Forty-second street. This portion is to be occupied by the offices and waiting-rooms of the New York and New Haven and the Shore Line railways. The southern portion of the west front is occupied by the offices and waiting-rooms of the New York, Harlem, and Albany Railway, and the remainder of this front by the offices and waiting-rooms of the Hudson River and New York Central railways. These roads are the only lines which enter the city, and they are here provided with a common terminus in the very heart of the metropolis. The waiting-rooms and offices are finished in hard wood, are handsomely frescoed, and are supplied with every convenience. The height of the roof of the main body of the depot is 100 feet from the ground; the apex of the central pavilion on Forty-second street is 160 feet from the ground.

The car-house constitutes the main body of the depot. It is lighted from the roof by day, and at night large reflectors, lighted by an electrical apparatus, illuminate the vast interior. The platforms between the tracks are composed of stone blocks. Each road has a particular portion assigned to it, and there is no confusion in any of the arrangements. The roof is supported by thirty-one handsome iron trusses, each weighing forty tons, and extending in an unbroken arch over the entire enclosure.   The glass plates in the roof measure 80,000 feet.   The interior of the car-house is painted in light colors, which harmonize well with the light which falls through the crystal roof.

About eighty trains enter and depart from this depot every day.   The running of these is regulated by the depot-master, who occupies an elevated position at the north end of the car-house, from which he can see the track for several miles.   A system of automatic signals governs the running of the trains through the city.

The building was projected by Commodore Vanderbilt. Ground was broken for it on the 15th of November, 1869, and it was ready for occupancy on the 9th of October, 1871.

LXXII.
PATENT DIVORCES.

It may not be generally known in other parts of the country, but it is very well understood in the city, that New York is the headquarters of a powerful Ring of corrupt and unscrupulous lawyers, whose business is to violate the law of the land, and procure by fraud divorces which will not be granted by any court after a fair and full hearing of the case. It may be asserted at the outset, that those who are fairly and justly entitled to such a separation, never seek it through the Divorce Ring.

In any issue of certain city newspapers, you will see such advertisements as the following:

ABSOLUTE DIVORCES LEGALLY OBTAINED, in New York, and States, where desertion. drunkenness, etc., etc., are sufficient cause. No publicity; no charge until divorce obtained; advice free. M— B——, attorney, 56 —— street.

The all-sufficient cause with these lawyers is the desire for a separation on the part of the husband or wife, and they never trouble themselves with questions of law or morality. The law of New York allows a divorce with the right to marry again, upon one ground only—that of adultery.

"The lawyers of the Divorce Ring are the pariahs of their profession—men who have been debarred in other States (sometimes in other countries) for detected malpractice; men who began life fairly, but sank into ignominy through dissipation, political failure, or natural vicious tendencies; men, even, who never opened a law-book before entering upon their present avocation, but gleaned a practical knowledge of the legal alternative of ' wedded woe ' by a course of training in the private detective's trade. These latter worthies often hire the use of practising lawyers' names. Occasionally they hire the said lawyers themselves to go through the mummeries of the courts for them ; and we could name one of our most eloquent and respectable criminal pleaders who, on a certain occasion at least, permitted himself to be nominally associated with one of the boldest operators of the Ring.

"The dens of the divorcers are situated chiefly on the thoroughfares most affected by lawyers of the highest caste, though even Broadway is not wholly exempt from them; and Wall street, Pine street, and especially Nassau street, contain a goodly number each. Without any ostentatious display of signs or identifications, they are generally furnished in the common law-office style, with substantial desks and chairs, shelves of law-books, and usually a shady private apartment for consultations. Sometimes the name upon the 'directory' of the building and name over the 'office' itself will be spelled differently, though conveying the same sound ; as though the proprietor thereof might have occasional use for a confusion of personalities. Along the stairs and hallways leading to these dens, at almost any hour of the day, from 10 A. M. to 3 P. M., may be met women in flashy finery and men with hats drawn down over their eyes—all manifestly gravitating, with more or less shamefacedness, towards the places in question. They may be dissolute actresses, seeking a spurious appearance of law to end an old alliance and prepare for a new one. They may be the frivolous, extravagant, reckless wives of poor clerks or hard-working mechanics, infatuatedly following out the first consequences of a matinee at the theatre and a 'Personal' in the *Herald*. They may be the worthless husbands of unsuspecting, faithful wives, who, by sickness, or some other unwitting provocation, have turned the unstable husbandly mind to thoughts of connubial pastures new and the advertising divorcers. They may be the 'lovers' of married women, who come to engage fabricated testimony and surreptitious unmarriage for the frail creatures whose virtue is still too cowardly to dare the more honest sin. They are *not* the wronged partners of marriage, who, by the mysterious chastising providence of outraged hearths and homes, are

49

compelled, in bitterest agony of soul, to invoke justice of the law for the honor based upon right and religion.

"The manufacture of 'a case' by the contrabandists of divorce is often such a marvel of unscrupulous audacity, that its very lawlessness constitutes in itself a kind of legal security. So wholly does it ignore all the conventionalities of mere legal evasion, as to virtually lapse into a barbarism, knowing neither law nor civilization. A young woman in flaunting jockey hat, extravagant 'chignon,' and gaudy dress, flirts into the den, and turns a bold, half-defiant face upon the rakish masculine figure at the principal desk. The figure looks up, a glance between the two tells the story, and the woman is invited to step into the consulting-room (if there be one), and give her husband's name and offence. A divorce will cost her say twenty-five, or fifty, or seventy-five dollars—in fact, whatever sum she can afford to pay for such a trifle. She can have it obtained for her in New York, or at the West, just as her husband's likelihood to pry into things, or her own taste in the matter, may render advisable. Not a word of the case can possibly get into the papers in either locality. She can charge 'intemperance,' or 'desertion,' or 'failure to support,' or whatever else she chooses; but, perhaps, it would be better to make it adultery, as that can be just as easily proved, and 'holds good in any State.' This point being decided, the young woman can go home, and there keep her luckless wretch of a husband properly in the dark until her 'decree' is ready for her. If the applicant is a man, the work is all the easier; for then even less art will be required to keep the unconscious 'party of the second part' in ignorance of the proceedings. The case is now quietly put on record in the proper court (if the 'suit' is to be 'tried' in New York), and a 'summons' prepared for service upon the 'defendant.' To serve this summons, any idle boy is called in from the street, and directed to take the paper to defendant's residence or place of business, and there serve it upon him. Away goes the boy, willing enough to earn fifty cents by this easy task, and is met upon the stoop of the residence, or before the door of the place of business, by a confederate of the divorce-

lawyer, who sharply asks what he wants. 'I want to see Mr.
——,' says the boy. 'I am Mr. ——,' returns the confederate,
who is thereupon served with the summons. Back hurries the
boy to the law-office, signs an affidavit that he has served the
paper upon defendant in person, is paid for the job, and goes
about his business. The time selected for the manœuvre is, of
course, adapted to what the 'plaintiff' has revealed of her husband's hours for home or for business; and, after the improvised
server of the 'summons' has once sworn to his affidavit and
disappeared, there is no such thing as ever finding him again!
A 'copy of the complaint' is 'served' in the same way; or,
the 'summons' is published once a week for a month in the
smallest type of the smallest obscure weekly paper to be found.
This latter device, however, is adopted only when the plaintiff
(having some moral scruples about too much perjury at once)
charges 'desertion,' and desires to appear quite ignorant of unnatural defendant's present place of abode. If, for any particular reason, the party seeking a divorce prefers a Western decree,
the 'lawyer,' or a clerk of his, starts at once for Indiana, or
some quiet county of Illinois; and, after hiring a room in some
tavern or farm-house in the name of his client (to establish the
requisite fact of residence!), gives the case into the hands of a
local attorney with whom he has a business partnership. This
Western branch of the trade has reached such licence that, not
long ago, a notorious practitioner of the Ring actually issued an
advertisement in a paper of New York, to the effect that he
had just returned to this city from the West with a fresh stock
of blank divorces! The wording was not literally thus, but
such was its obvious and only signification. Whether the
'trial' is to take place in New York or Indiana, however, there
is but one system commonly adopted in offering proof of the
truth of the complaint upon which a divorce is demanded.
Plaintiff's villanous attorney, after waiting a due length of
time for some response from the defendant in the case (!), asks
of the Court, as privately as possible, the appointment of a
referee.

  "His Honor the Court, upon learning that 'defendant' does

not oppose (of course not!), names a referee, who shall hear the testimony in the case, and submit a copy thereof, together with his decision thereon, to the Court for confirmation. Then, before the referee—who is to be properly feed for his officiation—go the divorce-lawyer and two or three shabby-genteel-looking 'witnesses,' who from thenceforth shall never be findable by mortal man again. The 'witnesses' swear to any thing and every thing—that they have seen and recognized defendant in highly improper houses with improper persons; that they know plaintiff to be pure, faithful, and shamefully misused in the marriage relation, etc., etc. As 'defendant,' not even aware that he or she *is* a 'defendant,' makes no appearance, either in person or by counsel, to combat this dreadful evidence, the referee must, of course, render decision for plaintiff—'the law awards it, and the Court doth give it.' The judge subsequently confirms this decision; a decree of full divorce is granted, in *due and full legal form,* to the triumphant plaintiff; and the 'defendant' is likely to become aware of the suit for the first time on that night."

The acts of the divorce Ring are no secrets in New York. Yet neither the judges nor the Bar Association make any efforts to rid the courts of such wretches. "A citizen of New York, whose misguided wife had secretly obtained a fraudulent divorce from him through such practice as we have described, and who, in turn, had successfully sued in the legitimate way for the dissolution of marriage thus forced upon him, sought to induce his legal adviser, a veteran metropolitan lawyer of the highest standing, to expose the infamous divorce 'Ring' before the courts, and demand, in behalf of his profession, that its practitioners should be at least disbarred. The response was, that the courts were presumed to be entirely ignorant of the fraudulent parts of the proceedings referred to; that the offenders could be 'cornered' only through a specific case in point against them, and, besides, that the referees in their cases were nearly all connected, either consanguinely or in bonds of partnership interest, with the judges who had appointed them, and before whom the motion for disbarment would probably come! For this last curious reason no lawyer could, consistently with his own best interests, inaugurate a movement likely to involve the whole referee system in its retributive effects.   A lawyer so doing might, when arguing future cases in court, find a certain apparent disposition of the Bench to show him less courtesy than on former occasions—to snub him, in fact, and thereby permanently prejudice his professional future likelihoods in that jurisdiction!"

LXXIII.
THE CROTON WATER WORKS.

THERE were many plans for supplying the city of New York with fresh water, previous to the adoption of the Croton Aqueduct scheme, but we have not the space to present them here.   They were all inadequate to the necessities of the city, and all in turn were thrown aside.   The most important was one for obtaining the water supply from the Bronx River.   It was believed that a daily supply of 3,000,000 gallons could be obtained from this stream, but nothing was done in the matter, and it was not until the prevalence of Asiatic Cholera in 1832 had impressed upon the people the necessity of a supply of pure water, nor until the great fire of 1837 had convinced them that they must have an abundance of water, that the scheme for supplying the city from the sources of the Croton River was definitely resolved upon.   De Witt Clinton gave his powerful support to the scheme, and the citizens at the municipal elections expressed themselves unqualifiedly in favor of a full supply of fresh water.   It was decided to obtain the supply from the Croton River, and in May, 1837, the work on the acqueduct which was to convey it to the city was actually begun, and on the 4th of July, 1842, the Croton water was distributed through the city.

The first step was to throw a massive dam across the Croton River, by means of which the Croton Lake was formed, the water being raised to a depth of forty feet by the obstruction. From this dam an aqueduct, constructed of brick, stone, and cement, conveys the water to the city, a distance of nearly forty miles.   It is arched above and below, and is seven and a half feet wide, and eight and a half feet high, with an inclination of

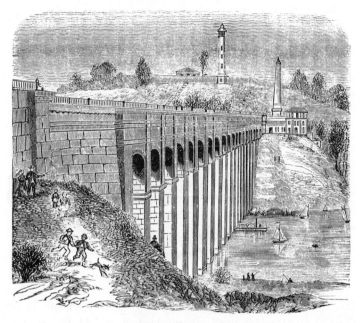

THE HIGH BRIDGE.

thirteen inches to the mile. It rests on the ground for a portion
of its course, and in other parts is supported by a series of stone
arches. It crosses twenty-five streams in Westchester County,
besides numerous brooks, which flow under it through culverts.
It is conveyed across the Harlem River by means of the High
Bridge. The water flows through vast iron pipes, which rest
upon the bridge. The bridge is a magnificent stone structure,
1450 feet long, with fifteen arches, the highest of which is one
hundred feet above high water mark. Its great height prevents
it from interfering with the navigation of the stream. The
High Bridge is one of the principal resorts in the suburbs of
New York. The structure itself is well worth seeing, and the
scenery is famed for its surpassing loveliness.

There are two large reservoirs at the city end of the bridge,
the "Storage Reservoir," and the "High Service," the latter of
which is designed for supplying the elevated section of Wash-

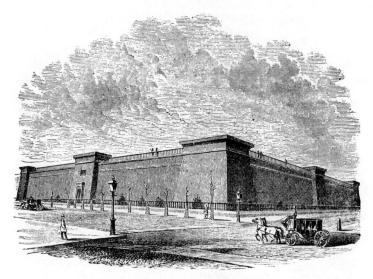

THE FIFTH AVENUE RESERVOIR.

ington Heights. From here to the distributing reservoirs in the Central Park, which have already been described, the distance is two and a quarter miles. The distributing reservoir for the principal part of the city is on Fifth Avenue, between Fortieth and Forty-second streets. It covers about four acres of ground, and is built of granite. It is forty feet above the street, is divided into two parts, and will hold 20,000,000 gallons of water. It is exactly forty-one miles from the Croton Lake.

The daily flow of water through the aqueduct is 60,000,000 gallons, its full capacity. The reservoirs hold over 2,000,000,000 gallons, or about fifteen days, supply. Nearly four hundred miles of main pipes distribute the water through the city, and supply it to 67,000 dwelling houses and stores, 1624 manufactories, 290 hospitals, prisons, schools, and public buildings, 307 churches, and 14 markets. There are 72 drinking hydrants, and a number of ornamental fountains in the city. The lakes and fountains in the Central Park are all formed by the Croton water, which is also supplied to the State Prison at Sing Sing, and the Institutions on Blackwell's, Randall's, and Ward's islands. The Croton River is one of the purest streams in the world. The water is bright and sparkling, and there is no sediment perceptible to the naked eye. Actual analysis has shown that the amount of impurity during an entire summer was but 4·45 grains in a gallon, or 7·63 parts in 100,000 parts.

The original cost of the aqueduct and reservoirs was about $9,000,000. Since then the increased supply, the new reservoirs, pipes, etc., have made the total amount upward of $40,000,000. The total receipts from the water tax since the opening of the aqueduct have amounted to about $22,000,000. The tax at present amounts to about $1,232,000 annually.

LXXIV.

EXCURSIONS.

THE suburbs of New York are very attractive, and excursions to nearly every point within reach of the city are made every day during the summer months. The fares are low, and a day may be pleasantly spent on the water by leaving the city about 8 o'clock in the morning and returning at 6 or 7 P. M.

One of the pleasantest excursions of this kind, is up the Hudson. One may go as far as West Point or Poughkeepsie, and enjoy the magnificent scenery of the famous river, or he may leave the boat at West Point, and spend an hour or two at that place before the arrival of the down boat. The steamers on the Hudson are the best of their kind, and afford every opportunity for enjoyment.

Staten Island, in New York Bay, seven miles from the city, and in full sight of it, offers many attractions to the pleasure seeker. There are several lines of steamers plying between the city and the towns on that island, and making hourly trips. The sail across the bay is delightful, and the fare is only ten or twelve cents each way.

Another trip, and one which should never be omitted by strangers visiting the city, is from Peck Slip up the East River to One-hundred-and-thirtieth street, or Harlem. The route lies along the entire East River front of the city, with Brooklyn, Williamsburg, and Long Island City on the opposite shores. Blackwell's, Randall's, and Ward's islands, with their magnificent edifices, are passed, and Hell Gate is an additional attraction. One is given a better idea of the size of New York and Brooklyn in this way, than in almost any other. Not the least of the attractions is the United States Navy Yard, at Brooklyn, an admirable

U. S. NAVY YARD, BROOKLYN.

view of which may be obtained from the deck of the steamer in passing it.   The boats run hourly from Peck Slip and Harlem. The fare is ten cents each way.   In the summer time there is a line of steamers plying between Harlem and the High Bridge, and connecting with the Peck Slip boats.

The towns on Long Island Sound are also connected with New York by lines of steamers.   These are among the pleasant objective points for excursionists within reach of the city.

The old route to Philadelphia, by way of South Amboy, offers another attraction.   The boat is a fine and powerful steamer, and makes two trips daily between New York and South Amboy.   Sometimes the route lies through the picturesque Kill Van Kull, or Staten Island Sound, or through the Narrows, into the Outer Bay, and around Staten Island into Raritan Bay.

WEST POINT.

The famous resorts of Rockaway and Coney Island are reached in from one to two hours by steamer. At either of these places a day may be spent on the sea shore. The surf-bathing is excellent at both, and each may also be reached by a railway. Of late years, Coney Island has become a favorite resort of the roughs of New York and Brooklyn, and, as a consequence, is not as attractive to respectable visitors as formerly.

Perhaps the pleasantest of all the excursions, except the trip up the Hudson, is the sail from the city to Sandy Hook and back on the Long Branch boats. These are magnificent steamers, and make several trips each day during the summer season. They connect at Sandy Hook with the railway to Long Branch. One may leave the city in the morning, spend the day at the Branch, enjoy a bath in the surf, and reach the New York pier again by 8 o'clock in the evening. The round trip fare is about two dollars.   The boats are provided with every luxury, and are famous for their excellent table.   A good band accompanies each, and discourses delicious music during the sail. The route lies down the harbor through the Narrows, and down the Lower Bay to Sandy Hook, in full sight of the Atlantic, and near enough to it to feel the deep swelling of its restless breast.   Those who do not care to visit Long Branch may make the round trip in four hours.

LXXV.
SAILORS IN NEW YORK.

IN the streets in the vicinity of the water, there are many buildings used as " Sailors' Boarding-houses." One would suppose that poor Jack needed a snug resting-place after his long and stormy voyages, but it is about the last thing he finds in New York. The houses for his accommodation are low, vile places. They are located in the filthiest sections of the city, and are never clean. Jack, however, is used to hard fare. He has spent six months, or it may be two years, in the damp and cheerless forecastle, and he will not grumble at the aspect of the only quarters available to him on shore. He has crowded with twenty men and boys into a space much smaller than the chamber assigned him, and he does not object to having half a dozen room mates. The bed is a wretched cot, but it is better than a bunk or a hammock, and Jack is not so used to cleanliness as to make him very fastidious.

The boarding-house has a flashy air. There are bright curtains at the windows, and the entire front is usually painted some gaudy color, and is adorned with a sign, with the name of the establishment in gilt letters. " The Sailor's Retreat," " Our House," " The Sailor's Welcome Home," " The Jolly Tar," and " The Flowing Sea Inn " are favorite names with these places. The entrance is generally low and narrow, and conducts the visitor to the main room, which is often the bar, of the house. This is a small, low-pitched apartment. The floor is sanded, and the ceiling is lined with tissue paper pendants cut in various designs. The mantelpiece is adorned with various seamen's trophies and curiosities from foreign lands, the majority of which have been stolen from the poor fellows, who brought them home for a different purpose. The bar is adorned with a multitude of bottles, decanters, and glasses, and the liquors give no indication to the eye of their deadly properties. A person accustomed to cross the ocean in the luxurious cabin of a Cunarder, would not find the place very attractive, but to Jack, who has never known anything better than the forecastle, it has many attractions, and he falls an easy victim to it.

The landlords of these places are simply the meanest of thieves and bullies. They charge a uniform price of about seven dollars per week, for which they give a mean bed in a dirty room occupied by five or six other persons, and three indifferent meals a day. They do not, however, reap their profits from their legitimate business. Their principal earnings are gained by their crimes.

They keep their runners in the harbor on the watch for ships coming in from long voyages. These board the vessels as soon as they reach the bay, and at once begin to extol the merits of their several establishments. They are adepts at their art, and before the vessel has cast anchor at her berth, they have secured one or more men apiece for their houses. They never leave them after this, but " stick to them " until they receive their wages, after which they conduct them to the boarding-house, and turn them over to the landlord. If the sailor is unwilling to promise to become a guest at the boarding-house, the runner has but little trouble in inducing him to " drop in and look at it." The great object is to get him within its doors. The first sense of freedom from the confinements of the ship is very grateful to Jack, and puts him in a good humor with himself and everybody else. This renders him the easier a victim.

When he has been brought within the portals of the boarding-house, the next step is to induce him to drink. Sailors are very tough, but even they cannot stand up against the effects of the poisonous liquors sold here. If the landlord is not able to induce the new-comer to drink, the " Jackal," or the porter, is called in. Jack never suspects the porter of any design upon him, but believes that the landlord is his only enemy, and the " Jackal " is usually successful. If it is found necessary to make quick work of the case, the liquor is drugged; but, as a general rule, it is poisonous enough to stupefy even a strong man in a very short while. When the victim is fairly helpless, he is conducted to his room. There may be other "boarders" in this apartment, but they are generally too drunk to notice what is going on. The doors are utterly without fastenings, and are oiled to prevent them from creaking. When all is quiet, and the victim is plunged in a heavy slumber, the "Jackal" creeps up the stairs, enters the room, and robs the poor fellow of whatever money or valuables he may have on his person. In the morning, when the sailor awakens, sick and disheartened, he discovers his loss. The landlord is full of sympathy for him, and is indignant that such an outrage should have been perpetrated beneath his roof. He has the house searched, and, if the sailor cannot be made drunk again, goes through the farce of causing the arrest of a "stool-pigeon," who is of course discharged for lack of evidence against him. Usually, however, the sailor is made drunk, and is gotten to sea again on a long voyage as soon as possible.

The various methods of forcing a sailor to sea are called "Shanghaiing." The practice is resorted to by landlords, to enable them to complete the crews which they have contracted to furnish to vessels. The owners and masters of these vessels are fully aware of the infamous manner in which men are procured for them, but say they must either connive at it, or let their vessels go to sea shorthanded. In "Shanghaiing" a sober man, resort is had to false promises. He is induced to go on board of a vessel, "to see how he likes her." He is then detained by force until the ship has left port. His true name is not entered on the list presented at the Custom House on the day before sailing, but he is passed under a fictitious name. When the wretches who carry on this business are very much pressed for men, they do not hesitate to waylay sailors, knock them senseless, and convey them on board vessels in this condition. They are not particular as to the qualifications of the men they ship as "able-bodied and thorough seamen." They sometimes abduct men who have never trod the deck of a ship before. During the war the notorious Thomas Hadden, of 374 Water street, induced a poor tailor to go on board of a ship by telling him that the crew wanted their clothes mended, and assured him that the "job" would give him employment for several days, and amply repay him for his trouble. The tailor, upon going on board, was at once set to work in the forecastle on a lot of dilapidated jackets, and Mr. Hadden at once went ashore. Immediately the cables were cast off, and the ship was towed out into the stream by a tug which had been held in readiness. The unsuspecting tailor continued his work, never noticing the motion of the ship, and it was not until she had crossed the bar, and gotten to sea, that he was aroused by the rough voice of the mate, commanding him to go to his duty on deck. Then, to his horror, he found that he was on his way to Canton. He returned, after a voyage of two years, and at once took measures to bring Hadden to justice. The wretch escaped, however, and was not seen again in Water street for three years. Mr. Hadden is now serving out a term of ten years imprisonment in the New Jersey Penitentiary, for grand larceny.

Usually, however, "Shanghaiing" is practised upon drunken sailors only. They are made drunk, as has been stated, immediately after the discovery of the loss of their wages, and are kept so until an opportunity presents itself for sending them to sea. Thus they are gotten rid of, care being taken to ship them only on voyages of two and three years duration. The landlords receive a premium on the men furnished by them. They also make out fictitious claims against the poor fellows, and pocket the three months' wages advanced by the owners or masters of the vessels on which the unfortunates are shipped.

Thus the sailor is plundered, made drunk, prevented from enjoying any other society on shore but that of thieves and the lowest prostitutes. It frequently happens that the poor fellow never receives the benefit of a single penny of his earnings, and never spends more than a week or ten days ashore between his voyages. Efforts have been made by conscientious ship-owners to put a stop to the outrages of the landlords, but each one has failed. The wretches have banded together, and have prevented

50

NEW YORK SEAMEN'S EXCHANGE BUILDING.

sailors from shipping, and in the end the ship-owners have been compelled to abandon the sailor to the mercy of his tyrants. Only a law of Congress, regulating sailors' boarding houses, according to the system now in use in England, will remedy the evil. Efforts are now being made to secure the passage, during the present session of Congress, of a bill, entitled the "Shipping Commissioners' Bill," which has received the sanction of the shipping merchants of New York, and which will effectually remedy the evils we have described.

The merchants of the city have also organized a "Seamen's Exchange," the objects of which are thus set forth by the Association:

"The objects of this Association shall be the moral, mental, and social improvement of seamen, to elevate their character and efficiency as a class, and to protect them from impositions and abuses at home and abroad.

"To build up such an organization of respectable seamen as will command the respect of the community, enable ship-owners to protect themselves from the imposition of worthless and disorderly characters claiming to be seamen, but disgracing the name, and secure for their vessels reliable and efficient crews; while at the same time the seaman will be enabled to select good ships and good officers, and thus secure good treatment."

They propose to attain these objects by the adoption of the following measures:

"To provide an exchange, reading-room, library, and savings-bank which shall be open to all seamen on the payment of a small annual subscription. To issue certificates of membership, and of character and capacity. To assert and maintain perfect liberty in the selection of boarding-houses, shipping-offices, and voyages. To refuse to pay or to receive 'bonus-money' for ships, or 'blood-money' for men, by which custom both ship-owners and seamen are sufferers. To supply vessels with crews without the intervention of any shipping-master should it become necessary. To discourage the system of advanced wages as the source of many evils and but few benefits. To keep a record of the name, age, character, and capacity, so far as can be ascertained, of every member of this Association; also, of the vessels in port, their class, owners or agents, and the voyages on which they are bound. To establish means by which seamen can receive afternoon and evening lessons in the common English branches and navigation. To encourage and assist every sailor in his efforts to improve his character and to save his hard-earned money for the benefit of himself and his family, and on all suitable occasions to give him such advice and information as his circumstances may seem to require."

Our engraving presents a view of the building now in course of erection by the Association.

LXXVI.

THE BALLET.

THE ballet seems at last to have found a home in New York, and to have become one of the permanent institutions of the great city,—witness the triumphs of the Black Crook, of Humpty Dumpty, and the spectacular plays of the Grand Opera House. It must be confessed that it is well done here. The Black Crook carries off the palm. Its ballets are the best arranged and the best executed, and its dancers are as good looking and attractive as ballet girls ever are.

There are several hundred girls and women in New York who earn their living by dancing in the ballets of the various theatres. The Black Crook alone employs about one hundred. Those who have seen these damsels in their glory, in the full glare of the foot and calcium lights, amidst the most gorgeous surroundings, and under the influence of delicious music, may have come to the conclusion that such a life must be very pleasant. They little know the experience of a ballet girl. "It's a hard life," said one of them, not long since, "and very little fun in it, if you're decent."

The ballet girl always appears on the bills as a miss, but some of them are married, and have to support helpless or worthless husbands. They are of all nationalities. The Premières are generally French or Italian—at least on the bills. These are usually excellent dancers, and are fond of their art. They are well paid, and as a rule save their money. Mdlle. Bona-fanti received $150 per week from the managers of Niblo's Theatre. Mdlle. Morlacchi also receives large sums. She is a sensible woman, and has invested her earnings in a pretty home in New England, where she spends her summers. Not more

THE BALLET.

then one or two in the same establishment receive such high pay, however. The salaries, as a rule, are small. The Secondas at Niblo's, the home of the Black Crook, receive from $50 to $100 per week. There are twelve coryphées who earn from $25 to $30 per week. Then follow the first, second, and third lines of the ballet, with wages ranging from $5 to $30 per week. The girls who march in the processions of female soldiers receive about $8 per week. The costumes, armor, etc., are furnished by the theatre, but there are many articles of dress which the girls are obliged to furnish at their own expense.

The ballet girl rises about eight o'clock in the morning, and is off to rehearsal by nine. A duller, more dreary sight than a rehearsal of a ballet by daylight, and in plain dress, cannot be imagined. The theatre is dark and gloomy, the stage not much lighter, and everything is in confusion. There is a smell of escaping gas in all parts of the building. Scattered about the stage are a number of girls and women in half skirts, with fleshings on their legs, and some of them with woollen hose drawn over the fleshings to keep them warm. They are terribly jaded and hollow eyed, and they seem incapable of being interested in anything. A very different set from the smiling, graceful houris of the evening before. At a given signal the music begins, and the girls commence a series of capers which seem utterly ridiculous. It is downright hard work for the girls, however; and those who are not engaged in leaping, or pirouetting, or wriggling, are leaning against the scenery and panting with fatigue. The leader of the ballet storms and swears at them, and is made frantic by every little mistake. The rehearsal occupies several hours. If there is a matinée that day, it is kept up until it is time for the girls to dress for that performance. Between the close of the matinée, and the opening of the evening performance, there is not much time for the tired girls to rest.

Upon assembling for the evening performance, the girls are dressed by a practical costumer, whose business it is to see that each one wears her costume properly. This arranged, they pass down to the painter's room, where their cheeks, ears, and nostrils are "touched up" by an artist. Their hair is dressed by another artist, and every defect of face and figure is overcome as far as is possible. Thus adorned, the dull and jaded girl of the morning becomes, under the magical influence of the footlights, a dazzling sprite, and the object of the admiration of the half-grown boys and brainless men who crowd the front rows of orchestra seats.

The performance is not over until near midnight. Then the dancer must change her dress, fold her stage dress carefully away, make up her bundle, and set out for home. The principal dancers, such as Bonafanti, and Morlacchi, of course, have an easier time than the ordinary ballet girls, but all work hard.

It is commonly supposed that the ballet-dancer is of necessity an impure woman. Too many of them are; but, as a class, they are much abused. They work hard, and do not have much leisure time, and deserve more sympathy than reproach. Men, especially, think that, because they appear on the stage in a state of semi-nudity, they are immodest and of easy virtue; and in New York there is a class of men, of nominal respectability, who appear to regard ballet-dancers as their legitimate prey. They exert all their arts to lead these poor girls astray, and are too often successful. There is not a ballet-dancer in the city but can tell many a tale of persecutions of this kind; and if ever the devil employed a legion of emissaries to do his work, they must be the grinning, leering men who occupy the front seats in the theatres during the ballet performances, and who spend their leisure time in seeking to compass the ballet-girl's ruin.

The ballet-girl, says Olive Logan, "is a dancer, and loves dancing as an art. That pose into which she now throws herself with such abandon, is not a vile pandering to the tastes of those giggling men in the orchestra stalls, but is an effort, which, to her idea, is as loving a tribute to a beloved art as a painter's dearest pencil touch is to him. I have seen these women burst into tears on leaving the stage, because they had observed men laughing among themselves, rolling their eyes about, and evidently making unworthy comments on the pretty creatures before them, whose whole heart was for the hour lovingly given over to Terpsichore. 'It is *they* who are bad,' said Mdlle. B—— to me, the other night; 'it is not we.'"

The majority of the ballet-dancers dwell with their parents, but many of those in the upper ranks of the profession like the freedom of Bleecker street, and reside in that thoroughfare. Thompson street also contains several boarding-houses patronized by dancers and burlesque actresses. A writer in the New York *World* gives the following clever sketch of the more prosperous ballet-girl at home:

"It was strictly a theatrical boarding-house, and all the young ladies were dancers. 'It would never do to have anybody else here. Mrs. Sullivan is Miss Jones's dresser at the "Adelphi," and she has kept house here some years. Her husband was an actor, and he went to California and never came back. She's a dear good woman, and treats us like her daughters.'

"'How many of you board here?'

"'Thirteen. All of them are high-priced dancers—no ballet and utility girls here. No, *sir!* We pay $10 to $15 a week for board. She treats us like her own family.'

" Miss Bell then suggested a tour of the house, offering to be the guide of such an exploration. Tripping down stairs with the elastic hop of a bird, she knocked at the door of the lower front chamber, and immediately ushered her companion into the room. It was large and elegant, and in exquisite order. One really beautiful girl was driving a sewing-machine before a window with the industry of a seamstress. Another was engaged in trimming a tiny pair of satin boots with beads of every color. She was short, small, and swarthy, her chief beauty being a languishing pair of black eyes. A third lay at full length on a small bed in an alcove, reading *Harper's Bazar* with the avidity of a milliner, or a lady of fashion. She was exceedingly pretty and ladylike. Two of them wore the inevitable white wrapper, while the third was fully dressed in a simple gray walking-suit. The lovely creature at the sewing-machine was Miss Ethel Lynn of the 'Lyceum;' the swarthy girl was Miss Lottie Taylor of the 'Gaiety,' and the third was another Miss Lynn, pseudo-sister of Ethel, with whom she 'worked,' but in reality a no-relation named Ellis. The three girls smiled prettily enough on learning their visitor's object, and the recumbent beauty regretted that it was. impossible, under the circumstances, to publish a picture of the scene.

"The next room was occupied by 'a very great swell,' the première danseuse of the 'Lyceum.' It contained a superb piano littered with stage properties, dresses, and general odds and ends. The furniture was of splendid quality, and large tinted photographs of prominent French 'professionals,' including an unusually prepossessing likeness of Schneider, decked the walls. Satin tights, exquisitely pink, hung out of a half-open trunk. The danseuse was seated at a small table, her own profuse golden hair coiled after an indolent fashion, while her diamonded fingers were hard at work saturating some superb yellow tresses in a saucerful of colorless fluid, a bleaching agent for continuing the lustre of blond hair. A clamorous parrot trolled a bar or two of ' Un Mari Sage' overhead, and a shaggy poodle lay couched in leonine fashion at her feet, munching a handsome though fractured fan. A well-directed kick of her dainty little slippered foot sent the sacrilegious animal flying on the entrance of the two invaders. This was Mademoiselle Helene Devereux, a young lady who twirled her toes for a salary scarcely less than that of the President of the United States. French by birth, she spoke English with a pure accent. She seemed much amused at the errand of her masculine visitor.

"'You want to see a première at home? Look at me now, dyeing my own hair. And see that dress there. I made it every bit myself. I get up every morning at 8. Some of the other lazy things in the house never think of breakfast till 10. But I turn out at 8; eat some breakfast; do all my mending; sort out my washing; go to rehearsal; practise new dances; come home to lunch; drive out to the Park; eat my dinner; go to the theatre; eat my supper, and go straight to bed. Can anybody live more properly? I don't think it possible. Mrs.

Sullivan says I'm a model. I don't give her the least bit of trouble, and she wouldn't part with me for anything. You ought to have been here just now, and seen little Vulfi of the "Melodeon." She makes $100 a night, and yet she doesn't dress any more stylishly than Mrs. Sullivan; and she never bought a jewel in her life. She supports a mother, and sends a brother to college in Florence. You people think we are fast. That's all nonsense. It is only the little dancers, *la canaille*, who can afford to be dissipated. I can't, I know that. I'm too tired after the theatre to think of going out on a spree, as they call it. Besides, it doesn't do for a dancer to be too cheap. It hurts her business.'

" 'Devereux's nice, isn't she?' said Miss Bell. 'She's very good, and she's plucky. A fellow once followed her home from rehearsal, chirping to her all the way. She said nothing, but went right on into the livery stable next door. The fellow went in after her, and she snatched a carriage whip out of the office, and, oh my! didn't she thrash him? Nobody interfered, and she whipped him till her arm ached. Ever since then she's been receiving dreadful letters, and so has Mrs. Sullivan. She can't find out who sends them, and she's never seen the fellow again.' "

LXXVII.

THE POOR OF NEW YORK.

I.

THE DESERVING POOR.

POVERTY is a terrible misfortune in any city. In New York it is frequently regarded as a crime. But whether the one or the other, it assumes here proportions which it does not reach in other American communities. The city is overrun with those who are classed as paupers, and in spite of the great efforts made to relieve them, their suffering is very great.

The deserving poor are numerous. They have been brought to their sad condition by misfortune. A laboring man may die and leave a widow with a number of small children dependent on her exertions. The lot of such is very hard. Sickness may strike down a father or mother, and thus deprive the remaining members of a family of their accustomed support, or men and women may be thrown out of work suddenly, or may be unable to procure employment. Again, a man may bring himself and his family to want by drunkenness. If the children are too young to earn their bread, the support of the family falls upon the wife. Whatever may be the cause of the misfortune, the lot of the poor in New York is very hard. Their homes are the most wretched tenement houses, and they are compelled to dwell among the most abandoned and criminal part of the population. No wonder poverty is so much dreaded here. The poor man has little, if any, chance of bettering his condition, and he is gradually forced down lower and lower in the scale of misery, until death steps in to relieve him, or he takes refuge in suicide.

THE POOR IN WINTER.

The Missionaries are constant in their labors among the poor. They shrink from no work, are deterred by no danger, but carry their spiritual and temporal relief into places from which the dainty pastors of fashionable churches shrink with disgust. They not only preach the Gospel to the poor, who would never hear it but for them, but they watch by the bed-sides of the sick and the dying, administer the last rites of religion to the believing pauper or the penitent criminal, and offer to the Great Judge the only appeal for mercy that is ever made in behalf of many a soul that dies in its sins. There is many a wretched home into which these men have carried the only joy that has ever entered its doors. Nor are they all men, for many of the most effective Missionaries are gentle and daintily nurtured women. A part of the Missionary's work is to distribute Bibles, tracts, and simple religious instruction. These are simple little documents, but they do a deal of good. They have reformed drunkards, converted the irreligious, shut the mouth of the swearer, and have brought peace to more than one heart. The work is done so silently and unpretendingly that few but those engaged in it know how great are its effects. They are encouraged by the evidences which they have, and continue their work gladly.

Thanks to the Missionaries, many of the deserving poor have been brought under the constant care of the Mission Establishments, from which they receive the assistance they need. Yet there are many who cannot be reached, or at least cannot be aided effectively. The officers of the Howard Mission relate many touching incidents of the suffering that has come under their notice.

There was among the inmates of the Mission, about a year ago, a girl named Rose ——. She was ten years old, and was so lame that she was unable to walk without crutches. When she became old enough to do anything, her mother, a drunken and depraved woman, sent her on the streets to sweep the crossings and beg. She managed to secure a little money, which she invested in "songs." She paid three-quarters of a cent for each "song," and sold them at a cent apiece. With her earnings she supported her mother. Their home was the back room of a cellar, into which no light ever shone, and their bed was a pile of rags. To reach this wretched spot, the little girl was compelled to pass through the front cellar, which was one of the vilest and most disgusting dens in the city.

The mother at length fell ill, and the child in despair applied to the Howard Mission for aid, which she received. Food and clothing were given to the mother, but they were of little use to her, as she died within two days. The breath had scarcely left her body, when the wretches who occupied the outer cellar stripped her of all her clothing, and left her naked. She was wrapped in an old sheet, put into a pine box, nailed up and buried in the potter's field, without the pretence of a funeral.

The little girl, now left alone, succeeded in obtaining some sewing. She worked on one occasion from Tuesday until Saturday, making eleven dozen leaves for trimming ladies' velvet cloaks. She furnished her own thread, and paid her own car fare. She received eight cents a dozen for the leaves, or eighty-eight cents in all, or less than the thread and car fare had actually cost her. The officers of the Howard Mission now came to her aid, and gave her a home in their blessed haven of rest.

One of the evening papers, about a year ago, contained the following "Incident of City Life:"

"In a cellar, No. 91 Cherry street, we found an Irish woman with five children, the oldest probably ten years old. Her husband had been out of work for nearly six months, and was suffering severely from bronchitis. There was no appearance of liquor about the place, and the Missionary who had visited them often said she was sure they did not drink. The woman was suffering severely from heart disease, and had a baby three weeks old. But what a place for a baby! There were two windows, two feet by two feet, next to the street, so splashed on the outside and stained by the dust and mud that they admitted but little light. A tidy housewife might say, Why don't the woman wash them? How can she stop to wash windows, with a baby three weeks old and four helplrss little ones besides, crying around her with hunger and cold? The floor had no

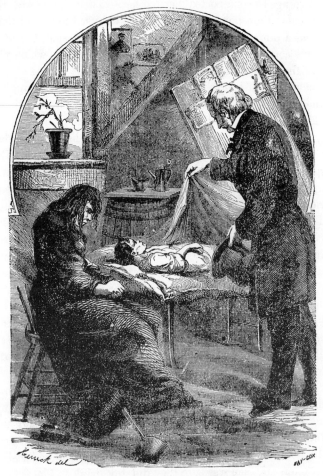

THE CITY MISSIONARY.

carpet. An old stove, which would not draw on account of some defect in the chimney of the house, had from time to time spread its clouds of smoke through the cellar—the only room—even when the baby was born. A few kettles, etc., stood around the floor, some crumbs of bread were on a shelf, but no sign of meat or vegetables. A wash-tub, containing half-washed clothing, stood near the middle of the room; there was a table, and a bedstead stood in a corner pretty well furnished—the bed clothing the gift of charity. In this the father, mother, babe, and perhaps a little boy two years old, slept. But the other children? O, they had some old bundles of rags on the floor, and here they were compelled to lie like pigs, with little or nothing to cover them. When it rained, the water from the street poured into this hole, and saturated the rags on which the children slept, and they had to lie there like poor little drowned rats, shivering and wailing till morning came, when they could go out and gather cinders enough to make a fire. The privilege of living in this place cost five dollars per month. And yet this woman was willing to talk about God, and believed in his goodness. She believed that he often visited that place. Yes, he does go down there when the good Miss —— from the Mission descends the slimy steps."

"I have been astounded," said a city clergyman to the writer, "to find so much genuine piety in the wretched places I visit. A few nights ago I was called to see a woman who was very ill. The messenger conducted me to a miserable cellar, where, on a bed of rags, I found a woman, about sixty years old, gasping for breath. She greeted me with feverish anxiety, and asked me if I thought it possible for her to get well; I told her I did not know, and as she seemed very ill, I sent the man who had been my conductor, to the nearest police station, to ask for medical aid. I asked her if she wished to live, she answered, ' No, unless it be God's will that I should.' Well, the reply startled me, for the tone was one of unquestioned resignation, and I had not expected to discover that virtue here. In reply to my questions she told me her story—a very common one—of a long life of bitter poverty, following close on a few years of happiness and comfort at the beginning of her womanhood. Her trial had been very hard, but she managed by God's grace to keep her soul pure and her conscience free from reproach.

"In a little while the physician I had sent for came in. He saw her condition at a glance, and turning to me said, in a low tone, that she would not live through the night, that she was

51

literally worn out. As low as he spoke, she overheard him. She clasped her bony hands exultantly, her poor wan face gleamed with joy, and she burst out in her thin, weak voice, into the words of the hymn:

> " ' Happy soul! thy days are ended,
> Leave thy trials here below:
> Go, by angel guards attended,
> To the breast of Jesus, go!'

" Well, she died that night, and I am sure she is in heaven now."

Great efforts are made by the organized charities of the city to relieve the sufferings of the deserving poor. Prominent among these charities is the "Association for Improving the Condition of the Poor." The object of the Society is to help them by enabling them to help themselves and gradually to lift them up out of the depths of poverty. The city is divided into small districts, each of which is in charge of a visitor, whose duty it is to seek out the deserving poor. All the assistance is given through these visitors, and nothing is done, except in extreme cases, until the true condition of the applicant is ascertained. Money is never given, and only such supplies as are not likely to be improperly used. Every recipient of the bounty of the Society is required to abstain from intoxicating liquors, to send young children to school, and to apprentice those of a suitable age. During the twenty-seven years of its existence, ending October 1st, 1870, the Society has expended in charities the sum of $1,203,767, and has given relief to 180,000 families, or 765,000 persons. The office of the Society is in the Bible House.

II.

THE BEGGARS.

BEGGING is a profession in New York. The deserving poor rarely come on the streets to seek aid, but the beggars crowd them, as they know the charitable institutions of the city would at once detect their imposture.   A short while ago the "Super-intendent of the Out-door Poor," said to a city merchant, " As a rule never give alms to a street beggar.   Send them to me when they accost you, and not one in fifty will dare to show his face in my office."

The New York beggars are mainly foreigners.   Scarcely an American is seen on the streets in this capacity.   Every year the number is increasing.   Foreigners who were professional beggars in their own countries, are coming over here to practise their trades, and these make New York their headquarters.   It is estimated that there are more professional beggars here than in all the other cities of the country combined.

Broadway, and especially Fourteenth street, Union Square, and the Fifth avenue are full of them.   They represent all forms of physical misfortune.   Some appear to have but one leg, others but one arm.   Some are blind, others horribly de-formed.   Some are genuine cripples, but the majority are sound in body.   They beg because the business is profitable, and they are too lazy to work.   The greater the semblance of distress, the more lucrative is their profession.   Women hire babies, and post themselves in the thoroughfares most frequented by ladies. They generally receive a considerable sum during the course of the day.   Others again provide themselves with a basket, in which they place a wretched display of shoestrings which no one is expected to buy, and station themselves in Broadway to attract the attention of the charitably disposed.   The most daring force their way into private houses and the hotels and demand assistance with the most brazen effrontery.   They hang on to you with the utmost determination, exposing the most disgusting sights to your gaze, and annoying you so much that you give them money in order to be rid of them.   They, in their turn, mark you well, and remember you when you pass them again.

Perhaps the most annoying of the street beggars are the children.   They frequent all parts of the city, but literally in-fest Fourteenth street and the lower part of the Fifth avenue. Many of them are driven into the streets by their parents to beg.   They have the most pitiful tales to tell if you will listen to them. There is one little girl who frequents Fourteenth street, whose "mother has just died and left seven small children," every day in the last two years. A gentleman was once accosted by two of these children, whose feet were bare, although the weather was very cold. Seizing each by the arm, he ordered them to put on their shoes and stockings. . His manner was so positive that they at once sat down on a door step, and producing their shoes and stockings from beneath their shawls, put them on. Many of these children support drunken or depraved parents by begging, and are soundly beaten by them if they return home at night without money. They grow up to a life of vagrancy. They soon learn to cheat and steal, and from such offences they pass rapidly into prostitution and crime.

Besides these street beggars, there are numbers of genteel, and doubtless well-meaning persons who make it their business to beg for others. They intrude upon you at the most inconvenient times, and venture into your private apartments with a freedom and assurance which positively amaze you. Refuse them, and they are insulting.

Then there are those who approach you by means of letters. They send you the most pitiful appeals for aid, and assure you that nothing but the direst necessity induces them to send you such a letter, and that they would not do so under any circumstances, were not they aware of your well-known charitable disposition. Some persons of known wealth receive as many as a dozen letters of this kind each day. They are, in ninety-nine cases out of a hundred, from impostors, and are properly consigned to the waste-basket.

Housekeepers have frequent applications every day for food. These are generally complied with, as, in all families of moderate size, there is much that must either be given or thrown away. Children and old people generally do this kind of begging. They come with long faces and pitiful voices, and ask for food in the most doleful tones. Grant their requests, and you will be amused at the cool manner in which they will produce large baskets, filled with provisions, and deposit your gift therein. Many Irish families find all their provisions in this way.

LXXVIII.

QUACK DOCTORS.

CARLYLE's savage description of the people of England—
"Eighteen millions of inhabitants, mostly fools"—is not ap-
plicable to his countrymen alone.   It may be regarded as
descriptive of the world at large, if the credulity, or to use a
more expressive term, "the gullibility" of men is to be taken
as a proof that they are "fools."   Many years ago a sharp-
witted scamp appeared in one of the European countries, and
offered for sale a pill which he declared to be a sure protection
against earthquakes.   Absurd as was the assertion, he sold large
quantities of his nostrum and grew rich upon the proceeds.
The credulity which enriched this man is still a marked characteristic of the human race, and often strikingly exhibits itself in
this country.   During the present winter a rumor went out that
a certain holy woman, highly venerated by the Roman Catholic
Church, had predicted on her death-bed, that during the month
of February, 1872, there would be three days of intense darkness over the world, in which many persons would perish, and
that this darkness would be so intense that no light but that
of a candle blessed by the Church could penetrate it.   A Roman
Catholic newspaper in Philadelphia ventured to print this
prophecy, and immediately the rush for consecrated candles was
so great on the part of the more ignorant members of that Church,
that the Bishop of the Diocese felt himself obliged to publicly
rebuke the superstition.   This credulity manifests itself in
nearly every form of life.   The quack doctors or medical impostors, to whom we shall devote this chapter, live upon it, and
do all in their power to encourage it.

There are quite a number of these men in New York.   They

offer to cure all manner of diseases, some for a small and others for a large sum. It has been discovered that some of these men carry on their business under two or three different names, often thus securing a double or triple share of their wretched business. The newspapers are full of their advertisements, many of which are unfit for the columns of a reputable journal. They cover the dead walls of the city with hideous pictures of disease and suffering, and flood the country with circulars and pamphlets setting forth the horrors of certain diseases, and giving an elaborate description of the symptoms by which they may be recognized. A clever physician has said that no man ever undertakes to look for defects in his physical system without finding them. The truth of the remark is proven by the fact that a very large number of persons, reading these descriptions of symptoms, many of which symptoms are common to a number of ills, come to the conclusion that they are affected in the manner stated by the quack. Great is the power of the imagination! so great, indeed, that many sound, healthy men are thus led to fancy themselves in need of medical attention. A short interview with some reputable physician would soon undeceive them, but they lay aside their good sense, and fall victims to their credulity. They think that as the quack has shown them where their trouble lies, he must needs have the power of curing them. They send their money to the author of the circular in question, and request a quantity of his medicine for the purpose of trying it. The nostrum is received in due time, and is accompanied by a second circular, in which the patient is coolly informed that he must not expect to be cured by one bottle, box, or package, as the case may be, but that five or six, or sometimes a dozen will be necessary to complete the cure, especially if the case is as desperate and stubborn as the letter applying for the medicine seems to indicate. Many are foolish enough to take the whole half dozen bottles or packages, and in the end are no better in health than they were at first. Indeed they are fortunate if they are not seriously injured by the doses they have taken. They are disheartened in nine cases out of ten, and are, at length, really in need of good medical advice. They have paid the quack more money than a good practitioner would demand for his services, and have only been injured by their folly.

It may be safely said that no honest and competent physician will undertake to treat cases by letter. *No one worthy of patronage will guarantee a cure in any case,* for an educated practitioner understands that cases are many and frequent where the best human skill may be exerted in vain. Further than this, a physician of merit will not advertise himself in the newspapers, except to announce the location of his office or residence. Such physicians are jealous of their personal and professional reputations, and are proud of their calling, which is justly esteemed one of the noblest on earth. They are men of humanity and learning, and they take more pleasure in relieving suffering than in making money. To those who have no money they give their services in the name of the Great Healer of all ills. They have no private remedies. Their knowledge is freely given to the scientific world that all men may be benefited by it, contenting themselves with the enjoyments of the fame of their discoveries.

The quack, however, is a different being. In some cases he has medical knowledge, in the majority of instances he is an ignoramus. His sole object is to make money, and he sells remedies which he knows to be worthless, and even vends drugs which he is sure will do positive harm in the majority of cases.

The best plan is never to answer a medical advertisement. There are regular physicians enough in the land, and if one is influenced by motives of economy, he is pursuing a mistaken course in dealing with the advertising quack doctors of New York. If there is real trouble, so much the greater is the need of the advice of an educated and conscientious physician. If concealment is desired, the patient is safe in the confidential relations which every honest physician observes towards those under his care. A man is simply a fool to swallow drugs or compounds of whose nature he is ignorant, or to subject himself to treatment at the hands of one who has no personal knowledge of his case.

The same credulity which makes the fortunes of quack

doctors, enriches the vendors of "Patent Medicines." The majority of the "specifics," "panaceas," etc., advertised in the newspapers are humbugs. They are generally made of drugs which can do no good, even if they do harm. Some are made of dangerous chemical substances, and nearly all contain articles which the majority of people are apt to abuse. The remedies advertised as cures for "private diseases" generally do nothing but keep the complaint at a fixed stage, and give it an opportunity to become chronic. The "Elixirs of Life," "Life Rejuvenators," "Vital Fluids," and other compounds sold to "revive worn out constitutions" are either dangerous poisons or worthless draughts. A prominent dealer in drugs once said to the writer that the progress of a certain "Bitters" could be traced across the continent, from Chicago to California "by the graves it had made." Bitters, "medicinal wines" and such liquors have no virtues worth speaking of. They either ruin the tone of the stomach, or produce habits of intemperance.

The "washes," "lotions," "toilet fluids," etc., are generally apt to produce skin diseases. They contain, in almost every instance, substances which are either directly or indirectly poisonous to the skin. The "tooth washes," "powders," and "dentifrices," are hurtful. They crack or wear away the enamel of the teeth, leave the nerve exposed, and cause the teeth to decay. If you are wise, dear reader, you will never use a dentifrice, unless you know what it is made of. The principal constituent of these dentifrices is a powerful acid, and there are some which contain large quantities of sulphuric acid, one single application of which will destroy the best teeth in the world. The "hair dyes," advertised under so many different names, contain such poisons as nitrate of silver, oxide of lead, acetate of lead, and sulphate of copper. These are fatal to the hair, and generally injure the scalp. The "ointments" and "unguents," for promoting the growth of whiskers and moustaches, are either perfumed and colored lard, or poisonous compounds, which contain quick lime, or corrosive sublimate, or some kindred substance. If you have any acquaintance who has ever used this means of covering his face with a manly down, ask him which came first, the beard, or a troublesome eruption on the face.

Dr. Harris, the recent Superintendent of the Board of Health of New York, has frequently pointed out the evils resulting from the use of these compounds. Dr. Sayre mentions several cases of fatal poisoning by the use of hair dye, which came under his notice.

The newspapers frequently contain such advertisements as the following :

A RETIRED PHYSICIAN, OF FORTY YEARS' practice, discovered, while in India, a sure remedy for consumption, bronchitis, colds, etc. Having relinquished his practice, he has no further use for the remedy, and will send it free on receipt of a three cent stamp to pay return postage.

Sometimes the advertiser is " A lady who has been cured of great nervous debility after many years of misery." Again, the advertiser is a " Retired clergyman," or a " Sufferer restored to health, and anxious to benefit his fellow men." In whatever form the announcement is made, the advertiser is usually one and the same person—an ignorant knave, who lives by his wits. He advertises largely in all parts of the land, spending thousands of dollars annually, and it would seem that even an idiot could understand that the most benevolent person could not afford so expensive a method of " benefiting his fellow men." Letters come to him by the hundred, from simpletons who have "taken his bait," asking for his valuable recipe. He sends the prescription, and notifies the party asking for it, that if the articles named in it cannot be procured by him at any drug store convenient to him, he, the " retired physician," " clergyman," or "nervous lady," will furnish them, upon application, at a certain sum (generally averaging five dollars), which he assures him is very cheap, as the drugs are rare and expensive. The articles named in the prescription are utterly unknown to any druggist in the world, and the names are the production of the quack's own brains, and, as a matter of course, the patient is unable to procure them at home, and sends an order for them with the price, to the " retired physician," " clergyman," or " nervous lady," and in return receives a nostrum compounded of drugs, which any apothecary could have furnished at one half the expense. In this way the " benevolence " of the quack is very profitable. Men have grown rich in this business, and it is carried on to an amazing extent in this city. It is done in violation of the law, and the benevolent individual not unfrequently falls into the hands of the police, but, as soon as released, he opens his business under a new name. As long as there are fools and dupes in the world, so long will the " retired physician " find an extensive practice.

LXXIX.

YOUNG MEN'S CHRISTIAN ASSOCIATION.

THE letters "Y. M. C. A." are familiar to every city and town of importance in the Union, and are well known to be the initials of one of the most praiseworthy organizations in the world. It is needless to enter into any general account of the Young Men's Christian Association, and I shall devote this chapter to a description of the means employed by that body to carry on its work in the metropolis. A writer in *Harper's Magazine* has aptly described the headquarters of the Association as a "Club House." "For such it is," he adds, "both in its appliances and its purposes, though consecrated neither to politics, as are some, to social festivities, degenerating too often into gambling and intemperance, as are others, nor to literature and polite society, as are one or two, but to the cause of good morals, of pure religion, and of Him who is the divine Inspirer of the one and the divine Founder of the other."

The building thus referred to is located on the southwest corner of Fourth avenue and Twenty-third street, and is one of the handsomest and most attractive edifices in the city. The locality is admirably chosen. It is in full sight of the Fifth avenue and the neighboring hotels, and but one block east of Madison Square. On the opposite side of Twenty-third street is the beautiful Academy of Design; diagonally opposite is the College of Physicians and Surgeons, and immediately across Fourth avenue is the splendid structure of St. Paul's Methodist Episcopal Church. It is but three minutes' walk from the stages and cars on Broadway, and two of the most important lines of street cars pass its doors. No better location could have been chosen.

YOUNG MEN'S CHRISTIAN ASSOCIATION HALL.

The building is five stories in height, and is constructed of dark New Jersey sandstone, from the Belleville quarries. It covers about one-third of an acre of ground, and has a frontage of one hundred and seventy-five feet on Twenty-third street, and eighty-three feet on the Fourth avenue. The architecture is of the French Renaissance style. The trimmings are of light Ohio stone, but the brown stone gives to the building its general aspect. The ground floor is occupied by handsome stores, and the fourth and fifth floors are devoted chiefly to artists' studios. These bring in an annual rental of about $12,000 or $13,000.

The second and third floors are used exclusively by the Association. At the head of the grand stairway which leads from the main entrance in Twenty-third street, is a large hall. On the left of this stairway is the main hall or lecture-room, one of the handsomest and most convenient public halls in the city. At the upper end is a fine platform with every convenience for lectures or concerts. The floor is provided with iron arm chairs, arranged after the manner of those in the parquet of Booth's Theatre. A large gallery extends around three sides of the hall, and is similarly provided with seats. The hall is two stories in height, is beautifully decorated, and will seat with comfort fifteen hundred people. On one side of the platform is a retiring room, and on the other is a large and handsomely decorated organ. This is one of the finest instruments in the city, and is a novelty in some respects, being furnished with a drum, a triangle, and a pair of cymbals. Organ concerts, lectures, and concerts by celebrated performers are given weekly during the fall and winter. On Sunday, religious services are held in the hall, the pastors of the different city churches officiating at the invitation of a committee of the Association in charge of these services.

On the opposite side of the main hall is the Reception Room of the Association, at one side of which is a door leading into the office of the Secretary, who is the executive officer. Adjoining the Reception Room are the Social Parlors and the Reading Room, in the latter of which the leading journals of the country are on file. The parlors are used for receptions and other social reunions of the members. From the Reception Room a flight of stairs leads directly down to the gymnasium and bowling-alley, where are to be found all the appliances for the development of "muscular Christianity" in its highest form.

On the third floor, which is on a level with the gallery of the Lecture Room, are rooms for prayer meetings, Bible classes, and week day classes for instruction in modern languages and other studies. Adjoining these is a handsome Library Room. The collection of books is increasing rapidly, and promises to be both valuable and useful.

Taken altogether, or in detail, the building and all its appointments are palatial. It is already the centre of a great and useful work, and offers many inducements to young men, especially to those who are living in the city, away from their

THE LIBRARY.

814

homes and families, and in the demoralizing atmosphere of the hotels and boarding-houses. The Association, however, does not content itself with merely offering these inducements to those who will seek its doors, but sends its members forth into the haunts of suffering and vice, and endeavors to win back those who have gone astray from the paths of virtue, and to alleviate the misery of those who are in distress.

LXXX.

CASTLE GARDEN.

NINE-TENTHS of the emigration from Europe to the United States is through the port of New York. In order to accommodate the vast number of arrivals, the Commissioners of Emigration have established a depot for the especial accommodation of this class.

The emigrant ships, both sailing vessels and steamers, anchor in the river after entering the port. They generally lie off their own piers, and wait for the Custom House boat to board them. As soon as this is done, and the necessary forms are gone through with, preparations are made to land the emigrants, who, with their baggage, are placed on board a small steamer and conveyed to Castle Garden, a round building which juts out into the water at the upper end of the Battery.

In the year 1807, work was begun on this building by order of the General Government, the site having been ceded by the city. It was intended to erect a strong fortification, to be called Castle Clinton, but, in 1820, it was discovered that the foundations were not strong enough to bear heavy ordnance, and Congress reconveyed the site to the city. The building was then completed as an opera house, and was used for several years for operatic and theatrical performances, concerts, and public receptions. It was the largest and most elegant hall in the country, and was the favorite resort of pleasure-seekers. Jenny Lind sang there, during her visit to the United States. It was used for public amusements until 1825, when, the wealth and fashion of the city having removed too high up town to make it profitable, it was leased to the Commissioners of Emigration as a landing-place for emigrants.

THE BATTERY AND CASTLE GARDEN.

817

This commission has the exclusive charge of the Landing Depot and its inmates. It is composed of six Commissioners, appointed by the Governor of the State. The Mayors of New York and Brooklyn, and the Presidents of the Irish and German Emigrant Societies, are members *ex-officio*. They are responsible to the Legislature for their acts.

The Landing Depot is fitted up with quarters for the emigrants and their baggage, and with various stores at which they can procure articles of necessity at moderate prices. As most of them come provided with some money, there is an exchange office in the enclosure, at which they can procure American currency for their foreign money. Many of them come furnished with railroad tickets to their destinations in the West, which they have purchased in Europe, but the majority buy their tickets in this city. There is an office for this purpose in the building, at which the agents of the various lines leading from the city to the Great West are prepared to sell tickets. No one is compelled to transact his business in the building, but all are advised to do so, as they will then be fairly treated ; while they are in danger of falling into the hands of swindlers outside. Attached to the establishment is an official, whose duty it is to furnish any information desired by the emigrants, and to advise them as to the boarding houses of the city which are worthy of their patronage. The keepers of these houses are held to a strict account of their treatment of their guests.

The majority of the emigrants go West in a few days after their arrival. Some have already decided on their place of future abode before leaving Europe, and others are influenced by the information they receive after reaching this country. Should they desire to remain in this city, they are frequently able to obtain employment, through the Labor Exchange connected with the Landing Depot, and by the same means many obtain work in other parts of the country—the Commissioners taking care that the contracts thus made are lawful and fair to both parties.

As we have said, the greater number of the emigrants arriv-

EMIGRANT HOSPITAL.

ing here have money when they come.   Others, who have been
able to raise only enough to reach this, to them, "land of
promise," or who have been swindled out of their funds by
sharpers in European ports, arrive here in the most destitute
condition.   These are a burden to the city and State at first,
and are at once sent to the Emigrant Refuge and Hospital.

This establishment is located on Ward's Island, in the Harlem
River, and consists of several large buildings for hospitals, nurseries, and other purposes.   It has a farm of one hundred and
six acres attached to it.   The destitute emigrants are sent to
this establishment, as soon as their condition is ascertained, and
cared for until they either obtain employment, or are provided
for by their friends in this country, or are sent to their original
destinations in the West at the expense of the Commissioners.
Medical attendance is provided at the Landing Depot, and is
free to all needing it.   Serious cases are sent to the hospital on
Ward's Island, where good medical skill and attendance are
furnished.

The number of emigrants at the Refuge sometimes amounts
to several hundred of all nationalities.   The Irish and Geman

elements predominate, and these being bitterly hostile to each other, the authorities are frequently compelled to adopt severe measures to prevent an open collision between them. In the winter of 1867–68, the Irish and German residents on the island came to blows, and a bloody riot immediately began between them, which was only quelled by the prompt arrival of a strong force of the City Police.

The Commissioners adopt every means in their power to prevent the inmates of the Landing Depot from falling into the hands of sharpers. Each emigrant in passing out of the enclosure for any purpose is required to apply for a permit, without which he cannot return, and no one is allowed, by the policeman on duty at the gate, to enter without permission from the proper authorities. In this way sharpers and swindlers are kept out of the enclosure, inside of which the emigrant is perfectly safe ; and when he ventures out he is warned of the dangers he will have to encounter the moment he passes the gateway.

The majority of the emigrants are unable to speak our language, and all are ignorant of the country, its laws, and customs. This makes them an easy prey to the villains who throng the Battery in wait for them.

Approaching these poor creatures, as they are gazing about them with the timidity and loneliness of strangers in a strange land, the scoundrels will accost them in their own language. Glad to hear the mother-tongue once more, the emigrant readily enters into conversation with the fellow, and reveals to him his destination, his plans, and the amount of money he has with him. The sharper after some pleasantries meant to lull the suspicions of his victim, offers to show him where he can purchase his railroad tickets at a lower rate than at the office in the Landing Depot, and if the emigrant is willing, conducts him to a house in Washington, Greenwich, West, or some neighboring street, where a confederate sells him the so-called railroad tickets and receives his money. He is then conducted back to the Battery by a different route, and the sharper leaves him. Upon inquiring at the office, he learns that his cheap tickets are so much worthless paper, and that he has been swindled out of his money, which may be his all. Of course he is unable to find the place where he was robbed, and has no redress for his loss.

Others again are led off, by persons who pretend to be friends, to take a friendly drink in a neighboring saloon. Their liquor is drugged, and they are soon rendered unconscious, when they are robbed of their money, valuables, and even their clothes, and turned out into the street in this condition, to be picked up by the police.

All sorts of worthless wares are palmed off upon them by unscrupulous wretches. They are drawn into gaming and are fleeced out of their money. Dozens of sharpers are on the watch for them, and woe to them if they fall into the hands of these wretches.

Women are prominent amongst the enemies of the emigrants. The proprietors of the dance-houses and brothels of the city send their agents to the Battery, to watch their opportunity to entice the fresh, healthy emigrant girls to their hells. They draw them away by promises of profitable employment, and other shams, and carry them off to the houses of their heartless masters and mistresses. There they are drugged and ruined, or in other ways literally forced into lives of shame.

LXXXI.
WORKING WOMEN.

It is said that there are more than forty thousand women and girls in New York dependent upon their own exertions for their support. This estimate includes the sewing women, factory girls, shop girls, female clerks, teachers, and governesses. They all labor under two common disadvantages. They are paid less for the same amount of work than men, and being more helpless than men are more at the mercy of unscrupulous employers. The female clerks and shop girls receive small wages, it is true, but they are generally paid regularly and honestly. The sewing women and factory hands are usually the most unfortunate, and these constitute the great bulk of the working women of New York. Many of these are married, or are widows with children dependent upon them for support.

The life of the New York working woman is very hard. She rises about daybreak, for she must have breakfast and be at her post by seven o'clock, if employed in a factory or workshop. At noon she has a brief intermission for dinner, and then resumes her work, which lasts until 6 o'clock in the evening. You may see them in the morning, thinly clad, weary and anxious, going in crowds to their work. They have few holidays except on Sunday, and but few pleasures at any time. Life with them is a constant struggle, and one in which they are always at a disadvantage. The sewing girls are in the majority, and there are two classes of these—those who work in the rooms of their employers and those who work at home. The former we have included in the general term of factory hands. The factory girls earn from two to four dollars a week, as a rule, a sum scarcely sufficient to keep body and soul together, but they

THE SEWING-GIRL'S HOME.

get their wages promptly and consider themselves fortunate. Men doing the same work would receive about twice as much.

The sewing women who work at home are worse off. They live in the poorer class of tenement houses, and are surrounded with discomfort of every kind. They work as hard as, if not harder than their sisters in the factories, and are even worse paid. They have not the advantage of being compelled to undertake the exercise of walking to and from the factories which the latter enjoy. They sit in their wretched rooms all day, and often late into the night, sewing for a miserable pittance, and for some scoundrel who will perhaps swindle them out of their hard earnings. For making blue cotton shirts, or "hickories" as they are called, a woman receives six cents apiece, and must furnish her own thread; for making linen coats she receives from fifteen to twenty cents apiece; for men's heavy overalls she gets sixty-two cents a dozen; for flannel shirts one dollar a dozen. These prices are not paid by the Jews alone, but by reputable Broadway dealers, men who style themselves "leading merchants." No wonder they pile up such large fortunes.

Now, in order to pay the rent of her bare and cheerless room, the sewing woman must make two whole shirts a day. Then she must do work enough to provide for her other expenses. She has to buy fuel in the winter, and kindling wood costs her three cents a bundle and coal fifteen cents a pail. Perhaps she has children, or a sick and helpless, or, worse still, a drunken husband to provide for. All out of her beggarly wages. Her food consists almost entirely of bread and potatoes, and sometimes she treats herself to the luxury of a cup of tea without milk or sugar. If she owns a sewing machine, and very few do, she can earn more than one who sews by hand, but constant work at the machine means a speedy breaking down of her health and a lingering death, or a transfer to the charity hospital.

Small as are her wages, the working woman is not always sure of receiving them. Some rascally employers—and one of the institutions to be mentioned further on, could give a long list of them—will, upon receiving the work, find fault with the sewing, and either deduct a part of the poor creature's wages for the alleged fault, or refuse point blank to pay her a cent. Others again will demand a deposit equal to the value of the materials taken home by the sewing women. Upon the return of the completed work, they will not only refuse the promised payment, alleging that the work is badly done, but will also refuse to return the money advanced by the woman. The wretch well knows that the woman is weak and helpless, and that she is ignorant of the mode of protecting herself. More than this, she has not the money to go to law.

These are simple facts, and not "sensational items." The records of the "Working Women's Protective Union" will corroborate them, and will furnish many others.

"Among the employés of a certain Israelitish manufacturer of straw goods in New York was a poor French woman, who, with her three small children, occupied apartments in a rear tenement house in Mulberry street. What renders this case of more than ordinary interest, is the fact that the lady had once been in affluent circumstances, and at one period of her life moved in the wealthiest circles of Paris. Misfortune befel her in the death of her husband, who was accidentally killed upon a railroad train. The bulk of the property of her deceased husband was seized upon by her creditors. The widow, however, succeeded in saving from the general wreck a few hundred dollars, and with this she emigrated to America, arriving here in the spring, and bringing with her three little children. Here she anticipated she would be enabled, with the aid of her superior education, to provide for herself and family. For several weeks her efforts at securing employment proved unavailing; but just before her last dollar was expended, she succeeded in forming a class in French, which she instructed for two months, at the expiration of which time she was deprived of this her only support—her pupils leaving her for the purpose of a summer's holiday at the fashionable watering-places. Other efforts were made to secure the position of teacher of languages (with several of which she is conversant), but all to no effect. Finally, reduced to absolute want, the lady was obliged to resort to manual labor in order to provide herself and little ones with bread.

Unused as she was to toil, her efforts to obtain employment were attended with little or no success. Day by day her case grew more desperate, until, at last, unable to pay the rent of her miserable attic apartment, she and her little ones were thrust into the street. Homeless and friendless, with not sufficient money wherewith to purchase a supper for herself and famishing little ones, the lady was forced to beg; which course, up to this time in her unfortunate career, she had looked upon as barely preferable to death itself. She had a few acquaintances among the parents of her former pupils, and to these she resolved to apply for aid. Her efforts in this direction were but a repetition of the old, old story. Her friends, who, during her prosperity, were lavishing their attentions on her, now, that misfortune had overtaken her, refused to recognize her, and thrust her from their doors without a penny. Fortune relented one day, and rewarded her efforts with a situation in a manufactory of straw goods. To be sure, the compensation was small; still, as bread enough might be secured in this manner to keep the wolf from the door until something better might present itself, she resolved to accept the terms of the straw manufacturer, and entered upon her duties. For a week or two the sum earned by the unfortunate lady was faithfully paid her, but on the third week the pusillanimous nature of the Jew cropped out. She had bargained to manufacture straw hats at eighty cents a dozen, or six and two-third cents each. At this rate, she managed to earn two dollars and fifty cents per week. Upon applying for her wages at the close of the third week, the employer informed her that he had discovered that six and two-thirds cents apiece was too large a compensation, and that from eighty cents he had resolved to reduce her pay to seventy cents per dozen, and accordingly presented her with her weekly payment, first deducting one dollar and forty cents from her wages. Pressed as she was for money, the lady refused to accept these terms, and at once set about seeking legal redress. Learning that at the 'Working Women's Union' of Bleecker street legal advice was furnished free of charge to such as herself, she laid her grievances before the officers of the institution, who at once placed the affair in the

hands of their legal adviser, who soon brought the rapacious
Israelite to terms.   At the time of her application to the institution the lady stated that she had been without fire, and, with
the exception of a small loaf or two of bread and what few
potatoes her children were enabled to gather from about the
stalls in several of the markets, without food for several days."
   The wrongs inflicted upon the working women are many.
"There are hoop-skirt manufactories where, in the incessant din
of machinery, girls stand upon weary feet all day long for fifty
cents.   There are photograph galleries—you pass them in Broadway admiringly—where girls 'mount' photographs in dark
rooms, which are hot in summer and cold in winter, for the same
money.   There are girls who make fans, who work in feathers,
who pick over and assort rags for paper warehouses, who act
as 'strippers' in tobacco shops, who make caps, and paper
boxes, and toys, and almost all imaginable things.   There are
milliners' girls, and bindery girls, and printers' girls—press-
feeders, bookfolders, hat-trimmers.   It is not to be supposed
that all these places are objectionable; it is not to be supposed
that all the places where sewing-girls work are objectionable;
but among each class there are very many—far too many—where
evils of the gravest character exist, where the poor girls are
wronged, the innocents suffer.   There are places where there are
not sufficient fires kept, in cold weather, and where the poor
girl, coming in wet and shivering from the storm, must go immediately to work, wet as she is, and so continue all day.   There
are places where the 'silent system' of prisons is rigidly enforced, where there are severe penalties for whispering to one's
neighbor, and where the windows are closely curtained, so that
no girl can look out upon the street; thus, in advance, inuring
the girls to the hardships of prison discipline, in view of the
possibility that they may some day become criminals!   There
are places where the employer treats his girls like slaves, in
every sense of the word.   Pause a moment, and reflect on all
that signifies.   As in the South 'as it was,' some of these girls
are given curses, and even blows, and even kicks; while others
are special favorites either of 'the boss,' or of some of his male

subordinates, and dress well, pay four dollars a week for board, and fare well generally—on a salary of three dollars a week."

Is it a wonder that so many of the working women and girls of New York glide into sin, with the hope of bettering their hard lot? And, when thrown out of work, with no food or shelter, save what can be obtained by begging or at the Station House, is it a wonder that they seek the concert saloons, in sheer desperation, or join the street walkers on Broadway?

But if the working woman has her persecutors, she has also her friends in the great city. One of the best institutions which have been organized for the protection and assistance of this class is the "Working Women's Protective Union," the head-quarters of which are in Bleecker street, a short distance east of Broadway. It is organized for the common benefit of all those women who obtain a livelihood by other employments than household services. It aids them:

"*First.* By securing legal protection from frauds and impositions free of expense. *Second.* By appeals, respectfully but urgently made, to employers for wages proportioned to the cost of living, and for such shortening of the hours of labor as is due to health and the requirements of household affairs. *Third.* By seeking new and appropriate spheres of labor in departments not now occupied by them. *Fourth.* By sustaining a registry system, through which those out of work may be assisted in finding employment. *Fifth.* By appeals to the community at large for that sympathy and support which is due to working women."

The members each contribute the sum of ten dollars annually to the support of the institution. Outside aid is also liberally given. The Union has done much good since its organization. It has compelled dishonest employers to fulfil their contracts with their operatives, and in one single week compelled the payment of the sum of three hundred and twenty-five dollars, which had been withheld by these scoundrels. Out of two hundred complaints against employers in a single year, it secured a fair settlement of nearly two-thirds. In 1869 it procured work for 3379 women and girls. It also looks after friendless and homeless women who seek its assistance, and helps them to secure employment.

STEWART'S HOME FOR WORKING WOMEN.

829

The "Home for Working Women," No. 45 Elizabeth street, is a massive brick building, six stories high, and will accommodate about five hundred boarders. It is supplied with a reading-room, a reception-room, a parlor, a restaurant, and a laundry. The upper floors are used as dormitories. The beds are neat and tidy, and are arranged in rows and separated from each other by white screens. The rooms are large and well ventilated, and the whole establishment is kept scrupulously clean and in perfect order. One dollar and twenty-five cents is the charge for a week's lodging and washing. The restaurant supplies meals of an excellent quality at an average cost of twenty-five cents. Lodgers are admitted until eleven o'clock at night at the price named. If they enter after that hour, they are charged twenty-five cents extra.

The Children's Aid Society conducts several lodging-houses for girls, one of which is located in Bleecker street, and the other at 27 St. Mark's Place. They furnish beds and meals to girls of all ages, at five cents each, while they have money, and give them for nothing where the applicant is found to be destitute. They have been tolerably successful thus far, and give promise of future usefulness.

There are several other associations, with similar objects, in operation in the city.

Mr. A. T. Stewart is now erecting, on Fourth avenue, a magnificent iron building, which is to be used as a "Home for Working Women." The building extends along the avenue, from Thirty-second to Thirty-third street, a distance of 192 feet, and has a depth of 205 feet. Including the central Mansard roofs, the building is eight stories in height. It is one of the finest edifices in the city, and will be provided with every convenience for the work to which it is destined. It will be capable of accommodating fifteen hundred boarders, and will be conducted on a plan similar to that of the "Home for Working Women" in Elizabeth street. It is not to be conducted as a charity. Each occupant is to pay a fixed sum per week; and it is believed that here this sum will not exceed two dollars a week for board, lodging, and washing.

LXXXII.

STREET VENDERS.

IT is not known how many stores, or places in which trade is conducted beneath the shelter of a roof, the city contains. They are numerous, but they are not sufficient for the wants of trade. The sellers overflow them and spread out into the streets and by-ways, with no roof above them but the blue sky. Some of these sellers are men, some women, and some mere children. Some have large stationary stands, others roam about with their wares in boxes, bags, or baskets in their hands. They sell all manner of wares. Watches, jewelry, newspapers, fruits, tobacco, cigars, candies, cakes, ice cream, lemonade, flowers, dogs, birds, —in short everything that can be carried in the hand—are sold by the Street Venders. The rich and the poor buy of them. The strolling vagrant picks up his scanty breakfast at one of these stands, and the millionaire buys an apple at another.

The eating and apple stands are mainly kept by women. The most of them are Irishwomen, and the big cap and dirty frill under the quilted bonnet are among the most common signs of such a stand. Some of these stands sell soups, some oysters, some coffee and hot cakes, some ice cream, and some merely fruits and apples. In Wall street they are kept by men, and pies and cakes form the staple articles of trade. Candies and nuts are sold exclusively by many. Such candies as are not to be had of any confectioner in town. Women never sell cigars or tobacco, though many of them never take their pipes from their mouths during business hours. Some of them offer ladies' hose and gentlemen's socks, and suspenders, yarns, worsted hoods, and gloves. A few women sell newspapers, but these are rapidly giving way to men.

SHOE LATCHETS!

"GLASS PUT IN!"

STREET VENDERS.

BALLOON MAN.

The newspaper stands are located principally on Broadway, in Wall street, and around the Post Office and the ferries. At some of them only the morning or evening journals are kept, but others offer all the weeklies and the illustrated papers as well.

The venders of cheap neckties and pocket book straps are mostly boys or very young men. They frequent the lower part of Broadway, which is also the favorite haunt of the venders of cheap jewelry. Pocket books of every description are sold at marvellously cheap prices, and photographs are displayed in such lavish quantities that you feel sure that every dealer in them has bankrupted himself in order to afford a free art exhibition to the crowd of little ragamuffins gathered around him. Toys of every contrivance adorn the stands above Canal street. The dealers in these articles are strong, ablebodied men, who prefer to stand on the side walks pulling the strings of a jumping jack, or making contortions with a toy contrived for that purpose, to a more manly way of earning their bread.

The balloon men, the penny whistle and pop gun dealers frequent the upper streets, where they are apt to be seen by children. The lame soldier sets up his stand anywhere, and deals principally in shoe strings, neckties, or in books and papers that no one ever reads. Towards Christmas large booths for the sale of toys are erected on some of the east and west side streets, at which a thriving business in toys and fire-works is carried on.

The Chinese candy and cigar sellers are to be found between the Astor House and the South Ferry. No one ever seems to buy from them, but they continue in the business, and thus afford proof positive that they have their customers.

The dog and bird men haunt the neighborhood of the Astor House and St. Nicholas hotels. They get high prices for their pets. Dogs sell readily. It is the fashion in New York to discourage the increase of families, and to attempt to satisfy the half-smothered maternal instinct by petting these dumb creatures.

Little girls are numerous among the street venders. They sell matches, tooth-picks, cigars, newspapers, songs and flowers.

53

The flower-girls are hideous little creatures, but their wares are beautiful and command a ready sale. These are made into hand bouquets, and buttonhole bouquets, and command from ten cents to several dollars each. When the day is wet and gloomy, and the slush and the mud of Broadway are thick over everything animate and inanimate, and the sensitive soul shrinks within itself at the sight of so much discomfort, the flower-girls do a good business. The flower-stands then constitute the most attractive objects on the street, and men are irresistibly drawn to them by the sight of their exquisite adornments. It is very pleasant at such times to have a bright, fragrant nosegay in one's buttonhole, or to carry a bouquet to one's home. On such days you may see hundreds of splashed and muddy men on the great thoroughfare, utterly hopeless of preserving any outward semblance of neatness, but each with his nosegay in his buttonhole; and as he glances down at it, from time to time, you may see his weary face soften and brighten, and an expression of cheerfulness steal over it, which renders him proof against even the depressing influences of the mud and the rain.

LXXXIII.
THE WHARVES.

No visitor to New York should omit visiting the wharves of the North and East rivers. A day may be profitably spent on the shore of each stream. The docks do not compare favorably with the massive structures of Liverpool, or London, or the other great seaports of the world. They are wretched, half decayed and dirty; but ere long they are to be replaced with a system of magnificent stone and iron piers, which will afford all the desired facilities, and render New York in this respect one of the best provided ports on the globe.

Beginning at the Battery on the North River side, we find first the pier of the famous Camden and Amboy Railway Company, from which passengers and freights are conveyed to the railway by steamer. Above this are the piers of the great European steamship lines, the coast steamers, and the steamboats plying between the city and the neighboring towns. The Boston boats, all of which run to points in Connecticut and Rhode Island, where they make connections with the railways to Boston, are fine steamers. Those of the Narragansett Steamship Company, the Bristol and Providence by name, are the most magnificent steamers in the world. They cost $1,250,000 apiece. They are simply floating palaces, as are also the Albany night boats. The foreign steamers are huge iron vessels, carrying thousands of tons of freight and hundreds of passengers. The sailing of one of these ships always draws a crowd to her pier, and though from five to eight of them leave the port every week, the attraction still continues.

The ferries to Jersey City and Hoboken are all located on this river, and are full of interest to the stranger. The Bethel,

BOAT STORES.

or floating chapel for seamen, is also worth visiting. The ice trade of the city is carried on on this front, the principal supply of that article being obtained along the river, about one hundred miles above the city.

The oyster boats, or boat stores, are peculiar to New York. They lie chiefly in the vicinity of Christopher street, and are sources of considerable profit to their owners. The Hay Scales are also curious objects. At the foot of Fifty-fourth street the numerous telegraph lines which connect New York with the States south of it, cross the Hudson. They gain the Jersey shore in the vicinity of the Elysian Fields at Hoboken, and thence continue their way to every part of the States mentioned.

The East River front is the terminus of the ferry lines to Brooklyn, Long Island City, and Hunter's Point. The shipping here consists almost entirely of sailing vessels. The craft plying between New York and the New England towns have their stations here, and here also are the California clippers. The huge Indiamen lie here receiving or discharging cargo.   The whole river front is covered with merchandise representing the products of every land under the sun.

The Floating Docks are among the principal sights of the East River, as are also the vast coal and ship yards. This stream will soon be spanned by an immense suspension bridge which is to connect the City Hall in New York with the City Hall in Brooklyn.   The total length of the bridge and its approaches is to be 5878 feet.   The bridge is to rest on cables, supported by massive stone towers at the water's edge on each side.   The span between these towers is to be 1616 feet.   From each tower the flooring is to be carried a further distance of 940 feet to the land approaches.   The New York approach is to be 1441 feet, and the Brooklyn approach 941 feet in length.   The approaches will, in some instances, be on a level with the tops of the houses in the cities through which they pass.   The total height of the bridge above the tide is to be 268 feet.   The work is now progressing rapidly, and will be completed in about three years.

Accidents are very common in every large port, but the peculiar construction of the New York ferry houses renders the number of cases of drowning doubly great. In order to guard against this, and to afford timely assistance to persons in danger of drowning, "rescue stations" have been established along the water front of the city.   There is one at each ferry house, and the others are located at the points where accidents are most likely to occur. These stations are each provided with a ladder of sufficient length to reach from the pier to the water at low tide, with hooks at one end, by means of which it is attached firmly to the pier; a boat hook fastened to a long pole; a life preserver or float, and a coil of rope.   These are merely deposited in a conspicuous place.   In case of accident, any one may use them for the purpose of rescuing a person in danger of drowning, but at other times it is punishable by law to interfere with them, or to remove them.   The station is in charge of the policeman attached to the "beat" in which it is located, and he has the exclusive right in the absence of one of his superior officers to direct all proceedings. At the same time, he is required to comply strictly with the law regulating such service on his part, and to render every assistance in his power. The law for the government of persons using the "rescue apparatus" is posted conspicuously by the side of the implements, as are also concise and simple directions as to the best method of attempting to resuscitate drowned persons. These stations have been of the greatest use since their establishment, and reflect the highest credit upon those who originated and introduced them.

LXXXIV.
THE MORGUE,

THERE stands on the shore of the East River, at the foot of Twenty-sixth street, a massive gray-stone building, known as Bellevue Hospital. Over the lowest door of the front, on the upper side of Twenty-sixth street, is a single word in gilt letters—MORGUE. This door marks the entrance to the Dead House of New York, one of the most repulsive, but most terribly fascinating places in the city. The place is named after the famous dead house of Paris, and the interior is arranged in exact imitation of it, except that it is smaller. It is a gloomy-looking place, this Morgue, and it is always crowded. Bodies found in the streets or in the harbor are brought here for identification. They are kept a certain length of time, usually from twenty-four to forty-eight hours, and if not claimed by relatives or friends, are buried at the expense of the city. Every article of clothing, every trinket, or other means of identification, found with a body, is carefully preserved, in the hope that it may lead to a discovery of the cause of the death.

The room is gloomy and cell-like in appearance. It is about twenty feet square. The floor is of brick tiles, and the walls are rough and heavy. The apartment is divided into two unequal portions by a partition of glass and iron. The smaller portion is used by the public. The remainder is devoted to the purposes of the establishment. Back of the glass screen are four stone tables on iron frames, each with its foot towards the glass. Stretched on these are lifeless naked forms, each covered with a sheet. A stream of cold water, from a movable jet, falls over the lifeless face of each and trickles over the senseless forms, warding off decay until the last moment, in the hope that

THE MORGUE.

some one to whom the dead man or woman was dear in life will come and claim the body. A vain hope, generally, for but few bodies are claimed. Nearly all go to the potter's field.

A fearful company, truly, as they lie there, cold and rigid, their ghastly features lighted by the chilly gleams which fall from the windows above. Here is the body of an infant, its little life of suffering over. It was found in an ash barrel in an alley. On the next slab is the form of a man who was evidently well to do in the world. He is a stranger to the city, the Superintendent tells you, and dropped in the streets from apoplexy. His friends will no doubt claim him before the day is over, as the articles found on his person have established his identity. The next table contains the body of a woman. She was young and must have been fair. She was found in the river, and as there are no marks of violence on her person, the presumption is that she sought her own destruction. "Such cases are becoming common," says the Superintendent in his matter of fact way. "They are very sad, but we see too many of them to think them romantic." A shudder comes over you as you gaze at the ghastly occupant of the last table. The dead man was evidently a gentleman, for he bears every mark of a person of good position in life. His purple, swollen features tell you plainly that he was taken from the river. There is a deep wound in his side, and marks of violence are numerous about his head and neck. You gaze at the Superintendent inquiringly, and even that cool, clear-headed official turns a shade paler as he answers, almost under his breath, "Murdered. For his money, doubtless."

On the walls back of the tables are suspended the clothing of the unfortunates, and of others who have preceded them. Maybe some friend will come along and recognize them, and the one who has been missing will be traced to this sad place. They form a strange collection, but they speak chiefly of poverty and suffering.

The dark waters of the rivers and bay send many an inmate to this gloomy room. The harbor police, making their early morning rounds, find some dark object floating in the waters.

It is scarcely light enough to distinguish it, but the men know well what it is. They are accustomed to such things. They grapple it and tow it in silent horror past the long lines of shipping, and pause only when the Morgue looms up coldly before them in the uncertain light of the breaking day. The still form is lifted out of the water, and carried swiftly into the gloomy building. It is laid on the marble slab, stripped, covered with a sheet, the water is turned on, and the room is deserted and silent again.

So many come here on their way to their long homes. The average number is about two hundred per year. You can scarcely take up a city newspaper without finding one or more advertisements of persons "lost." Many of them come here. Many are never heard of again. The waters which encompass the city keep well the secrets confided to them, and neither the Morgue nor the Police books can tell the fate of all the missing. Strangers visiting the city often venture into the chosen haunts of crime "to see the sights," and in so doing place themselves in the power of the most desperate and reckless villains. Human life is held so cheap here, and murder has become such a profession, that no respectable person is safe who ventures into these localities. You may often see at the Morgue, where the majority of the bodies show marks of violence, the lifeless forms of those who but a few days before left their pleasant homes in other portions of the country to see the metropolis. A visit to a concert saloon or a dance house, merely from what they consider the most innocent curiosity, has sealed their doom. A glass of drugged liquor has destroyed their power of self-protection, and even without this they have been assaulted. They are helpless, and they have paid with their lives the price of their "innocent curiosity." Then the River and the Morgue complete the story; or perhaps the River keeps its secret, and the dead man's name goes down on the long list of the missing.

Strangers, and all others who would see New York, should content themselves with its innocent sights and amusements. Those who seek to pass beneath the shadow wilfully take their lives in their hands.

LXXXV.
THE CUSTOM HOUSE.

THE Custom House is one of the most prominent and interesting places in New York. It is one of the largest in the country, and is provided with every facility for the prompt despatch of the vast business transacted in it. Five-sixths of all the duties on imports collected in the United States are received here.

The Custom House building was formerly the Merchants' Exchange. It is one of the handsomest structures in the city, and its purchase cost the General Government one million of dollars in gold. The building is constructed of solid granite, with a fine portico and colonnade in front. It is fire-proof throughout. It occupies the entire block bounded by Wall street, Exchange Place, William street, and Hanover street. Its dimensions are a depth of two hundred feet, a frontage of one hundred and forty-four feet, and a rear breadth of one hundred and seventy-one feet. The top of the central dome is one hundred and twenty-four feet from the ground. The main entrance is on Wall street, but there are entrances on every side. The Rotunda occupies the space beneath the central dome, and is one of the finest interiors in the country.

Within the Rotunda are arranged rows of desks, running parallel with the walls. These are occupied by four "deputy collectors," three "chief clerks," five "entry clerks," two "bond clerks," the "foreign clearance clerk" and his assistant, and by those whose duties bring them most commonly in contact with the merchants, shippers, commanders of vessels, etc., in the ordinary routine of the business of the port. The Collector and the higher officials have handsome offices in other parts of the building.

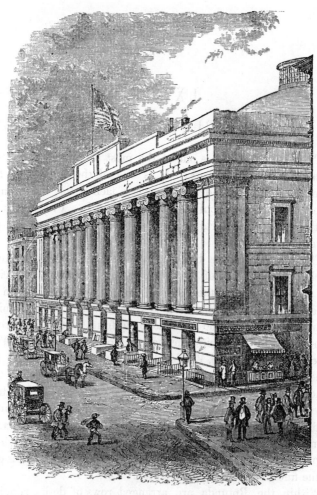

THE CUSTOM HOUSE.

There are about 1100 clerks attached to the Custom House, whose total wages amount to about $3,000,000 per annum. The legal salary of the Collector is $6000 per annum, but his fees and perquisites make up an actual income of five or six times that amount. The Collectorship of this port is the best paying office within the gift of the Government. Colonel

Thorpe thus sums up the duties of the various officers of the port:

"The Collector shall receive all reports, manifests, and documents to be made or exhibited on the entry of any ship or vessel; shall record, on books to be kept for that purpose, all manifests; shall receive the entries of all ships or vessels, and of the goods, wares, and merchandise imported in them; shall estimate the amount of the duties payable thereupon, indorsing said amount on the respective entries; shall receive all moneys paid for duties, and take all bonds for securing the payment thereof; shall, with the approbation of the Secretary of the Treasury, employ proper personages—weighers, gaugers, measurers, and inspectors—at the port within his district.

"The Naval Officer shall receive *copies* of all manifests and entries; shall estimate the duties on all goods, wares, and merchandise subject to duty (and no duties shall be received without such estimate), and shall keep a separate record thereof; and shall *countersign* all permits, clearances, certificates, debentures, and other documents granted by the Collector. He shall also examine the Collector's abstract of duties, his accounts, receipts, bonds, and expenditures, and, if found correct, shall certify the same.

"The Surveyor shall superintend and direct all inspectors, weighers, measurers, and gaugers; shall visit and inspect the ships and vessels; shall return in writing every morning to the Collector the name and nationality of all vessels which shall have arrived from foreign ports; shall examine all goods, wares, and merchandise imported, to see that they agree with the inspector's return; and shall see that all goods intended for exportation correspond with the entries, and permits granted therefor; and the said Surveyor shall, in all cases, be subject to the Collector.

"The Appraisers' department is simply for the purpose of deciding the market values and dutiable character of all goods imported, so that the imposts can be laid with correctness. Other than this, it has no connection with the Custom House."

There is located at the Battery, an old white building, surmounted by a light tower.   This is the Barge office, and is the
headquarters of the Inspectors attached to the Surveyor's office,
who are under the orders of Mr. John L. Van Buskirk, now
nearly 89 years of age, and who has been "Assistant to the
surveyor" for many years.   The arrivals of all ships are reported from the telegraph station at Sandy Hook, and as soon
as it is announced at the barge office that a steamer or ship
"from foreign ports" is off soundings, two Inspectors are placed
on a revenue cutter, and sent down to take charge of the
arriving vessel.   From the moment they set foot on the vessel's
deck, they are in supreme control of the cargo and passengers.
One would think from the manner in which many of them
conduct themselves toward passengers, that an American citizen
coming home from abroad has no rights but such as the Inspector chooses to accord him.   Certainly the joy which an
American feels in returning to his own home is very effectually
dampened by the contrast which he is compelled to draw between the courtesy and fairness of the customs officials of European lands, and the insolence and brutality of those into whose
clutches he falls upon entering the port of New York.   The Inspectors examine the baggage of the cabin passengers, collect the
imposts on dutiable articles, and send them ashore.   They then
send the steerage passengers to Castle Garden where they are
examined.   After this, the ship is allowed to go alongside of
her pier, where her cargo is discharged under their inspection,
and carted to the Bonded Warehouses of the United States, for
appraisement and collection of duties.

Passing goods through the Custom House is a troublesome
and intricate undertaking, and most merchants employ a Broker
to perform that duty for them.   A novice might spend hours
in wandering about the labyrinths of the huge building, trying to find the proper officials.   The broker knows every
nook and corner in the establishment, and where to find the
proper men, and moreover manages to secure the good will of
the officials so that he is never kept waiting, but is given every
facility for the despatch of his business.   The fee for "passing

an entry " is five dollars. Sometimes a broker will pass fifty different entries in a single day, thus earning $250. Some brokers make handsome fortunes in their business. When there is a dispute between the government and the importer as to the value of the goods or the amount of the duty, the broker's work is tedious and slow. The large importing houses have their regular brokers at stated salaries.

LXXXVI.

MISSING.

IT is a common and almost meaningless remark, that one has to be careful to avoid being lost in New York, but the words "Lost in New York" have a deeper meaning than the thoughtless speakers imagine. If the curious would know the full force of these words, let them go to the Police Headquarters, in Mulberry street, and ask for the "Bureau for the Recovery of Lost Persons." The records of this bureau abound in stories of mystery, of sorrow, and of crime.

As many as seven hundred people have been reported as "lost," to this bureau, in a single year, and it is believed that this does not include all the disappearances. Many of those so reported are found, as in the cases of old persons and children, but many disappear forever. Others who are recovered by their friends are never reported as found to the bureau, and consequently remain on its books as missing.

When a person is reported "Missing" to this bureau, a description of the age, height, figure, whiskers, if any, color of eyes, dress, hair, the place where last seen, the habits and disposition of the person, is given to the official in charge, who enters it in the register. When the returns of the Morgue, which are sent to the Police authorities every twenty-four hours, are received, they are compared with the descriptions in the register, and in this way bodies are often identified. Five or six hundred cards with the description of the missing person are printed, and sent to the various police precincts, with orders to the commanding officers to make a vigilant search for the person so described. Advertisements are also inserted in the newspapers describing the missing ones. Many of the estrays are children, and these are usually recovered within twenty-four hours. These little ones usually fall directly into the hands of the police, and are taken at once to the station house.

THE SIGHTS AND SENSATIONS OF NEW YORK.

THE FATE OF HUNDREDS OF YOUNG MEN.

1. LEAVING HOME FOR NEW YORK. 2. IN A FASHIONABLE SALOON AMONGST THE WAITER GIRLS
—THE ROAD TO RUIN. 3. DRINKING WITH "THE FANCY"—IN THE HANDS OF GAMBLERS. 4. MUR-
DERED AND ROBBED BY HIS "FANCY" COMPANIONS.—5. HIS BODY FOUND BY THE HARBOR POLICE.

852 LIGHTS AND SHADOWS OF NEW YORK LIFE; OR,

If not claimed there, they are sent at nightfall to Police Head-quarters, where they are cared for until their friends come for them.

Many of the missing are men—strangers to the city. They have come here on business or for pleasure, and have under-taken to see the sights of New York. They have drowned their senses in liquor, and have fallen into the hands of the thieves and murderers, who are ever on the watch for such as they. They have been robbed and murdered, thrown into the river, from which they sometimes find their way to the Morgue. Or perhaps they have followed some street walker to her den, there to fall victims to the knife or club of her accomplice. The river is close at hand, and it hides its secrets well. Year after year the same thing goes on, and men pay with their lives the price of their impure curiosity. The street walker still finds her victim ready to follow her to her den, for "he knoweth not that the dead are there: and that her guests are in the depths of hell. He goeth after her straightway, as an ox goeth to the slaughter, or as a fool to the correction of the stocks. Till a dart strike through his liver, and knoweth not that it is for his life. She hath cast down many wounded; yea, many strong men have been slain by her. Her house is the way to hell, going down to the chambers of death."

Year after year the waters cast up their dead, and the Morgue is filled with those who are known to the police as "missing." Men and women, the victims of the assassin, and those who are tired of life, find their way to the ghastly tables of the dead house; but they are not all. There are long rows of names in the dreary register of the police against which the entry "found" is never written. What has become of them, whether they are living or dead, no one knows. They were "lost in New York," and they are practically dead to those interested in knowing their fate. Year after year the sad list lengthens.

In many a far off home there is mourning for some loved one. Years have passed away since the sorrow came upon these mourners, but the cloud still hangs over them. Their loved one was "lost in New York." That is all they know—all they will ever know.

DO YOU WANT TO MAKE MONEY?

No business pays so well as an agency for popular Histories, and Illustrated Bibles and Biblical works, for they are the class of books that every intelligent person wants, and is always ready to buy. The only difficulty in the matter is to secure a *Valuable and Popular Series of Books,* and such pre-eminently are the works that we are now publishing. No series published will compare with them in *real value, interest, and popularity.*

☞ Being the most extensive subscription book Publishers in the United States, and having four houses, we can afford to sell books cheaper and pay Agents more liberal commissions than any other company.

Our books do not pass through the hands of General Agents, (as nearly all other subscription works do,) therefore we are enabled to give our canvassers the *extra per cent.* which other publishers allow to General Agents. Experienced canvassers will see the advantages of dealing directly with the publishers.

☞ By engaging in this business young men will *educate* themselves in that knowledge of the country, and of men and things, which is acquired only by traveling and observation, and which is recognized by all as essential to every business man.

Old agents, and all others who want the *Best Paying Agencies,* will please send for circulars and see our terms, and compare them and the character of our works, with those of other publishers.

Address,   **NATIONAL PUBLISHING CO.,**

At either of the following Places, (whichever is nearest to you):

19 North Seventh Street, Philadelphia, Pa.,
181 West Madison Street, Chicago, Ill.,
178 Elm Street, Cincinnati, Ohio,
410 Market Street, St. Louis, Mo.

☞ The following pages contain a Catalogue of some of our most valuable and popular Works, a specimen copy of either of which will be sent by mail, postage paid, to any address, on receipt of price.

LIFE IN UTAH;

OR, THE

MYSTERIES AND CRIMES OF MORMONISM.

BEING AN EXPOSÉ

)F THEIR SECRET RITES AND CEREMONIES; WITH A FULL AND AU-
THENTIC HISTORY OF POLYGAMY AND THE MORMON SECT
FROM ITS ORIGIN TO THE PRESENT TIME.

By J. H. BEADLE,

EDITOR OF THE SALT LAKE REPORTER, AND UTAH CORRESPONDENT OF THE
CINCINNATI COMMERCIAL.

ILLUSTRATED WITH 34 FINE ENGRAVINGS.

For more than thirty years the world has been horrified, startled and perplexed by th udacity and success of a sect calling themselves Mormons. Though founded in fraud, this sect has succeeded in spite of all opposition, until it is to-day the standing reproach of our country.

Several works have appeared, purporting to be exposures of the secret rites and myste-ries of this strange sect, but *none* have been complete, and few authentic. At present the demand for a work of this kind· is greatly increased by the determination of the General Government to put in force active and decisive measures against those people who calling themselves Saints have violated every law of God and man.

The Author's long residence in Utah; his position as editor of the leading journal of that Territory; his spirited defence of the cause of morality against Mormon treason and licentiousness, and his own sufferings at their hands, peculiarly qualify him for this task. Mormonism has been productive of so many dark and strange mysteries—so many terrible crimes that few can comprehend, without an intimate knowledge of it, how much wicked-ness it has to answer for, and what a standing menace to order and society it is.

THE WORK TREATS OF

Mormonism; its origin and history, and shows how, founded on imposture, it has grown by deceit and crime. It shows how JOE SMITH was enabled to deceive and cheat his followers; how by leading them on from crime to crime, and enticing them with licentious baits, he succeeded in maintaining his influence over them.

Of crime and lawlessness in Utah; showing the Mormon leaders in their true light, as thieves, murderers and assassins; how human life is every day taken in Utah; explain-ing and illustrating the infamous doctrine of killing a man to save his soul; and pre-senting a catalogue of crimes and horrors at which even the coolest and calmest reader will turn pale. It tells of frightful massacres of whole trains of emigrants, how they are murdered for their property, and how that property thus obtained, is seen daily in the possession of the Mormon leaders.

Of the Mormon religion, its infamous and heathenish character, its multitude of gods, it abominable doctrines and practices, revealing many strange mysteries and outrageous ceremonies.

Of the *Endowment* or initiation ceremonies, showing how obscene and disgusting they are; how female modesty is outraged in them, and how licentiousness is taught as a part of their religious creed.

Of the spiritual wife doctrine, showing how a woman may have more than one living hus-band and accord to each the same privileges; how women are debauched and degraded; how they are required to prostitute themselves "for religion's sake;" showing the terri-ble results of polygamy and sin.

The high praise which this work has received from members of Congress, and Govern-ment officials to whom it was submitted, and by whom its publication was urged as a duty to the country, stamps it as no ordinary work, but as one of the most powerful and thrilling books ever published. It is comprised in one large octavo volume of 540 pages, illustrated and embellished with 34 fine engravings, and furnished to subscribers,

Elegartly bound in Extra Fine English Cloth, - at $2.75 per Copy.
" " Fine Leather, (Library Style,) at $3.25 " "

AGENTS WANTED. Address, NATIONAL PUBLISHING CO.,

Philadelphia, Pa., Chicago, Ill., St. Louis, Mo., or Atlanta, Ga.

NEW ILLUSTRATED
Devotional & Practical
FAMILY BIBLE,
With over **450** Fine Scripture Illustrations.

In addition to the Old and New Testaments, Apocrypha, Concordance and Psalms in Metre, it contains a large amount of explanatory matter, compiled with great care, and furnishing a complete encyclopedia of Biblical knowledge.

The following are among its leading features:

1. A History of all the existing Religious Denominations in the world, and the various Sects, both ancient and modern.

2. A complete and practical household Dictionary of the Bible, comprising its Antiquities, Biography, Geography and Natural History, carefully abridged from the distinguished and popular author, William Smith, LL. D. Expounding every subject mentioned in the Bible; giving the most comprehensive, correct, and useful information possible, and guiding all to a higher appreciation of the correctness, authority and harmony of the Holy Scriptures.

3. A beautiful Lithographic Family Record; A very elegant and unique Marriage Certificate; and a Photographic Album for Sixteen Portraits.

4. Over **450** fine Scripture Illustrations, accurately showing the Manners and Customs of the Period, Biblical Antiquities and Scenery, Natural History, etc.; the Wanderings in the Wilderness, showing the Camp of the Israelites, Standards of the Twelve Tribes, etc.; Illustrations of the Tabernacle, and Solomon's Temple; Topographical Sketch of the Holy Land, with Maps and Panoramic Views of the Country as occupied by the different Tribes, etc., etc.

5. A Table of Contents of the Old and New Testaments, so arranged that any subject or occurrence mentioned in the Bible can be readily referred to.

6. Nearly One Hundred Thousand Marginal References and Readings arranged in the centre of the page.

7. A History of the Translation of the Bible; and Chronology of the Books of the New Testament, with the Times and Places at which they were written.

8. A Harmony of the Four Gospels, and Analysis of the Old and New Testaments.
